Camping is the way to go! Our trip was wonderful. Many thanks to your book (the cover is now two layers of tape, due to use!). Loved Europe and decided to stay...plan to travel further for two more years.

Leslie Carter, Kent, Wa.

Camp, camp, camp! It's the most fun, really! Also inexpensive! We averaged $2.00 a night camping. Met many fine Europeans and Americans. Had a wonderful, wonderful time. Wouldn't have missed it for the world. If I could say to someone thinking of going to Europe, I would only say--DO IT, DO IT, DO IT--it is the experience of a lifetime. Thanks for a great guidebook! It was really all we needed.

Kathy Carlson, Gardena, Ca.

Thanks for writing such a great guidebook! It always came through for us.

Kris and Ted Bushek, Eugene, Oregon

A friend and I left last June for our first trip to Europe, and have used your book quite often as our guide. We've found it to be full of the information that nobody else tells us, but that is vital to getting around and keeping our sanity. Your book saved us a lot of time and money, and often we simply could not have found a camp without it. We would use your book again, and will recommend it to our friends.

Frances Packer, Los Altos Hills, Ca.

Thanks for publishing such a terrific book. It made our trip much more enjoyable and with fewer worries. We enjoyed the trip so much that we plan to take another as soon as possible.

Mr. and Mrs. Robert K. Cooper, Batavia, Ill.

Two years ago I used your first edition during a very enjoyable trip to Europe. It was a big help. This summer I am taking another trip to Europe, this time for the entire summer, and I want to get the latest edition of your book. Thank you very much, and please keep up the good work.

Scott Taylor, Ames Iowa

How to Camp Europe by Train

with car-camping supplement

LENORE BAKEN

Additional copies of this book may be obtained by mail by
sending name, address and a check for $7.95 per copy to
Ariel Publications, P.O. Box 255, Mercer Island, Wa.
98040. (Washington State residents please add sales tax.)

We would like to gratefully acknowledge the assistance of
many fine people in the tourist offices and railroad offices,
both here and abroad, who gave so generously of their time
and knowledge.

We wish to thank the following travelers who wrote to us
following their trip and gave so much valuable information.

Kris and Ted Bushek, Eugene, Oregon; Kathy Carlson,
Gardena, California; Leslie Carter, Kent, Washington;
Linda Clark, Decatur, Georgia; Mr. and Mrs. Robert Cooper,
Batavia, Illinois; Lee Diamond, Far Rockaway, New York;
Janet Dutton, Overland Park, Kansas; Philip Jones, West
Chester, Pennsylvania; Frances Packer, Los Altos Hills,
California; Ray R. Rylander, Colorado Springs, Colorado;
Eric R. Wolterstorff, New Haven, Connecticut; Peggy Redelfs,
St. Louis, Missouri; Louise Miller, Scottsdale, Arizona; Rob
Rubin, San Diego, California; Clyde and Mary Anna Anderson,
St. Louis, Missouri; Harold C. Parkerson, Franklin, North
Carolina; Bonnie and Doug Robinson, Brandon, Vermont; Gary
Wing, San Francisco, California; Sara Dolph, Austin, Texas,
Kevin Cassity, Anchorage, Alaska; Bob Skiffington, Woonsocket,
Rhode Island; Jack Visscher, Fremont, Michigan.

ISBN 0-917656-04-0 795
Library of Congress Catalog Card #74-28580

Published by Ariel Publications, P.O. Box 255,
Mercer Island, Washington 98040

contents

Antibes 192, Biot 193, St. Paul 194, Vence 195, Nice 195, Le
Lavandou 195, Annecy 195, Chamonix 197, Rheims 199,
Hendaye 200, Valence 200, Grenoble 202, Mulhouse 202,
Strasbourg 203, Le Havre 203, Cherbourg 205, Dijon 205

Let's Camp Europe by Train

CAMPING IS MORE than just a way to beat the cost of a hotel or hostel and gas. Campgrounds are very informal places where Europeans, being on vacation themselves, have the time and interest to visit with you. Camping puts you in touch with the real Europe and the real Europeans--not just maids and waitresses, and with other camping Americans who will be glad to swap information with you. Most campgrounds are in very pleasant surroundings, some exceptionally so.

"My favorite campground was at Cala Levado, near Tossa de Mar, Costa Brava, Spain. Gorgeous camp--in all different levels on the hill above the coast. Good facilities--very private camp spaces. Clean and nice." (Leslie Carter)

"We loved the location of Camp Firenze, Florence, Italy--in an olive grove, near Piazzale Michelangelo practically downtown, and on a bus line. The view from Camping Reichenau, Innsbruck, Austria, was of the Inn River and the magnificent mountains surrounding Innsbruck. Camping Fontana Bianche, Syracuse, Sicily, was in an almond grove across the street from a beach with some of the most beautiful water I have ever seen." (Linda Clark)

"We stayed at dozens of beautiful campgrounds but we especially liked Le Pylone campground in Biot, France. The grounds were well organized and well taken care of. The van and trailer campers had their area and tent campers had their own area away from the noise of most autos. The sites were pleasingly large and grassy. They were divided by a few small trees on either side. Also, for privacy, each section of sites was divided by waist-high hedges. The campground's location was a great help to us. The train station was only a few blocks away so taking excursions up and down the coast was incredibly easy." (Mr. and Mrs. Robert Cooper)

At 75¢ to $3.00 a night per person, camping is the cheapest way to tour, yet it frees you from that constant dreary search for a hotel and the dormitory accommodations and curfews of a hostel. Camping gives you the option of home cooking, and puts you in company with others who have similar ideas about spending.

One of the best things about camping in Europe is that you don't need to have a car! In Europe, lots and lots of people travel by train and they do it all the time. Unlike the United States, the European continent is uniquely suitable for camping by train because of its superb modern dense railway network, unlimited mileage train passes, capital city campgrounds on municipal bus lines, and village campgrounds within walking distance of the train station. Train travel is fast and excellent between large cities--Paris to Brussels takes two hours and 20 minutes, and Milan to Geneva is a four hour trip. Trains find their way into the smallest hamlet and will take you off-the-beaten-track into the picturesque villages you have come to see.

The government-subsidized railroads of 16 European countries have banded together to offer two convenient train passes which provide for un- limited travel for a specified time period. The Eurailpass includes travel on all the super-deluxe Trans Europe Express trains and first class seats on other trains. It costs $650 for three months, $530 for two months, $390 for one month, $320 for 21 days and $250 for 15 days. The Eurail Youthpass can be bought by persons under 26 years of age for unlimited travel in second class for $350 for two months and $270 for one month.

The advantage of a train pass with itinerary planning is that a tour needn't be planned to obtain the most efficient method of routing to save on gas and driving time. The passes allow you to make plans with an eye to the weather (which means avoiding heat waves in summer) or to summer festivals, and to crisscross the continent without being penalized by addi- tional costs. They are also ideal for basing yourself in one city and making day trips from there. The railpasses are particularly good for the itinerary that encompasses the breadth of Western Europe and for the traveler who wants the grand introduction to the continent by visiting all the capitals from Helsinki to Athens to Lisbon.

Railpasses too expensive? By concentrating your efforts in one or two countries such as France, Spain or Italy, not over $100 for second class train fare need be spent and you can still have the time of your life for 1-1/2 to 2 months!

It's easy to camp Europe by train because of the availability of mini- weight camping equipment originally designed for backpackers. A nylon backpacking tent for two persons weighs a mere six pounds, a down-filled sleeping bag registers at under three pounds and an air mattress at three pounds. The usual large city train station anchors one end of the city's most important shopping street, and city buses wait at the station entrance. The station itself is akin to a small shopping center and offers such vital addi- tional services as an official tourist information office and a bank that cashes travelers checks and stays open long hours.

Riding the trains and camping is ideal for friends, couples, a person traveling alone (go!), parent and child and small families--anyone regard- less of age who is willing to carry a backpack. But driving has advantages for the family traveling with a baby, the large family where train fares can total the cost of a vehicle and gas, and for people who want a lot of privacy, who can't see themselves with a backpack, or who can bankroll the superior comforts of a camping van. A van is more comfortable than a tent and car but rental costs are higher and gas mileage poorer. The high cost of gas notwithstanding--around $2-3.00 a gallon, the main disadvantage of driving is contending with city traffic and locating campgrounds within cities. After that, the vehicle can be left at camp to avoid traffic congestion and inadequate parking downtown. Though driving is pleasant in the countryside and familiar on freeways, the time is better spent reading up on the next city, writing and relaxing on the train. A car can become just another one of those bothersome possessions, curtailing your freedom and encapsulating you from the people. "We think train camping greatly outweighs car camping. The trains, for the most part, were clean, comfortable, and fast. We wouldn't have liked to pay the gasoline prices or deal with the sometimes outrageous traffic in cities." (Mr. and Mrs. Robert Cooper)

We have done it both ways, and have always had a good time, and you will too no matter how you go.

HOW MUCH WILL I NEED TO CAMP WITH A RAILPASS?

Excluding airfare and train costs (and adjusting for inflation), you will need $9-20 a day per person. For example, a 24 year old man traveled for 150 days and spent $2,000--an average of $13 a day. Two people in their late thirties toured 90 days costing them less than $1500 which averages $8.50 a day each. A 24 year old student stayed 45 days and spent $600--an average of $13.50 per day. A husband and wife in their late fifties traveled for 59 days, spent $2430 for both, averaging a little over $20 a day per person. A newly married couple stayed 77 days and spent a total of $2100 or $13.64 a day each. Two people traveled one month for $750--an average of $12.50 a day each. One traveler toured two months and spent $600 or $10 a day. A couple spent one month on $1200, averaging $20 a day.

The money goes for food, entrance fees, going out, city transportation, guidebooks, buying things and campground fees. Most people spend more the first few days of their trip until they get the hang of it. The $9-20 a day mentioned above is an average figure which means that some days a person will live on less and other days more. Travelers report their biggest mistake is staying in pensions or inexpensive hotels at the beginning instead of camping from the start. Don't stay in a third class hotel when you can be enjoying yourself at a first class campground.

TRAVELING WITH CHILDREN. There are special considerations if you're traveling as a family. Taking the train repeatedly would be too much to cope with if you have an infant. Infants require too much special equipment and parents need the privacy of a car to minimize the added psychological strain of a baby crying in public. (We camped by car and tent in 1976 with our 8-month old, 4 and 6 year olds and I think that traveling by train would be too difficult for a family of that configuration, but camping with a tent--or better yet a van--is great!) We would say nix on a toddler too, because he just doesn't walk fast enough and you will be walking a great deal when taking the train. Surely a car would be more comfortable. With a toddler, the parents would have to carry his things in addition to their own, plus a folding stroller would be an absolute necessity unless one parent could carry all the equipment and the other backpack the child. The only advantages of the train would be the toddler being able to walk around and a toilet always close at hand.

It would be possible to take the train with a preschooler who is used to backpacking in the woods and can walk long distances without tiring, but unless you are the exceptional family who has acquired the walking habit, don't travel by train unless you're prepared to carry your child occasionally. The train comes into its own for family travel when there is only one child or the children are seven to eleven and still young enough to get the Eurailpass at half price, but old enough to carry their own belongings or most of them anyway. In this instance, children seem to enjoy riding a train rather than being confined to a car. Train-camping is wonderful for the single parent family, and the one who has left daddy at home, because it is cheaper and easier than having a car.

Besides the fun of traveling together, the main advantage for parents in traveling with children is that the children serve as ice-breakers. Everyone has a friendly smile or word for a baby or toddler, and older children make friends with other children at the campground and then you meet their parents.

Linda Clark of Decatur, Georgia, returned the post-trip questionnaire from which we learned that she had traveled by train and camping with her husband and their 21 month old daughter. We wrote to her and asked if she could tell us how she did it so we could include it in this edition of the book. We thank her very much for replying and we share this valuable information with you.

"Thank you for your interest in our trip to Europe. It's always nice to think over fun times, and who ever tires of giving verbal slide shows of a vacation? I just hope I don't bore you with my verbosity."

"Our daughter, Cathy, was introduced to camping at a young age-- six months to be exact. Her first experience with camping was a short trip to a state park which culminated in a very wet tent (We hadn't used it in a long time and it had been growing holes.) and my fear that we were going to be the cause of our baby's death from exposure. But of course she survived and the following summer we took a camping trip up the east coast and into Canada. Cathy did very well on both these trips and seemed to enjoy herself."

"By the beginning of her second cummer, Cathy was an old pro at camping. She probably adapted to adverse conditions, such as dampness and cold, at least as well as Ed and I did and I had realized by that time that a little dirt wouldn't hurt her. I would recommend that anyone planning to take a young child camping in Europe have some "practice sessions" first. I suppose this should also apply to adults."

"Of course camping by train is more difficult than camping by car when you can pack along many of the comforts of home and drive right up to a campsite. Not having a car in Europe presented us with the problem of what to do with our "home" and all the things we would have to take along for Cathy. We had close to 100 pounds of luggage, a horrible amount I'll readily admit. Because of this weight, we put the load on wheels. Ed rigged up a two-wheeled golf cart to which he tied an old backpack filled with our heaviest equipment. Then he bundled our sleeping bags and tent together and tied them on top of the pack. We hung the duffle bag containing Cathy's and my clothes on the cart handle to balance the load. Ed then pulled or pushed the golf cart while I pushed Cathy in her "Umbroller" - type stroller and sometimes carried along a small bag of groceries. Most of the time Cathy rode in her stroller, but in bad weather or when she was going through a rebellious day, I carried her. She didn't do too much walking when we were on our way to set up camp. Usually we were anxious to set up camp."

"The golf cart arrangement was at times unwieldy and occasionally a real pain to cope with, especially when we faced long rows of stairs and were rushed to catch a train. Those were the times we wished we had the freedom of movement backpacks would have offered. But for hauling a lot of weight over far stretches of smooth sidewalks, it was ideal. It held up with only minor repairs until our very last day. We were headed for the train station into London from our campground in Kent when the cart finally collapsed completely -- beyond repair. We had to borrow a wheelbarrow to get all of our baggage to the station. If we ever use a golf cart to carry all our equipment again, we will use a stronger one and be more careful not to roll it down stairs and off high curbs. It is a fairly good method to use, but apparently not too popular. We got some amused stares, because as far as we could tell, we had the only golf cart traveling around Europe that summer!"

"In retrospect, we must have been able to get along with less baggage, even though our standard line whenever we go on a trip now is, "We took less than this to Europe for nine weeks!" But if we had packed less, we could have gotten along with two backpacks and taken turns carrying Cathy or pushing her in her stroller."

"We had first class Eurailpasses so we usually found ample room in train compartments. Only on a few of the more popular trains did we have any trouble. I remember one ride in particular, from Rome to Nice. The cars going to Nice were completely packed. We were unfortunate enough to find ourselves in the same compartment as a middle-age American woman who, when I sat down across from her with Cathy (some 5 or 10 minutes before Ed got on the train) turned to her husband and made some very rude remarks about having to spend the night with a squalling baby. Cathy was sound asleep at the time. I don't know whether she had realized I spoke English or not, but when I said, "I beg your pardon," she gave me a hostile look. Her husband, however, looked embarrassed and apologized for his wife's behavior. The tension was too high for me to want to stay there all night, so we moved down to a first class compartment at the other end of the train. That car was only going as far as the Italian-French border. We checked the time table and discovered that the train would not be separating until mid-morning and that the ride from the border to Nice was a short one. We climbed into that car, had a compartment (with plusher seats than the one we had started out in) completely to ourselves, stretched out, and enjoyed a restful night. The next morning we moved over to one of the cars continuing on to Nice and, although they were very crowded, we did manage to find two seats together. The train we took from Madrid to Granada was terribly crowded also. Ditto the one from Paris to Lucerne, a trip Ed spent sleeping in the hall. But most of the time we shared compartments with no more than three other people."

"We frequently used the old trick of taking night trains. That, of course, gave us "free" lodging and we usually arrived in a city in the morning so that a day was not wasted in transport."

"The American woman's reaction to Cathy was the only one like it we experienced during our whole trip. If anyone else had similar thoughts, they were civil enough not to express them within our hearing. In fact, most people seemed to enjoy talking with us and playing with Cathy. Luckily Cathy slept soundly most of the time and all but twice (on the Spanish and Parisian trains) had room to stretch out on the seats. She seemed to like to watch the passing scenery and to explore the trains. Ed and I took turns keeping her amused. We took her for walks on the train, played with her, and read to her quite a bit. She has always enjoyed books and now, at age three, can read for herself most children's books up to about the fifth grade level. We packed along two colorful children's dictionaries (The Cat in the Hat Beginner Dictionary and A Golden Picture Dictionary). These had a lot of action in them and many short stories or scenarios. We also took along a Richard Scarry book for the same reasons. Although these books were large and relatively heavy, they probably hold a child's interest over a longer period of time than does a short, single-story book. We did take a few of those, however, and it was during that trip that we found Cathy would listen to us tell her a story -- that she didn't always need pictures and words on paper."

"We took along a few toys for Cathy: a doll, a small ball, paper and crayons, and some other little toys. We bought dolls in the native costumes of each of the countries we visited, so Cathy had a growing collection of things to play with. Another thing we did was to take pictures of her grandparents, aunts, uncles, cousins and friends before we left Atlanta. We put these into one of those small pocket-size albums and took it along so she could remember those people. I think she liked looking at the photographs and talking about them. This was somewhat comforting to her maternal grandmother who hated not being able to see her for so long and who was sure Cathy would forget many of the people who loved her after being gone for so long."

"Cathy was still in diapers. We used disposable ones, starting off with a package of American ones but switching to the European style after discovering the cost of Pampers in Europe. The European disposable diaper was a pad approximately ten inches long that fit into a pair of plastic pants that snapped on the sides. A Canadian pediatrician camping beside us in Venice seemed to think they were better than the kind we have here because their more abbreviated size and ventilation holes allowed more circulation of air to reach the body. But they looked awfully hot and uncomfortable at times."

"Cathy was breastfed until whe was 18 months old and at the time, it seemed much easier for me to wean her to a bottle. She drank from a cup at meals, but when going to sleep, she seemed to "need" a bottle. Most of the time in Europe that was no problem, we just bought a container of milk and gave it to her. But when faced with a long train trip or no convenient way to get milk, we carried packets of dry milk. The water in Europe rarely gave us trouble, so we carried a plastic container of it most everywhere we went. When a long train trip would lead to the spoiling of milk, we simply mixed some dry milk with water we had carried on board the train.

In that way Cathy could have her bottle of milk when she got sleepy. "

"As to her clothing, we had to take many more changes for her than for us. She was closer to the ground and picked up more dirt, especially in Naples where she reminded us of the character in Pigpen in the Peanuts comic strip. She would be coated with dirt within 5 minutes of leaving the tent."

"For the hot southern countries, we dressed her in shorts and sundresses, sandals, and a sun bonnet. She had been exposed to the sun before we left home, so sunburn was not really a problem. For the northern countries, we packed a jacket with a hood, long pants, socks and tennis shoes."

"When we went sightseeing, we always took along a small lightweight nylon pack filled with diapers, a change of clothing for Cathy, our camera, maps and guidebooks, and lunch. This we hung over the back of the stroller. The stroller also came in handy when we went grocery shopping. We were able to put the groceries in the seat of the stroller and let Cathy walk or be carried."

"Sightseeing can be slow with a toddler. We found Cathy was more interested in natural history museums than in art museums. Sometimes Ed and I took turns roaming through exhibits while the other lagged behind with Cathy or read or played with her. That might not be the ideal way to see a museum (certainly not the quickest!), but we accepted the fact that Cathy wasn't interested in everything and shouldn't have been expected to be. Also, we believe in spending much time with a young child."

"Our days were often relaxed because Cathy was with us. We sometimes spent an hour or so at a playground or sat in a park or square while Cathy looked at flowers or chased pigeons. These times were probably good for all three of us. It's hard to keep up a frantic pace for nine weeks."

"Cathy rarely seemed bored and although she regretably didn't understand the significance of some of the things we visited, she seemed interested in much of it. One notable exception was the old Roman ruins in Italy. She invariably went to sleep whenever we started to explore some and didn't wake up until we were about to leave. It was almost as though she was making some sort of statement about what she considered their worth to be."

"You are so right about her opening the door for us when it came to making new friends. People everywhere, with the exception of those in Paris and some of the northern German towns, went out of their way to talk with her. In southern Germany, I believe most elderly people must carry candy in their pockets to give to children. A few times people approached us to ask if they could photograph Cathy, one photographer following her around Dam Square in Amsterdam for a good 20 minutes while she chased pigeons. I recall a young couple in Rome asking us if they could pose for a picture with Cathy. All these incidents flattered us and I feel it was good for Cathy to receive affection from other people, particularly as her grandparents were so far away. I also feel it was good for her to be exposed to different nationalities and languages. She has learned at an early age that the world is populated by people of different colors, backgrounds, and languages and that none of these characteristics need be deterrents to friendship."

"Having a toddler along on our trip slowed us down somewhat and other people taking small children would be wise to make allowances for a more relaxed pace. In slowing us down, though, Cathy taught us how to appreciate some of the simpler things along the way, such as a pretty garden (seeing the parts as well as the whole) and the parade of people that passes through a park on a summer afternoon. When we got too wound up with trying to get somewhere in a hurry, she would often do something that would put things in their proper perspective and remind us that the world would not fall apart if we didn't see everything in the guidebook in one day. In short, she learned a lot and she taught us a few lessons as well. All things considered, it was a great experience and we usually had lots of fun. Camping gave us the opportunity to talk with a lot of interesting people, sharing experiences and information and sometimes a bottle of wine or bit of food. We would not hesitate to do it all again if we were able."

"I hope I have helped you a little, though my suggestions don't seem that extaordinary. You've brightened my day by giving me a change to express some of my thoughts about our trip to Europe."

"Think we'll get out the slides tonight.........."

Linda Clark's letter gives a good picture of what it is actually like to travel with a young child, and I hope it will allay any fears that parents might have about taking a young child to Europe.

GROUP CAMPING. For nine summers, Denise and Ed Ferry have taken a group of high school students camping through Europe by private motor-coach. They will organize and direct a camping trip tailored to your group's specific requirements. Write to them at Tent 'n' Trek, 152 Henry Street, San Francisco, Ca. 94114.

I See by Your Papers that You are a Tourist

AIRLINE TICKET AND PASSPORT are the essential documents to obtain before you go. The Eurailpass and Eurail Youthpass must be purchased in the United States. The International Student Identity Card can save substantial money because it entitles the student to reduced rates at musems. Be sure to get it if you qualify. A national museum ticket, Britain's Open to View Ticket would be worthwhile depending upon how extensively you plan to travel there. A Camping Carnet is NOT necessary. Our family of five camped without all one summer and were never turned away! Save your $14. Consider being immunized before you go, and accident and sickness insurance is recommended. If Eastern Europe figures in your plans, time is saved by obtaining visas in the U.S. Except for an initial supply of the proper currency for your first country abroad, money should be carried in travelers checks.

AIRFARES. Within a matter of hours you'll be there when you fly. Airfare offers the greatest single opportunity to save money on your trip. To do so requires that you do your homework by calling a number of airlines and doing some comparison shopping. When you call, state at the outset that you want to go the cheapest way possible and after the airline clerk tells you a fare, then be sure to ask if there is any cheaper fare. If you just call an airline and ask "what does it cost to fly from this city to that city," normally the airline personnel will tell you about the most frequently used type of fare and may not volunteer information about stand-by fares or similar fares which are used to fill up the plane and give lower fares in exchange for some inconvenience. Now that the International Air Transport Association no longer sets fares for its members, there are so many different types and their shelf-life is not always very long so we are not going into them here because the information would be out-dated too quickly.

But in general for most all fares, children 2-11 pay half fare and infants under 2 pay 10%. An eleven-year-old who becomes twelve while in Europe, still qualifies for the child rate. The prices of all types of fares vary according to season with lowest price in low season and highest price in high season: Low season: to and from Europe-- Nov-Mar.
Shoulder season: to Europe--Apr, May, Sept, Oct.
from Europe--Apr, May, June, Oct.
High season: to Europe--June, July, August.
from Europe--July, Aug, Sept.

16

The important thing is to call an airline early and make reservations as the best departure dates for the lowest fares sell out quickly. Call at least three months in advance for the best selection. If airline fares are rising, reserving a seat before the first of the year for the summer's travel may net you the old rate, depending on airline policy. When traveling with a baby, be sure to tell the airline when the reservation is made so a "skycot" will be provided, which is a type of bassinet that clamps securely to the ceiling bulkhead above your seat.

Student Travel Services CIEE/SOFA offer flights from New York, Chicago, Los Angeles and San Francisco which are open to anyone. Their free booklet can be obtained by writing to:

777 United Nations Plaza 236 North Santa Cruz, #314
New York, N.Y. 10017 Los Gatos, Ca 95030

Icelandic Airlines has regularly scheduled flights between New York and Luxembourg. Its address is 630 Fifth Ave., New York, N. Y. 10020. Laker Airways flies from New York and Los Angeles.

Remember to tie the sleeping bag securely to your pack, and it doesn't hurt to tie the whole thing up in rope like a package so nothing comes loose during baggage handling. Put your pocket knife in your pack. The actual flight will be more enjoyable if you plan ahead for your personal comfort. Clothing should be loose and non-restrictive. Omit any item that will impede circulation any more than prolonged sitting already does. During take-off, pressure in your ears may be relieved by swallowing repeatedly, chewing gum or sucking candy. To counteract prolonged sitting, give your feet and

leg muscles relief with five minutes of exercise every hour. Feet sometimes swell during the long flight in which case roomy shoes to begin with are a blessing. The swelling soon disappears once you are up and about.

Jet lag is like adjusting to daylight savings time except more so. Flying to Europe means passing through several time zones. This puts you ahead about five or six hours from the East Coast and eight or nine hours from the West Coast. You loose a third of your day BESIDES travel time of six to ten hours. Once in Europe, you find the natives eating and sleeping five to nine hours ahead of what you feel like doing. Accordingly, you must adjust your activities to the sun's position and eat dinner just because the sun is on the western horizon regardless of what your internal clock says. In practical terms, this means your body will feel like staying up late and sleeping in. When you would be eating breakfast at home, it will be mid-afternoon abroad. When you would usually be going to bed, in Europe it will be time for breakfast. THE EARLIER YOU GET UP IN THE U.S., THE LEAST AMOUNT OF ADJUSTING YOU'LL HAVE TO DO.

Remember to reconfirm your return flight at least three days (72 hours) before scheduled departure time. It can be done as soon as you arrive in Europe, which gets it out of the way.

PASSPORT A passport costs $10 plus a $5 execution fee, and the cost of two photographs. It is valid for five years and non-renewable. Each adult and child must have his own passport.

If you live in Boston, Cambridge, Chicago, Detroit, Honolulu, Houston, Los Angeles, Miami, New Orleans, New York, Philadelphia, San Francisco, Seattle or Washington D.C., apply in person at the local U.S. Passport

Agency. If you live outside these areas, certain clerks of court and post
offices are authorized to issue passports. A quick call to the local court-
house or post office will determine this.

Take these with you when you apply: (1) Two identical photographs,
2"x 2", in black and white or color, with the person wearing street clothes
but no hat, and facing the camera with white or light gray background behind.
From top of head to chin must be no less than one inch nor more than 1-3/8
inch. Photo must have been taken within six months. Extra passport photos
are handy to use for required pictures for the Student Identity Card and visas
for Eastern Europe (two per country).

(2) One of the following "proof of citizenship" papers: a previous
passport, a certified birth certificate (write to Vital Statistics, Division of
Department of Public Health, in the county in which you were born and
enclose $4), baptismal certificate issued within one year of birth, or
naturalization certificate.

(3) One piece of signed identification with description or photo such as
previous passport, driver's license, or university or government identification card. A birth certificate alone is acceptable for children.

To sum up, take two photos, birth certificate, and driver's license or
student body card, and $15 (check acceptable) to the passport office. Fill
out an application form upon arrival and submit it, photos and identification
papers to the clerk. Passport will be mailed to you in about two weeks, but
allow a month to be safe. (You must have your passport to apply for visas
for Eastern Europe, and passport number must be entered on the Eurailpass
and Eurail Youthpass.)

If you have a passport no more than eight years old, it is possible in
most cases to obtain a new one by mail for only the $10 fee. Get form
DSP-82, "Application for Passport by Mail," from passport office, court or
post office.

To replace a lost passport in Europe (unlikely), contact any U.S.
embassy or consulate to obtain a temporary one. Be sure to take along
someone who knows you as this person must complete an affidavit swearing
to your U.S. citizenship.

If you anticipate applying for visas for Eastern Europe, get your passport early as it must be sent in turn, along with visa application form,
photos and fee, to each country's embassy. The passport is returned with a
visa stamped in it.

EURAILPASS. Eurailpass is a wallet-sized card that entitles the bearer to
unlimited use of first class train coaches throughout 16 European countries
for a specified time period. A three month pass costs $650, two months--
$530, one month--$390, 21 days-- $320, and 15 days--$250. Children from
four through eleven pay half these amounts while those under four go free.
The price of the pass has gone up about five percent at the first of each year
in the past. From the day you buy it, you have six months to begin using it.
Seat reservations are not included and cost about $1.50 each when and if
necessary.

Here's what you get with Eurailpass. (1) First class travel. Most
European trains carry both first and second class coaches. Cars of the
usual international train are divided into enclosed seating compartments with
a corridor next to one set of windows. Each compartment is entered

by a sliding door. Inside are two rows of seats facing each other. Nowadays both first and second class coaches have only three seats abreast. The only difference between first and second class is that there is more leg room in a first class compartment as well as wider windows. On some minor rail routes and on commuter trains, there is only one class (second).

(2) TEE trains. Trans Europe Express (TEE) trains are the best in Europe. The Eurailpass holder will try to schedule one in whenever one goes where he wants. These are the newest and most modern trains in Europe and have better seating than our airplanes. Almost all are air-conditioned. Were you to buy a ticket for a TEE in Europe, you would have to pay a supplement besides the usual first class fare for that distance. TEE trains are included with the Eurailpass at no extra charge.

(3) Convenience. Except for the initial train ride when the date must be stamped on the Eurailpass to indicate the beginning of the use period, the pass is used by simply boarding the desired train, finding a seat and showing the pass when a conductor checks tickets sometime during the journey. If you were to purchase each individual train ticket within Europe, about a half hour could be wasted for each ticket in finding the right line and standing in it awhile. You simply hop aboard with Eurailpass. The only line waiting to do will be in making reservations but only a very few will be needed.

(4) Mistake proof. Should you board the wrong train or be in the wrong coach when the train splits with each half going in a different direction, then only time is lost not money.

(5) Bonuses. Some alternative means of transportation are included with the Eurailpass. A complete listing is given in the Eurailpass folder distributed free by any travel agent but the following are the most important. The Rhine Steamers are usually billed as the "Castles on the Rhine" boat trip in the tour folders. You get the same thing for no extra cost by simply getting off the train at a town on the Rhine River and transferring to a boat for awhile. Romantic Road Europabus, between Frankfurt and Munich, is a worthwhile trip for the change of pace it provides, and to see the medieval walled town of Rothenburg. Castle Road Europabus goes from Nuremberg and Mannheim with notable visits to Heidelberg and Rothenburg. (Try to take "Romantic Road" at least.) Some lake ferries are included such as those on the Lakes of Geneva, Zurich and Lucerne in Switzerland, or you might like to try the river steamer on the Danube between Vienna and the small town of Melk, the most interesting section. The best bonuses are ship passage between Brindisi, Italy and Patras, Greece; Stockholm, Sweden and Helsinki, Finland; and Rosslare, Ireland; and Le Havre or Cherbourg, France.

(6) Commuter trains. Eurailpass saves money on transportation within some cities when commuter trains can be used to get to the campground. In a few cities, the subway is operated by the government railroads and hence is included in Eurailpass. This is true for Copenhagen, Naples and the S-Bahn in Stuttgart, Munich, Hamburg, Cologne and other German cities.

(7) Itinerary flexibility. Since additional miles cost no more with Eurailpass, an itinerary can be planned according to train timetables and the convenience of the journey rather than on a straight mileage basis. You

can crisscross the continent to include special festivals at no extra cost,
and plan your trip to get the best weather, rather than starting at one point
and making a circular tour.

Though the three month Eurailpass is a good value for those planning
a trip which encompasses European capitals from Stockholm to Vienna and
Athens to Madrid, a less extensive itinerary on the shorter passes might
not warrant its purchase. If you are in doubt, send your itinerary to a
U.S. office of a European railroad (see itinerary planning) and have it calculated using second class fares. Train fares in general are higher in
Scandinavia and northern Europe than in France and southern Europe.

Eurailpass regulations require that the pass be bought outside of
Europe. A passport number is required to have the pass issued. It can be
purchased by mail from a U.S. office of a European railroad or through a
travel agent. Its period of validity begins on the first day of use. Eurailpass is refundable only if unused and then a ten percent service charge is
deducted. Once used, no refunds are made if lost or stolen (rare). Before
boarding the train for the initial use of the pass, take it to the ticket window
and have the date recorded on it. The clerk will also enter the expiration
date. Don't leave the window without checking the accuracy of the dates.
Your pass is valid up to midnight on the last day of the use period. Passport
must be shown along with the Eurailpass when the train conductor goes from
compartment to compartment checking tickets.

The pass is valid on the national railroads of Austria, Belgium,
Denmark, Finland, France, West Germany, Greece, Italy, Luxembourg,
Netherlands, Norway, Portugal, Spain, Sweden, Switzerland, and Ireland.

EURAIL YOUTHPASS. Eurail Youthpass can be bought by anyone under
26 and its first day of use must occur before the 26th birthday. The cost
is $350 for two months and $270 for one month. It gives unlimited travel in
the same countries as does the Eurailpass but in the second class cars. The
pass can only be bought outside of Europe. Almost all the bonuses of the
Eurailpass are included in the Eurail Youthpass with the most notable exception being that the express service on the Rhine River can't be taken without
paying a supplement but there are other boats to take anyway. This pass is
an excellent value but you should be aware of what it doesn't give you. You
cannot ride all of the second class coaches in Spain, Portugal, Austria and
Italy without paying a supplement. It is the express trains that require a
supplement (20 AS for Austria for example) but there are always non-
express trains which are only slightly slower and for which a supplement is
not required. Supplements are required to ride the Talgo and TER trains in
Spain for example. The Talgo is the Spanish equivalent to the TEE train
(which has no second class seats) but it has second class seats. Of course,
you also cannot ride the TEE trains or in first class   coaches. Second
class is generally more crowded than first, especially in summer. Otherwise please read the Eurailpass paragraphs as the rest of the information
applies.

Leslie Carter writes: "Personally I recommend the first class
Eurail. We were _very_ glad we had first class--_less crowded_-- second class
was always full--frequently people were standing--no hope to sleep in second
class. First class we were often able to stretch out and sleep at night,
always got a seat except once in Italy it was so packed the aisles were full.

Don't bother with couchettes--they're not worth the money. Reservations
are rarely necessary (we never made one)."
    In Scandinavian countries and in The Netherlands, Belgium, Germany,
Switzerland, Austria and parts of France, second class is not much different than first. On international trains for eight to ten hour journeys,
second class is more crowded and a reservation may be needed. In Spain
and Italy, a supplement must be paid to take their deluxe trains, but the
amount isn't large and the Eurail Youthpass holder is fortunate that these
countries carry second class on their luxury trains.

INTER-RAIL CARD. An Inter-Rail Card is available to anyone under 26
years of age at trains stations in Europe. Valid for one month, it entitles
the holder to unlimited second class train travel in 21 countries, except in
the country in which the ticket is bought only a 50 percent reduction is given.
Then there are no extra charges except on a few special trains. A detailed
folder comes with the Inter-Rail Ticket. The cost is approximately $215.
The countries are Austria, Belgium, Denmark, West Germany, Finland,
France, Greece, Great Britain, Hungary, Ireland, Italy, Luxembourg,
Morocco, The Netherlands, Portugal, Romania, Spain, Sweden,
Switzerland, Norway and Yugoslavia. It also gives 50 percent discount on
the Hook of Holland-Harwich cross-channel ferry line.

INTER-RAIL SENIOR CARD. This pass is available to all persons of 65
years of age or over. It's valid for one month on the national railways of
Switzerland, France, West Germany, Italy, Austria, Luxembourg, Belgium,
The Netherlands, Denmark, Sweden, Norway, Finland, Yugoslavia,
Romania, Greece, Spain and Portugal. It is bought at train stations of
participating countries. It is good for only a 50 percent discount on trains
of the country in which the pass is purchased. Cost is about $215 for second
class and $300 for first class which includes TEE trains.

EURAIL TICKET. If you aren't going to buy one of the rail passes and plan
to buy point-to-point train tickets instead, the Eurail Ticket is what you get
if you buy the tickets here before you go instead of when you get to Europe.
There are certain advantages of doing so, namely a six month validity
period is given instead of the two month which is standard in Europe, and
the convenience of pre-paying and not having to contend with buying tickets
in foreign countries. Also the rates are set at the beginning of each year
and the Eurailtariff is used for the entire year despite currency fluctuations
(which benefits us if the dollar falls). Of course, to buy a Eurail Ticket
requires that you have your exact itinerary figured when the ticket is bought.
A passenger is allowed to make any stopover en route with his ticket within
the validity period of six months. It is also not necessary to have the tickets
validated at any of the stations where the trip is interrupted. The only thing
the traveler has to do is to make sure he keeps the tickets in his possession
which have not been used. The price of the ticket is based on the regular
price of tickets, either first or second class, less any discounts that may
apply to that particular journey such as a reduction for a circular trip. A
seat reservation can be made in the U.S. for $1.50 per seat plus $1.00 telex
charge when necessary.
    There is also a Eurailtariff for groups which offers a discount of about

30 percent when at least 10 to 24 people travel together and they reach in some cases 50 percent when 25 or more travel together. Also many European railroads offer a youth group rate which is close to 50 percent for a minimum of ten people under 21 years of age which includes one adult chaperon. For further information, contact the U.S. office of a European railroad (see itinerary planning for addresses).

On tickets bought in the U.S., children from four through eleven years of age pay half. Those under four travel free. It used to be that the age limits for when a child qualified for half price varied by country in Europe but the German Federal Railroad says that "the reduction for children is uniform in most countries of Europe and children from 4 through 11 pay half fares. The only exception today are Austria and Switzerland where the age limits are 16 for half-fare tickets." The gist of this is that on tickets bought in the U.S. the upper limit is eleven, whereas if tickets are bought in Austria and Switzerland, the limit of 16 is applied. (Please note, this information supersedes that given under "trains" in the individual country chapters.)

SPECIAL PASSES FOR BRITAIN.   The Brit-Rail Pass, Youth Pass and Senior Citizen Pass must be purchased in North America. They cannot be bought in Great Britain. The passes give unlimited travel on the railways in England, Wales and Scotland and are valid on the "Sealink" ships to the Isle of Wight and on the Lake Windermere pleasure steamers. The pass is validated at the station from which you make your first journey. Children 5 through 15 pay half. Those under 5 are free. Youth Pass is only available to those from 14 through 25 Senior Citizen Pass gives those who are 65 or over first class travel at the regular economy rate. Adult pass costs $140-- 7 days, $210--14 days, $260--21 days, $299--1 month for first class. Adult economy pass costs $99--7 days, $150--14 days, $190--21 days, and $225-- 1 month. Youth economy pass costs $86--7 days, $133--14 days, $169--21 days and $199--1 month. A Seapass Supplement may be bought which adds a one way or round trip ticket for travel across the channel which is outside of the validity period. A Continental Seapass Supplement costs $25 one way or $50 round trip. A similar Ireland Seapass Supplement cost $38 one way and $75 round trip. There is a special 10 day Highlands and Islands Travel Pass for unlimited economy class train travel and some bus and shipping lines in the far north and west of Scotland plus rail access from Edinburgh and Glasgow, for $113--10 days and $68--5 days, no reduction for a child.

Considerably cheaper than Brit-Rail passes is the Coachmaster Pass which is valid for unlimited travel on the National Express Motorcoach network and some local bus services and city sightseeing excursions. No charge is made for seat reservations, but only one seat reservation "Journey Ticket" can be made for any one particular journey. It is sold for 8, 15, 22 and 29 days and can be bought in Britain. The bus network is more extensive than the rail network in Britain.

A Brit Express Travelcard is available for either 5 or 10 days of express coach (bus) travel during any 28 day period. The ticket allows unlimited point-to-point travel between over 60 main towns and cities in England, Scotland and Wales. Once marked off for a specific date, the pass may be used on as many journeys as required on that day. Cost is

25 British pounds for 5 days and 40 pounds for 10 days. It can be bought from the National Travel Office at Victoria Coach Station, London SW1. Information on all passes can be obtained in the U.S. from BritRail Travel, 630 Third Ave., N.Y., N.Y. 10017; 510 West Sixth St., Los Angeles, CA 90014; and 333 North Michigan Ave., Chicago, IL 60601.

INTERNATIONAL STUDENT IDENTITY CARD (ISIC). Full-time (12 semester hours) college students of any age are eligible to buy this student identification card. Students showing the card are entitled to substantial discounts on sightseeing admission fees and some other benefits. Be certain to obtain it if you qualify. Card is valid for 15 months from October of one year to December of the next, and costs $3.00 from Student Travel Services. (See addresses under "Airfares.")

INTERNATIONAL SCHOLAR IDENTITY CARD. For high school students, this card is obtained for $3.00 from Student Travel Services.

BRITISH "OPEN TO VIEW" TICKET. Good at more than 500 attractions in Britain, this tickets costs $19 for adults and $9.50 for children 5 through 15. It is valid for one month starting on first day of use. Send check to Brit Rail office listed above. The ticket is worth its price for anyone planning to tour the British Isles, but you won't get enough use out of it to warrant its purchase for a visit to London and one other city. The ticket gives admission in London to the Tower of London, Hampton Court Palace, and such lesser attractions as Kew Palace, Banqueting House and Carlyle's House. In Edinburgh, the ticket is good for the important attractions of Edinburgh Castle, Palace of Holyrood House and Blair Castle. Included are other notable sights throughout Britain such as Shakespeare's birthplace, Stonehenge, Winston Churchill's Chartwell and 20 stately homes of the nobility.

MEDICAL INSURANCE AND IMMUNIZATIONS. Medical insurance is a worthwhile investment. The best kind covers sickness as well as accident as the former is many times more likely to occur than the latter. The first step is to check your present policy to see if its coverage extends to Europe. Take a claim form with you to Europe, just in case. Special travelers insurance is available from many firms and any travel agent will sell you some although the premium will be higher than that available from student or special interest groups. The Student Travel Service (see "airfares") has some at good rates which are available to anyone--not just students.

A smallpox shot is no longer needed to return to the United States, but it's well to keep up ones immunizations anyway. County health departments usually provide shots free as do some university health centers. Ask their advice, but the usual are smallpox, typhoid-paratyphoid, tetanus-diptheria and polio. Start getting shots several months before departure so they can be spaced apart. Check with your doctor if you're in the early months of pregnancy or there is the possibility of pregnancy because shots may be harmful. Most children already have had these shots.

VISAS FOR EASTERN EUROPE. A Eurailpass or Eurail Youthpass holder might like to include Budapest, Prague or a Yugoslavian coastal city (which wasn't too badly damaged in the 1979 earthquake) on his itinerary. Prague and Budapest are only a few hours away from Vienna by train and a train pass is good right up to the border. Yugoslavia is but a hour away from Venice. All Eastern European countries have campgrounds and, except for having to pay for a visa in Poland, Czechoslovakia and Hungary, Eastern Europe provides the opportunity to flex one's itinerary and let the budget recover in less heavily promoted and cheaper Eastern Europe.

A visa is an entry permit that is rubber stamped onto a page in your passport. There are several kinds of visas, namely (1) a Transit Visa for those just passing through which allows a stay of up to 48 hours in the country, (2) a Single Entry Visa which allows the traveler to enter and exit from the country once, but to stay up to 30 or 90 days in the interim, and (3) Double Entry Visa which means you can enter two times, but it costs more. It's best to get each visa from the proper embassy in the U.S., but visas can also be obtained from an embassy or consulate in Western Europe and at some borders (but usually not on the train) for sometimes an extra charge.

The first step in getting a visa is to apply for your passport. While that's being processed, write to each country's embassy or tourist office and ask for a visa application form for each adult and child over 15. Once your passport arrives, send it off with the completed application form, fee (if any) and photos (if any) to one of the Eastern European countries on your itinerary. Allow sufficient time as it may take up to ten days for each visa which must be sent for successively as the passport must be included. Regular mail is perfectly safe.

You must not take any Eastern European currency with you except where certain small amounts are legally permitted such as Hungary. Then it is to your advantage to take in the legally permitted amount as the exchange rate in Western Europe is much better than the official rate given within the country.

Bulgaria.   No visa is necessary for a 48 hour to 59 day visit if you have prepaid more than 48 hours worth of accommodations--which means you must exchange about $10 a day for a minimum of three days into Bulgarian currency "vouchers" outside of the country. Otherwise if you don't want to prepay,   then you must buy an entry visa for $14.00 which allows you into the country and can spend as little as you like. Visa application forms are available from The Bulgarian Tourist Office, 50 East 42nd, New York, N. Y. 10017.

Czechoslovakia. Write to the Czechoslovak Embassy, Visa Section, 3900 Linnean Avenue, N.W., Washington, D.C. 20008 for visa application forms.   Two photos are required and the fee is $10.   Daily minimum.

Poland.   Write to the Polish National Tourist Office, 500 Fifth Ave., New York, N. Y. 10110   or 333 N. Michigan Avenue, Chicago, Ill. 60601, for visa application forms.   A visa costs $12 and there are minimum currency exchange regulations for each day of your stay. Regular tourists must exchange $15 a day, students between 16 and 24 and campers must exchange $7 a day.   These "exchange orders" must be obtained before a visa is given. As not too many Americans camp in Poland, it is easier to obtain camping vouchers and a visa in London.

Hungary.   Write to the Embassy of the Hungarian People's Republic, 3910 Shoemaker Street N.W., Washington, D.C. 20008 for visa application forms.   A visa costs $6.00 and two passport photos are required.   No minimum amount must be spent.

Romania. The Romanian visa is free and no photos are required, but there is a minimum daily exchange requirement. Write to Embassy of the Socialist Republic of Romania, 1607 23rd Street N.W., Washington, D.C. 20008.

Yugoslavia. Visa is free and no photos are needed. It can be obtained in advance or at the border. Write to Yugoslav Consulate General, 488 Madison Avenue, New York, N. Y. 10022, or 1375 Sutter St, Suite 406, San Francisco, CA 94109. You may import 1000 dinars in 100 D notes or less. This is to your advantage as a higher exchange rate is given by banks outside of Yugoslavia.

TRAVELERS CHECKS. Travelers checks are safe, convenient and easy to use. All brands are readily accepted and refunds are readily given once you find the respective office or bank that's open. Payment of the one percent fee to buy travelers checks can usually be avoided by calling savings and loan associations to discover which ones give checks "free" with an account. Denominations in which to buy checks depends on your estimate of daily expenses and length of time spent in any one country. Funds should be mostly in $50 and $20 checks with a few $10 ones. American Express sells foreign currency travelers checks for the German deutschmark (DM50, DM100, etc.), Swiss franc (SF50, SF100, etc.), British pound and French franc. Dollar travelers checks can be exchanged in Europe for checks of those currencies at American Express offices. If the dollar is falling rather than rising, buying checks in either deutschmarks or Swiss francs could save some money. (A fee is charged in the U.S. to reconvert foreign travelers checks to U.S. currency.) For an extended stay abroad, it's handy to know that American Express or Cook's will exchange large denomination travelers checks into small ones at no extra cost.

In Europe, aim to exchange from dollar travelers checks into local currency only that amount which you anticipate spending within that country as an exchange fee is levied with every exchange transaction.

What to Bring

CAMPING EQUIPMENT, CLOTHING, toiletries, cooking equipment, travel documents and literature, a few odds and ends and a backpack to put them all in are what you will need. CHOOSE THE LIGHTEST AND MOST COMPACT VERSION OF EACH. Everything should weigh no more than about 20 pounds:

Tent (eg. Half Dome--weight split with another)	3	lbs.
Sleeping bag (down fillied plus stuffing bag)	3-1/4	lbs.
Air mattress (nylon)	3	lbs.
Backpack	3-1/2	lbs.
Clothing and toiletries	3	lbs.
Cooking equipment	2	lbs.
Travel literature and miscellaneous	2	lbs.
Total	19-3/4	lbs.

Also needed is something in which to carry money, travelers checks, passport, railpasses and such. This could be a purse, shopping bag, athletic bag or what have you, but the outside zipper pockets on a backpack must NOT be used for safety's sake. For camping equipment the basic necessities are tent, sleeping bag, air mattress or pad, flashlight and backpack. If you are buying new, please do lots of comparison shopping first.

CHOOSING YOUR TENT   Look for a two-person, lightweight, backpacking tent designed for lowland camping. The total weight of one of these wonders ranges from three to seven pounds! The tent frame is sectional and the entire tent folds into a very small package. The most commonly found design is an A-frame and provides for sitting height only. American-made are superior to European in fabric strength, lightness and convenience of design.   You will get the best value for your money if you think of the tent as a lasting useful possession and can pay $100-$200 for it. But don't let those prices put you off as adequate tents are available in the $30 range. Usually the cheaper tents are either of uncoated nylon which soaks through in the rain or of coated nylon which causes condensation to form inside the tent. Because of the temperature differential inside and outside the tent, water collects in droplets on the inside of the roof and walls to eventually drip on the inhabitants and be soaked up by sleeping bags and gear rubbing against the walls. But a coated nylon tent will work out so long as the door and window (if there is one hopefully) are left uncovered at night to provide adequate ventilation. Even so, some minor condensation can be expected. At the campground, the tent can be erected to face a hedge, bushes or the backside of another tent to assure privacy.

The most comfortable tent for all temperatures is the uncoated nylon tent with a rainfly. A rainfly is a separate roof which is suspended a few inches over the top of the tent which keeps the tent dry during rains and also acts as a sunshade in hotter climates. A common problem with all nylon tents of the A-frame style where the tent is slung between two end poles is the tendency of nylon fabric to stretch when wet. A sagging tent makes interior space even smaller so periodic tightening of tent lines is necessary. Do this by retying lines to tent stakes by hand or by adding a shock cord or cord tightening device to the lines. The best place to shop for a backpacking tent is through backpacking or mountaineering specialty shops. For example, Recreational Equipment, Inc., Box C-88125, Seattle, Wa. 98188, publishes a summer catalog in March and a winter one in December which have pictures and detailed descriptions and comparisons of backpacking equipment. This firm is organized as a consumer co-operative and pays yearly patronage dividends figured as a percentage of each member's purchases over the past year. The dividend rate has been about 10 percent. The co-op has 340,000 members and lifetime membership costs $5. It has retail outlets in Seattle, Portland, Berkeley and Torrance. Write for its free mailorder catalog. All examples of equipment mentioned in this chapter can be obtained there unless otherwise noted.

Recreational Equipment sells an economy A-frame tent for $39 made of coated nylon, measuring 58" x 81" x 42" high, weighing 3-1/4 lbs and requiring stakes. Both door and opposing window are screened which is advantageous when leaving them uncovered at night to avoid condensation. This tent is perfectly suitable, but far superior in convenience and comfort are the R.E.I. Half Dome (our first choice), Light Dimension Tent and Eureka Timberline.

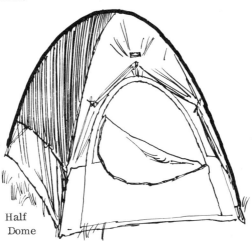

Half
Dome

R.E.I. half dome features exterior framing of curvable fiberglass rods which eliminates the need for tent lines and staking. The nylon tent can be lifted and moved after assembling. It weighs only 6 lbs. 4 oz. including rainfly, is 52" high at the center where the fiberlass ribs meet with a 55 x 86" floor area and has a very spacious interior for a backpack tent. Price is $124.95. R.E.I. also manufactures a three-person trail dome that weighs 7 lbs. 6 oz. and costs more. The LIGHT DIMENSION tent uses a Gore-Tex laminate fabric that is "as waterproof as coated nylon but at the same time breathes (passes water vapor) as readily as ventile cloth." It weighs only 3-3/4 lbs., sleeps two, uses two shock-loaded fiberglass poles, only three stakes and is megaphone shaped. Its light weight and compactness are achieved because the properties of Gore-Tex eliminate the need for a rainfly. (Follow directions for sealing seams.) Cost is $295. Tent is available only at Early Winters, Ltd., 110 PreFontaine Place S., Seattle, Wa. 98104. Write for literature. EUREKA TIMBERLINE is a two-person A-frame with exterior framework which makes it free-standing and eliminates staking. Rainfly included, 7 lbs. 14 oz., $119.95.   Of these tents, our first choice is R.E.I. half dome. If your tent needs stakes, the best kind should be light, firm holding in dirt and easily pushed down by hand. A thin wire stake is usually easier to push down than a plastic one. K-Kote Seam Sealer can be brushed on seams of a coated nylon rainfly to prevent leakage during rain.

SELECTING YOUR SLEEPING BAG   The requirements of moderate warmth, lightness in weight and compactibility limit the choice of sleeping bag to those filled with goose down, duck down, one of the new generation of high-loft polyester fiberfills such as Dacron Holofill, or a combination of these. Goose down is better than duck down, but it costs more. A synthetic is cheaper than both. Down is the most lightweight and compact and is our first choice. It is also highest in price, has a tendency to compact when slept upon thereby losing its warmth and needs special care in laundering. The advantages of the new synthetics are their even warmth provided by the non-separable batting rather than large pockets of feathers in which all the feathers may end up in one corner, their slowness in soaking up water, ease in washing, quickness in drying and lower price. On the other hand, a synthetic bag is heavier and bulkier. Some bags are designed for camping in winter, so be certain to buy one meant for lowland backpacking. A down bag should have about 1-1/2 to 2 lbs. of feathers.

Here is a sampling of sleeping bags from Recreational Equipment, Inc. All are barrel shaped, which is midway between a mummy bag and straight rectangular bag. All have full length zippers that zip open flat or can be used to zip two bags together. Mt. Baker bag costs $54.95, weighs 4-1/4 lbs., is filled with Dacron Holofill II and made of ripstop nylon. Its stuffing bag is 9" in diameter, 20" long and weighs 3-1/4 oz. Bugaboo bag costs $119.95, weighs 3 lbs. 8 oz., is filled with 1 lb. 10 oz. of a mixture of 60% duck down and 40% feathers, has slant tube construction, and is made of nylon taffeta outside and nylsilk fabric inside. Stuffing bag is included. The New Monarch bag costs $195, weighs 4 lb. 1 oz., is filled with goose down, has slant tube construction, is lined with trinyl nylon, covered with nylon taffeta and has stuff bag.   A drawstring clamp (nylon toggle) is convenient for securing stuffing bag tie strings. A stuffing bag resembles a tiny duffel bag into which the sleeping bag is pushed for compacting as much as possible. After removing a down bag from its stuffer, restore its insulating ability by fluffing it up. A bag can be kept cleaner by using a liner or snapping a cloth onto the equivalent pillow portion.

AIR MATTRESS or SLEEPING PAD   Necessary for comfort and as a barrier against sometimes damp ground, either an air mattress or sleeping pad will do. A pad is a better insulator than an air mattress but the latter is softer and more comfortable. A pad costs $6, but a Therm-a-Rest mattress combines both types, is self-inflating, but costs $47.95.

FLASHLIGHT   Take one per tent. Get a small, lightweight flashlight with a powerful beam. The most vulnerable part is the switch. Whatever your choice, the long life alkaline or cadmium sulfide batteries are better than the cheaper carbon-zinc ones. A good American-made flashlight is the small plastic   three-ounce Mallory Duracell compact flashlight. It throws a 250-foot beam, takes two "AA" alkaline batteries and costs under $3.00.

BACKPACK   If you have to carry 20 or so pounds, a backpack is the easiest way of doing so. A well-designed pack will distribute the weight factor between shoulders and hips (with shoulders carrying the larger portion) and leave your hands free. A backpack is carried close to the body and its 15-inch width does not protrude any more than the person carrying it which gives good crowd manuverability. In selecting your pack, choose a rigid frame backpack (not a frameless rucksack) that weighs no more than four pounds. It should be of coated nylon to be waterproof (NOT canvas) and have either two or three small pockets sewn on the outside or the main bag divided into two compartments inside to prevent belongings from becoming jumbled. Zippers on pockets should be covered with the same waterproof material as rest of the bag. If pack doesn't come with built-in padded shoulderstraps, buy a pair of removable straps to help cushion the load. Packs are sized according to height rather than frame and length of pack increases proportionately but width remains the same.   Packs with interior frames are less bulky and easier to fit into luggage lockers. Exterior framed packs are cooler as there is air space between pack and back.

READERS' SUGGESTIONS   (What would you have done differently?)
"Brought higher quality camping gear as we were wet and cold at times." Janet Dutton, Overland Park, Kansas.   "We would have left our old sleeping bags at home and taken down ones instead. We found the northern countries very cold and down bags would have helped. They also would have been lighter and more compact than the ones we took." Linda Clark, Decatur, Georgia.   "Buy the absolute best tent and sleeping bag you can afford. We took a lightweight two-man tent, which sagged and got wet in the rain. Needed is a tent large enough to sit up and play cards if it starts to rain and you want to stay inside your tent." Kathy Carlson, Gardena, California.

CLOTHING   The amount of clothing needed depends on how often you want to wash. Minimum is two sets, one to wear and another to handwash at the campground, but it's a nuisance to have to wash every night. The following list is based on the principle that underwear is changed daily but an outer garment can survive two or three days without being washed. Clothing never gets as clean with handwashing and white synthetics turn gray after a month of this. Sometimes a camp will have an automatic washer and self-service washers and dryers are available in cities.   All-nylon clothing can be very uncomfortable in Greece and southern Europe. SHOES are the MOST

important item that you'll be taking as they affect your comfort the most. Be
sure they are not brand new but have been broken in at least three weeks
before you leave. The sole should be of spongy material such as crepe or
rubber. This is of the utmost importance for comfort as the terrain varies
from cobblestones, pavement, dirt, rocks, wood and stone to hard marble
which can be slippery when wet. Shoes should be a little roomy in width as
extensive walking builds up foot muscles and the flight to Europe may cause
some temporary swelling.

Clothing List (includes clothing worn)
1 pair shoes   (with crepe or rubber soles)
2-3 outfits   (whatever)
4-5 underwear and socks (cotton socks absorb perspiration best)
1 cardigan sweater
1 jacket or raincoat
3 handkerchiefs   (or tissues)
nightwear (optional)
bathing suit
rubber thongs (for the shower) or athlete's foot ointment (optional)

If you plan to do some hiking, lug-soled shoes or boots, suitable socks
and a warmer jacket with hood should be brought. The above list is
for summer.

TOILETRIES KIT   Bring a durable plastic bag with string or loop attached
to hang in washroom or shower stall. Here is a suggested list of contents.
toothbrush and toothpaste
dental tape
drinking glass   (small soft plastic)
soap in leakproof plastic container (Ivory can be used as dish and
    clothes washing detergent too or take a small bottle of Ivory liquid)
washcloth and hand towel (thin, cheap kind--handtowel doubles as bath
    towel, put washcloth in plastic bag
shampoo   (small amount)
1/3 roll toilet paper in plastic bag (remove cardboard center)
comb
cosmetics and starter supply of sanitary napkins or tampons for women
shaving gear (if any) for men, note: Both voltage and socket differ in
    Europe. On the continent, 220 volts is normally found. The outlet
    is round and requires a round plug (75¢ in hardware stores in US).
    To attach a 110 volt razor to a 220 volt outlet requires attaching a
    resistor cord ($2.00) which converts the voltage. Resistor cord
    comes with the correct round plug. Remington and Norelco market
    electric shavers which can be manually set for either 110 or 220
    volt current. You will still need a round plug to go with it. Britain
    is a case apart with a variety of voltages and plugs.

FOOD EQUIPMENT   This basic equipment is essential for everybody.
pocketknife with can-opener (or buy Swiss Army knife in Europe)
spoon
plastic bowl and glass or cup
WATER BOTTLE   (pint or quart-size for carrying water on trains)

nylon folding shopping bag or equivalent (or buy string bag in Europe)
a ready-to-eat snack for first meal in Europe

The following items are optional depending on your plans for cooking. If you
already have the cooking equipment take it with you--otherwise it can be
bought in Europe.

5-10 plastic bags (assorted sizes)
2-3 waxed paper bags that our French bread comes in (to keep the
French bread you'll buy in Europe clean)
matches (not given free in Europe)
freeze-dried coffee or tea (both are heavily taxed in Europe, but tea
is cheap in Britain)
lightweight backpack fry pan and sauce pan
pancake turner
fork
soup spoon (omit teaspoon)
tiny amounts of any seasonings you use including a meat tenderizer
dishtowel
scouring pad and plastic bag
one-burner backpacking stove of European make - Please note: stove
fuel is prohibited from airplanes--be sure your stove is empty.
Fuel can be bought in Europe.

TRAVEL DOCUMENTS AND LITERATURE
airline tickets
Eurailpass or Eurail Youthpass or train tickets
passport (tape card with passport number, date and place of issuance
inside purse or wallet as you are asked repeatedly for this)
travelers checks (pack receipt which lists numbers separately)
international student identity card, if qualified
Italian Museum Pass
2-3 personal checks
Visa card or similar if you have one
5 - $1 bills and 3 - $5 bills (leave US coins at home)
currency for the country in which you arrive
extra coin purse for storing leftover money from countries that you'll
be revisiting (or small plastic bags and twists)
2-3 manilla envelopes for mailing home guidebooks and literature after
you've used them
this guidebook
free "Eurail" booklet and "Eurailmap"
other material

ODDS AND ENDS
bandages (5-10 assorted)
sunburn preventive (small size)
asperin (optional)
sunglasses
prescription for eye glasses or spare pair (takes 10 days to have
glasses made)
nail clippers or small blunt end scissors (sold in baby departments)
few safety pins or needle and thread

air mattress repair kit (optional)
cold water soap powder or liquid (optional)
ballpoint pen
address list
camera and film (optional)   alarm clock   (optional)

The airport screening device DOES harm film. Request a physical inspection for the bag with film. To avoid paying duty on European made articles taken with you, register them with customs at the airport or take along sales receipt. We also recommend packing in 3-6 cans of tuna and meat and a jar of peanut butter which are much cheaper here and will save you a lot on food in northern Europe. These will be used up within a week or two so you won't be carrying them forever but they will help conserve money for the first few days of your trip while you're getting your bearings! If you arrive in Britain, save them for across the channel.

The final step is to secure your pack to withstand the rigors of airline baggage handling. We recommend placing the entire pack within two layers of the large-type lawn cleanup plastic bags and then tying rope around the whole thing to hold it together.

READERS' SUGGESTIONS   What would you have left out...?   "A few clothes. Though we were very glad we had a warm jacket -- up in the mountains and this Fall it got cold a few places." Leslie Carter, Kent, Washington.   "Polyester pants--I wore jeans and skirts--never really needed to dress formally and skirts were great for summer wear. I would have brought a raincoat and light jacket instead of sweater. Clothes need to be of a type which can be washed easily and hung out to dry--dark prints and colors are a must. Travel light! My idea of clothes to take is 2 pair jeans, 4 or 5 underpants, 2 pair socks, 1 pair shorts, 1 or 2 skirts, 2 t-shirt tops, 1 long-sleeved turtleneck, 1 lightweight jacket (with hood preferably) and 1 plastic raincoat! A pair of sandals and a pair of walking shoes. All matchable, of course." Kathy Carlson, Gardena, California   "Your list of what to bring should be followed. We found we kicked ourselves plenty of times when we needed something but didn't have it because we thought it would take up too much room, etc. We would have bought a backpacker stove and cooking equipment in the U.S. before we left. At first we ate at restaurants which became very expensive. We bought the stove and cooking equipment in Salzburg, Austria. We found that we not only saved money but also had a variety of meals. Supermarkets were available as much as restaurants were." Mr. and Mrs. Robert Cooper, Batavia, Illinois. "We also brought four-function calculators which were cheap on sale at home for gifts to helpful folk in Eastern Europe. Bring printed cards with name and address for quick exchange with new-found friends. Ground cloth is most essential. We enjoyed having a small transistor radio--for local music and Armed Forces network (turned volume very low)." Kris and Ted Bushek, Eugene, Oregon.

CAR AND VAN CAMPING   Car and van campers will probably want to add to the lists for backpackers but shouldn't get carried away! Keep in mind that added possessions require increased organization. Additional clothing means using self-service laundries more, washing by hand less, and taking more time to pack, sort and re-pack. The only indispensable extra items for car and van campers are a collapsible 2-5 gallon plastic water container with handle and spout, and a whisk broom or child's broom. For car-campers, stove, table (about $30) and chairs (about $6 each) can be bought in Europe. We purchased a collapsible table for what would now be about 150 francs from La Hutte camping store chain in France in which the slatted wood top rolled into a cylinder and the base folded up and tucked inside the rolled table top. Ingenious! Substitute duffel bags for suitcases for efficient loading of a car and easy storage in a van. But remember, the key to happy traveling is few belongings.

As most everything is cheaper in the U.S., you may wish to take along some food and paper products which can be left in one place in the car or van until needed. We would suggest canned meats, tuna fish, peanut butter, juice mixes, anything dehydrated and perhaps tissues, paper towels and one roll of toilet paper.

Only recently have front seatbelts been legally required in many European countries and rear seatbelts are practically unheard of. When traveling with children, take baby's car seat with you (it will cost at least twice as much in Europe) and buy seatbelts in the U.S. for each child and for baby's carseat and have them installed in Europe. We learned this the hard way when our travel agent assured us that we could get rear seatbelts installed in our rental car and we wasted two days trying unsuccessfully to have this done. We could have had them installed if we had brought them with us but we couldn't buy any in France.

CHILDREN   If traveling by car or van, each child should have his own bag to keep toys and trip accummulations together. Don't bring many toys from home as he will collect some in Europe. Keep clothing to a minimum too as it's easier to handwash a needed item than to pack and re-pack dirty clothes. At minimum a child should have 1 pair sandals, 1 pair walking shoes for rainy weather, 3-5 outfits, 5-7 underpants/shorts and socks, 1-2 under-shirts, sweater, water-repellent jacket with hood, pajamas and bathing suit. The amount of clothing should be reduced for children who are backpacking.

Now for babies, the type of diaper that is available everywhere--camp-store, street market, grocery store--resembles an oversized obstetrical pad and costs about 20¢ each. This diaper tucks inside waterproof pants. The Pampers type of diaper is available in every country too, but mainly at phar-macies at a cost of about 30-40¢ each. Formulas and baby food are sold in pharmacies and supermarkets and cost about a third to a half more than ours. For bedding for our 8-month-old, I took along a blue foam pad (available at backpacking stores) which slipped inside a king-size pillow case. She wore a sleeper to bed and had a warm blanket. A backpack is far better than a travel stroller for carrying baby because of all the steps going up to build-ings and down to subways--and because much of the terrain isn't smooth pavement but cobblestones, grass, dirt, sand and rocks.   Packing list:

2 safety pins, disposable diapers	jacket or bunting
4-7 waterproof diaper covers	plastic bags for soiled diapers
1 sleeper plus warm hat	feeding needs
1 sweater	rectal thermometer
5 outfits plus sunbonnet	baby asperin, Desitin ointment
2-4 undershirts	favorite toy
blanket	washcloth, towel

The Best Laid Plans of..

SKETCHING AN ITINERARY. To plan or not to plan an itinerary is really a matter of personality, time and interest. It may sound fashionably romantic to blow with the wind and be guided by the inspiration of the moment and doing it this way leaves much to be covered for your second trip. An itinerary is best thought of as a travel program of where you would like to go and in what order which you plan for yourself at leisure before you go and use as a basis of departure once you get over there. It is much easier to evaluate touring possibilities here rather than once on vacation when time is at a premium and the sirens beckon. Go with an itinerary in mind, but feel free to tamper with it or throw it out completely once you are abroad. The main advantage of planning before you go, besides the fun of it, is that it acquaints you with unfamiliar names, monetary systems and train schedules which gives you a headstart once you get there.

CAMPING SEASONS. July and August are the height of the camping season throughout Europe. The good weather usually stretches out at either end to include June and September, though temperature and rainfall in these months fluctuates just like at home. Destinations in northern Scandinavia (i.e above the Arctic Circle) should be scheduled for July and August, the warmest time. Northern Europe can be rather cold and/or rainy in May and October and camping can be uncomfortable though capital city campgrounds remain open all year around. May and October are fine months for camping in southern Europe, including the south of France, Spain except for the northern coast, Portugal, Italy except for the Alps, Yugoslavia, Greece, Turkey and Morocco. Winter camping is possible on the island of Sicily in Italy, on the Costa del Sol in southern Spain, in the Algave in southern Portugal, and in Greece, Turkey and Morocco.

Summer weather in Europe varies from year to year just like at home. For instance, the summer of 1975 was notably rainy throughout Europe while the following summer in 1976 a continent-wide drought occurred. Railpasses give you the freedom to change your plans according to the week by week weather situation, and even in a rainy year there is always southern Europe and Greece to which to escape. Traveler Kathy Carlson advises: "I think an itinerary should be planned with keeping in mind that northern countries have a lot of rain and southern countries have a lot of sun. I love California, so preferring sun I would recommend Spain, Italy, Greece, southern France and Germany for better weather and camping. "

PRICE LEVEL. It is possible to reduce living costs or increase your standard of living by spending most of your time in the less expensive countries. This would be worthwhile only if you didn't have a Eurailpass or Eurail Youthpass. If you have either of these, then you'll never have a cheaper opportunity to visit the higher-priced countries than by train pass and campground and now is the time to do it. It's indeed difficult to rank countries by price level as so many different factors enter that may make one city more or less expensive than another regardless of country.

Group I. Of the highest priced countries, Switzerland tops the list. The problem is that its currency is so strong that it takes more dollars to buy it. West Germany, Sweden, The Netherlands, Norway, Belgium, Denmark and Finland are also in this group. Camping in these countries will cost about $2-3 per person. Food is high and these are the countries in which to cook or eat in cafeterias.

Group II. Camping costs are less in France, often $1.00 a night, but food costs are more like Group I countries. Austria, Italy, Great Britain and Spain are similarly priced where camping averages $1-2 per person. Food and camping are the cheapest in Portugal.

Group III. Yugoslavia is cheaper yet as is Eastern Europe generally.

Group IV. Greece is cheapest along with Morocco and Turkey.

SIGHTSEEING STRATEGIES. In planning what you want to accomplish in a day, bear in mind that the two main sightseeing periods available are from about 9:30 am until noon and from 1:30-4:30 pm. Upon arrival in a region, city, town or museum, do things in priority order. This way what you don't get done will be relatively unimportant to you personally. Try doing the free things first. Most often whether or not admission is charged depends more on whether it's subsidized by the state rather than on quality of attraction. Aim for variety within each day and throughout the trip. Then be sure to quit an activity while you're still ahead. If you stay at a museum until you're famished, you make easy prey for the first restaurant that comes along. Try to alternate museum hopping with physical activity. A visit to a small town or resort interspaced between capitals gives some restful counterpoint to your journey. There is nothing like a small village to clear the cobwebs for another siege on the city and its geographical complexities.

Be selective. It's only natural to want to do everything and go everywhere but having gone once you will return. Unless you already know that a particular civilization, period or era mesmerizes you, then for general cultural purposes be content with only one or two of the best examples of the period. Some civilizations left many more monuments than other equally important periods. Try to see choice morsels from the greatest span of time that you can. Avoid too many three-star duplications from prolific periods. The caves used by prehistoric man are about the earliest in time that you can get in Europe.

To avoid frustration, allow at least five days for either Paris or Rome and their environs.

Try to go where most of the tourists aren't if your trip is in July and August. There are such places and they are rewarding. Many inland medium sized towns fall into this category when most Americans are visiting only the capitals, and Europeans have migrated to sunny beaches for their holiday. The Perigord in France, famous for its fine cuisine, is an excellent such region. Here are the caves where early man lived and left his paintings on the walls, picturesque cliff-hanging villages, and good examples of ancient fortified towns. And it's one of the cheaper regions of France.

Try to go in months other than July and August. This is not feasible for most people, but camping is possible in late spring or early fall. You save all the way down the line from off-season airfares to discounted camp fees and less expensive daily specials offered in restaurants. Also avoided is the budget depleting need for cool refreshment that constantly crops up during the "hot" months of July and August. However disadvantages of traveling off-season are shortened museum hours, closure of some campgrounds and services, and rain and cold in northern Europe.

The best and most painless remembrance of things past is a visit to a museum town. It's great fun to go exploring in these perfectly preserved ancient towns with their logical geographical structure. They are extraordinarily relaxing, the town plans make such good sense, and they are always "picturebook." Rothenburg in Germany, Bruges in Belgium, and Carcassonne in France are well-known examples but there are many other less famous ones.

Include the contemporary world in your trip. Much contemporary sculpture and architecture is interesting, beautiful and worthwhile. Suburban communities built around "open spaces" are a vision of what's to come. Should Vienna be on your itinerary, why not take the train to nearby Budapest for a glimpse of Eastern Europe?

CIVILIZATIONS AND PERIODS. To refresh your memory, here's a brief outline of the ancient civilizations and modern historical periods which have left their monuments throughout Europe. After each are listed only a few of the many examples of the period that are found in Europe. Try to incorporate a few examples from many periods into your itinerary. And note that the more spectacular the past culture, the better the sightseeing. In modern terms that means France, Italy, Spain and Greece.

Prehistory
Caves of Lascaux, France (closed)
Caves of Les Eyzies, France (open)
Caves of Altamira, Santillana del Mar, Spain (open)

Greek Civilization (classical architecture)
Doric order
Temple of Poseidon, Paestum, Italy
Temple of Concord, Agrigento, Sicily, Italy
Temple of Segesta, Sicily, Italy
Ionic order
Temple of Fortuna Virile, Rome, Italy
Corinthian order
Maison Carree, Nimes, France

Etruscan Civilization (only sculpture remains)
Etruscan Museum, Rome

Roman Civilization (arches and cupolas)
Arch of Titus, Rome

Pompeii, Italy
Coliseum, Rome
Pantheon, Rome
Amphitheater, Verona, Italy
Acqueduct, Segovia, Spain

Byzantine
(Architectural style originating in Constantinople, then capital of the
Eastern Roman Empire.)
St. Mark's Cathedral, Venice
St. Vitale Cathedral, Ravenna, Italy (capital of Byzantine art)
Basilica of St. Apollinaris, Ravenna, Italy

Romanesque
(Eleventh and twelfth centuries, medieval style)
Cathedral, Pisa, Italy
Cathedral San Ambroglio, Milan
Autun Cathedral, Autun (Burgundy), France
Madeleine, Vezelay (Languedoc), France
Cathedral, Salamanca, Spain

Gothic
(Twelfth to fifteenth centuries, diagonally ribbed vaulting and flying
buttresses; textbook examples are Cathedral of Chartres, France,
and Notre Dame in Paris; other countries had ethnic variations.)
Duomo, Milan, Italy
Cathedral, Burgos, Spain
St. Stephens Cathedral, Vienna
Cathedral, Cologne, Germany
Cathedral, Antwerp, Belgium
Salisbury Cathedral, England

Renaissance
(Fifteenth and sixteenth centuries, incorporated elements of Greek
and Roman architecture into new forms.)
St. Peter's, Rome
Palazzo Vendramin, Venice
Pazzi Chapel, Florence
Chambord, Loire Valley, France
El Escorial, Spain
Antwerp Town Hall, The Netherlands
Heidelberg Castle, Germany

French Classical
(Seventeenth century)
Versailles, France

Baroque
(Seventeenth and eighteenth centuries, florid)
Trevi Fountain, Rome
St. Agnese Cathedral, Rome
Plaza Mayor, Salamanca, Spain
Belvedere Palace, Vienna, Austria

Neo-classical
(Late 18th and early 19th centuries)
Palais Royal, Paris
Prado, Madrid
Hyde Park Corner Arch, London
Brandenburger Tor, Berlin

DOING YOUR HOMEWORK. The best advice comes from Post-trip
questionnaires sent to us by travelers upon their return.
"Read while still in U.S. on what you want to see. A lot of time is
wasted going to places of little interest--using purely the tourist office information." Philip Jones
What would you have done differently? "Not much except not be
worried about things. We went with a very sketchy itinerary--open for much
change. I'd do the same again. I like to feel free to take whatever oppor-
tunities come up. Before I came to Europe I didn't know what to expect--now
I wouldn't worry about anything--everything came off well--people everywhere were unbelievably friendly and helpful--many offers by families asking
us if we'd like to stay for dinner and the night. People were great. Only
thing I might change is to have done more reading on more places first.
To know more what I wanted to see and where. It's a little late to read this
when you get to the city. Much more enjoyable to know a little about the
places you go and what they have to offer." Leslie Carter
"We recommend to learn a little history about the places and sights
you plan to see beforehand. To have a better understanding leads to a fuller
and more enjoyable trip." What would you have done differently? "We
would have tried to learn a foreign language(s) so that we could communicate
with others better. We would have researched areas better so we could have
understood their history and/or significance." Also, "If a person goes to
Europe wanting to see a lot of cities, he should be prepared to deal with
frantic paces, crowds, and higher prices among other things." Mr. and Mrs.
Robert Cooper
"What we would have done differently is another question. We would
have spent about twice as long. I didn't expect to like Spain as much as I did
and could have easily spent a month exploring it. We also would have liked
to have seen more of Sicily. I had wanted to go to Morocco, but as we were
running out of time and had not gone to Paris or London by that time, we had
to omit it." Also, "Our favorite city was London because of all the
museums and other things to see there and because of the good transportation
system. The next time we go, our daughter will be older and we'll take in
some of the plays. Paris and Florence are very close runners-up for me
because of the art found there and the beauty of Paris itself. I liked Venice
a lot, also, and thought it had a very romantic atmosphere. My husband
liked Munich and Paris just a little less than London. He was very interested
in the Deutsches Museum (science) found in Munich. Cathy liked the beach
and amusement park near Camping Badalona-Playa near Barcelona and also
any city that had pretty flower gardens, natural history museums, and wide
plazas with lots of pigeons to chase." Linda Clark

SOURCES OF INFORMATION. The library, national tourist offices, U.S.
representatives of the European railroads and bookstores all offer material
to help plan your trip.

Public Library. First off, visit the library and hunt up the non-fiction section starting at Dewey #914. Here is where the general travel books about Europe begin. The first books cover the entire European continent, and then starting with 914.2, books are exclusively about one or another European country or city. Listed are Dewey call numbers. (Some libraries use Library of Congress numbers.)

914.	General travel books about Europe
914.2	Britain, Ireland
914.3	Germany, Netherlands, Belgium, Luxembourg
914.4	France
914.5	Italy
914.6	Spain, Portugal
914.7	U.S.S.R.
914.8	Scandinavia
914.9	Other countries

Maps for individual cities and countries are usually kept in a pamphlet file. Travel books with the emphasis on art and architecture are found in the art section in 700's.

National Tourist Offices. The government of each country maintains one or more tourist offices in the U.S. and Canada to encourage people to visit its country. They are literally a goldmine of free material. After you have an idea about where you want to go, send off a postcard to the respective tourist office requesting specific information. There is no charge for material, and probably each office has at least a hundred different brochures and maps on various subjects and cities. After writing a tourist office, you will receive gorgeous full-color leaflets extolling the photogenic wonders of the respective country. More important are the free country and city maps, list of campgrounds, and railroad schedules. These should be specifically requested along with anything else you might be interested in such as hiking, children's sightseeing attractions, food, wine, etc.

Austrian State Tourist Dept.
545 Fifth Avenue
New York, N.Y. 10017

200 E. Randolph
Chicago, Illinois 60601

3440 Wilshire Blvd. #515
Los Angeles, Ca 90010

1007 N.W. 24th Avenue
Portland, Oregon 97210

Belgian National Tourist Office
745 Fifth Avenue
New York, N. Y. 10022

Bulgarian Tourist Office
50 East 42nd Street
New York, N. Y. 10017

British Tourist Authority
680 Fifth Avenue
New York, N.Y. 10022

John Hancock Center, Suite #2450
875 North Michigan Avenue
Chicago, Illinois 60611

612 South Flower Street
Los Angeles, Ca 90017

Cedok-Czechoslovak Travel Bureau
10 East 40th Street
New York, N. Y. 10016

Danish National Tourist Board
75 Rockefeller Plaza
New York, N.Y. 10019

3440 Wilshire Blvd.
Los Angeles, CA 90010

Finnish National Tourist Office
75 Rockefeller Plaza
New York, N. Y. 10019

French Government Tourist Office
610 Fifth Avenue
New York, N. Y. 10020

9401 Wilshire Blvd.
Beverly Hills, CA 90212

645 North Michigan Avenue, #430
Chicago, IL 60611

German National Tourist Office
630 Fifth Avenue
New York, N. Y. 10020

104 South Michigan Avenue
Chicago, IL 60603

700 S. Flower Street, #1714
Los Angeles, CA 90017

Greek National Tourist Organization
Olympic Tower
645 Fifth Avenue
New York, N. Y. 10022

168 North Michigan Avenue
Chicago, IL 60601

611 West Sixth Street
Los Angeles, CA 90017

Embassy of the Hungarian People's
Republic
3910 Shoemaker Street Northwest
Washington D. C. 20008

Irish Tourist Board
590 Fifth Avenue
New York, N. Y. 10036

230 North Michigan Avenue
Chicago, IL 60611

360 Post Street, #801
San Francisco, CA 94108

Italian Government Travel Office
630 Fifth Avenue
New York, N. Y. 10020

500 North Michigan Avenue
Chicago, IL 60611

360 Post Street, Suite 801
San Francisco, CA 94108

360 Post Street, Suite 801
San Francisco, CA 94108

Netherlands National Tourist Office
576 Fifth Avenue
New York, N. Y. 10036

681 Market Street
San Francisco, CA 94105

Norwegian National Tourist Office
75 Rockefeller Plaza
New York, N. Y. 10019

Polish National Tourist Office
500 Fifth Avenue
New York, N. Y. 10110

Portuguese National Tourist Office
548 Fifth Avenue
New York, N. Y. 10036

Spanish National Tourist Office
665 Fifth Avenue
New York, N. Y. 10022

845 North Michigan Avenue
Chicago, IL 60611

I Hallidie Plaza
San Francisco, CA 94102

Swedish National Tourist Office
75 Rockefeller Plaza
New York, N. Y. 10019

Swiss National Tourist Office
608 Fifth Avenue
New York, N. Y. 10020

104 South Michigan Avenue
Chicago, IL 60603

250 Stockton Street
San Francisco, CA 94108

Turkish Tourism Office
821 United Nations Plaza
New York, N. Y. 10017

Yugoslav State Tourist Office
630 Fifth Avenue
New York, N. Y. 10022

Europe<u>an Railroad Offices.</u> Be sure to write to one of the offices
below to obtain the very good free booklet "Eurail," which lists all Trans
Europ Express train schedules and international train schedules. There are
also some schedules for trains within each country. Every person who plans
to go by train should get this schedule, which is valid for the summer season
from May 28th until September 30th. The Eurailpass and Eurail Youthpass
can be ordered from these offices as well as special single country passes
(see under "trains" in the respective country for a listing). The German
Federal Railroad office also sells the Austria Ticket and Finnrailpass. All
offices listed sell the Eurailpass, Eurail Youthpass, and Eurail Ticket for
individuals and groups. Each office has brochures about the special train
passes offered in its country.

BELGIUM
Belgian National Railroads
720 Fifth Avenue
New York, N. Y. 10019
(212) 582-1750

FRANCE
French National Railroads
610 Fifth Avenue
New York, N. Y. 10020
(212) 582-2110

2121 Ponce de Leon Blvd.
Coral Gables, Fla. 33134
(305) 445-8648

11 East Adams Street
Chicago, Ill. 60603
(312) 427-8691

9465 Wilshire Blvd.
Beverly Hills, Calif. 90212
(213) 274-6934

360 Post Street on Union Square
San Francisco, Calif. 94108
(415) 982-1993

1500 Stanley Street
Montreal H3A 1R3, P. Q., Canada
(514) 288-8255

GERMANY
German Federal Railroad
630 Fifth Avenue, Suite 1418
New York, N. Y. 10020
(212) 977-9300

45 Richmond Street West, Suite 706
Toronto M5H 1Z2, Ont., Canada
(416) 364-2214

1121 Walker Street
Houston, Texas 77002
(713) 224-8781

GREAT BRITAIN
Britrail Travel International Inc.
270 Madison Avenue
New York, N. Y. 10016
(212) 725-7700

510 West Sixth Street
Los Angeles, Calif. 90014
(213) 626-5104

333 North Michigan Avenue
Chicago, Ill. 60601
(312) 263-1910

55 Eglinton Avenue East
Toronto M4P 1G8, Ont., Canada
(416) 486-8766

409 Granville Street
Vancouver V6C 1T2, B. C., Canada
(604) 683-6896

ITALY
Italian State Railways
500 Fifth Avenue
New York, N. Y. 10036
(212) 354-9783

333 North Michigan Avenue
Chicago, Ill. 60601
(312) 332-5334

5670 Wilshire Blvd., Suite 2025
Los Angeles, Calif. 90036
(213) 938-2921

323 Geary Street
San Francisco, Calif. 94102
(415) 362-3559

2055 Peel Street, Suite 102
Montreal 110, H3A 1V4,
P. Q., Canada
(514) 845-9101

111 Richmond Street West,
Suite 419
Toronto M5H 2G4, Ont., Canada
(416) 364-4724

40 West Fourth Street, Suite 1313
Dayton, Ohio 45402
(513) 222-0909

NETHERLANDS
Netherlands Railways
576 Fifth Avenue
New York, N. Y. 10036
(212) 245-5320

681 Market Street, Suite 941
San Francisco, Calif. 94105
(415) 781-3387

Royal Trust Tower, Suite 3310
P. O. Box 311
Toronto Dominion Center
Toronto M5K 1K2, Ont., Canada
(416) 364-5339

SWITZERLAND
Swiss Federal Railways
The Swiss Center
608 Fifth Avenue
New York, N. Y. 10020
(212) 757-5944

<u>Thomas Cook International Timetable.</u> Each country's railroad
publishes a book(s) of local and Europe-wide train schedules that is sold at
train information offices or magazine kiosks in train stations abroad. Each
costs about $3. 00. Additionally, most railroads offer free schedules for
individual runs which are available from train information or racks. The
traveler can get all the schedule information he needs without paying anything, but there is one good all-encompassing source which you might consider buying. This is the THOMAS COOK INTERNATIONAL TIMETABLE
which is 9-1/2"x 6-1/4"x 3/4", weighs 15 ounces, contains 536 pages and
costs $15. 95 (1982) or $16. 95 (1983), which includes postage and handling,
from Forsyth Travel Libary, Dept. CET, Box 2975, Shawnee Mission,
Kansas 66201
        This timetable is published in London on the first day of each month.
The June, July, August and September issues contain the Continental summer train schedules. The issues from October to May contain winter
schedules. The issues from February to May contain an advance European

summer service supplement to enable users of the timetable to plan summer itineraries before the complete summer timetable is published. The April and May issues contain winter schedules adjusted to daylight savings time in Europe from the first weekend in April. The May issue also contains summer services in Britain. Each issue contains 800 tables of rail schedules in the 24-hour clock over every main line railway and grouped according to country, a separate section listing all TEE trains, a separate section listing all express international routes, rail maps for each country with schedule number indicated on the route for quick reference, schedules for passenger ferries on the Rhine, Danube, Gota Canal and Swiss and Italian lakes, ferry schedules for all crossings in Europe including Stockholm to Finland, Brindisi to Greece, and Britain, Ireland, Scandinavia and throughout the Mediterranean, cross-channel hovercraft services with connections to and from London and Paris, train services between European cities and their international airports, list of geographical names with corresponding English lnaguage names, list of principal towns not served by rail and their nearest rail gateway, comparative international times in Europe with dates of daylight saving time where adopted, list of Thomas Cook offices, an index listing European towns and page number of rail schedule, list of holidays for each country, some schedules for Swiss buses and trains operated by private companies, small maps showing the train stations within a city when there is more than one (for selected cities), and an explanation of symbols used in the schedules. The timetable does not include schedules for all of the small rail routes such as those taken to some of the chateaux of the Loire, those on the Pelopponnese in Greece, and the line to Paestum in Italy. It does not include schedules for local trains (commuter trains) out of large cities. Not all rail lines are indicated on its rail maps. It does not give prices. But, all in all, it can be a very valuable aid in planning your trip, and in having up-to-date train schedules at your fingertips while traveling.

Forsyth Travel Library. A good organization to know about, the Forsyth Travel Library handles travel books, maps and aids exclusively and has a whole warehouse full of them from which it fills mail-orders on the same day the order is received! It carries all Michelin guides and maps, Nagel Encyclopedia Guides, and city and area maps by Falk, Hallwag and Kummerley+Frey, among others. Forsyth Travel Library is also the sole agent for the importation of the Thomas Cook International Timetable which is air-freighted to them upon its publication on the first of each month. Send 25¢ in coin or a stamped self-addressed legal size envelope for a complete listing and description of their travel guides and maps. The address is Forsyth Travel Library, Dept. CET, P.O. Box 2975, Shawnee Mission, Kansas 66201. (They also carry the book you are reading.) Their new mail-order phone number is (913) 384-0496 and books can be charged to your bankcard.

Travel Guides. For language help, we prefer the Berlitz "Pocket Dictionary Plus Menu Reader" because it contains the phonetic pronunciation of foreign words. They cost $1.95 in the U.S. and 50 pence in Britain, and are published in Lausanne, Switzerland for each of the European languages. (Note: this is not the Berlitz phrase guide but the dictionary.)

For sightseeing, we prefer the Michelin series of tall slender green guides published by the French Michelin Tire Company. The guides cover museums, monuments, architecture, natural formations, viewpoints, history, art, food and wines, and include maps of the area and towns and suggested itineraries. Cities and attractions are rated from 0 to 3 stars according to importance. The guides' only deficiency is their lack of coverage of 20th century architecture and art. These guides come in an English language edition for Switzerland, West Germany, Italy, Austria and Spain, and for the cities of London and Paris. Separate guides are issued for each region in France. Those with English editions are Brittany, Chateaux of the Loire, Dordogne, French Riviera and Normandy. These guides retail in the U.S. at $7.95 each, but can be bought in France and throughout Europe at department stores, American Express offices, museum shops, etc. for at least 40% less than their U.S. price. Then each can be mailed home from Europe under the cheap "book rate."

For motorists, Michelin red guides take many of the wrinkles out of touring. These guidebooks list and rate restaurants and hotels, and most importantly, contain city, town and regional maps. They are available for France, Germany, Great Britain & Ireland, Italy, Spain & Portugal, and Benelux (Belgium, Netherlands and Luxembourg) in hardback only and retail from $9.95 to $11.95 here or about 40% less in Europe. Issued only for France, the Michelin, "Camping Caravanning en France," lists and rates campgrounds, indicates facilities and prices, and best of all, includes maps locating the campgrounds for many cities and towns. This costs $5.95 in the U.S. or about 40% less in France. Michelin also issues a series of maps, countrywide and smaller scale area ones which are indispensable to the motorist and cost from $1.95-2.95 here and much less in Europe. Rail lines and train stations are located on their regional maps. For orders of 25 items or more, the Michelin importer in the U.S. grants a 20% discount plus postage. Write to them at Michelin Guides and Maps, P. O. Box 5022, New Hyde Park, N.Y., N.Y. 11040 for a list of guides and maps.

Camping guidebooks are written with the car-camper in mind and are not worth carrying along for the backpacker with a railpass. "Europa Camping and Caravanning" has been published annually for many years and is reliable. The German publication lists campsites and motels and provides an English translation of the basic text. We carried along the Rand McNally "European Campgrounds and Trailer Parks" guide when we traveled by car but found its directions inadequate.

For hikers, there are three small volumes on hiking in the mountains, published by Sierra Club Books, Box 7959, Rincon Annex, San Francisco, Ca 94120. They are "Foot-loose in the Swiss Alps" by Reifsnyder ($7.15), "Hut Hopping in the Austrian Alps" by Reifsnyder ($4.45) and "Huts and Hikes in the Dolomites" by Rudner ($4.45). More recently written is 100 Hikes in the Alps by Ira Spring and Harvey Edwards, $7.95 from the publisher: The Mountaineers, 719 Pine Street, Seattle, WA 98101. The book contains maps and directions for 100 hikes from easy to difficult.

The European Ways of Life

UPON ARRIVAL IN EUROPE, proceed inside the terminal where you must wait until the baggage is brought in. If an airline counter is in the area, this is a good time to take care of reconfirming your return flight. Once you are in possession of your backpack, proceed to the customs line marked "nothing to declare." The first thing you do after clearing customs is locate the tourist information office and ask for a map of the city and public transportation system, sightseeing information and other material, and verify directions to the campground. If you didn't bring along some of the country's currency, then find the airport bank office and change some money.

CURRENCY CONVERSION

"Change" is the French word for exchanging one country's money for the kind another country uses. On a sign the word "change" is usually followed by its Spanish equivalent "cambio" and the German "wechsel." Whenever those words or "bureau de change," "sportello cambio," "la oficina de cambio," or "wechselschalter" appear, you are notified that the establishment will cash travelers checks and change dollars into a foreign currency. The rate of exchange is how much foreign currency you get for one U.S. dollar before an exchange fee, if any, is deducted. There is both a free market rate that fluctuates daily according to supply and demand, and an official rate that is government set and held. However some governments float, within set limits, the official rate so it too responds to fluctuations in the money market.

You can shop around for exchange rates which usually vary from bank to bank within a country. Hotels, shops and restaurants will also change money but always give a much lower rate than a bank. The currency exchange policy at American Express offices in Europe is "there is a cost for this service which is included in the rate of exchange you receive. In some countries there are also government or banking association imposed taxes or handling charges." Usually a flat fee of about 50¢ per transaction is deducted before the clerk hands you the money so you try to change money infrequently. Sometimes a fee is avoided by changing travelers checks at correspondent banks abroad of the issuing company. The exchange rate is listed on the large readerboard on the wall of exchange offices. The exchange clerk in an American Express office or branch bank office in a train station usually speaks English so you can ask about a fee. A passport is required to cash a travelers check. Exchange only the amount that you expect to need for any one country up to the amount you feel comfortable in carrying. When the clerk changes the travelers check into large bills, hand them back and ask for smaller ones as money is spent in fairly small amounts with a meal being about the largest outgo at any one time. To simplify keeping track of your money and avoid being shortchanged (rare) when spending it, be sure to get small bills when cashing a travelers check. If you have money left over from a country, save it to exchange when you cash a travelers check. Some exchange offices will change both bills and coins--others won't bother with small change under 25¢ or will fail to convert it. Try to spend nickel and dime equivalents before leaving the country.

The thoughtful traveler who respects his money will do these things: (1) Learn the value of the currency. Know the bill that is equivalent to our dollar. Know the coin that is worth about 25¢. (2) Always pay for a purchase with the bill or coin that allows the smallest amount of change to be given. Pay in exact change when possible. (3) Count your change before leaving the counter or vendor. If there is a discrepancy, state it immediately. You will receive either an explanation or the remainder of the change. If you don't follow these rules, there will be some occasion in your traveling life when you will wonder if you were shortchanged even though you probably weren't.

As an emergency safeguard, tuck one travelers check somewhere deep in your pack so all your money and travelers checks won't be together. To obtain a refund for lost travelers checks, apply to the correspondent bank of the issuing company. The procedure for American Express travelers checks is "on weekdays, you can get a full refund by going to the nearest office of American Express Company, its subsidiaries or representatives. On weekends and holidays, in key travel areas you can get an Emergency Refund. Contact Avis Rent A Car for the address of its nearest office where you can get up to $100 to tide you over until the next business day."

If you need more money than what you've brought along, remember that you can pay for a purchase being mailed to your home with a personal check because the store can hold the merchandise until the check clears. Otherwise consider check cashing privileges of credit cards. American Express, Visa, Pan American and TWA cards entitle the holder to a certain amount for a fee immediately from a European office. A visa card can be used at any bank with a VISA sign on it for the amount of your credit line, but you are restricted to $500 or less at any one transaction. Usual set-up charges and interest rate apply. However the brochure states "the exchange rate utilized by Visa banks to convert from a foreign currency to U.S. dollars (the interbank bid rate plus a margin of up to 1/4 of 1%) usually affords cardholders a more favorable exchange rate than otherwise available." The rate is that in effect when the transaction is processed by the clearing bank. The following banks give cash advances: Belgium, Bank of America; Denmark, Handelsbanken; Finland, Luottokunta-Kreditlaget at Heikkilantie 10, Helsinki; France, Banque Nationale de Paris, Credit Commercial de France, Credit Industriel et Commercial, Credit Lyonnais, Credit du Nord, Societe Generale and Carte Bleue affiliated banks, Bank of America, Bankers Trust Company, Banque Canadienne Nationale; Greece, Commercial Bank of Greece, Bank of America; Italy, Banca d'America e d'Italia and affiliated banks, Bankers Trust Company; Norway, Bergen Bank A/S, Christiania Bank og Kreditkasse, Den norske Creditbank; Portugal, Banco Pinto and Sotto Mayor; Spain, Banco de Bilbao, Banco del Comercio, Banco Industrial de Bilbao; Sweden, Conto Foretagen (Linnegatan 48A, Stockholm); Switzerland, Corner Banca S. A., Bank of America; The Netherlands, Bank of America; United Kingdom, Barclays Bank Ltd., Bank of America, Bank of Credit and Commerce, Bankers Trust Company, First National Bank of Chicago, Rainier National Bank, Wells Fargo Bank; West Germany, Bankhaus Centrale Credit, Bank of America; Andorra, Banc Internacional; Austria, Bank of America, Luxembourg, Bank of America.

Cashing a personal check in Europe takes about 10 days because the bank must contact your stateside bank before it will pay you. Things can be speeded up if you're willing to pay a cable charge of about $10. Or you can write directly to your hometown bank, enclosing the account number, and ask that a specified sum be sent to you care of an affiliate bank in the city in Europe which you specify. Be sure to include a European address for yourself so your bank can notify you of the name and address of the bank to which they sent the money.

Funds can be received in currency or travelers checks from an American Express Company office in Europe through its foreign remittance service. This service is available only from regular company offices with foreign exchange desks, not travel representative offices. The simplest way is to write home and ask that arrangements be made with the local American Express office for money to be sent in care of a designated American Express office in Europe. Choose an office in a capital city--all are company offices--which you plan to visit in ten days to two weeks to allow sufficient time for money to arrive. Allow three weeks for Spain. Specify if you want travelers checks or currency. The fee is about $2.25 plus travelers check fee if applicable. To get money faster, money can be cabled through American Express in three days for about $10. Another way is for someone at home to mail you an American Express Money Order, or obtain an emergency cash transfer on his credit card for you.

LE CAMPING

The arbiters of the French language, that group of elite Frenchmen who are official guardians of the virginity of "le francais," wish the phrase "le camping" would disappear. It is not (quelle horreur!) pure French but to them another incidence of that creeping disease termed "franglais." But the American abroad is grateful that the word "camping" remains recognizable regardless of language. The international symbol to denote a campground is the outline of a tent. Sometimes the distance to the campground is indicated in meters. These signs will lead you to an immense variety of campgrounds in Europe. Many have been

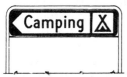

placed in breathtaking surroundings and command a view of spectacular mountains, the bright lights of a city, or a river, sea or lake. In Oslo, Ekeberg Campground spreads on a hillside overlooking downtown Oslo and in Paris, the campground nestles beside the Seine River adjacent to the lovely Bois de Boulogne park. In the Loire Valley, the chateau region of France, campers look up from their island campground, L'Ile d'Or, towards floodlit Amboise Castle across the river.

Upon arrival at a campground, first go into the office to register. The attendant will ask for your passport and record your name and address as required by law regardless of where you stay, and return your passport to you. Sometimes the clerk will keep your passport and fill out the government forms in his slow period so remember to retrieve it before going into town. Sometimes you will be asked to complete the registration form. Below is an example of a camp registration form used in Blere, France.

FICHE DE VOYAGEUR	VILLE DE BLÉRÉ ——— Camping Municipal	Nombre d'enfants de moins de 15 ans accompagnant le chef de famille : _____ *Accompanying children under 15* *Zahl der Kinder unter 15 Jahren die den Familienvorstand begleiten*
NOM : _____ *Name in capital letters* (écrire en majuscules) *Name (in Druckschrift)* **Nom de jeune fille :** _____ *Maiden name* *Madchen Name* **Prénoms :** _____ *Christian names* *Vorname* **Né le :** _____ à _____ *Date and place of birth* *Geburtsort - Datum* **Département** (ou Pays pour l'étranger) : _____ *Country* *Für Auslander Angabe des Geburtslandes* **Profession :** _____ *Occupation* *Beruf* **Domicile habituel :** _____ *Permanent address* *Gewohnlicher Wohnort* **NATIONALITÉ :** *Nationality* *Nationalitat* T. S. V. P. (Please turn over - Bitte wenden)		**PIÈCE D'IDENTITÉ PRODUITE** Nature : _____ ———— Pour les étrangers seulement ———— *(For aliens only)* - *(Nur für Auslander)* **CARTE D'IDENTITÉ OU PASSEPORT** CERTIFICATE OF IDENTITY OR PASSPORT *(cross out word not available)* AUSWEIS - PASS N° _____ **délivré le :** _____ *Issued on - Ausgestellt den* à _____ **par** _____ *at* *by* *in* *durch* **Date d'entrée en France :** _____ *Date of arrival in France* *Datum der Einreise in Frankreich* _____ **le** _____ Signature *Unterschrift*

Usually you pay upon arrival so if you don't know how long you'll be staying, pay for one night and then pay again the next day if staying over. Sometimes there is a flat camping fee per tent or per adult, but most often the daily camping fee is the sum total of small separate charges for each adult, child, tent, car, van, motorcycle, trailer and hook-up. In a few camps a small tent is charged less than a large one. Sometimes a small visitor's tax is charged. Camp fees range from about 50¢ to as much as $5.00 for two persons with a tent but the average is about $3-$5 for two. The registration clerk will give you a receipt and a tag to hang on your tent to show that you've paid. The tag is turned back into the office when you leave.

Tent camping sites are rarely assigned. In fact individual tent sites are usually not marked and you are free to choose your spot in the camping area which is usually flat and grassy with bushes, trees and narrow roads. No tables are provided nor are open fires permitted. The nearby building you see is most likely the restrooms and shower rooms. Commonly, the sinks have only cold water and sometimes a charge is made for a hot water shower and then often it is equipped with a coin operated meter which gives you about two to five minutes of hot water for about 25-50¢. Electrical outlets and mirrors are provided in the washbasin area with the usual voltage of the country. If uncertain how your razor will react, first switch it onto the high voltage setting and plug it in. If it runs slowly, switch on low voltage and try again. This avoids burning out the motor. Some campgrounds will have a separate room for washing dishes and another room for laundry with sinks and a washing machine and possibly a dryer. Some camps have a day room for relaxation and other facilities might include a childrens' playground, hotplates for cooking (free or small charge), refrigerator, swimming pool or boat rentals. Stamps are sold at the office which usually has an outgoing box for mail. A food store may be available where fresh bread, pastry, rolls, milk, butter, cheese, margarine, cooking oil, eggs, yoghurt, coffee and canned goods may be bought. Some camping supplies may be sold, the most useful being stove fuel. During off-season, the store may be closed even though the camp remains open. Many camps have some sort of a snack bar and some even a restaurant. Before leaving for the day, investigate take-out food possibilities for your evening meal. Some offer rotisseried chicken but the order must be placed in the morning.

European campgrounds are classified both by their national government and by organizations issuing campground guides. A government will classify its country's campgrounds to maintain standards and set fees. Campgrounds with more facilities are allowed to charge more. Guidebook compilers rate campgrounds according to criteria important to vacationing Europeans. Since most Europeans go to the beach and stay put for several weeks, guidebooks focus on auxiliary facilities. In effect these two systems give similar ratings. Brochures issued by the national tourist offices give the government rating which is your clue to the prices charged. Highest category may be termed deluxe or three stars and these campgrounds may have extensive facilities making them resemble a small shopping center. Prices get progressively lower and facilities fewer with lower categories, but even the lowest category camp will have a clean grassy area, running water and some form of toilet. Virtually all campgrounds are enclosed by a fence. We advise ignoring the ratings and choosing a camp by its convenience to the train station and prices charged.

Most campgrounds have rules which you would pretty much expect like don't pick the flowers and shrubs, turn off the lights, no loud noise after 10 pm and don't litter. However a few are unexpected like don't hang your laundry from the tent lines but use the drying area provided and if you arrive after 11 pm you must leave your car outside the camp and walk in. The most important thing to remember is to CAMP from the very first day--you'll be glad you did!

READERS SUGGESTIONS   What would you have left out? "Left out all pensions." Janet Dutton, Overland Park, Kansas. "If campground operator claims he is full--argue for awhile, they usually give in to a person with backpack while turning cars away." Philip Jones, West Chester, Pa. "Camp whenever possible. We found that it is very easy to become accustomed to the comfort of hotels. The more hotels you stay in the faster the money goes." Mr. and Mrs. Robert Cooper, Batavia, Illinois.

48

EUROPEAN TRAINS

In sleek modern coaches of the marvelous European railway network, you will glide from one city center to another in less time than you could fly or drive. The wonder is that this same network finds its way into the most idyllic out-of-the-way hamlet through the most breathtaking scenery in every country in Europe. The railway is the dominant mode of transportation on the continent and is well organized and easy to use.

THE STATION The European train station is an institution in itself. The main station is most always downtown and the main shopping street often begins at its entrance. The bus terminal is usally across the street or within a block or two. The station is always a bustling place with folks coming and going at all hours and some large stations resemble an abbreviated shopping mall. Every capital city station offers multiple services which stay open quite late. You may find (1),several eating places ranging from restaurant service to buffet and snack bar; (2) money exchange office with English-speaking personnel; (3) train information office for obtaining information on train schedules, free abridged timetables of trains departing from that city and sometimes seat reservations; (4) ticket windows for buying tickets and sometimes for obtaining seat reservations; (5) sometimes a special window or office solely for seat reservations; (6) tourist information office; (7) hotel reservations counter where assistant will reserve a room for a fee; (8) waiting rooms, usually one each for first and second class; (9) temporary luggage storage facilities with attendant; (10) coin-operated lockers for temporary luggage storage; (11) restrooms; (12) newstand and candy counter; and (13) big readerboard listing train arrivals and departures by track number.

Upon arrival in a city or town, first seek out the tourist information office for a free map of the city and other material and to verify directions to the campground. Remember to ask specifically for everything you want. Don't discuss a general subject and assume the clerk will volunteer any free maps and literature that may be helpful. Some do but many don't. Ask "have you a map of the city?" and then check to make certain it's a detailed street map not one that just shows main streets. If it's the latter, ask for a more detailed map and then ask for a map which shows bus and tram routes as these are usually on a separate map. Among items these offices stock (all free) are road maps of the country, abridged railway schedules, lists of campgrounds, restaurants, museums, suggested excursions around the city and what's happening in that city for that month or week. They also will likely have a brochure on such exotica as gliding, wine tasting, sailing and salt mine tours and a capital city office will generally have a brochure for each other town or region in that country. Pick them up now so you can read them on the train on your way there.

Most stations have two kinds of temporary luggage storage facilities. First, rows of coin-operated lockers in two sizes are scattered throughout the station. Luggage can be left for 24 hours after which it will be removed to the attended baggage check office. As the small size costs about 50-60¢ but a backpack usually requires the larger size at about $1.00, it is usually cheaper to check a pack at the attended baggage check which charges on a per piece basis. These places are called "deposito bagagli" in Italian, "gepackverwahrung" in German speaking countries, "depot de bagages" in

France and "la oficina de equipajes" in Spain. The checking service normally is open long hours but closing time is generally posted. Charge is similar to small coin-operated lockers and is based on either a 24-hour period or midnight as the start of a new fee day. Lines sometimes form during the peak demand time of late afternoon.

The train information office ("bureau de renseignements," "auskunfts-buro," "oficina de informacion," "ufficio informazioni") personnel will look up train schedules for you but sometimes there are long lines and it is easier to do it yourself by reading the timetables provided in the station. Sometimes individual timetables for single trains are available and sometimes booklets of the important international trains are given free. Otherwise or in addition, timetables for arrivals and departures for that particular train station are posted within the station. These usually are large sheets of paper hung on the walls. Time are given using the 24-hour clock which is the same as ours up to noon and then becomes 13:00 for 1 pm, 14:00 for 2 pm and so forth until 24:00 midnight. Departures are printed on yellow paper in most countries whereas arrivals are on white. Different train schedules are generally in effect for "working day trains" which run Monday through Saturday and for trains operating on Sundays and holidays. When checking schedules, be sure to note the station from which the train departs. This is given in parenthesis following the name of the city. Most large cities have more than one station and often a train will only stop at one station within a city. The station is indicated in "Cook's Timetable," and the free, "The Best Trains in Europe." This information can also be obtained from train information at the stations and from the conductor on board who also knows track numbers for connecting trains.   It is important to know in advance at what station you want to get off because if the train stops at two stations, you'll want to get off at the "central" (meaning downtown) station, and if the train only stops at a suburban station, you need to know this to get off there as the next stop will be in another town.

To get on board the right train, first consult the large readerboard which is usually suspended from the ceiling or on the wall of every large station. It lists arriving and departing trains and gives the most accurate information as it includes any last minute changes that may have been made. The right half of the board lists departures by kind of train, originating city, destination, time of departure and track number of train. Scan the board until you recognize your train. Make a mental note of track number. Track is "quai" in French, "glies" in German, "spoor, spor and spar" in Dutch, Norwegian and Swedish respectively, "perron" in Danish, "voie" in Flemish (Belgium), "binario" in Italian and "anden" in Spanish. Signs point the way to the tracks. Track number is prominently displayed from a post in front of each track. Walk along beside the coaches of your train and note markings on side of cars. Number "1" means seats are first class. Number "2" designates second class seats. Sometimes a car is half first and half second class and each end is so designated. Yellow markings also indicate first class. Each coach has a removable metal nameplate in a slot on the side of the coach by the door. The first line states the city where the train began its run. The most important intermediate stops are listed on the middle line and final destination is on the bottom line. For example:

ROMA   (or)   ROMA

Firenze - Bologna   Firenze - Bologna

VENEZIA   MILANO

This means the originating point is Rome. Florence and Bologna are largest city stops enroute though stops are likely elsewhere too (look in the schedule for them). Venice is the final destination for the coach with the first nameplate and Milan for the second. What happens in Europe is that coaches destined for different cities may be strung together as the train leaves the city and run together until they must part to reach their final destinations. In the example above, after the train reaches Bologna the coaches going to Venice are attached to another engine and each train proceeds on its way. The important thing to remember is that trains can split midway in their journey so you obviously must be in the coach going to your destination. You can usually tell when a train is splitting because it happens in the switching yard and you can feel the coach being pushed or pulled and another engine being connected. Inside each coach by the door is a nameplate bearing the destination city. Always make a mental note to check the destination card for your coach. This is important because you will often board one coach, but continue on to another from inside as you seek a vacant seat. We did this once and ended up in Venice rather than Milan, but at least with a train pass only time was lost. (Had we a ticket, the conductor would have noted our error and sent us to the proper coach.) One final point, when traveling between Puttgarden, Germany and Rodby, Denmark (to or from Copenhagen), the train rolls onto the ferry and then everyone gets off to go upstairs during the crossing. Be sure to make note of where your train coach is because this is where some passengers upon returning have to scramble to find theirs.

RESERVATIONS   In large stations there may be a separate window for seat reservations but often a seat reservation is made at a ticket window or in the train information office. It may be helpful to write down the name of the train you want, date of departure (Europeans write the day BEFORE the month such as 10-6-80 for June 10, 1980) and time of departure using the 24-hour clock. Fee for each reservation is about $1-$1.50 depending upon country. Usually a reservation can also be made at a travel agency for the same fee. When is a reservation necessary? That's a hard one to answer and the suggestions given here should be refined when you get there by talking to others who may have just come from where you're going. In general, second class is more crowded than first and reservations will be needed more often. Trains are less crowded during the week and traveling against holiday traffic (which leaves town on Friday night and Saturday and returns Sunday evening). Trains are usually crowded during the weekend of national holidays. But always there are some people with reservations who are traveling short distances and their seats will be available later. Another approach if there isn't a seat is to find the dining or bar coach and order a beverage.

Trans-Europe Express (TEE) trains are Europe's finest and connect the heart of Europe (France, Germany, Switzerland, Italy, Belgium and The Netherlands) during daytime runs. Almost all are air-conditioned and Common Market businessmen find them faster and more certain than an airplane and the downtown terminal more convenient. TEE is a supplement-fare train for normal-paying passengers--that is the businessman must pay

the price of a first class ticket plus a supplement. Eurailpass includes TEE
trains at no extra cost and these should be first choice, but the usual TEE
departs between 7 and 9 am so an alarm clock may be necessary. Is a
reservation necessary? The policy stated on the "Eurail Map" folder given
with the railpasses is "except for sleepers or couchettes and on some
TEEs or name trains, no reservation is required to board trains." Cook's
timetable states the policy as "prior reservation is obligatory for travel by
most TEE trains, but the train conductor can allocate places if accommodation is still available." But in Cook's timetable listings, the notation "reservation required" (R) is noted for all TEE trains and this symbol should be
evaluated in light of the first statement. For instance, Cook's timetable
#268 for TEE L'Arbalete between Basle and Zurich has the "reservation re-
quired" symbol on it, but the Swiss timetable states that for local travel
within Switzerland a reservation cannot be made but the TEE train can be
used if you can find a seat. In our experience on TEE trains throughout
Europe, if you arrive without a reservation and can find an unreserved seat
or "no show" then you're on. A reservation card will be tucked into the
pocket on the seat or inserted into the holder on the compartment door if the
seat is reserved. The reservation card notes the cities between which the
person is traveling so you can occupy that seat until the train arrives at the
city indicated or after the person with the reservation gets off. A reservation is less likely to be needed in the heart of Europe traveling between the
German and Swiss cities on the Rhine, Amsterdam, Brussels and Paris
because several TEE trains ply these routes.

International Express Trains make a continuous journey through
several countries and always carry both first and second class. They stop
at main cities only. These trains used to be filled by northern Europeans
coming or going from southern European vacations but nowadays most of
them fly so these trains are generally used for somewhat shorter journeys
by Europeans and Americans. Reservations might be needed for second
class on these trains perhaps in Scandinavia, Italy and Austria. Most
countries have fast inter-city trains that provide good rail connections among
the most important cities within a country. Reservations are not needed on
these trains but occasionally the country demands it as for certain trains in
Denmark and Sweden. Reservations are never needed for slower trains that
stop at most towns nor for suburban commuter trains of large cities. We
advise reservations on the Talgo, TER and ELT in Spain and on the train you
take to make ferry connections in Brindisi, Italy and for the ferry to Greece.

Throughout Europe lines at the reservation window are shortest Monday through Thursday mornings. Avoid noontime, immediately after work
and Friday afternoon through Sunday night. You can register your preference
for a smoking or non-smoking compartment and for the window seat which
has a small table between the two people next to it. On Talgo and some TEE
trains having airplane type seating rather than the usual compartments of
6 persons in first and 8 in second, both window seat and side of aisle can be
reserved. Seat reservations can be made in the U.S. up to two months in
advance from the European railroads for $1.50 plus $1.00 telex charge.

ABOARD THE TRAIN Restrooms are located at both ends of each railroad
car and they are uni-sex. You can easily tell if someone is in there because

as the latch is locked from inside a sign appears outside just above the handle signed "ocupado" or similar. Sometimes this notice is conveyed by a space of red color on the lock, and occasionally a neon sign lights above the door to signal the availability of the restroom. Water in restrooms is never safe to drink and this is clearly marked by the word "non-potable." (Be certain to point this out to children.) The water is for hand-washing only. On long overnight runs, toilet paper may run out so a small personal supply is handy. The restroom also contains mirror, shaver outlet and paper towels. There are both smoking and non-smoking compartments on a train and this is indicated by a sign on the door. Seats are adjustable into a reclining position which makes overnight journeys better. During the day, putting ones feet on an unoccupied seat across from you is considered rather appalling manners by a European. If you would like to open the window, it's polite to ask the others before doing so. If you are a smoker in a non-smoking compartment, merely step outside into the hallway when you wish to smoke but never do so in a non-smoking compartment. The usual train has double-decker racks above the seats for your luggage. When searching for a vacant seat, it's well to ask at the door of the compartment if the seat is vacant before claiming it.

Most TEE and international express trains have dining facilities, but the price of dinner is so high (about $14) that few Americans use them. However in case you're interested it goes like this. On a train with seating in compartments, the dining captain comes down the corridor taking reservations for first and second sittings in the dining car. On TEE trains with a middle aisle, the meal is served airplane-style except servings are made from a cart and fine china, wine goblets and linen are used for the multi-course meal. The first rule of budget travel on European trains is to bring along something to eat and drink. ALWAYS carry a pint-size or bigger filled water bottle. Try to pick up some fruit, bread, cheese or slices of luncheon meat at your usual cheap source of nourishment before getting to the station. Usual food sold at the station is fruit at an exhobitant per piece price and candy bars. Sometimes a cold boxed lunch can be bought for about $2.50 but we think you are better off assembling your own from the public market or supermarket. Coming aboard empty-handed doesn't mean starvation, but having to pay more than you wish. Snack carts roll up and down aisles on some trains with sandwiches, soft drinks and beer. Larger versions of these carts are on the platform as the train makes five to ten minute station stops and you can buy something from the train window if you have the right kind of money. The timetable indicates how long the train stops at intermediate points and sometimes there is time to dash in to buy something. Just remember to note track number. On returning hop aboard closest car and find your seat from within. Make a standing arrangement with your traveling companions as to procedure to follow if anyone should miss the train. Always, each should carry own train pass, passport and travelers checks.

There are three ways to sleep on trains. (1) Curl up on your seat (seats recline) or stretch across three seats in an empty compartment, (2) reserve a couchette, and (3) get a sleeper. Most campers will make do with the first but I'll explain the others so you don't think you're missing anything. For $7.50,   a couchette can be reserved for either first or second class and consists of a special first or second class car with compartmented seating of three across which converts to sleeping platforms stacked three high at night. Everyone in the compartment agrees on bedtime, converts the seats to beds and then goes to bed with his clothes on as there is no privacy. For border crossings, the customs official wakes you to ask for your passport. Reserving a couchette guarantees that your compartment will be full while merely taking a seat gives you a sporting chance that maybe there will be only two or three of you in the compartment.   A sleeper (Wagon-Lit or Mitropa Car) costs about $18 and gives you a made-up bed in a sleeper car so you can undress, and a porter will take your passport so you can sleep through customs.

When it's time to get off the train, watch out the window for the name of the station as the train is pulling in. You will have a few minutes between seeing the station name and having to get off. Once in the station, find tourist information to ask for a map, verify directions to the campground and ask for any other information.

STATION SIGNS

Train information	Tickets	Seat reservations
Currency exchange	Post office	Public phone
Entrance	Exit	Women's restroom
Restroom	Men's restroom	Car rentals
Drinking water	Don't drink water	Luggage storage
Luggage lockers	Baggage registration	Pick up baggage
Waiting room	Snack bar	Restaurant
Smoking permitted	No smoking	Lost and found

READERS' SUGGESTIONS   "Don't worry about train reservations except in Spain and Scandinavia. We rode numerous 3/4ths empty TEE trains in France, Germany and Belgium." Philip Jones, W. Chester, Pa.   "Second class trains are overcrowded in Italy and Spain. Figure out least crowded time to travel beforehand in these countries. Buy plenty of food and drink to take on the train as food is expensive--a coke can cost over $1 in places." Kathy Carlson, Gardena, California   "A lot of time you can spot the camp from the train window. My wife and I were travelling Chur to St. Moritz, and we were passing through Filisur, and she saw a bunch of tents and cara-

vans. 'Oh, what a lovely place! Let's stop.' We had about five seconds to
get off the train, and it was easy to find our way through the village down to
the camp along the river. And it was a wonderful place. We never did get to
St. Moritz that trip. Filisur? No American has ever heard of Filisur, much
less ever stopped there." Ray R. Rylander, Colorado Springs, Colorado
"Use trains to get away from big cities on day trips, for example Normandy
and Chateau (Loire) region from Paris. It is much less of a hassle than
packing everything up and finding a new campground." Philip Jones, W.
Chester, Pa.

LE SPORT

When driving a car in Europe, the single most important rule to remember is that TRAFFIC COMING FROM THE RIGHT HAS PRIORITY, unless otherwise signed. This means that when two drivers who are each on a non-priority road are about to intersect, the driver coming from the right has "right of way." He can cut in front of the person already on the road to enter it. That's his right, unlike in the U.S. where we look both ways to be sure there is no oncoming traffic. So look to your right when approaching intersections and crossroads and be prepared to yield to the car entering from your right. Europe does not have as many traffic signals as we are used to, so remember that at unsignaled and unsigned normal four-way intersections, you look to the right and stop only if a car is coming. Trust the driver on the left to stop as you go through.

This general rule is not in effect on PRIORITY roads which are usually main highways where the driver already on the road has "right of way." Road maps and signs indicate a priority road. Don't assume that you're on a priority road just because it's wider. Be alert for approaching traffic from the right unless certain you're on a priority road. Now when you want to enter a priority road, don't try to merge onto it depending on the good will of the driver on the priority road to allow you to squeeze in. He won't, so be certain the road is clear before entering.

European cities have one-way streets, traffic signals and pedestrian crosswalks just like at home. What we don't have are circular multi-intersections that can be astounding to the uniniated during rush hour. A multi-intersection (circus or roundabout) is where five to eight side and main streets converge at different points onto a three to five lane width pavement which encircles a fountain or monument. Traffic always moves one way--counter clockwise around the circle. That is, you turn right to enter and turn right again to exit. It's really a very logical device where traffic keeps moving and you get where you are going without resorting to traffic lights. Priority on the right rule is its effective backbone. ALWAYS GIVE WAY TO THE CAR ENTERING ON YOUR RIGHT even though you are already in the roundabout. Keep looking to your right and assume the driver to your left is watching out for you. To say it again, Americans who are used to merging onto freeways and yielding to on-going traffic must remember that they now have the right-of-way when MERGING but must YIELD the right-of-way to the merging car on the right when already in the circular intersection. This is very important--if you see a car with a dented right fender, chances are the driver is an American tourist.

International road signs are used throughout Europe and particularly the triangular signs should be memorized BEFORE arriving. Even so, tape a copy of the road signs inside your car for quick reference. Triangular signs give warning and any sign outlined in red is important. Memorize the "do not enter" sign, a red circle with white horizontal bar across the middle as Europe has many one-way streets. Our interstate highway system is similar to the international highways in Europe which are designated by letter E plus number on a green or black background. For example, E1 extends from Britain to Italy and E5 from Belgium to Turkey. For speed alone, the best roads are freeways, called "autobahn" in Germany, "autostrade" in Italy and "autosnelwegens" in The Netherlands for example. In France, Italy and Spain, these are toll roads where the charge is based on mileage plus engine size. For every freeway, there exists a less crowded secondary road, more scenic but slower. On the highway, headlights are flashed to alert the driver in front that you intend to pass. During daylight, a driver might honk his horn to let you know he is passing. France and Denmark have the three lane highway where the center lane is the passing lane. On some roads the middle lane is used by both directions of traffic while on other roads, signs indicate the direction of traffic which is to use the passing lane. Tolls are collected for some mountain passes and tunnels. Some are railway tunnels where you drive onto a train and are conveyed through the tunnel. Cars are driven directly onto ferries. Scandinavian ferries are cheaper outside of July and August.

Parking is either hard to find or expensive on weekdays downtown in large cities. We recommend leaving the car at camp and taking the bus or tram. Parking regulations vary by city but are usually marked on the street. Parking meters are used, but some French cities use the blue zone system in which a cardboard disc is placed in the window to show when you left. Elsewhere parking may only be allowed on one side of the street and the side changes according to odd or even-numbered days. Gas is called petrol, essence, benzina or benzin at the Shell, Esso, Caltex or other gas station. Top grade is "super" and sold by liter (4 liters equal 1 U.S. gallon approximately) or amount.

U.S. Gallons	Liters
.26	1
.53	2
.79	3
1.06	4
1.32	5
1.58	6
1.85	7
2.11	8
2.38	9
2.64	10
5.28	20
7.93	30
10.57	40
13.21	50
26.42	100

1 Imperial Gallon equals 5 U.S. Quarts

WARNING SIGNS

Dangerous bend   Double bend   Right bend

Cross roads   Intersection w/minor road   Merging traffic   Road narrows   Uneven road   Slippery road

Round-about   Give way   Dangerous descent   Road work   Tunnel   Opening bridge

Level crossing with barrier   Level crossing without barrier   Pedestrians   Children   Two-way traffic   Falling rocks

Traffic signals ahead   Animals   Other dangers   Danger! Train

56

REGULATIVE SIGNS

Road closed | No entry | No right turn

No U-turns | No entry for motorcars | No entry for motorcycles | No entry for all motor vehicles | No entry for bicycles | No entry for pedestrians

No overtaking | End of no overtaking | Maximum load | Axle weight limit | Width limit | Height limit

Maximum speed limit | End of speed limit | End of all restrictions | Halt sign | Customs | No stopping

No parking | Priority to oncoming vehicles | Use of horns prohibited | Direction obligatory | Motorway exit | Priority road | End of priority road

A LOAF OF BREAD
A HUNK OF CHEESE
A JUG OF WINE
AND THE EUROPEAN COW

A last stand for national character is being made in the kitchens of each European nation. Apart from the cross-continent favorite of steak and french fries, the rest of the foods which make up the menu are rooted deep in each nation's history. The tumultuousness of the past has gone a long way in determining current quality of cuisine offered by each country. By and large, the best eating is in areas where life still revolves around the land, and the cooking is not as good in countries most dislocated by industry. The farmhouse tradition of good eating supported by the intense interest of Frenchmen for whom food must rank number one on the gallic hierarchy of pleasures has made France a country to which many go to eat, or rather "dine." What we consider "gourmet" is everyday fare in France. You can eat gourmet cooking at virtually any restaurant in the French countryside (note exception of Paris) and at a great range in price. On a cheaper menu you might be served exquisitely prepared lentils and a small portion of meat as the entree, but the cooking skill will be tops. This also means that eating well does not require dressing up. The variety of cuisine in Europe is exciting and each country offers good eating.

Of course food fashions travel, and the trend is for dishes which have long been European staples to catch the fancy of the American public. U.S. processors develop them for domestic consumption and then parrot them back over to Europe where they are called "those subfoods from America" at the same time that Europe's affluent daughters rush to the supermarket to buy these "chic" snacks and convenience foods. Imitations of America like Wimpy's or Le Drugstore are invariably dissapointing. Most Americans side with the European elders and lust after the chance to eat authentic and try such delights as "coquilles St. Jacques" and original Neapolitan pizza on their homeground. A visit to Naples will give you a chance to compare U.S. frozen pizza, the number two bestseller after orange juice in the frozen food sweepstakes with the original. The subtleness of taste and texture didn't quite make it across the ocean and through the test kitchens. Truly, eating in Europe is a treat!

Food will be your number one expense in Europe assuming your train fare is prepaid. But here is where costs become flexible because a camper has a choice between eating out and eating in. Theoretically one could prepare all his own meals, but this would mean missing out on some of the enjoyment of a European vacation. If possible, we recommend eating one meal a day in a restaurant perhaps in Southern Europe but always only in a cafeteria in Switzerland, Belgium, Holland, Denmark, Germany, Norway and Sweden except for a "special" meal. We suggest starting the day with breakfast at the campground, drawing upon fresh milk and bread from the campground store. We advise making the noon meal the biggest one by taking the "table d'hote" menu at a restaurant in Southern Europe or the "daily special" in cafeterias in Northern Europe. Then make supper a lighter meal by visiting the delicatessen and buying a selection of prepared foods for "le pique-nique," or cook a meal from scratch in the campground. Of course this arrangement can be altered to fit your daily touring needs as well as for savoring more restaurant meals in countries whose cuisine you especially appreciate. Camp cooking will give you a greater variety of foods as well as save money in Northern Europe where inexpensive prepared food is generally limited in variety. In Southern Europe, restaurants are cheaper in smaller towns.

The number one rule for budget eating is to omit soft drinks and canned fruit juices as they are very expensive, and to drink water with cafeteria meals in Northern Europe because beverages are generally about twice the cost from a grocery store, though there are some exceptions. The second rule is to control the American habit of buying ice cream cones which can cost from 50¢ to $1 each. (We found this difficult.) The third rule is to buy food at the public market whenever possible because it is anywhere from a third to a half less than at small shops and at least 25 percent less than in most supermarkets but sometimes supermarket "specials" in Northern Europe are less than the market. The public market is generally called the "open market" in Europe (though sometimes it is covered). Large cities have several markets and the biggest one will be open Monday through Saturday morning at least and sometimes Saturday afternoon. Smaller neighborhood markets may operate only two or three times a week or a street market may be set up and operating at 7 am and be completely gone by 11 am. In a small town the market is usually in the central square by the oldest church and may be open one or two days a week. Upon arrival in a new town, always ask the tourist office where the market is and when it is open. Anything can be bought in small amounts, like two eggs or a handful of olives from the barrel. Paper bags are not given away American-style so remember to bring a shopping bag. Fruits and vegetables are handed to you unwrapped. Food is sold by gram and kilo rather than ounce and pound, except in Britain. One-half kilo (500 grams) is a little over one pound. One hundred grams is a little less than 1/4 pound or about three ounces. One kilo (1000 grams) equals 2.2 pounds. Liquids are sold by liter. One liter is about a quart. One U.S. gallon equals 3-3/4 liters. The British gallon is larger than ours.

For camp cooking, you will need to buy a small one-burner backpack stove or use the hotplates provided at some campgrounds. Sometimes a small charge is made to use a hotplate and not every campground has them. One-burner backpack stoves are widely used in Europe and are fueled by butane, propane, white gas or kerosene. The advantages of butane and propane are their non-spillable cartridge form, lack of odor, relative safety, compactness and clean-burning qualities of emitting less carbon monoxide and other pollutants. Butane is under less pressure than propane and hence the steel cartridge casing can be thinner. Butane will not burn when temperature is less than 20 degrees above zero. White gas and kerosene stoves are messy to use and fuel is not as readily obtainable. All stove fuel is prohibited from airplanes. The French-made Camping Gaz International is the most popular brand of stoves. Different models take either a disposable cartridge or a refillable cylinder. The small disposable cartridge contains 10 ounces of butane gas and burns up to 3-1/2 hours. As the cartridge empties, pressure begins to fall and only low heat is available towards the end. Each cartridge costs about $1-$1.25. Similar equipment is manufactured under the Garcia brand. The bright blue Bluet S 200 one-burner model costs about $13. It operates by placing the fuel cartridge in cartridge holder and screwing stove to top of cartridge. Wheel valve is opened and escaping gas is lighted with a match. (Have match ready when wheel is turned or collected gas might explode while a match is found.) Flame size is regulated by opening and closing the valve. Instruction leaflet in eleven languages is included. Never unscrew upper part of stove while any butane gas remains in the cartridge. Burn up fuel and throw away cartridge before boarding airplane to come home. At some camp stores, gas stations and sporting goods stores, a used cartridge can be turned in for a small discount on a new one. The Lotus is a newer model with low square shape and more stability in its four-bar grill cooking surface. It uses a cylinder fuel cartridge. Cartridges are available in the U.S. too. Swedish stoves Optimus, Primus and Svea burn white gas or kerosene.

A camp meal without cooking can easily be put together by a visit to a delicatessen to select small amounts (say 100 grams worth) of freshly prepared salads, cooked vegetables, meat spread (pate) and perhaps a rotisseried chicken. Many supermarkets have wonderfully large delicatessen sections where a hot cooked chicken comes in a foil bag. Supermarkets are commonly located in the basement of department stores.

Fresh fragant bread may be the staff of life, but in Europe it is the saviour of your budget as well. It is reasonable in France, Britain, Italy, Austria, Spain, Portugal and Greece, moderate elsewhere and rather high in Scandinavia. Most European governments would fall if the price of bread became too high. Bread costs about 50¢ to $1 a loaf and possibly less in Greece. In France, Italy, Spain, Portugal and Greece, bread is sold unwrapped from shelves or baskets according to size and popped into your shopping bag. We save paper and plastic bags that our French bread comes in at home and take them along to use on such occasions. When first bought, French bread should be slipped into the paper bag so that the crust will remain crisp and the moistness of the interior will not migrate into the crust. Bread goes stale quickly, especially after being broken open so we keep leftover bread in a plastic bag where the crust softens but the interior remains edible. Northern European countries sell sliced and wrapped bread. Each country bakes a variety of bread but the type of bread eaten by the common man is always the cheapest. Basically this means French bread in Southern Europe, rye bread in Northern Europe and white sliced sandwich bread in Britain.

Eggs, cheese, yogurt and refrigerated custard are reasonable in price and a good source of protein. Both eggs and cheese make a good addition to breakfast. Cheese is served for breakfast in Scandinavia, Germany and Holland and as a pre-dessert course in France. Entering a cheese shop is bewildering in the variety of cheese resting behind the counter. If you are unsure of your tastes, the best policy is to buy 100 grams worth. As cheese isn't taken out of the cheese cellar and sold until its ripe, try to eat it within a few hours or sooner in hot weather. However, hard type cheese keeps longer if the temperature is not too warm. Cheese is sold in the supermarkets wrapped in plastic just like ours and you can even find Kraft cheese there. Dutch and Danish packaged cheeses are distributed throughout Europe.

Of beef, veal, pork, poultry and fish, the latter is the cheapest but it is hard to use without refrigeration. The fish market is apart from the other markets and is logically found on the waterfront. It opens early in the morning and the day's catch may well be sold by mid-morning. The European chicken is a plump flavorful bird and one of our favorites. Rotisseried chicken is a popular item that you will see often. These chickens are cooked on a giant rotisserie where about seven rows of plump chickens revolve on long skewers, each row suspended above another row with the cooking element behind. Each newly-to-be-roasted row of birds is placed on the top rack where their juices baste the fowls beneath and so on down to the bottom row. The chickens that are almost done hang on the bottom rack, with a trough beneath to catch juices for basting. To fill an order, a chicken is removed from the bottom spit, hacked in half or kept whole as ordered and slipped into a foil-lined bag. One chicken serves three adults and costs about $3-$5 each. Veal is cheaper than beef, particularly in Italy and Spain. Little veal is sold in the U.S. because of high prices and limited production, so Europe is your opportunity to indulge. High quality veal is pale pink and fine grained, devoid of natural fat covering or marbling. It comes from a five to twelve-week-old milk fed calf. Red or rosy flesh indicates the calf was older and was put to pasture. As veal isn't much used in the U.S., a few cooking suggestions might be helpful. Cuts of interest are chops, steaks, loin and ground veal which are easily cooked in a frying pan with butter until the juices turn from rosy pink to yellow. After initial browning, add chopped onion or mashed garlic clove and cook a few minutes before pouring over the meat a third cup of white wine to bring out the flavor. Cover and finish cooking until juices run yellow. Remove meat and put in a little water and boullion cube, and boil down to make a sauce. Sliced mushrooms added with onion and garlic give extra flavor. Veal hamburger lacks fat and is improved by mixing in pork sausage. Beef costs more in Europe than here, but shrinks less because growth-inducing hormones aren't used as much. Cuts differ with the French dividing the carcass according to muscle separation rather than across the grain.

Fruits and vegetables should be washed before eating. Prices vary according to season and locality and some on-the-spot price comparisons will let you know the best buy at the moment. Fruit is somewhat expensive in Northern Europe but you can get your fill in Italy, Spain and especially Greece. Europeans commonly eat fruit for dessert.

Milk is a best buy in Europe and especially in Scandinavia. In small towns of Greece, Portugal and Spain, check for a pasteurization label. We drink the water throughout Europe and have suffered no ill effects, but bottled water is sold inexpensively in Southern Europe in grocery stores. Two fizzless brands are Evian and Vitelli. If you need a water bottle for the train, bottled mineral water is sold in non-returnable plastic bottles which make good ones. All soft drinks are expensive and best done without. Wine is a reasonable buy in wine producing and drinking countries such as France, Italy, Spain and Greece. Belgium, Germany, Holland and Scandinavia are noted beer countries. Price is less in a grocery store than cafe, but is taxed in either case. Coffee drinkers are advised to bring some instant, or better yet, the more compact and lighter freeze-dried coffee from home as it is expensive and heavily taxed in Europe. So is tea, except in Britain.

In northern Europe, a cafeteria represents considerable saving over a restaurant and is a fine buy. Switzerland and Germany have the cafeteria counter which culminates in stand-up tables, but the more common cafeteria is similar to the U.S. Both department stores and supermarkets often have a cafeteria. A cafeteria meal costs about $3-$4 in northern Europe, less so in southern Europe.

For meals in southern Europe, we recommend eating in a restaurant for the noon meal rather than in the evening. It is the "table d'hote" lunch which vies for the patronage of the businessman, bureaucrat, shopgirl and officeworker on his lunch hour. This is the daily special which changes each day, incorporates seasonal foods and is served more quickly than anything on the regular menu. It goes by a different name in each country such as "menu a '25' franc" in France or "el pranzo" in Italy. Usually it will be listed on a half-page dittoed sheet sometimes attached to the regular menu and sometimes not. Though often the regular menu is multi-lingual or else there is a separate English one, the table d'hote menu isn't translated from its native language in most cases. A weekday is the best time for this lunch but sometimes one might be available on Saturdays for shoppers. On Sundays, restaurants are geared for the family weekend outing trade and the selected meal is more expensive as it usually incorporates more costly ingredients. Normally, this meal consists of three courses. Taxes and service may not be included in the price, but the menu will indicate this. If beverage is included the menu will state that for example a quarter liter of wine is included. Probably you will have your choice of red or white house wine that varies with quality of the restaurant but is always pleasant. Individual carafes are filled from a big barrel in back. Another menu custom is the government regulated "tourist menu" offered in several countries. The rules are uniform within each country and the quoted price is always all-inclusive of beverage, service, cover and taxes. The meal is several courses as stipulated by law and the diner is given a selection for each course and of beverage usually. Virtually every European restaurant posts its a la carte, table d'hote and tourist menu outside near the door and you will quickly get in the habit of menu shopping before deciding to enter. You should look for what entree is included and at what price when menu shopping for whether you find the entree appealing on the table d'hote menu will usually determine if you stay. Normally the locals know the best values. Follow a trail of officeworkers into a restaurant to discover a good value in eating for that particular area. Aim for a 1:00 pm lunch in most countries. You will need $3-$5 for this meal. To help keep costs in line in a restaurant, reserve coffee and other beverages except maybe wine when it's reasonable for back at camp where they're cheaper. Do this for dessert too if it's not included in the set price. Water isn't automatically placed on the table like at home and you must ask for it. Make it known that you want tap water as Europeans drink bottled mineral water with wine and food and it hurts the waiter to see you depart from custom.

Much of the cost of the meal will depend upon your selection of entree. Beef is always the most expensive entree except for shellfish and other exotica. Don't bother with steaks as nothing compares with the best American steakhouses. However, steak and french fries are THE continent-wide favorite and the combination is found on most menus. Most times this steak is a thin filet that has been pounded tender and fried which results in satisfactory fare as long as the price is moderate. Chicken and veal are a real treat in Europe where chickens are plump and flavorful, unlike those scrawny tasteless things we get in the supermarket in the U.S., and veal is actually LESS expensive than beef. Fish is reasonable and always excellent so long as it's perfectly fresh, which it will be even inland. Eel is a particularly good and reasonable choice. Subtle sauces and fresh herb seasonings are the treats in southern European cooking. Except in an unnervingly expensive haute cuisine-type restaurant where each item is ordered separately and not a morsel is thrown in free, the entree will come garnished with a vegetable or two at least. Most often it will be the lowly but vitamin and mineral packed potato. Except in extremely high-priced restaurants, larger portions are served in first class restaurants rather than cheaper ones. In a few places, the bread in the bread basket that is automatically placed on the table is not included with the meal but a small sum is charged for each piece eaten.

When a guidebook starts talking about food specialties, it can mean any of several things. There are regional specialties, seasonal specialties, "house" specialties and specialties in which "haute cuisine" is implicit. Then again there are specialty dishes, specialty ingredients and specialty sauces. A specialty recommended in a guidebook can be an ephemeral thing--not easily found, and if found, not easily paid for. Many specialties lie in the stellar haute cuisine category, incorporating expensive ingredients such as crustaceans, truffles or goose liver into cost profligating labor intense sauces. Summertime is not the best time of year to play the specialty game as many ingredients appear only in other months. For instance, the Dutch stew "hochepot" is served in colder months only. Each region within a country has certain dishes for which the ingredients are grown and raised locally in that particular climate and which become known as regional specialties. These are offered in restaurants, but also can be found in delicatessens for much less. These should be tasted when the traveler is in the appropriate region, but also can be found imported to other places or approximations prepared. But honestly, the dishes found on the table d'hote menu utilize the regional and seasonal produce and protein source, so you are bound to get a feel for the food merely by ordering the daily special without hunting down a recommended specialty which invariably costs more.

In the average restaurant in a wine drinking nation, the house wine is a good buy and always pleasant. For a celebration meal, you may want to order a bottle of wine and consult the cellar master or "sommelier" (som-nee-lay) in France. As there are always suitable bottles in both lower and higher price ranges, it helps if you give him some idea of how fine a wine you want. If the wine steward is in doubt about your means, he'll probably recommend the higher priced wine both because it's better and because he wouldn't want to insult your taste by recommending a lesser and cheaper wine. If his suggestion is too expensive, ask him to suggest something cheaper. He gets tipped (75¢) regardless of whether you just tell him what you want or confer with him over the matter so you might as well see what his expertise would recommend. Another way is to look at the bottles on the tables around you and order one after checking the price. Sometimes the cheapest vintage on the list has been very carefully selected and is a good value. If you haven't finished the bottle, you can ask the waiter if you can take it with you.

There is no cheap way to drink hard liquor in a bar or restaurant. The least expensive way is to buy a bottle in the duty free store at the airport and have it at the campground. An alternative is to try the local favorite which is usually strong. In Scandinavia, it's aquavit which is colorless and 100 proof. In Germany, it's Asbach Uralt through whose plant incidentally you can get a free guided tour and tasting in Rudesheim on the Rhine River. The east Indian Arrac is downed in The Netherlands or else try gin. Calvados, distilled from apples, would be your choice in France. However, Europeans customarily drink something a little softer for their before-dinner drink (if any) and the bite isn't unmanageable if local custom is followed. The aperitif takes the limelight and usually falls in the category of a fortified wine such as vermouth or sherry. Some examples are Campari, Suisse, Byrrh or Dubonnet. In Spain, a glass of red wine is common and elsewhere a glass of white might be ordered. Brandy or liqueur follow dinner. In Spain, try Fundador. In Greece, ask for Metaxa. Try kirsch, a wine distilled from cherries, in Switzerland. It's cognac, aramagnac or as a last resort, eau de ville, the cheapest and coarsest, in France.

To be prepared for paying the bill, make a mental tally of the menu prices as you order to have some basis of comparison when you finally receive the bill. This is simplified if you've ordered the table d'hote or tourist menu, but requires a little more work for a la carte. Sometimes the bill has been added wrong or an extra dish put on that wasn't served. If you sense that something is wrong, take the time to look over the bill carefully making sure it's not some legitimate charge like an extra amount for bread, service or taxes. Usually the waiter's handwriting is illegible to Americans so you will have to ask him about a particular item. Call any possible error to the waiter's attention and he'll either explain the charge or correct it matter-of-factly. When paying the bill, try to give the exact amount or slightly over to facilitate counting change. Tipping is taken care of by the charge for service which is included in the tourist menu price and mandatorily added onto your bill by the waiter. Rarely is a 12 or 15 percent service charge not included or added, in which case a 10 to 15 percent tip is in order. Normally a menu will state a mandatory service charge at the bottom if there is one. Even when a service charge has been added, you will notice one or two

people leaving small change behind. This never amounts to more than five
percent of the bill and is a small extra tip.

READERS' SUGGESTIONS   "Buy a small camp stove and cook your own food
in northern countries. Enjoy ethnic dishes when you do decide to eat out."
Kathy Carlson, Gardena, Ca. "For food we recommend shopping in supermarkets and open markets whenever possible and to use a backpacker stove
to cook it on. The money you'll save is great and the meals can be very delicious." Mr. and Mrs. Robert Cooper, Batavia, Illinois   "Restaurants were
MUCH less expensive in small towns and people friendlier." Philip Jones,
W. Chester, Pa.

EUROPEAN CUSTOMS

MANNERS European manners vary slightly from ours in several respects.
It's standard procedure to say "good morning" or "good afternoon" when
entering a small shop, bakery, train compartment or other small physical
space with few people. Those present return the greeting but it's not considered a prelude to conversation. In France it's impolite to greet a person
with a "good morning" for instance without adding "mademoiselle, madame
or monsieur" after it. During an introduction on a social occasion, a
European will shake hands when meeting and usually say his name simul-
taneously rather than say "how do you do." During the conversation, whereas
an American may be more apt to state the literal truth and be very direct, the
European tends to avoid this if it might hurt someone's feelings. Europeans
don't ask personal questions such as "what do you do for a living" or "how
many children do you have," but are more likely to comment on an item from
the newspaper or a sports event. A European appreciates a sincere favorable
comment on his country. In public places, the European tends to keep his
voice pitched low and never shouts across open spaces. European children
tend to play less exuberantly, not expect quite so much attention from their
parents and not run around so freely in public.

FRIENDLY LOCALS   In tourist areas in southern Europe, you may be
approached by a resident who starts a conversation. Most likely he wants
nothing more than a chance to practice his English with you. Occasionally
he may be a professional guide who would like to engage you as a client. In
this case, he will let you know and will be glad to show his government
license if requested. The professional guides are extremely knowledgeable
in history and the fine arts and usually have an engaging personality as well.
Rates are government regulated but always ask the price in advance.

CITY PUBLIC TRANSPORTATION SYSTEMS   These are well developed,
efficient and frequent. Each system has its own deviations, but generally the
name on the front of the bus is its destination. Two names indicate both the
beginning and end of the run. To make sure that you are on the right bus and
going in the right direction, as you enter say the destination you want in a
questioning manner and the driver will call out your stop when it's time to get
off. Tickets are usually sold at the back or in the last car of a bus or tram
or from the increasingly prevalent automatic vending machines at the stops.
If you don't notice the locals buying tickets it's because they have weekly
passes which are shown only if an inspector gets aboard. Some trams and
buses operate on the honor system where a machine dispenses your ticket
and you show it only if an inspector happens to be on board. The subway is

always the fastest and least complicated way of getting around but you miss the scenery.

WRITING HOME   The aerogram is the bargain here. It's a one-page airmail letter that is bought at the post office, written upon, and dropped in the mailbox in the country in which it was purchased. Cost varies from 30¢ to 45¢.

RECEIVING U.S. NEWS ABROAD   Major cities have streetside kiosks which stock current English language publications. (The kiosk is, in fact, a small drugstore and has a multitude of minor essentials like writing paper, maps and candy for sale.) English language newspapers are also found in lobbies of major hotels.   The reading matter most frequently purchased by Americans is the "International Herald Tribune" which is sold in all large cities for about 40¢ to 50¢ a copy. "The London Times" is also widely available. Some cities such as Rome and Brussels publish a local daily English language paper aimed at the local foreign colony which includes listings of current events in the city that would be of interest to travelers as well.

WASHING CLOTHES   Expect to use cold water when washing clothing by hand at the campground. Soap flakes are sold at the camp store or you may prefer to pack along some cold water soap powder of the type made for washing woolens. Any white nylon underwear will turn gray in a month of washings by hand. Britain has soft water but hard water is more likely on the continent. Javel water is an inexpensive bleach that is sold in small plastic bags in France and added to hand laundry. If the campground has a washing machine, the store will sell detergent. Often there isn't a dryer but only a centrifuge which gives the clothing a good spin to get rid of excess water so clothing must be hung on the lines to dry. Self-service laundries in cities usually have a machine to dispense detergent. It helps to take along some change, but usually there will be either a change machine or attendant.

RESTROOMS   Public toilets are found in all the usual places and are not difficult to find until you need one. Museums, railroad stations, restaurants, department stores and municipal buildings all offer haven in addition to city-run ones which are often in the main square. It's well to know in an emergency that virtually every hotel has public facilities in an out-of-the-way spot on the first or second floor. Exact location is never obvious so you have to ask. Sometimes a small fee is charged for use of the toilet and is collected by the honor system and the visual aid reminder of a small saucer on a table or counter. About 15¢ to 25¢ is expected. It's considered discourteous to enter a small, family-run cafe or establishment for the sole purpose of using the toilet and then to leave without buying something. Hot and cold faucets are often reversed in Europe. An embossed "C" stands for hot. A red dot means hot and a blue dot means cold.

MOVIES   You can always park yourself or older children in a movie. In Europe the show starts at set hours just like ours, but a ticket is bought for a specific seat and show. Different seats sell at different prices with the cheapest being closest to the screen. Before buying a ticket, check to see if the American or British movie is dubbed or merely subtitled. Subtitled movies are prevalent in northern Europe and particularly Scandinavia where a large portion of the populace speaks English.

POLLUTION   Europe has not escaped pollution of its oceans, seas and lakes any more than we. Many sewer systems of coastal towns empty untreated sewage into the sea. Just because you see vacationing Europeans swimming in questionable waters doesn't mean it's safe. Safety is assured in the cold oceanic waters off northern Europe, but swimming in parts of the warm Mediterranean and Adriatic near metropolitan or resort areas, and in the Rhine, Rhone and Po Rivers is risky.

OCEAN BEACHES   Apart from pollution, beaches may be unsafe because of tidal action. If a desirable-looking beach is little used, there may be a reason so inquire first at the tourist office. Some beaches are posted, particularly on the Atlantic.

CROSSING THE STREET   Sometimes in southern Europe, getting across the street is hard. The timid wait for a stout Italian housewife to cross and tag along as she shunts across the street shouting epithets at her countrymen who calculate risks very finely and stop at the last possible moment. Check for underground passageways under traffic swirling around monuments. Towards northern Europe, frequency of traffic lights seemingly increases in direct proportion to number of bicycles. Watch out for them. When in Britain, remember to LOOK RIGHT before crossing the street as traffic comes from the opposite direction. Tram tracks run in odd places in Budapest and a tram whooshes by just when you think you're on a sidewalk.

HIGH ALTITUDE SICKNESS   If you plan any excursions up high mountains in the Alps, there is a slight possibility of experiencing high altitude sickness with symptoms of breathing difficulty, faintness or headache. Sit down until you adjust or take the next lift down and wait in the inevitable cafe for your companions.

MEDICAL HELP   Competent medical help is never far away. Some campgrounds have a doctor on call, or you can get the name of an English-speaking one from an American consulate 24 hours a day, tourist office or leading hotel. Costs are lower than in the U.S. The American Hospital in Paris has an out-patient department. French pharmacists prepare prescriptions, but also are trained to dress wounds, treat burns, set bones and give first aid. A pharmacy sells asperin, sanitary napkins, tampons (often behind the counter), baby food and diapers. American-trained dentists and dental methods are reputedly superior to European ones and worth seeking should need arise.

SAFETY OF FOOD AND WATER   Whether or not water is safe depends on its source. In large cities and throughout northern Europe, water comes from a central supply that is watched by authorities. In primitive areas and in small towns in Italy and Spain, the source may be a well and therefore may be questionable. Egg provides a fertile medium for bacterial growth so be cautious about keeping egg fillings like custards for very long without refrigeration. Avoid shellfish whose beds are in polluted waters such as near Venice. Ice cream sold from vending carts without means of refrigeration beyond ice should be avoided, but ice cream sold in stores, cafes or restaurants is alright. Know in advance what to do if children get diahrrea. Our doctor recommends a liquid diet of a carrot soup so we pack along a can of carrot juice just in case. Ask your doctor and bring along one of whatever he recommends.

DATE AND TIME   Europeans write the date with the day preceding month such as 1 June 1980 for our June 1, 1980. Europeans write number 7 with a

bar across it like this 7 to distinguish it from number 1.
Europe uses the 24-hour clock where our 1:00 pm becomes
13:00, our 2:00 pm becomes 14:00 and so forth until midnight or 24:00.

SHOPPING

U.S. Customs allows each adult and child to bring into the United
States $300 retail value worth of goods duty-free. A family may combine its
exemptions.   Each adult may include one quart of liquor in this amount.
An additional $600 worth may be brought in at a flat duty rate of 10 percent.
After that regular duty rates apply, which vary according to type of item and
may be higher or lower than 10 percent. No duty is assessed on saffron,
truffles (canned), postage stamps, works of art, antiques (minimum age 100
years--obtain proof of age from dealer), hand done copies of art and all
books. Books are cheaply mailed home under "book rate." Special high duty
rates of typically 70 percent are assessed items made in Eastern Europe,
but can be brought in duty-free within the $300 allowance or at 10 percent if
between $300 and $600. Only one bottle of perfume of each brand trade-
marked in the U.S. can be brought in. Don't attempt to carry home fruits,
vegetables, plant cuttings, seed, perishable meats (including cured and
cooked items) or unprocessed plant products. These are forbidden entry. If
you bring in cheese, expect to be the last one through customs because additional time is needed to clear it. Canned or processed food, bakery products,
and "commercially canned meat, sterilized by heat in hermetically sealed
cans and shelf stable without refrigeration" are admissible. U.S. Customs
allows gift packages worth up to $25 retail to be mailed duty-free to someone
in the United States as long as no more than one gift package for the same
address goes through customs on the same day. Mark it "unsolicited gift--
value under $25. "

The best values are generally found in department stores, flea markets,
street markets and trade fairs. Avoid small souvenir shops--lowest prices for
souvenirs are in the cheapest department stores. Value-added tax is a percentage tax included in the retail price of goods. Usually the tax is deducted
from any purchase mailed out of the country or is reimbursed if the correct
forms are completed when the tourist leaves the country. It's not worth
bothering about unless total purchases from a single store amount to $20.
There is always a leading department store with the highest prices and then
cheaper department stores with lower prices.   The basement supermarket
in the second or third class department store often has good values as does
its cafeteria. When buying gifts, try to select small weightless ones such as
saffron, truffles, Swiss Army knife or perfume. Flea markets are fun to
browse but hard to find something to buy. They are the place to shop for the
whimsical antique item of small size and price. Good buys are found only on
items currently out of fashion. Best time to shop is when weather is terrible
and business is slow like fall or winter. Otherwise get there when the market
opens and preferably on the day new merchandise arrives. Dealers charge
what they think traffic will bear so show no enthusiasm, bargain but be prepared to give up the item or pay the price if the dealer won't come down.

AUSTRIA

The Austrian national anthem is by Mozart. Prices remain lower here than in northern Europe. Austria is not a member of the Common Market and is not subject to its agricultural agreements. (State Treaty signed after World War II declared neutral political status for Austria between East and West-- hence Austria cannot join the Common Market.)

CURRENCY   Austrian schilling. Each schilling is worth about 6¢. There are about 16 schillings to the U.S. dollar in 1981.

WEATHER   June to September is camping season. Prepare for occasional rainfall.

CAMPING   Tourist office booklet "Camping" lists campgrounds and indicates whether a bus stop is nearby. A tax of 8% plus 1 shilling is levied throughout Austria. Fees generally range from 20-30 schillings per night per person with no extra charge for the tent. According to regulations, "camping is not restricted to the camping areas, but should one camp on private property, it is first necessary to obtain permission from the owner."

TRAINS   Austrian Federal Railway (OBB) is very good and the mountainous routes are particularly scenic though a little slower. Price reductions include half-price for children 6-15 years old, free for under 6 years and 20-25% discount for groups of ten or more. An Austria Ticket is sold which is valid for unlimited travel on all Austrian Railroad lines (federal, state and private, including "corridor trains" running through Germany between Salzburg and Kufstein), all Austrian bus lines operated by the Austrian Postal Service and the Austrian Federal Railways (but not city transit buses and trams), scheduled boats on Lake Constance and Lake St. Wolfgang, and the Schafberg and Schneeberg mountain railways. This ticket also gives a 50% discount on upstream trips on Danube Steamboats, a 7-50% discount on various aerial trams and chair lifts in mountain resorts, and free admission to Austria's nine casinos. Austria Ticket costs 1500 AS for 9 days and 2100 AS for 16 days, second class. First class is also available. Children under 6 are free and those 6-23 pay half-price. The Austria Ticket is sold

68

by German Federal Railroads, 630 Fifth Ave., N.Y., N.Y. 10020 and in Austria at all railroad stations. Women 60 and over and men 65 and over can buy a Half-Fare Train Pass for 140 schillings, valid for one calendar year, which entitles them to purchase all Austrian Railways train tickets and bus tickets for half price. TEE trains are not included but the Transalpin and Vindobona expresses are upon payment of 20 schillings one way. Half-fare passes may only be bought in Austria and are sold at train stations. Sample fares are: Vienna to Innsbruck $33, Vienna to Salzburg $20, Salzburg to Innsbruck $17.

Eurail Youthpass holders must pay a supplement of 20 AS (schillings) on Express trains but there are always other trains available on the same routes. Included in Eurail and Eurail Youthpass are all buses operated by the Austrian Federal Railway (OBB)--not postal buses, and boat and cogwheel railway trips as follows. Ferry boats between Passau and Vienna, operated by Gesellschaft. Cog-wheel railways St. Wolfgang - Schafbergspitze (see Salzkammergut) and Puchberg am Schneeberg-Hochschneeberg. The latter is reached by train from Vienna's South Station to Wiener Neustadt, a town south of Vienna. Then a local train is taken to transfer point for cog-railway (22 km) to Puchberg am Schneeberg which climbs Schneeberg mountain (6,806 ft.), highest peak in lower Austria from which there is a fine view, including rock walls. Railpass holders receive a 50% discount on steamers on Lake Constance (Bodensee), shared by Austria, Germany and Switzerland, and a popular resort area with swimming, sailing, waterskiing and summer cultural events. The area has good train access from Innsbruck, Zurich and Stuttgart, and many campgrounds.

Trains are classified TEE, Ex (Expresszug-international express trains), TS (Triebwagenschnellzug-long distance express trains), D (general express trains), TE (Triebwageneileilzug-semi fast train), and E (Eilzuggeneral semi-fast train). A supplement of 20 AS is collected for trains marked EX, TS and D except for Eurailpass and tickets issued outside of Austria. "Corridor" trains are "Korridorzuge" which have to pass through Germany or Italy to reach another part of Austria. It is not possible to get off or on in Germany or Italy on these trains.

The only TEE train which goes to Austria is the "Mediolanum" which leaves Munich at 3:35 pm, arrives in Innsbruck at 5:25 pm, and then continues to Milan, arriving at 10:45 pm. The former TEE train "Prinz Eugen" is now classified as a German inter-city train and carries both first and second class between Frankfurt and Vienna. The Transalpin Express is famous for its scenery and goes from Vienna to Paris. Train routes which cross the mountains to enter Italy are also scenic, although tunnels may be used on some crossings.

About seat reservations, Francis Packer advises "can't recommend night train from Stuttgart--noisy and crowded. Get seat reservations!" Months are given in Roman numerals in timetables. Abbreviations:

ab - leaves at	werktags - weekdays	mo - monday
an - arrives at	fahrzeit - traveling time	di - tuesday
bis - until, to	bergfahrt - upward journey	mi - wed.
und ab - and from	talfahrt - downward journey	do - thursday
nur - only	berg und talfahrt - round trip	fr - friday
preis - price	verkehrt nur an - runs only on	sa - saturday
von - from	platzkartenpflichter zug -	so - sunday
taglich - daily	reservation required	

Taktfahrplan West

Wien –
Salzburg–Wien

Wien Westbf	ab	7.00	9.00	11.00	15.00	17.00	19.00
St. Pölten Hbf	an	7.41		11.41		17.41	19.41
	ab	7.42		11.42		17.42	19.42
St. Valentin	an					18.36	
	ab					18.37	
Linz Hbf	an	8.53	10.53	12.53	16.53	18.53	20.53
	ab	8.55	10.55	12.55	16.55	18.55	20.55
Wels	an	9.10		13.10	17.10	19.10	21.10
	ab	9.11		13.11	17.11	19.11	21.11
Attnang-Puchh.	an	9.30		13.30	17.30	19.30	21.30
	ab	9.32		13.32	17.32	19.32	21.32
Salzburg Hbf	an	10.20	12.08	14.20	18.23	20.20	22.19

Salzburg Hbf	an		8.28	10.37	12.37	14.37	16.38
	ab	6.40	8.40	10.40	12.40	14.40	16.40
Vöcklamarkt	an		9.14				
	ab		9.15				
Attnang-Puchh.	an	7.27	9.27	11.27	13.27	15.27	17.27
	ab	7.29	9.29	11.29	13.29	15.29	17.29
Wels	an	7.47	9.47	11.47	13.47	15.47	17.47
	ab	7.48	9.48	11.48	13.48	15.48	17.48
Linz Hbf	an	8.03	10.03	12.03	14.03	16.03	18.03
	ab	8.05	10.05	12.05	14.05	16.05	18.05
St. Valentin	an	8.20					
	ab	8.21					
St. Pölten Hbf	an	9.14	11.14	13.14	15.14	17.14	19.14
	ab	9.15	11.15	13.15	15.15	17.15	19.15
Wien Westbf	an	10.00	12.00	14.00	16.00	18.00	20.00

Neu: Taktfahrplan Süd

Wien –
Graz–Wien

Wien Südbf	ab	7.00	9.00	11.00		15.00	17.00	19.00
Wr. Neustadt	an	7.29	9.29	11.29		15.29	17.29	19.29
	ab	7.30	9.30	11.30		15.30	17.30	19.30
Semmering	ab			12.15				20.15
Mürzzuschlag	an	8.27	10.27	12.27		16.27	18.27	20.27
	ab	8.28	10.28	12.28		16.28	18.28	20.28
Kindberg	ab							20.44
Kapfenberg	ab			12.53				20.53
Bruck a. d. Mur	an	8.58	10.58	12.58		16.58	18.58	20.58
	ab	9.00	11.00	13.00		17.00	19.00	21.00
Frohnleiten	ab							21.20
Graz Hbf	an	9.35	11.35	13.35		17.35	19.35	21.40

Graz Hbf	ab	6.20	8.20	10.20	12.20	14.20	16.20	18.20	20.20
Frohnleiten	ab	6.39							
Bruck a.d. Mur	an	6.56	8.56	10.56	12.56	14.56	16.56	18.56	20.56
	ab	6.58	8.58	10.58	12.58	14.58	16.58	18.58	20.58
Kapfenberg	ab	7.03				15.03			21.03
Kindberg	ab	7.12				15.12			
Mürzzuschlag	an	7.29	9.29	11.29	13.29	15.29	17.29	19.29	21.29
	ab	7.30	9.30	11.30	13.30	15.30	17.30	19.30	21.30
Semmering	ab	7.44	9.44			15.44			21.44
Wr. Neustadt	an	8.29	10.29	12.29	14.29	16.29	18.29	20.29	22.29
	ab	8.30	10.30	12.30	14.30	16.30	18.30	20.30	22.30
Baden	ab					16.44			
Meidling	an	8.59	10.59			16.59		20.59	
Wien Südbf	an	9.05	11.05	13.05	15.05	17.05	19.05	21.05	23.05

FOOD   In 1981, one liter of milk was 10.20 AS, 500 grams of bread, 6 AS, and one whole cooked chicken, 70 AS.

Mountainous Austria has excellent water. Foodstores are open 7-6:30 on weekdays and close at 2:30 on Saturday. (In Vienna, train station food stores close at midnight.) Feinkost is a delicatessen. Pastry shops (kaffeehaus) have take-out and sit-down service of rolls, pastries, cakes, coffee, tea and hot chocolate with or without whipped cream (schlagobers). Coffee is served in many different combinations of coffee, milk and whipped cream. Cafes are busiest between 3-5pm for jause (YOW-sah). Sitting for a hour over your order and writing letters or reading a newspaper is perfectly proper. Alternatively, a basement keller or beisel serves wine or beer. "Seidel" is 3/10th liter and "krugel" a half-liter of draft beer. "Viertel" is 1/4 liter of house wine. Austrian white wines are considered better than reds. Gasthaus, beisel and keller establishments serve meals as do first

70

class restaurants. Best clue to pegging price level is to check the cost of "weiner schnitzel" (breaded veal cutlet). Daily special is called "menus." "Garni" means accompanied with a vegetable, usually potato. Any dessert can be ordered "mit schlag" (with whipped cream).

HIKING   Trails are excellent. Paths are marked by colored signs on trees and rocks. Alpine huts provide beds and meals for about 60 schillings each. You can eat in a hut without staying there. The Austrian Alpine Club is at Wilhelm-Greil-Strasse 15, A-6020, Innsbruck. Maps are available that indicate colored trail signs and location of huts. Innsbruck and Zell-am-see are two towns with good trails nearby. "Gruss Gott" (God greets you) is the most commonly heard greeting when hiking. Provide for cool evenings and sudden rain. Mountain Rambles in Austria is free from U.S. tourist office.

SHOPPING   We quote from tourist office publication: "Foreign visitors can reclaim value added tax (VAT) paid on goods bought in Austria but intended for use or consumption abroad. If buyer presents his passport at time of purchase, salesman will make out a receipt with bearer's name and address, showing amount of VAT paid separately. He will also fill out the official form code numbered U 34. The receipt, the form, and the goods involved should be presented to Austrian customs on leaving the country; departure is then confirmed with stamp on relevant section of U 34 form. When receipt and form are sent back to the shop where the purchase was made, the VAT will be transferred by cheque to any specified bank account."

GRAZ

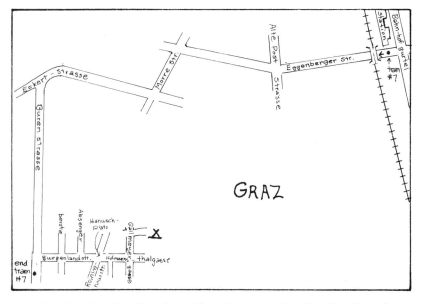

Camping directions for Graz (grats) have been contributed by Ray Rylander as follows. "(1) Take tram #7 east from hauptbahnhof to Hauptplatz. Change to tram #4 or 5 going north and ride to Robert Stolz Gasse. A very poor excuse for a campingplatz is up the hill and to the right. (2) A much better campingplatz: take tram #7 west from hauptbahnhof to its end. Walk east on Burgenlandstrasse, crossing Reininghausstrasse at an angle to Hanuschplatz. Continue east along Hofmannsthalgasse and turn left on Gallmeyergasse. Good campingplatz is off to the right, down in a little dale." (See map.)

INNSBRUCK

Innsbruck (EENS-brook), capital of the Tyrol, is a good railway gateway to hiking and climbing country. Its tourist office has sent information on new free guided hiking tours which look like an excellent way to learn the ropes for European hiking. Here's how it works. Anyone who is staying three days in Innsbruck gets free membership in "Club Innsbruck" with benefits of free guided hiking tours and discounts for shops and museums. The hiking tours are offered daily from June 1 to September 30 and include free bus transportation to and from the start of the hike. Twenty-five different day hikes are planned, each one having about four to six hours of actual hiking time. Participants must sign up for the tour at the tourist office by 4 pm the day before. The next day the group meets in front of the convention center at 8:30 am, equipped with raincoat or jacket, hat, sunglasses, food for enroute, dried fruit, canned drink and some money as some hikes involve a cablecar lift. Each hike passes by an Inn where more food may be purchased. Return time is set between 4 and 6 pm. Bonnie and Doug Robinson report, "enjoyed Innsbruck for its "Club Innsbruck." Excellent hiking opportunity and great fun with friendly tour guides. We camped there for 3 nights and became eligible. They provide you with rucksacks, hiking boots (well worn), and raincoats if you need them. Our trip consisted of a 45 minute free bus ride into the mountains and inexpensive short chairlift ride. Hiked through incredible scenery that we wouldn't have been able to see otherwise."

TRAIN STATION   Hauptbahnhof, main station, is four blocks from main shopping street, Maria Theresien Str. and five blocks from the old town centering on Herzog Friedrich Str. Buses leave from Sudtiroler Platz in front of train station. Within station are "Jugendwarteraum" (youth information center), post office, and currency exchange (in main hall open daily 9:15 am-1:30 pm and 3-7:45 pm, in departure hall open daily 7:30 am-8:30pm). Hauptbahnhof handles international traffic. Smaller stations, Bahnhof-Hotting and Westbahnhof serve suburbs, small towns and villages. Local trains can often be used instead of bus or tram to explore city's outskirts.

TOURIST INFORMATION   Tourist office, verkehrsverein, is five blocks from train station at Burggraben 3 (open M-F 8-12 & 2-5:30, Sa 9-12). It has a very good leaflet "Innsbruck" which contains a map of the town, map of environs marked with hiking trails and huts, description of 15 marked trails in the area, suggestions for longer mountain hikes, list of cog-wheel railways and cablecars, and weekly program of musical events. Hikers should visit Alpine Auskunft information office, Bozner Platz 7 (2 blocks from station), to purchase larger, topographical map.

CAMPGROUNDS   Camping Reichenau (Stadt Campingplatz) is on Reichenauer Str. beside the Inn River, and is the most convenient. Open Apr 15-Oct 15. Take bus "R" across from station. Buses leave station at

72

about 10 minute intervals except every 30 minutes after 8:05 pm. On weekends, bus leaves every 15 minutes at five minutes past the hour. Bus stops
at camp entrance. Hot showers, store, snack bar and cooking facilities.
Adult/28 AS, student/25 AS, tent/free. This camp was picked by Linda Clark
as having best scenery: "There were some picnic tables here and view we
got from ours was of the Inn River and the magnificent mountains surrounding." Frances Packer contributes: "Very nice facilities, must pay extra to
cook or have hot shower (6 AS)."
     Camping Innsbruck-West can be reached by bus "Lk" (Kranebitten)
from Bozner Platz. Adult/28 AS, child under 10/22 AS, tent/20 AS, tax/4 AS.
     Camping Seewirt, in Amras, can be reached by bus "K" from the
station. Bus stops close to camp. Adult/28 AS, child 5-12/22 AS, tent/
20 AS, tax/4 AS per person.

PUBLIC TRANSPORTATION   Trams and buses cost 10 AS for one ride,
5 tickets for 37 AS, or 10 tickets for 70 AS.

FOOD   Market is in the Markthalle at Marktgraben and Herzog-Sigm.-
Ufer. Open M-F 7-6:30 and Sa 7-1.

SIGHTSEEING   Sightseeing divides into (1) exploring the old town with a
visit to Hofburg Castle (open M-Sa 9-4, about adult/10 AS, student and child/
2 AS) and the fine Tyrolean Art Museum, (2) ascending the heights by cog-
wheel railway and chairlift, (3) hiking, and (4) attending a Tyrolean musical
program. Tyrolean Folk Art Museum (Tiroler Volkskunst Museum) shows
22 authentic peasant home and inn interiors from several regions of Austria
and Germany, and peasant attire. It is on Universitats Str. and open M-Sa
9-12 & 2-5 and Su 9-12, adult/15 AS.
     Hungerburg Vista is reached by trolley bus "C" from Bozner-platz or
tram #1 to Hungerburg funicular. Hungerburgbahn (24 AS roundtrip) goes to
Hungerburg mountain (2,838 ft.) where a cableway to Seegrube begins which
connects with another that continues to Hafelekar (7,700 ft.). (Railpasses
entitle you to a 20% discount on cableway prices.) From the top, a trail
follows a mountain ridge unveiling views of more mountains and glaciers of
Zillertal and Stubai. Both Seegrube and Hafelekar have hotels with dining
facilities but it's cheaper to pack a lunch.
     To Bergisel, take tram #1 in direction of Bergisel from Anichstrasse
and ride to last stop. Bergisel is a memorial to Tyrolese killed in battle,
with a good view of Innsbruck and Nordkette mountain range in background.
Here also is the Regimental Museum of the famous Emperor's Riflemen
which is open 8-6, adult/10 AS, student/5 AS. Bergisel is starting point for
several marked and numbered hikes (see day hikes below). It is also possible
to go from here to Ambras Castle via the Mittelberger railway (line 6) to
Igls. Castle is open May-Sept 10-4, closed Tuesday, guided tour every half
hour, adult/10 AS. Schloss Ambras was built on a projecting rock and is the
dominant landmark for the surrounding valley. Castle is considered one of
the finest Renaissance palaces in Austria. Inside a collection of weaponry
from 15th to 18th centuries is displayed. There is also a "Chamber of Artifacts and Marvels." Grounds are landscaped with ponds and waterfalls. To
return to Innsbruck, take tram #3, bus "K" or line 6 of Mittelberger Railway
(Mittelgebirgsbahn).
     Day Hikes. There are 15 marked and numbered hiking trails through

the woods and villages near Innsbruck. Trails are numbered and marked in blue and white. Tourist office free leaflet "Innsbruck" outlines all 15 and more detailed maps can be bought here. Alpine Auskunft office on Boznerplatz sells the topographical map (Freytag-Berndt-Wanderkarte map to scale of 1:100:000, sheet 3 of Innsbruck Environs).

Hike #1. Tummelplatzweg and Castle Ambras. One hour. Trail starts at Bergisel, passes war cemetary (Tummelplatz) and leads to Castle Ambras. Return to main railway station in Innsbruck by tram #3, bus "K" or line 6 of Mittelgebirgsbahn.

Hike #2. Bederlungerweg. All day hike starting in Bergisel and ending in the interesting town of Solbad Hall from which you can return to Innsbruck by train or bus. Trail parallels hike #1 in the beginning and then branches for an easy ascent to village of Aldrans and Herzsee (lake) for 1-3/4 hours. From lake, trail continues to towns of Judenstein, Rinn and Tulfes (2 hours), reaching Solbad Hall in another hour.

Hike #7. Hottinger-Bild-Weg. Trail starts at Hotting bus stop, "Grosser Gott," in northeastern Innsbruck. Trail leads by Schlotthof and Planotzenhof (huts) to Hottinger Bild (hut) in one hour. Here are connecting paths (1) to Gramartboden (hut) or (2) the longer route by Stangensteig to Kerschbuchhof (railway station) and then to Kranebitten (bus stop). Latter branch is hike #8, the Stangensteig.

Hike #14. Rosnerweg. Trail leaves from Hungerburg at end of Hungerburgbahn (12 AS one way). Going in easterly direction towards Arzler Alms trail branches to Herzwiesenweg about 1-1/2 hours out and then meets connecting trail to Rumer Alms 2 hours. Return trip is easy descent to town of Rum with bus stop for return to Innsbruck.

Overnight hikes. Provide yourself with lug soled shoes or boots, jacket resistant to wind and rain (sudden), sunglasses and sun burn preventive cream. Trails are marked. Maps should be bought from Alpine Auskunft. Following two hikes take AVKarwendel map, 1:25,000, western sheet. Hikes can be made in one day, but are for experienced hikers only. ALL HIKERS SHOULD GET IN TOUCH with Alpine Auskunft for the latest news on trail and weather conditions before starting. It is imperative that climbers carry proper and good climbing equipment.

Reith Bei Seefeld (3,395 ft.) to Reither Spitz (7,831 ft.) and back. Allow 4 hours for the ascent plus return time. First take Mittenwald train to Reith bei Seefeld. From Seefeld Station, pick up the trail at the church. Path heads across the meadow and begins to climb through the woods until a little before Rauhenkopf where trail turns left to Schartlehner Inn and follows Schoasgrat ridge to Nordlinger Hutte (food available) at 7,385 ft. and another hour. Path continues to follow the ridge, climbing 500 more feet to peak of Reither Spitz which takes about 30 minutes hiking time. From the peak, the view is of Karwendel mountains and glaciers of Zillertal and Stubai. Mieming and Lechtal mountains are to the west. Return to Seefeld by same trail.

Hungerburg to Sattelspitze. Allow 5 hours. All trails are marked. Take the Hungerburgbahn to Hungerburg and then Nordketten cablecar to Seegrube (6,287 ft.) which costs 78 AS for both (less reduction with railpass). The trail climbs steadily for about a hour, then follows the ridge to top of Sattelspitze (7,824 ft.) in a half hour. Panoramic view. Take the same trail back to the spring before Seegrube. Then rather than returning to Seegrube, follow the trail down past Hottinger Alm (hut) and Umbruckler Alm (hut) to Hungerburg.

LAUNDROMAT   EFEF-Wascherei is at Amraser Str. 15, open M-F 7:45-6:00. Frances Packer reports one is on Burgerstrasse.

READERS' SUGGESTIONS   "Skip Innsbruck unless you like hiking, and then only if the weather is good." (Frances Packer)   "We would recommend seeing Neuschwanstein, "Mad" King Ludwig II's castle in Fussen, Germany. It was like stepping into a fairy tale: winding stairs, romantic murals of knights, fair damsels and wizards, hidden rooms, high towers, and a crashing waterfall in a ravine outside. We would not, however, recommend going there from Innsbruck, which looks very close on a map. We decided to make a day-trip to Fussen from Innsbruck and got there 5-1/2 hours later after a train ride and two bus trips. We missed the last bus back and had to go all the way to Munich to catch a train to Innsbruck. We got back to camp at 3:00 am! We're not sorry we went because the castle was enchanting and the trip through the mountains between Innsbruck and Garmisch-Partenkirchen was beautiful. But we would suggest to anyone interested that the trip to Fussen be made from Munich. It's only a few hours. Save the mountains around Garmisch for another day." (Linda Clark)

HIKES IN TYROL BETWEEN INNSBRUCK AND SALZBURG

Many small towns along the Arlberg Express train route are good starting points for hikes in the valleys and mountains. Always check with the tourist office for trail and weather conditions and have proper maps and gear.

SCHARNITZ   From Innsbruck, take Mittenwald railway line which passes through Seefeld and continues to Scharnitz. Many trails begin from here into the Karwendel mountains. Shorter trips are available, but there is a 4 day hike through Karwendel Valley punctuated by a visit to a mountain hut each day. First hut is Karwendel, second is Falken and third, Lamsenjoch. Trail ends at Achensee (lake and town). Take local train to Jenbach on main railway line between Innsbruck and Salzburg. Topographical maps can be bought from Alpine Auskunft in Innsbruck. For the experienced hiker only.

KELLERJOCH MOUNTAIN   Trail leaves from picturesque town of Schwaz, 17 miles from Innsbruck in direction of Salzburg. No campground in Schwaz, but there's camping near swimming pool in Solbad Hall, on railway line five miles before Schwaz. Camp has store, snack bar and hot showers. Trail to Kellerjoch mountain (7,700 ft.) from Schwaz is termed "moderately easy."

ZILLERTAL ALPS   From Jenbach, 22 miles from Innsbruck in direction of Salzburg, a narrow gauge railroad runs for 20 miles into the Zillertal Alps. Several hikes are available--Tuxer waterfalls and glacier of Gefrorene Wand, trail through Zemmtal Valley to Berliner Hut at 6,750 ft., or an all day hike to Plauener Hut at 7,700 feet in the Zillergrund.

RATTENBERG   Seven miles from Jenbach, Rattenberg is an interesting old town with a one hour trail to Reintaler lakes for swimming.

WESTENDORF   Ten miles before Kitzbuhel is Westendorf, where a chairlift to Alpenrosenhaus at 5,250 ft. is start of several trails. In KITZBUHEL, Camping Schwarzsee, is a 40 minute walk or take bus from station plus 5 minute walk. Free hot showers, washing machine, adult/38 AS, tent/25.

ZELL-AM-SEE (SEL-ahm-zay) Take cable railroad from Zell-am-see to Schmittenhohe (6,457 ft.), starting point of many trails including Pinzgauer Path which runs mostly at 6,000 feet and has good views. In Zell-am-see, Stadtgemeinde Camping is by lake and has hot showers, store, snack bar and bus stop.

KLAGENFURT

Camping Strandbad Klagenfurt is within a municipal recreational-cultural park called "Hobbyland." Take bus A (direction Annabichl) which begins its run in front of the train station, and leaves on the hour and 7, 15, 22, 30, 37, 45 and 52 minutes past each hour. The bus travels along Bahnhof Strasse for 7 blocks and then turns left on Paradeiser Strasse, pasts Neuer Platz, then right onto Dr. Hermanng Strasse, then get off in one block at Heiligengeistplatz. Change to bus S which originates at Heiligengeistplatz, leaves at 22 and 52 minutes past each hour, and travels on Villacher Strasse for about 20 blocks until it reaches Europa Park (Hobbyland) and the campground, and terminates. Camp has hot showers/5 AS, money exchange, store, restaurant, washing machine/10 AS, adult/32 AS, tent/free. Within the park are zoo, museums, planetarium, beach, mini-golf, pond, outdoor chessboard, and start of 9 km trail along Lake Worthersee.

Open market is at Benediktiner-Platz, two blocks from Neuer Platz and tourist office.

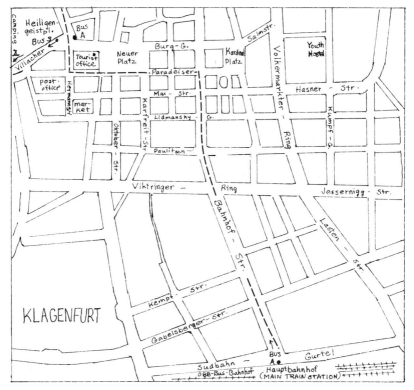

76

LINZ

From Ray Rylander: "Take tram #3
from hauptbahnhof two stops to
Blumauer Platz (Wienerstrasse).
Change to tram #1 and ride it south
one stop (just under the underpass)
at Unionstrasse. Change to trolleybus #41 for long, roundabout ride
to Eichendorfstrasse. Campingplatz
is on the right. Good store on the
left."

READERS' SUGGESTIONS

"My favorite place in Austria is
Obertraun--50 meters from the
station in a farmer's cow pasture."
Editor's note: Obertraum is near
Bad Aussee, southeast of Salzburg
and on the rail line Linz - Stainach
Irdning. "The little camping place
in Hallstatt in Ober Austria, where
early man first learned to dig in the
earth for minerals, lies across the
lake from the town, and you must
take the lake boat. Very, very
primitive--an outdoor john, and you
must pull water from a well in a
bucket, but the camp is free, if you
shut the gate behind you and don't
let the cows in. There's the lake
for swimming." Ray R. Rylander
Editor's note: Hallstatt is one
train stop after Obertraun in the
direction of Bad Ischl.

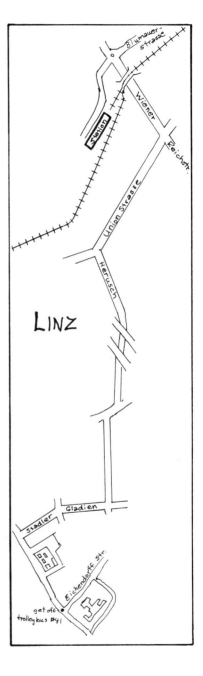

ST. WOLFGANG

Southeast of Salzburg, the Salzkammergut region is noted for limestone mountains and many lakes. Wolfgang See (lake) is the best known. The area is beautiful with many trails giving access to the interior. (Higher than average rainfall in this area though.) Rail passes give free use of steamers which connect the towns on Lake Wolfgang, and rack railway from town of St. Wolfgang to Schafbergspitze (mountain). Allow about 4 hours for the Schafbergspitze trip which includes a 2 hour cog-wheel railway journey and sightseeing time at the top. Train departs several times daily. Try to sit on left hand side going up. From the summit is a good view of the many lakes in the area. Bus from Salzburg (40 km) passes by two campgrounds about 1 km from St. Wolfgang. Camping Appesbach, adult/33 AS, tent/20 AS, is closest. Camping Berau is slightly farther away towards Stroble, has washing machine/40 AS, dryer/25 AS, hot shower/10 AS, adult/28 AS, tent/ 20 AS, tax/4 AS per person. The closest town served by the railways is Bad Ischl which is about 15 km from St. Wolfgang and connected by bus.

SALZBURG

Salzburg (ZAHLTS-bork) hosts the Mozart Festival during August when the town becomes filled to capacity. You'll be able to squeeze in at least one of the eight campgrounds around town, but festival tickets are harder to come by at the last moment. Write ahead to Austrian tourist office for schedule and prices if you're interested.

TRAIN STATION   Train station (hauptbahnhof) has a tourist office (informationsdienst), exchange office (wechselstube) and post office. Station is 12 blocks from Makartplatz, center of downtown, and within walking distance of the municipal campground. Salzburg's second train station is Bahnhof Gnigl.

TOURIST INFORMATION (Informationsdienst)   There are several offices, but the most convenient is at train station. Ask for town map, bus route map, two page sightseeing bochure and addenda "Visiting Hours and Fees for Sights of Salzburg City." Club Young Austria organizes tours for youth groups of members under 27. Typical arrangements offered are for 3, 4 or 7 days, with music workshops for choirs and orchestras and special interest programs such as folklore. Write in advance at Alpenstrasse 102; 5020 Salzburg, Austria.

CAMPGROUNDS   Stadtcamping, Bayerhamer Str. 14 A and several blocks east of the station, is the most conveniently situated for train-campers. Camp can be reached by taking the pedestrian overpass at north end of terminal which puts you across from the station on Lastenstrasse. Turn left on Lastenstrasse and walk a half block until street is intersected (45-degree angle) by Weiserhofstrasse. Turn right on Weiserhofstrasse and then left on Breitenfelderstrasse for one block. Turn right on Bayerhamerstrasse. Or, take the car route by walking on Rainerstrasse south to underpass. Turn left on Gabelsbergstrasse and follow signs. (See map next page.) Open May 15 to Oct 31. Camp is fairly crowded in July and August. Hot showers (5 AS), store, snack bar. July and August fees are about adult/25 AS, child 4-14/ 20 AS, tax 8% plus 1 AS. Lower fees are charged at other times. To reach "old town" from camp, walk to bus stop on Bayerhamerstrasse and

Sterneckstrasse. Take bus "G" in direction of Kongresshaus (not Lengfelden) and ride to Kongresshaus, the last stop. Next door are Mirabel Park and Castle. Transfer to bus #3 or 5 at Kongresshaus bus stop. These buses travel beside Mirabel Park before crossing Salzach River to "old town." Rathaus bus stop is first stop across river. Camp to downtown is a 15 minute walk. We didn't see any in July, but Ray Rylander writes: "And you didn't mention the slugs at Stadtcamping Salzburg. Great big ones that crawl up the tent at night. The first time with the wife, we left in the middle of the night. The next time with the boy, we put a saucer of beer in front of the tent, and the next morning--25 or 30 drunk slugs!"

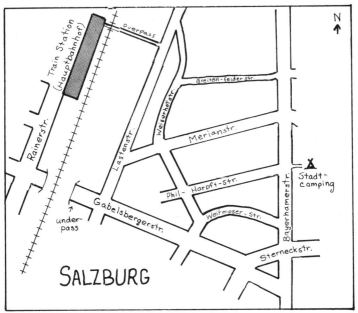

Camping Ost-Gnigl, Parcherstrasse 4, is near Bahnhof Gnigl. Open Apr 15-Oct 15. From main station, Hauptbahnhof, local trains leave for Gnigl station only every couple of hours. From Bahnhof Gnigl, walk south-west for one block to Aglassingerstrasse. In third block is a tourist office. Two blocks farther, Aglassingerstrasse is renamed Parscherstrasse and the camp is on this street near the athletic field. Or, take bus #4 from Makartplatz. To get downtown, walk two blocks north to where Minneshei-merstrasse intersects with Aglassingerstrasse (near tourist office) to bus stop. Take bus #4 (direction Leifering Spitz) which first goes to Makartplatz in the newer part of town before crossing the river to the old town. Camp has hot showers, store, snack bar, no cooking facilities, fees slightly less than Stadtcamping.

CITY TRANSPORTATION   Single bus ticket costs about adult/10 AS, but you can save 1/3 by buying a 5 ride card (5 Fahrten Karte Erwachsene) for 37 AS or a 10 ride card (10 Fahrten Karte Erwachsene) for 70 AS. Children under 15 and luggage pay 5 AS per ride or 18 AS for a 5 ride card and 36 AS for a 10 ride card. The 5 and 10 ride cards MUST be bought before boarding the bus from a ticket agency or tobacconist with the sign "Fahrschein Vorvekauf" and picture of bus in the middle. Bus driver only sells single tickets. Most buses have no conductor. Each person is responsible for cancelling his ticket in the machine inside the door. Bell rings as ticket is cancelled. Each ticket is good for one transfer. A map of bus lines "Salzburger Stadtwerk-Verkehrsbetriebe" is free from tourist office.

FOOD   Public markets are at Gruenmarkt on Universitatsplatz in the old town, open M-Sa 7:30-4; and on Schrannemarkt, outside Andrakirche, and open Thursday morning. Restaurant meals are cheaper in areas outside the central area. You can beat the prices downtown by buying coldcuts at a "feinkost" and eating in a park. In the old town, not far from the market on Universitatsplatz, is the restaurant complex Sternbrau at Getreidegasse 34. Its self-service section has the cheapest food. Tables outside on the terrace are for self-service too. This restaurant butchers its own meat and prepares sausages right on the premises.

SIGHTSEEING   A walking tour of Salzburg takes the full day, and then you may wish to visit Schloss Hellbrunn. Walking Tour. From Stadtcamping, walk ten blocks to Schloss Mirabell to explore the grounds, not missing the statues of the funny fat dwarfs. The park has many out-of-the-way spots for picnics. From Schloss Mirabell, walk to Makartplatz, the central square. Cross over Staatsbrucke (bridge) to the old town (inner stadt) to make the obligatory pilgrimage to Mozart's birthplace (Geburtshaus) at Getreidegasse 9. The market is nearby on Universitatsplatz. Continue to Mozartplatz (center of town) where chimes play at 7 am, 11 am and 6pm. A tourist office is on Mozartplatz. Continue past the Cathedral to base of funicular ascending to fortress Hohensalzburg, that imposing structure on the hill that lends Salzburg much of its character. Funicular leaves every 10 minutes from 7:30 am-11 pm, June-August, with shorter hours rest of year. The fortress was started in 1077 and continually enlarged until 1681. Guided tours through some historically preserved rooms, castle of Museum of Medieval Art and Rainer Museum are given May-Sept, daily 9-5:30 at 15 minute intervals. About adult/14 AS, student/10 AS, child/3 AS. Tours of residence are July-Oct M-F 9-12 & 2-5, SaSu 10-12; Nov-June M-F 10-12 & 2-4, SaSu 10-12, about adult/8 AS, student and child/1.50 AS.

Schloss Hellbrunn, castle and grounds, are termed "manneristic early Baroque style." Located south of Salzburg, take bus "H" from main station which stops downtown before proceeding to Schloss Hellbrunn. Bus operates June 15-Sept 14 only. Ride is 20 minutes. Castle and grounds are open Apr-Oct. Castle is open May-Aug daily 8-6, shorter hours rest of year. In July and August, park is open Monday and Friday evenings until 8:30 pm when admission is about adult/25 AS, child/12 AS. Regular admission is about adult/20 AS, child/10 AS. There are guided tours of the castle from June through August. Garden is famous for its trick fountains that occasionally sprinkle spectators unexpectedly, and as an example of a Baroque ornamental garden with grottoes and a rock theater. Alpine zoo is adjacent. Salzburg Folklore Museum is in Monatsschlosschen, built in 1615, in the garden. Some castle rooms are unique and ingeniously planned.

80

LE POTPOURRI   A Self-service laundry is across the square from the
Hauptbahnhof.   Need medical attention?   Go to Landescrankenhause,
University medical outpatient clinic, for least complicated approach to
medical care at reasonable cost.

VIENNA (WIEN)

The architecture of Vienna (Wien in German) is basically Baroque and the
city can be adequately viewed in three days although there's plenty to do if
you have more time. If you have come this far, you might consider going
a little further to visit close-by Budapest in Hungary. Stop at IBUSZ office,
26 Kaerntnerstrasse near the opera, first thing as a visa takes 2-3 days to
process.
    Vienna is best visualized as a pebble thrown in the water with the
concentric circles expanding outward. The inner ring is the old quarter
where most of the sightseeing is. It's surrounded by Ringstrasse, which
refers both to a boulevard and a circular tram route. Pedestrians use underpasses to cross the Ring. Many public buildings, such as the opera, city
hall and parliament are found along the Ring. Beyond is later growth of
Vienna with light industry, newer shopping areas and train stations. Next
are residential areas, and finally campgrounds and the Vienna Woods are
located 7 to 10 kilometers from the center. Vienna Woods is a large natural
forest park with trails, and is open to the public.

TRAIN STATIONS   Two main ones are Wien-Westbahnhof (west station) and
Wien-Sudbahnhof (south station). Westbahnhof serves Scandinavia, Germany,
and northern Europe in general, plus the Austrian towns of Salzburg and
Innsbruck. Tourist Office is on upper level and is open daily 6:15 am-11 pm.
Exchange office is open daily 7 am-10 pm. Sudbahnhof carries traffic from
Italy and southern Austria such as Graz and Villach. Tourist Office is open
daily 6:30 am-10 pm. Exchange office is open daily 6:30 am-10 pm. A train
leaves Vienna from each station at 7, 9, and 11 am and 3, 5 and 7 pm. A
third station, Wien- Mitte (central station), serves East Germany and
Czechoslovakia.   Free with railpass is the bus operated by Austrian Federal
Railway between City Air Terminal and Schwechat Airport, from 6 am to
7 pm.

TOURIST OFFICE   Both main stations have one. For downtown Vienna, try
the tourist office in Opernpassage, the small shopping center in the underground passage beneath the Ring in front of the Opera House. Office is open
9-7 and sells a good "Guide to the Sights of Vienna" for 15 AS. Restrooms
are in passage too. For best prices for musical events, purchase tickets
at Rathaus box office where you'll pay about 80 AS rather than the 100 AS
at the tourist office and other places.

CAMPGROUNDS   Vienna have five, four of which are accessible to public
transportation.

Camping Wien-
West I and Wien-
West II are munici-
pal campgrounds at
Huttelbergstrasse
40 and 80, about
6 km from downtown.
From Westbahnhof,
take tram #52
(marked Baumparten)
to last stop. Trans-
fer to tram #49
(Hutteldorf) to last
stop. Change to bus
52 B and get off at
second stop. Tram
ticket costs adult/
12 AS, child/6 AS
and is good for both
transfers. Another
way is to take a local
train from Westbahn-
hof, get off at
Hutteldorf-Hacking
Station and take bus
#52 B to campground.
From Sudbahnhof,
take tram #18
(Urban Loritz-Platz)
to last stop. Trans-

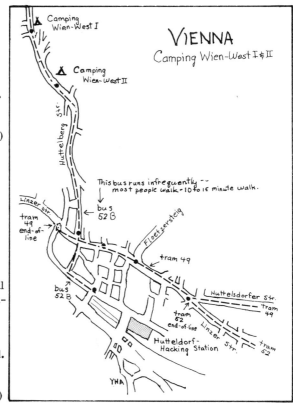

fer to tram #49 (Hutteldorf) to last stop. Change to bus #52 B and get off at
second stop. Bus stop is next to camp entrance. (See map.) Both camps
have hot showers, store, post office and washing machines (30 AS). Postal
address for Wien-I is Campingplatz der Stadt-Wien, Wien-West I,
Huttelbergstrasse 40, 1140 Wien, Austria. Camp fee is adult/26 AS. To
go back downtown, continue on tram #49 to the end. Francis Packer adds:
"Camping Wien-West II -- can walk from end of tram #49 since bus 52 A is
infrequent. Has free stoves, money exchange, directions in English for
trams to various sites." Editor's note: In verifying the information in this
edition, the Vienna Tourist Office corrected bus 52 A to be bus 52 B. Ray
Rylander comments: "Camping Wien-West in der nahe Hutteldorf is OK. It
is a large campingplatz with every facility you need, and easy to get to from
the Autobahn, the S-bahn, and tram line 49. It is very popular, usually very
crowded, also very noisy. I hacked it there for 2 nights, and then went looking for the other camping places in Wien. The one I chose was Stadt Camping
Wien Sud in Rodaun. Tiny, off the beaten path and hard to get to, but quiet.
And the people are more friendly."

Camping Wien-Sud Rodaun is open all year. Here are Ray Rylander's
directions. "Ok, there are several ways to get there if you are afoot in Wien.
From the Westbahnhof (and most people coming to Vienna by train get off at

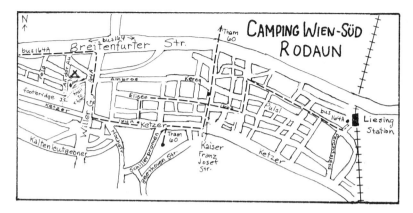

this station) go out the main door and to the right. The big street roaring by
is Mariahilfer Strasse. Go out to the tram island and catch a tram #58, going
away from town with the sign-board "Unter St. Veit". Ride it out past the
Technical Museum on the right and Schloss Schonbrunn on the left. Get off at
Kennedy-Brucke, where the tram makes a big loop around a kiosk. Walk
across the way and change to a tram #60 "Rodaun." Ride it to the end--a
beautiful tram ride. Arriving in Rodaun, the tram makes a left turn off
Ketzergasse to the end station. Walk back to Ketzergasse and turn left toward
the Wienerwald. Cross Willergasse, where most of the traffic turns. Beyond
this intersection, Ketzergasse dwindles down to a narrow lane, hardly wide
enough for 2 cars to pass. Apartments on the left, first little shops, and
then forest on the right. Then you will notice a little stream on the right.
Then a little footbridge. Turn right and cross it, and you will find yourself
on the street, "An der Au." Walk a little ways farther and there is the
campingplatz entrance."

"A free non-heated swimming bad (pool), free hot water showers, a
little restaurant, and a little store (but a cheaper one is across the creek).
And quiet! But if you can't stand the ducks that quack on the lake, you better go back to Wien-West and listen to diesel buses and yelling hippies."

"There are other ways of getting there, like take the S-bahn (from
Sudbahnhof, for example) to Liesing Station, and then catch the Kalksburg
bus #164, which goes along Breitenfurterstrasse. Get off an An der Au and
walk south a couple of blocks. If you come in at Franz Joseph Bahnhof, go out
main door and catch a tram #5 and ride to its end station at Mariahilfer-
strasse, change to line 58, and
proceed as from Westbahnhof."
Bus 164 A also leaves from
Liesing Station. Harold
Parkerson reports, " a
putzerei (automatic washer and
dryer) at 366 Ketzer Gasse
within walking distance of
campground (wash 47 AS,
dry 54 AS).

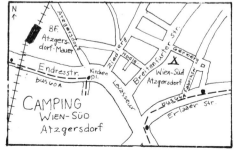

Camping Wien-Sud
Atzgersdorf, Breitenfurter-

strasse 269, is open May-Sept. Take the schnellbahn from Sud or Meidling Stations to Atzgersdorf-Mauer Station. Then a short walk. (See map.) Sud Station is at Sudbahnhof. Campground has trees, hot showers, cooking facilities, store and restaurant.

CITY TRANSPORTATION   There are trams, buses, "schnellbahn" (subway), "stadtbahn", "badnerbahn", U-Bahn (under construction) and local stations of the OBB (Austrian Railways and included in train passes.) Tourist office map, "Wiener Stadtweke, Berkehrsbetriebe," shows public transportation routes and locations of campgrounds. Single fare for tram, bus, metropolitan railway (stadtbahn) and schnellbahn is 12 AS. The cost is reduced to 8.60 AS each if a 5-ticket book is bought for 43 AS. A 24 hour ticket costs 43 AS and a "3 Day Vienna Ticket" costs 55 AS (the best buy). Ticket books and 24 hour ticket can be bought in most tobacconist shops. The 3 day ticket can be bought from any tourist office. All three tickets can be bought from any office of Wiener Verkehrsbetriebe, city transport office. A single ticket allows transfers in any direction on any form of public transportation.

These are the train lines of the OBB (Austrian Railways) in Vienna. One line goes north from Franz-Josefs Bahnhof and stops at Heiligenstadt, Nussdorf, Kahlenbergerdorf, Klosterneuburg, Klosterneuburg-Weidling, and Klosterneuburg-Kierling on its way to Tullin. Another line goes west from Westbahnhof and stops at Penzing, Hutteldorf-Hacking, Hadersdof-Weidlingen, Weidlingau-Wurzbachtal, Purkersdorf-Sanatorium and Unter-Purkersdorf. Two lines leave from Sudbahnhof, one stops at Simmeringer Hauptstr., Stdlt. Brucke Lusthaus, Lobau, Stadlau and branches north and east. The north branch stops at Kagran, Gerasdorf and continues to Laa a. d. Thaya. The eastern branch stops at Erzherzog Karl-Strasse, Hirschstetten Aspern, and continues to Marchegg. The other line from Sudbahnhof goes to Simmering (Ostbahn), Kledering and towards Bruck a. d. L. Trains out of Meidling Station stop at Inzersdorf Ort and Inzersdorf Metzgerwerk in the direction of Wiener Neustadt. From Landstr. Station, trains stop at Rennweg, Simmering (Aspangbahn), Zentralfriedhof, Kl. Schwechat Gross, Schwechat-Flughafen Wien in the direction of Wolfsthal. There is another line out of Sudbahnhof which goes to Meidling Station but after Meidling, the next three stops Hetzendorf, Atzgersdorf-Maurer (campground) and Liesing (campground) are classified as Schnellbahn stops, but the ones after Liesing are OBB stops again. They are Perchtoldsdorf, Modling, Guntramsdorf, and Gumpoldskirchen.

FOOD   Vienna has 17 public food markets scattered throughout the city. Hours are M-F 6 am-6:30 pm, Sa 6 am-2 pm. Schwendermarkt, Schwendergasse and Reichsapfelgasse, is on tram lines 52 and 58, and passed as one goes to Camping Wien-West or Wien Sud Rodaun from West-Bahnhof (station). After boarding the tram from in front of the station, get off at the fourth stop and then walk back one block past Holler Strasse to Reidhsapfelgasse. Meiselmarkt, Meiselstrasse and Wurmsergasse, is on tram line 49 when taken from Wien-West Camping into town without transferring to tram 52. Get off at John Strasse, a main intersection, and walk forward one block to Wurmsergasse. Market is about 14 blocks from West Bahnhof.

Markets closer to the "ring" are Karmelitermarkt, Krummbaumgasse and Im Werd, which is outside the "ring" across Salztorbk bridge and then

a three block walk; Augustinermarkt, Landstrasse Hauptstrasse and Erd-
bergstrasse, is outside the "ring", one block from Landstrasse Station;
Karolinenmarkt, St. Elisabeth Platz, is by the Cathedral of the same name,
four or five blocks from Sud Bahnhof; Naschmarkt is located along parallel
avenues Linke Wienzeile and Rechte Wienzeile at Getreidemarkt, outside
the "ring' about seven blocks from the Opera House。
    BILLA and LOWA grocery store chains have the best prices and good
quality. Wurst sold at sausage stands is generally priced per 100 grams.

SIGHTSEEING   Kunsthistorisches Museum is Vienna's museum of fine arts
at 1 Maria Theresien-Platz near Hofburg. Stadtbahn and schnellbahn:
Karlsplatz, tram: all circular lines. Open Tu-F 10-3, SaSu 9-1, Tuesday
and Friday evenings 7-10 pm. Adult/20 AS, student/free, groups/10 AS.
    Schonbrunn Palace is in the southwest sector of Vienna far beyond the
Ring, but not as far as the campgrounds. From camp Wien-West, take
bus #52 B to last stop at Hutteldorf-Hacking Station of Austrian Railways.
Nearby is city subway (stadtbahn) terminal station Hutteldorf Hacking. Take
it and get off at fifth stop, Schonbrunn. From Camping Wien-Sud, ride tram
#60 to last stop. Palace is open daily 8-5, although the grounds don't close
until 8 pm. Castle is shown by guided tour only. Tour hours are 9-12 and
1-4. Adult/20 AS, student/5 AS. The summer palace of the Hapsburgs,
Schonbrunn is a white and gold, ornate rococo affair set with formal Baroque
gardens.
    Belvedere Palace is near Sudbahnhof. From camp Wien-West, take
bus #52 B and get off at second stop. Transfer to tram #49 and get off at
Urban Loritz-Platz. Change to tram #18 and get off at Belvedere, just beyond
Sudbahnhof. Address is Prinz Eugen Strasse 27. Open Tu-Sa 10-4, Su 9-12,
Friday until 7 pm. Adult/10 AS.   Palace houses three art collections: 20th
Century Gallery, Baroque, and Medieval Galleries.
    The Danube River between Krems and Melk, 85 km from Vienna, is
the most scenic part and has castles, terraced vineyards and orchards.
Steamers depart from Praterkai on the Danube in Vienna. (Tourist office is
on pier.) Steamers operated by Erste Donau-Dampfschiffahrts-Gesellschaft
between Passau and Vienna are free with train pass. (Delphin plying between
Linz and Vienna is excluded.) For a day trip, ride the train to Melk, visit
its Baroque Benedictine Abbey--largest monastery north of the Alps, and
take the 3:10 pm boat back to Vienna. Trains leave from Westbahnhof for
Linz and stop at Melk on the way at 9:05 am, 9:10, and 12:20 pm for the hour
trip. Other trains leave Westbahnhof for Selzthal and stop at Melk on the way
at   7:35 and 9:10 am.

SHOPPING   Flea Market, Naschmarkt, is Saturday 7-6. Dorotheum is the
national auction house, administered by the government, where reasonably-
priced goods can sometimes be bought. Located at Dorotheergasse 17, the
doors open M-F 10-4, Sa 8:30-12。 The procedure is to go early in the week
to look over the goods and then to return towards the end of the week to bid
as items go on the block. You pay bid plus two percent fee.

TRAIN SCHEDULES   The Transalpin Express, a scenic train ride which
crosses the Alps lengthwise, goes between Basel, Zurich, Innsbruck,
Salzburg and Vienna. It leaves Basel at 9:52 am and arrives in Vienna at
9 pm. It leaves Vienna Westbahnhof at 9 am and arrives in Basel at 7:46 pm.

Cook's Timetable mark   this run as "reservation required," whether or not
this is actually the case, I don't know. It carries both first and second class.
To Budapest, the Wiener-Walzer Express leaves Vienna Westbahnhof
at 9:20 am and arrives in Budapest (Keleti) at 1:45 pm. Rail passes are good
only to the border. A ticket can be purchased for the remainder (from
Hegyeshalom to Budapest) at the train station in Vienna before leaving, or at
the border where it can be paid for in the Hungarian currency forints. (See
Hungary chapter about bringing in the legally allowed amount of forints which
are bought cheaply from any bank in Vienna--as it is this allowance which
makes Hungary cheap.) Danube hydrofoils make the run Vienna-Budapest in
about 6-1/2 hours with the return journey upstream about a hour faster. It
leaves weekdays from Vienna at DDSG quay at 2:30 pm, arriving in Budapest
at 7:10 pm. It leaves Budapest at 8 am and arrives in Vienna at 1:30 pm.
To Prague, the Vindobona Express leaves Vienna Mitte Station at 9:20
in the morning and arrives in Prague (main station) at 3:04 pm. Returning it
leaves Prague at 2:54 pm, arriving in Vienna at 9 pm. Railpasses are good
to the border at Gmund, but a ticket must be bought for the remaining 183 km.
It can be bought in Vienna before you go. Other trains ply this route, including an overnight one, but they are slower. Reservation is required on the
Vindobona, according to Cook's Timetable.

LICENSE PLATE CODE

An easy way to learn the nationality of your camping
neighbors is to glance at the white oval sticker on their car.
Each country has a different set of abbreviations.

A	Austria
B	Belgium
CH	Switzerland
CS	Czechoslovakia
D	Germany
DK	Denmark
E	Spain
F	France (a '75' means Paris)
GB	Great Britain
GR	Greece
H	Hungary
I	Italy
IRL	Ireland
L	Luxumbourg
N	Norway
NL	The Netherlands
P	Portugal
PL	Poland
S	Sweden
SF	Finland
YU	Yugoslavia
TR	Turkey

ATTENTION!!!   The railway schedules given in this book are
for planning purposes only. They are meant to give the reader
some idea of train frequency and length of journey. Please check
all departure times in a current timetable or at the station.

The directions given on how to reach campgrounds should be
double-checked with the tourist office in the respective city.
Sometimes a campground will have been closed or the bus or
tram route changed.

Pronunciation of place names is given phonetically in parenthesis following the name.

PACK TOO HEAVY?   Mark the envelope "printed matter," "impresos,"
"imprimes," or "drucksache" to cheaply mail home tourist literature.

BELGIUM

This small country has the best snack food in Europe--the Belgian waffle--
and excellent train service. We would put Bruges, a lovely medieval walled
town, first on our list and then we would choose among Antwerp, Brussels
and Gent.

CURRENCY   Belgian franc. Each franc is worth about 2-3/4¢. One dollar
equals about 37 francs (F). Value-added tax is deducted from purchases
sent out of the country.

WEATHER   Generally like the Pacific Northwest, except June is the
sunniest month with the warmest weather. July and August are also good
though an occasional rainfall might come. Nights are cool. Camping in May
and September in a tent is more wet and cold. High season is July 15-August
15 and any summer weekend on the coast.

CAMPING   Belgian tourist office will send you the brochure, "Camping
1981" which is a partial listing of campgrounds. Many towns have camps
that aren't listed in the brochure. Brochure gives distance from bus stop.

TRAINS   Belgium National Railways (SNCB) maintains a dense railway
network and frequent service. A railpass holder could set up headquarters
in one city and make day excursions from there as Antwerp to Brussels takes
only 29 minutes, Brussels to Gent 32 minutes and Brussels to Bruges, one
hour. Trains depart about every 30 minutes to and from these main cities
during rush hours and about hourly at other times. Railway information
offices give free railway schedules. All stations have coin-operated luggage
lockers costing 10 or 15 francs and taking two or three 5 franc coins. The
attended baggage check costs about 15 francs for 24 hours. Belgium is a bi-
lingual country and railway signs are posted in Dutch and French. Arrival
is "aankomst" or "arrivee", departure is "vertrek" or "depart" and track
is "spoor" or "voie."

Tourist Season Tickets are sold for second class travel for five days for 1130 F, 10 days for 1490 F and 15 days for 2120 F of unlimited travel for 5, 10 or 15 days within a 16 day validity period. A Half-Price Card valid for one month allows rail tickets to be purchased at half price and costs 410 F second class. Groups of 10 receive a 25% reduction, groups of 20 which are traveling more than 100 kilometers receive a 50% reduction or pay a maximum of 380 F per person. Groups of 10 under 21 years of age receive 50% off with the maximum fare payable being 253 F in second class. These tickets are sold at all major train stations in Belgium or write Handelsagentschap N.M.B.S., Frankrijk Straat 85, B-1070 Brussels, Belgium. Also available is a Benelux Tourrail ticket which gives unlimited train travel in Belgium, The Netherlands and Luxembourg for 2180 F second class for ten days within a 16 day period. Cost is 1670 F for persons 12 to 25 years old.

BELGIUM TO BRITAIN Cheapest way to go from Ostend to London is the night crossing by ship combined with second class rail to London for which a ticket is 980 F. By day, Ostend to Dover or Folkestone costs 794 F and Ostend to London (ship plus train) costs 1304 F. Hydrofoil is 350 F extra.

FOOD Food is cheapest in the open markets and supermarkets. One liter of milk costs 19-20 F, 500 gram loaf of bread costs 20-21 F and one whole hot cooked chicken "to go" costs about 150 F in 1981. Belgium's national cuisine is very good and the place to sample it is in the small towns rather than Brussels, Antwerp, Gent or Bruges where prices are higher. Meal hours are noon to 2 and 7-9 pm. The "plat du jour" from the noontime menu of a department store cafeteria is good value. The most popular dish among Belgians is a thin steak filet and french fries (biftek et frites). Belgians eat more potatoes per family than any other nationality in Europe. The next most favored vegetable is endive (witloof or chicorees) served roasted or as a salad. Brussels sprouts (choux de Bruxelles) are often seen. Good entrees include "waterzooi poulet" (chicken stew), "waterzooi poisson" (fish stew), "poularde Bruxelloise" (chicken), "carbonnades flamandes" (beef stew), "tomates aux crevettes" (shrimp stuffed tomatoes) and "anguilles au vert" (eel). "Lapin" or "lievre aux pruneaux" (rabbit or hare with prunes) is commonly eaten in Flanders (Bruges or Gent). A recurring appetizer is "fondue au fromage" (cheese croquette served with fried parsley). Beer is the national drink as Belgium has almost no vineyards. "Biere de table" is light beer. Strong Orval beer is made by Trappist monks.

CHILDREN Babysitters are listed in the phone book under "Babysit Service." "Bureau de Placement" at any university maintains a list of sitters. In Flemish-speaking regions, movies are shown in the original language with subtitles whereas dubbing is usual in French-speaking areas. There are children's matinees.

ANTWERP (ANTWERPEN, ANVERS)

Belgium's biggest port, Antwerp is 50 miles from the sea on the River Schelde. Brussels is 30 minutes away by twice-hourly train. In 1983 Antwerp hosts the Biennial Exhibition of Contemporary Sculpture which was outstanding the year we saw it and definitely worth a special trip for modern art enthusiasts.

TRAIN STATIONS Main station is Central Station located about ten blocks from downtown and the riverfront. Station exchange office is near the restaurant. Further away from downtown, Berchem Station is on the Brussels line, and TEEs and international expresses on the route Rotterdam, Antwerp, Brussels and Paris stop only at Berchem Station. Some of the other trains on this line stop only at Central Station while others stop at both. Trains to Gent stop at both stations and go at least once an hour.

TOURIST OFFICE   It's in front of Central Station on Koningin Astridplein and is open daily. Main office is at Suikerrui 19 near the Steenplein. The tourist office city map contains a compendium of helpful sightseeing information. It also stocks a free bus and tram map and sells tickets, 8 rides for 85 F.

CAMPGROUNDS   Best is the municipal camp, STEDELIJK KAMPEER-TERREIN, Jan Van Rijswijcklaan 193, which is located just off that street behind the Building Center. Open Apr-Sept. Take tram #2 or bus #27 (19 F) from Koningin Astridplein in front of Central Station. Hot showers in modern restroom building, no store or restaurant but about a ten minute walk from a suburban mainstreet with shops. Capacity is 170 persons on a flat, grassy field. Adult/25 F, child/free, tent/25 F. CAMPING DE MOLEN at St. Ann's Beach (St. Annastrand) on the left river bank. Take bus #36 (19 F) from Koningin Astridplein in front of Central Station. Snack bar, cold showers only. Adult/25 F, child to 15/free, tent/ 25 F.

FOOD   Public market is on Oude Vaartplaats (off Frankrijklei) on Saturday 10-4 and Sunday 9-1. Sarma Supermarket downtown has an inexpensive cafeteria. Two main department stores, both with restaurants, are Innovation on corner of Meir and Otto Veniusstraat, and Grand Bazar, Groenplaats and Eiermarkt.

SIGHTSEEING   MIDDELHEIMPARK, Middelheimlaan 59, is a 15-minute walk from the municipal campground or take tram #15 or bus #17, 27 or 32 from Central Station. Open daily 10-sunset. Free. The permanent collection of pieces by Rodin, Maillol and others is set among the trees but the super exciting part is when the Biennial Exhibition of Contemporary Sculpture is held in odd-numbered years across the road from the other. During the Exhibition an entry charge of adult/25 F, adult under 25/15 F, child/free is made and is well worth it.

PLANTIN-MORETUS Museum, 22 Vrijdagmarkt, is a 16th century patrician house with the original printing shop intact. Open daily 10-5, free. Tram #3, 2 or 15 from Central Station. RUBENS HOUSE and GARDENS is the artist's luxurious 1610 villa now open to the public as a museum. Open 10-5, free, tram #2 and 15 from Central Station or one kilometer walk. STEEN CASTLE on the waterfront houses the maritime museum, National Scheepvaartmuseum. Open daily 10-5, free, tram #2, 3, 10, 11 or 15 from Central Station. The PORT itself is third largest in the world with 3167 acres of docks, 18 dry docks and 6 locks. Flandria Excursion boats offer tours of the port and River Schelde for about adult/ 160F and child under 12/120 F starting at 10 am and 2 pm. Another Flandria boat goes to Flushing in The Netherlands by motoring down the River Scheldt and across to the island of Walcheren to visit the picturesque towns of Middlebug and Flushing (Vlissingen). All boats leave from Steenplein. St. Anna tunnel, the pedestrian and bicycle underpass beneath the River Scheldt, is one block away on your left as you face the river from Steenplein and leads to a modern district.

GROTE MARKT, focal point of the old town, is lined with the Town

Hall (Stadhuis) and Gothic and Flemish Renaissance Guild Houses. Take
tram # 2, 3, 10, 11 or 15 from Central Station. The important and enormous
Gothic OUR LADY CATHEDRAL rings with Carillion Concerts on Friday
11:30 am and Monday 9 pm from June-Sept.
ROYAL GALLERY OF FINE ARTS (Koninklijk Museum Voor Schone
Kunsten), Leopold de Waelplaats about ten blocks from Grote Markt, shows
an excellent collection of Flemish primitives and 16th and 17th century
painters. Contemporary art is also shown and Belgium's foremost modern
artist, Ensor, is represented by his reputed best work, "Entry of Christ
into Brussels." BROUWERSHEUIS, Adriaan Brouwerstraat 20, is the
original brewers' house constructed to supply pure water to the breweries
and is now a museum showing the original hydraulic works. Open 10-5, free.
MAYER VAN DEN BERGH MUSEUM, Lange Gaastruisstraat 19, has a small
collection of choice paintings. Open 10-5, free. VOLKSKUNDEMUSEUM
(regional ethnology) shows folklore and has a puppet theater. Open 10-5, free.
HET VLEESHUIS MUSEUM (Butcher's House), Vleeshouwersstraat 38-40,
contains musical instruments and weaponry. Open 10-5, free. The world-
famous ZOO beside Central Station has an aquarium, dolphin tank, museum
of natural history, planetarium and modern reptile house. Open 8:30-5:30,
adult/160 F. A diamond exhibition at the Veiligheidsmuseum, 28-30
Jezusstraat, is open 10-5 and gives demonstrations 2-5 pm weekends, free.

ARDENNES

The Ardennes (ahr-DEN) is an area south of the Meuse River noted for its
natural beauty which is revealed to the traveler by simply taking a train
through the area. Jemelle, the gateway town, can be reached via Namur or
Liege. From Jemele the journey continues to Han-sur-Less through a
national forest and wildlife preserve and beside a grotto where waters of the
Lesse River alternately go underground and resurface. A while later the
train passes through Rochefort grottos enroute to Luxembourg.

BOKRIJK

Belgium's outdoor museum of historic rural buildings from the Flemish-
speaking part of Belgium is in Bokrijk, a 75-minute train ride from
Brussels. The farms, stables, thatched roofs and windmills are part of a
larger recreation complex including four restaurants or snack bars, trails,
arboretum, museum of natural science, lakes, rose garden, deer reserve,
and playground which has an immense wading pool with water slide, climbing
bars, twinned roller coaster slide and swings. Open daily Apr-Oct 10-6, 70 F.
Train line is Brussels-Landen-Hasselt-Bokrijk-Genk. Get off at Bokrijk
Station which is at park entrance.

BRUGES (BRUGGE)

Bruges (pronounced broozh) is a choice medieval and renaissance town that
is very convenient to the main rail routes of Europe. The city is an hour
train ride from Brussels and a 14-minute ride from Ostend on the English
Channel. A very rich and important city in the 13th to 15th centuries, the
town went into decline when its shipping route filled with silt. Allow a day for
this very pleasant and tranquil walking town, but pack along lunch as there
are no inexpensive restaurants in the area in which you'll be concentrating

your efforts. A sack lunch can be supplemented by freshly cooked french fries served in a paper cone "to go" from a vending truck on the Markt. (Benches surround the inner square.)

TRAIN STATION   Railway information is open Mar-Sept, M-Sa 8-7 and Su 8:30-12 & 2-6:30. About a 15 minute walk from the station will bring you to the Markt, the central and most impressive square of Bruges. Maps of the town are on signposts.

TOURIST OFFICE   Dienst voor Toerisme is in the halles (#7) on the Markt and open Apr-Sept, M-F 9-8, Sa-Su 9:30-12:30 & 2-8. Ask for its brochure which contains a map of three walking itineraries and its larger, fold-out map of town. Tourist office will change money on weekends when banks are closed.

CAMPGROUNDS   ST. MICHIEL CAMPING, Tillegemstraat 29, open all year, is reached by bus #7 (St. Michiels) (16 F) from behind the station. Hot showers, restaurant, beer garden, store. Adult/38 F, child/21 F, tent/50 F. LAC LOPPEN CAMPING, Lac 10, is on the lake in the village of Zedelgem. Open all year. Take bus #66B (Brugge-Roeselare) from station. "Must walk 1/4 mile down road to right after bus lets you off. Supermarket at bus stop is best," Frances Packer, Los Altos, Ca. Hot showers, restaurant, beer garden, store. Adult/50 F, child/30 F, tent/50 F.

FOOD   Public market is Saturday morning on the Markt. Sarma cafeteria, Steenstraat 73-75, open daily including Sundays, has meals in the 95-250 F range which is about the cheapest available in Bruges itself. Sarma is located near St. Saviour's Cathedral and near the square Simon Stevinplein, about half-way between the train station and the Markt.

SIGHTSEEING   The MARKT, focal point of Bruges, is of similar characterization though smaller than the "Grand Place" in Brussels. Its notable gothic tower, the Belfry, can be climbed for a view of the town. Open Apr-Sept, daily 9:30-12 & 2-6, shorter hours rest of year, adult/ 20 F. Below the tower is a 14th century market house, now offices and the tourist office. Historic guild houses surround the square.

     Though the town is a museum in itself and wandering around is sufficient attraction, you may still wish to visit a few museums in Bruges. A central museum ticket, good for entrance into the Groeninge, Arentshuis, Gruuthuse and Memling museums, is 100 F and sold at each museum and the tourist office. General museum hours are Apr-Sept, daily 10-12 & 1:45-6.   GROENINGE MUSEUM on Dyver Canal is nearest the square and a fine arts museum. Highlight is the collection of early Flemish masters which are displayed in separate rooms with one important work to each. In the 17th century, every painter in Bruges was required to belong to the Corporation of Painters and Saddlemakers. The museum started when dissidents formed their own Academy requiring each to donate a painting as dues. In this museum are the most reproduced panels of van Eyck, Memling and Bosch. Adult/40 F. Close by is the GRUUTHUSE Museum which displays period rooms including an interesting kitchen, and silver, lace, china and musical instruments within its 15th century mansion. Adult/40 F. ST. JOHN'S HOSPITAL has the important HANS MEMLING Museum, adult/40 F including entry to Old Dispensary.

     BEGUINAGE, home of nuns is a tranquil spot open M-Sa 10-12 & 1:45-

6, Su 10:30-12 & 1:45-6. No charge for visiting the grounds, and the house which costs 30 F to enter is of minor interest. Virgin and Child sculpture of MICHELANGELO may be seen in the south transcept of the Church of Our Lady, open Apr-Sept 10-12 & 2:30-6, closed Sunday mornings. Also of interest are the Van Eyck Square in the "old quarter," fish market, Gothic Basilica of the Holy Blood and the lace makers on Walplein. LACE CENTER on Balstraat is a lace-making school which can be visited M, Tu, Th 2-6 and W, Sa 2-4. BOAT TRIPS on the canals last 35 minutes and cost adult/90 F and child under 14/40 F. Boats leave from several docks such as the one beside the Town Hall on the Burg. Canals and Historical monuments are floodlit nightly from May through September. HORSE DRAWN CABS leave from the Markt in front of the Belfry Tower, 300 F per cab for 40 minutes. FLEA MARKET is on Dyver on Saturday afternoon and Sunday. Flower Market is on Burg Square Saturday and Wednesday morning. CARILLION concerts peal from the Markt, June 15-Sept M, W, Sa 9-10 pm, Su 11:45 am-12:30 pm. Rest of year: W, Sa, Su 11:45 am.

Reader's Suggestion: "Rent bikes--need to get out into the countryside. Belgium is particularly good for bicycles. We rented bikes in Bruges and rode to Zeebruges--very enjoyable for an afternoon." Philip Jones, W. Chester, Pa. Rent bikes at train stations for 120 F (or 95 F with train ticket) per day. Bike can be returned to any train station in Belgium.

(BRUSSELS   (BRUXELLES)

If you haven't time for anything else in Brussels, at least try to stop off to see the illuminated "Grand Place" at night--it's only a few blocks from Central Station.

AIRPORT   In Zaventem, nine miles from downtown, the airport has currency exchange, tourist information, restaurant, hotel and daycare (open 7 am - 10 pm daily for children under 12). Airport is connected by train with Central Station in downtown Brussels. Fare is 42 F including luggage or free with railpass. Trains leave every 20 minutes and stop mid-way at Gare du Nord Station. Entire trip takes 18 minutes. Follow signs in airport to railroad platform. No tipping.

TRAIN STATIONS   Brussels has three main stations, Brussel-Noord (Bruxelles Nord), the downtown station Brussel-Centraal (Gare Centrale) and Brussel-Zuid (Bruxelles Midi). Though all three stations are connected and trains zip through the heart of Brussels underground, INTERNATIONAL TRAINS may not stop at Central Station but only at the other two. Local trains stop at all three so it's always easy to get to Central Station from the other two stations. MIDI Station is the largest with the most facilities and

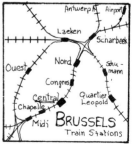

bus connections. Services include exchange office, seat reservations, train information and lockers. At the train information office, pick up their brochure on one day rail excursions called "A beautiful day at..."

TOURIST INFORMATION   Main office is at 61, rue du Marche-aux-herbes, which is near the Grand Place, the central square. Open June-Sept, M-F 9-8, SaSu 9-7; Oct-May daily 9-6. "General Plan of Brussels and Suburbs" has campgrounds marked. "Plan du Reseau" shows bus, tram and subway routes. Request its excellent brochure on the Grand Place, and "Brussels Guide" which lists museum hours. The office also stocks information on the other cities and towns in Belgium.

CAMPGROUNDS   CAMPING BEERSEL, Ukkelsesteenweg 75 in suburb of Beersel, is open all year. Take tram #55 from Nord or Midi Stations (or local train from any station) to Uccle-Calevoet. Change to bus "UB" outside of Uccle-Calevoet Station to Beersel. Camp is 100 meters'from bus stop. Hot showers, store, adult/23 F, child/12 F, tent/17 F. Camp is 9 km to the south of Brussels.

CAMPING PROVINCIAAL DOMEIN, Provinciaal Domein 6 in Huizingen, 13 km to the south of Brussels, is open Mar 15-Sept 30. Take a local train to Huizingen Station which is 1 km from camp, or to Buizingen Station which is 1.2 km away. There is also a bus which stops 200 meters from the camp. No hot showers; store and restaurant are .5 km away; adult/30 F, child/ free, tent/free.

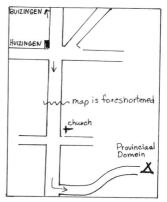

CAMPING GRIMBERGEN, Veldkantstraat 64 in Grimbergen, 13 km north of Brussels, is open Apr 1-Oct 31. From Station Nord, take bus G (not bus G because it goes in the other direction) and get out at the Barcelle Kerk (church) bus stop. Cold showers only, 1 km to store and restaurant, adult/25 F, child/25 F, tent/ 16.5 F.

CAMPING PAUL ROSMANT, Warandeberg 52 in Wezembeek-Oppem, 10 km east of Brussels, is open Apr 1-Oct 31. Adult/35 F, child/18 F, tent/ 35 F.

CITY TRANSPORTATION   Subway (metro), pre-metro (tram lines which run underground), trams and yellow buses are part of the STIB (Societes des Transports Intercommunaux de Bruxelle) network. There are also orange suburban S.N.C.V. buses. A one day tourist ticket is sold by the tourist office, in railway stations, in newspaper kiosks in metro stations and from drivers of S.N.C.V. buses (orange buses in the Brussels area). Cost is 55 F for one day of unlimited travel on metro, pre-metro, tram, yellow buses and orange buses within the Brussels area. Have the ticket stamped by the automatic machine or collector from starting your day's travels.

Price of a single ticket is 23 F payable to the driver of a bus or tram, or at the ticket office at a metro entrance. A card good for 10 rides costs 130 F and is sold in metro ticket offices and some newspaper kiosks. Cards valid for 5 rides cost 85 F and are only sold on trams and buses. Have the card punched in the machines at metro entrances or near the front door of buses and trams.   Transfers are free but you must remember to pick up a transfer ticket by pushing the button marked "transit" at the entrance to metro stations or near the entrance door of trams and buses.

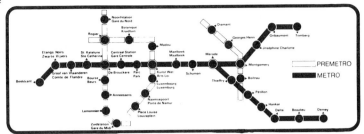

Metro stations are marked by a big M in white on a blue background.
Tram and bus stops are indicated by red and white or blue and white signs.
Previously mentioned tickets are for the STIB network and do not include the
suburban orange S. N. C. V. buses except for those within Brussels when
using the one day ticket. Ordinary local trains can be used to some extent
in the greater Brussels area.

FOOD   Market is on Place St. Catherine about 11 blocks from Central
Station. Open daily 8-6. Numerous small food shops are nearby. Department
stores offer a noon fixed-price meal. Au Bon Marche, across from Place
Rogier on corner of Rue Neuve and Boulevard du Jardin Botanique, five
blocks south of Nord Station, has a cafeteria on its fourth floor. Its Self-Service Express offers a set menu between 11 am-2:30 pm, M-Sa. Cafeteria is
open 11-6 and to 9 pm on Friday. Noprix department store, 32 Rue du
Marche aux Poulets, a fairly short seven blocks west of Central Station, has
a second floor cafeteria. Sarma department store, 17 Rue Neuve and about
nine blocks northwest of Central Station has a cheaper menu, open M-F 11:30
to 3. Mister G. B. Cafeteria chain has a good branch at Porte de Namur,
about 10 blocks south of Central Station at metro stop Pte de Namur. This
large modern operation is open 8 am-10 pm. SNACKS--be sure to try the
waffles(gaufres) sold in department stores. Vending carts selling mussels
and tiny shish-ka-bobs line Petite Rue au Beurre near Place de la Bourse
in the evenings.

SIGHTSEEING   GRAND PLACE is the top attraction and worth a return
visit when it's illuminated at night. The most important building in the square
is Hotel de Ville (Town Hall), a most imposing example of Gothic architecture. MUSEE de L'ART ANCIEN, 3 Rue de la Regence, five blocks south of
Central Station, has a good collection of Old Masters including outstanding
works by Breughel and Bosch. Open T-Su 10-5, adult/5 F or free Saturday
afternoon and Sunday, student/free, groups/2.5 F. One hour guided tour
in English if you write ahead. Subway is Parc Royal or bus route, Place
Royale.
    ROYAL CENTRAL AFRICAN MUSEUM, Leuvensesteenweg 13 in
Tervuren, has a fine group of African art and departments of zoology,
anthropology, etc. which cover every phase of African life and history. Open
daily 9-5:30, free, take tram #44 from Central Station or tram #45 from
Midi Station to last stop. MUSEE d'ART MODERNE, Place Royale, shows
mostly 19th and 20th century Belgium paintings and some contemporary
French, German, English and Dutch paintings and sculpture. Open Tu-Su
10-12 & 1-5, adult/ 5 F. ATOMIUM in Heysel, symbol of the Brussels World
Fair, can be reached by tram #18 from Porte de Namur. The huge BOIS DE
LA CAMBRE park has trails threading through its pruned woods.

GENT (GHENT)

Gent is Belgium's second great medieval museum town. In contrast to
Bruges, the old parts in Gent are mixed with the new thriving city so sightseeing is not so self-contained. Musical performances are given in the great
medieval buildings of the town during the Festival of Flanders which occurs
during August, September and October.

TRAIN STATIONS   St. Peter's Station (St.-Pietersstation), located at the
K. Maria-Hendrikaplein (square), contains a regional tourist office (Feder-
atie voor Toerisme in Oost-Vlaanderen), and is where international trains
stop. Dampoort Station (Dampoortstation) is closer to downtown, used for
local trains and does not have a tourist office.

TOURIST OFFICE   Dienst voor Toerisme is at Borluutstraat 9, downtown
(open M-F 9-12:30 & 1:30-5); and at Graaf Van Vlaanderenplein (on the exit
of highways E3-E5) and within easy reach of St. Peter's Station (bus 70 or
71 (open daily 9-7).   The office sells a detailed color brochure for 20 F.

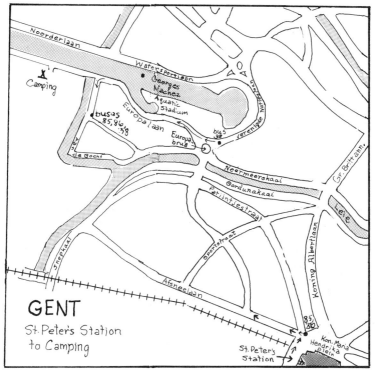

CAMPGROUNDS   Blaarmeersen Camping, Zuiderlaan 12, was new in 1979
and is rated four stars by the Belgian Tourist Association. Open Mar 1 -
Oct 10. From St. Peter's Station take bus 85 or 86 to last stop. From
Dampoort Station, take bus 70 or 71 to St. Peter's Station (last stop) and
change to bus 85 or 86 to last stop. Or else, take bus 30, 31 or 17 to the
Koornmarkt and there change to bus 38 to last stop. Then camp is a few
minutes by foot. The camp is in a suburban area of high rises, and the

modern Georges Nachez Aquatic Stadium is on the same side of the river. Hot showers, store, snack bar, adult/35 F, child/25 F, tent/40 F.

PUBLIC TRANSPORTATION   A single bus or tram ticket is 17 F, or 18 F including transfer. Six tickets are sold for 57 F.

FOOD   Fruit and vegetable market is at Groentenmarkt, open M-F, 7-1 and Sa 7 am-7 pm. Chickens and rabbits are sold at Oude Beestenmarkt on Friday 7-1.

SIGHTSEEING   OLD QUARTER centers around St. Baafsplein and Koornmarkt. On St. Baafsplein is St. Baafskathedraal (St. Bavo's Cathedral) with its 15th century tower. Inside is the masterpiece, "The Adoration of the Mystic Lamb," by the van Eyck brothers. At the other end of the square is the Belfry and Cloth Hall, a towered building dating from the turn of the 14th century. In the Cloth Hall, a 20-minute historical audio-visual show, "Ghent and Charles V," is given in English using a model of Ghent as it was 400 years ago. Continuous performances daily 8:30-11:30 and 1-5:30 for 15 F.
    From St. Baafsplein, walk to Botermarkt, anchored by the Town Hall (15th century Gothic and 17th century Renaissance) with flags flying from it. In Koornmarkt, oldest of the old, St. Nicholas Church dates from the 13th century. Behind Koornmarkt on Graslei Street, facing the canal sits a row of guild houses with decorated facades and stair-stepped roofs. Guild House of the Grain Measurers (1698) is the one with wreathlike decoration near the peak of its front. To its right is Guild House of the Free Boatmen (1531). Tiny house of the Toll Collector (1682) flanks its left. Grain Warehouse (1200) is next to it followed by First Grain Measurer's House. The building with a top looking like candles on a tiered birthday cake is the Mason's Guild House dating from 1526.
    MUSEUM OF FOLKLORE, three blocks from Koornmarkt, recreates life around 1900 with 18 Flemish houses, room settings and mannikins showing people at work. St. Michael's Church is across St. Michielshelling bridge near St. Nicholas Church. The former was started in 1440 and completed in 1648 and now shows 17th century art. CASTLE OF THE COUNTS (Gravensteen) was built in 1180 by the Count of Flanders, Philip of Alsace, and is located four blocks north of Koornmarkt on St. Veerleplein.
    Grouped together are CITADEL PARK, SPORTS STADIUM, MUSEUM OF FINE ARTS and FLORALIA PALACE. From near camp, take bus #51 to last stop or bus #52 or 54 to Museum of Fine Arts (Museum voor Schone Kunsten). Museum is noted for its Flemish School (15th-20th centuries) and has the Bosch works, "The Bearing of the Cross" and "St. Hieronymus."
    Flower market, Kouter, operates daily 7-1. Bird market on Prof. Laurentplein is open Sunday 7-1 and the Pet market on Oude Beestenmarkt is open Sunday 7-1.

SHOPPING   Flea market on the Beverhoutplein near St. Jacob's Church is open Friday 7-1 and Saturday 7-6.

OSTEND (OOSTENDE)

The cheapest crossing from Ostend to Dover, Britain, is any ship leaving Dover between 9 pm and 5:59 am. On these crossings a combined ticket for the crossing plus connecting train to London is 980 F. (This compares with

a fare of 1,304 F during the daytime. These large car-ferry ships depart
Ostend at 11 pm (not Sat and until Sept. 26), 2:00 am (Tu-Sa, June 2-Sept 26),
and 5:00 am (June 2-Sept 26). Daytime sailings are at 8:00 am, 11:00 am,
2:00 pm, 5:00 pm and 8:00 pm. Crossing time is 3 3/4 hours. The entire
journey from Ostend to London takes about 5 hours. For the same rates, you
can go from Ostend to London via Folkestone instead of Dover, except that
the trip takes about 6 hours and 15 minutes and departs at 1:45 am (June 1-
Sept 26) and 5:15 am (weekdays June 1-Sept 30). Children from 4 to 14 pay
half these prices.

Taking the Jetfoil (hydrofoil) shortens the actual sea crossing to 40
minutes but a supplement of 350 F per person regardless of age is assessed
on top of the ship ferry price. This price structure makes the cheapest Jetfoil the 9:04 pm departure with London arrival at 10:36 pm. However, for
Jetfoil crossings passengers must check in 45 minutes before departure to
be processed for customs. (On the ship ferries, passengers go through
customs while on board.)

Tickets can be bought at the Belgian Railways office, outside the train
station at Natienkaai 2, or at the Maritime Transport office, Natienkaai 5.
Sealink operates the ferry and jetfoil crossings and their ship ferry docks
are next to the train station while the jetfoil departure point is across the
water at Vuurtorenook.

TOURIST INFORMATION office
is in Festival Hall on Wapenplein, a 6 block walk or bus 5
from the station. Summer hours
are M-Sa 9-1 & 2-8, Su 10-1 &
2-8.

CAMPGROUNDS   Four camps
can be reached by bus 6 (direction Raversijde, not Stene)
from the train station. De Kal-
kaert, Fleriskotstraat 8; Ostend
Camping, Nieuwpoortsesteen-
weg 514; Petit Bruxelles,
Duinenstraat 93; and Ramon,
Duinenstraat 127 are all resort
camps and charge about adult/
40-60 F, tent/40-50 F.

CITY TRANSPORTATION
Information office is at Brand-
ariskaai, near the station.
Tram 1 travels between Ostend
and nearby resort of Knokke.
Tram 2 goes between Ostend
and resort town of DePanne.
City buses cost 16 F, and trams
20-75 F according to distance.
One day and 5 day tourist cards
are sold.

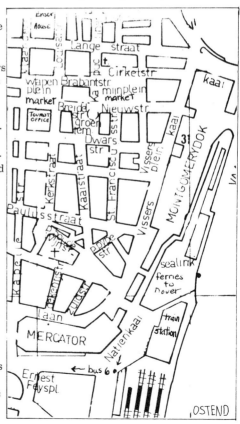

FOOD Markets are held starting at 8:00 am in the mornings of Thursday (the main day), Saturday and Monday on the Wapenplein, the Groentemarkt and the Mijnplein. An old-fashioned picturesque fish market is held on the Visserskaai each morning. The modern fish market is in the "minque" across the channel from the station. Bus #3 goes there from Marie-Joseplein. From campgrounds, change to bus #3 at the Town Hall. Market is best on Monday, Tuesday, Wednesday and Friday mornings.

SIGHTSEEING Ensor Museum, 27 Vlaanderenstraat, is the house where James Ensor, Belgium's foremost modern painter, worked and lived. Open Wed-Mo 10-12 & 2-5, adult/20 F. North Sea Aquarium, Visserskaai, is open daily 10-12:30 & 2-6, adult/20 F. Six hikes are marked by orange hexagonal signs and range from 6 to 80 kms.

SWIMMING Swimming conditions are indicated by color of pennant on the beach. Green means safe, yellow that swimming can be dangerous but is still permitted, and red that swimming is prohibited. Indoor-outdoor pools with heated salt water are near Thermal Institute on K. Astridlaan. Open in summer M-F 8:15-12:00 & 1:00-7:30, SaSu 9-12:30 & 2-6:30.

CHILDREN At the Dolphin Club, on the beach next to the Lido, there is day-care for children up to 14 years old for 150 F per day.

BRITAIN

Great Britain is where you can read all the signs even though you can't understand everything they say. Remember to LOCK RIGHT when crossing streets.
Britain is a bargain when compared with northern European countries, so if
this is your arrival country, save those cans of tuna and peanut butter for
across the Channel.

CURRENCY   Pound(£)is divided into 100 new pence (p). One pound is worth
$1.90.

WEATHER   Variable. June days can be sunny or they can be cold, damp
and rainy. July and August are more reliably warm.

CAMPING   Camping is very popular in Britain and British campers are
very friendly. British camps generally charge a flat fee rather than separate charges for each person, tent and car. This is the
type of sign used and it indicates whether the camp is
only for tents, for both tents and caravans (trailers) or
only for caravans.

TRAINS   Eurailpass and Eurail Youthpass are not valid for Great
Britain. British Rail offers similar BritRail passes, and a Brit Express
Travelcard for unlimited travel on buses is also sold. Please refer to
Chapter "Before you Go." A Family Railcard is sold in Britain. One adult
pays full fare and second adult plus up to four children pay about $1.25 per
trip, except at peak travel hours. Card is valid one year and costs about

$40. There are also day-return, weekend return and one month return rail tickets where the return portion of the trip is sharply discounted that are sold in Britain. A bus ticket costs less than half the train ticket.

DRIVING In Britain, cars are driven on the opposite ("wrong") side of the road and hence the steering wheel is on the right hand side of the car. U.S. driver's license is accepted.

OPEN TO VIEW TICKET With this ticket costing $19 you can visit 560 stately homes, castles and palaces including Stonehenge, Edinburgh Castle and Shakespeare's birthplace. (See chapter "Before You Go.")

FOOD The best prepared food value is fish and chips. In 1974, the government began to subsidize six basic food items: milk, butter, bulk cheese, bread, tea and household flour. Milk can be kept for a month and the date on it indicates the last day it can be used, but once opened the milk must be used within 24 hours or refrigerated. One quart milk costs 39p, bread 42p.

CROSSING THE CHANNEL Crossing time is reduced to 40 minutes by taking the hydrofoil. Hoverlloyd crosses between Ramsgate and Calais and Seaspeed Hovercraft between Dover and Calais or Boulogne. About 15-21 crossings daily. Craft accommodate 250-400 passengers and 35-50 cars. Hoverlloyd offers a "youth single fare" for ages 3-18 plus students up to 26 and 10% discount for groups of 10 full-fare passengers. No reduction for round trip. Hoverlloyd has a special fare where a driver pays for the car and is allowed up to five free passengers. Sometimes a driver with extra room will let you ride free or a person might offer to pay part of the fare. This must be done before the driver buys a ticket. A good value is the Express Coach Service from London which leaves London (Britannia Air/ Coach Terminal, Kings Cross, 250 Pentonville Road) at fifteen minutes past the hour between 8:15 am and 2:15 pm and arrives in Calais four hours and 25 minutes later. Most companies sell tickets for trucks that include one free passenger. Also, if you sail you can ask around the marina at Dover and offer to crew for a boat crossing the channel.

LONDON

A wonderful town with superb theater at a bargain, friendly and polite people and a lot to do, no visitor will want to miss London.

AIRPORTS The British Airports Authority owns and manages seven airports in the United Kingdom of which Heathrow, Gatwick and Stansted are in the London area. Heathrow is the busiest international airport in the world and handles over 23 million passengers each year. Upon arrival from abroad you will pass through Immigration and passport control and then go to the Baggage Reclaim area where your luggage is put onto a conveyor belt or revolving table which shows the number of your flight. When going through Customs, enter the green line if you've nothing to declare. An Information desk in each terminal is open 7 am- 10 pm and provides tourist literature. There is a bank in each terminal and the Barclays Bank in the arrival terminal (#3) is open daily for 24 hours. For passengers leaving Britain, a duty free supermarket is available upon presentation of your airline boarding card or ticket. Each terminal has a temporary baggage storage counter which is open 24 hours a day and costs 30 pence a day. You may be asked to open your luggage for security reasons. In terminal 1 and terminal 2 there are daycare facilities for mothers with young children. Each is staffed by a children's nurse and facilities are provided for feeding and changing babies and a play area is provided for children up to age 8. No charge. An unstaffed mothers' room is in terminal 3 and is open from 8 am - 8 pm and can be opened at other hours by asking an airline staff member. Porters whose services are free and free self-service baggage carts are provided in the terminals. Each terminal has a post office and eating facilities. In the roof gardens of the Queen's Building, you can watch the planes take off and land and there is a children's playground. Admission is adult/20 p and child 3-15/ 10 p. British Airways, Air Canada, Pan Am and TWA have executive lounges in terminal 3. TO GET TO LONDON, take the underground (subway) which is the end-station on the Picadilly Line. To Piccadilly Circus in downtown London, from where you take the bus to Crystal Palace Camping, takes 47 minutes and costs about £1. To Liverpool Street for the bus to Hackney Camping requires a change of subway at Holborn and takes 61 minutes for a fare of about £1.10. Trains run every 4-10 minutes between 5:07 am (6:48 Su) and 11:50 pm (10:51 Su). The first arrival from downtown London is at 6:30 am (Su 8:18 am) and the last at 12:53 am (Su 12:18 am). Airline buses are also available and cost about 30 pence more.

GATWICK is Britain's second most important airport. Upon arrival from abroad go through immigration and passport control and then go to the "buffer" lounge where you wait until the television monitors show your flight number. This means your luggage has been unloaded onto the circular tables in the baggage reclaim area. Then get in the green line for Customs if you've nothing to declare. In the international arrival hall there is an information desk that stocks tourist literature and a bank that is open 24 hours a day in summer. The duty-free supermarket is in the international departures lounge after the passport control station. An airline boarding card must be shown when making purchases. Temporary luggage storage is available 24 hours a day. There are two free "mother's rooms" called nurseries. One is in the international arrivals hall and the other in the departures lounge. There are free self-service baggage carts and the help of porters is free. A post office is in the international arrivals area. TO GET TO DOWNTOWN LONDON, take a British Rail train from the station outside the terminal building. Trains leave every 15 minutes during the day and hourly throughout the night for Victoria Station in London.

Stansted Airport is used by some flights arriving from the U.S. After passing the immigration and passport control officer, proceed to the baggage area to select your bags from the turntable. Get in the green customs line if you've nothing to declare. There is a Barclays Bank in the terminal whose opening hours vary according to demand. There is a duty-free shop and a free mothers' room (nursery). Porters carry baggage for free and there are free baggage carts available. Transportation to London is not as good as at Heathrow and Gatwick Airports. Normally the airline upon whose flight you have arrived will have made arrangements for a bus to take its passengers into London. Otherwise, the airport advises the best way is to take a taxi the four miles to British Rail's Bishop's Stortford Station from which a train goes to Liverpool Street Station in London where you can get the underground (subway). There is a Stansted train station but connections are better from

Bishop's Stortford Station. London is 34 miles from Stansted Airport.

TRAIN STATIONS   London has several but the most important is VICTORIA Station which handles departures for the European continent. The station's tourist information is near platform 15 and the nearby Thomas Cook "Bureau de Change" is open daily 7:45 am - 10 pm. National Travel Ltd. (NBC), open daily 8 am - 9 pm, gives information on long-distance buses and sells the Coach Master ticket. Because of the bomb scares, luggage lockers are not in use but the "Left Luggage Department" is available for 35 pence for small articles and 50 pence for large ones for the first 24 hours.

CAMPGROUNDS   London has eight or more campgrounds in the general vicinity. Cheapest and best appears to be HACKNEY CAMPING, Millfields Road, Hackney Marshes, London E5, open mid-June to end of August and reserved for overseas visitors only. The camp only takes tents, has room for 200 of them and charges about £1 per person. From London take the underground to Liverpool Street and then bus 22 A to Mandeville Road and walk over bridge. From Victoria Station, take bus 11 to Liverpool Street and then bus 22 A to Mandeville Road. It's a level grass site with facilities of hot showers, laundry and store. Frances Packer writes "Crystal Palace Campground--easy to get to, very crowded and gravelly. We found a much better one: Hackney Camping on Mandeville Road. Bus 11 from Victoria to Bus 22A at Liverpool Street. Green field, good shop, hot showers. All tents--not campers (R.V.'s, etc.). On the way to campground try "Quality Fish Mart" around the corner from Wimpy's, Graham Road, Hackney. Best fish and chips we found and huge portions."

CRYSTAL PALACE CAMPGROUND, Caravan Harbor, North Parade in Crystal Palace Park in southern part of London, is beside the Crystal Palace TV transmission tower. Open all year. From outside Victoria Train Station take bus 2B (direction Crystal) to the campground. You can also take a local British Rail train from inside Victoria Station. Trains leave every 20 minutes and the fare is 84 p. If you will be coming back into London that day it's cheaper to buy a "day return" fare which is a round trip fare valid one day. Get off at Crystal Palace Train Station which is about a fifteen minute walk from camp (see map next page). Turn right as you come out of Crystal Palace Station onto road. Go to top of hill and turn right. Camp is on

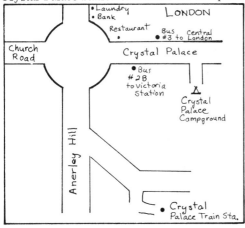

right side before high television tower is reached. From Victoria Coach Station, walk on Buckingham Palace Road to Victoria Railway Station and then take either bus 2B or train as above. From Heathrow Airport, take the underground (subway) to Piccadilly and then change to bus 3 on Regents Street to Crystal Palace. From Gatwick Airport, take the train to Victoria Station and proceed as on previous page.   Eric Wolterstorff writes "The camp can be reached directly by train from Gatwick Airport without going into Victoria Station.   Some trains from Gatwick stop at Crystal Palace, otherwise one must transfer; check the schedules in Gatwick Station.   From Crystal Palace to Victoria Station, trains leave every 15 minutes and take 20-25 minutes.   The day return adult fare was 96 p in 1981."

To go downtown from camp, take double-decker bus #3 into Fleet Street or Piccadilly Circus, a 30 minute ride.   Route is Crystal Palace, West Dulwich, Herne Hill, Brixton, Kennington, Lambeth Bridge, Westminster, Trafalgar Square, Piccadilly Circus, Oxford Circus, Great Portland Town and Camden Town.

Mailing address for the campground is Crystal Palace Campground, Crystal Palace Parade; London S. E. 19. 1 UF GREAT BRITAIN.   No reservations taken.   Office sells guidebooks, go-as-you-please and red-rover tickets.   Camp has hot water in sinks, hot showers, laundry and store. Adult/£ 1. 25 flat fee.   Nearby is self-service laundry and inexpensive restaurant.

ABBEY WOOD CAMPGROUND,   Co-operative Woods Camping and Caravan Site is about 6 km from central London on Federation Road in Abbey Wood, a southeastern section of London.   Take British Rail train from Charing Cross to Abbey Wood Station.   From Victoria Station to Charing Cross, take Circle or District Line underground from Victoria Station to third stop, Charing Cross. After 9:30 am, a day return (round-trip) rail ticket from Charing Cross to Abbey Wood is £1.18.   Also bus 177 from Greenwich goes near the campground.   Site is sloping and grassy with hot showers, store, adult/£1.25. Laundromat is a five minute walk away.

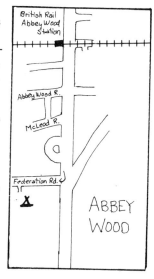

EASTWAY CAMPING SITE, Temple Mills Lane, Leyton, E. 15.   Open April to September 30.   Take the underground to Leyton Station (Central Line) and then it's a 15 minute walk.   By British Rail, Stratford Station is on British Rail Eastern Region (London Main Line Station, Liverpool Street and the campground is about a 20 minute walk.   (Stratford Station is also a stop on the underground.)   By bus, # 6, 30 and 236 all pass close by.   The camp is six miles from downtown London and is a level grassy site, part of a 40 acre park containing a cycle track.   Hot showers, nightly fee/£ 1. 25.   (See map next page.)

GRANGE FARM LEISURE CENTER, High Road, Chigwell, Essex, 1G7 6 DP, England.   The campground is 12 miles from downtown London situated in rural surroundings on 90 acres.   Closest underground station is Chigwell (Central Line) which is one mile from camp and a 40 minute ride

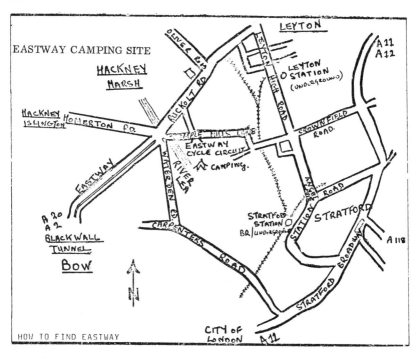

EASTWAY CAMPING SITE

HACKNEY MARSH

HOW TO FIND EASTWAY

from downtown London. Store, dormitories for group accommodation, 600 individual camp sites separated by trees and hedges, hot water in sinks, free hot showers, washing machines and driers, television, reading room, recreation hall with ping-pong, two swimming pools, take-out meals, children's play area. Site fee is £ 2 (6/22-9/6) and £1.50 rest of year plus 60 p per person over 5 years in high season and 50 p other times.

the bus stop sign has "request" written on it. To "request" you ring the bell on the bus or wave your arms at the bus stop. RED ARROW BUSES are downtown shuttle buses with a flat fare of 20 pence. No reduction for children and you must have 2, 5 and 10 pence coins available for coin-in-slot entry gate. Buses stop only where indicated by special blue plates at stops. A RED ROVER bus ticket costs adult/£ 2.10 and child under 16/60p, and is valid one day on all red buses. It's sold at London Transport Enquiry Offices at underground stations at Piccadilly Circus, Oxford Circus, King's Cross, Euston, Victoria and St. Jame's Park. This is a good value, especially if you stay at Hackney or Crystal Palace Camping which can both be reached by bus. Free bus maps are given at London Transport Enquiry Offices.

In the subway stations are easy-to-read fare charts telling what price ticket to buy from the automatic vending machine before boarding train. Children 5-15 pay about half. Save ticket to show at exit if necessary. "Day tube return" (one day round trip) tickets save about 20% and are valid anytime on weekends and after 9:30 am weekdays. They are sold at subway stations. Free subway maps are given at London Transport Offices.

"GO AS YOU PLEASE" tickets are sold for 3, 4 or 7 days and give unlimited travel on all of London's Red Buses and over the entire Underground system (except to a few outlying stations--beyond Northwood, Harrow and Wealdstone, and Debden). It's sold at the London Tourist Board offices such as the one in Victoria Station for: 3 day ticket, adult/£10.50, child under 16/£3.50; 4 days, adult/£13.00, child/£4.50; and 7 days, adult/ £18.50, child/£6.50. A one day Central Tube Rover ticket for unlimited underground travel costs adult/£ 2.90, child under 16/£1.10.

For British Rail trains, the cheapest fare is called "day return" and is a round trip fare in which both directions of travel must be used on the same day. "Return" fare is a regular round trip ticket. "Single" is a regular one-way ticket.

London Country Green Line buses serve Suburban London but can be boarded in downtown London. A Green Line bus will take you to Windsor Castle and other outlying attractions. A "Golden Rover" ticket is sold which allows unlimited travel for one day. On Mondays to Fridays, they cannot be purchased before 9 am. "Outback" tickets are about 40% cheaper than two single tickets and are day return tickets except if you buy one on Saturday the return portion can be used the next day. They are sold on London Country buses or Green Line coaches, but not before 9 am on Mondays to Fridays. Route map is available from office on Eccleston Bridge, Victoria or in Victoria Coach Station.

FOOD   Food is reasonable and a meal at a simple restaurant can be had for £ 2.00. "Nicholson's Guide to London" lists many restaurants in the $5 range that are very good and this is the best practical guide to London. Expensive but worth it is The Carvery at the Regent Palace Hotel (Piccadilly underground) that serves a buffet lunch and dinner with excellent meats and attractive surroundings. The procedure is to sit down at a table first and be served an appetizer by a waitress. Then you serve yourself from U-shaped tables laden with freshly roasted meats, vegetables, salads and hot Yorkshire puddings (popovers). A leg of lamb, roast beef (one each of rare, medium and well) and pork roast are available. Waitress serves dessert. Open for lunch, M-Sa 12-2:30 and for dinner M-F 5:30-8:30. Cost is about

£7. Another Carvery is in the Cumberland Hotel at Marble Arch.

SIGHTSEEING   "Museums and Art Galleries in and near London" lists museums, hours, prices, contents and bus and underground directions and costs 5 p. from London Transport Enquiry Offices (see buses). The Michelin green guide for London is excellent for historical and cultural background and what to see. Michelin-rated three star attractions are as follows. TOWER of London, open M-Sa 9:30-5 & Su 2-5, Tower Hill underground or buses 9A, 42 or 78, June 25-Aug 26: adult/£ 2.50, before June 25 and after August 26: adult/£ 2.00, child/£ 1. Royal Fusiliers Museum is 10 p extra. Crown Jewels entry is adult/60p child/20p. Services at the Chapel Royal are held on Sunday at 9:15 am and 11 am and weekdays at 5:15 pm except August. For free entry contact the Yeoman Warder at the main gate about 30 minutes ahead. Free tours of the Tower are given half-hourly and start from the Middle Tower, close to the main entrance. The 700-year old ceremonial locking of the main gate of the Tower occurs nightly by the chief warden and an escort of guards at 9:50 pm but be there before 9:35 pm. Free passes can be obtained by writing to The Resident Governor, Queen's House, H.M. Tower of London EC 3, Great Britain. The Changing of the Guard takes place at 11:30 am on days when there is a Guard change at Buckingham Palace. Ask at tourist office. There are Gun Salutes at the Tower of 62 guns at 1 pm by the Honorable Artillery Company from Tower Wharf on April 21 (Queen's birthday), June 2 (Coronation Day), June 10 (Prince Philip's birthday) and August 4 (Queen Mother's birthday). Weekdays at the Tower are less crowded than weekends.

British Museum, Holborn or Tottenham Court Road Stations or many buses, M-Sa 10-6, Su 2-6. The City including St. Paul's Cathedral, Hampton Court (Palace and Gardens), M-Sa 9:30-6 & Su 11-6, State apartments, about 50 p. Science Museum, Exhibition Road in Kensington, M-Sa 10-6 & Su 2:30-6, has seven acres worth of exhibits such as locks and fire starting in the basement; mechanical, hot air, gas, oil, electrical energy on the ground floor; machines, meteorology, astronomy on the first floor up; photography on second floor; and optics, acoustics and geophysics on third floor. Victoria and Albert Museum, South Kensington Station or bus #14 from Piccadilly, M-Sa 10-5:50 & Su 2:30-5:50. Kew Royal Botanic Gardens, daily 10-8. National Gallery, M-Sa 10-6 and in June-Sept Tu & Th to 9 pm. Tate Gallery (includes a good modern section), M-Sa 10-6 & Su 2-6, Pimlico Station. Palace of Westminster, Sa 10-5 & M, Tu, Th in Aug & Th in Sept. Westminster Abbey, M-Sa 8-6, Su 8-7:30 & W to 8 pm. Zoo, daily 10-6. Windsor Castle, #700 express Green Line Coach from Victoria Coach Station. Greenwich by boat from Westminster or the Tower for one hour trip to Greenwich Pier or trains leave from Charing Cross, Waterloo and Cannon Street for 20 minute trip. Buses also go there. To see are National Maritime Museum daily 10-6; Cutty Sark, M-Sa 11-6, Su 2:30-6 and Old Royal Observatory.

Michelin-rated two star attractions are Courtauld Institute Galleries, London University in Courtauld-Warburg Building, Woburn Square, bus #14 from Piccadilly Circus or Goodge Street or Russel Square Stations, M-Sa 10-5 & Su 2-5, which shows French impressionists and modern art. Chelsea District. Buckingham Palace. Ham House which has been restored to its 1678 appearance and is owned by the National Trust, Tu-Su 2-6. Kenwood House, 18th century gentleman's country house, daily 10-7. Hyde Park and

Kensington Palace.

THEATER   Buy tickets at theater box offices rather than through a broker
to save money. Even cheaper is to arrive at the theater one hour before the
box office opens and stand in line. Remaining unsold tickets for that day's
performances are sold cheaply on a first-come first-served basis. For instance, the National Theater opens at 8:30 am so be in line at 7:30. Covent
Garden opens at 10 am so get there at 9 am. The cheapest seat is fine.
"Time Out magazine a must," say Kris and Ted Bushek, Eugene, Oregon.

SHOPPING Value added tax (TVA) is deducted from anything sent home or
delivered to departing plane. Camping equipment is sold at the Youth Hostel
Association store, 29 John Adam St., London W. C. 2. John Lewis chain of
department stores will not be undersold. Marks and Spencer is good for
children's clothes. Irish knit sweaters are purchased more cheaply outside
of London in the countryside.

CHILDREN   London offers excellent children's theater. Call "children's
London" listed in phone book to hear a weekly updated recording. For babysitters, there's Child-minders, who charge a membership fee of around £3
and then an hourly charge. Universal Aunts charges a basic fee per appointment plus an hourly fee. Daycare center, Walton, at Knightsbridge, takes
children from 8 am-5:45 pm including lunch. For all these services, figure
on paying $2.50 - $3.50 an hour. Campground personnel may know of someone not connected with an agency who would be cheaper.

EDINBURGH

Edinburgh is a lovely city in the beautiful green countryside. The outgoing
Scots are a delight to encounter and their exuberant English is very easily
understood unless you find yourself so captivated by the lilt that you forget
to listen! If you have arrived in Glasgow, move on to Edinburgh immediately
as Glasgow is industrial and of little interest.   From May to October, a bus
runs daily between Prestwick Airport and Edinburgh. From Prestwick, the
bus leaves at 10 am and arrives in Edinburgh at 12:10 pm. From Edinburgh,
the bus leaves platform A, St. Andrews Square Bus Station at 9 am, arriving
at Prestwick at 11:10 am. Fare is about £5.50. An airline bus connects
with scheduled flight arrivals and departures to and from Anderston Cross
bus depot in Glasgow. Fare is about £3.00. If you use this service from
Glasgow you should be at Anderston Cross bus depot two and a quarter hours
before scheduled flight departure time. If you miss the bus, you can walk
a half-mile to Prestwick Station and take the train to Glasgow. Trains leave
Prestwick Station at 22 minutes and 50 minutes past each hour with the last
train leaving at 10:22 pm. Sunday service is less. The train costs about 50 p
less than the Airport bus but even cheaper is a local bus to Glasgow which
runs about every half hour. Once in Glasgow, there is hourly bus service to
Edinburgh and train service on the half-hour for the 45-minute ride to
Edinburgh. At Prestwick Airport there is a Scottish Tourist Board counter
and a Clydesdale Bank (M-F 6 am - 7 pm, SaSu 6 am-5 pm) on the main con-
course. Airport porters carry baggage for free and free baggage carts are
available to use. In the main terminal is a free mothers' room where a baby
can be fed and changed and young children can play. There is a duty-free shop.

The International Festival of Drama and Music is held annually during three weeks from late August to early September. Besides theater companies and world-famous orchestras, the festival includes art exhibits, film festival, military tattoo and theater productions by student groups playing on the Festival "Fringe." The best procedure is to get the program and subsequently order tickets from the British Tourist Authority in the U.S. or directly from the Festival Society Office, 21 Market Street, Edinburgh, United Kingdom. But don't write until April 1 when the program and tickets become available.

TOURIST INFORMATION   City of Edinburgh Tourist Information and Accommodation Service is at 5 Waverly Bridge next to train station. City map has bus routes and places of interest marked.

CAMPGROUNDS   Camping Muirhouse, 37 Marine Drive, is open April-Sept. Hot showers, store. During Festival reserve in advance by writing City of Edinburgh Parks and Recreation Department, 27 York Place, Edinburgh EH 1 3HP, Britain. From bus station, take bus #16 from nearby York Place and ride to last stop at Silverknowes. From train station, walk on Market Street to The Mound (street) and take bus #27 going north (direction Silverknowes) to last stop. Camp is on the Firth of Forth (bay).

"In Edinburgh, we stayed at Little French Caravan Park on Old Dalkieth Road. Open from April to October. Take bus #33 from North Bridge

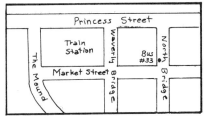

(see map). The park has a store, hot showers were free and sinks had hot water. The grounds were large and grassy," Mr. & Mrs. Robert Cooper. (Cost is £2 +V.A.T. for two people.)

SIGHTSEEING   Top priority is the Royal Mile spreading between Edinburgh Castle and Holyrood Palace. The Military Tattoo performed in the Castle courtyard is famous. Bring raincoats. National Gallery, The Mound near Waverly train station shows El Greco's "St. Jerome," English and European paintings and a group of French impressionists. Open M-Sa 10-5 & Su 2-5. Restrooms outside rooms IV and XIV.

DOVER

Hawthorn Farm Campground is the closest camp to the channel ferries. Open March through October. Brit Rail's Martin Mill Station, at which all London trains from Charing Cross stop, is 300 yards from camp. The Station has a post office. The camp has a store, hot showers, separate tent area, and fees of adult/£1, child to 14/45p.

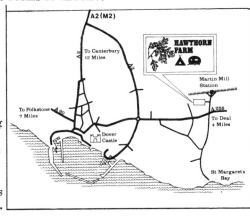

WALES

"Another campground that is within walking distance of the train station is at Betws-y-Coed, Wales," Philip Jones, W.Chester, PA. Famed for its beauty, the small village of Betws-y-Coed is set in a green valley surrounded by forested hills in the Snowdon Region of North Wales. Trains leave Euston Station in London destined for Llandudno on the London-Chester-Holyhead line about ten times daily. The trip is about four hours to Llandudno Junction which is the stop before Llandudno. (Some of these trains require a change at Crewe which is about one hour and ten minutes out of London.) At Llandudno Junction, change trains to the Llandudno-Bl. Ffestiniog-Porthmadog line, and Betws-y-Coed is a half-hour ride and the first stop on that train after Llandudno Junction. Seven trains run each day on this line.

DENMARK

"There is a lovely land
That proudly spreads her beeches
Beside the Baltic strand,

A land that curves in hill and dale
That men have named old Denmark
And this is Freia's hall."
Danish National Anthem

Though Denmark is one of the smallest countries in the world, it encompasses several hundred islands besides its mainland peninsula, Jutland (YOO-lan). During the Ice Age, glaciers carried Norway's topsoil south, dumping it on Denmark's chalk foundation and assuring its future as a prosperous agricultural country. Though Copenhagen is its glittering star, Denmark is predominantly farmland and the visitor is encouraged to break out of the city and pass through the neatly tended agricultural lands of Jutland and Fyn. Try to see one of these three interesting old villages: Ribe (see Esbjerg), Ebeltoft (see Arhus) or Kerteminde (see Odense). Legoland in Billund is obligatory for families with young children.

CURRENCY   Danish krone is divided into 100 ore. There are about 7 kroner (crown-nur) to $1.00. Each krone is worth about 14¢. MOMS (mumps) is the 20 to 25 percent value added tax included in the prices of goods and services. The amount is deducted on any item sent out of the country and it is also possible to get the tax refunded if upon departure you submit the required forms.

WEATHER   June through August is the warmest period, though September can be pleasant too. Brief periods of rain sometimes come amidst sunny

112

skies, but the duration is often less than half an hour. Evenings are chilly at times. July and August are high season.

CAMPING   Whenever he can, a Dane will take off for the beach or go camping. The 500 approved Danish camping sites require the International Camping Carnet or Danish Camping Card. The latter can be bought for 17 kr at any campground, is valid for a year for the whole family and carries third party liability insurance. A camping pass for groups costs 40 kr for up to 15 people. Usual camping fee is 18 kr per adult and half price for children to 14 years of age. Occasionally an extra charge may be made for car, tent or van. Tourist office in U.S. issues a pamphlet, "Camping and Youth Hostels," that includes a map of the country marked with campsites, a listing and official government classification. Official Danish camping guidebook, "Campingpladser I Danmark," is sold in bookstores in Denmark for 30 kr. This guide is very helpful for extensive touring by car because it contains a map of each city and town with campgrounds and most important entry roads marked, and a brief capsule in English of the town's most important attractions. Camp facilities and fees are given and an English translation of symbols and general information are supplied.

YOUTH HOSTELS (Vandrerhjem)   Denmark has about 80 youth hostels, many of which provide "family rooms" for families with children up to 15 years. Family rooms should be reserved by writing ahead as demand is heavy. Youth Hostel card is necessary, but there is no age limit and motorists are welcome. Charges in 1981 were 20-29 kr per person per night so this is more expensive than camping but would be very helpful for an off-season trip. Free tourist office in U.S. publication, "Camping and Youth Hostels," lists names, addresses, number of beds and family rooms, and distance from train station, bus stop and beach.

TRAINS   Danish State Railways (DSB) operate the trains. Some routes involve a ferry crossing for which the train rolls onto the ferry and passengers get off to go above deck. Duty-free shops and the "kolde bord" (all-you-can-eat buffet, a good value) are only available on ferries connecting Denmark to other countries, i.e. Denmark-Germany (Rodby-Puttgarten, Gedser-Warnemunde), and Denmark-Sweden (Helsingor-Helsingborg). Fastest and best trains are LYNTOG (LUEEN-taw) trains. These travel the route Copenhagen, Odense, Kolding and then the train splits with some cars continuing west to Esbjerg and Struer and the rest going south to Sonderborg and the German border.
    Intercity trains are fast modern trains on the main city-to-city routes within Denmark. Each second-class compartment has six seats rather than the standard eight. Intercity trains leave every hour on the hour between 6 am and 9 pm from Copenhagen to Arhus, and 15 minutes past each hour from 5:15 am to 7:15 pm from Arhus to Copenhagen. Trip is five hours. Intercity train service is scheduled also between Fredericia and Flensborg, Fredericia and Esbjerg, Vejle-Herning-Thisted-Skanderborg-Silkeborg, and Arhus-Alborg-Frederikshavn. Trains go to many other Danish towns too and where the trains leave off the buses take over.
    Seat reservation costs 5 kr. Reservation is mandatory on Ⓛ Lyntog (express through) trains and "ic" Intercity trains only when traveling on the "Great Belt" ferry. "Great Belt" refers to ferry crossing between islands of Sjaelland and Fyn. For instance, the "Great Belt" ferry route is taken

when traveling between Copenhagen and Odense. Reservations may be advised for international trains in summer.   On train fares, children 4-12 pay half and those under 4 ride free.   Reductions are given for persons over 65 and groups.   A group must consist of a minimum of three persons and age doesn't matter.   A group of three receives a 20 percent discount, 4- 9 persons get 30 percent off, 10-25 persons get 53 percent off.   Senior citizens can purchase roundtrip tickets for the one-way fare for journeys taken Monday through Friday, as well as Saturday until 2 pm and Sunday until 2 pm except Christmas and Easter holidays.   Transporting your bicycle with you costs 6. 20 kr for 1-100 km trips and 12. 40 kr for over 100 km.

Sold in Danish train stations are a one month ticket valid for unlimited travel on trains, buses and ferries for $144 second class; child 4 through 11 pays half fare; and a "Take Five" ticket valid for unlimited travel on trains, buses and ferries for any five days within a 17 day period for $144 second class, child half price.

A Scandinavian Nordturist Pass is sold in Scandinavia at train stations and is valid for unlimited rail travel in Denmark, Finland, Norway and Sweden for 21 days for $179 and one month for $219.   Children 4 through 11 pay half, and the prices given are for second class.

Train information offices have free schedule leaflets covering individual routes, and a free 104-page booklet, "Fjerntrafik, udland," which gives important international European routes.   For about 7 kr, the information offices sell the DSB KOREPLAN, a 1-1/4 inch thick 815 page paperback listing all train, ferry and intercity bus schedules for the entire country including fares, giving 30 maps with train and bus routes indicated and small inset maps giving the relation of train station to bus station for some cities.   The following symbols are used in Danish timetables.

Weekdays	⚒		Does not run daily	⸗
Sundays and Holidays (Public Holidays in Denmark: 25.XII., 26.XII. 1978, 1.I., 12.IV., 13.IV., 16.IV., 11.V. and 24.V. 1979)			Train does not stop at this station	ǀ
	†		Change	*
			Trans-Europ-Express. 1. cl. only	𝔗𝔈𝔈
Weekdays except Saturdays	Ⓐ		Through carriages	
Daily except Saturdays	Ⓑ			
Saturdays, Sundays and Holidays	Ⓒ		Ferry and boat connection	
Mondays	①		Frontier station with passport and customs control	🏠
Tuesdays	②			
Wednesdays	③		Departure	af
Thursdays	④		Arrival	an
Fridays	⑤		only	kun
Saturdays	⑥		not	ikke
Sundays	⑦		except	undtagen

These words are found in train stations:

afgang   - departure   koreplan - timetable
ankomst - arrival   oplysning - information
banegarden - railstation   pladsbestillingen -reservations
billetkontoret - ticket office   perron - track
indang - entrance   udang - exit

Included in Eurailpass and Eurail Youthpass are ferry crossings Arhus to Kalundborg, Knudshoved to Halsskov, Nyborg to Korsor, Fynshav to Bojken; ferry crossing Rodby Faerge to Puttgarden (Federal Republic of Germany); ferry crossings operated by the Danish and Swedish State Railways between Helsingor and Helsingborg, Sweden; ferry crossings operated

114

by Stena Sessan Linjen between Frederikshavn, Denmark and Goteborg, Sweden. A reduction of 20 percent is granted on normal fares of Steamship Company DFDS between Esbjerg and Harwich, Esbjerg and Newcastle, Esbjerg and Far Oer Islands, and Copenhagen and Oslo.

DRIVING   Roads are flat and good. Denmark has the center passing lane used by cars passing in both directions. Car reservations for any ferry are made free at any railroad station, or the camp attendant may be willing to call in the reservation. In 1981, regular gas cost $3.31 per gallon.

FOOD   Food production is a principal industry of Denmark. Main exports are livestock, bacon, meat, butter, eggs, cheese, milk, cereals and lard. Canned meat, condensed milk, sugar and canned fish are produced. Denmark is the largest exporter of pork products in the world.

To control costs for meals, the best strategy is to buy take-out rotisseried chicken, cook at camp, and drink plenty of the delicous and reasonably priced milk. In a cafeteria, "dagens ret" signifies the daily special. Good values are also found in a "platte." Smorrebord, the small open-faced sandwiches which are a Danish specialty, are not necessarily the best value for lunch. If you come upon a "koldbord" (cold table) that is reasonably priced, try to indulge because you're entitled to limitless servings from platters of bread, butter, cheese, meat and often a hot dish. Danish pastry is called "wienerbrod", and bakeries are open Sunday morning to sell you pastry and a glass of milk. Danish dairy products are outstanding. Whole milk is "sod maelk;" skim milk is "skummet maelk." In 1981, one liter milk cost 3.90 kr, 500 grams rye bread (which is less than white) cost 4-7 kr, and one whole hot cooked chicken cost 28-30 kr.

CHILDREN   "Barn" is child and "born" is children. Special compartments for mothers who are traveling with children under 4 years of age are provided on international express trains. Some stations have special mother's rooms with a table for changing baby. About diapers, Tumbling brand "Ble og snip i eet" are like Pampers. Tumbling #1 (green box) is for birth to 11 pounds (til born op til 5 kg), day or night (day-og natble). Tumbling #2 (red package) is for 5-10 kg (12-22 lbs) daytime and #2 blue package is the same weight but for night. Tumbling #3 (purple) is for over 22 pounds (10 kg) day or night. Ble (diaper) is pronounced BLEE. Strip type diaper without the plastic cover is also available and cheaper.

COPENHAGEN (KOBENHAVN)

Flying into Copenhagen over the North Sea, we could look down on checker-boards of growing green fields and freshly plowed soil punctuated by stretches of brilliant yellow mustard fields and a few red tile farmhouse roofs. Soon the suburbs appeared and we were set down at Copenhagen Airport. Copenhagen means "merchant's harbor." Old Copenhagen has lived for 800 years. Some of its original fortified walls and moats can be seen in the city's parks.

AIRPORT   Copenhagen Airport (Lufthavn) is on Amager Island, 10 km from downtown Copenhagen. Arriving here on an international flight is very easy. Upon arrival, connecting flight reservations should be confirmed at one of the check-in counters for transfer passengers. Passengers staying in

Copenhagen will find baggage carts at no cost in the arrival hall. A moving sidewalk connects the arrival-departure area with the main transit hall with lounges, restaurants, stores and post office. "Rest cabins" (private rooms) can be rented until your connecting flight at the information desk for a fee of 60 kr. In the transit hall, beyond the information desk and delicatessen counter, are three "nursery" rooms on the right hand side of the hall. The doors are marked "Nursery 1" and "Nursery II" and inside the latter are two separate rooms. A lock is on the inside of each door. Each wood-paneled room is about 7 by 21 feet and equipped with crib (slightly smaller than full size) made up with clean sheets, adult size cot, loveseat, 2-1/2 foot square wood coffee table, long stainless counter with handwashing sink and recessed baby bathtub backed by white tile, mirror, paper cups, towels, disposable diapers and a bathroom. These rooms are free of charge for families with a baby or young children--just ask for the key at the information desk.

On the return flight, two hours should be allowed for checking baggage, passing through security check and shopping at the duty-free store.

In front of the airport, bus #32 goes to Raadhuspladsen in downtown Copenhagen.

TRAIN STATION   Main station is Kobenhavn H, located downtown next door to Tivoli amusement/cultural center and across the street from SAS Terminal. All banks charge 18 kr to cash a travelers check, except American Express charges 8 kr for its own brand only. Hovedbanegard, station restaurant, serves a smorgasbord for about 59 kr, and child 6-12 is half price. Also inside station are shoe repair stand and S-tog (subway) station whose trains are included in railpasses. Tourist office is in separate building outside station. Many buses leave from Radhuspladsen (Town Hall Square), three blocks away. To get there, leave station and walk forward past the open well where trains pass beneath the city, then turn right on main street, Verterbrogade, and walk three blocks.

TOURIST OFFICE   Danmarks Turistrad, Banegardspladsen 2, is outside train station on left of open well. Open May-June M-Sa 9-7, July-Aug M-Sa 9-9 & Su 9-1, Sept M-Sa 9-7 & Su 9-1, Oct-Apr M-F 9-5 & Sa 9-12. Its Copenhagen map has buses and subways marked. Brochure on hikes in the suburban forests and lake areas is available. While you're here, ask for a leaflet on any other Danish town on your itinerary.

CAMPGROUNDS   Of all the big cities in Europe, Copenhagen is the most generously supplied with campgrounds. Seven camps are found within 25 km of downtown and all are served by public transportation. All are members of the Danish Camping Union, except for Dragor Camping, and charge adult/ 18 kr and child/9 kr. Camps are open 7 am to 10 pm for new arrivals except as noted. Absalon Camping is reached via S-tog (subway), free with railpasses. Sundbyvester Camping requires least walking for backpackers. Bellahoj Camping is closest in.

ABSALON CAMPING, Korsdalsvej in Rodovre district, 9 km from train station. Mailing address: Korsdalsvej, DK-2610, Rodovre. Open all year. From train station, take S-tog , linie B to Brondbyoster Station. Then a six block walk to camp (see map). By car, camp is visible on left-hand side of A1 (Roskildevej) coming from Roskilde enroute to Copenhagen. Hot showers, hot water in dishwashing sinks, gas burners, store, washing machine,

(15.25 kr including soap), dryer (5 kr), dayroom, playground. Leslie Carter says "We
liked Absalon Camping--fantastic facilities!
Huge bathrooms, many showers (free and hot),
clothes washing room, iron, cooking facilities,
television room even. Big camp too!
SUNDBYVESTER CAMPING, Konge-
lundsvej 54 (DK 2300 Copenhagen S) in Sundbyvester District on Amager Island, 6 km
from downtown. Open about April 6 to first
weekend in September. From train station,
take bus #13 (direction Sundbyvester Plads)
from Bernstoftsgade near the station (see
map on next page) to Amagerfaelledve,
which is five blocks after crossing the river.
Transfer to bus #31 (direction Finderup or
Noragersmindevej). Get off at Veilands
Allee, immediately in front of camp. Irma
Supermarket is across from camp. By car,
follow signs to airport (Lufthavn). This will
get you to Amager Island. But after crossing the river and passing Bella Center
(convention center) on the right, watch for
camping signs. Once into built-up area

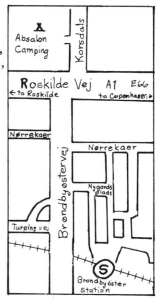

again, turn right onto Kongelunds Vej. Camp is in fourth block on right.
Narrow entrance is immediately before gas station--Irma Supermarket is on
left. The grassy area of the camp is subdivided by hedges and trees into
areas large enough for about 8 tents. There are free hot showers, hot water
in dishwashing sinks, free gas burners, playground equipment, outdoor
tables and chairs, dayroom with television, and hot dog stand. Manager
speaks English, changes money, and makes appointments to use the washer
and dryer. At your appointment time, go to the office as the manager has to
start the washer. Laundry room has a large tub with hot water for handwash-

ing clothing. Store is open 7-12
& 2-10. Vending machine outside
dispenses hot coffee, hot chocolate, soup and tea. A vending
machine freezer for packaged
liquid ice works on an exchange
basis. You insert your melted
liquid ice package and an already
frozen one comes out immediately.
To go downtown from camp, take
bus #31 across street from camp
and ride to Kongens Torv, the
last stop.

BELLAHOJ CAMPING
(BELL-lah-hoy), Hvidkildevej 64
(DK-2400 Copenhagen NV) in
Bronshoj district, is 5 km from
downtown. Open about last week

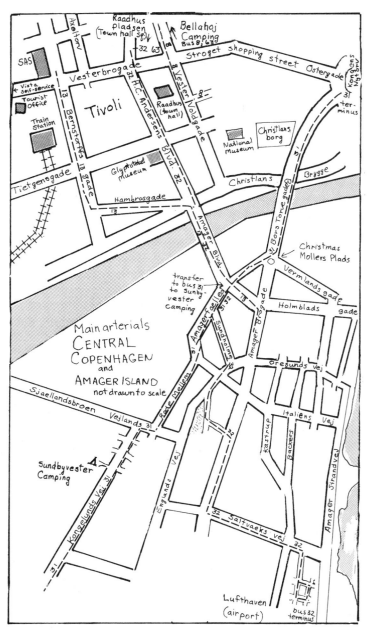

in June through August. From train station, walk to Radhuspladsen (Town
Hall Square) three blocks from station and take bus #8 (direction Tingbjerg)
or #63 (direction Vaerebroparken), and get off at bus stop Hareskovvej.
Cross the street and you'll see the camp ahead with a cyclone fence around
it. The entrance is on the opposite side of the park. Walk towards your left

as you face the fence, a 10-15 minute walk. By car from Roskilde on A 1, watch for a lake (Damhus Soen) on your left. Immediately beyond it, turn left onto Peter Bangs Vej. Go 3 blocks. At main intersection, angle left onto Grondals Park Vej (the most important street). Follow this road as it successively is renamed Rebild Vej and Hulgards Vej. (If in doubt, follow bus #21.) Turn left at Hvidkildevej. Go one block. Turn right on Bellahojvej. By car on E 4 (north or south), stay on ring road (freeway) as far as Gladsaxe. Exit onto Hareskovvej in direction of downtown (centrum). At important 5-way intersection, turn right onto Bellahojvej. Camp is on left. Campsite is a flat grassy area with few trees. English is spoken in the office. Camp has hot showers, store, dishwashing sinks with hot water, and cooking facilities.

STRANDMOLLEN CAMPING, Strandvejen, 2930 Klampenborg on edge of Deer Park (Jaegersborg Woods) which is laced with trails, and about 14 km from Copenhagen. Mailing address is Strandvejen, DK-2942 Skodsborg. The camp is for tents only. Cars and vans must be parked outside. Open about May 15 through August. From train station, take S-tog to Klampenborg Station, which is 3 km from camp. Outside station, change to bus #188 (direction Helsingor). Bus stops at camp. By car from Helsingor on A 3, exit at Naerum and go east on Skodsborg Vej to district of Skodsborg. When you come to the sea, turn right (south) onto Strand Vejen. Camp has hot showers, hot water in dishwashing sinks, dayroom, playground, no store.

NAERUM CAMPING, Ravnebakken, DK-2850 Naerum, is 15 km north of downtown. Open April to first weekend in September. From train station, take S-tog to Jaegersborg Station. Change to train to Naerum Station, the terminus. About 1 km walk to camp (see map). By car from Helsingor on A 3, exit at Naerum. Cross first main street, Skodsborg Vej, onto Lange-bjerg (going south). Camp is about 8 blocks away and is signed. Camp has hot showers, hot water in dishwashing sinks, cooking facilities, playground, store, washing machine (15.25 kr including soap), and drying lines.

HUNDIGE CAMPING, Hundige Strandvej 47 & 72, is about 19 km from downtown. Mailing address is Hundige Strandvej 47 & 72, 2670 Greve Strand, DK-Denmark. Open about May 10 -Sept 9. From train station take S-tog to Hundige Station, and change to bus #121. Get off at "Lejrklubben Danmark." This is a large, well-organized permanent campsite with space for temporary guests. Store is near camp. Camp has hot showers, cold water in dishwashing sinks and playground.

UNDINEGARDENS CAMPING is about 25 km from downtown. Mailing address is Ganlose, DK-2760 Maalov. Open all year. From train station, take S-tog to Farum Station and change to bus #332 (4 kr). Get off at Undinevej. Walk 10 minutes to camp. Campground is beautifully situated near Lake Bastrup, has access to the lake, and is one portion of a farm operated by owner Ivar Petersen. Hot showers, cooking facilities, store.

DRAGOR CAMPING, Sdr. Strandve in the picturesque village of Dragor on Amager Island, 14 km from downtown. Open May-Aug. This is Dragor's municipal camp and it is not a member of the Danish Camping Union. It's an open camp on the beach and, though fenced, beach visitors must use the camp restrooms. Cars and vans must be parked outside. From train station, take bus #30 or 33 from Radhuspladsen. By car, follow signs to airport (lufthavn) to get to Amager Island. Dragor is a quaint old seaport on the southeast tip of the island. Camp facilities are minimal. Cold water only, no showers, store stocked with few items, playground. Do visit Dragor as its old quarter is officially protected and kept as it was when the town flourished as an important fishing port.

CITY TRANSPORTATION S-trains (S-tog) are part of the Danish State Railway and are covered by Eurailpass and Eurail Youthpass. Much money can be saved by taking the S-tog to the nearest station and walking from there. Stations give free schedules and maps. The train station, Kobenhavn H at which you arrive in Copenhagen, is the main terminal for S-tog. Many buses leave from Radhuspladsen (RAWTH-hoose-PLAH-sehn), Town Hall Square, which is about three blocks from train station. All bus and rail lines in Copenhagen and North Sealand use the same tickets. Cost depends on how many zones you travel through. Tickets are sold on the buses and at the S-tog stations. The cheapest ticket is a 3-zone ticket. It's cheaper to buy multi-ride cards which are available for 3, 6 and unlimited zones, and can be shared among you. The cards should be stamped in the automatic machine when boarding a bus, or in the yellow machine at train stations. Each stamp is good for 1 person for 1, 1-1/2 or 2 hours use on both trains and buses. Children between 5 and 12 pay about half on a child ticket or card.

DRIVING Copenhagen has a ring road, highway E 4, which bypasses the downtown area. For street parking, there are either parking meters or parking marked "P-Skive Pabudt" where parking is free but a cardboard disc must be used. Disc is free at gas stations, post offices and most banks. Set disc to next quarter hour and place face forward on dashboard nearest the curb. You can then park for one hour unless a longer time limit is shown on the sign. Parking meters and disc areas are only in effect M-F 9-6 & Sa 9-1 unless otherwise stated. "Stopforbud" means no stopping at all. "Parkering forbudt" means no parking. Times given state hours of no parking. "Datostop" and "datoparkering" mean parking is allowed only on one side of the street. Parking is allowed on side of street with even numbered street numbers on even numbered days and odd street numbers on odd days.

FOOD Tourist office has a list of cafeterias. A reasonable one within walking distance of the train station is VISTA Restaurant (cafeteria), at Vesterbrogade 40 which is at Vesterbros Torv, a five minute walk. After leaving station, walk forward past train well to main street, Vesterbrogade, and turn left. Vista is about 6 blocks away, across the street and on the second floor (first floor up) of the building. Open daily 9-8. Daily menu (dagens ret) served 11-8 is offered in four price ranges. Pitchers of water are available. Both daily and a la carte menu are translated into English.

Irma Grill, in Irma Supermarket in Rodovre shopping center (Rodovre Centrum), is a 5 minute drive or bus ride (#13) from Absalon Camping. (See map next page.) Rodovre Centrum is in the suburbs, direction Rodovre from Korsdals and Valhojs Alle. It is also 4 long blocks off A 1 from Roskilde. Traveling towards Copenhagen, after passing Absalon Camping on the left, in 5 blocks turn left at first main street, Tarn Vej. Rodovre Centrum is on the right. Irma Grill features a super modern yellow,

120

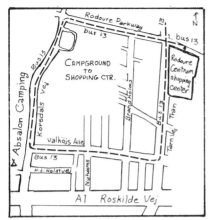

orange, red and blue graphic decor in its cafeteria. Regular menu is printed on placemats at the tables. Lunchtime daily special (mormors middag) is also offered to children as "borneportion." Other menu items include 1/2 chicken (1/2 stegt kylling) weighing 425 and served with french fries, and a buffet. For the buffet, the meal cost is the cost of a hot entree such as fish filet, liver and bacon, or hamburger patty as indicated by a price stick on each platter. Price given is for one piece (stk.) of meat or fish plus one slice bread, butter, and all you want of the surrounding condiments such as pickled beets, sliced cucumbers and onions. A bowlful of tossed green salad costs extra.

Smorgasbord refers to a buffet from which you serve yourself as much as you wish. Smorrebord are multiple varieties of open-faced sandwiches. However, the platters from which you make your selections for smorgasbord contain the ingredients to concoct your own smorrebord, that is sandwiches, at your table. A Dane eats from a smorgasbord by first selecting a fish item and eating it before returning to the buffet for meat, pickles, vegetables and so forth. All of these dishes are served cold, though one or two hot dishes such as a casserole of meatballs may be available. An attractive smorgasbord is served in the train station restaurant at a reasonable price for a smorgasbord which is always fairly expensive.

SIGHTSEEING   TIVOLI, one block from train station, is open May- Sept 15 with admission about 10 kr. Basically a smaller and more intimate Danish version of a stateside civic entertainment center, Tivoli encompasses much inviting open space around a meandering lake, several small outdoor stages, a modern concert theater, gourmet restaurants and an amusement park. Multi-colored lighting at night adds fairytale enchantment to an already delightful setting. Lots of free entertainment in the evening: variety acts on outdoor stage in the gardens start at 7 pm, mime to left of entrance at 7:30 pm and ballet at 9:30 pm. Symphony in the theater begins at 8 or 9 pm depending upon the day of the week. Tivoli Boy Guards parade on Saturday and Sunday at 6:30 and 8:30 pm. Evenings are chilly; food is expensive.

NY CARLSBERG GLYPTOTEK MUSEUM on Dantes Plads, across from rear entrance of Tivoli, is a private foundation with well-planned exhibits showing the development of art from the Egyptians and Mesopotamians through the Romans, and modern French and Danish art. Gauguin and Degas are well represented in the modern art galleries with about 25 paintings and 3 woodcuts by Gauguin, and paintings and a set of 73 bronzes by Degas. Open May-Sept Tu-Su 10-4, Oct-Apr Tu-Sa 12-3 & Su 10-4. Adult/ 10 kr, child/free, Wed & Sun free. One hour guided tour in English available to groups if arranged in advance. Restroom in basement.

ROYAL MUSEUM OF FINE ARTS (Statens Museum for Kunst), 1307 Solvgade, contains art from many periods, much of it Danish; and a fairly large group of 20th century French works. Modern Danish art is shown in the annex at 18 Kastelsvej. The Department of Prints and Drawings rotates the works of Picasso, Rembrandt, Daumier and others. Open Tu-Su 10-5 plus late 10pm closing on Wed. Dept. of Prints and Drawings is open Tu-Su 10-5 and Wed. to 8pm. Free admission. S-tog to Osterport or Norreport.

CHRISTIANSBORG PALACE (kres-tee-ahnz-borh) opens its Royal Reception Rooms from Apr-Oct Tu-Su for guided tours at noon, 2 and 4pm. Admission 10 kr.

TOJHUSMUSSET (Royal Arsenal Museum), 3 Tojhusgade near Christiansborg Palace contains a huge collection of military items housed in a 16th century armoury. Cannons are on first floor; guns, swords, armor and artillery on second; and uniforms on third. My husband and son spent four engrossing hours here until they closed the doors. Open May-Sept M-Sa 1-4 & Su 10-4, Oct-Apr M-Sa 1-3 & Su 11-4. Free admission, free checking, toilets by entry room.

ROSENBORG CASTLE COLLECTIONS, Ostervoldgade 4a. Built as a summer palace for King Christian IV between 1606 and 1617, this small Renaissance style castle now serves as a museum of the history of the Danish kings. The collections comprise arms, family portraits, crown jewels, royal costumes, Venetian glass, silver, furniture, an ivory coronation chair, 3 life-size silver lions and an elaborately decorated Gothic drinking horn made in 1470. The palace is surrounded by a park. Open May-Oct 11-3, shorter hours the rest of year. Adult/12 kr.

ZOOLOGICAL MUSEUM, 15 Universitetsparken, is reached by bus #43 from vicinity of Holmens Church (easy transfer from bus #31 from Sundbyvester Camping). Also bus #24 or 84 from Norreport Station. This is the best zoological museum we've seen from an originality of design standpoint. It's at the other end of the spectrum from the old-style stuffed birds and animals behind glass type. The Danes have recreated the environment of the spot-lighted birds and animals. You can hear the wind blowing in the arctic and the sounds of a swamp, view what goes on underwater or feel musk ox fur over ice to see how well it insulates. A person doesn't just go from room to room to see this but follows a self-guided tour that winds and twists. Open May-Sept 10-5, Oct-Apr M-F 1-5pm & Sa-Su 10-5. Free. Guidebook in English costs 2.50 kr. There is an unsupervised playroom about half-way through the exhibits but I can't imagine any child preferring it to the animals. Free parking behind Museum.

FRILANDSMUSEET (Open-air Museum), 100 Kongevejen, is reached by Lyngby S-train to Sorgenfri or bus #84 from Norreport. Museum is within two blocks of A5. It is a collection of original old houses and cottages brought from different parts of Denmark. Old-time skills such as lace-making, pottery, weaving, dyeing and candle making are demonstrated. See free tourist office pamphlet, "This Week", for schedule. Free guided tours in English are given on Thursday at 2pm and Sunday at 11am. Open April 15-Sept Tu-Su 10-5, Oct 1-14 Tu-Su 10-3, Oct 15-Apr 14 Su 10-3. Adult/3 kr, child/1 kr. (Agricultural Museum is across the street.)

NATIONAL MUSEUM, Frederiksholm Kanal, is open Su 10-4. Parts of museum are open other days. Be sure to go when Prehistoric and Greenland exhibits are open. Adult/free.

Special interest museums and sights of Copenhagen encompass antiques, working models of motor-ships, brewing, plant observatory, musical instruments, Oriental handicrafts, film, model theaters, World War II, lightship, Danish art, town history, toys, medicine, mechanical music, minerals, fossils and meteorites, boat models, post office, rose garden with 250 varieties, reptiles, works of Danish sculptor Thorvaldsen and zoo. Information is in "This Week" from tourist office.

Two examples of new pre-planned communities are Askerod reached by S-train A to Hundie and Farum Midtpunkt located at S-train station of same name. Inexpensive guided walking tours are described in the brochure "Copenhagen on Foot" from the tourist office. During July and August, the Guide-Ring offers tours in English (1-1/2 to 2 hours) for about adult/12 kr, ages 12-25/6 kr and under 12/free. The Guide-Ring says what every camper knows that "the best way to see a town is by foot! You can cover the old parts of Copenhagen in a few leisurely walks (no rush). We walk through narrow streets and look into court yards, preferably seeking things which are difficult to see from a bus or to find on one's own." Tours cover Heart of the City, The Old Canals, The Noble City, Christianshavn, Flowers and Arts, Christian IV's Castle and Garden, and From Stone Age to Vikings.

ROSKILDE. Trains leave Copenhagen Train Station for the 20 minute ride to Roskilde two or three times an hour. By car it's 31 km west of Copenhagen on A 1. Tourist office in Roskilde is seven blocks from train station. One block from tourist office is the medieval Cathedral, open Apr-Sept M-Sa 9-5:45 & Su 12:30-5:45, Oct-Mar M-Sa 10-3:45, Su 12:30-3:45. Adult/2 kr, child/.50 kr. From the Cathedral, a 15 minute walk brings you to the Viking Ship Museum which exhibits five viking ships from 1000 A.D. and shows an English language film on how the ships were recovered and restored. The film is shown when museum personnel feel enough English speaking visitors are present. Showing is announced over loudspeaker. The modern museum is at the edge of a fjord and a long walk from the station. Bus #307 to Hillerod leaves from the train station at 10 minutes past the hour and the driver will let you off near the museum and then it's a 5 minute walk. Open June-Aug daily 9-6, Sept-Oct & Apr-May daily 9-5, Nov-Mar daily 10-4. Adult 21-65/10 kr, ages 6-21 & over 65/3 kr, reductions for groups. A nice wood and sand playground is on the opposite side of the museum from the parking lot. Oldtidsbyen (Arkaeologisk Forsogscenter) west of nearby Lejre, is a reconstructed prehistoric settlement with houses, well, fences and fields seeded with crops grown during that time. By car go via Ledreborg manor house to Herthadalen. Trains leave Roskilde for Lejre at 31 mintues past each hour. Outside Lejre train take bus #233 to Oldtisbyen and the Arkaeologisk Forsogscenter. Open June 21-Aug 8 daily 10-5, and May - Sept 26 daily 10-5. A castle, Ledreborg Slot, is also in Lejre. In Roskilde, Vigen Strandparks Camping, 5 km north of downtown in a beach park off A 6 (direction Frederikssund), can be reached from Roskilde station by bus #602 (direction Veddelev/Riso) which leaves at 37 and 7 minutes past the hour. Bus fare is 4 kr or 11 rides for 40 kr. Camp is about 1 km from bus stop. Open Apr 11-Sept 13, hot showers, hot water in dishwashing sinks, store, cooking burners, playground. Public MARKET in Roskilde is held Wednesday and Saturday in Staendertorvet, the town's central square.

FREE TOURS. Mr. and Mrs. Robert Cooper recommend "When in Copenhagen be sure to include a free guided tour through Tuborg breweries. An unlimited supply of the finished product was tasted at the end of the tour.

A bus can be taken from town hall square." Tuborg Brewery is located at Strandvejen 54, open for tours M-F 8:30-2:30, and reached by buses #1 and 21. Carlsberg Brewery also offers tours. Holmegard Glassworks offers free tours M-F 9-1:30 & Sa-Sun 11 & 3. Take the train to Naestved which leaves Copenhagen at 8:43 (ar. 10:11), 10:42 (ar. 12:09). Then take bus #75 (Fensmarkt). Bus leaves Naestved at 11:10 am, 12:20 (not Sun.), 1:55 pm and returns at 2:15, 3:05 and 5:30 pm. Trains leave Naestved for Copenhagen at 3:56 and 5:41 pm. The town of Naestved has some interesting old half-timbered houses. In particular, see Boderne where one house is now a crafts museum. (The Glass factory is closed for three weeks in July.)

GILLELEJE. Janet Dutton writes that her favorite town was "Gilleleje, a fishing village 60 minutes from Copenhagen." The town is at the extreme northern tip of this island Sjaelland and can be reached from Helsingor or Hillerod. The rail line to the town is marked "private" on the train schedule so ask in advance whether it's included in railpasses.

SHOPPING   Value-added tax of 20-25 percent is deducted from any purchase sent out of the country. Bring drapery measurements, reupholstering requirements, dining room table size, etc. as fabrics are outstanding. Some Scandinavian furniture such as safari chairs knock down into small enough packages to be sent regular parcel post. For larger shipments inquire as to shipping costs and brokerage fees in advance. The normal procedure is to pay for the transportation costs (as quoted by the firm's shipping agency at time of purchase) on arrival of the goods in the U.S. port city. By picking up the shipment in the U.S. port city yourself, a brokerage charge can be avoided.

Stroget (stroy-et) is the tourist shopping street prohibited to traffic in downtown Copenhagen. At the Kongens Nytorv end is its most outstanding store, ILLUMS BOLIGHUS, a visual delight in home furnishings. Also good but smaller, Den Permanente, Vesterbrogade, offers jury-screened merchandise of furniture, fabrics, dinnerware, toys and more. The average Dane shops at IKEA, a large furniture complex in Tastrup for good quality and reasonable prices. The huge multi-level store is visible from A 1 (Roskilde Vej) in Tastrup. Open M 11-7:30, T-Th 11-5:30, F 11-7:30 & Sa 7-2. Free catalog. Free supervised playroom for 3-7 year olds which features a giant twisting slide ending in a pile of styrofoam balls. Cafeteria served a roast beef dinner for 24.75 kr the day we were there. Ikea can also be reached by S-train to Tastrup and then about a 30 minute walk or bus #199 from outside Tastrup Station.

CHILDREN   Below is a partial list of free supervised playgrounds in public parks. Ostre Anlaeg, Solvtorvet, Osterport Station is in vicinity of Kunst Museum. Skydebanen behind Kobenhavns Bymuseum (history of Copenhagen), is at Vesterbrogade 59, 7 blocks or 15 minute walk west of train station. Christianshavns Vold, at Torvegade on Amager Island, is on bus route #31 from Sundbyvester Camping to downtown. Faelledparken at Norre Alle/Borgmester Jensesn Alle, is in vicinity of Zoological Museum. This one has a traffic kindergarten of kiddy cars and road signs, and a swimming pool.

TRAIN SCHEDULES   Trains leave Copenhage for Odense on the hour and the trip takes about two hours.   An alternative to the inter-city train between Arhus and Copenhagen is the route via Kalundborg which doesn't require a reservation fee be paid as would be necessary for the Nyborg-Korsor

124

crossing. Trains leave Kobenhavn H. Station at 7:30 am (daily from about
June 12-Aug 19, otherwise daily except Sunday) (ar. 12:23 pm), 9:55 am
(ar. 2:55 pm), 2:55 pm (daily from about May 28-Aug 18, otherwise daily
except Sat) (ar. 8 pm), 5:20 pm (ar. 9:58 pm). The train reaches Kalundborg
in 2 hours 20 minutes where you must get off the train and walk onto the
ferry which departs 8 minutes later. In about 3 hours and 10 minutes, the
ferry arrives at Arhus Harbor Station from which a train goes to Arhus Station downtown, a 15 minute trip.

To Oslo, trains go via Helsingor and Helsingborg between which there
is a 15 minute ferry. Trains leave Kobenhavn H. at 6:51 am (ar. Oslo East
4:49 pm), 12:34 pm (ar. Oslo East 9:50 pm) and 11 pm (ar. Oslo East 9 am).

To Stockholm, trains go via Helsingor and Helsingborg between which
there is a 15 minute ferry. Trains leave Kobenhavn H. at 7:34 am (ar. 3:44pm),
9:19 am (ar. 5:44 pm), 3:19 pm (ar. 11:20 pm), 9:19 pm (daily from about May
28-Sept 30, otherwise daily except Sat.) (ar. 7:44 am) and 11:19 pm (ar.
8:44 am).

To Hamburg and Cologne, trains leave Kobenhavn H. at 7:20 am (ar.
Hamburg Hbf 12:21 pm, Hamburg Altona 12:46 pm), 10:15 am "intercity" (former TEE) train (ar. Hamburg Hbf 3:03 pm, ar. Cologne 7:53 pm), 1:20 pm
(ar. Hamburg Hbf 6:28 pm), 3:20 pm (ar. Hamburg Hbf 8:34 pm) and later
departures.

HUMLEBAEK AND HELSINGOR

Trains leave Kobenhavn H Station at least twice hourly for the 45 minute trip
to Helsingor, north of Copenhagen. Humlebaek is a stop on the same line 36
minutes from Copenhagen.

HUMLEBAEK. Louisiana Museum (Louisiana Museet), Gl. Strandvej
13. Open daily 10-5. Adult/15 kr, student and senior citizen/6 kr, child under
16/free. Free drawing room for children with paper and crayons to left of
entrance. This is Denmark's prime museum of modern art. An excellent
collection of modern European paintings is shown indoors, and sculpture is
mounted outdoors within a park overlooking the sound. The original museum
building was the home over a hundred years ago of a Danish nobleman who
successively married three times, each time to a woman named Louise. The
new contemporary structure is linked with this original manor house by a
series of covered walks. Museum shop has a good selection of reproductions
and frames for sale. Museum is a 15 minute walk from Humlebaek Station or
a shorter bus ride.

HELSINGOR (Elsinore). Kronberg Castle of Hamlet fame is within
walking distance of the ferry dock. Between town and ferry dock, a camping
sign is posted near the Hamlet Hotel and the camp is within walking distance.
To Helsingborg, Sweden, ferries leave every 15 minutes for the 20 minute
crossing. Ferry lines DSB and SJ are included in railpasses, Sundbusser and
LB-Faerger are not. Cars including driver cost 100 kr one way in May-Sept
and less in Oct-Apr. Adult/10 kr, child 6-11/half price, child under 6/free,
bicycle/free. Camping van to 6 meters in length and driver cost 145 kr.

ODENSE

On the island of Fyn, Odense (OH-then-seh) is two hours from Copenhagen on the Lyntog, high speed diesel train.

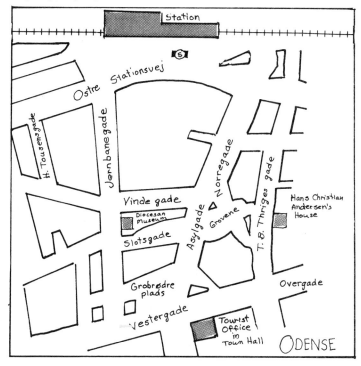

Tourist office is in the Town Hall, 7 blocks from train station. Open June 15-Aug M-Sa 9-8 & Su 10-12 & 6-8. Tours of Town Hall at 2 pm M-F, tickets from tourist office. Autocamp Hunderup, Odensevej 102 in southern part of city, is reached by bus #1 from outside train station. Fare is 4 kr. Camp is 5 minute walk from bus stop. Camp has excellent facilities, hot showers, store, washing machine, free hotplates. Public market is on Sortebrodre Torv in general area of Hans Christian Andersen's home, and open Wednesday and Saturday mornings. Funen Village (Den Fynske Landsby) at Sejerskovvej is an outdoor museum of peasant houses, farms and workshops showing Danish pastoral life of the 18th and 19th centuries. Open May 9-5:30, June-Aug 15 9-6:30, Aug 16-Sept 9-4:30. Adult/3 kr, child/.50 kr. Take bus 2 from train station or 5 minute walk from camp. Tivoli amusement park, Sdr. Boulevard 304, is open May-Sept from 2-11 pm.

KERTEMINDE, 25 km from Odense, is an interesting old town with picturesque old houses on Langegade and old general shops which is now a fishing port and summer resort. Most important attraction is at nearby Ladby, an 8 minute bus ride, and burial place for a 1100 year old Viking Ship, 72 feet long and 9 feet wide which has been preserved along with the Viking Chief, his weapons and belongings including four hunting dogs and 11 horses. From Odense, buses take three different routes to Kerteminde. If you wish to stop off at Ladby on the way, take the bus marked "Odense-Kolstrup-Kerteminde" which leaves M-F at 8:00 am, 12:10, 2:05 and 5:10 pm; Saturday at 12:10 and 2:05 pm; and Sunday at 2:05 and 10:20 pm. Other buses leave at 7:45, 9:25, 10:35, 11:05 am, noon, 2:10, 3:10, 4:20, 5:20, 7:20, 9:25 and 11:30 pm. These buses leave from rutebilstation (bus station) behind the train station. Trip is 35-50 minutes.

In Kerteminde, the municipal campground "Kerteminde Camping" is open May-Sept 15, and is 2 km from the bus station. It has hot showers, hot water in sinks, cooking burners, playground, washing machine and dayroom.

JUTLAND (JYLLAND) PENINSULA

Jutland (yoo-lan) is the largest land mass of Denmark, the top of the European continent that reaches northwards from Germany. Arhus, Denmark's second city, is here and its recreated old town of tradesmen's shops is exceptional. Children love Jutland for Legoland at Billund. Viking remnants, picturesque small towns and sandy beaches complete the picture. We will start at the southern part and proceed west and north. See introductory train section for schedules.

HADERSLEV   Located on highway A 10/E 3 and served by a connecting bus from train station of Vojens, Haderslev has an ancient city center and open air museum with a wonderful old mill to climb. Bus stops at tiny Haderslev by station downtown. Tourist office, Apotekergade 1 near the Cathedral, is open May 15-Sept 15 M-F 9:30-5:30 & Sa 9-12. Closes at 4:30 pm weekdays during rest of year. A former orphans home has been made into a new youth hostel which is down by Haderslev Lake in very beautiful surroundings. A sightseeing boat from the hostel dock runs 5 times daily to the city center. Address is Erlevvej 34. Haderslev Kommune Campingpladsen is at the white water tower, 1.5 km from the station (see map next page). The camp backs up to highway A 10/E 3, but cannot be entered directly from it. Follow signs from A 10/E 3. Camp has cold water in sinks, free hot showers, gas cooking burners and small store. Town market is at Gravene, Th & F, 7 am-noon.

Haderslev Museum, Astrupvej 48, built in 1977, shows archaeological finds from the area, including the young girl from Skrudstrup with typical clothes and coiffure of the period. Tape recorder in each room commentates in English at the sound of a kroner. Best part of museum is across the street outside where four buildings, a fine mill, church bell and well can be found. First is the 16th century Bole house in which both people and small animals shared the premises around a central fireplace. An elaborate half-timbered farmhouse, dating from 1750-1800 shows utensils of the period including a churn whose energy was supplied by a dog hitched to a wheel. Agricultural tools are shown in a barn from the village of Osby. Open Tu-F 10-5 and Sa Su noon-5. . Adult/2 kr, child/.60 kr. Free Nov-Apr. Helpful free handout in English is given. The interesting medieval quarter of Haderslev is explained in the leaflet "Stadtwanderung in Haderslev " from the

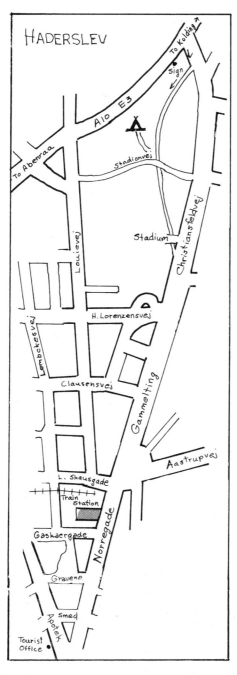

tourist office.

KOLDING   A main crossroads of the Jutland peninsula, Kolding boasts a
20 acre plant conservatory (Geografisk
Have og Rosenhaven) with 2,000 plants
from all over the world grouped according
to origin. Rare specimens include a
pigeon tree from SzeTschwan province
and a water spruce from China. There is
also a children's playground. Open May-
Oct 9 from 9 am-sunset. Adult/2.50 kr,
child/free. LEGOLAND in Billund can
be reached in 1 hour by bus from bus
station next to train station. Bus leaves
M-F at 9:05 am, 2:00, 5:10 pm, Saturday
at 9:05 am, noon, 5:00 pm and Sunday at
10:05 am, noon, 8:00 pm (check times).
    Kolding tourist office, Helligkors-
gade 18, is open July-Aug 15 M-F 9-6, Sa 9-1. Aug 16-June M-F 9-5, Sa
9-12. Campground, Turistforeningens Lejrplads, Ndr. Ringvej, open April-
Sept, and a 15 minute walk from the train station. Outside the station, you
turn right and then go straight ahead. (Follow arrows on map.) There is
also a bus #2 which picks up next to the post office and the fare is 4 kr. For
drivers, the camp is off highway 1. Hot showers, small store, hot water in
dishwashing sinks, cooking burners, playground, adult/16 kr, child (0-11)/
8 kr. KFUM (YMCA) Cafeteria, Bredgate 12-14 (see map) is a good value.
Driving from Haderslev, you will notice a large institutional building with
KFUM letters on the facade on the left hand side of highway 10 before reaching the business district. Cafeteria is upstairs; restrooms downstairs.

ESBJERG This is the largest town on the
west coast of Jutland peninsula. Train and
bus stations are next to each other downtown. Tourist office, Skolegade 33, three
blocks from station, is open M-F 9-5 &
Sa 9-12.
    Strandskovens Camping (Kommu-
nens Lejrplads ved Strandskoven), Gl.
Vardevej 76 next to stadium in Idraets
park, is within walking distance of station
or take bus # 1, 9, 11 or 12 from train
station. Camp has hot showers, store,
washing machine, playground, snack bar,
hot water for dishwashing, cooking burners, swimming pool and wading pool.
    Youth hostel (Vandrerhjem), Kirk-
egade 51, is four blocks from station.
    Steen Favor supermarket is at
Parkvej 124, Droob supermarket is at
Kongensgade 18 and Fotex is on Smedgad.
Daily catch of Denmark's largest fishing
fleet is auctioned at Fish Auction Hall
(Auktionshal) starting at 7 am.

Fishery and Maritime Museum and Aquarium, Tarphagevej, is open June 16-Aug 15 daily 10-8, Aug 16-June 15 M-F 10-5 & Sa-Su 10-6. Museum was built in 1968 to exhibit fishing equipment, boat models and examples of small boats. Esbjerg Museum, Finsensgade 1, open daily 10-4, shows regional historical items with emphasis on former peasant life, and manor farms. Kunstpavillionen, near water tower in Havnegade is a new museum of modern art with collection of Danish pictorial canvasses, sculpture, graphic and ceramic works. Open June 15- Aug 15 M-F 10-5 & Sa-Su 10-6, Aug 16-June 14 M-F 10-12 & 2-5 and Sa-Su 10-6. Admission charge.

RIBE   South of Esbjerg, Denmark's oldest town Ribe enjoyed its greatest prosperity in the Viking Era and Middle Ages as a trading port. It has kept its medieval atmosphere. Train station and bus station are next to each other on the east side of town. Ribe is about a 40 minute train ride from Esbjerg via Bramming in the direction of Tonder on the German border. Tourist office, Overdammen, a street off the main square Torvet about six blocks from the station, has a good leaflet giving a building by building description of the old town.

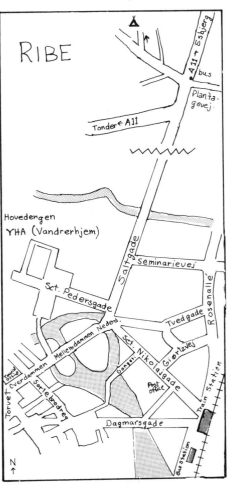

Municipal CAMP (turistforeningens lejrplads), Farupvej, is outside and north of Ribe, about 2 km from train station. There is a bus from the train station to the crossroads of A 11 and Plantagevej. By car, the camp is signed from highway 11. Camp has hot showers, store, cooking burners, hot water in dishwashing sinks and playground. Adult/ 18 kr, child/ 9 kr.

Youth hostel (vandrerhjem) at Hovedengen five blocks from the station has family rooms.

VEJLE   The town is on a fjord and the closest gateway city to Legoland in Billund. Bus Station (Rutebilstation) for buses to Legoland is beside train station (see map next page). Trip is 40 minutes and bus stops at Legoland before stopping in Billund.   Bus 912 (Vejle-Grinsted-Varde) costs about 15 kr and leaves at 5:30, 6:20, 8:20, 9:20 and 11:05 am, and 1:20, 2:10, 3:20, 4:20, 5:20, 8:20 and 11:05 pm.

Tourist office in Vejle is at Havnegade 1 and open June-Aug M-F 9-6 &

130

Sa 9-1. (Closes 1 hour earlier rest of year.) Vejle Communens Lejrplads

(camp) is on Norremarksvej, 3 km from train station. It is a 30 minute \
walk or bus #4 from opposite the train station to Norremarken (and campground.) Bus leaves on the hour and half-hour, costs 4 kr, and get off at the
stadium. Large attractive site, hot showers, cooking burners, adult/18 kr,
child/9 kr, washing machine/10 kr, dryer/5 kr.
      Market is W & Sa at Ved Anlaeget. Cafeteria in Fotex Department Store
is at Norregade 17-19. Deer Park is in Norreskoven, 10 minute walk from
campground.

LEGOLAND, BILLUND   Billund is a tiny town with good bus service from
Vejle and Kolding and an airport served by SAS. Danish families flock here
to enjoy the utterly charming Legoland amusement park where all rides and
dioramas are constructed of ..... you guessed it! Our children loved it,
thought it very special, and back home told their friends.   We enjoyed it
too. Open May 1 to last Sunday in September, 10 am-9 pm. Approximate
prices: adult/18 kr, child 3 and up/10 kr, child under 3/free, groups/half-
price. Some rides are charged "per car" (pr. voon) rather than by person.
Safariland ride, about 7 kr per car which holds two children, sends young-
sters through the jungle of Lego giraffes and Lego vultures in Lego jeeps.
Lego train, about adult/5 kr child/ 3 kr, minibade (boat ride) about 6 kr
per boat, maximum 2 persons, and goldmine ride for about 7 kr are others.
Miniature Lego dioramas can be seen throughout the park featuring famous
Danish castles and manor houses, typical Swedish scenery from Daisland to
Norway, Norwegian town with stave church, a working harbor, miniature
Amsterdam and more. Then there is Legoredo, a Scandinavian version of a
western town, a traffic school for children 8-14, free marionette theater
with hourly performances, free doll museum, free cultural exhibit on Green-

land (this may change), free bandstand performances and free play equipment area.

You can bring your own food and eat at the thoughtfully provided picnic
tables at the rear of Legoland or get yours from a hot dog stand, cafeteria
or restaurant. Hot dog costs about 7 kr   and a beef sandwich about 10 kr.
Be sure to visit the cafeteria in the front of the park to see the miniature
replica of the Taj Mahal.

Restrooms are in the cafeteria and at the rear of Legoland where
there is also a baby-changing room. At the far back of the park behind
"Legeplads" are tables and benches under cover with sunken circular baskets
of all shapes and sizes of Legos, free for anyone to play with. This is where
everyone headed during the frequent though short-lived spurts of rainfall
throughout the otherwise sunny June afternoon that we were there. The Lego
Toyshop sells everything the Lego factory makes at list prices. (For that
matter, we never found them discounted anywhere in Denmark nor did we
find them cheaper than in the U.S.) If you have the foresight to bring in
your address list, postcards can be mailed in the postal box in the toyshop
and will receive a special Legoland postmark. Money exchange is next to
information office. Free parking is outside.

Billunds Communes Campingplads, across the street from Legoland,
is open May-Sept 15. Hot showers, store, hot water in dishwashing sinks,
cooking burners, washing machine and playground. Adult/18 kr, child/9 kr.

Buses leave Legoland for Vejle M-F at 6:50, 8:08, 10:08 am, 1:00,
1:55, 3:55, 5:55, 6:58 and 9:56 pm; Sa at 9:03, 10:25 am, 1:00 (6/20-8/8),
2:25, 4:05, 6:58 and 9:56 pm; and Su at 9:03, 10:25 am, 1:00 (6/20-8/8),
2:25, 4:00, 6:30, 7:05, 9:05 and 9:55 pm. Buses leave Billund Bus Station for
Kolding about three times daily. (Check all times.)

ARHUS (aw-hoose)   Denmark's second city shouldn't be overlooked for
here you can visit "The Old Town" comprising 60 authentic tradesmen's
shops and buildings, and Moesgard Prehistoric Museum. Main station,

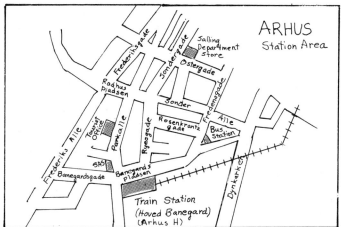

Arhus H Station, is downtown. Train information is open 8-7, currency exchange M-Sa 8 am-9:30 pm & Su 2-9:30 pm, baggage check, supermarket
open daily 8 am-midnight and restaurant serving, for example, two fish

132

filets and vegetables for 24.75 kr. Secondary train stations are Arhus
Havnestation serving the ferry docks and Arhus O Station near the waterfront. From Arhus H Station to Arhus Havnestation (ferries to Samso and
Kalundborg) is about a 5 minute walk. Bus Station (Rutebilstation) is two
blocks from Arhus H. Station.

Tourist information is two blocks from Arhus H Station in the Town
Hall at base of tower. Open June-Aug daily 9-9, Sept-May M-F 9-6 and Sa
9-12. SAS, Banegaardsplads 16, one block from Arhus H Station, is open
M-F 9-5 and Sa 9-12. Arhus is well-signed for tourists.

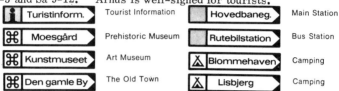

Turistinform.	Tourist Information	
Moesgård	Prehistoric Museum	
Kunstmuseet	Art Museum	
Den gamle By	The Old Town	
Hovedbaneg.	Main Station	
Rutebilstation	Bus Station	
Blommehaven	Camping	
Lisbjerg	Camping	

Camping BLOMMEHAVEN (Plum Forest) is 6 km from downtown in a
beautiful setting near the sea. From Arhus H Station, bus #19 leaves from
the square in front opposite the station building at 5 minutes past each hour.
Fare is 4 kr, enter at back and pay upon leaving. Bus stop is in front of camp.
By car, the camp is south of Arhus in Marselisborg Skov (forest)--follow the
signs "Camping Blommehaven" all the way through the forest. The route is
by Strandvejen (road). Open May-Sept 15. Hot showers, store, hot water in
dishwashing sinks, cooking burners, washing machine. Adult/ 14kr, child/
7 kr. Camp is starting point of 7 kilometer trail which follows the sea, passing by Moesgard Beach and then inland to Moesgard Forest Mill (Skovmolle)
Restaurant, next to a 300 year old water mill. Path returns to camp via
woods. Trail is well-marked with yellow signs. From the restaurant, it's
possible to walk to the Moesgard Prehistoric Museum.

Camping ARHUS NORD is 8 km north of town on A 10, beyond Lisbjerg.
Open all year. Take bus #54 from Bus Station, two blocks from main station.
Bus fare is 6 kr. Camp has hot showers (1 kr), hot water in two sinks in
main washroom building (25 ore) and table for changing baby, brushes
attached to sinks for extra do-it-yourself cleaning, quite small store at
office, swimming pool (child under 7 not allowed), wading pool, swings,
teeter totter, dayroom, cooking burners, washing machine (ask). Adult/
18 kr, child/ 9 kr.

Youth Hostel (Vandrehjemmet) is 3 km from downtown on outskirts of
Risskov at Marienlund. From Arhus H Station, take bus #1 or 2 (direction
Marienlund) to last stop. Then walk northeast on Marienlunsvej for three
blocks to hostel. Open all year, 161 beds, family rooms.

Fotex department store downtown sells one-plate meals for 25 kr in
its upstairs cafeteria and has a supermarket in the basement. Cafeteria at
the University has good meals for about 19 kr.

DEN GAMLE BY (The Old Town) entrance is at intersection of Warm-
ingsvej and Viborgvej. Follow signs or take bus #3 from Arhus H Station.
The Old Town is part of the Botanical Gardens and open for strolling all day
and into the evening, admission free. However the buildings are open only
10-5 daily. Office sells tickets for adult/8 kr and child under 12/free which
gives entry and guided tour in English of your choice of five buildings. Be
sure to pick up a free ticket for children under 12 as it's necessary for
entry into buildings. Guidebook costs 6 kr. Picnic tables in Tea Garden are

available for visitors who bring their own food. Otherwise food purchased in the park or at the restaurant is expensive. Buildings of the old town have been arranged to recreate a typical Danish market town of 1600-1850. Those open for whole day or most of it are: Mayor's Residence, Textile Collection, Aalborg Mansion, Clock Museum, Apothecary, Holst's Mansion, Customshouse, Post Office (can buy stamps and letters are postmarked "The Old Town"), Bakery, Potter at work in Mansard Warehouse, Wine Cellar. Other buildings are open only when a tour is scheduled. Two tours detailing the way things used to be made are offered every half-hour. At 10 am & 2 pm: tour #1 Pinmaker's and Candlemaker's Workshops, Cooper's Workshop, Shoemaker's Workshop--tour #2 Theater. At 10:30 am & 2:30 pm: tour #1 Tobacco Factory, Rope Walk--tour #2 School, Turner's Workshop. At 11 am & 3 pm: tour #1 Carpenter's Workshop, Painter's, Joiner's and Woodcarver's Workshops--tour #2 Tannery, Sadler's Workshop. Noon & 4 pm: tour #1 Gardener's House, Mill--tour #2 Post Office, Brewery. At 12:30 & 4:30 pm: Blacksmith's Workshops, Hatter's Shop. At 1 & 4:30 pm: Dye Works, Barbershop and Glazier's Workshops. At 1:30 pm: tour #1 Distillery, Bakery, Engraver's Workshop, Bookbinder's and Basketmaker's--tour #2 Printer's Workshop, Wood Engraver's Workshop, Stove Collection.

MOESGARD PREHISTORIC MUSEUM is at Moesgard, 6 km south of Arhus. Bus #6 (Moesgard) from Arhus H Station to last stop at museum entrance. Open daily 8-5, adult/6 kr, student, groups of 10 or more/3 kr, child/2 kr. Play equipment, minimal snack bar (weiner 6 kr). Museum is installed in an attractive red-brick manor farm of 1784 and contains well-displayed weapons, rune stones and the 4th century body termed "Grauballe Man" found well-preserved in a nearby bog. In the ethnography section, an Afghanistan exhibit comprises rooms arranged to resemble a "souk" with winding passageways, sound effects, smells, and a house which make an extremely effective presentation of Afghanistan culture. On grazing land behind the manor house, a trail leads past a Thai house on stilts and farther along there are viking age stones and reconstructions of viking age buildings. "Prehistoric Pathway" booklet for sale at museum entrance, and map of trail on wall are available.

Other sights in Arhus include Arhus Cathedral dating from 1201, the crypt underneath the Church of our Lady dating back to 1060 and the oldest vaulted church in Scandinavia, Fire Brigade Museum which is the largest museum of its kind in the world, Arhus Art Museum with a good collection of Danish paintings from 1770 to present, Natural History Museum and Tivoli amusement park. Tourist office has folder on opening times and locations. Each year beginning the first weekend in September, Arhus' Festival lasts for nine days with ballet, theater, opera, concerts and sports events.

Bus #20 leaves from the Tourist Office daily from June 15-Sept 9 at 11 am and 1:00 pm for a 2 hour tour with English speaking guide for 20 kr, which includes 24 hours of unlimited travel on city buses.

Ebeltoft, 47 km from Arhus, is a small interesting town with the Frigate "Jylland" moored in its small boat harbor. This man-of-war was used in the Battle of Helgoland in 1864 and can now be toured. Adult/6 kr, child 6 and up/3 kr. Buses leave Arhus Rutebilstation for Ebeltoft at 15 minutes past every hour between 8:15 am and 6:15 pm for the hour and a half trip. If you have a trainpass, it's cheaper to take the train to Morke and then a bus to Ebeltoft. Best train would be the 10:02 am departure from Arhus H Station

134

for Grena which arrives at Morke at 10:43 am. A bus leaves Morke at
10:47 am and arrives in Ebeltoft at 11:35 am. Returning, leave Ebeltoft Rutebilstation at 4:25 or 6:25 pm to arrive in Morke at 5:15 or 7:15 pm. Trains
leave Morke for Arhus at 6:50 or 8:46 pm (except Sat) and at 6:13 and 9:11pm
on Saturday. (Check all times.)

Shopping hours in Arhus are M-Th 9-5:30, F 9-8, Sa 9-1.

SILKEBORG (SIL-ke-bork) is in a favorite Danish vacation area of "highlands" (such as there are in flat Denmark) and many small lakes. Train Station is on Drewsensvej downtown. Tourist Office, Torvet 9, is five blocks

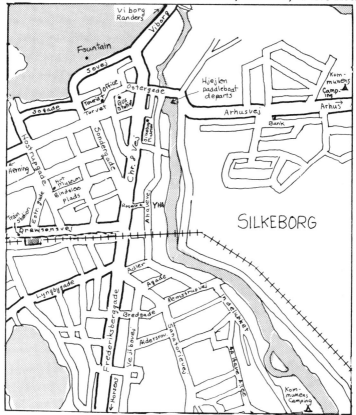

from train station. Open July-Aug 10 M-F 9-6, Sa 9-1 & 4-6, Su 10-12.
Aug 11-June 30 M-F 9-5, Sa 9-12. Kommunens Campingplads, Arhusvej
(upper right corner on map), open Apr 15-Sept 15, is 2 km from train station
on road to Arhus. Hot showers, store, playground, cooking burners. Kommunens Lejrplads "Indeluckket" (campground) is in a spruce plantation 2 km
from train station (see lower right corner of map). Open May 15-Sept. This
site is older and smaller than the first-mentioned. Similar facilities, but
next to Indeluckket park with playground. Youth Hostel, Ahavevej 55, is 5
blocks from train station. Fotex department store cafeteria, is on Torvet
near Tourist Office.

Lake Tours on 220 year old "Hjejlens" paddleboat steamer leave at

daily at 10:00 am and 1:45 pm between July 1 and August 6, and on Sunday
only in June and the rest of August. Non-stop tour is one hour and costs
adult/20 kr, child 4-14/10 kr. Motorboats traverse the lake on a regular
schedule. All tickets, except non-stop tour, allow stopovers at any landing
stage. Departures for Himmelbjerget (viewpoint with 80-foot tower) are at
10:00, 11:00 am, 1:45, 2:45 pm daily June-Aug. Return trip is at 12:15,
1:15, 4:00 and 5:00 pm.
    The 2200 year old head of Tollund man found in a peat bog is the most
notable exhibit of the Cultural Museum, Hovedgarden. The facial features
are remarkably well-preserved and give a rare glimpse of what men looked
like long ago. Open May-Oct daily 10-12 & 1-5. Shorter hours rest of year.
Adult/5 kr, child/1 kr. Art Museum, Hostrupsgade 41, shows Asger Jorns'
works, Cobra group (Appel, etc.) and modern European art. Open May-Oct
daily 10-12 & 2-5. Shorter hours rest of year. Adult/4 kr, child/1 kr. Lang-
so's Fountain, large with colored lights, turns on at twilight and off at 11 pm
in summer.

HOBRO   Outside Hobro is Fyrkat, site of a 1000 year old Viking castle in
Onsild river valley. The only thing that's left is a circular rampart made of
earth. Posts have been installed to indicate the position of dwellings but the
majority is left for the imagination which is given a needed nudge by drawings
of what must have been. New modern restrooms in entry building. No bus
goes to Fyrkat which is about 3 km from the train station and about a 45
minute walk.
    Train station is outside downtown area. Tourist Office is downtown at
Havnegade 2. Gattenborg Camping, Skivevej, is southwest of town. Get
directions from Tourist Office about a trail that goes through Byparken to
Skivevej and through a nature preserve to camp. About a 20 minute walk. Hot
showers, private sinks, changing table for infants, playground with play-
house, store, snack bar (hot dogs, ice cream, rotisseried chickens), kitchen
with four burners, sinks with hot water, tables and chairs. One division of
the subdivided camping area is modeled after Fyrkat castle with circular
enclosures of tenting area. Trail from camp leads to town heated swimming
pool and wading pool. Youth Hostel "Strandpromenaden," Nedre-Strandvej
21, is one kilometer from train station close to downtown area. Open May-
Sept 15. Ten family cottages.

AALBORG (OL-bor)   This is the fourth largest city in Denmark. Train
Station is downtown. Bus Station is on John F. Kennedy Plads, across the
plaza on the right as you leave train station. Tourist Office, 8 Oesteraagade,
is seven blocks from train station. Upon leaving station, cross John F.
Kennedy Plads (plaza) in front and turn left on mainstreet Boulevarden
Oesteraagade and go seven blocks. Tourist Office is on right hand side. Open
July-Aug 15 M-F 9-9, Sa 9-3 & 7-9, Su 10-12 & 7-9, Aug 16-June M-F
9-5, Sa 9-12.
    "Strandparken" campground is on western outskirts of Alborg, near
the fjord and the outdoor swimming pool. Take bus #2 opposite the train
station. Open May 15-Sept, adult/14 kr, child/7 kr. By car coming from
Frederikshavn, two blocks after crossing the bridge, turn right onto mainstreet Borgergade and follow signs. From Hobro, pass through downtown
area by following signs to Frederikshavn, but turn left onto Borgergade

before crossing the fjord. "Moelleparken" camping is open May-Sept 15.
Take bus #8 opposite the train station. By car from Hobro, follow signs to
Aalborg until seeing camping signs (turn left on Moelleparkvej which is before downtown Aalborg). From Frederikshavn, pass through downtown by
following signs to Hobro and turn right onto Moelleparkvej. Hot showers,
washing machine, store, hot water in dishwashing sinks, cook facilities and
refrigerator, playground, adult/14 kr, child/7 kr. Youth hostel is 500
meters from camping "Molleparken."

North Jutland Museum of Art, 50 Kong Christians Alle, is within walking distance of train station. Designed by Finnish architects Elissa and
Alvar Aalto, the striking building contains works from 1890 to present.
Lindholm Hills (Hoje) has viking burial grounds with 682 graves, many of
which are stone ships. Fifteen houses have been excavated from a village
of 1000 A.D. Also see the picturesque parts of the city with narrow pedestrians only streets and 150-400 year old well preserved houses. Ask for
leaflet from Tourist Office. Market is W & Sa 7-2 on Aagade, near station.

FREDERIKSHAVN   The town has ferry connections to Goteborg, Sweden
and Larvik and Oslo, Norway. Make ferry reservations at least 24 hours in
advance for cars. Reservations are free--ask at tourist office of the town
you're in. If you haven't a reservation, there still may be some space even
if it's fully booked because of "no shows." There is a special line for cars
waiting to see if room becomes available. Tell the attendant you want to
wait and see if you can get on. After your car is in line, then dispatch someone to ticket office to buy tickets. If you do not get on or choose not to wait,
make car reservation at office. Currency exchange is in ticket office. Only
Stena Sessan Line is included in Eurailpass and Eurail Youthpass. You will
need to walk from train station to ferry dock, about a ten minute walk (see
map next page). For drivers, prices are cut to about half before about
June 20th and after about August 8th. Between those two periods is "high
season" and the cost is car/193 kr, adult/96 kr, student/82 kr, child/48 kr.
Special prices are in effect for a car plus all passengers on the 4:00 am,
8:00 am, and 10:15 pm sailings. Crossing is 3 hours and 15 minutes.

The best food values in Scandinavia are found on the international
ferries. Be sure to bypass the cafeteria until you come to the dining room
where the "Koldt bord" is available from about 11 am to 3 pm. The "Koldt
bord" is a huge buffet for a set price and offers different sorts of herring
and perhaps some other kind of fish, an assortment of coldcuts ("palaeg")
to put on a variety of breads, butter, a few hot dishes, and perhaps cheese
with crackers, and fruit. The price does not include beverage. Less
expensive than the koldt bord is the typical Danish breakfast ("morgenmad")
which is a help yourself buffet served in the dining room also. You're
entitled to unlimited servings but be sure to have everything you want on
your plate and in your glass by about 45 minutes after the ferry leaves as
the buffet table is cleared at 9:00 am to be reopened at 10:00 am for another
buffet. At the 8:00 am koldt bord, cheese, sausage, Danish pastry, assort-
of breads, crackers, butter, jams, herring, liverpaste, corn flakes, milk,
coffee, hot chocolate, sugar and cream are served. Beverages are
included in the price.

Tourist office, Brotorvet 1, is open M-F 9-5, Sa 9-12, except in July
(open M-Sa 8:30 am-10:30 pm, Su 11-8:30).

NORDSTRAND CAMPING, Apholmenvej 40, is about a 30 minute walk north of the train station and dock area. Open May-Sept. Camp is large and modern with room for 1500 people. Facilities include 2 restroom buildings, one heated by a combination of electrical and solar energy, which contain 64 hot showers, wash basins with hot water, 60 flush toilets plus 8 more for the handicapped, 2 baby bathing rooms, 4 washing machines and dryers, 40 electric hotplates; youth center with games and color television; grocery store, cafeteria which seats 80 (open June 15-Aug 15 9 am-10 pm); 10 cabins sleeping 4 (70 kr plus camping fee); and two children's play areas. Adult/ 18 kr, child/9 kr.

Bus #2 from Sondergade goes to youth hostel or can walk 14 blocks.

Fish auction is on pier V, M-Sa at 7:30 am. Fotex Cafeteria, Havnegade 4, is open M-W 8:30-5:30, Th 8:30-6, F 8:30-8, Sa 8-1. Schou Epa Cafeteria, Danmarksgade 74, is open M-Th 9-5, F 9-7, and Sa 9-1. No open market.

Krudttarnsmuseet, on way to campground, is open 10-5, adult/2 kr, child/1 kr. The round gun tower, part of a larger fortification built in 1686-1690, contains weapons and uniforms from that period. Bangsbo Museum, Dronning Margrethesvej, is open 10-5, adult/3 kr, child/1 kr. Take bus 1 or 2 from Kirkepladsen. The historical museum is a manor house from 1364, barn from 1630 housing wagons and farming tools, a ship

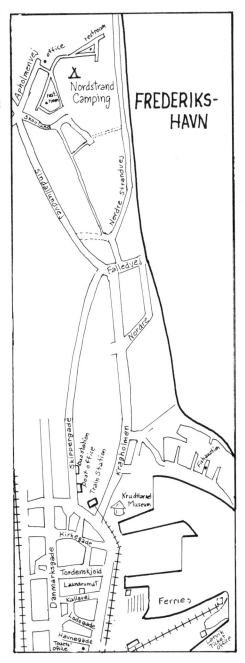

FREDERIKS-HAVN

138

from the middle ages, and period rooms. Jernalderkaeldrene, Logten
Mark, Bronderslevvej, (open all day and free) are late Celtic Iron Age
cellars of stone construction containing several small almost oval rooms.
Jaettestuen, Blakshojgard, Gaerum, (open all day, adult/1 kr) is a notable
burial grave with a large burial room from the later Stone Age.
Kunstmuseum, Kallsvej/Danmarksgade (open T, Th, Sa, Su 10-5; W 12-7;
adult/3 kr, child/free) shows changing eshibitions of modern art.

FINLAND

What's happening in contemporary design is happening in Finland, or rather Suomi as the Finns call it. Finland is a camping country where most campgrounds come complete with sauna! The Midnight Sun turns night into day during summer which simplifies finding a campground late at night. June 21 is Finnish Flag Day.

CURRENCY   Finnish markka (Fmk) is divided into 100 penni. There are about 43 markka to a U.S. dollar in 1981. One Fmk equals about 23¢.

WEATHER   In southern Finland, it's warm enough to camp from June through August, and in northern Finland from about the last week in June through the first three weeks in August.

FERRIES TO STOCKHOLM   Included in Eurailpass and Eurail Youthpass is deck passage on Silja Line ships between Finland and Stockholm as follows.   Helsinki (So. Harbor-Helsingfors) to Stockholm (Vartan): lv. Helsinki daily 6 pm (ar. 9 am). Turku (Abo) to Stockholm (Vartan): lv. 7:30 pm daily beginning June 1 (ar. 8:00 am), and lv. 9:30 pm daily (ar. 7:00 am--the ship is faster).   Turku (Abo) to Aland Islands (Mariehamn) to Stockholm (Vartan): lv 10:30 am daily beginning about May 16 (ar. Mariehamn 4:15 pm, Stockholm 8:30 pm).   Daytime passage unveils the many islands enroute.   These large 6,000-12,000 ton car ferries offer movies, duty-free shop, cocktail lounge with live music, and a dining room which serves smorgasbord for lunch and dinner.   Make reservations at Silja Line offices, E. Makasiinikatu 4, Helsinki 13. Silja Line ticket office is at Etelaesplanadi 14. Children under 12 are free on every ferry line.

TRAINS   Finnish State Railways (VR) operate the trains. There are about 6000 kilometers of track in Finland, and where the trains don't go, the buses do. It is necessary to change trains at the Swedish-Finnish border as the tracks are of a different width. A seat reservation costing 10 Fmk is mandatory for fast express trains (EP). On other trains no seat reservation is required but if you want one it costs 5 Fmk. Trains for which a seat reservation are required are marked $\boxed{R}$ on the schedules in the stations.

Children under 4 travel free and those between 4 and 11 pay half. Families of a minimum of three receive 20% off on fares. Groups of at least 10 get 20% off. A "Tourist Ticket" is sold which includes rail, air, bus and boat travel, and is purchased in train stations and travel agencies in Finland. A Finnrail Pass is sold in the U.S. which gives unlimited rail travel for 1, 2 or 3 weeks for 220 Fmk, 320 Fmk and 430 Fmk, respectively. This same pass is sold in train stations in Finland where it is called a Holiday Ticket.

A sleeper (3 berths per compartment) in second class costs 28 Fmk and must be reserved in advance.

aikataulut   - timetable
lahto   - departure
laiturilta   - track
lippuluukku - ticket office
matkalippujen - reservations
neuvontatoimist - information

odotussali - checkroom
rautatieasemalle - train station
saapuminen - arrival
sisaan - entrance
ulos - exit

CAMPING   Campgrounds are well-equipped, spacious and in beautiful natural surroundings. Most every town has one. Usually there is a flat fee per night per single individual or per family. Always tightly close your tent when leaving for the day as unexpected showers (though brief) are not uncommon. Tourist office has a pamphlet listing campsites. Camps listed in this book are open June-August except as noted. Many camps are open only during the three summer months. The basic fee includes the use of showers, cooking facilities and washing facilities, where provided. Sauna is charged extra. A national camping card is sold for 4 Fmk and can be bought at the first site which requires it.

FOOD   As always, cheapest place to buy food is at the open market. Lunch is normally eaten between 11 am and 2 pm, and dinner from 5-6 pm. Staples of the Finnish diet include milk, butter, potatoes, fish, meat, rye bread, and fresh berries in season. "Lihapullia" is meatballs, "piirakka" is meat and rice filled egg pancakes, and "kalakukko" is fish pie. "Lappi" is a mild semi-soft white cheese similar to mozzarella in taste and cooking properties and is reasonably priced. "Voileipapoyta" is akin to smorgasbord, a buffet of many different fish dishes, meat and salad specialties. Cafeterias are "baari" and "grilli." "Grilli-kioski" and "shaslik-grilli" are fast-food places serving hot grilled meats like shish-ke-bob.

In 1981, one liter milk cost 2.39 Fmk, one loaf of wheat bread weighing about 350 grams cost 3.50 Fmk, one 400 gram loaf of rye bread cost 2.50 Fmk, and one grilled chicken cost 22 Fmk per kilogram.

HELSINKI

Planned on a grand scale, Helsinki has a number of monumental buildings to use as landmarks.

TRAIN STATION   Central terminal was built in 1919 by Saarinen and has exchange office, hotel booking service (which also functions as a tourist office), cafeteria, luggage lockers and baggage check.

TOURIST INFORMATION   Helsinki City Tourist Office, Pohjoisesplanadi 19, is near Market Square and close to where ferries arrive. Ferry docks are South Harbor Passenger Pavillion and Katajanokka Terminal, the former is used by Silja Line ferries. "Matkailutoimisto" is tourist office.

CAMPGROUND   Rastila Campground is 13 km east of the city center. Open May 15-Sept 15. From Railway Square, Rautatientorilta (street) near station, take bus #96 or 96 V from platform 13. By car, go on Itainen moottoritie, Meripellontie and across Vuosaari Bridge to Rastila district. Camp has hot showers, cooking facilities, restaurant, row boats and rental cabins (16 cabins sleeping 4 each at 75 Fmk a day and 4 cabins for 2 persons at 50 Fmk a day). Campground charges are 12 Fmk for a single person or 24 Fmk for car, tent, trailer and people altogether, per day.

CITY TRANSPORTATION   Bus and tram cost 3.50 Fmk per adult and 1.40 Fmk per child for a single ticket. It's much cheaper to buy a book of 10 tickets for adult/30 Fmk, child/ 7 Fmk. Transfers in any direction can be made within one hour. Tourist Ticket, good for 24 hours beginning with first ride, costs 18 Fmk and is sold by tourist office or on bus or tram. Tram 3 T is a sightseeing tour with commentary in English, operating from 10 am-3 pm and 6-8 pm Monday through Fridays and 9 am - 8 pm on weekends during summer only. Tram 3 T starts from Market Square (Kauppatori) near ferry pier.

FOOD   Market is on Market Square (Kauppatori), open M-Sa 7 am-2 pm. Other markets are at Hietalahti, Hakaniemi and Toolo. "Voileipapoyta" is served in the restaurants of Hotel Helsinki, Hotel Hesperia, Hotel Vaakuna, Hotel Klaus Kurki and Hotel Torni and in the restaurants Kappeli and Kellarikrouvi. The price is between 35-40 Fmk.

SIGHTSEEING   Ask tourist office for its excellent brochures "Sights In and Around Helsinki" and "Helsinki's Four Tourist Islands." Things to see include the National Museum, National Theater and Art Museum, Congress and Concert Hall by Alvar Aalto and the Olympic Stadium. Didrichsen Art Museum (Didrichsenin Taldemuseo), at Grano, is open Wednesday and Sunday from 2-4 pm. Take bus # 194 or 195 from platform 50 or #192 from platform 51 at bus station. Get off at second stop on island of Kuusisaari (Grano) which is a 20 minute ride. Museum costs adult/3 Fmk, child/1 Fmk. Museum is the personal collection of the owners and shown in their countryhome. Art from many countries and periods and sculpture have been collected.

TOILETS   Usually the doors are marked with pictures--man or woman/ rooster or hen! Sometimes the word "naisille" for woman or "miehille" for man is printed.

TRAIN SCHEDULES   To Turku trains leave at 7:32, 9:10 am, 12:40, 4:02, 6:02 and 9:12 pm (runs daily May 27-Sept 2, otherwise only M-F, Su). The 6:02 pm departure arrives at Turku Harbor at 9:12 pm to connect with ferry.

Trains to Tampere leave at 6:10, 7:00, 8:00, 9:05, 10:00, 11:00 am, 1:00, 2:00, 3:30, 4:00 (reservation required), 5:30, 6:00, 6:10, 7:00, and 10:05 pm. Trip is 2 to 2-1/2 hours. Lapponia Express requires a reservation as indicated above and costs 10 Fmk.

Trains to Jyvaskyla leave at 8:00, 10:00 am, 1:00 and 6:10 pm. About a 4 hour trip.

Trains to Seinajoki leave at 7:00, 10:00 am, 4:00 (reservation required), 6:00, 7:00, 8:10 and 10:00 pm. Trip is about 4 hours.

Trains to Oulu leave at 7:00, 10:00 am, 4:00 (reservation required), 7:00, 8:10, and 10:00 pm. Trip is 7-1/2 to 9-1/2 hours.

To go from Helsinki to Narvik, Norway in one fell swoop take the 10:00 evening departure from Helsinki which arrives in Tornio at the Finnish border at 9:45 am. The train arrives at Haparanda, the Swedish border town at which you must change trains because Swedish tracks are narrower, at 8:55 in the morning Swedish time. Swedish trains leave Haparanda at 10:20 am and 3:25 pm arriving in Boden at 12:55 pm and 6:00 pm, respectively. At Boden you must change trains. A train leaves Boden at 3:10 pm and arrives in Gallivare (where there is a campground) at 5:25 pm and Narvik at 10:20 pm which is still light enough to pitch a tent.

TURKU (ABO in Swedish)

Turku, Finland's oldest city, is where the ferry arrives via the Aland Islands. The ferry stops at Mariehamn (Maarianhamina), an unspoiled town with the Pommern, 4-masted barque and now a museum ship, in its harbor. At Mariehamn, Aland Islands, is Grona Udden Camping, open May 15-Aug.

In TURKU, tourist offices are in the Silja Terminal at the harbor, in the market square, (open M-F 8:30-8:00, Sa 8:30-6:00, Su 8:30-3:00) and at Kasityolaiskatu 4. CAMPING RUISSALO is 10 km from downtown. From the harbor, take bus #1 to the market place and then take bus #8 by the Orthodox church by the market place to the campground. Camp shares the lovely island of Ruissalo with a Botanical Garden and recreation area. Open June-Aug, hot showers, sauna, cooking facilities, restaurant, store, swimming, rental cabins, one person/15 Fmk, family/30 Fmk. BUS FARE is 2.50 Fmk, or 24 hour tourist ticket for 8 Fmk. OPEN MARKET at Market Square is open M-Sa 7-2. Covered market closes at 5 pm. YOUTH HOSTEL, 39 Linnankatu, is reached by bus #3 from train station or bus #1 from harbor, 15 Fmk per person. SIGHTSEEING includes Turku castle which has an armory, historical museum, atmospheric prison and Fire Brigade Museum; Handicrafts Museum; and an Art Gallery.

Trains leave Turku for Helsinki at 7:00 am, 8:47 am, 10:15 am, 12:15 pm, 3:45 pm, 5:25 pm and 8:45 pm. Direct connection from the harbor on arrival of ferries.

VALKEAKOSKI

Valkeakoski, 35 km from Tampere, is home of the Voipaala Art Center comprising exhibition areas and classrooms sponsored by the Finnish League of Visual Arts, and the Kauppilanmaki Outdoor Museum which depicts life of paper mill workers from 1870-1920. Nearest train station is 20 km away in Toijala on the route Helsinki-Tampere. Hourly bus costing 6.20 Fmk goes from Toijala to Valkeakoski. Camping Apianlahti is then a 300 meter walk

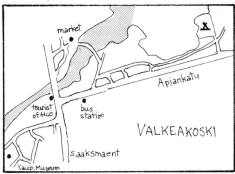

from bus station (see map). Camp costs a flat fee of 20 Fmk per tent and has store, hot showers, hot water in sinks, beach sauna, washing machine, rental boats, cooking facilities, swimming, and cabins for rent. Food market is on Tuesday and Friday and is within walking distance of camp. Kaùppilanmaki Outdoor Museum, within walking distance of bus station, contains five original houses plus a smoke-sauna, out-house and workers' meeting house. Special program is given at 2 pm on Sunday in summer and this is the best time to visit. Voipaala Art Center hosts the National Summer Exhibition from June-August daily 11-6. Also of interest is the Emil Wikstrom Museum, open May-Sept daily 11-7 except closes 5 pm Mondays.

TAMPERE

Finland's second largest city is situated on an isthmus between two lakes. Tourist Office (Kaupungin Matkailu) is at A. Kiven Katu 14B, open June-Aug M-F 8:30-6, Sa 8:30-2, Su 1-2 and Sept-May M-F 8:30-4. Campground is at Harmala, 5 km from the station. Take bus #1 from main street bridge (see map), about 300 meters from train station.

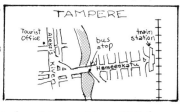

Fare is 3.50 Fmk for a single ticket but a booklet of ten tickets can be bought on the bus for 21 Fmk. The bus stops 200 meters from the camp and there is a big sign on the right side of the street. The camp is 200 meters to the right. Camp charges 28 Fmk per tent for everybody or 14 Fmk for a single person. Sauna costs 10 Fmk, and washing machine, 10 Fmk. Hot showers, cooking facilities and outdoor games are free. Rental cabins for 3 persons cost 60 Fmk and for 4 persons cost from 75 Fmk. Camp also has a television room and store. Tourist information is available on the site.

There are two open markets, Tammelantori and Laukontori, which are open M-Sa 7 am-1 pm. On the mainstreet (Hameenkatu) is a market hall open M-F 8-5 and Sa 8-2 (in summer on Sa 8-1).

Municipal Museum in Hatenpaa Manor, a 19th century oriental-Renaissance building, shows industrial exhibits, local artifacts and period rooms. In Sarkanniemi Recreation Center there is an aquarium, planetarium, observation tower, children's zoo and amusement park. There is also a modern art gallery, natural science museum, doll and costume museum and technical museum.

Trains leave Tampere for Helsinki at least once an hour. For Seinajoki, trains leave at 8:55 am, 12:15 pm, 6:00 pm (reservation required), 8:10 pm and 9:47 pm. The ride is about 1-1/2 to 2 hours. For Jyvaskyla, trains leave at 10:20 am, 12:15 pm, 3:05 (not SatO and 8:30 pm for the 1-1/2 to two hour trip.

JYVASKYLA

The renowned Finnish architect Alvar Aalto spent his adolescense and began his career in Jyvaskyla. Pick up an architectural map from the tourist office for a tour of his many buildings which include the Central Finland Museum (1960), Alvar Aalto Museum (1973), Police Station (1970), College of Education (1957) and Student Union Building. Tourist office is near train station (see map).

Tuomiojarvi Camping is about 2 km from the train station. The easiest way to get there is to go by foot through the center of town. But if you want, you can walk to the bus station (see map) and take bus #22, 23, 32, 34 or 35 to campground. Bus stops just outside camp. The camp costs 25 Fmk per tent, car and family altogether, 12.50 Fmk for one person. Camp is open June- Aug, and has hot showers, hot water in sinks, large store (open 8 am- 10 pm), sauna and cooking facilities.

Market (M-Sa 7-2) is marked on map.

Trains to Tampere leave at 9 am, 2:08,, 4:50 and 6:40 pm (not Sat) for 1-3/4 hour trip.

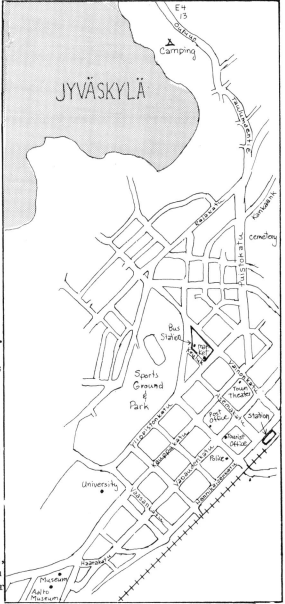

SEINAJOKI

Founded in 1960, Seinajoki is a junction for five railways and is famous for its downtown area designed by Alvar Aalto. Tourist Office is in train station. Camping Tornava, 3.5 km from the station is reached by bus #1 from Rautatiekatu (street) on left of station as you go out (see map). Bus leaves at 6:05, 7:05, 8:05, 9:10 and ten minutes past each hour until 10:10 pm. Bus costs 2.80 Fmk, and stops near camp entrance. Camp is open June-August and charges a flat fee of 24 Fmks for a tent or 12 Fmks for a single person. There are hot showers, hot water in sinks, cooking facilities, restaurant, fishing, washing machine, and store. The camp is part of Tornava Center, a former manor estate, which now comprises forest, hostel, agricultural museum, outdoor museum, powder museum in a powder mill, summer theater, beach and athletic field.

Open market is three blocks from train station and operates 7-2. Also within 1-3 blocks of the station are 6 supermarkets, open about 9-8. Designed by Alvar Aalto, the administrative and cultural center comprises Lakeuden Risti (church), parish center, town hall, library (2) and house of state offices. The area is 5 blocks from the station and map from Tourist Office shows locations. The industrial areas of the town are interesting for their modern design as are the totally pre-planned residential communities of Kivisto, Kasperi and Katajalaakso.

Trains go south to Tampere, Toijala and Helsinki at 8:05, 10:50 am (reservation required), 4:45 pm, 5:45 pm (Su only), and 7:50 pm. The trip to Helsinki is about 4 hours. For Turku, change trains at Toijala which is a half hour beyond Tampere. Trains go north to Oulu at 10:45 am and 2:07 pm. Trip is about 4 hours.

OULU

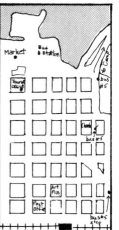

Oulu, largest city in Northern Finland, is situated at mouth of Oulu River. The modernity of its university and medical centers contrasts with the nearby village of Ii, reminiscent of the Middle Ages.

Tourist Office (Kaup. matkailu toimisto) at Torikatu 14 towards the waterfront is 8 blocks from the train station (see map). Open M-F 9-7 & Sa 9-1. The office publishes an excellent English language folder with a good map.

Nallikari Camping, the most popular camp in Finland, logs in 38,000 visitors a year, about a third being foreigners. The last two weeks in July are its busiest period during which it registered a record 1,975 visitors in one day. The camp is in a birch grove next to the sea with a sandy beach. Open June-August. It is 4 km from downtown Oulu. Take bus #5 (bus stop is on one-way street Heikinkatu, 3

146

blocks from station--see map) to camp entrance. The resort camp has hot showers, hot water in sinks, cooking facilities, restaurant, store, miniature golf, volleyball, exercises under the direction of a physical fitness instructor, a woman to supervise children, 45 cabins for rent and a disco one kilometer away. Its sauna costs 12 Fmk. Camp costs 24 Fmk per tent or 12 Fmk for a single person.

Open market, Kauppahalli, is downtown on the waterfront. Fish is sold in the Market Hall. Turkansaari, an island outdoor museum of 22 buildings from olden times, including a church dating from 1694 and an authentic tar pit from the days when northern Finland produced a large amount of the tar needed for 18th and 19th century sailing ships. Museum is open 11 am-9 pm. Boat for Turkansaari leaves from dock near bridge of Pohjantie (highway E 4) which crosses River Oulu. Boat leaves June 1-15 Tu-Sa at 6 pm and Su at 11:30 am & 4 pm, June 16-Aug 14 Tu-Sa at 2 & 6 pm and Su at 11 am, 3 & 6 pm, Aug 16-31 Tu-Sa at 5 pm and Su at 11:30 am & 4 pm. Trip takes 3 hours with 1-1/2 hours spent at the museum.

Koskikeskus, designed by Alvar Aalto, includes North Ostrobothnia Museum, Art Museum, modern University Hospital and University of Oulu. Sightseeing tour of Oulu leaves campground at 1:30 pm Mon-Sat during July. Hailuoto, island off Oulu with good beaches, is reached by free 20 minute ferry from Oulu. Ii (Iin Hamina), 37 km north of Oulu, is a picturesque fishing village with narrow alleys and small wooden dwellings seemingly perched one on top of another above the harbor of what once flourished as a market and trading center during the Middle Ages. A campground is within walking distance. Take local train from Oulu (direction Kemi).

To go to Sweden take the 8:00 am train to Haparanda which arrives there at 8:55 am Swedish time which is an hour earlier. Trains leave Haparanda at 10:20 am and 3:25 pm for Boden. At Boden you can take a train at 3:10 pm which arrives in Narvik, Norway at 10:22 pm, or you can go to Stockholm by taking the 6:20 pm train which arrives at 8:15 am. The connections are better if you want to go straight to Malmo, Sweden: leave Haparanda at 11:20 am, ar. Boden 12:55 pm (change trains), lv. Boden 1:15 pm, ar. Malmo 9:41 am the next day, ar. Helsingborg 10:15 am, ar. Copenhagen 11:51 am.

From Oulu to Seinajoki, trains leave at 7 am (reservation required), 12:15 and 4:00 pm for the 3-1/2 to 4 hour trip. These same trains continue on to Tampere and Helsinki.

FRANCE

Everyone loves France. To the tourist, the virtues of France are delicious food, great cheese, good wines, wonderful ancient walled towns in the countryside, magnificent chateaux, gardens and furniture, superb collections of modern art, and the animation and "joie de vivre" of the French people. In general, the French seem to be a little more lighthearted on the average than other Europeans which may stem from the French point of view of life that nothing could be so bad that it couldn't be worse. Many people who have lived in France, and especially in Paris, feel the hallmark of French society is tolerance of the French to let people be themselves. The French tend to think in gray, rather than the black and white of an adversary mentality, and are realistic and practical. Individual liberty is given highest priority.

Bargains in France are her incomparable bread, restaurant meals in the countryside and hairdressers. Whereas Britain seems to have a travel agency in every block, in France you'll find a coiffeur. The typical Frenchwoman has great respect for her crowning glory, doesn't mess around with it and goes to the hairdresser weekly. If it gets dirty before she can get there, she covers it up with a hat. (A while back we took a tour of the wine producers in the Bordeaux area with a very attractive Frenchwoman as our guide. She drove us in her small French car and when leaving the Chateau de Rothschild inadvertently backed the car into a tree. This upset her greatly, which we understood until she explained it was because her car would have to be in the repair garage and how then could she get to the hairdresser's!)

France is also the home of the world's most attractive ugly women--
in fact the French have a term for it, "une jolie laide." Most Frenchwomen
make the best of what they have and this form of respect for oneself and the
natural endowment of things, be it food, wine or personality, is wonderfully
prevalent in France.

Incidentally, some travelers (chiefly older) seem to associate the word
French solely with sex and indeed the world's most elegant nudity is available in Paris. But at the risk of demolishing reputations, we must report
that many observers of the Paris scene will swear food comes first on the
list of a Frenchman's pleasures, and they aren't sure just where "l'amour"
would rank--possibly somewhere among the joys of driving his car as fast
as he can and the pleasures of doing the tax collector out of some money.

The French priority? If you must do France once-over-lightly, five
days in Paris, one day in Chenonceaux (chateau of the Loire), one day in
Les Eyzies (prehistoric capital), one day in Carcasonne (medieval fortified
town), and a visit to the new spectacular Vasarely Museum in Aix-en-
Provence might be considered. Of course this would miss the Riviera with
its modern art collections, wonderful Annecy and Chamonix in the French
Alps, the Roman ruins of Arles, Nimes and Orange, many other castles of
the Loire, tours of champagne-makers in Rheims as well as the other
French provinces, each worth visiting.

Michelin guidebooks take many of the wrinkles out of touring. Drivers
may wish to buy its "Camping Caravanning en France" for its lists of campgrounds and helpful maps. Its series of regional sightseeing guides with
green covers are indispensable for understanding what you're seeing and
are available in English editions for Paris, Chateaux of the Loire, Brittany,
Normandy and Cote D'Azur (Riviera). The red "Michelin Guide France" has
maps of every city and town of any size as well as hotel and restaurant listings and will save many a headache for drivers. Buy all Michelin guides and
maps in France as the cost is at least 40 percent below U.S. retail.

CURRENCY   Currency exchange is "bureau de change." The currency
is French francs. Each franc is divided into 100 centimes. There are about
5.7 francs (F) to one dollar. Each franc is worth about 18¢. We got a better
rate of exchange in the U.S. than we did in France.

WEATHER   Camping weather in Paris is best from June to September.
Camping on the Riviera is pleasant from May into October, with September
and October being warmer than May. August is the most crowded time in
the resort areas of France as this is the month of the great escape for the
Frenchman. Try to avoid it, but don't worry if you can't--just stay put at
the beginning and end of the month when the French are on the move.

CAMPING   There are 3600 campgrounds in France. The French Tourist
Office will send you regional listings of campgrounds, the map "Go Camping
in France" and the brochure "Castels et Camping Caravanning" which lists
deluxe camps on the estate of a chateau. At the French Touring Club's
camps in France you can obtain free their "Directory of Campgrounds" or
"Indicateur du Camping Caravanning" for the current year which lists camps
and prices and indicates whether camps can be reached by bus or train.

French campgrounds are a bargain compared to those in Switzerland and northern Europe. The average nightly campground fee is about 3-5 F (54¢-90¢) per person and 2-5 F (36¢-90¢) per tent (emplacement) and per car. Children under 7 usually pay half price. Fee is higher at deluxe camps. According to law, charges must be posted at camp entrance. Most French camps do not furnish toilet paper and over half of the camps we used had hole-in-the-floor toilets. However the camps in Paris and many others have conventional toilets. Deluxe camps generally have conventional toilets, toilet paper, and hot water in the wash basins. No camping carnet is needed in France except for the State Forests (in which you are unlikely to camp). A passport is accepted even when a sign states "license exigee" (camping permit needed). Here is a French camping vocabulary:

redevance - charge	reduction - discount
par personne - per person	distribution d'eau chaude compris-
auto - car	price includes hot water
tente - tent	plats cuisines - take-out food
caravan - trailer	infirmerie - first aid
taxe de sejour - residence tax	glacieres - ice chest
demi-tarif - half price	depot de glace a rafraichir - ice
douche chaude - hot shower	location - for rent
piscine chauffee - swimming pool	machines a laver - washing machine
aucune redevance - no charge	rechauds a gaz - gas stoves
hors saison - out of season	material de camping - equipment

TRAINS   French National Railroads (SNCF or Societe Nationale des Chemins de Fer Francais) are excellent. The best railway lines radiate outwards from Paris like spokes of a wheel. Keep this in mind when planning an itinerary as criss-crossing the hinterlands is slower. The world speed record of 236 mph is held by the French railroads by its TVG--train a grade vitesse (of great speed)--model, introduced in September, 1981. The low-slung orange, gray and white "Flying Peacock" makes the 265 mile Paris to Lyon run in 2-1/2 hours, chopping 1 hour and 48 minutes off the previous time for a TEE. In 1983, the TGV track will reach Marseille to make the Paris-Marseille run in 4 hours and 50 minutes, 2 hours shorter than before. Developing the new system has cost SNCF 1.6 billion dollars since 1970. Each train carries a single unit of 8 cars, holding 386 passengers in first class, and 275 in second. The TGV needs 2 miles to stop when going 162 mph so a special track was built without any track crossings. The TVG is energy efficient and uses about the same amount of fuel as conventional trains, and much less than car or plane on a per passenger basis. The railroads are electric and thus reduce the country's dependence on foreign oil using instead France's hydroelectric and nuclear energy. Other European countries are likely to buy trains and a European network of TGV trains is predicted.

A "France Vacances" ticket is sold by French National Railroads, 610 Fifth Avenue, N. Y., N.Y. 10020. In 1981, the ticket for second class cost $115 for 7 days, $150 for 15 days, and $230 for 1 month. A child 4 through 11 pays about 60%. France Vacances includes unlimited train travel, 4 or 7 days of public transportation in Paris, admission to Pompidou Museum in Paris, and 10% discount on SNCF bus sightseeing tours.

The following special tickets can only be purchased in France. Get them at any railroad station in France. On the French Tourist Ticket, travelers making a circular or round-trip route of at least 1500 kilometers within France are eligible for a 20 percent discount. The exact itinerary must be submitted and all stopovers indicated at time the ticket is purchased. The ticket must start and end from the same point, a minimum of five days must be spent before using the return portion, leaving France is acceptable as long as the same border point is used to return, the ticket is valid for two months and children 4 through 9 pay half-price. On the French Family Ticket the first two adults pay full fare, the other adults pay 1/4th fare and children 4 through 9 pay 1/8th fare. Grandparents and babysitters are considered part of a family. The route must be a round-trip or circular trip of at least 300 kilometers (187 miles). Ticket is valid for 40 days with two renewals of 20 days each for a 10 percent supplement being possible. On "Group Tickets" 10-23 people traveling together receive 20% off and 24 or more 30% off. One free conductor ticket is issued for 15 paying passengers. "Carte Vermeil" is available to women over 60 and men over 65 for 28 F that entitles them to a 30% reduction on most railway tickets. Not valid on holidays or weekends.

For price comparison purposes, we have figured the fare on the French Tourist Ticket (Billet Touristique) on the following itinerary based on a 1979 price of 3.3 francs per 10 kilometers second class.

Paris-Orleans-Beaugency-Blois-Amboise-Tours (235 km)
     Sidetrip: Tours- Azay-le-Rideau - Chinon - Tours (98 km)
     Sidetrip: Tours-Chenonceaux-Tours (60 km)

Tours-Loches, Loches-Chateauroux by bus same price, Chateauroux-Limoges-Perigueux-Niversac-Les Eyzies-Agen-Carcasonne-Montpellier-Nimes-Arles-Marseilles-Cannes-Antibes-Nice (1185 km)

Nice-Digne-St. Auban-Veynes-Grenoble-Aix-les-Bains-Annecy-Chamonix (590 km)

Chamonix-Paris (600 km)

This itinerary totals 2768 km and costs approximately $175 on the Tourist Ticket valid for two months. For an additional 10 percent the validity can be extended one month.

Included in Eurailpass and Eurail Youthpass are ferry crossings from Rosslare, Ireland to either Le Havre or Cherbourg, France. Port taxes are extra and must be paid in French francs. The ferry leaves Le Havre daily except Tuesdays and Saturdays at 6:00 pm and arrives in Rosslare at 2:00 pm the next day,--a 21 hour crossing. The ferry leaves Cherbourg on Tuesday and Saturday at 9:00 pm and arrives in Rosslare at 2:00pm the next day.   (There is a one hour time difference between Ireland and France.) A reservation charge of $5.00 plus a $3.00 supplement is paid if you want the cheapest berth, which is in a 6-berth cabin with washbasin on the lower deck. This rate is not available on "Saint Patrick" ferry; its cheapest berth is in a 4-berth cabin and costs $10 supplement plus $5 reservation fee. Otherwise you are entitled to deck class on the luxurious ships which have lounges, a discotheque, movies on closed circuit television, snack bar, duty free shop, and restaurant (breakfast $6, lunch $8, dinner

$11--don't forget to stock your larder). During July and August a reservation may be necessary. Passengers must check in not less than one hour before sailing time. Between October 1 and March 31, the only sailings are from Le Havre on Tuesday, Thursday and Saturday. Ships are St. Patrick and St. Gillian, carrying 1,040 and 1,500 passengers.

Of French trains, TVG and TEE are best, then come international expresses and "rapides" which serve France internally. Lower down in the hierarchy are "expresses" that are slower than "rapides." At bottom are local trains, "direct" ones don't stop at every station and "omnibus" do. Seat reservation costs about 5 F at a train station. On tickets purchased in France, children four through nine travel at half fare. Under four are free. Validity of a regular ticket varies from 10 to 30 days. Stopovers are free. Ticket must be validated in the orange machine on the platform before getting on. From Paris to destinations within 50 miles, special Sunday one-day excursion tickets and 3-day weekend tickets are discounted 30-50%.

Free train schedules for individual routes are available in racks in the train stations. SNCF publish the official timetables in 10 volumes. Volume A "Indicateur Renseignements Generaux" gives European-wide schedules and is given free when any other schedule A is purchased. The other schedules cost from 15-20 francs at train station newspaper kiosks. They are #A1 "Horaires du reseau de l'Est" (covering eastern France), #A2 "Horaires du reseau du Nord" (covering northern France), #A3 "Horaires du reseau de l'Ouest" (covering western France), #A4 "Horaires du reseau du Sud-Ouest" (covering southwestern France), #A5 "Horaires du reseau du Sud-Est" (covering southeastern France), #B1 "Horaires de la banlieue de Paris-Est" (covering suburban lines east of Paris), #B2 "Horaires de la banlieue de Paris-Nord" (covering suburban lines north of Paris), #B3 "Horaires de la banlieue de Paris-Ouest" (covering suburban lines west of Paris) and #B4 "Horaires de la banlieue de Paris-Sud" (covering suburban lines south of Paris).

Station restaurants (buffets de gare) in France serve very good food and the French go there just like they would to a regular restaurant. Automatic lockers in the station are 29"deep, 12" wide and 17" high and take 2 one-franc coins for 24 hours. Large size is twice as wide and takes one 5 franc coin.

la gare (lah-gar) - station	a, de - to, from
quai - track	lundi - monday
banlieue - local train departures	mardi - tuesday
bureau de change - exchange office	mercredi - wednesday
renseignement - train information	jeudi - thursday
voiture - car	vendredi - friday
non fumeurs - no smoking	samedi - saturday
fumeurs - smoking allowed	dimanche - sunday
salle d'attente - waiting room	arrivee - arrival
consigne - baggage storage	depart - departure
arret facultatif -stops on signal	arret obligatoire - stops

Symbols and abbreviations used in French timetables are listed on the next page.

Trains not running daily throughout the period of the timetable ....

Supplement payable for travel on this train

Mondays (Holidays or not)	①
Tuesdays —	②
Wednesdays —	③
Thursdays —	④
Fridays —	⑤
Saturdays —	⑥
Sundays	⑦
Sundays and Public Holidays only (2)	†
Not Sundays and Public Holidays (2)	✕
Not Sundays, Saturdays and Holidays	Ⓐ
Sundays excepted (Holidays or not)	Ⓑ
Saturdays, Sundays and Holidays	©

Trans Europ Express High-speed train for which a supplement is payable .... ⓉⒺⒺ
Bus same tariff as S.N.C.F. .... ⟲⟳

Through carriages	⟺
Sleeping car (Wagon-lits Co) (full bedding facilities)	⛏
Couchettes sleeping berths (1 st or 2nd cl.)	⊨

In the list of stations = Dining room (hot meals and drinks)
In the timetable columns = Full meal and service

In « Tableau des voitures directes » = Restaurant car or carriage with restaurant service } ✕

In the list of stations = Refreshment room (cold meals and drinks)
In the timetable columns = Snack

In « Tableau des voitures directes » = Light refreshments available (Minibar) } ⊻

Self-service, Gril-Express, Gril-Bar	⊗
Bar-car	⊠
Tray-meals available	⊿
Meals available at passenger's seat............	⋈
Immigration or customs formalities............	⌸

Regular steamer service..................... ⌁
Stations accepting telegrams .... ⌺

Arrival .... A
Station unstaffed for the issue of tickets, and for handling registered baggage, such facilities being then dealt with by train staff, with certain restrictions (3) .... ⊙

Station unstaffed on Sundays and Public Holidays only, for the facilities indicated against the symbol ⊙ above, such facilities being then dealt with by train staff, with certain restrictions (3)........ ⊚

Station unstaffed on Saturdays, Sundays and Public Holidays only, for the facilities indicated against the symbol ⊙ above, such facilities being then dealt with by train staff, with certain restrictions (3)................................... △

'(1) Indications concerning stations and trains are also applicable to the bus-stops and to the buses.
(2) The legal Public Holidays are : January 1. Easter Monday, May 1, Ascension Day Whit Monday, July 14, August 15, November 1, November 11, Christmas Day.
(3) Passengers with luggage are requested to help with its handling if need be.

DRIVING   What every French driver has embedded in his brain so deeply that the response is automatic is PRIORITY ON THE RIGHT (priorite a droite). While driving in French cities, you must constantly remind yourself of this unsigned rule that is followed absolutely without any slowing down or hesitation by all French people. PRIORITY ON THE RIGHT IS IN EFFECT AT ANY UNSIGNED INTERSECTION. This means that if you are driving through an unsigned intersection and a car is entering the intersection from the street on your right, then YOU MUST YIELD TO THAT CAR EVEN IF THE STREET HE IS ON IS A SIDESTREET and EVEN IF YOU THINK YOU'RE GOING TO GET TO THE INTERSECTION SLIGHTLY AHEAD OF HIM. Conversely, if you're coming from the right, hesitating or slowing down is not necessary as the Frenchman on the left will reliably yield to you.

Priority on the right is in effect at every multi-intersection where traffic from several streets flows into a one-way circular junction. Traffic entering the roundabout from the right has priority. Traffic in the roundabout must yield to traffic entering from the right.

Most large cities have a ring-road or freeway that circles around the outlying parts of a city and must be left to reach downtown. Unless a large or moderately sized city is a sightseeing destination, the best strategy is to avoid traffic congestion by weaving your way between towns of any size by using the less important roads, all of which are paved. Parking lights, rather than headlights, are used in cities where overhead illumination is provided. Headlights are used on dark streets as warning signals. Headlight beams are lowered when another car approaches on the highway. A parking disc (disque obligatoire) is necessary for designated parking areas and is given free from tourist office. It is set at time you park. Gas is "essence" and diesel fuel is "gas oil. " Gas is purchased by asking for 40 or 50 francs worth for example or for a fill-up.

"Autoroutes" are toll freeways. "Peage" in white on a blue background indicates an entry to an autoroute. Autoroute entrances are automated where you stop and push a button which releases a ticket which is turned in at the exit to determine the toll. Sample tolls: Frejus to Gardane (outside Aix-en-Provence) is 18 F, Salon-de-Provence to Valance is 19 F and Champery to Annecy is 3 F. Rest stops along autoroutes have gas stations, restrooms and restaurants. Gas stations sell maps and accessories. Restrooms have a special compartment in the women's with padded counter and sink for changing baby and a small toilet for young children. This is called a "nursery." At the chain of Jacques Borel restaurants you can get "croque monsieur" grilled cheese sandwiches, ham sandwiches and so forth but the preferable strategy is to avoid eating on the autoroutes by finding a restaurant in a small town. Emergency phones are placed at intervals along the freeways.

"Routes Nationales" are generally four lanes with numerous side roads and are heavily traveled. "N" plus number roads are in good repair and excellent for tourists as Routes Nationales carry most of the traffic. "D" plus number are good well signed secondary roads. "VO" plus number are fairly minor roads some of which are quite good. All roads are very well signed and getting lost is difficult. Again, we recommend bypassing cities and medium sized towns by taking secondary roads to navigate between and around them, rather than getting caught in traffic. In France, road signs are given by destination rather than by number so when setting off have in mind names of the immediate small town and further along large town.

A solid line must not be crossed and means no passing. A road marked "passage protege" gives right-of-way to those already on the road. Side-streets will have a stop sign at the entrance to this type of road. Accidents occur most frequently during the first week in August, Sundays, and between 6 and 7 pm. Tuesday, wednesday and thursday are the most accident free. Here are some road signs for the curious as the international traffic signs will see you through.

cassis - bump ahead

chute de pierres - watch out for fallen stones

defense de doubler - no passing other vehicles

defense de klaxonner - use of horns forbidden

double sens - two-way traffic

deviation - detour

feu - traffic light

fin de chantier - end of construction zone

fin d'interdiction de depasser - end of no-passing zone

goudron - tar

gravillons - gravel

gravillons roulants - loose rocks

impasse - dead-end street

interdiction de parquer or interdiction de stationner - no parking

passage a niveau - level crossing

pietons - pedestrians

piste cyclable - bicycle path

poids lourds - heavy trucks

pont coupe - bridge out of order

priorite en face - first car to enter narrow road has right-of-way

ralentir, ralentissez - go slowly

route barree - route barricaded

secours routier - first-aid

sens interdit - do not enter

sens obligatoire - go this way

sens unique - one-way traffic

serrez a droite - merge right

signaux sonores interdit - no honking

154

stationnement autorise jours pairs (impairs) - parking on even (uneven) days of month allowed	Un train peut ·en cacher un autre - the train you see can hide another train behind it voie ferree - railroad voie retrecie - narrow road
tenez votre droite - keep to the right tournons brusques - hairpin turns	voie sans issue - dead-end street

BICYCLING   An excellent source of itineraries for bicycling in France is "La France A Bicyclette" by The Touring Club of France. Maps, directions and descriptions are given for 74 self-contained routes covering all the best places in France. Though the text is in French, the maps and distances are easily comprehended by the non-French reader. Book also lists sources of bicycle rentals including 35 train stations where a bicycle rents for 11 F a half day or 16 F a full day.   A deposit of 50 F is required. Train stations renting bikes in towns mentioned in this book are: Aix-en-Provence, Annecy, Antibes, Blois, Cannes, Juan-les-Pins and Nimes.   The 191-page paperback was published in 1975 by Flammarion, 26 rue Racine, 75278 Paris Cedex 06 and sold in bookstores in France for 17 F.

FOOD   In 1981, one liter of milk cost from 2.25-3.25 F, 500 grams bread from 3.00-4.50 F and a whole hot cooked chicken from 23-30 F.
    Food is the superlative of French civilization. Here is where gastronomy has reached the status of a fine art. And here is where we ate one meal a day in a restaurant. Considering the high quality of cooking, we found restaurant meals to be good value compared to what's available in the U.S. but you'll need to be able to spend at least $5 to discover this. If you do, try to eat the noon meal in a restaurant and settle for a camp meal of perhaps bread, cheese and fruit for dinner. You can never go wrong by patronizing the cheapest Michelin-listed restaurant and the full meal will cost between 21-28 F. We also were successful eating in restaurants on the road where the parking lot was full of trucks. These places usually had 17-20 F menus. Another good approach is to ask the tourist office for its free list of restaurants (every tourist office has one and menu prices are given) and seek out the ones with the cheapest menu, usually about 17-20 F. These places usually had a worker clientele and were away from the downtown area, but often not too far from the station--usually in the opposite direction from downtown. Occasionally a listed restaurant turned out to be a pizza place in which a small pizza cost the same as a full menu elsewhere so we went elsewhere. The only clearly sub-standard food we had in France was at a Mammouth shopping center cafeteria though it was cheap enough. The other meal that was slightly disappointing was when we went to the restaurant next door to a Michelin-listed one when the latter's menu turned out to be too expensive. The restaurant next door had a 25 F menu but the quality of cooking was far below what we had come to expect from Michelin-listed restaurants in that price range. From our experiences we concluded that if you plan to pay 21 F or over for a meal, be sure to patronize a Michelin-listed one, but

if a restaurant has a less expensive menu, then it's probably an excellent
value and you still won't be disappointed.

If it's the height of the dining hour (12-2 or 7:30-9:30), a good restaurant should be fairly full. The only problem is a "complet" sign may already
be hanging in the window signifying that no more diners can be accommo-
dated. Avoid restaurants with an employee stationed outside the door. The
recommendation of a policeman, shop girl, campground attendant or any
local person can be relied upon. A small, family-run restaurant will be
better value than a middle class establishment. There may be only two or
three menu selections, but each one will be good. Don't judge a restaurant
by its exterior but by amount of patronage. If a restaurant lacks a posted
outside menu, it's very expensive no matter how it looks. A "brasserie"
sometimes indicates a less expensive restaurant.

Always order the "menu" which is a three or four course meal at a
set price, never a la carte. The exception to this might be ordering an omelet for a child. The custom in France is for the house specialties, those
items on which the restaurant has built its reputation, to be printed on the
menu in red. These items are never the cheapest offerings on the menu and
usually fall in the higher price ranges but they are always very, very good.
On the "menu" hors d'oeuvres are the first course. Most common is a combination plate of sliced tomatoes, sliced cucumbers which have been left to
drain in "gros sel" (crystal salt), never "sel fin" as that would not "fatiguer"
them properly, and lightly dressed potatoes with parsley. Appetizers are
freshly prepared for the noontime meal, whereas sometimes soup is the
first course for the evening meal. The entree follows and is normally garnished (garni) with a vegetable. Fruit, ice cream (glace) and caramel custard are usually the dessert choices. If there are four courses, a fish dish
or omelet will precede the entree, a salad will follow it, or a cheese platter
will be served before dessert. The waiter presents the cheese tray with
good-sized wedges of five or six varieties on it for your inspection. The
custom is to indicate perhaps two from which you would like a slice but it's
acceptable to ask for even three. However we have asked for very small
pieces of four or five when types were unfamiliar to us and we had yet to
discover our favorites. The waiters have always been courteous at such
times, though this isn't supposed to be the thing to do. Most cheeses are
served as a triangular wedge which is correctly eaten by cutting off sequen-
tial wedges (like slicing a pie) always starting from the same point. Coffee
is served after dessert and the French commonly go elsewhere for it. Incidentally butter is not served with the basket of French bread. If radishes
are part of the appetizer, butter will accompany them. To ask for the check,
say "l'addition, s'il vous plaît."

Good basic entrees include "pot au feu" (pot roast), "boeuf bourguig-
non" (beef stew), "blanquette de veau" (veal stew) and "poulet a la chasseur"
(chicken in tomato sauce and shallots). The best way to get acquainted with
French menu terms is to peruse the two volumes by Julia Child, et al.,
"Mastering the Art of French Cooking." The French cook with butter and
peanut oil mostly with walnut oil sometimes in salad dressing. Olive oil is
used very successfully in the south of France. The words "a la florentine"
mean with spinach, and "a l'alsacienne" indicates sauerkraut. Sunday lunch
is the most important meal of the week for the French and will be taken at
as good a restaurant as can be afforded. This is when you will see families

eating out together.

Most milk is pasteurized but not always. Do check as French children aren't reared on milk as ours are. Tap water (eau nature) is safe even in small towns but the French feel it lacks "joie de vivre" and prefer mineral water for its taste, carbonation or special mineral properties. "Evian" is the standard non-carbonated mineral water. Lemonade is "citron presse." Whole milk is "lait entiere" and skim milk is "lait ecreme." The tourist office will send you a very good publication "Wines of France." Most restaurants stock a house wine (vin ordinaire) that comes in either red or white, can be ordered by quarter, half or whole liter and is served in a carafe. "Vin compris" on the menu means a certain portion of house wine is included in the menu price.

When grocery shopping, sidewalk markets are cheapest. Remember to say "Bonjour, Madame" and "Au Revoir, Mademoiselle" when shopping at the market and small shops. Bread is baked three times a day and sold according to weight in grams in a "boulangerie." The crusty bread with chewy interior is made of soft wheat, yeast and coarse salt and baked in brick ovens. In the food category, it is the best value in France and the only inexpensive snack item. That Marie Antoinette's supposed comment on the hungry--"Let them eat cake"--triggered a revolution attests to the deliciousness of the stuff. Actually the price of bread has started to rise after the newly elected French government in 1978 started a program to streamline the economy by getting rid of subsidies. The price of bread had been fixed by the state since 1791 when the Revolution's leaders, before beheading Antoinette, resolved that the Staff of Life would never again be out of reach of the poor. Before the revolution, a laborer spent 50 percent of his wages on bread. French royalty, forever aware of the political dangers of a bread shortage, tried to set up a dependable supply system but it depended on the weather so the price of bread could double overnight. Bread riots were almost a yearly event and the victims were usually the bakers who were beaten and even lynched. But in one instance, the lieutenant governor of St. Denis, near Paris, was chased up a church steeple and stabbed to death for pompously informing the crowd that "one does not sell bread to rabble for two sous a loaf." The monarchy reacted to the bread riots sometimes severely as in the instance when 50 people were hanged. But today bread consumes only 3 percent of a French household's budget. The bereted, mustashioed baker peddling loaves from a pushcart has about disappeared today but the bread is still as good as ever. Wonderfully delicious but more expensive than bread for breakfast is the croissant. A croissant costs from 1.50- 2.50 F each depending on the neighborhood and whether it's made with butter. The bakery also sells a variation on the croissant which has the same flaky pastry wrapped around a thin stick of chocolate.

Meat is expensive. Beef is particularly high and does not cost that much more when served in a restaurant as when bought at the market. Meat is divided according to muscle separation as in Belgium and Switzerland. Listed are approximate French equivalents to U.S. cuts of meat.

Beef	
cote premier - prime rib	grumeau - brisket
entrecote - sirloin steak	tranche carree - bottom round
faux-filet - tenderloin	piece ronde - eye of round
tenderloin - t-bone	flanchet - flank
	hache - hamburger

Pork	jambon - ham
cote premiere - loin chop	lard - bacon
filet - loin	sous epaule - shoulder

A "charcuterie" sells cooked meats such as pork, ham, chicken, roast beef, meat loaf, veal, pate and terrines (ground meat mixtures) and various side dishes, all delicious. There are always several varieties of pate (pah-TAY), each based on a different meat or combination of ingredients. Most expensive is "pate de foie gras" (pah-TAY duh fwah grah) which is made from diseased liver of geese locked up in the attics under gabled eaves. A "cremerie" sells a great variety of cheese. Chevre are goat milk cheeses, small and round with a natural green-gray covering. Cabecous d'Aurie is a dry goat cheese reputedly favored by Yul Brynner if you care. A "patisserie" sells cakes, croissants, creme puffs and such but no bread. A "confiserie" sells candy and ice cream. An "epicerie" is a small grocery store. Supermarkets are usually chains such as Co-op, Monoprix, or Prisunic and it was in these supermarkets in France where the idea of plain labeling began.

French canned foods make good gifts to take home. Foods listed here come canned or bottled and are available in large cities. Most are processed in the Perigord area and Perigueux is a good place to buy them if you happen to be there. First on the list must come truffles, the tuber that grows wild in the mountains and is used for flavoring somewhat in the manner of mushrooms. Now is the time to buy them if you've ever wanted to try some because they are an accelerating rarity. In 1945, 1800 tons were found but in 1970 only 120 tons were sniffed out by the dogs and female pigs who find them underground near roots of oak trees. Truffles cannot be cultivated as they do not reproduce in the usual way. Besides enhancing the flavor of dishes, truffles reputedly have certain antibiotic qualities, tone up the system, and have aphrodisiacal properties as well. (Supposedly Louis XIV ate a pound a day.) Other products include "pate en croute" (liver paste in crust), "roulade de foie gras," poulet aux champignons" (chicken with mushrooms), "terrine de lievre aux cerneaux" (with walnut kernels), "foie de porc" (pork liver paste), "galantine de dinde" (of turkey), "cassoulet" (bean and meat casserole), sauce "Perigueux" and various kinds of canned meats, mushrooms, snails and vegetables. French liqueurs include "cerise" (cherry), "framboise" (raspberry and excellent), "pruneaux" (prune), "abricot" (apricot), "l'eau de vie de prune" (plum) and "la creme de noix" (walnut).

SHOPPING   A "droguerie" sells household goods like clothespins and detergent not drugs as you might expect. A drugstore is a "farmacie" and sells prescriptions and baby food and diapers. TVA is the value added tax which amounts to about 15 percent and is deducted from any item mailed out of the country. The discount is also given for goods taken with you if they total 400 F worth from a single store. When you leave France, you must hand your receipt to French customs who will add its stamp. Customs will return the receipt to the store and the store will send you the amount of the discount through a bank. If you wish to go through this, be sure to ask about it at the store as the necessary papers must be completed. When leaving by train, check the list below for the proper procedure. From Paris St. Lazare Station on special boat trains and all international trains for Britain, passengers must report to customs at le Havre, Cherbourg, Calais, Dieppe or Dunkerque. From Gare du Nord, on TEE #71 and 73 (Paris-Brussels-Amsterdam), passengers must report to Gare du Nord customs; on Paris-Scandinavia trains check at Jeumont Station; on Paris-Copenhagen trains check between Jeumont and Charleroi; on the Nord-Express check at Saint-Quentin and Maubeuge. From Gare de l'Est on L'Arbalete #65, passengers much report to Gare de l'Est customs; on Alberg Express report to customs who board the train when it stops at Basle Station (French side); on Orient-Express. and trains from Paris to Munich, check at Strasbourg or between Strasbourg and Kehl. From Gare de Lyon on Lombardie-Express, Cisalpin #13, Simplon Express Direct-Orient, passengers should report to the French customs official during the journey between Frasne and Vallorbe or at Vallobe Station. From Austerlitz Station on all trains stopping at Hendaye, report to customs at Hendaye Station. From Marseille on the TEE Ligure, check between Monaco and Ventimiglia. From other cities, rail travelers must have the paper stamped by customs either at the station or by a customs official enroute or at the border station if the train stops long enough.

CHILDREN   The most expensive but most convenient place to buy diapers is at a "farmacie." It's almost impossible to pass through a small French town without noticing one. The cheapest place to buy diapers is at a street market and next best is a department store. Diaper is "couche nuit" (coosh nwee). The most commonly found kind and the cheapest looks like an oversized obstetrical pad. Coated nylon or plastic outer pants are needed to go with them. These worked very well on our 8-month old baby girl. Cost is about 16 F for 30 at a pharmacie or about 13 F for 50 at an outdoor market. Night diapers "coussineige speciales nuit" cost about 16 F for 35 in a plastic bag at a street market. The Pampers kind of diaper is called "complet" and costs about 20 F for 15. Some large resort-type campgrounds on the coasts offer daycare for children for about 5 F a half day. These "garderie d'enfants" operate only in the high season, usually from mid-July through August. In restaurants sometimes a cover charge of 2-4 F is assessed if a child is sharing the "menu" (full meal) of an adult. French hotel rooms are charged by the room so no extra is added if children sleep on the floor in sleeping bags.

LE POTPOURRI   The French have high standards of politeness and "monsieur," "madame" or "mademoiselle" is always appended to any short answer or request you give. For instance always say "Bonjour, monsieur," "Oui, madame," or "Non, mademoiselle." You will hear yourself addressed this way many times and will be rewarded with friendship and better service if you follow suit. When in a restaurant, add "s'il vous plait, madame" when making a request.

It's not considered good manners to go in and use the restroom of a small family cafe without buying something. Tip usherettes and cloakroom attendants 1/2 - 1 F, museum attendants who give you special service get 1 F and the girl who washes your hair 1/2-1 F. Toilet attendant gets about 1/2 F.

Summertime holidays are July 14 (Bastille Day with celebrations in Paris and throughout France) and August 15 (Assumption Day).

Main floor of a building is "rez-de-chaussee" and marked "RC" in an elevator. The "first floor" is what we would consider the second.

In a French Postoffice (PTT) many things can go wrong and many of the "fontionnaires" seem to start shaking their heads "no" before you even reach the window. A package must be two kilos or under, except for books which may weigh three kilos. Oversized packages may not be accepted. Stamps are sold at tobacco shops and that's where most people buy them. "Poste Restante" (P.O.) is effective in France. Mail is picked up at the main postoffice by showing a passport and paying a small fee for each letter. Look for the special window for this. Letters can be forwarded by paying a fee and completing the form "Ordre De Reexpedition, 755 A" which must be signed on the back.

As far as calling home, the standard joke in France is "The French are divided into two categories: those waiting to have a telephone installed and those waiting to get a dial tone. "

PARIS

Paris offers the greatest breadth of prices in Europe from the ultra plush (whence cometh its reputation) to the inexpensive good value. Because the average French person wants his money's worth and has a developed aesthetic sense, Paris offers a very wide range of moderately priced hotels and restaurants. The camper is the luckiest of all as Paris and suburbs are well endowed with campgrounds and the "metro" (subway) is reasonable when tickets are purchased in groups of ten.

AEROPORT CHARLES DeGAULLE   This ultra-modern airport is located near Roissy-en-France 27 km from Paris. Free airport guide in French is available at AP information on floor (etage) "arrivee." Nursery is on floor (etage) "transfert-satellites" near satellite 3. Roissy Rail was instituted in 1976 to provide swift rail transportation between the airport and Gare du Nord in Paris. Trip takes 30 minutes and costs about 15 F, second class. Eurailpass and Eurail Youthpass can be used but an additional 1.50 F (about) must be paid for the connecting bus between the train terminal near the airport and the airport entrance. Connecting bus to Roissy-Aeroport Station for the train to Paris leaves from floor (etage) "arrivee," "porte 30" every 15 minutes between 5:06 am and 1:05 am. When traveling from Paris to the airport on a railpass, buy the bus ticket from ticket window inside Roissy-Aeroport Station before proceeding outside to bus.

To/from Camping Le Tremblay. If you don't have a railpass or don't want to start the validity period but plan to stay at Camping Le Tremblay, then take bus RATP #351 from outside floor (etage) "boutiquaire". Bus leaves from shelter outside and to right of exit every 30 minutes from 6:35 am to 9:10 pm for the 50-60 minute trip to Nation metro (subway) station. Bus stops three times enroute. Fare is 9.50 F or 6 tickets from a carnet (see public transportation).

To/from Versailles or Bois de Boulogne campgrounds. Bus RATP #350 travels from the airport to Gare de l'Est in Paris in 50-60 minutes. Fare is 9.50 F or 6 tickets from a carnet (see public transportation). Bus leaves every 15-20 minutes between 6:13 am and 11:50 pm from floor (etage) "boutiquaire" at airport. Bus leaves from shelter outside and to right of exit. If you're going to the camps at Bois de Boulogne or Versailles, get off at Porte de la Chapelle, three stops before Gare de l'Est for more

direct metro access. Another way to get to Gare des Invalides more directly for those going to Versailles campground is to take the Air France limousine from floor (etage) "Arrivee," portes 32-34. Service runs every 20
minutes from 7:20 am to 11:20 pm and costs 18 F for the 50 minute trip
to Gare des Invalides. Take the limo to Porte Maillot for Boulogne Camping.

ORLY AIRPORT   Orly/Rail goes from Orly Airport to Quai D'Orsay in
Paris, stopping at Austerlitz Station (get off here if going to Camping Le
Tremblay) and Pont S. Michel on the way. Also available are Cars Air
France (airport limousine) to Gare des Invalides and RATP bus #215 to
place Denfert-Rochereau.

TRAIN STATIONS   Paris has six. Gare du NORD serves Flanders, Artois
and Picardie within France and Belgium, The Netherlands, Great Britain,
Germany, Scandinavia, Poland and the U.S.S.R. There is a direct connection to trains going to the Riviera or Spain via Hendaye for certain trains
that arrive at Gare du Nord. Welcome Information Office is near Interna-
tional Arrivals platform, open M-Sa 8:30 am-10 pm.
    Gare de l'EST serves Champagne, Lorraine, Vosges and Alsace within
France, and Switzerland, Italy, Germany, Austria and Eastern Europe.
Welcome Information Office is open M-Sa 7-1 & 5-11.
    Gare de LYON serves Burgundy, Savoy, Dauphine, Provence, Riviera,
Corsica, Auvergne and Languedoc, and Switzerland, Italy, Yugoslavia,
Greece, Bulgaria, Turkey and Great Britain. Exchange office is open daily.
Tourist Office is open M-Sa 6:30-12:30 & 5-11.
    Gare d'AUSTERLITZ serves the Loire Valley, Auvergne, Atlantic
Coast, Basque country, Pyrenees and Languedoc, and the Roussillon pro-
vinces of Spain and Portugal.
    Gare MONTPARNASSE serves the Paris suburbs and the Atlantic
Coast. Gare ST. LAZARE serves Normandy and Great Britain. Each station
is connected to every other station by metro and bus. For certain trains,
a special bus waits outside the station to whisk passengers to the connecting
train at another station. There is regular inter-station bus service between
Austerlitz, Est, Nord and St. Lazare.

TOURIST INFORMATION   L'Office de Tourisme de Paris, 127 avenue des
Champs-Elysees is open daily 9 am-10 pm. Branch offices are in Nord,
Lyon and Est train stations, Aerogare des Invalides (air terminal) open
M-Sa 9 am- 10 pm, and Palais des Congres at Porte Maillot open M-Sa 11-6.
Best free map of the city is given by Galeries Lafayette department store in
its folder "Welcome to Paris."

CAMPGROUNDS   One is within Paris and five more are in outlying areas
but accessible by public transportation. Parc de Camping Paris-Ouest-
BOIS DE BOULOGNE (bow-LONE-yuh) is the official name of the Paris
campground. It is also called Camp du T.C.F. for Touring Club of France.
Camp is at far western edge of 2500 acre Bois de Boulogne (park) next to
Seine River and near eastern edge of Pont de Suresnes (bridge). It is not
shown on tourist office map as that shows only eastern part of park. It is
indicated as "Camp du T.C.F." on map of Bois de Boulogne in Michelin
green guide for Paris. The camp is on street "Alle du Bord de L'Eau"
across from "Jeu de Polo." This camp is wall-to-wall tents in summer
but space will be found for a camper on foot with a small tent. Drivers

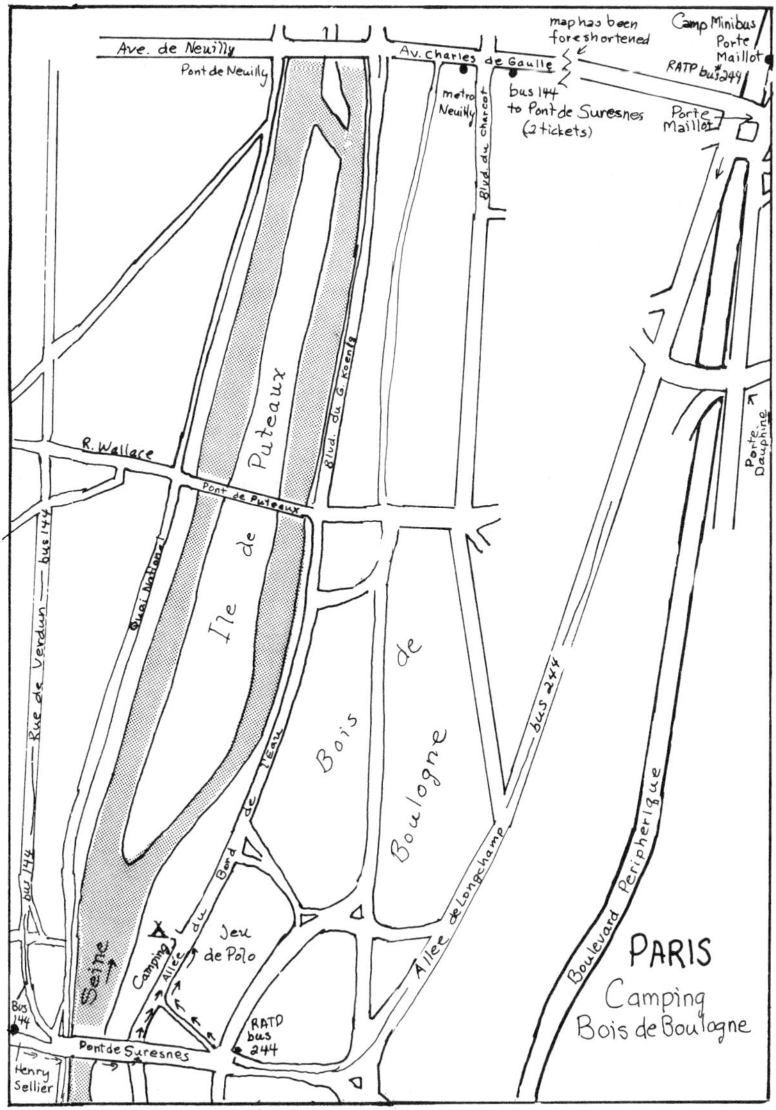
Ave. de Neuilly
Pont de Neuilly
Av. Charles de Gaulle
map has been foreshortened
Camp Minibus Porte Maillot
RATP bus #244
metro Neuilly
Blvd. du Charcot
bus 144 to Pont de Suresnes (2 tickets)
Porte Maillot
R. Wallace
Pont de Puteaux
Blvd. du G. Koenig
Ile de Puteaux
Quai National
Rue de Verdun
bus 144
Porte Dauphine
Bois de Boulogne
bus 244
Boulevard Peripherique
Allee de Longchamp
Allee du Bord de l'Eau
Jeu de Polo
Camping
Seine
PARIS
Camping Bois de Boulogne
Bus 144
Pont de Suresnes
RATP bus 244
Henry Sellier

should plan to arrive in the morning to find space. To get there, take the metro (subway) to Porte Maillot, then RATP bus 244, which goes down Alee de Longchamps and stops on the road to Pont de Suresnes, just south of the polo grounds. From here, walk 5 minutes northwest up the diagonal road along the edge of the polo grounds to Allee du bord de l'eau. Bus 244 also runs at night as bus 244 N. The camp runs a minibus (van) shuttle service between Porte Maillot station and the campground, which costs a high 6 F, and operates during summer only from 8 am–1 am. Catch the bus at the bus stop over the Peripherique Road. Alternatively, you can take regular city bus #144 (144N is night service) from Pont de Neuilly metro station (watch the signs at Pont de Neuilly to exit on the correct side of the street) to one block from the Pont de Suresnes. (Ask the driver to let you know when to get off.)   By car from (1) A 1 (Autoroute du Nord) take Blvd. Peripherique (direction Ouest) until you reach the Bois de Boulogne exit. It is well-signed. Follow signs to camp. (2) From A 6 (Autoroute du Sud), take Blvd. Peripherique (direction Ouest) until Porte Dauphine exit. Follow signs to camp at exit. (3) From A 10, A 11, F 18 from Pont de Sevres, while on the bridge (Pont de Sevre) stay in right hand lane as you need to take second road on right, signed Neuilly-sur-Seine. This road turns to the north and runs parallel with the Seine River until reaching the camp. (4) From A 13 (Autoroute de l'Ouest) after the Saint-Cloud Tunnel continue towards Paris, but immediately after crossing the Seine River, turn right at the sign "Bois de Boulogne," the first turn-off. This road joins one next to Seine River which leads to camp.

The nine-acre camp is open all year. On the grounds are a small grocery-variety store, snack bar serving soft drinks and hot plates (french fries and chicken for example), automatic washing machine and dryer, pay telephone and office which sells stamps and has a large map of Paris posted outside. Guided tours of Paris leave from the office and reservations are made there. Fees are adult pedestrians/4 F, adult with car/5.50 F, tent/ 4 F, hot shower/1 F (buy slug at office for about 3 minutes worth).

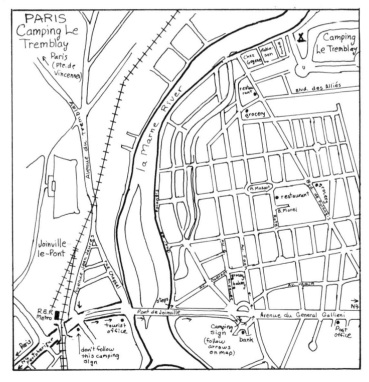

Camping Paris Est-LE TREMBLAY (trahng-bler) in Joinville-le-Pont (shown-veel-lah-pahnt) is a fairly new camp operated by the Touring Club of

Franc. The camp is attractively sited on the left bank of the Marne River
between Pont de Joinville (bridge) and Pont de Nogent (bridge). Joinville is
an affluent suburb. You pass through tree lined residential streets on the
way to camp. Large beautiful homes, modern apartments and an athletic
club line the opposite shore. No camping carnet is needed despite the sign
and French guidebook indications. Space is always available. To get there,
take the metro to Nation. Change to RER line (direction Boissy St. Leger)
and get off at fourth stop, Joinville-le-Pont. From downtown Paris to Joinville is a 45 minute ride. The 4 and 7 day Tourist Tickets (see public transportation) include the RER system and are a fairly good value if you stay
here. Otherwise, a single metro ticket is only good until Nation metro station and then a special ticket must be bought for the RER line ride to Joinville. RER tickets are priced according to distance traveled, and sold individually, by five ticket carnet, or combination metro-RER ticket, for either
first or second class. Tickets are purchased from yellow machines in stations. (1) Push the button for Joinville-le-Pont (or other destination). (2)
Push button corresponding to type of ticket desired--top two buttons are for
"cartes hebdomadaires" (weekly cards--not the tourist ticket), middle buttons are for individual tickets, first or second class, "plein tarif" (full fare)
or "demi-tarif" (half-fare). Lower buttons are for carnets, first or second
class. When this is done the amount due lights up in upper left hand corner
of machine. (3) Insert coins (10¢, 20¢, 1/2 F, 1 F, 5 F or 10 F). If the red
light appears in upper left hand corner, no change is available and the exact
amount must be inserted. (4) Ticket and change (if any) come out buttom
from separate chutes. Tickets are checked by inserting the ticket in slot in
automatic barrier before passing through. Red light indicates invalid ticket.
A free booklet in English, "Have you Heard about the RER?" is available at
station information offices.

After getting off at Joinville Station (which is marked SNCF outside),
follow signs to autobus #306, or go to information sign, turn left and go out
doors at left. Walk up ramp. This brings you to Avenue Jean Jaures and N 4.
You will see two camping signs. DON'T turn right but go straight ahead to
bridge. Follow camping sign with "Touring Club de France" at bottom. The
other sign is for a different camp. After crossing the bridge, backpackers
can reach camp by several ways such as walking beside the river or by following road signs. Camp is a 20 minute walk from Joinville Station.

By car from (1) A 1 (Autoroute du Nord), at Porte de la Chapelle, take
Peripherique Est to Port de Vincennes exit. This exit will take you to Joinville. In Joinville only follow camp signs with T. C. F. or Touring Club de
France at the bottom. Following a sign without this indication will lead you
astray to another camp. Get in right hand lane as you approach Joinville
bridge. IMMEDIATELY after the bridge a campground sign will direct you
to turn right. Follow signs to camp. (2) From A 6 (Autoroute du Sud), take
Peripherique Est to Porte de Bercy exit. Then go in direction of Nancy (N4)
until the town of Joinville. Now ONLY follow camping signs with T.C.F. or
Touring Club de France at the bottom. Continue on N 4 across Joinville
bridge, but get in right hand lane as you must turn right IMMEDIATELY
after bridge. Follow signs to camp. (3) From A 13 (Autoroute de l'Ouest)
take Peripherique Sud to Porte de Bercy exit. Follow signs to Nancy (N 4)
and proceed under #2 above. (4) Approaching Paris from Nancy, two hundred
meters after angling onto Avenue du General Gallieni in Champigny-sur-

164

Marne, turn right onto boulevard Polangis and follow camp signs.
An English-speaking person usually is working in the office. Free
T.C.F. campground directory and tourist literature is available there. The
camp is grassy and partly shaded. The new autoroute will pass on a ridge
behind it when construction is completed. Restrooms have individual sink
cubicles with cold water only, hot showers, and sinks outside building for
washing clothes. Store at campground stocks lettuce, tomatoes, yoghurt,
cheese, butter, ham, weiners, oranges, apples, bananas, croissants,
brioches, dessert tarts and bread. Snack bar sells hot dogs, croque monsieur (grilled cheese sandwich), fries, rotisseried chicken, coffee and
orange juice. "Poulet frites" is chicken and fries, "saucisses frites" is
weiner and fries and "oeufs frites" is egg and fries. Fees are about adult/
3.60 F, child uner 7/1.80 F, tent or van/3 F, car/2 F, tax/.25 F each.
Next door to camp are miniature golf (18 holes for about 8 F), boats for rent
("location bateaux pedalos") and Robinson Discotheque, Restaurant and Ter-
rasse. Its snack bar sells fries, mussels ("moules") and sandwiches ("pate,
fromages, saucissons"--liverwurst, cheese or weiner) and the discotheque
costs about 30 F for a "consummation ordinaire" (beverage) including service which in reality is the entry cost. Next to Robinson is Bar-Dancing Chez
Gegene.

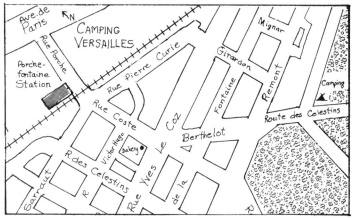

VERSAILLES campground (Terrain Municipal de Campisme) is in the
Porchefontaine district of Versailles and is open Apr-Oct. To get there, go
to the SNCF (French Railways) Invalides Station which is about two blocks
from Invalides metro station. SNCF Invalides Station faces the river side of
the Air France building, near bridge (pont) Alexandre III. At the station,
follow signs "S.N.C.F. Versailles-Rive Gauche." (The two main stations
of Versailles are called Gare Rive Gauche (left bank) and Gare Rive Droite
(right bank) but we are only concerned with Rive Gauche Station as it serves
a commuter line from Invalides Station in Paris.) Trains leave every 15
minutes from both ends during rush hours and less frequently late at night
for the 25 minute trip. Train is free with railpass or else about 3 F one way.
GET OFF AT STATION DE PORCHEFONTAINE which is BEFORE Rive
Gauche Station in Versailles. The Station is well signed so you can't miss it
if you're looking out the window. Campground is a 7 minute walk from

Station de Porchefontaine (see map). Another way to get from Paris to Versailles campground which is especially good for holders of Tourist Tickets is to take bus #171 from outside Pont de Sevres metro station. Trip takes about 15 minutes. Ask to be let off near camp. Bus fare is three tickets from a carnet. (Train fare without a pass is 8 F.) Camp has unisex, hole-in-floor toilets (other camps have conventional) which are distributed around camp in small builamgs rather than in the central shower and washing facility near camp entrance, hot showers (1.90 F), hot water in sinks in main building (no sinks with toilets), no store at camp or restaurants in immediate area so take train to Versailles for meals. Fees are adult/ 5.40 F, child/ 4.05 F, child under 4/free, tent/1.50 F, car/1.30 F. There is a reduction of 30 centimes from Sept 16 and before June 15. Market in Porchefontaine operates Wednesday and Saturday. "Marche Notre Dame" market at Place du Marche about 6 blocks north of Rive Gauche Station in Versailles is open Tuesday and Friday. Bakery is at corner of Rue Coste and Rue Yves (see map) which is passed on way to Porchefontaine Station. Versailles Palace is about 4 blocks from Rive Gauche Station.

CAMPING INTER-NATIONAL is in town of Maisons-Lafitte on rue Johnson on an island (I'lle de la Commune) in the Seine River outside Paris. Open all year, hot showers, hot water in wash basins, laundry tub with hot water, automatic washing machine, store, restaurant, food to take out, proprietor speaks English. Take a commuter train (banlieue) from Gare St. Lazare in Paris to

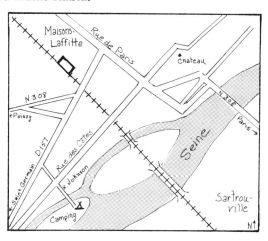

Maisons-Laffitte Station which is about a 30 minute ride. The cost is 5 F or free with railpass. Then there is about a 20 minute walk (see map). Fees include hot water and are about adult/7.50 F, child to 7/4.50 F, tent/7 F. If you have a Tourist Ticket, take RATP bus #262 from Puteaux (RER Station La Defense) to end of line. Then about a 20 minute walk to camp.

CITY TRANSPORTATION   Paris can't possibly be seen without taking the metro (subway). If you have a little extra time for the ride and to figure out which bus to take, Paris buses give a good non-subterranean view of the city. Tourist office map includes metro and bus map and how to get to important monuments and museums. The important point to remember for the metro and bus is that each line is identified by both a number and its terminal point. Children under 12 travel at half fare. The best buy is the "carnet" (CAR-nay) of ten yellow second class tickets for 17.50F. A single second class ticket (une deuxieme) costs 3 F. A ticket is good for a trip on the metro no matter how long you travel or how many times you change lines except on one or two extended suburban lines. Tickets are interchangeably

166

valid on buses as well. But on buses, the city is divided into zones and one ticket is good for 2 zones and 2 tickets are reqired for 3 or more zones of travel. A Tourist Ticket called "billet de tourisme" or R.A.T.P. cards are sold for 35 F--2 days, 53F--4 days and 88F--7 days, for unlimited use of first class metro cars, R.E.R., and R.A.T.P. Parisian and suburban (banlieue) buses. The card can be bought in advance from the French National Railroads in the U.S. or at railway stations and 50 metro stations in Paris. Also sold at metro stations are a ticket good for 2 trips per day for 6 consecutive days for 14 F, and a monthly ticket ("la carte orange") for unlimited trips on metro, commuter railway lines, Paris and suburban buses. Cost is based on a zone system, 85 F for a 2 zone ticket up to 213 F for a 5 zone ticket. (Rates given are for second class tickets--first class tickets are also available.)

The METRO is marvelously efficient and very simple to use. Each station has a large map of metro lines and each line is a different color. In principal stations maps are electrified. You have only to push a button indicating your destination and the proper metro line and change points (correspondances) light up. Remember to note terminus of line. A map is also provided within each metro car. Tickets are sold by machine or at ticket windows and you stamp your own ticket in the slot as you go through the entry gate. Date and entry number are recorded on the back in the machine. First class cars (painted yellow in middle of train) stop at the painted section in the middle of the platform. Rest of train is second class which is cheaper and perfectly fine though a little crowded during rush hour. Certain seats close to the doors are reserved for war invalids and are so marked. When changing trains (correspondance points), the mechanical gate is timed to arrival and departure of trains. Gate opens immediately after a train has left and closes again just as another enters the station. Always wait for the next train and never try to squish through as gate is closing. (Gate prevents would-be passengers from rushing through a closing train door.) Each station is three minutes apart, including time spent getting on and off. Board quickly and get off immediately. Turn door handle on train to open. Exits are well marked with signs directing you topside to each side of the street. (For Bois de Boulogne Camping take line 1 direction Pont de Neuilly to Porte Maillot for camp bus or Neuilly (Pont de) for city bus.)

The R.E.R. has two lines A and B which are divided into sections and priced according to distance traveled. Inside Paris itself the price is the same as on the Metro.

First BUS in the morning leaves at 6:30 am and the last bus is 9 pm except on certain lines which run till 12:30 am. Name on front of bus is destination. If there are two names, one is the starting point and the other the terminus. On side of bus and on sign at bus stops (arret), route is indicated by station names and time of last run is given. During rush hours, take a number from dispenser on signpost. When bus stops, conductor calls first for invalids, persons over 65 and mothers with more than four children. Then he reaches down and takes a number from someone in front and calls it. Anyone with a lower number gets on the bus. Then he calls another number and procedure is repeated. "Complet" sign is put up when bus is full. Ring for next stop when you want to get off. Signal to driver from bus stop if you want that bus. Paris has two double-decker buses which give a good view of the city and are worthwhile if you have a Tourist Ticket. Bus #94 leaves from the left bank of Gare Montparnasse, travels to the right bank and terminates at Le Vallois. Bus #53 departs from Place de l'Opera (Opera House) and goes to Porte d'Asnieres. Bus "PC" (pay-say) circles Paris.

DRIVING IN PARIS   Once you get there you will no doubt decide to leave your car at camp and take public transportation within Paris. It's easy to spend half a day getting out of Paris when you want to leave so here are some suggestions. In general, it's best to get on the Boulevard Peripherique, the ring-road around Paris, and exit for your destination. As an example, here is how to go from Camping Le Tremblay to Orleans. (1) At Joinville-le-Pont take route marked Pte. de Bercy. This is well signed at the bridge. (2) Follow large sign above highway marked Paris, Bd. Peripherique. (3) Follow large sign above highway marked Peripherique Sud, Direction Rouen, Lyon. This is clogged with traffic and slow but the best way. Stay in right hand two lanes. (4) Sign with Chartres, Orleans--get in lane indicated. (5) Take Porte d'Orleans exit, the next one after Porte d'Italie. Exit sign is marked Chartres, Orleans. (6) On A 6, get in far right lane and exit from A 6 at sign Chartres, Orleans. (7) Another highway and exit again Chartres, Orleans. (8) You are on A 10 and Orleans is 110 km away. (9) Can continue on freeway to Orleans or exit onto R.N. 20 for Orleans.

If you take R.N. 20 and need a place to eat, watch for restaurants where 20-30 trucks are pulled off the road between noon and 2 pm. These restaurants are usually cheaper than any listed in Michelin. We visited Restaurant S. Michel in Etampes which had a 25 F menu including service and wine. To get there, take first exit for Etampes. Restaurant is on left hand side about a kilometer from exit (see map). First course was radish, butter, tomato, lettuce and cucumber; or pate; or eggs with mayonnaise dressing. Main course offered kidney, steak or porkchop in tomato sauce served with french fries, peas or green beans. Chevre (goat) or camembert were the cheese course selections. Dessert was ice cream. To return to R.N. 20, turn right at Les Acacias Restaurant and you will see a short dirt access road leading to the highway. Access is marked by two "yield" signs only.

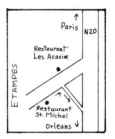

FOOD   Good street markets (open 7am- 1 pm closed Mon) are Rue de Buci (metro Odeon), rue Mouffetar (metro Censier-Daubenton) and rue Lepic (metro Blanche) and Cite Retiro (metro Madeleine). Restaurants are cheaper on the Left Bank (try around Place St.-Michel) and in outlying areas--try to avoid the downtown area for meals. Otherwise downtown department stores have supermarkets in their basements. Here is an example of a reasonable restaurant close to Ourcq Metro station on the Eglise de Pantin line. La Couronne D'Or, Restaurant Chinois, 140 Avenue Jean-Jaures, is open daily 12-4:40 & 7-10:30 pm. It has nice decor and red linen tablecloths and napkins. 30 F menu described below is served 12-4:30 pm except on Saturday. First course: choice of "potage poulet vermicelles" (vermicelli soup with mushrooms, sliced chicken and ham on top), "salade chinois" (bean sprouts lightly dressed with strips of tender chicken and ham on top) or "pate imperial". Main course: choice of "crevettes sautees aux legumes" (deep fried shrimp with sauce and tomato, lettuce and celery), "crevettes au carry" (shrimp in curry sauce), "poulet aux champignons noirs" (chicken with kelp)

or "seiche sautee aux legumes" (curled strips of intestine or other variety meat with green pepper). (The waiter looked surprised when we ordered the latter and I understood why when we got it but it was very good--Dennis, my husband, said.) A bowl of steamed rice is included (riz compris). Dessert choices were apple, orange or banana (fruits de saison) or a large half-inch thick cookie with almond on top (gateau aux amande). Beverage was included (boisson compris)--your choice of 1/4 liter wine, 25 cl. of beer, half-bottle (demi) mineral water or tea (the au jasmin).

SIGHTSEEING   We recommend buying the green Michelin guide "Paris and The Principal Sights Near By,"sold at American Express, department stores and bookstores for about 20 F. Be sure to get the English edition. If the guide is deficient in any respect, it is probably in lack of coverage for 20th century monuments. Five days is the minimum amount of time needed for Paris and its environs such as Versailles and Chartres. Most museums are open 10-12 and 2-5 and are closed Tuesday. Most are half price (demi-tarif) on Sundays and holidays. For Versailles (ver-SIGH), follow directions for Versailles campground but get off at last stop which is a short walk from the Chateau. Trains leave from Montparnasse Station about once an hour for Chartres (SHAR-tr) for the hour-long trip to see the Cathedral. Be sure to get the tourist office's publication "Paris Ile de France" which lists all monuments and museums, tells how to get there and gives opening times. Below are scattered notes on sightseeing in Paris.

Les Invalides Sound and Light Show presents an English version at 9 and 11 pm, Easter to November, in the courtyard. Show lasts about 45 minutes and costs about 13 F for adults and 9 F for children under 12. We mention the small Jeu de Paume museum in Tuileries Gardens, Place de la Concorde (metro Concorde) to be certain it doesn't get overlooked. Open 9:45-5:15, closed Tuesday, adult/7 F, student/3.50 F, half-price on Sunday. It houses all the best impressionist paintings. Not to be missed is The Centre d'Art et de Culture Georges-Pompidou, an unusual complex devoted to the 20th century and containing the National Museum of Modern Art, public library, Centre for Industrial Creation, and I.R.C.A.M. where musicians and artists research a new musical alphabet. Metro stops are Rambuteau or Hotel de Ville, R.E.R. is Chatelet-Halles. Other modern Paris landmarks are the Centre International de Paris at Porte Maillot, Montparnasse Tower and a new city to the west of Paris, La Defense on R.E.R. La Defense. Of secondary importance to the Georges Pompidou collection which was formed by gleaning works from the national art museums to show the history of modern art from its birth with 2000 works on permanent display, is the Musee National d'Art Moderne, 11 avenue du President-Wilson (metro Iena), open 9:45-5:15, closed Tuesday. Adult/9 F, student/4.50 F. Musee Marmottan (Institut de France), 2 rue Louis-Boilly (metro La Muette), open 10-6, closed Monday, has an impressionist collection in the basement. Unesco Building (metro Gambronne) has a Japanese stone garden by Noguchi and decorations by Picasso, Moore, Miro and Calder. Guided tours of the Louvre in English are given at 10:30 am and 3 pm except Tuesday and Sunday, starting from the Bureau d'Informations, salle (room) du Manege and lasting 1-1/2 hours for adult/9 F, student/4.50 F. Paris has a museum on almost every subject, all listed in the tourist office booklet mentioned above.

For children, in the   Bois de Boulogne (park) is the Jardin d'Accli-
mation, a playground for children 4-12. Activities open in the afternoon and
zoo is next door. Take the metro to Sablons. Other parks with good playgrounds are Champ de Mars at the foot of the Eiffel Tower, Jardins des
Champs-Elysees (metro Champs-Elysees Clemenceau) and Jardin du
Luxembourg at Boulevard St.-Michel on the Left Bank (puppet show).
Comedie Francaise has matinee performances children enjoy if they are
already familiar with the story. Here is where French children develop the
critical eye and ear that turns them into the demanding audience in adulthood
which maintains the excellent standards of acting prevalent in France. Metro
is Palais-Royal, closed July and August. Shows designed and produced by
children are given at Theater du Petit Monde, 252 Fg. Saint-Honore on Wed
and Sun. Children's movies are shown at Studio Marigny, Carre Marigny.

Ermenonville Center of Jean Richard is a French version of an amusement park featuring a Moroccan market and restaurant, desert with live
camel rides, Normandy farm and a Western town a la francaise. It's located
in Ermenonville 40 km north of Paris. Take the train from Gare du Nord to
Plessis-Belleville. Change to bus to Ermenonville, 6 km away. Or take a
bus from Stalingrad metro station which leaves from #5, Quai de Seine at
10:30 am and returns at 4:30 and 5:30 pm. Round trip fare is about 20 F.
Park is open M-Sa 11-7 and Su 10-8 from May to September. Entrance is
about 6 F for adults and 4 F for children. A Touring Club of France campground is adjacent.

SHOPPING   Paris has marvelous department stores of which Galeries
Lafayette near the Opera is the most outstanding. Camping equipment is
sold in every department store but La Hutte chain of camping and sporting
goods stores offer a wide selection and reasonable prices. La Hutte locations
are: 53-55 rue C.-Bernard (metro Censier Daubenten), 87 blvd. Voltaire
(metro St. Amboise), 72 blvd. de Grenelle (metro Dupleix), 66 bis rue St.-
Didier (metro Boissiere) and 173 ave. de Versailles (metro Pte. St. Cloud).
Camping equipment in U.S. is cheaper but La Hutte sells a table of wood
slats (80 cm square) on metal legs of unique design where legs fold and slats
are rolled around them for a cylindrical package for about 150 F.

Museum shops offer low-cost reproductions which are available to you
at the same price a dealer must pay to stock them in his shop. The Louvre
shop has a wide selection just off the main entrance, and in Laboratoire de
la Chalcopraphie you can get prints from copperplates and woodcuts done by
Van Dyke, Matisse, Vlaminck and so forth for about $8 and up. Their cate-
log costs about 6 F and mail orders are accepted. Address is Quai du Louvre,
Paris 75001. Musee de Sevres sells porcelain figures made from original
18th century molds.

Hotel Drouot antique auction house is on the corner of Rue Chauchat
and Rue Rossini near Opera Comique in the 9th arrondisement. This is the
auction house of Paris which holds over 4,000 auctions a year. Less valuable
items are consigned to one section. These have often been seized to pay off
bad debts or are the belongings of an estate. Middle class Frenchwomen
come here to look over the miscellaneous collection of goods and to make a
bid if something appeals to them. Most pieces are not sold individually but
by lot which is usually a basket filled with odds and ends, all of which are
not visible. Some go for as little as 50 F. Valuable items carry a guarantee

170

of authenticity and are sold individually. Each is listed in the official catalog and if an item turns out not to be authentic, the auction house will refund your money. This policy is unique in the world of auctions and not found anywhere else. The buyer pays a commission to the auction house of about 16 percent on items selling for up to about $300 and less for items over that amount. Open M-Sa 10 am-11 pm, auctions held M-Sa 2-6 pm.

Used books in English are sold at Shakespeare and Co., 37 Rue de la Bucherie (metro St. Michel).

BABYSITTERS Student babysitters: Alliance Francaise, 101 bd. Raspail, 75006 Paris, 222-25-28; Operation Biberon, 26 Faubourg St.-Jacques, 75014 Paris, 033-25-44; Centre Regional Des Oeuvres Universitaires et Scolaires, 39 av. George-Bernanos, 326-07-49. Other babysitters: Kid Service, 17 rue Moliere, 266-07-61, Nurses Service, 33 rue Fortuny, 622-26-22, SOS Santel, 655-25-35.

LE POTPOURRI The American Hospital, 63 Blvd. Victor-Hugo in Neuilly, has an outpatient department that accepts walk-ins, but the wait may be long. Bring a snack along as the area is devoid of food stores and the hospital restaurant only serves full-course meals. Most Post Offices are closed Saturday afternoon and all day Sunday, but the one on Champs-Elysees near Avenue George V is open in the evening every day.

TRAIN SCHEDULES To Valley of the Loire. Trains leave from Austerlitz Station and go to Les Aubrais just outside Orleans. You must check the schedule beforehand or ask the conductor enroute to find out if the train goes into Orleans or if you must change trains at Les Aubrais. Most through trains to Tours leave Les Aubrais and then follow the Loire River stopping only at Blois and St. Pierre-des-Corps before Tours. Some of these trains stop at Beaugency, Onzain and Amboise too but if you want to get off there you must be sure to take a train which makes those stops. Otherwise get off at Blois or St. Pierre-des-Corps and take a local from there. Trains which stop at all these small towns leave Austerlitz at 9:06 am, 1:38 and 5:17 pm for the about two hour trip to Amboise for example. The relationship of St. Pierre-des-Corps to Tours is similar to that between Les Aubrais and Orleans. If you are going to Tours to make a connection with another train, you can merely get off at St. Pierre-des-Corps and make the connection there if you wish. For those wishing a through train to Tours, trains leave Austerlitz at 7:51 am (TEE) (ar. 9:22 am), 8:40 am (ar. 10:45 am), 9:10 am (ar. 11:10 am), 11:25 am (ar. 1:21 pm), 2:00 pm (ar. 4:02 pm), 4:45 pm (ar. 6:55 pm), 5:20 pm (ar. 6:49 pm) and later trains. At Tours you can make connections to Azay-le-Rideau, Chinon, Chenonceaux and Loches. Of these four towns, only the train to Chenonceaux can be boarded at St. Pierre-des-Corps as well.

To the Riviera, trains leave Gare de Lyon for Antibes at 9:57 am (ar. 7:43 pm), 1:15 pm TEE (ar. 10:14 pm), 7:26 pm (ar. 6:22 am), 8:48 pm (ar. 7:45 am) plus TVG trains.

To Le Havre and Cherbourg, trains leave from St. Lazare Station about once an hour for the 2-3 hour trip.

To Calais, trains leave from Nord Station for the 3 hour trip.

To Madrid, trains leave Austerlitz Station at 8:00 pm which is the Puerta del Sol on which a change of train isn't necessary at the border as through cars Paris-Madrid are jacked up at Hendaye and the wheel width adjusted to fit Spanish tracks (ar. Madrid Chamartin 8:55 am), 9:55 pm, change at Irun 7:14 am (ar. Madrid Chamartin 4:29 pm), 6:45 am, change to Talgo at Irun 2:32 pm (ar. Madrid Chamartin 9:58 pm) and 1:54 pm, change at Irun 9:31 pm (ar. Madrid Chamartin 9:10 am). Reservation advised.

To Barcelona Termino Station, trains leave Austerlitz Station at 7:41 am TEE, change trains in Narbonne 3:36 pm (ar. 9:02 pm), 9:38 am (ar. 11:25 pm), 8:00 pm (ar. 9:48 am), 9:00 pm (ar. 9:01 pm). All trains require a change of train at Port Bou except the 9:00 pm departure.

To northern Germany, Belgium and The Netherlands, trains leave Gare du Nord six or eight times daily including several TEE trains. No reservation needed.

CHATEAUX OF THE LOIRE

The Val de Loire (lwah), about a two hour train ride from Paris, stretches only 50 miles along the River Loire but contains a density of over 100 castles, cathedrals and curiosities representing seven centuries from the Middle Ages to the 18th century. This area was the seat of power during the 15th and 16th centuries when the kings and queens of France and the lesser ruling nobility built their castles here. You can see fortified strongholds, the original sleeping beauty castle (whence came Disneyland's inspiration), Chenonceaux (travel poster castle which spans a river), the only existing example of a 16th century formal French garden, and nightly illuminations. The food is great, this being the "garden of France," and wines are pleasant. The river yields salmon, pike and carp which are sauced and served at reasonable prices. The area is comprised mostly of small towns, each having grown around a castle, and this makes it easy to find one's way. In large cities where remnants of the past are interwoven among the developments of the day, getting any sort of "feeling" for a past period is difficult. Here the past comes alive in the lovely French countryside.

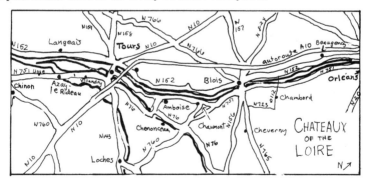

The Michelin green guide "Chateaux of the Loire" in English gives historical information and small maps of the towns. Chateaux are generally open 9-12 and 2-7 in summer and charge about 8 F. Often you are not allowed to wander at will but will be escorted in an English-speaking group with a guide. The following places can be reached by train: Angers, Azay-le-Rideau, Beaugency, Blois, Bourges, Chambord, Cheverny, Chinon,

Fontevrault, Gien, Langeais, Loches, Lude, Orleans, Saumur, Usse,
Villandry and Amboise. Michelin map #64 yellow Angers-Orleans shows
train lines and stations. Which chateaux should be given priority? The
Castle of Chenonceaux is seducer for the region, built over the River Cher
with graceful curves of arches predominating. Chambord is an immense
440 room elaborate 16th century castle. Chateau of Villandry houses a fine
arts museum, but its elaborately coiffed 16th century formal gardens are of
more interest. Loches is of an entirely different character, a fortified
stronghold built during the Middle Ages. In contrast the Chateau of Cheverny
appears as a sober looking 17th century mansion with period interior. Azay-
le-Rideau is the sleeping beauty castle prototype. If you can manage it, be
at your first chateau when it opens to beat the tour buses. All of the most
important chateaux are floodlit evenings. Sound and Light shows of Chenonceaux and Amboise have an English version. Guided bus tours, visiting three
or four chateaux at a time, leave from Blois and Tours train stations for
about 40-45 F but these can all be done more cheaply on your own.

ORLEANS (or-lay-AHn) The town is Michelin rated 1 star and is a large
business center with lower prices in department stores than Paris. Many
trains from Paris do not come all the way into Orleans but only go as far
as Les Aubrais. From Les Aubrais, connecting trains go to Orleans.
Tourist office is outside station ahead towards the right and sells Michelin
maps. Market is off Place du Chatelet, open all day to 6 or 7 pm, Tuesday
through Saturday and on Sunday morning. Restaurant prices are very com-
petitive for the area if not slightly lower than in smaller towns. La Hutte
camping store is 61 Rue Bannier. Camping Gaston-Marchand at St. Jean de
la Ruelle can be reached by busline B (ligne B) S. E. M. T. A. O. Reseau Urbain D'Orleans (direction Roche Aux Fees) from the station (Place Albert
1er). Ask driver to let you off but it's about the 13th or 14th stop.

BEAUGENCY (BO-sjahn-see) Michelin rated 2 star, the old town gives a
good glimpse of the Middle Ages. Beaugency is 25 miles from Orleans or
35 minutes by train. A 15 minute walk from the station brings you to a
beautifully situated camp on the banks of the Loire. Tourist office is at Pl.
du Martroi. Camping Municipal "Val de Flux, " on Loire River across from
the town (see map next page) is open April-Sept. Hole-in-floor toilets with
one conventional toilet, individual sink stalls with cold water, hot showers,
outdoor dishwashing sinks, swings, merry-go-round, teeter totter, attractive wooded site, grass cover, view of bridge with arches, sand dunes and
jetty. Minor annoyance--swarms of tiny bugs and cotton from cottonwood
trees. English spoken by both man and woman in office. Loud speaker
system for paging campers. Snack bar "buvette de la plage" is open July and
August. Adult/ 3 F, child under 7/1 F, car and tent or van/3 F. Mailing address is 45190 Beaugency, France. Mail will be held for you.

BLOIS (blwah)   A Michelin 3 star town, the chateau is a 10 minute walk
from the train station.   Three campgrounds are out-of-town but inconven-
ient for backpackers. Here is an excellent restaurant choice for drivers.
Restaurant La Pompadour is at Menars, 8 km outside Blois on the river
side of N 142. Closed Wednesday. It's listed in Michelin, has wonderful food
and is a good value.   On the 30 F menu I had two ham slices garnished with
tomato, lettuce and foil-wrapped butter; an entree of excellent quenelles

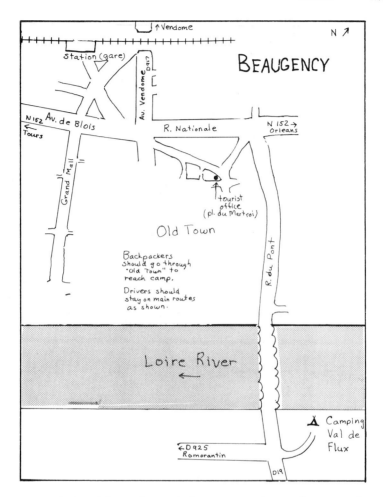

which are cylindrical fish cakes with cheese sauce, browned on top and served with parslied potatoes and lemon wedges; and my choice of chocolate eclair, ice cream or cake for dessert. On the 35 F menu, the first course was either cold crab with mayonnaise, lemon, tomato and lettuce or hot crayfish in sauce, the entree was veal in sauce with potatoes and green beans, a cheese platter was presented and the same choices were given for dessert as on the 30 F menu. Service and taxes were extra.

CHAUMONT-Sur-Loire   Michelin rated 2 stars, the beautifully sited 16th century chateau is set within a large park. The train goes to Onzain, a town across the Loire River from Chaumont s. Loire (see map next page). From Onzain train station (which is actually between the Loire and the town of Onzain), to the chateau is 1.7 km. Camping Grosse-Greve is beneath the bridge spanning the Loire, east of the chateau. Open March-Sept. Turn left upon leaving Onzain station, then turn left again and cross railroad tracks. Go straight ahead and cross bridge over Loire. Camping is by the

Loire on left. To reach chateau, turn right at end of bridge and entrance to chateau is at main intersection. On the grounds are two foot bridges that are connected by stairs within a hollowed out tree trunk.

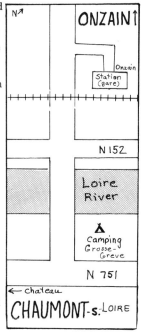

AMBOISE (ahn-BWAZ) Michelin 2 star, the town has a historically important chateau. Train station is across Loire River from the "old town." Tourist office, syndicat d'Initiative, is at quai General de Gaulle. Camping L'Ille d'Or is on an island in the middle of the Loire River directly across from the chateau. Evening brings a tentside view of illuminated ramparts and castle. Camp is about a 20 minute walk from station (see map below). Space is always available in the 25 acre camp. Hole-in-floor toilets, sinks with cold water, hot showers (open 8-12 & 4-8, 180 F), day room, two slides, wading pool, climbing bars, swings, merry-go-round, town swimming pool and tennis courts share the grounds. Adult/3.50 F, tent/3 F, car/3 F. Market is across from tourist office next to river and is open Friday and Sunday 7-5. Boulangerie (bakery) is on right as you turn left off bridge to campground.

TOURS (tour) This is the largest town in an area where time is best spent in the villages. Rail travelers

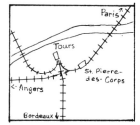

may need to change trains here but are advised to continue to a small town to camp. Drivers can circumnavigate Tours by taking country roads or by driving straight through on the highway. Tourist office is outside train station in round glass building across the street. Station restaurant, Relais Buffet Gare, is Michelin listed and has a 35 F menu including service but not beverage. Restaurant has nice decor centering around a

garden mural and large plants, pink linen tablecloths and napkins,and waiters
in green vests. The 35 F menu gave a choice of soup or pate, then roast
chicken, and either cheese or dessert of caramel custard or ice cream. On
the day we were there, for 40 F you could have "rillettes" or "quenelles"
(a cylindrical hot fish mousse piece with sauce and fluted half-moon pastry
as garnish) as the first course; veal, guinea hen (pintadeau) or salmon as
the main course; and either cheese or dessert of caramel custard, ice
cream or fresh strawberries. The guinea hen was served roasted with
small morel mushrooms, tiny onions and hot crisp shoestring potatoes. A
side dish of french fries came with all entrees. A cover charge of 3 F is
made for a child who shares a "menu" with an adult.

Trains leave Tours for Azay-le-Rideau and Chinon (direction Thouars)
at 9:27 am daily 6/25 -9/12, 12:13 & 6:26 pm for the half-hour trip to Azay-
le-Rideau and hour trip to Chinon.

Trains leave Tours for Chenonceaux-Chisseaux (direction Vierzon)
at 12:20, 4:41 and 6:35 pm. Trains pick up at St.-Pierre-des-Corps about
five minutes later. The trip takes about 36 minutes.

Trains leave Tours for Loches at 12:26 (not sat) , 5:13 and 6:41 pm (not
Sun) for the hour trip.

To get to Les Eyzies in one day, you must leave Tours at 9:13 am TEE
or 9:40 am for Poitiers. (Both departures pick up at St.-Pierre-des-Corps
about 5 minutes later.) TEE arrives Poitiers at 10:01 and the other train
at 10:44 am. Change trains. Trains leave Poitiers for Limoges at 10:10 and
11:58 am (ar. 12:40 and 2:01 pm). Trains leave Limoges for Les Eyzies at
1:23 and 5:49 pm (ar. 3:28 and 7:43 pm).

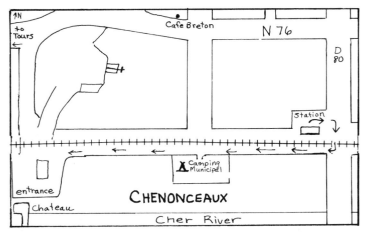

CHENONCEAUX (shen-on-SEW)   The chateaux rates Michelin 3 stars.
Don't miss. Train station is between the towns of Chenonceaux and
Chisseaux and is called "Chenonceaux-Chisseaux." In station is a map showing two possible ways to walk to the castle and the location of the campground.
From station to camp is about 1-1/2 km and the chateau is about half a kilometer farther on (see map above). Camping Municipal is an attractive but
very small camp. Hole-in-floor toilets, hot shower, dishwashing and
clothes washing sinks, clothesline, slide, teeter totter. Adult/ 3 F, child to
7/1.50 F, tent and car/3 F.   Frances Packer says "Very nice to camp

176

here in September-empty! (Free hot showers). Note-only train to Vierzon in
the morning is at 6:24 am, might consider leaving in evening." If camp is
full (possibly August), car-campers may wish to go to the large municipal
(stade) camp in nearby Blere. Open Easter-Sept, conventional toilets, hot
showers, day room, climbing bars, slide, merry-go-round, teeter totter,
adult/2.80 F, child under 15/1.40 F, tent/2.80 F. There is a Sound and
Light show in English in the evening at Chenonceaux. Cafe Gateau Breton
on N76 in Chenonceaux is listed in Michelin and has a 25 F menu.
    Trains leave for Tours at 9:56 am and 1:15 pm, about a half hour trip.
    To Les Eyzies, take the early morning 6:56 departure to Tours and
then refer to Tours for rest of schedule.

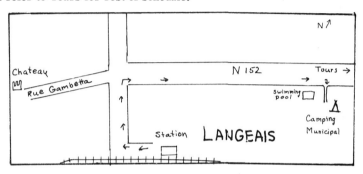

LANGEAIS (lahn-SJAY)   Rated Michelin two star, the 15th century chateau
was built within only four to five years and no remodeling has been done.
It's a five minute walk from station to chateau (see map). Castle interior is
shown in group tours--meanwhile the gardens are yours to enjoy until sum-
moned by a bell. Tour is in French but a written translation in English is
provided. Camping Municipal is off N152 on road to Tours (see map), near
a small lake and town swimming pool. Camp is 1.2 km to chateau and less to
train station. Modern white restroom building with conventional toilets, free
hot showers, one with sink and bidet in the women's; adult/2.60 F, tent/
2.70 F, open June 1-Sept 15 only.   Langeais is the station after Cinq-
Mars on the rail line from Tours (direction Saumur). Trains leave Tours
at 9:37, 11:52 am, 2:34, 4:56 (except Sat), 6:21, 8:10 pm for the approximately 25 minute trip to Langeais. Trains leave Langeais for Tours at 7:04 (except Sun), 7:24 (Sun only), 10:26 am, 1:39, 3:09, 4:41, 5:35, 6:32 (except
Sat), 7:28 (Sun only) and 8:39 pm.

AZAY-LE-RIDEAU (ah-zeh-leh-ree-DOH)   Rated Michelin 2 star. Chateau
d'Azay is a beautiful Renaissance chateau, smaller than Chenonceaux. Sound
and Light show 9-10:45 pm for about adult/10 F. Camping Parc du Sabot, east
of chateau (see map next page) is off D 84 and next to Indre River. Next
door is town swimming pool. Open Apr-Sept. From train station, which is
outside town to the west, to chateau is 1.6 km and the camp is an additional
five minute walk. The entire way is level ground or slightly downhill. New
restrooms were built in 1976. Conventional toilets, sinks with hot and cold
water, hot showers (charge), ice machine with ice cubes in day room across
from office, swings, teeter totter, slide, sandpit.
    Trains leave for Tours at 7:08 am, 1:21, 4:41 daily 6/25-9/12, and
8:08 pm. Trains leave for Chinon at 8:45 (Sun only), 9:50 daily 6/25-9/12,

12:46, 6:58 and 8:50 (Fri only).

CHINON (she-KNOWN) Michelin 2 star. This is
the Middle Ages and the chateau is a stern
medieval fortress overlooking an old town which
is extremely evocative of the period. Chateau is
1 km from the station and can be reached by
walking up the hill through the old town. Open
9-12 and 2-5. Adult/5 F, child, student/2.50 F,
groups of 20/4 F. Camping Municipal de L'ile
Auger is beside Vienne River near the bridge,
and across the river from the old town (see map
next page). Open Mar 15-Oct 15. Camp is 1.5
km from train station. New restroom building
next to older one. Conventional toilets, cold
water in sinks, merry-go-round, swings,
sandpit, climbing bars. Automatic washing
machine is installed annually in May for the
summer season and then removed for the winter because Indre River floods and camp is
submerged. Clotheslines are under the building on stilts. Gallon of ice cubes is sold for
1 F at 11 am and 5 pm at office. Man in office
speaks English and said he would never turn
people with a small tent away. Bakery, cafe,
canoe and paddle boat rentals nearby. Adult/
3 F, child/1.50 F, tent/3 F, car/free.

Public market is all day Thursday and
morning only on Saturday in town square by
tourist office. Boule d'Or Restaurant is
Michelin listed with 30 F menu, closed Mon.
If you have a car, Auberge Jeanne d'Arc on
road coming from Langeais is on left side of
road BEFORE reaching Chinon. Michelin
listed, dinner is served starting at 7:30 pm.
Nice interior, homelike, fireplace and plants.
On the 28 F menu we had our choice of soup,
"pate en croute" or "extremeses" (tomato,
cauliflower, two slices sausage, butter).
Main course selections were veal, sauteed
trout in butter, and filet of cod in scallop
shell with cheese on top, followed by choice
of salad, cheese or dessert (ice cream or
"creme caramel"--caramel custard).

Trains to Tours leave at 6:34 am,
12:48, 4:20 daily 6/25-9/12, 7:38 pm and
stop at Azay-le-Rideau on the way.

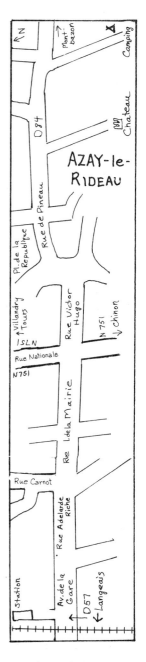

LOCHES (low-SHAY) Michelin 3 star medieval town, castle and fortifica-
tions. Camping Municipal is on N 143 south of old town, next to a stadium
and on shore of Indre River. Chateau is visible from camp. Train station to

178

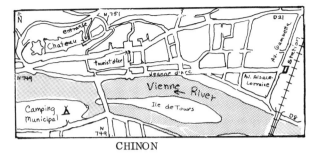

CHINON

LOCHES

campground is .8 km (see map at right). In same building as office are conventional toilets in tile-lined toilet
stalls, good hot showers with small bench and hook to
hang clothes, cold water in sinks. In another building
are more showers and semi-private sinks. Camp is a
grassy field next door to town swimming pool, tennis
and basketball courts. Adult/2.50 F, child under 7/1 F,
tent and car/2.50 F Large Bravo Supermarket is just
outside town on N 143 in direction of Chateauroux, if you have a car.

Trains leave for Tours at 6:30 (not Sun), 7:35 am and 7:50 pm. The
7:32 am departure will get to Tours in time to connect with train to Poitiers
and then to Les Eyzies.

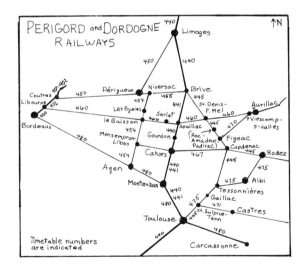

PERIGORD (Center of Prehistory)

Perigord is a wonderful off-the-beaten-track area with cliff-hanging towns,
caves where prehistoric man dwelt and marvelous food. Rail entry points
are Perigueux or Brive, the latter a stop on TEE le Capitole between Paris
and Toulouse. For drivers, Michelin map (yellow) #75, Bordeaux-Tulle.

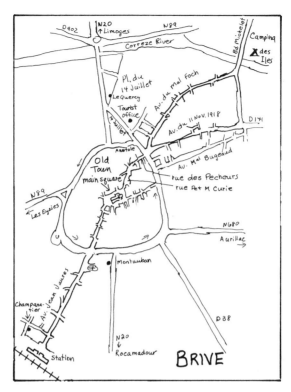

BRIVE-LA-GAILLARDE   Camping des Iles, Boulevard Michelet, is on shore of Correze River about a 30 minute walk from train station. Camp has swimming pool and store. Adult/ 6 F, tent/3.50 F, car/3.50 F. Michelin listed restaurants with 45 F or under menus: Champanatier, 15 r. Dumyrat one block from station; Montauban, 6 ave. E.-Herriot just outside old town, and cheapest; Le Quercy, pl. 14-Juillet, vicinity of tourist office. Open market is on Tuesday, Thursday and Saturday on pl. 14-Juillet and so is Tourist Office, open July-Aug M-Sa 9-8, Sept-June M-Sa 10-12 & 2-5:30.

To Les Eyzies, take the train to Niversac which leaves Brive at 5:55 am, 1:12 pm and 6:07 pm. One hour trip. Trains leave Niversac (direction Le Buisson or Agen) for Les Eyzies at 7:25 am, 12:25, 3:00 and 7:14 pm for the 30 minute trip. The 6:07 pm departure from Brive is the last one that will make the 7:18 pm departure for Les Eyzies.

PERIGUEUX   The town is a relatively large city (50,000) in the Dordogne and a gateway city to Les Eyzies, prehistoric capital. Perigueux's Musee de Perigord, open 10-12 and 2-5 (3 F), exhibits prehistoric finds of tools and a skeleton of early man. Similar items are displayed in the museum of Les Eyzies. It's best to continue onto tiny Les Eyzies for the night as its camp is only a ten minute walk from the train station, but buy some food to take along as grocery shopping is very limited (one tiny store) in Les Eyzies though restaurants are available.

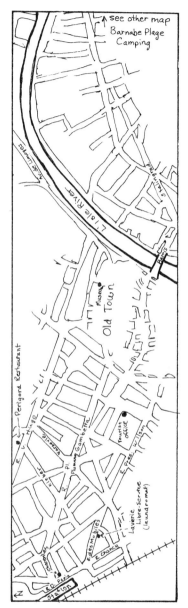

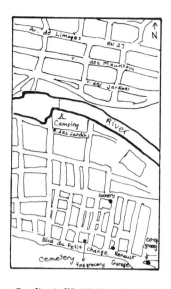

Syndicat d'Initiative is at 1 Av. Aquitaine (see map). Tourist office for the whole region is at 15 rue Wilson. Camping Barnabe Plage is 2 km east of on Isle River. Camping is on both sides of river but main portion with facilities is on east shore. Boat on pulley crosses to other side (.80 F each with maximum charge of 6 persons). From train station, first walk to tourist office for a map and then continue on to the camp, about a 30 minute walk. Camp is beautifully situated with a beach in front and short falls nearby where early morning fishermen cast their lines. Large white round building has a large courtyard with tables under the trees, and becomes a teenage gathering spot at night. Ping-pong, shuffleboard, row boats, pedal boats (hour/ 19 F), miniature golf. Ice is .50 F a bag. Ring bell on sign and attendant will come and indicate where to camp. Attendant is usually working in cafe in round white building. Campsites are separated by hedges. There are a variety of restrooms, both hole-in-floor and conventional toilets, some individual wash basin stalls, hot showers with handheld shower head (1 F for 15 minutes hot water). Adult/4.80 F, child/ 2.40 F, tent/5.60 F. Have to leave by 5 pm or pay for another night.

Michelin recommended Chez Marcel, 37 ave. Limoges, has a 35 F menu. Take boat across river from camp and walk three blocks straight ahead to ave. Limoges. Charentes, 16 r. D.-Papin, Michelin recommended,

40 F menu, is across from train station (see map). Perigord, 74 r. Victor Hugo, 6 blocks from station, Michelin listed, has a 35 F menu: soup, tomato salad, pate or sardines; roast veal, pork chops or tongue; cheese or dessert; not including beverage or service ("service non compris a l'appreciation de la clientele"). Quarter liter wine is 2.50 F, a la carte steak-frites (steak-fries) about 20 F.

A self-service laundry is Laverie Libre-Service, 3 r. Des Mobiles-de-Coulmeis, 3 blocks from station. Open 9-7, closed 12:30-2 for lunch break and Sunday and Monday. One load white and colored clothes-- 10 F, nylon and wool-- 9 F. Smaller machines than in U.S. Mandatory use of their soap for .20 F a scoop. Each load takes two scoops, except one scoop for nylons and wools. Wash cycle takes 35 minutes. Large dryers hold three washer loads.

Trains leave Perigueux for Les Eyzies (direction Agen) at 7:14 am, 12:13 pm, 2:51 pm and 7:02 pm for the 30-40 minute trip.

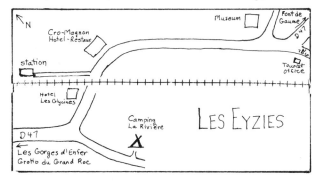

LES-EYZIES-DE-TAYAC   Les Eyzies is a wonderful tiny village in the Perigord and center of prehistorical finds in France. Don't miss. The town is on the Paris-Agen railway line. Tourist office is on main road across from turn-off for museum and will change money. Try to bring some groceries with you to Les Eyzies as there is only one small grocery store. Camping La Riviere is 1/4 km from station. At end of narrow road leading from station, turn right onto highway D47 and walk until you see camping sign. Then turn left. Camp is a grassy field around a large house in which you can get cooked meals. Hot showers, badminton, horse rides, room with double bed/ 40 F, with twin beds/55 F, camping adult/4 F, tent/4 F, breakfast/8 F.

The Perigord is a noted area for eating and this tiny town has two Michelin one-star restaurants. Cro-Magnon on left of station road has a 55 F menu and in town near the museum is Centenaire with similar prices. Three other restaurants are Michelin listed. Across the railroad tracks from Cro-Magnon is Les Glycines with a 53 F menu. On this menu we received (1) julienne carrots dressed in vinegar and oil, lightly dressed cucumbers, small slice of pate, and individual foil-wrapped butter portions; (2) omelette made with herbs; (3) quarter chicken with delicious mushroom sauce and french fries; (4) green salad tossed at the table immediately before being served and (5) creme caramel (custard) with fan-shaped wafer. Service was included. Half-liter wine in carafe costs 6 F. Centre Restaurant and France are also Michelin listed with similar prices.

Musee National de Prehistoire is half a kilometer from train station.

182

After emerging from station road onto highway, go towards your left passing by Cro-Magnon Hotel and continuing until museum sign. Open daily 9:30-12 & 2-6. Adult/ 5 F. Guidebook in English 7 F. Museum contains excavation finds from various caves, photographs of drawings in some caves and an entire piece of rock with an embedded relief sculpture.

Grotte de Font-de-Gaume (fohn-duh-GOH-meh) is 1.5 km from train station. Follow directions to Prehistory Museum, but continue on main road until sign to Sarlat. Follow signs to Sarlat and cave is on right hand side of road just outside Les Eyzies. Open daily except Tuesday, 9-11 & 2-5. Adult/ 8 F, persons 18-25/4 F, student and child/ 1 F. Bag of souvenir rocks/ 9 F. Visitors are taken through the cave in groups with commentary in French. Cave is electrically lighted and neither cold nor damp. Parts are narrow and low so we took the baby out of her backpack and carried her in our arms. Cave interior contains somewhat faded pictures of animals on the walls drawn by prehistoric man and is worthwhile seeing. Cave is much more extensive than the short distance covered by the tour.

Several attractions are in the opposite direction from the train station and on the main road (D47 direction Perigueux) beyond the turn-off to camp. Musee de la Speleologie, open July-Sept, daily 9-12 and 2-6, is the closest. Next comes Les Gorges d'Enfer with prehistoric caves and rock-shelters within an animal preserve, open 9-7, adult/11 F, child 6-14/6 F. Caves were used by Neanderthal and Cro-Magnon man. Trails lead to 8 sites classified as historical monuments. Bison, Prejalski horse and a wild donkey of same species that lived in prehistoric times live in animal reserve. There is also sort of a semi-enclosed zoo. The third attraction and the furthest from the station at 1.5 km is Le Grand Roc, a natural cavern of crystal formations. Open daily 9-12 and 2-6, except no lunch break is taken in August. Adult/10 F, child/5 F.

Guided tours in English leave from tourist office, July-Sept at 9:30 am and 2:30 pm, which visit the Museum of Prehistory first and then a bus takes participants to the main sites and caves in the area including La Grotte des Combarelles which is opened exclusively for this tour. Tours end at 12:30 and 5:30 pm. Cost is adult/23 F.

Trains leave Les Eyzies for Perigueux at 8:32, 11:59 am, 4:00, 8:24 and 10:55 pm. The last departure arrives in Paris Austerlitz at 5:44 am.

To Carcasonne, the best way is to leave Les Eyzies at 7:55 am (ar. Agen 10:00 am), change trains, lv. Agen 1:01 pm (ar. Carcasonne 3:04 pm). If you wish to spend the layover time in Toulouse instead of Agen, a train for Toulouse-Matabiau leaves at 10:10 am from Agen and the train for Carcasonne leaves Toulouse-Matabiau at 2:13 pm. The alternative is to leave Les Eyzies at 3:22 pm (ar. Agen 5:12 pm), change trains, lv. Agen 5:28 pm (ar. Toulouse-Matabiau 6:35 pm, ar. Carcasonne 7:34 pm).

SARLAT -la-Caneda   Sarlat is a picturesque medieval town but backpackers may wish to skip it because the closest camp is one kilometer uphill from the old town while the train station is outside of town at the opposite end. Tourist office is in old town. Camping Les Perieres, 1 km N.E. on road #47, is a deluxe camp with terraced campsites, conventional toilets, hot water in sinks, free hot showers, children's swimming pool, swings, game room with table tennis and billards, sitting room, library, sports area for tennis and volleyball. Small store with milk, bread (get there early in morning) and some staples. Adult/10 F, tent and car/9 F,

TOULOUSE

Camping Les Violettes, 9 km from Toulouse on N 113 towards Narbonne, is a first category camp. From Toulouse Matabiau Station, walk to bus station which is one block north of train station on the same side of the street, Boulevard de la Gare. (With your back to the station, turn right.) Take bus to Narbonne. Fare is 6.50 F and there are 11 departures each day. A bus stop is in front of the camp. Camp has hot showers, lounge, restaurant, take-out meals. Adult/7 F, tent/7 F. St. Sernin Cathedral, the top attraction, is 7 blocks from station. Walk forward from station across bridge 4 blocks to Strasbourg, turn right, go one block, turn left.

TARN (ALBI and CASTRES)

Please refer to railway map under Perigord. Albi and Castres are most directly reached via Toulouse. Change at St. Sulpice for Castres.

Toulouse to St. Sulpice to Albi (direction Rodez)

lv. Toulouse	10:07	12:25	1:53	5:38	6:53
ar. St. Sulpice	10:34	12:46	2:18	5:59	7:16
Ar. Albi (ville)	11:12	1:27	2:58		7:59

St. Sulpice to Castres (direction St. Pons)

lv. St. Sulpice	2:21	6:00	7:23 pm
ar. Castres	3:01	6:38	8:04

ALBI   A fairly large town, Albi has a Michelin rated 3 star cathedral, and a Toulouse-Lautrec museum. Tourist office is across from cathedral which is next to Musee Toulouse-Lautrec in Palais de la Berbie in main square of town--a 15 minute walk from train station.
Camping Parc de Caussels is 2 km east of Albi by N 99 and D 100 in direction of St.-Juery. Turn left to camp just before Mammouth shopping center. Well signed. From train station take bus # 6 which will be going to your right as you face the train station. Get off in about 6 blocks at the central bus stop on Place J. Jaures. Change to bus #3 (direction Cantepau) and ride for about 1 km and get off just before Mammouth shopping center on your left. Camp is five minute walk from bus stop (see map). Camp is wooded hilly site, conventional toilets, private sinks, free hot showers, eight stainless steel sinks for dishwashing, store, swings and basketball hoops. Town swimming pool is adjacent. Cost is 22 F for car, tent and 2 persons; 50% reduction granted for pedestrians.

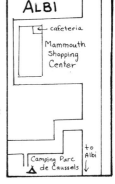

Musee Toulouse-Lautrec, open daily 10-12 and 2-6 except opens at 9:00 am in July and August. Adult/8 F, student and groups/4 F, child under 15/free. Restroom on each floor. One hour guided tour for groups in English if arrangements are made in advance. The turretted fortress-like castle of the Archbishops who ruled Albi from the 13th century to the time of the revolution now houses this museum. The Comtesse de Toulouse-Lautrec donated her son's paintings following his death in 1901. Other gifts made over

184

the years have resulted in 13 rooms on the first floor containing the artist's paintings, posters and memorabilia, the largest collection of his works in one place. The museum is excellent for following the development of Lautrec since boyhood. His sketches show that he was accomplished by the age of nine. Upstairs in the contemporary section are woodcuts from a book by Gauguin, nine paintings by Dufy, a Roualt, Utrillo, two Bonnards, three Vuillard and two by Matisse. The castle, built between the 13th and 18th centuries, overlooks the Tarn River. A beautiful formal garden and grape arbor in the rear is open to the public. A wonderful view of this can be seen from the circular balcony protruding off the Lautrec section of the museum. Museum store sells large poster reproductions for 15 F and postcard reproductions for 1 F.

Across from camp the Mammouth shopping center has a supermarket, store (including camping goods), snack concessions such as a creperie and an upstairs cafeteria. Restrooms are on outdoor balcony. Cafeteria is open 11:30-2 and 6:30-9:30. Cooking is very inferior for France, but not expensive. High chairs are available. Take a glass as you go through the line and then fill a carafe full of water near the seating area. Half chicken and fries/ 17.50 F, hamburger (rare) in tomato sauce with mashed potatoes/ 13 F, desserts/2.30-4.50 F. In town, cheapest Michelin listed restaurant is Relais Gascon et Aub. Landaise, 1 rue Balzac, closed Monday, about a 33 F menu. Unlisted train station restaurant, Restaurant Couronne, 77 rue Croix-Verte and Hotel Fouillade (Lavergne), 12 Place Fernand-Pelloutier, have cheaper menus. Market (Halles) is 1 block from tourist office.

CASTRES   Built on each side of the Agout River and once the site of a Roman defense station, Castres is a fine town in the Tarn district. In the 1619 Bishop's Palace with lovely formal French gardens is the Goya Museum. Banks are closed on Monday. Tourist office, place Alsace-Lorraine, is open Monday afternoon to Saturday from 9-12 and 2-7.

Camping Gravieyras, avenue de Roquecourbe on the shore of l'Agout River, is just off highway D 89 in the direction of Vabre or Burlats. From train station, camp is about a 20 minute walk. The small camp has restrooms and showers but no store. Adult/ 2.30 F, child 4-7/1.15 F, tent/ 1 F, car/1 F.

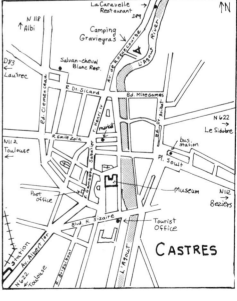

Good market is on Place Jean Jaures. Michelin listed restaurant is La Caravelle, 150 av. Roquecourbe, open June 15-Sept 15, 40 F menu. Less expensive and good is Salvan Cheval Blanc, 28 pl. d'Albinque, 35 F menu.

Musee Goya, well sited in a castle overlooking the river (see map), is open Tu-Sa 9-12 & 2-6 and Su 10-12 & 2-6. Adult/5 F, child/2.50 F, child under 7/free, student and groups/4 F. Pass through first rooms quickly as Goya's works are farther along in the last three rooms of Musee Goya wing. His 24 drawings of "The Disasters of War" hang in a nook. Goya's humorous "Les Caprices" series take up a separate room. Others are his "Los Proverbios" series: Sottise Feminine, Sottise de Frayeur, Sottise de Niais, and Sottise Ridicule; and a bullfight-toreador group, "La Taureaumachie." His drawings and portraits are a mastery of social commentary. Museum shop sells a packet of ten postcard reproductions of "The Caprices of Goya" for 5 F and the same of "La Tauromachie."

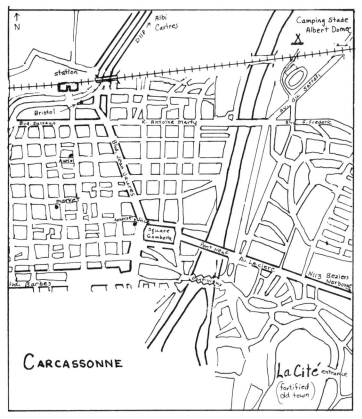

CARCASSONNE   Don't miss Carcassonne, a superb medieval walled town in the south of France near the Spanish border. Ramparts are complete with 50 towers dating from the 5th, 12th and 13th centuries. Choicest item within the old town is Basilique St. Nazaire's best ever 14th and 16th century stained glass windows.   Train station is in lower and newer town and you must walk up the hill to the old town (la cite) on the bluff. Tourist office has a branch next to the station, and at Porte Narbonnaise in La Cite which are open summer only. Main office is on Boulevard Camille-Pelletan, M-Sa 9-12 & 2-8, Su 10-12 in summer and changes money when banks are closed.

Camping Stade Albert Domec is on right bank of river and behind stadium, about a 15 minute walk from station (see map). Camp is beyond stadium but go into stadium entrance and walk towards left around stadium to entrance ahead. Well signed. Trailers and tents are segregated, wooded tent area, hole-in-floor toilets, row of sinks, one hot shower with two sinks, swings, teeter totter, slide, merry-go-round. Adult/ 3.80 F, tent/2.90 F, car/2.90 F.

Market days are Tuesday, Thursday and Saturday (morning only) on Rue de Verdun (see map). Cheapest Michelin listed restaurants are Bristol, across river from station, and Aurio (closed Sat), 52 rue 4-September, both with about a 35 F menu (see map). Tourist office list gives names of several with 25-30 F menus.

La Cite can be reached by car by taking the road leading to Narbonne and the "montee Combeleran." Large parking lot at entrance. On foot from the station takes about 20 minutes. Stop by tourist office and get its brochure on La Cite (lah sit-TAY). There is no charge for entering the old city but highly recommended is the hour tour which leaves from Chateau Comtal daily between 9-12 and 2-6 for adult/8 F, child/2 F, student/4 F, half price on Sunday. The tour lets you inside the ramparts where you can walk on the lists, the grassy boulevard between the two walls.

To Barcelona, the two through trains from Carcassonne leave at 5:56 am (ar. 11:56 am) and 6:09 pm (ar. 11:25 pm). It's also possible to take a train to Narbonne and wait there for trains coming from Marseilles and going to Barcelona. Trains leave Carcassonne for Narbonne at 7:10 (ar. 7:40), 8:21 (ar. 8:55), 9:51 (ar. 10:21), 11:00 am (ar. 11:35 am), 1:06 pm-- not daily--(ar. 1:41pm), 1:34--daily June 24-Sept 24--(ar. 2:05), 2:59 (ar. 3:36), 5:58 (ar. 6:28), 7:31 pm (ar. 8:09) plus later trains.

Trains leave Narbonne for Barcelona (must change trains at Port Bou) at 8:09 am (ar. Port Bou 9:38, lv. Port Bou 10:10, ar. Barcelona 12:55 pm), 11:40 (ar. Port Bou 1:17 pm, lv. 1:45 pm, ar. Barcelona 3:54 pm), 4:05 pm (ar. Port Bou 7:05, lv. 7:25, ar. Barcelona 10:17 pm), 5:04 pm (ar. Port Bou 6:55 pm, lv. 7:15 pm, ar. Barcelona 10:17 pm), 5:17 pm TEE (ar. Barcelona 9:02 pm, no change of trains), and 6:54 pm (ar. Port Bou 9:03 pm, lv. 9:20 pm, ar. Barcelona 11:30 pm). All trains arrive at Barcelona Termino Station.

BEZIERS, MONTPELLIER, LA GRANDE MOTTE

BEZIERS (bay-zee-A)   Beziers is in southern France. Autoroute (freeway) begins at Narbonne and costs 3 F to Beziers, but take N 9 instead if you want to see the Celtic settlement which is 8 km from Beziers off N 9 (direction Narbonne). The OPPIDUM d'ENSERUNE is the most complete pre-Roman Celtic settlement in France. From the sign "Oppidum d'Enserune" on N 9, the small hill of the one-time village can be seen and the sign directs you to the road which stretches 3 km to it. Open daily 8-12 and 2-6. The settlement was abandoned in the process of the Roman conquest. Lower parts of dwellings with grain storage amphora in place can be seen and some ramparts remain. There is a wonderful view of natural bowl in surrounding countryside. Museum (adult/5 F, student and child 7-18/2.50 F) shows pottery, coins, pestle and mortars, bracelets and other jewelry, small sculpture, tools (combs for carding wool), dice, oil lamps and swords. There are cases full of bits and pieces which attest to the French habit of showing everything they find.

MONTPELLIER (mohn-pay-lee-A)   This is the gateway to fantastic La Grande Motte. Train travelers should rail to Montpellier and then take the bus from Gare Routiere, a half-block from train station. Bus is operated by Les Courriers du Midi. Montpellier to La Grande Motte is 20 km or 45 minutes. Take any bus in the direction of La Grande Motte, Le Grau-du-Roi, Port Camargue or Aigues-Mortes. A bus leaves about every hour. Fare is 9 F one way.

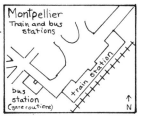

Tourist office is on place de la Comedie. From train station, walk on rue Maguelone two blocks to main intersection. Tourist office is towards the left, across blvd. Victor Hugo. Open M-Sa 9-12 & 2-6:15 and open also July-Sept 15 until 7 pm and is open Sunday 10-12. Tourist office will change money.

Camping Municipal, Ave. St. Auohe de Novigens, is open all year. From train station take bus #8 (direction Rimbaud) from rue Maguelone near station. Bus leaves every 30 minutes, adult/1.50 F, child under 4/free. Can buy 6 tickets for 5.50 F. Ride is 25 minutes and camp is 50 meters from bus stop. Camp has hot showers (1.10 F), store and snack bar.

There are three food markets. One is two blocks from train station at end of rue Republique. Main market is at place Jean Jaures and open Tuesday to Friday mornings and all day Saturday. Musee Fabre, 13 rue Montpellier, is open Tu-Su 9-12 & 2-5, and is a fine arts museum. Self-service laundry is on rue Seranne, two blocks from train station. From station, turn right onto J. Ferry for one block, left on Rue de Verdun for one block and right on rue Seranne. Closed Sunday.

LA GRANDE MOTTE   This is a completely pre-planned, surrealistic French resort on the Mediterranean that is worth seeing. When the Bank of America pyramid in San Francisco goes home, this is where it will come. The hotels look like they belong on the cover of a science fiction magazine. French fantasy is fantastic and I urge you to come. This is a simple matter for drivers. La Grande Motte is 21 km from Montpellier. If you take the autoroute from Beziers, exit Montpellier Est for La Grande Motte. Toll is 12 F. There is also a slower inland route and more scenic coastal road. Train travelers please see directions under "Montpellier." Alternatively but less conveniently, La Grande Motte can be reached by train from Nimes to Le-Grau-du-Roi and then by bus for the 10 minute ride to La Grande Motte. Trains leave Nimes at 8:55 am (ar. 9:45), 11:52 (ar. 12:59pm), 1:11 (ar. 2:16) and 6:45 pm (ar. 7:43 pm). Buses leave Le-Grau-du-Roi at 10:44 and 11:15 am and 1:00, 2:00, 4:15, 5:15, 5:40, 6:50 and 7:40pm.

Tourist office is open daily including holidays from 9 am- 8 pm without lunch break. Excursions are listed on bulletin board. Map, bus schedule, sailing school and children's daycare (July and August only) information is available. Each year the village hosts a jazz festival beginning on July 15.

Seven campgrounds are next to each other and a 10-20 minute walk to center of community. Camping Le Garden is closest. Le Garden, Louis

188

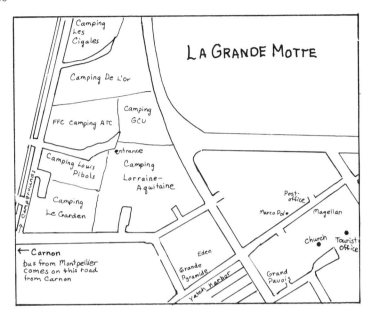

Pibols and l'Or are all highest category camps. Campsites are marked and numbered. Fees are about 30-40 F for 1-2 persons and 40-52 F for 3-4 persons including hot water in sinks and showers. All are recently built and have modern restrooms with individual sink cubicles with hot water, hot showers, and conventional toilets, hot water in dish and clothes washing rooms, store and dayroom. Camping de l'Or has a circular main building with wedge-shaped rooms used for dormitories, dayrooms with tables and chairs, daycare in July and August, and a store. Camping Les Cigales has fewer facilities and charges less. On Le Grande Motte side of neighboring resort Le-Grau-du-Roi, is Camping Boucanet which fronts on the beach and costs less than the deluxe camps of Le Grand Motte. Take bus to Le-Grau-du-Roi but ask to get off at the camp which is before the town.

Food is somewhat expensive in the resort and it is advisable to bring along some groceries. Tourist office says pizza places and snack bars are least expensive places to eat: Pizzeria La Caleche-Avenue du Casino, Pizzeria Mercure-Immeuble Saint-Clair, Restaurant Helvetia-Centre Commercial Neptune, and Snack-Bar Richelieu-Centre Commercial Miramar. For those who are splurging in France, the cheapest Michelin listed restaurants are L'Estrambord with unusual decor and about a 40 F menu, and Le Yam's, quai d'Honneur with about a 45 F menu.

Discovering all the fantastic architecture in the resort will take 1-2 hours and the beach is wide and sandy. An excursion can be made to Aigues-Mortes (egg-mort) with its intact ramparts. The town can be reached by bus all the way, or by bus to Le-Grau-du-Roi and then train to Aigues-Mortes. Bus leaves La Grande Motte at 6:50 am (ar. 7:10) and 7:10 pm (ar. 7:30). Bus leaves Aigues-Mortes for Le-Grau-du-Roi at 6:34 am (ar. 6:55) and 7:30 pm (ar. 7:50). Train leaves Le-Grau-du-Roi at 10:09 am (except at 10:26 am between about June 27 and Aug 29), 12:53, 6:07 (between about June 12 and Sept 13) and 9:24 pm (between about June 27 and Aug 29) for the

6-9 minute trip to Aigues-Mortes. Train leaves Aigues-Mortes at 9:39 or
9:50 am, 12:37, 2:07 (about June 12-Sept 13 only) and 7:37 pm. Last bus
leaves from Le-Grau-du-Roi for Le Grande Motte at 7:40 pm.

PROVENCE

Provence is the center of Roman monuments in France. Avignon is five
hours and 40 minutes from Paris on TEE Mistral which averages 82 miles
an hour. For drivers, the area is covered by Michelin map #93 Lyon-
Marseille (yellow). Avignon might be used as an excursion base as camps
aren't available that can be reached by public transport in Arles, Nimes,
Orange and Pont-du-Gard.

AVIGNON   Train station is just outside town walls at Porte de la
Republique. Mainstreet Cours Jean Jaures extends perpendicularly from in
front of station and is
within the ramparts.
In third block on right
is tourist office,
"Maison du Tourisme
et du Vin."
    Camping Bagatelle
is on l'ile de Barthe-
lasses, 2 km north off
road to Nimes and
about a 30 minute walk
from station. Palace
of Popes and original
bridge of Avignon can
be seen from camp.
Free hot showers,
store, snack bar,
washing machine
(8 F), dryer, adult/
5.50 F, tent/3 F.

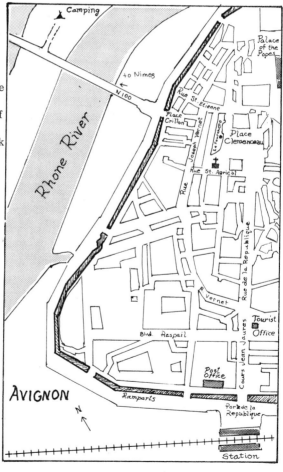

Market is on
Place Pie. Auberge
de France, 28 pl.
Horloge, south of
Palace of the Popes
is Michelin 1 star
with a 45 F menu. It's
small and is closed
Wednesday evening,
Thursday and about
June 9-26. Also
Michelin listed are
La Fourchette, 7 r.
Racine, closed Sun-
day, Monday and month of June, and Aub. Pont St.-Benezet, 48 quai la
Ligne, closed Wednesday.

Palace of the Popes (Palais des Papes) offers a guided tour in English. There is also Musee Calvet and Petit Palais Museum with 14th and 15th century Italian paintings.

ARLES   Here are Roman ruins and Museum Reattu with works by Picasso. Arles is a compact town and easy to walk around. No campground for backpackers. Most everything of interest is about a 10-15 minute walk from the station. A ticket good for all monuments is sold at any monument for about adult/18 F, reduction for students. Arles' most famous site, the Roman Arena, is open 8:30-12:30 and 2-7, closed Monday, adult/4 F if bought individually. Bullfights are held in the arena each Sunday at 9:30 pm, beginning in June. Adult/15 or 25 F, child/5 F. See also: Theater Antique, Cloitre St. Trophime and les Alyscamps. Musee Reattu, 8:30-12:15 and 2-6:45, adult 4 F, child/free, shows many of Picasso's paintings and drawings in the last two rooms.   Two Michelin listed restaurants which are located between the station and monuments are Le Tambourin, 65 r. A. -Pichot, closed Sat., about 33 F menu, and across the street, Brasserie Provencale, 38 r. A.- Pichot, closed Sun, about a 35 F menu.

NIMES   Famous for its monuments from the Roman occupation of Gaul, its Maison Carree, within walking distance of the station, is called the "gem of Roman architecture in France." It dates from the Augustan age, a small beautiful temple only 27 by 13 yards in dimension. Also see arena. No campground. (If you have limited time, Arles is more attractive than Nimes.)

ORANGE   In the best preserved of all Roman theaters in France, plays and concerts are given in summer.

PONT-du-GARD   No mortar was used in placing the precisely cut blocks for this Roman aqueduct, 19 centuries old. Take bus to Remoulins from Avignon. No train.

AIX-EN-PROVENCE   Brand new and don't miss is the "Fondation Vasarely" (vahz-sah-HEE-lee), Ave. Marcel Pagnol, Jas de Bouffan, built on the outskirts of Aix (ikes) as a showcase for the op artist. This is not a museum in the sense of hanging pictures already created by an artist, but an environment designed especially for the works planned by Vasarely for the "Fondation." The result is superb and a living experience in op art. His gigantic pieces, some woven like a tapestry and others made of an assortment of materials, completely engulf the visitor. The Fondation is still vividly remembered by our 4 and 6 year olds. Open 10-5 and in summer to 6 pm, closed Tuesday, adult/8 F, student/4 F. A bus goes to the Fondation from near the tourist office. Tourist office is at place du General deGaulle, open 8-5 and to 10 pm July-Sept. From train station, go straight ahead two blocks and turn left on Victor Hugo and go three blocks to Place deGaulle. By car, if you take the "autoroute du Soleil" freeway at Salon, payment of 3 F at entrance outside of Salon (direction Aix-en-Provence) is required. (Three 1 F pieces are thrown into a bin.) Take Aix-Ouest (west) exit and you'll see the building on a hill on the city side of the freeway. It appears silver and black marked with alternating black and silver circles. A gray V modern sculpture by the freeway marks the exit. Also, museum shop sells reproductions for 20-96 F, and signed and numbered lithographs for 300-3600 F. AIROTEL CAMPING CHANTECLER, Val St. Andre, is 2 km from train station. Take bus #3 from station, then a 10 min walk. Hot showers, store, washing machine, swimming pool, adult/12 F, tent/15 F.

RIVIERA

The Riviera has a large colony of artists and writers, and its most important attraction besides its beaches which can be pebbly, narrow and crowded is the collection of contemporary art found in the towns. Camping season extends from May into October and any campground that fronts directly on the beach will likely have been filled by prior reservation in August. Beaches can become polluted during the summer months. Purification plants are being built and in the past local authorities have closed a beach if it became really bad. There are a few free public beaches, otherwise admission consists of renting a chair and umbrella for 5-25 F a day. Incidentally, it's accepted to change into your swim suit directly on the beach under a big towel with a hole in the middle. The Ile du Levant, an island off the coast at St. Tropez (san-tro-PEH), is devoted to nude sunbathing and living except for having to wear "le minimum" in the village, and you can go there too, although you will blend in best if you are physically attractive.

The best strategy for seeing the Riviera for those with a railpass is to base yourself in one town and make day excursions from there. The TEEs and international expresses stop at San Rafael, Cannes, Antibes and Nice, and from these towns local trains depart for the villages.

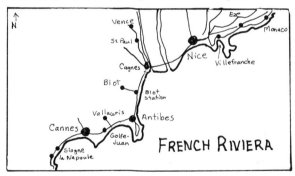

ST. RAPHAEL (san-rah-feh-EL)   Neither town nor camp is particularly recommended but train schedules may force you to spend the night here. Tourist office is on right when leaving station. Camping Beausejour, on main

road N 98 (direction Cannes), is closest. From train station take bus (direction Cannes) from bus station to left of train station. In 2 km get off at the bridge. Camp is across road from beach. Hot showers, individual washrooms, hole-in-floor toilets and some seat-less conventional types, store, car wash, swings, slide, washing machine (9 F, attendant will put in soap and start machine, one hour cycle, no dryer).

CANNES (can) "Accueil de France" tourist office is in station. Ranch Camping is 8 km west of Cannes. Take bus #6 or 10 from bus station near l'Hotel de Ville (city hall), 500 meters from train station. Bus stops at camp. Free hot showers, store, restaurant, by reservation in July and August, Sept-June 2 people/30 F, July-Aug 2 people/46 F. Market in Cannes, "marche Forville," is 1 block north of l'Hotel de Ville, open Tu-Sa 7-1. Cannes-la-Boca Station is by the beach in suburban Cannes.

LA NAPOULE   Don't get off train at La Napoule for these two camps, but at station "Pinede de la Siagne" between La Napoule and Cannes. Station is not a building but merely a shelter with a sign. To reach the station from the ground, note sign on steps leading to station. Be sure to go up the Nice side to go to Cannes since crossing the tracks is not allowed. Camping La Siagne (see-ahg-nay), open April-Sept, is 200 meters from Gare (Pinede) La Siagne. Camp is wooded, hole-in-floor toilets, hot showers (1.90 F), store, adult/4.50 F, child under 5/ 2.25 F, tent and car/ 5.50 F. Camping du Bosquet, also within a five minute walk from Pinede de la Siagne, has both hole-in-floor and conventional toilets and similar prices.

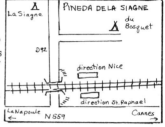

Trains leave Pinede de la Siagne for Cannes at 6:53 am, 9:16, 11:52, 2:24pm and 7:02 pm.

VALLAURIS   To get there, take the train to Golfe Juan (the closest) or Cannes and then a bus from either train station to Vallauris. There are about 20 buses a day. Picasso's noted painting, "War and Peace," is in the 16th century Castle of Monks of the Lerins Islands (now called Musee National d'Art Moderne). It covers three sides of the crypt walls in the chapel. In the central square is Picasso's bronze sculpture, "Man with a Sheep." The Museum is open 10-12 and 2-5. The town hosts a permanent exhibition of pottery, some of it by Picasso, at A.V.E.C., 15 rue Sicard, open 10-12 and 2:30-7 in summer. Madoura, a store, sells authorized copies of Picasso's pottery. In even-numbered years, the Ceramic Arts Biennial of international scope is held. Michelin listed restaurants include Sports Hotel, rue de la Gendarmerie, about 35 F menu, and Le Vallauris, Ave. G. Clemenceau, about a 39 F menu.

ANTIBES (on-TEEB)   Tourist office is in Place DeGaulle. From station, turn right on main street, Robert Soleau, which leads to Place DeGaulle in five blocks. Ask for map and English language booklet, "Rendevous A Antibes, Juan-les-Pins (zwahn-lay-PAN)," which tells of town history and sightseeing. Antibes' campgrounds are by the train station of Biot, a four minute train ride from Antibes. See Biot. Banque de Paris et des Pays-Bas at Vauban Harbor near Antibes train station is open every day including Sundays and holidays from 9-4. Market is at Place Massena, one block inland from Musee Picasso, open mornings.   Liberator, 30 ave. R.-Soleau, has about a 35 F menu. Musee Picasso, Chateau Grimaldi, contains 175 works done by Picasso during his stay in Antibes in 1946 and which he donated to the town. Museum is behind the ramparts and faces the sea in the older part of town, about a 15 minute walk from the station. Open July-Sept 10-12 & 3-7; Oct-June, daily except Tu, 10-12 & 2-6. Antibes also has an archaeological museum and Naval and Napoleonic Museum.

BIOT (bee-AWT) Biot makes a good excursion base for the Riviera, as it's 11 km from Nice and 9 km from Cannes with about hourly train service in both directions. Persons arriving via a TEE or international train should get off in Antibes and take a local train or bus for the 4 minute ride to Biot Station. Five campgrounds are within 500 meters of Biot Station, and these camps are more deluxe than those at La Siagne.

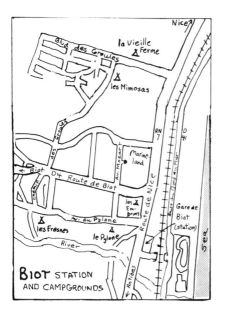

Closest are Les Embruns and Le Pylone. Les Embruns, open Apr-Sept, has free hot showers, hot water in sinks, store, snack bar. Le Pylone, Route de Biot, has free hot showers, hot water in sinks, store, snack bar. The manager, Mr. Pauget, reports that this campground is now being reserved solely for groups from Britain, but that he hopes to have expanded the campground for 1982, in which case it will be open again to individual campers. Camp is open Apr 15-Oct 15. Les Mimosas, chemin des Groules by Parc de Vaugrenier, is 500 meters from Biot Station. Free hot showers, store, hot water in sinks, cooked meals to go. La Vieille Ferme Boulevard des Groules, has free hot showers, store, washing machine, hot water in sinks. Les Fresnes, quai de la Brague, and open Easter-Sept, has hot showers, store, cooked meals to go. Of these camps, Le Pylone is the best but they are all very good. Mr. & Mrs. Robert Cooper comment, "We stayed in dozens of beautiful campgrounds but we especially like Le Pylone. The grounds were well organized and well taken care of. Tent campers had their own area away from the noise of most autos. The sites were divided by a few small trees on either side, and each section was divided by waist-high hedges."

From Biot Station, trains going in the direction of Marseille stop at Antibes, Juan-les-Pins, Golfe-Juan Vallauis, Cannes, Cannes-la-Bocca, Pinede-de-la-Siagne, Mandelieu-la-Napoule, Theoule-sur-Mer, Le Trayas, Antheor-Cap-Roux, Agay, Le Dramont, Boulouris-sur-Mer and St. Raphael Valescure. Trains run from 6:22 am to 11:22 pm. Some trains go only as far as Cannes-La-Bocca.

Trains going in the direction of Ventimiglia stop at Villeneuve-Loubet-Plage, Cagnes-sur-Mer, Cros-de-Cagnes, St. Laurent-du-Var, Nice St.-Augustin, Nice-Ville (downtown), Nice-Riquier, Villefranche-sur-Mer, Beaulieu-sur-Mer, Eze, Cap d'Ail, Monaco, Cap-Martin-Roquebrune,

Carnoles and Menton (mahn-TOHN). Trains leave Biot Station at 6:43*, 7:24, 12:43 (request stop), 1:30*, 2:52, 3:34, 4:40, 6:00, 7:01, 7:38 (request stop), 8:37 and 10:24 pm *. Note: *indicates trains going only as far as Nice-ville. "Request stop" means you must let the conductor at the train station know that you wish to take that train so he can signal the train to stop. On these same trains, if you wish to get off at Eze or Cap d'Ail, the conductor must be notified on the train.

Musee National Fernan Leger is 1.9 km from Biot train station <u>uphill</u>. Follow signs on route de Biot. Just before museum is Camping l'Eden. Museum is open 10-12 and 2-6, closed Monday, adult/7 F, student and child 12-15/3.50 F, child under 12/free, art students with card/free, groups of 20 persons/3.50 F each. Museum is a white contemporary structure built especially for Leger's works. Guide to Museum/1 F, poster of museum/10 F, reproductions/50 F, signed lithographs/300 F, ceramic plates/100 F, silk scarves/200 F.

SAINT PAUL DE VENCE (s an -pohl-deh-VAHNS)   Called St. Paul for short, the town is 7 km from Cagnes-sur-Mer and 4.5 km from Vence. Buses leave from Gare Routiere in Nice or (preferably because it's closer) from S.N.C.F. station in Cagnes-sur-Mer and pass by St. Paul on their way to Vence. Buses leave Cagnes at 8:10*, 9:20, 10:20, 11:20, 11:35*am, 1:50, 2:55*, 2:50, 3:50, 4:45*, 4:50, 5:50*, 6:05, 6:55*, 7:10, 7:40 and 8:05 pm. Note: * indicates bus picks up at bus stop at the mairie not at station. Tell the driver you want off at St. Paul. The town itself is a picturesque medieval fortified village with ramparts that can be walked upon. Foundation Maeght (mag) is outside town on a hillside. Bring your lunch. The goal of Marguerite and Aime Maeght in creating the Foundation was to achieve a "total environ-ment" for modern art. This was attained by the skillful blending of terraces, sculpture, pools and gardens into a rich natural setting. The Foundation includes an amphitheater (concerts, theater and ballet in summer), chapel with stained glass windows by Braque and Ubac, library, movie theater, theater for the performing arts, artists' accommodations and workspace for creating lithography, etchings and ceramics. Besides the galleries showing paintings, sculpture, mosaics and glass; the artists Braque, Chagall, Kandinsky, Miro and Giacometti each have a room dedicated to him. Owning the Maeght Gallery in Paris gave Mr. and Mrs. Maeght the opportunity to purchase some of the best works of the foremost modern artists of our time. Represented are Bonnard, Matisse, Leger, Bazaine, Bram Van Velde, Tal Coat, Palazuelo, Gonzalez, Hartung, Adami, Soulages, Messagier, Zadkine, Richier, Arp, Rebeyrolle, Tapies and Chillida, many of which are not yet well known in the U.S. The Foundation is open 10-12:30 and 3-7 in summer and closes at 6 pm rest of year. Adult/10 F, student and child/7 F. If coming by car, don't park at first parking lot but drive up hill and park closer to museum. Foundation's sales room is outstanding with several hundred reproductions for 10 F and up. Small reproductions of works by Chagall, Giacometti, Kandinsky, and Miro sell for 5 F. Lithographs sell for 120-150 F, signed lithographs by modern artists for 250 F and up. For example a Calder lithograph (#11 of an edition of 150) is priced at 800 F. An unsigned but num-bered Braque lithograph sells for 150 F. Signed Miro lithographs sell for 8,000 F and up, unsigned Miro lithograph plus book in French is priced at 150 F (a value) and there is a similar offering by Calder.

VENCE (vahns)   Take same bus from Cagnes-sur-Mer as given under St.
Paul. Trip is 40 minutes. Matisse thought the Chapel of the Rosary, built
under his direction in 1950, was his best work. The graphic interior is done
with black outlines on white ceramic tile walls, and the stained glass windows
of blue, green and yellow are of modern design. Open Tuesday and Thursday,
10-11:30 and 2:30-5:30. The bus to Vence lets you off at place du Grand-
Jardin which is also the location of the tourist office. The chapel is outside
town and about a half hour walk--ask about buses.

NICE (neece)   Nice has reasonable restaurants, a good supermarket and
department stores. There is no campground but it's an easy commute from
Biot Station campgrounds (see Biot) or other camps in vicinity. Train station
is at edge of shopping area and seven blocks from Prisunic department store
and its excellent supermarket. Tourist office is outside station on left.
Nice's second station, Chemin de fer de Provence, 33 Ave. rue Malaussena,
seven blocks from main station (SNCF), handles local trains of Chemin de
fer de Provence. Market is at Place Massena. Matisse Museum and Musee
National Marc Chagall are in hills surrounding Nice and reachable by bus
#15 or 15-A which picks up across from Galeries Lafayette department store
on Ave. Jean Medecin, towards waterfront end. Matisse Museum is closed
Monday, Chagall Museum closed Tuesday. Bus tickets are cheaper by the
carnet.

VILLEFRANCHE-SUR-MER   The town is on the main train line just beyond
Nice heading towards Monaco. Jean Cocteau's frescoes decorate walls of
Chapelle St.-Pierre (Fishermen's Chapel), open 9-12 and 2-7.

LE LAVANDOU   Leslie Carter writes: "Le Lavandou--riotous fun! Small
town on the Riviera. I loved it because of all the people--the whole feeling of
the place. People were wild, crazy and fun. Wild drivers, great discos
(though expensive), beautiful beaches and beautiful people. Crepes! Very
pretty countryside--not so commercialized as Nice, Cannes, etc.--smaller
and nicer."   To reach Le Lavandou, take a bus operated by Chemin de Fer
de Provence from train station in St. Raphael. St. Tropez is an earlier stop
on the same route. The trip is 2 hours, 65 km.   Trains leave at 7:30,
8:51, 11:55 am*, 1:30*, 3:20*, 4:48* and 6:50 pm*(daily only between July 1-
Sept 5). Note: *indicates a change of trains must be made at Cavalaire. More
departures than listed are available to St. Tropez only. Closest campground,
St. Pons, is inland, 1 km south of Le Lavandou. The camp has hot showers,
store, dayroom.

HAUTE SAVOIE (FRENCH ALPS)

The Haute Savoie (oh suh-VWAH) is often overlooked by Americans who go
to Switzerland to see the Alps. But France is equally good and cheaper because the narrow gauge railway leading to Chamonix is included in railpasses
and French campgrounds are cheaper.

ANNECY   A wonderful off-the-beaten-track medium sized town, Annecy
is on a clear blue lake in the French Alps. Tourist office (see map next
page) is about a 10 minute walk from train station. In Annecy, Le Belvedere
camping is 1.5 km south on road to Semnoz but we don't recommend it for

196

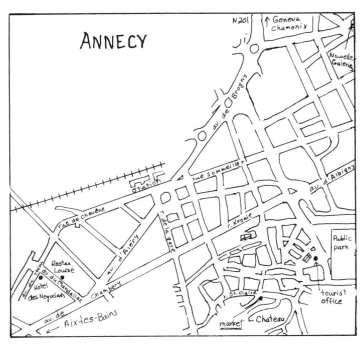

backpackers as it's at least a 30 minute uphill walk and no bus goes there.
It's far better to take bus from train station or tourist office to a camp on
the lake at a small village (see map). At Bout-du-Lac, Camping International du Lac Bleu, is a two minute walk from bus stop. Open Easter-Sept, the clean hedged camp is on the water with mostly Dutch and British clientele with their daysailers and inflatables. Free hot showers, cold water in sinks, no individual sink compartments, hole-in-floor toilets with one conventional, store, ping-pong, swimming, dock, rocky beach. Adult/6 F, child under 7/3.50 F, tent/3.75 F, car/3.80 F.

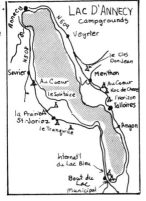

A five minute walk further on is Camping Municipal, open June 15-Aug, hot showers, play equipment and cheaper than Lac Bleu. A restaurant is between these two camps. For other camps see map at right.

Bus fare to Bout du Lac is about 6 F. All buses leave from train station and then go to Hotel de Ville (city hall) by tourist office before getting on lakeshore road. Bus stops at all small towns before the destination unless otherwise noted below. Bus driver will stop at camps between towns on request. Annecy to St. Jorioz (20 minute ride): 7:05 (not Sun), 8:00, 9:45 am (July-Sept 14 only), 12:05, 1:50 (July-Sept 14), 5:10, 6:10, 7:10 pm.
Annecy to Angon (25 minute ride): 7:45, 8:25, 11:00 (July-Sept 4), 11:20 am (except July-Sept 4), 12:05 (July-Sept 4 except Sun), 2:15, 4:45, 6:30 (July-

Sept 4), 7:05 (except July-Sept 4), 7:30 pm (July-Sept 4). Annecy to Bout-du-Lac (direction Albertville, 30 minute ride): 10:15, 11:15 am, 1:50, 4:15, 6:15, 7:20 pm.

Market in Annecy is Tuesday and Friday mornings on rue St.-Claire at Pont-Morens (bridge). Restaurant Louise, 16 Ave. Mandallaz, near train station (see map) was one of our best values in France, huge servings. Closed Sunday. The bar is in front--pass through kitchen to get to restaurant in back. Menu of about 25 F without beverage, of beet salad, braised beef and mashed potatoes and gravy, followed by choice of cheese, fruit or ice cream (two scoops). The plat du jour costs about 20 F for just the meat and potatoes. Three minute walk from Restaurant Louise, the Hotel des Negociants has about a 30 F menu of crudites (appetizers), steak and fries, cheese and dessert, service included, drink extra.

Sightseeing consists of the arcaded old town of Annecy, the beautiful lake and Les Gorges du Fier, 12 minutes away by train. For the latter, get off at Lovagny Station on Aix-les-Bains line. A boardwalk has been con-structed over the gully. For shopping, Nouvelle Galeries department store (see map) is open 9:30-12:30 and 2:30-7:30 daily except Sunday and Friday night until 10 pm. Restaurant inside is open 9:30 am -10 pm with about a 25 F menu and 15 F, 17 F and 20 F "plat du jour." Michelin maps and guides are discounted here.

To Chamonix, trains leave Annecy 7:16 am (ar. 9:47 am), 9:33 am (ar. 12:05 pm), 12:32 pm (ar. 2:45 pm), 1:37 pm (ar. 3:57 pm), 3:17 pm (ar. 5:55 pm). A change of train at St. Gervais-le-Fayet is required for the ride through the valley up to Chamonix.

CHAMONIX-MONT-BLANC (sha-mo-NEE)   See map next page. Chamonix is best approached from the French side via Aix-les-Bains and Annecy be-cause the train trip is included in the railpasses and the scenery is still won-derful. If you go via Martigny in Switzerland, a private railway fare must be paid between Martigny and Chamonix. In Chamonix, the tourist office is at place de l'Eglise, but plan to get off at train station nearest to intended camp-ground. Camps are within walking distance of stations. Also, a bus connects Chamonix with the other villages in the valley. Destinations are signed by altitude.

Camping Les Rosieres, 1.5 km NE of Chamonix Station, take bus from station towards Les Praz, free hot showers. Camping L'ille des Barrats, open June-Sept 20, 1 km south of Chamonix, get off at Les Moussoux Station, hot showers, cafe. At Les Bossons (get off at station Les Bossons), 3.5 km from Chamonix, Les Bossons camping is the closest and is in the village, 100 meters from Arve River, view of Mont Blanc, open May-Sept, hot showers. Further away on route du Tremplin are Les Deux Glaciers, rte. du Tremplin-Olympique, terraced campsites, hot showers, hot water in sinks, store open July-Aug; Les Cimes, open June-Sept 15, on rte. du Tremplin-Olympique, hot showers, store open July-Aug; and Les Verneys, rte du Tremplin-Olympique, view of the glacier and Mont Blanc, hot showers. At Praz-de-Chamonix, 2.5 km from Chamonix (get off at Les Praz Station), La Mer de Glace camping is open July-Aug, hot showers, and Les Drus camping has a view of Mont Blanc, hot showers and store. At Les Houches, Clair de Lune camping is 1 km east of Les Houches, open June 15-Sept 15, hot showers, by reservation only in August; and Le Petit Pont camping, 2 km

198

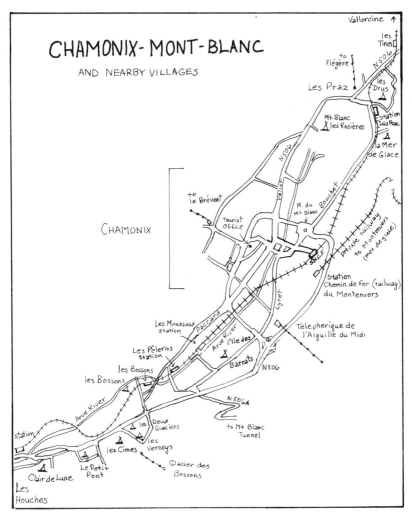

east of Les Houches, view of Mont Blanc, open June 15-Sept 15, hot showers, ping pong. Of the campgrounds, Les Deux Glaciers is open all year around and is rated the highest and is the most expensive at about 11 F for two persons including hot water. The simplest camps are L'ille des Barrats and Les Bossons. Most of the other camps charge about 7 F per person and 5 F per "emplacement" (tent).

Discount coupons are available for the cable-cars in the area--ask at the tourist office or campground. You can save money by riding up and walking down--but don't do this on L'Aiguille du Midi. Ask what time of day is best to go up because local people know the cloud patterns for predicting the weather. L'Aiguille du Midi telepherique takes you up to the Mont Blanc massif and costs around 35 F with coupon. Telepherique du Brevant is about half the cost and goes **high**   enough to view the Mont Blanc mountain range

from across the valley. Also Michelin rated 3 stars is Mer de Glace
(glacier) and le Montenvers, a 20 minute 6 km trip via private railway from
Chamonix. Many trails are in the area, some not too difficult, and tourist
office sells a trail map.

SNCF trains go as far as the village of Vallorcine which is the end
of railpass validity. For Annecy, trains leave Chamonix at 9:01am (ar.
11:15), 11:19 am (ar. 2:03 pm), 2:30 pm (ar. 4:54), 3:29 pm (ar. 5:47),
5:09 pm (ar. 7:40). Change trains at St.-Gervais-le-Fayet.

CHAMPAGNE

RHEIMS, REIMS (rans)   This is champagne country and the champagne
makers offer free guided tours through their plants and cellars. Tourist
office main branch is at 3 boulevard de la Paix, a 10 block walk from the
station or take bus "C" from in front and get off at Place A. Briand. Another
office is on rue Chanzy near the Cathedral, open 9-12:30 and 2-6:30 and
until 8:30 pm in July and August. Ask for city map and list of champagne
houses.

Camping de Champagne, in Domaine des Essillards on Avenue Hoche
on the outskirts of town, is open Easter-Sept 30. Take bus Z from the
Theater, which is 7 blocks from the station, to the campground. Free hot
showers, adult/7 F, site/7 F. Bus fare is 2.40 F or 10 tickets for 12 F.

Market takes place each day but at scattered locations. Monday: Place
St. Thomas, ave. de Laon (to rear of station across Pont de Laon), buslines
A and C. Tuesday: place Saint-Maurice and boulevard Pommery, between
camp and downtown on busline D. Wednesday: Halles Centrales, 50 rue de
Mars, centrally located downtown near Place de l'Hotel de Ville (city hall).
Others are at Z.U.P. Chatillons (place des Argonauts) and at Quartier Croix
Rouge near university. Thursday: boulevard Carteret, east of downtown on
buslines B and C; and place Luton. Friday: Halles Centrales, Z.U.P. Neuf-
chatel, and boulevard du President Wilson and rue Maison Blanche, west of
camp and away from downtown on buslines A and G. Saturday: Halles
Centrales. Sunday: ave. Jean Jaures which begins at Place Briand in eastern
part of downtown on busline B and in vicinity of tourist office; and at Quartier
Saint Anne.

Ten champagne cellars and manufacturing plants offer free guided
tours in English to visitors. Several end the tour with a very generous tasting of the product. Tourist office has brochure listing locations of champagne
houses. If you visit two or three, take notice of size of bubble (called bead)
as this indicates amount of sugar added and care taken during second fer-
mentation. Smaller the bead, the better the champagne. Mumm, 34 rue du
Champ-de-Mars, M-F 9-11:15 and 2-5 with no lunch break taken in July and
August, is the largest and most modern. The tour is probably the most complete as far as detailed information is concerned. Free champagne at the end.
(Prior to the tour you are asked your preference as to dryness and the
appropriately chilled tenth awaits you at the finish.) Piper Heidsieck, 51
boulevard Henry-Vasnier, daily 9-11:30 and 2-5:30, gives you a tour through
the cellars on a miniature train with open cars. Veuve Clicquot-Ponsardin,
1 place des Droits de l'Homme, across from campground, M-F 9-11:30 and
2:15-4:30, Sa 2:15-5:30 pm. Taittinger, 9 place Saint-Nicaise, daily 9-11
and 2-5. Ruinart Pere et Fils, 4 rue des Crayeres, M-F 9-11 and 2:30-4.

Pommery and Greno, 5 place du General Gourand, M-F 9-11:15 and 2:15-4:30, Sa 2:15-5:30 pm. Lanson, 48 rue de Courlancy, July 1-Sept 15 M-F 9-11 and 2-5. Bessarat de Bellefon, Allee du Vignoble, M-F 9-12 and 2-5, closed August. Heidsieck and C. Monopole, 83 rue Doquebert, M-F 9-11 and 2:10-4:30, Sa-Su 2:30-4:30 pm, closed August. Henriot, 3 place des Droits de l'Homme, M-F 8:30-11:30 and 2-5:30. Jacquart, 5 rue Gosset, daily 9-11 and 2-7 by appointment.

Cathedral of Notre-Dame, 13th century masterpiece of Gothic art, was purposely designed for coronation of royalty. Here is where Joan of Arc's crusade achieved its mission with the coronation of Charles VII. France's kings from Clovis to Charles X were crowned here. Tourist office outside. Musee Saint Denis, in Abbey Saint-Denis at 8 rue Chanzy near the Cathedral is open 10-12 and 2-6, closed Tuesday. The province's fine arts museum has a notable ancient tapestry collection and paintings from 15th century onward.

BASQUE REGION

HENDAYE on the Atlantic coast on the French side of the Spanish-French border is good for a day of relaxation. Get off the international express train at Hendaye and change to the local shuttle train that goes to Hendaye-Plage Station (beach station). Camping Sascoenea, rue des Lilas, is a 10 minute walk (see map). Camp is on slope overlooking ocean, open Easter-Sept, hot showers, hole-in-floor toilets with one conventional, terraced campsites, store, cafe, adult/ 7 F including hot water, tent/ 5 F, car/3 F. Sandy beach is a 15 minute walk. Camping Alturan, though farther from station, is even more attractively situated being only 100 meters from the beach, and is slightly cheaper than Camping Sascoenea. Both have a terraced camping area for tents. The fine sand

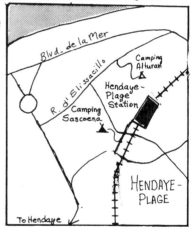

beach of Hendaye-Plage is nearly two miles and safe with a gentle slope. Restaurants are cheaper in Hendaye than Hendaye-Plage. Shuttle train service between Hendaye and San Sebastian in Spain is available several times daily.

OTHER CITIES

VALENCE (between Lyon and Avignon) Tourist office is 3 blocks from train station--turn right when leaving station. Camping L'Eperviere is across the street from the international youth "Centre de L'Eperviere," 2 km from the station. No bus. Open all year, hot showers, store, adult/ 5.50 F, tent/3 F, car/3 F. In the "Centre" is a cafeteria available to campers. Its low 1981 prices are "repas complet" which includes a main course with meat and vegetable, cheese, dessert, and drink for 22 F, or 10 meal tickets for 210 F. A "plat du jour" (entree only) costs 13 F.

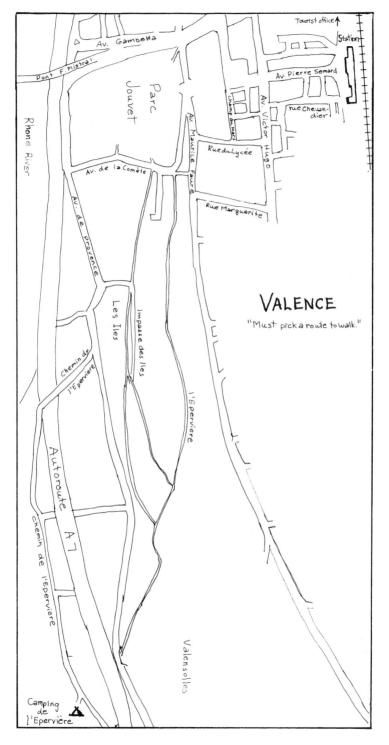

Tourist office↑

Station

Av. Gambetta

Pont F. Mistral

Av. Pierre Semard

rue Chevan-dier

Parc Jouvet

Av. Victor Hugo

Rue du Lycée

Rhone River

Av. Maurice Faure

Rue Marguerite

Av. de la Comète

VALENCE

"Must pick a route to walk."

Av. de Provence

Les Iles

Impasse des Iles

l'Eperviere

Chemin de l'Eperviere

Autoroute A 7

Chemin de l'Eperviere

Valensolles

Camping de l'Eperviere

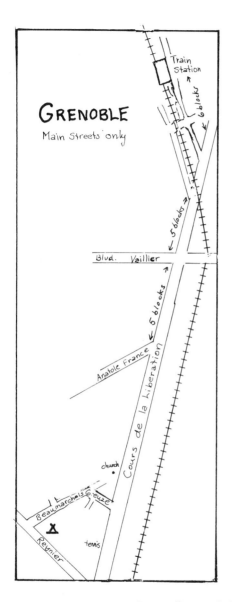

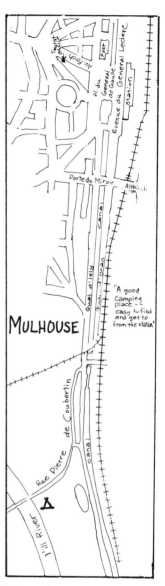

GRENOBLE   Municipal camp "Le Bachelard" is on Avenue Beaumarchais.
Ray Rylander reports, "there are bus lines but it's best to walk." Camp
has hot showers, store, adult/2.80 F, tent/1.50 F, car/1.50 F.

MULHOUSE   There is frequent train service between Mulhouse and Basel,
Switzerland.   It is possible to stay at this camp and make the 30 minute
commute to Basel. Camping L'Ill, rue Pierre-de-Coubertin on the shore
of L'Ill River, is open Easter –Oct 15. It's a very good camp within about

a 20 minute walk from the station. Ray Rylander calls it "easy to find and get to from the station. Hot showers, store. Tourist office is one block from the station. Go out of the station and cross the canal in front, find Avenue Mar.-Foch which is the street that goes north from the east (right) side of the landscaped area. Tourist office is at end of block on left side of street.

STRASBOURG   Tourist office is across from the front of the station. Camping La Montagne Verte, 2 rue Robert-Forrer, is within town. Ray Rylander says, "unless you know good French, it's best to walk. Camp has hot showers.

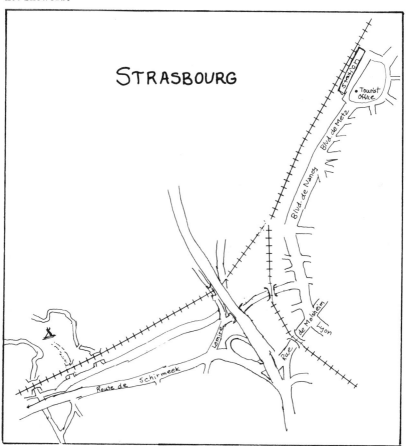

LE HAVRE   Two train stations are Gare Centrale and Gare Maritime. Tourist office is in Place de la Hotel de Ville, 11 blocks west of Central Train Station. Municipal campground Foret de Montgeon is an excellent campsite within the Montgeon Forest and Park.   From Central Station, the camp is 4 km.   Take bus #5 from in front of the Station and get off at the "Cimetiere du Nord." (See map.)   Then a 1 km 300 meter walk through the Park.   Store, free hot showers, lounge, adult/6 F, tent/4 F.   Market is

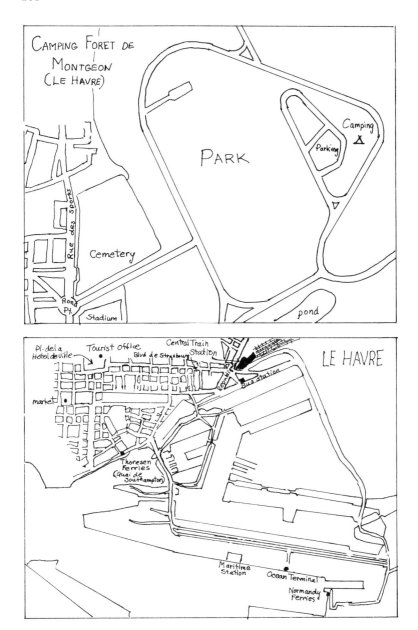

CAMPING FORET DE MONTGEON (LE HAVRE)

PARK

Camping

Parking

Rue des Sports

Cemetery

Rond Pt.

Stadium

pond

Pl. de la Hotel de ville

Tourist office

Central Train Station

Blvd de Strasbourg

LE HAVRE

Bus station

market

Thoresen Ferries (Quai de Southampton)

Maritime Station

Ocean Terminal

Normandy Ferries

on Rue Voltaire, 3 blocks south of Place de l'Hotel de Ville. See introductory section for France for Irish Continental Line departure times. The ferry arrives from Rosslare, Ireland, at 3 pm. A train leaves at 5:10 pm and arrives Paris St. Lazare Station at 7:12 pm.

CHERBOURG   Train Station (central) is 5 blocks from tourist office.
Maritime train station is next to ferry dock。 Camping Municipal is off Rue
de l'Abbaye, within town and walking distance。 This is a small simple camp
and please check to make sure it still exists. Otherwise, Camping
Municipal de la Saline is on a street jutting perpendicularly off D 901 to the
west of town。 Free hot showers。 Market is 4 blocks from tourist office。
(See introductory section on France for Irish Continental Lines departure
times.) To continue to Paris after arriving by sea in Cherbourg at 11 am,
take the train which leaves at 1:58 pm and arrives in Paris St。 Laz are Station at 5:10 pm.

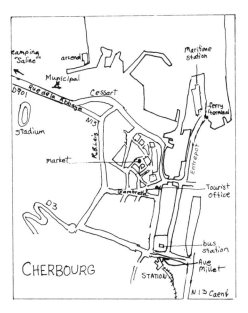

DIJON   Eric Wolsterstorff reports, "The tourist office is at Place Darcy,
east of the train station down Avenue Marechal Foch (M-Sa 9-12, 2-9; Su 10-
12, 3-7). There one can pick up a guide to the city and a bus map. The city
center is lovely, with extensive pedestrian areas。 The Maille store, 32 rue
de la Liberte, displays a beautiful variety of famous Dijon mustards as well
as other sauces and chutneys. There are many Hotels (i. e。 urban palaces)
from the Burgundian heyday in the 15-16th centuries. The Musee des Beaux
Arts (daily 9-12, 2-6, partly closed tuesday; 2 F, free Su) has the Robert
Campin Nativity, Melchior Broederlam's diptych, and the Claus Sluter
sculptures for the tombs of the Dukes of Burgundy. Other Sluter works
nearby include the Moses Well (Puit de Moise) and Chapel Portal, which he
executed for the Chartreuse de Champmol. The monastery being no longer
extant, these two monuments are now located in the grounds of a psychiatric
hospital, free admission. From the train station, follow the signs 800
meters west down Avenue Albert Premier, or take bus 12 or 18."

     "Camping Municipal du Lac--the camp is about 2 km down the same
road, at 43 Ave. Albert Premier, which is also the N-5 route to Sens. Take
bus 18 which originates at the station."

PRONUNCIATION OF FRENCH WORDS

Arles	arl
Avignon	ah-veen-yawn
Brittany	bruh-TAN-yuh
Burgundy	boor-GAWN-yuh
(Bourgogne)	
Caen	kahn
Calais	ka-LEH
Chambord	shahn-bawr
Cherbourg	shehr-BOOR
Corsica (Corse)	kawrss
Cote d'Azur	koht da zeur
Fontainbleau	fohn-ten-BLOH
Geneva	zhuh-nehv
LeHavre	luh AHV-ruh
Lyons	lee-AWN
Marseilles	mar-SAY-yuh
Meus	muhz
Mont St. Michel	maun sen mee-
Nantes	nahnt /SHEHL
Rhone	rohn
Saint Cloud	sen cloo
Saint Malo	sen ma-loh
Strasbourg	strahz-boor
Touraine	too-REHN
Versailles	vehr-SAH-yuh

PARIS

L'Arc de Triomphe	lark duh tree-awnf
La Palais de Chaillot	luh paleh duh shah-yoh
La Conciergerie	la Kawn-see-ehr-zhree
L'Hotel des Invalides	loh-tel day zen-vah-leed
Ile de la Cite	eel duh la see-TAY
La Louvre	luh loov-ruh
La Madeleine	lah mad-lehn
Montparnasse	MAWN pahr nass
Montmarte	mawn-MAR-truh
L'Opera	loh-pay-rah
Le Pantheon	luh pahn-tay-awn
Les Quais	lay kay
Le Palais du Luxembourg	luh pa-leh dew lewk-sahn-
La Sainte-Chapelle	la sent shah-pehl /boor
La Tour Eiffel	la toor ay-fehl
Les Tuileries	lay twee-luh-ree

GERMANY

Castles on the Rhine, medieval Rothenburg, rococo castles of "mad" King Ludwig of Bavaria and modern cities oriented toward the pedestrian, all speak of Germany.

CURRENCY   German mark (Deutsch Mark) is abbreviated DM. One DM equals 44¢ in 1981. There are 2.2 DM to one U.S. dollar. Each German mark is divided into 100 pfennig.

WEATHER   Camping weather stretches from June through September. Rain is always possible in northern Germany and mountain areas.

CAMPING   Tourist office publishes "Camping 1979-80," which contains a map with campgrounds marked, and a listing. Information given is very rudimentary: general rating, basic facilties, noise level, and dates of opening. Nightly fee ranges from adult/2-4 DM, child/1-3 DM, tent/2-4 DM and car/2-4 DM.

TRAINS   German trains are excellent. The German Federal Railroad (abbreviated DB for Deutsche Bundesbahn) carries 1.5 billion passengers annually. Reservations are never needed for travel within Germany because trains run very frequently--for instance, there are over 20 direct trains between Cologne and Frankfurt each day. Germanrail, as the German Federal Railroad has been slicked up to be called in its English language brochures, also operates buses, passenger ferries and commuter trains, almost all of which are included in Eurailpass and Eurail Youthpass. Children under 4 ride free. Those 4-11 inclusive pay half fare. Children 4-13 inclusive pay half fare on ferry boats.

Germanrail offers a Tourist Card which gives unlimited travel on all scheduled trains in Germany for 9 days, first class for $165, second class for $120, and 16 days first class for $220, second class $165. You also get reduced rates on the steamers on the Rhine and Moselle Rivers, and a free trip on the Romantic Road bus to Rothenburg as well as other bonuses. Unique with this ticket is the cut-rate price of 28 DM for second class roundtrip fare to Berlin plus a free city sightseeing tour by bus. This ticket should be bought from a German Federal Railroad office in the U.S.

Other special rail plans which are available at train stations in Germany include a Senior Citizen Ticket (Senioren Pass) for women of 60 and men of 65 which entitles the holder to purchase all rail tickets at half price. Pass A costs 60 DM and allows either first or second class travel on Tuesday, Wednesday or Thursday only. Pass B costs 110 DM and allows travel on any day. Tickets on buses operated by Germanrail and the German Post Office can be bought at a discount. The "Junior Pass" allows people from 12 to 23 to buy rail tickets at half price for travel any time for 110 DM.

German trains are classified as TEE, IC (fast deluxe inter-city trains within Germany), D (all other express services), and E (semi-fast trains). A local or commuter train is called "Nahverkehrszug." From Hamburg to Copenhagen takes 4-1/2 hours. From Cologne to Amsterdam--2-3/4 hours, to Brussels--2-1/2 hours, and to Paris--4-3/4 hours. From Frankfurt to Amsterdam takes 6 hours, to Paris--7 hours, to Zurich--5 hours. From Munich to Innsbruck takes 1-3/4 hours, to Salzburg--1-3/4 hours and to Vienna--5-1/2 hours. Germanrail office in the U.S. will send you the free German Railroad schedule, "Schnellzug Fahrplan."

A seat reservation costs 2.50 DM when made in Germany. If it is a weekend and likely to be crowded, go to the station early and check the departures board for a last minute train that may have been added to carry the overload in summer. Extra trains usually leave either a few minutes before or after the regularly scheduled train. Reservations for buses of the German Federal Railroad are made at the train reservation window of the train station and often the bus leaves from outside the train station.

When boarding a train, note class designation, routing and final destination to be sure you board the right car. As some German trains split enroute, it's obviously important that you sit in a coach whose destination coincides with your own. Free baggage carts (koffer-kulis) are provided at the larger stations. Coin-operated lockers cost 1 DM for small and 1.50 DM for the large size for 24 hours. Train stations are well-organized with helpful pictorial signs.

| zug - train | gleis - track | abfahrt - departures |
| wagen - car | platz - seat | ankunft - arrivals |

reisedatum - date of departure	bis - until
abfahrtszeit - time of departure	So - sunday
auskunft - train information	Mo - monday
platzkarte - seat reservations	Di - tuesday
ab - departure time	Mi - wednesday
an - arrival time	Do - thursday
taglich - daily service	Fr - friday
nur - except	Sa - saturday

The "Romantic Road" Eurapabus is included in Eurailpass and Eurail Youthpass, and goes between Frankfurt and Munich. The trip varies the train riding a bit and lets you see Germany from the road. The highlight of the ride is the two hour stop in Rothenburg, a fascinating old walled village of the Middle Ages, now designated a museum town. This town on the Tauber River was a free city of the Holy Roman Empire from 1274 to 1803. Its architecture is mostly Gothic and Renaissance and the town is definitely worth seeing. (Camping Tauber Idyll is 3 km north of Rothenburg on Romantische Strasse, open Apr-Oct, hot showers, store--but two hours is sufficient to see the town.) A reservation (free) is necessary for the bus and can be made at the seat reservations office or train ticket window at a train station. In Frankfurt, Eurapabus office is outside the train station. You may stop off overnight or join the bus from another town enroute, but this should be indicated when the reservation is made. The bus operates every day in both directions from April to October. An English speaking hostess provides sightseeing commentary enroute. The journey breaks for two hours in Rothenburg and about one hour in its sister medieval town, Dinkelsbuhl. (Dinkelsbuhl is not so determinedly picturesque as Rothenburg and its architecture is more relaxed. A campground is outside the walls across the moat beyond Wornitz Castle, and within walking distance.) The time in Dinkelsbuhl is sufficient for sightseeing provided you have packed a lunch to eat enroute so precious layover time can be used to see the town.

The "Romantic Road" bus leaves Wiesbaden from Hotel Nassauer Hof at 7 am, and departs Frankfurt from outside Central Station at 8:15 am. Bus arrives in Wurzburg at 10:00 am, spends from 11:30-1:45 in Rothenburg, arrives in Dinkelsbuhl at 2:30 pm and leaves at 3:30 pm. Augsburg is reached at 5:35 pm and Munich at 6:55 pm at Central Station. From Munich to Frankfurt/Wiesbaden, the bus leaves from outside the Hauptbahnhof (main station) on the right side as you face it (see map under "Munich") at 9 am. Bus arrives in Augsburg at 10:10 am. From 12:35 to 2:15 is spent in Dinkelsbuhl. Rothenburg is reached at 3:15 and left at 5 pm. Bus arrives in Wurzburg at 6:10 pm and at Frankfurt's Central Station at 8 pm. Arrival in Wiesbaden (Hotel Nassauer Hof) is at 8:45 pm.

Railpasses are also valid on certain ferry passenger boats on the Rhine River (see Rhine River: Koblenz to Bingen) and Mosel River; ferry crossings from Puttgarden to Rodby, Denmark; and on most of the bus lines of the integrated bus transport Post/Railroad bus union of which the "Romantic Road" bus is an example. Railpass holders receive a 50% reduction on regular steamer services of German Federal Railroad on Lake Constance. The S-bahn has been constructed by the German Federal Railroads in several cities to link the suburbs with the downtown center and these DB trains are included in the Eurail and Eurail Youthpass.

The following map shows the inter-city rail network within Germany.
Service is frequent enough on these lines that reservations shouldn't be
necessary. Please note that this is not a map of the complete rail routes
in Germany, but only the most important routes. (Courtesy GermanRail)

INTERCITY

DRIVING   Germany's freeways are called "autobahnen" and are marked
with blue signs. Speed limit is 140 km/h (81 mph). Rest areas are marked
"Parkplatz" and have tables and garbage cans but not always toilets.
"Ausfahrt" means exit. Autobahn that is parallel with the Rhine River is
clogged with trucks, but they stay in the right hand lane so traffic still
moves speedily.   Remember to keep to the right and use the left lane only
when passing. Service areas have been built along the autobahnen that
include gas station, restaurant, restrooms and usually a play equipment

area for children.

Main highways and smaller roads are marked with yellow signs. Speed limit is 100 km/h (62 mph). Sightseeing attractions within cities have white signs. Speed limit in cities is 50 km/h (31 mph).

TOURIST OFFICE   Called Verkehrsamt.

FOOD   In 1981, one liter of milk ranges from 1 DM to 1.30 with about 1.10 DM being about average, 500 grams of bread cost about 1.40 DM and one whole hot cooked chicken about 8 DM. Grocery prices are lowest in the public market. Supermarkets and food sections of department stores have the next best prices and have weekly specials just like in the U.S. "Backereien" is a bakery and it often sells coffee too. Milk and cheese are bought at a "molkereien." "Konditoreien" are cafe type pastry shops that sometimes have sit-down tables, but the pastry usually costs more than at a backereien.

Whole milk is "voll milch," skim milk is "magermilch." Apple juice (apfelsaft) and apple cider (appelwoi) are widely available, sometimes packed in liter milk-type cartons. The Rhine and Mosel are famous for their fine wines, but bottled ones are expensive. It is helpful to know that all restaurants have an open table wine (offenen wien) which is pleasant and cheaper. You can order a glass (pokal or glas) or a carafe. Wine is sold in the supermarket too.

As far as dining out, the food situation in Germany is similar to that in the United States. Small fast food places like a bratwurst eaterie or a Schnell-Imbiss serve a limited menu, reliably and reasonably. Wurst (sausage like frankfurters) comes in many varieties with pork bratwurst being the most common and the German equivalent of our short-order hamburger. Small bratwurst places dot every German city. In most of these, you order from the counter and then take your sausage and roll to standing height tables, add your own mustard (senf) and eat. A more extensive menu is found at a Schnell-Imbiss. Here's where you can pick up a rotisseried chicken, french fries, salad and more to take out or eat at standing height tables.

Because restaurants are expensive (and you should save your restaurant money for France), most meals will probably be taken at department store cafeterias or fast-food places. A department store usually has its cheapest cafeteria in the basement and often the food is consumed at standing height tables. If you do eat in a restaurant, most offer a daily special called "tellergericht, gedeck, sonder angebot or tages spezialitaten" at the noontime meal. Price on the menu normally includes the sales tax (mehrwertsteuer) and service charge (bedienung). When ordering from the regular menu, keep in mind that those items listed under "fleischgerichte" or "fertige speisen" are already prepared and can be served quickly. The German takes his heaviest meal at lunchtime. The evening meal will be lighter and perhaps a casserole or sandwiches will be served. Waitress is addressed as "fraulein" and waiter as "herr ober."

SHOPPING   Shopping hours are usually 9-6:30 with an early 2 pm closing on Saturday. German goods are very costly but can still be a good buy if a high quality camera or binocular with high rate of duty is bought and imported into U.S. under your tourist exemption. Amount of savings will depend almost entirely upon amount of import duty a U.S. store would have had to pay. To have the value added tax refunded, save all sales receipts and have them stamped by German customs as you leave the country. Then mail stamped receipts back to the store, and it's the store's responsibility to refund the money. Tell the store that you will be doing this so it will give you the correct forms. When entering a small shop, the custom is to greet the clerk with a "guten tag" or equivalent, and to say "auf wiederschen" as you leave.

HIKING   Hiking is very popular in Germany and a list of hostels, huts and lookout towers can be obtained from Verband Deutscher Gevirgs-und Wandervereine, D7 Stuttgart 1, Hospitalstrasse 21b, West Germany.

BICYCLING   Bicycles are rented at about 300 train stations for 8 DM a day. Train ticket holders receive a 50% reduction.

PRONUNCIATION OF PLACE NAMES   Aachen (AH-ken), Augsburg (OUKS-bork), Baden Baden (BAH-dun BAH-dun), Bayreuth (by-ROIT), Braunschweig (BRAWN-schvike), Cologne (kuh-LONE), Garmisch Partenkirchen (GAR-mish PAR-ten-kir-ken), Mainz (mynts), Mannheim (MAN-hyme), Munich (MYOO-nik), Oberammergau (oh-ber-AHM-er-go), Schwabisch-Hall (SHVA-bish-HAHL), Stuttgart (STUT-gahrt), Trier (treer), Westphalia (west-FAY-lyah), Wiesbaden (VEES-bah-den), Wurzburg (VURTS-bork).

CASTLES ON THE RHINE ** BINGEN TO KOBLENZ

Rail passes are valid on ferry passenger boats operated by Koln-Dusseldorfer-Deutsche Rheinschiffahrt (KD line) on regularly scheduled runs on the Rhine River between Dusseldorf and Frankfurt. Hydrofoil Rheinpfeil is not included. Schedule is available from tourist office. Most scenic portion is between Koblenz and Bingen which takes 2-3/4 hours downstream (Bingen to Koblenz) or 4-3/4 hours upstream. Once a day express service called "schnell-fahrt" leaves Bingen at 10:30 am and arrives in Koblenz at Rheinwerft near Deutsches Eck at 1:15 pm. Several small towns along the Rhine have a campground accessible to backpackers who wish to stop overnight. Directions are included for Bacharach, St. Goar, St. Goarshausen and Boppard. Below are boat schedules for about June 20 to August 29. Schnellfahrt (express) service is the same in other months, but ordinary service is curtailed. Eurail Youthpass holders must pay a supplement for Schnellfahrt service. Boats stop at more towns than listed below. (* is schnellfahrt.)

MAINZ TO KOBLENZ

Mainz Am Rathaus	* 8:45		9:00	10:15	11:00		
Rudesheim	10:15	9:50	10:35	11:50	12:35	2:00	4:20
Bingen	10:30	10:15	10:50	12:05	12:50	2:15	4:35
Bacharach	11:10	11:06	11:41	12:45	1:41	3:06	5:25
St. Goar	11:40	-	12:25	1:15	-	-	6:05
St. Goarshausen	-	11:55	-	1:20	2:30	3:55	6:15
Boppard	12:20	12:35	1:05	-	3:37	5:02	7:22
Koblenz	1:15	1:40	-	-	4:15	7:40	8:00

KOBLENZ TO MAINZ   *

Koblenz	7:30	9:00	-	-	12:30	2:00	2:30
Boppard	9:05	10:35	-	1:35	2:05	3:25	4:05
St. Goars-							
hausen	10:05	11:40	1:35	2:35	3:05	4:20	5:05
St. Goar	10:15	11:45	1:45	2:45	3:15	4:25	5:15
Bacharach	11:15	12:48	2:45	3:45	4:15	5:20	6:15
Bingen	12:40	2:10	4:00	5:10	5:40	6:35	7:40
Rudesheim	12:50	2:20	4:15	5:25	5:55	6:50	7:50
Mainz							
Am Rathaus	-	-	6:05	7:25	7:55	8:50	-

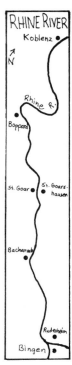

KOBLENZ (Coblence)   Tourist office is in round building
across from station. Use pedestrian underpass. Open M-Sa
8:30-8:00, Su 1-7. Post office is outside station to right. Bus
#1 (1.20 DM) from in front of three small shops in the plaza
in front of the train station, terminates at Deutsches Eck,
from which the ferry dock, Rhein werft, is a short distance.
Camping Rhein-Mosel is opposite the Deutsches Eck monument at the confluence of the Rhine and Mosel Rivers. To
get there from where the passenger ferry lets you off at
Rhein werft, walk to the Deutsches Eck monument and then
go past it and then walk down to the Mosel River where you
will see a tiny dock where you must wait for the motorboat
to come from across the river and take you across to the
camp. A fee is charged for the ride. Last boat leaves at 7 pm.
Ray Rylander contributed these directions to the camp from
the train station. "Take bus #4 from Hauptbahnhof to Schwarzerweg and
walk. Beautiful place right on the river. Stop at Koblenz when you miss the
train to Luxembourg. (After drinking that wonderful Mosel wine you may not
want to go on to Luxembourg!)"

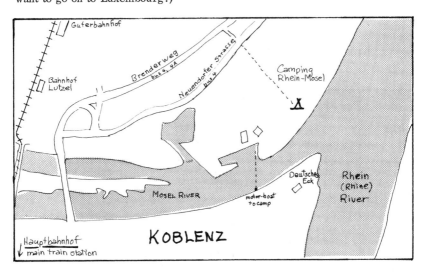

KOBLENZ

BOPPARD   Camping Sonneneck is north of town, 5 km from Boppard
Station, isolated from ferry dock, town and restaurants. Camp is located
between highway and river. Local train stop is "Ohlenberg," but we don't
know what kind of service it has, if any. Backpackers are advised to spend
the night at a more convenient camp.

ST. GOAR   This is a small town with Burg Rheinfels (castle). Camping
Loreleyblock, on Bundestrasse (the main riverside highway) is on the southern edge of town. Camp is 1 km from train station or ferry dock. From station, walk to river and turn right onto Bundestrasse (highway). Camp is
directly on beach--not as good as camp at Bacharach. Burg Rheinfels is
open daily 9-6, adult/2 DM, child/1 DM, student, groups/.75 DM.

ST. GOARSHAUSEN   Camping is on Rhine River north of town about 1 km
from ferry dock.

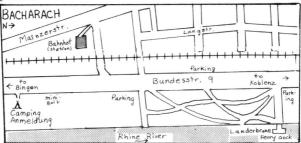

BACHARACH   This small village has Camping Anmeldung which is 200
meters from the station (bahnhof) or 1/2 km from ferry boat dock (lande-
brucke). Camp is next to Rhine River, windy, some trees, good restroom
facilities, store, modern restaurant with terrace overlooking the Rhine.
Camp fees are about adult over 18/3.00 DM, child 12-18/2 DM, child under
12/1.50 DM, car or van/3.00 DM.

BINGEN   Trains from Mainz and Cologne stop at Bingen Bahnhof. Across
street on right is tourist office (verkehrsamt), open M-Sa 9-7, Su 9-12.
Ferry dock for Rhine excursion boats is three blocks away. Campground is
east of town on Rhine River in suburb of Kempten. Bus to Kempten leaves
every 20 minutes across the street from the station. Ride is 10 minutes plus
there is a five minute walk to the camp. Bingen's second and less important
station is called Bingen-Bingerbruck. For a more picturesque evening, you
might want to take the ferry across the river to Rudesheim which has narrow
alleys, overhanging houses with flower boxes and lots of wine taverns. The
town is not authentic as it was built up after the war, but it was nicely done
and attracts lots of merry-makers. There is a free tour through a distillery.
You must walk to its campground at the edge of town. Frances Packer
writes: "We got off the Rhine steamer here around 7 pm. They have a wine
festival for a week (started Sept 5). Very nice! "
      Stopping at any small town on the Rhine or Mosel Rivers between July
and mid-October, posters announcing the dates of a nearby Wine Festival
will be posted on the train station walls. Though called this, the date
usually has no relation to the actural harvest which occurs between mid-
September and November depending on the weather.

BERLIN

Ray Fylander who spent two weeks in Berlin gave us this information. "From Berlin-Zoo, take U-Bahn to <u>Ruhleben</u> (end of line). Change to bus #35 and ride about 30 minutes to Krampnitzer Weg. Walk about 1.5 km down the road to the Wall and the very excellent camping-platz is on the left at end of road. During rush hours, another little bus (#35 E) will halve the walking. Sometimes there is a lot of noise from the other side of the Wall: shouting and dogs barking, etc., but this is the only year round camping in Berlin."

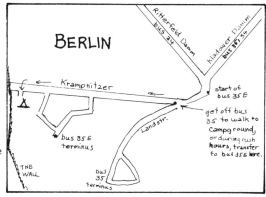

Eric Wolterstorff adds "City information is in Europaplatz near the train station, Berlin-Zoo (walk east past the ruined Gedachtnisskirche). Public transportation maps cost 1 DM at the tourist office or at a public transport kiosk. One can purchase 2-day and 4-day tourist tickets for 13 DM and 24 DM, respectively, or a 5-ride Sammelkarte for 7.20 DM. Single tickets, allowing unlimited transfers in one direction for 1-1/2 hours, cost 1.70 DM. The tourist office has an inadequate but helpful map with important sights marked, and a comprehensive list of museums. These many superb museums are open 9-5 except Monday. All those which are state run, as part of the Preussischekulturbesitz, are free."

"Camping Cladow, Krampnitzer Weg 111-117, open year round, is the one mentioned in the book. Under the complicated charge system, I paid 8.79 DM per night. The camp is a long way from the center of town, but the facilities are excellent and it's a pleasant place to stay. Bus 35E is just a shuttle connecting to the main route 35. One should check the posted schedule by the bus stops, since 35E doesn't run very often. When it does run, it is designed to drop one opposite the stop for bus 35 a few minutes before a bus is scheduled to depart for Ruhleben."

COLOGNE (KOLN)

Cologne is a busy railway junction with over 200 international connections and a huge terminal. Cathedral (Dom) and most important museums are within walking distance of the station.

TRAIN STATION   The terminal is very busy with many people, shops and snack counters. Train information is open daily 6 am-10 pm. Exchange office is open M-Sa 7 am-9 pm, Su 8 am-9 pm. Pedestrian shopping street, Hohe Strasse, begins two blocks from station on other side of Cathedral.

TOURIST INFORMATION   Not located within the station, the tourist office is outside opposite the main entrance of the Cathedral. Open M-Sa 8 am-10:30 pm.

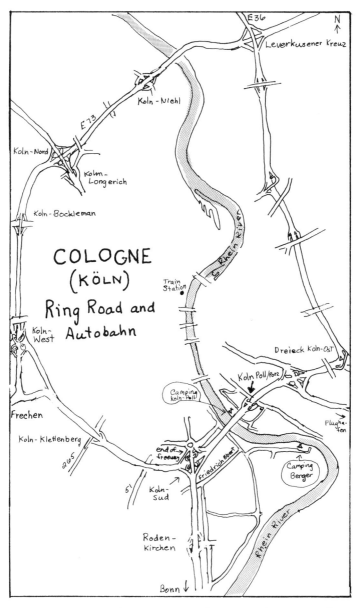

COLOGNE
(KÖLN)
Ring Road and
Autobahn

CAMPGROUNDS Koln- Poll Camping, Weidenweg, is the municipal campground (Stadtischer Familienzeltplatz) for families. Open May–Oct 10. Best
way is to take subway line 16 from inside train station to Marienburg and
then walk across the autobahn bridge. Once across, look for stairs to
the land below. Alternatively, you can take subway 9, 11, 12 or 16 to Neumarkt, change to tram #7 and get off at Drehbrucke stop. Camp is next to
the autobahn (Rodenkirchener Brucke) bridge. By car, the autobahn coming

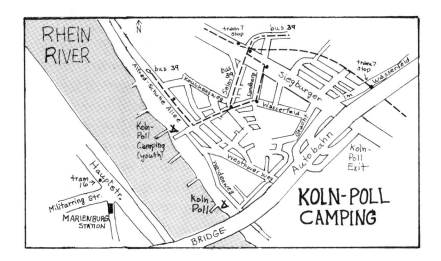

from Bonn connects with the ring road before reaching downtown. At the
ring road where the autobahn ends (before it peters out and leaves you in the
city), go in the direction of the airport, Flughafen, but get off at first exit,
"Poll, " across the Rhine River. Hot showers, store, washing machine.
    Koln-Poll Camping, Alfred-Schutte-Allee nearby Koln-Poll Camping,
is the municipal campground (Jugendzeltplatz) for young people. Open July-
Sept 15. Same directions as for previous camp, but if you take tram #7,
transfer to bus #39 which will bring you closer to camp.
    Camping Berger, in Rodenkirchen at Uferstrasse 53 A, is open all year.
Take subway #16 from inside train station and get off Marienburg. Change to
tram #16 (direction Rodenkirchen) which stops on Hauptstrasse, the road that
parallels the Rhine, and ride to terminus. (You should be traveling with
the Rhine River on your leftside.) By car on the autobahn coming from Bonn,
take Rodenkirchen exit which is before the autobahn connects with the ring
road. Hot showers, store, restaurant, washing machine.

YOUTH, HOSTELS   Jugendherberge-Konrad Adenauer Ufer. Take back
exit from railway station and walk as far as the Rhine embankment, turn left,
follow Rhine embankment to Elsa Brandstromstrasse. About 20 minutes walk.
    Jugendherberge Koln-Deutz, Siegesstrasse. Take back exit from train
station and walk towards the Rhine River (about two blocks) and cross the
river on the bridge (Hohenzollernbrucke). After crossing the bridge, in about
one long block you come to the main intersection Ottoplatz. Cross Ottoplatz.
If train stops at Koln-Deutz station, get off there and cross Ottoplatz in front.

CITY TRANSPORTATION   Buses, trams and U-Bahn are integrated into
one system. A ticket office is in the train station. Trams and buses have
no conductor and tickets are sold from vending machines at stops, and
validated in the machine on the bus or tram, which stamps date, hour and
direction on the ticket. Transfers are allowed in same direction within one
hour. Fare is adult/2 DM, child/1 DM, or 3 adult tickets/4 DM, 4 child
tickets/3 DM. There are also many commuter trains operated by the railroad.

FOOD   Supermarkets are in the basement of department stores Kaufhalle
and Kaufhog on Hohe Strasse (pedestrian shopping street near station); and
Hertie and Karstadt department stores are near Neumarkt.

SIGHTSEEING   This 2000 year old city founded by the Romans displays art
treasures and monuments from every period in its well done museums.
(Ask for tourist office illustrated map, and consider purchasing their
visitor's guide "Koln" for .50 DM which gives history and museum information.)
    Focal point of the city is the large Cathedral next to the train station.
Begun in 1248 and completed in 1880, this world-famous Gothic building contains many art treasures such as the Golden Shrine of the Magi (12th century).
Open 5:45 am-7:30 pm. In summer, organ concerts Tuesday evenings.
Guided tours in German starting from the altar M-F 10, 11, 2:30, 3:30 and 4.
    Romano-Germanic Museum on the southside of the Cathedral cost 25
million marks to build in 1974. The building, display methods and contents
are all worth seeing. Two of its most prized possessions are the Dionysos
mosaic (2nd century A. D) and the 40 foot high funeral monument of Poblicius
(1st century A. D.). Innovative display techniques include the use of T-bars
of steel painted in pompeian red, instead of the usual stone or marble bases,
for head sculptures and fragments. Life-sized copies of the exterior of a
Roman guard tower and Roman coach are shown. In each department, color
slides give background information on the exhibits.
    Wallraf-Richartz Museum/Museum Ludwig, An der Rechteshule, are
open Tu-Su 10-5, Tu & Th to 8 pm. Here are paintings from the Middle Ages
to present with one of the most complete selections of European modern art
in Germany, including the pop art of the Ludwig collection.
    Josef-Haubrich Kunsthalle near Neumarkt is worth checking for special
large-scale exhibitions of ancient or modern art. Museums are open daily
10-5, except Mondays , and cost adult/2 DM, child/1 DM.
    The beautifully designed Cologne opera house on Offenbachplatz offers
its cheapest seats for 10 DM, which may be available even on the day of the
performance.

DUISBURG

North of Cologne, Duisburg is an industrial city with many wonderful free
museums, but no campground. Tourist office is across from train station.
Duisburg's outstanding museum of modern sculpture opened in 1964 is only
500 meters from the train station. Horten Department store is diagonally
across from the museum. The city has very frequent train service and worth
visiting for its museums and modern areas. Youth Hostel is in Duisburg
Wedau and can be reached by bus #934 or 944 from train station.

Wilhelm-Lehmbruck Museum, Friedrich-Wilhelm Strasse 40 is open
W, Th, Sa, Su 10-5; Tu & F 2-10 pm. Free entry. Checking-room (for your
pack) and restrooms are downstairs under the lobby. The sales desk has a
free color postcard of Brancusi sculpture, free small reproduction of drawing by Paul Klee, posters for 1 DM, large Picasso poster reproduction for
5 DM, signed lithographs starting at 10 DM, catalogs for .50-2.50 DM and
good reproductions for 6 DM. The striking steel and concrete museum is

within a city park (benches available). Even
if the museum building is closed, most of
the sculpture can still be seen by walking
around outside, and children enjoy the
ponds among the sculptures. Some inside
walls are textured cement that looks like
rough hewed lumber. Lots of Lembruck's
nude sculptures (male and female) are in
this area. Other walls have white rocks
embedded in cement. One small room has a
wall sculpture in movable units that can be
rearranged by the visitor. There is a far-
out piece by Gunther Vecker of a square
white block covered with nails, and a
tableau of five wounded and dead figures by
Duane Hanson, 1967, called "Vietnam
Piece." A painting of wild creatures by Max
Ernst caught the attention of our 4 year old
son. Lots of well known names are represented here such as Giacometti, Barlach,
Brancusi, Hepworth and Moore; and there's
even a roomful of Paul Klee's pictures, but

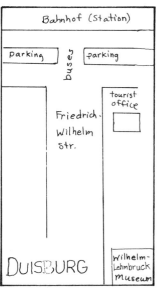

even more works are by lesser known artists which should give the Wilhelm-
Lehmbruck Museum some sort of distinction in the broad representation of
artists category.

FRANKFURT

This may well be your arrival city as its airport is one of the largest in the
world and used by 14 million persons each year. Otherwise we would skip it.

AIRPORT (Flughafen)   There is a train station right at the airport to
whisk you wherever you want to go, quickly and in style! The Eurailpass,
Eurail Youthpass and GermanRail Tourist Card may be validated at the ticket
office in the Airport railway station which is across from the customs exit.
Otherwise, obtain a ticket before entering the train at the ticket office in
arrival hall B or at ticket vending machines which have instructions in
English. One-way second class ticket costs about 1.50 DM to Frankfurt
main station (Hauptbahnhof). Trains also go directly to Mainz in 25 minutes
and Wiesbaden in 40 minutes with about hourly service. In 1978, the airport railway station also began offering direct rail connections to Cologne,
Darmstadt, Dusseldorf, Ludwigshafen, Mannheim and Saarbruecken in addition to Mainz and Wiesbaden. These longer distance trains are specially
marked with light and dark blue stripes around the cars and the friendly
slogan: "Ihr Zug zum Flug" (your train to the plane).

TRAIN STATION (Hauptbahnhof)   The station has many facilities including exchange office, train information window (auskunft), seat reservations office (around the corner from windows 10 and 11) and restaurants. Eurapabus office is outside. Tourist office, verkehrsverein, is in the north wing. Trams leave from Bahnhofplatz in front of station which is reached through the underground passage under the station plaza.

TOURIST INFORMATION   Train station office is opposite track 23, M-Sa 8 am-10 pm, Su 9:30 am-8 pm. Hauptwache station office, level B, M-F 9-6.

CAMPGROUNDS   Camping Niederrader Ufer, Alte Schleuse, is closest. Take tram #15 from main station. Get off at Heinrich-Hofmann-Strasse. Camp has hot showers, snack bar, store. Camping Heddernheim is at Sandelmuhl. Hot showers, snack bar, store. Ray Rylander has camped at both and says: "From the Frankfurt Flughafen, you can take the local S-bahn into town to the main Hauptbahnhof - the S 14 line. From there (as you say in your book), take the tram 15 to the Niederrad Camping platz. (But I walked, it is so close). A good place, right on the river. But for the Heddernheim Camping Platz, from the Hauptbahnhof, you must either: (1) change to S-bahn lines S1, S2, S3... (any of them) to S6 in the direction of "Hauptwache." At Hauptwache, change to U-bahn lines U1, U2, or U3, and ride out to Heddernheim Station. The camp is just a short walk away up the Sandelmuhle. Or (2) from Hauptbahnhof, change to U-bahn line U 5, and get off at the very first stop "Theaterplatz," where you change for U-bahn lines U 1, U 2, or U 3 as before.   Niederrad is the better camping place, but the people at Heddernheim are more friendly. The manager, a Frau Thacker, is a wonderful old lady."   Camping Heddernheim is open all year.

Eric Wolterstorff adds, "the tourist office in the train station has free U-Bahn/S-Bahn guides and city maps, as well as an excellent comprehensive map of all city transportation. At DM 6, the 24-hour ticket is a bargain if one has to get around the city. Don't be a Schwarzfahrer; there are frequent ticket inspections. Camping Niederrader. Take tram 15 or 19 from the station. Get off across the river just after passing under the train trestle. The camp is just west of the tracks, where they cross the river. The walk is about 30 minutes without the tram, and may not be entirely safe as the station is on the edge of one of Germany's most crime-ridden areas. I found the camp grim and unfriendly; I was charged DM 6 per night for a small plot of gravel immediately next to a permanently docked vacation trailer."

YOUTH HOSTEL, situated at Deutschherrnufer 12, is reached by bus #46 from the station.

CITY TRANSPORTATION   There are buses, trams, U-Bahn and S-Bahn. S-Bahn is free with Eurailpasses. Single ticket is 1.30 DM, except 1.60 DM during rush hours. Ticket books give a discount. 24-hour ticket costs 6 DM.

FOOD   Fruit and vegetable market is the Kleinmarkthalle downtown, and is open 9-6. Department stores are on Rossmarkt and Zeil streets.

SIGHTSEEING   Art gallery, Stadel'sches Kunstinstitute, shows both Old

Masters and contemporary works, and is free on Sunday from 10-5. Frankfurt Zoo is open 8 am-sunset, with admission about 3 DM or free on Sunday. Take tram #3, 9 or 15--main gate is at Alfred-Brehm-Platz. Sachsenhausen is the old quarter of Frankfurt on the other side of the Main River. Get there by crossing the Alte Brucke (old bridge). Here is where the wine taverns are where the drink is apple wine. Intercontinental Hotel, 43 Wilhelm-Leuschner Strasse near the river and about four blocks from the station, has decorations by Picasso inside.

FREIBURG

Thanks go to Ray Rylander for this information: "From Hauptbahnhof (main station), take tram #3 or 4 (going toward the direction Littenweiler--right or south from station). Get off at Messehalle --big buildings and parking lot on right. Go down under street and north (left) on Hirzbergstrasse past a church and a school--across a little creek and then to the left again along Str. Average campingplatz is on the right up the hill. Many good hikes from Freiburg into the Schwartzwald."

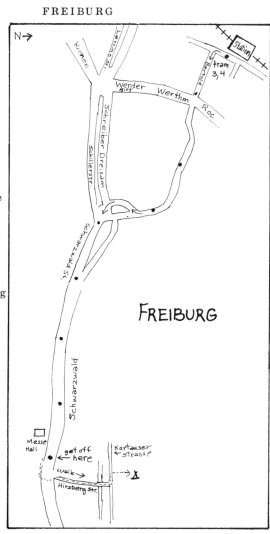

222

GARMISCH - PARTENKIRCHEN

Garmisch-Partenkirchen is pronounced GAR-mish PAR-ten-kir-ken. Ray Rylander advises: "Take the bus along Zugspitzerstrasse to Grainaurweg. Excellent camping with store nearby and free showers."

HAMBURG

Hamburg is a green city with even more canals than Venice. It has a well-developed industry, is a major trade center, and international seaport and, after New York, the second largest consular city in the world. It's a worthwhile stopover on the way to Copenhagen.

TRAIN STATIONS   Hamburg has three important ones. Hauptbahnhof is the main station, Hamburg-Altona and Hamburg-Dammtor are the others. The S-Bahn (free with railpasses) uses tracks 1 and 2 of the main station. Main station is connected to Hamburg-Altona Station by S-Bahn. Hauptbahnhof is the principal point of arrival and departure for long distance trains. Exchange office is open 6:30 am-11 pm. The Hotel Accommodation Service (Hotelnachweis der FVZ) of the Tourist Office (Hachmannplatz exit) is open 7 am-11:30pm and has tourist information. Other side of station funnels into Glockengiesserwall, pedestrian tunnel to Spitalerstrasse, and shopping street, Moenckeberg-strasse.

TOURIST INFORMATION   Main office (Fremdenverkehrszentrale Hamburg e. V.) is outside station in Bieberhaus on Hachmannplatz.

GARMISCH-PARTENKIRCHEN

map has been foreshortened

CAMPGROUNDS   Most convenient camps are on Kieler Strasse near the zoo (Tierpark) and have beer gardens attached. The following two camps can be reached from the main station by subway U 2 to "schlump" and then by bus #182. S-Bahn has a line to this part of the city, Eidelstedt, but the bus goes much closer to the camps and is preferable. Camping Anders is in Hamburg-Eidelstedt at 650 Kieler

Strasse. Adult/3 DM child/1 DM, tent/from 3 DM. Camping Bruning is in Hamburg-Stellingen at Kronsaalsweg 861, Kieler Strasse. Adult/3 DM, child/1 DM, tent/from 3.50 DM.   Camping Buchholz has been closed.

Mr. and Mrs. Robert Cooper have sent these excellent directions to Camping Anders: "Take bus #188 from Steinerplatz outside main station to last stop. Change to bus #183 which will take you to Kieler Strasse. The campground is a five minute walk. The total time spent on buses was forty minutes. General information about the campground--small store and restaurant, hot shower (.50 DM), small sand-box, swings, washer, cooking plates and sinks to hand wash clothes. To return to Hauptbahnhof--5 minute walk to bus stop marked Reichsbahn Strasse. Take bus #182 to last stop marked Sternschanze. On the right side of street you will see U Schump. This is the U-Bahn. Take U 2, Gleis 4, to Hauptbahnhof Nord. The bus ticket costs 1.50 DM--transferable in same direction for two hours."

CITY TRANSPORTATION   Hamburg has a very well developed subway system with six of its nine most important lines being on the S-Bahn which is included in railpasses. The other three are U-Bahn lines, plus there are three suburban lines run by private companies that tack onto the end of the S-Bahn or U-Bahn. Tourist office has a subway map. All buses leave from Steintor Platz outside main station. Fares vary from 1-2 DM for adults, with average fare being 1.50 DM. Children up to 12 years pay .70 DM on all routes.

HVV (Hamburg Transport Association) is a group of eight companies using the same tickets. Hence a ticket can be used interchangeably on sub-way, bus or on regular boat services on the Alster and around the harbor. HVV sells a Tourist Ticket for 6 DM valid from 9 am of the day of issue until 4:30 am the following day on all buses, trams, subways within zone 2, and Hadag harbor ferries and Alster steamers (but not the harbor or Alster sightseeing tours).   Buy it at the Tourist Information or Hotel Accommodation Service.

FOOD   Market is near the main station at the market halls. Open M-F 12-6, Sa 10-4. Suburban markets are held twice weekly. Fish Market sells more than just fish and has become a minor flea market. Open Sunday morning from 6-9:30. No license is needed to sell there. Department stores are on Moeckebergstrasse.

SIGHTSEEING   Admission to state-owned museums is adult/1 DM, child/ .50 DM, Wednesday/free. Museums are closed Monday. Contemporary art is conveniently grouped in three museums in one block of Glockengiesser-wall, two blocks from Hauptbahnhof (station). Hamburg Art Gallery (Hamburger Kunsthalle) has French Impressionists and works by Klee, Friedrich and Runge. Open Tu-Su 10-5, Wednesday to 7 pm. Kunstverein next door holds exhibitions of modern artists and in the past has featured the works of Picasso, Klee and Rauschenberg. Open Tu-Su 10-6, Wednesday to 8 pm. Adult/2 DM. Kunsthaus on Ferdinandstor and next to the Art Gallery, houses contemporary paintings, sculpture and graphic art. Open Tu-Su 10-6, Wednesday to 8 pm. Adult/2 DM.

Museum of Fine Arts and Crafts, on Steintorplatz across from the station, contains European arts and crafts from pre-history to present, art of Near and Far East and graphic art and folk art collections. Open Tu-Su 10-5, Wednesday to 7 pm.

Museum of Hamburg's History (Museum fuer Hamburgische Geschichte) at Holstenwall 24 (towards St. Pauli-Landungsbruecken where harbor tours leave), contains a navigation section with models of ships from the Vikings to modern day ocean liners, model of Hammaburg Castle and a large model railway. Open Tu-Su 10-5. Take U-Bahn to St. Pauli station.

Outdoor Museum Kiekebert, at Ehestorf near Hamburg, is a large moorland farm with sheep-fold, draw-well, beehives and baking oven. Open M-F 8-5, SaSu 10-6.

Hamburg Zoo (Hagenbecks. Tierpark) is a privately owned zoo in Stellingen. Take U-Bahn to Tierpark station. Adult/8 DM, child 3-14/4 DM. Open 8 am to sunset. A cage-less zoo with open-air enclosures, its Tropical House (Troparium) and new Dolphin Pool are well known.

St. Michaelis Church (St. Michaelis Kirche) is the most important Baroque church in northern Germany. It's near Ost-West-Strasse. The steeple can be reached by elevator (1.50 DM) or 400 stairs. Open M-Sa 9-5:30, Su 11:30-5:30, in summer on Friday and Saturday until 11pm. Adult/ 1 DM, child to 14/.60 DM.

Fernsehturm (television tower) on Rentzerstrasse has an observation deck 433 feet high. Open 9-5:30 daily. Elevator fee is adult/3 DM, child under 12/1.50 DM. Planten un Blomen Park is open 7 am- 8 pm, free. Take U-Bahn to Dammtor station. Conducted tours of City Hall are given in English every hour M-F 10-3, SaSu 10-1. Adult/1 DM, child under 14/ .50 DM. No tours when official programs are in progress.

City Nord is Hamburg's new 200 acre business park housing the administrative headquarters of Esso, BP, Shell, B.A.T., etc. Thirty office blocks are next to Stadtpark, 5 km from downtown. Take S-Bahn to Ruben-kamp station. St. Pauli-Landungsbruecken is lined with restaurants, shops and offices which are supported by six floating ferro-concrete pontoons, 2,625 feet long. The pontoons rise and fall about nine feet with the tidal movement. (U-Bahn to St. Pauli.) Between this street and the shipyards on Steinwerder is the old Elbtunnel that was burrowed 70 feet beneath the Elbe River and is used for cars and pedestrians.

MUNICH (MUNCHEN)

The revitalization of the old town into a pedestrian sector, Fussganger, won Munich the American Institute of Architects Award for community architec-ture in 1974. Munich is pronounced MYOO-nik. The Deutsches Museum is one of Europe's finest science museums. You can see the antithesis of the intimacy of the French workingman's neighborhood cafe in the gigantic beer halls of Munich where comaraderie is served up en masse.

TRAIN STATION (Hauptbahnhof)   See map next page. This large terminal has food stalls (including rotisseried chicken across from the tracks), cafeteria, exchange office, tourist office, pharmacy and post office. The main post office which is open 24 hours is across the street from the station. Starnberger Station (Bahnhof) is attached and handles trains to nearby towns and villages. For example, a train goes from here to Schloss Neuschwan-stein. Less important is Ostbahnhof (east station) which is linked by S-Bahn to Hauptbahnhof. Europabus to Rothenburg leaves daily 9 am from platform #23 on Arnulfstrasse outside Starnberger Bahnhof by main station. The bus

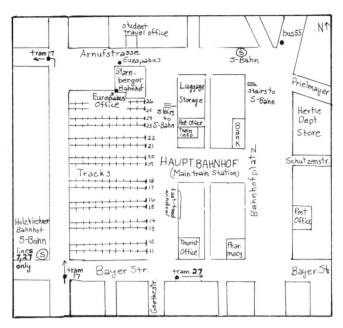

is included in Eurail and Eurail Youthpass but there is a 2 DM charge per
suitcase. A seat MUST be reserved at Europabus Office (Deutsch Touring
Gmbh) in Starnberger Station.

TOURIST INFORMATION   Fremdenverkehrsamt is in the train station at
the Bayerstrasse exit. Open 8 am- 11 pm. Map costs .30 DM (30 pfennig) but
the most helpful city brochure in Europe, "Young People's Guide to Munich,"
is free and everyone regardless of age should ask for it. Also free are
"Combined Transport in Munich-- Travel Fare and Tickets," "Verkehs-
linienplan--Staat and Region," and "Rendevous with Munich" all dealing with
public transportation; "Castles in Bavaria," and leaflets on both campgrounds.

CAMPGROUNDS   Camping Thalkirchen (thal-kir-ken) is across the river
from Hellabrunn Zoo (tierpark) about 4 km south of downtown. Open May–Oct.
From Hauptbahnhof, go out door by tourist office, turn right and walk to S-
Bahn Station (see map). (Don't follow signs to S- Bahn.) Take line 7 or 27 to
fifth stop Siemenswerke. Trains leave on the hour and every 20 minutes except
Sunday, every 40 minutes. Ride is 10-12 min.   Walk east on Rupert-Mayer
Strasse and follow map (on next page) to camp--about 1. 8 km or 25 minutes.
Or, ride tram #14 or 27 from right of station in direction of arrow on map
above. Get off at Sendlinger-Tor-platz, the second stop. Change to bus #57
which is in front of U-Bahn station and ride to last stop. Turn to your right
as you get off bus, walk about 100 meters, turn left, cross railroad tracks
and turn right. (Follow arrows on map on next page.) It's about a 20 minute
walk to camp. You will pass signs for bus #57 but driver said bus doesn't
go down that far.
    By car on autobahn from Salzburg, exit onto Chiemgau Strasse (section

226

of ring road) going
west. From Innsbruck,
camp is signed from
highway and is only 5
minutes off main road.
From Garmisch-
Partenkirchen, exit
onto Boschetsrieder
Strasse going east.
(This is before the
ring road is reached.)
From Stuttgart, the
Obermenzing camp is
more easily reached.

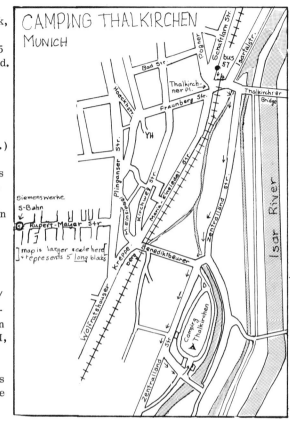

Camp has hot
showers (1 DM in coin
slot for 8 minutes),
private sink stalls,
washer and dryer,
snack bar, cooking
facilities. Adult/
3.50 DM, child 2-12/
2.00DM, tent/ 2.00-
3.00DM depending on
size, van/4-5.50 DM,
car/2 DM. Reserva-
tions are taken for
groups only. Address
is Zentrallandstrasse
49, D-8000 Munchen
70, West Germany.
Mail for campers can also be sent here.

Camping Obermenzing is further from downtown at Lochhausener
Strasse 59 in Obermenzing district, northwest of main station. It's off the
beginning of the Stuttgart autobahn and within a park. Open all year. From
Hauptbahnhof, take S-Bahn (green line S 2, direction Petershausen) to
Obermenzing Station. Camp is 2-1/2 km from here. Change to bus #75
(direction Karlsfeld) and get off at Lochhausener Strasse, the fifth stop.
Walk on Lochhausener Strasse to the park and follow signs to camp. Or,
take tram #17 from near Hauptbahnhof in the direction of arrow on map on
previous page. Get off at Amalienburgstrasse. Change to bus #75 (direction
Karlsfeld) to Lochhausener Strasse. By car, follow signs "Autobahn
Stuttgart." Camp is at entrance to autobahn, about a 20 minute drive from
downtown Munich. Camp has hot showers, sinks with hot water and divided
by privacy curtains, cooking facilities, store, cafe, washer and dryer, and
tents and cabins for rent.

"Our favorite city was Munchen. We really like camping at Obermenzing. The transportation was great and we had many pleasurable hours sightseeing and shopping," report Mr. and Mrs. Robert Cooper. Linda Clark
voted Camping Obermenzing for the best facilities: "I liked having sinks
with free hot water and privacy curtains. It made bathing my little girl very

easy (she doesn't like showers at all). We also appreciated having stoves and a laundromat (albeit expensive). This campground was far from town, however."

Ray Rylander has two suggestions for other camps: "In Munchen, Camping Thalkirchen is simply terrible, especially during Oktoberfest time. Take S-Bahn #5 from Hauptbahnhof to Hechendorf, and a somewhat more primitive camp is about 1 km away around the head of Pilsensee (lake), again over footbridges and along paths (you can go around by the road, but it is longer). A better camp is about 2 km away on narby Worthsee, but over a hill from Hechendorf. Both are about 20 minutes from Munchen by the S-Bahn, which is, as you mentioned, free to railpass holders."

CITY TRANSPORTATION   Munich's trams, buses and two subways, S-Bahn and U-Bahn, are coordinated. Same ticket is valid for each and connecting bus and tram wait at subway entrance. S-Bahn is free with railpass and will get you within walking distance of most everywhere. Tickets are sold from vending machines indicated by a white K on a light green background. There are single tickets, strip tickets and a 24 hour ticket. Buy a single ticket from the machine "Einzelfahrkarten." Each costs a minimum of 1.50 DM which is a 2 zone ticket good as far as the second zone as indicated on the maps. Both camps are within these two zones as are most tourist attractions. Children 4-15 pay a reduced rate for up to four zones of travel. Push the button for the number of zones you need and the price will light up. Insert money and ticket comes out. The strip ticket is cheaper. There are three kinds. The small ticket (blue) costs 5 DM for 6 strips. The large ticket (green) costs 10 DM for 12 tickets.   The red K ticket (especially good for tourists) costs 4.50 DM for 8 tickets, or basically three rides, but each ride can't be longer than two fare zones. All tickets include free transfers within two hours in the same direction.   Children 4-15 use the same red K strip ticket, but in their case one strip is good for a four zone ride. Minimum fare regardless of ticket or distance is two strips, even for a one zone ride. The 24 hour ticket begins at the time of your first trip. The 6 DM ticket is blue and valid for the first two zones. The 10 DM ticket is green and includes greater Munich out to the countryside (but the S-Bahn will get you there too). The 24 hour ticket and strip tickets are sold from mehrfahrtenkarten machine in Hauptbahnhof. Tourist office and travel agencies sell the 24 hour ticket too.

Before boarding tram, bus or subway, cancel ticket in machine at the stop, indicated by a black E on yellow background. To open door of vehicle, push button on right. Refer to tourist office map "Verkehrslinienplan Stadt and Region."   Remember, S-Bahn is free with Eurailpasses.

MUNICH ORIENTATION   Core of downtown is the Fussgangerbereich, a pedestrian mall that stretches for a half-mile from the Stachus (Karlsplatz) down Neuhauser Strasse and Kaufinger Strasse to Marienplatz, center of the old town (alstadt). The area is dotted with tulip-filled planters, shrubbery, vending carts, modern lighting, benches, and a 16-foot high illuminated fountain. Within the area are department stores Karstadt, Kaufhof, Neckermann and Oberpollinger (the most expensive), shops and historical buildings. Pedestrian underpasses (stairs and escalators) and underground shopping malls connect the "people only" area with surrounding streets of cars and shops. Both Marienplatz square and Stacchus shopping mall have a subway terminal where U-Bahn and S-Bahn lines criss-cross.

FOOD   Market (viktualienmarkt) is three blocks from Marienplatz and
open Monday–Saturday, 8–3.   Kaufhof department store sells groceries,
delicatessen items and meals in its basement. The basement cafeteria has
a daily special (sonder angebot) and stand-up tables. Murr Butcher and
Delicatessen is at 7 Rosenstrasse, one block from Marienplatz. Herties
department store near Hauptbahnhof has a basement cafeteria which is
divided into several "limited menu" lines, and stand-up tables. Schuler
Bufeteria, corner of Zweigstrasse and Bayerstrasse near Stachus, has a
wurst stand outside.

SIGHTSEEING   Deutches Museum is the largest science and technical
museum in the world. Great for kids too with airplanes to clamber over,
levers to pull and countless demonstrations. To get there from Camping
Thalkirchen, return to Sendlinger-Tor-Platz and take tram#18, or take
S-Bahn to Isartorplatz station. Museum is on Isarinsel, island in Isar River.
Open daily 9-5. Adult/3 DM, child and student/1 DM. Illustrated guide in
English is sold at bookshop by main entrance. Museum has 300 rooms on the
subjects of (1) mining and metallurgical techniques (walk through salt and
coal mines, casting of metals such as aluminun at 10:30 and 2:30, ground
floor; (2) engines; (3) electricity (high voltage plant demonstrations at 11,
2 and 4, ground floor); (4) cars; (5) trains (model railroad, 10 am and each
hour following, ground floor); (6) planes (from WWI and later to climb on);
(7) chemistry (plastics made at 11:30 and 3:30, second floor); (8) astronomy
(Zeiss Planetarium at 10, 12, 2 and 4, sixth floor, and observatory at 12 and
3, sixth floor); (9) meteorology; (10) watchmaking; (11) musical instruments (16th-18th century keyboard instruments demonstrated);   (12) marine
navigation (full size ship); (13) physics (pull handles and work levers that
demonstrate basic laws); and (14) aeronautics (history of development of
rocket, space vehicles). Restaurant (moderate for Germany) is on right,
up stairs from entrance. Best to bring food along.
      Alte Pinakothek is Munich's fine arts gallery with paintings from 14th
through 18th centuries. Works by Breughel, Durer, Cranach, Giotto,
Holbein, Da Vinci, Rubens, van Dyck, Rembrandt, Valesquez, El Greco and
others. Open Tu-Su 9-4:30, Tu & Th 7-9 pm. Adult/3. 00 DM, Sunday/free.
Take tram #18 from Stachus or Sendlinger-Tor-Platz.
      Haus der Kunst, 1 Prinzregenternstrasse, shows works from 18th to
20th centuries including those of Cezanne, Van Gogh, Monet and Gauguin.
Museum is divided into three sections, each with a separate admission fee.
Sections to the left as you face the building are Neue Pinakothek and Neue
Staatsgalerie, open Tu-Su 9-4:30, Th 7-9 pm. Adult/2. 50 DM, sunday/free.
Exhibitions are held at far right of building. Take bus #55 from front of
Hauptbahnhof.
      Galerie im Lenbachhaus, 33 Luisenstrasse, is within walking distance
of Alte Pinakothek. Shown are modern works with extensive group of
Kandinsky's paintings and small collection of Klee's hanging in new wing.
Open Tu-Su 9-4:30. Adult/1. 50 DM, student and child/. 50 DM, sunday/free.
Take tram #18 from Stachus to Brienner Strasse.
      Residenzmuseum shows period rooms from four centuries. Open Tu-
Sa 9-12:30 and 1:30-5, Su 10-1. Adult/2 DM. Take S-Bahn to Marienplatz.
      Olympic Village is reached by U-Bahn line 3 to Olympia zentrum.
Olympiaturm tower is open 8 am to midnight and costs about adult/3 DM,

child over 5 years/2 DM.

Schloss Neuschwanstein, travel poster cliff-perching castle of King Ludwig II, was built in Fussen from 1868-1886 in a scenic mountain area above Poellatgorge. Sumptuous furnishings inside. Open daily 8:30-5:30. (Refer to Linda Clark's comments under Innsbruck.) Take train from Starnberger Station to Fussen (2-1/2 hour trip) and then it's a 5 minute ride by bus or you can walk.

Dachau Concentration Camp Museum is at Dachau, about 16 km from Munich. Take S-Bahn line 2 (direction Peterhausen) to Dachau Station. Change to bus 1 or 3 to museum memorial, Gedenkstatle. Bus fare is adult/ 1 DM, student/.70 DM. Museum is free. At 11:30 am and 3:30 pm, an English language film is shown. Not for young children. (Open 9-5.)

Neuperlach Community (of possible interest to students of architecture or urban planning) is a new housing development plus shopping mall which accommodates 80,000 people. Take S-Bahn line 1 to Neuperlach Sud, or take bus #56 from Sendlinger-Tor-Platz to Anzinger Strasse. Change to tram #24 or bus #95 or 195.

Additional museums, castles and sights are listed in "Munich, This Month," which costs 1 DM from tourist office.

BEER, BANDS AND BELCHES   Any first timer to Munich will want to include an evening visit to one of the great beer halls sponsored by Hofbrau, Lowenbrau, Spatenbrau, Hackerbrau, Augustinerbrau or Pschorrbrau beer companies. Hofbrauhaus, at Platzl 9 downtown, is the liveliest. Each beer hall serves food in several restaurants, beer, brass bands in lederhosen, costumed waitresses, group singing, belching and smoke in generous quantities and in great fun. The French Michelin Guide refers to the "extraordinary atmosphere" and "astonishing spectacle." The noisiest, most boisterous room is the ground floor of Hofbrauhaus where a half liter of beer is "eine halb," and a whole liter, "eine mass." Light beer is "hell" and dark is "dunkel."

OKTERBERFEST is the last two weeks in September, or specifically from the third Saturday in September to the first Sunday in October. Parades are held during the first weekend. At 11 am on the first Saturday, the opening parade features marchers, bands and horses pulling gaily decorated gigantic beer kegs. Parade route starts on Josephspitalstrasse and goes to the festi- val grounds at Theresien Meadow. Grandstand seats are sold for about 10 DM but the parade can be watched free from the sidewalk just as easily. That night there is usually a folklore entertainment with dancing, singing and music by groups who have come to town to be in the parade, at Circus Krone on Marsstrasse 43 starting at 8 pm. Ticket should be bought from ABR ticket office in Stacchus. Admission is about 8-16 DM. The next day, Sunday, the best parade called "Octoberfest Costume and Marksmen's Procession" starts at 10 am at Max II Memorial, later passing through the old town on its way to the festival grounds.

At the fairgrounds are mammoth canvas tents, each functioning as a portable beer hall with lederhosen-garbed brass band on a revolving stage in the middle, and long narrow tables filled with merry-makers all around. Beer is served in one liter steins and huge signs translated into six languages warn not to steal the steins. Waitresses carry six to eight steins in one hand and will also manage to bring an order of rotisseried chicken. Everyone stands, links arms and joins in the singing. As the evening draws late, an elderly man faints in the aisle and the medical man comes. It's an exercise in mass convivality and worth seeing, but go on a weekend evening when things are the liveliest. Theresien-Wiese fairgrounds are within walking distance of the Hauptbahnhof or take tram #2.

SHOPPING   Auer Dult, Munich's flea market and garage sale, is held thrice yearly for one week in early April, early August and mid-October in Mariahilfsplatz (beyond Deutches Museum) and across the Isar River. Here is where householders sell their cast-offs and the general public and dealers come to see what they can find.

STUTTGART

Stuttgart (STUT-gahrt) is green and airy with 60 percent of the land reserved as open space for parks, gardens and woods.

TRAIN STATION (Hauptbahnhof)   The station is right downtown. Exchange office is open M-Sa 7:45 am-9 pm and Su 8:30 am- 8 pm. Tourist office is outside in an underground passage. Bus terminal is at side of main station's tower, with entrance through the park. Tram terminal is second level underground. A large park, Schlossgarten, with fountains, lakes and playgrounds, extends for almost 4 km beside the station.   Park is divided into three sections, Oberer Schlossgarten, Mittlerer Schlossgarten and Unterer Schlossgarten.   In front of station, Kocnigstrasse is a one mile long shopping street, an attractive pedestrian mall. In its middle is the historical Schlossplatz (Palace Square).

TOURIST INFORMATION   Tourist office is located in the Klett-Passage, underground, in front of Hauptbahnhof. Open M-Sa 8:30 am-10 pm, Su 11-8. Ask for city map, "Museums in Stuttgart," "Theaters in Stuttgart," and tram and bus map.

CAMPGROUND   Camping Cannstatter Wasen is a private camp located across the Neckar River in Stuttgart-Bad Cannstatt, next to where the Cannstatter Volksfest, autumn festival, is held.   Open all year. From main station, take S-Bahn (included in railpasses), line S 1 (direction of Plochingen) to Bad Cannstatt. Trip is only five minutes.   Get off in Bad Cannstatt (Eisenbahn station). Then camp is a 25 minute walk in the direction of the river (see map next page).   Or, another convenient way is by tram #1 or 2   from Staatsgalerie. To reach Staatsgalerie, turn left as you leave the station and walk through the park on Schiller-strasse which leads into the tram intersection. (Both trams also pick up at Charlottenplatz, but this is farther from the station.)   Get off at Mercedes Strasse after tram crosses Neckar River.   Camp has hot showers, store. Adult/3.80 DM, child 2-12/2.00 DM, tent/3 DM, car/2.75 DM.

CITY TRANSPORTATION   A dense network of S-Bahn trains, trams and buses is available. A single ride for the whole city area costs a flat rate of 1.70 DM. Tickets can be bought in multiples at savings.   A 24 hour ticket is 5.50 DM, (children 2.50 DM) and gives unlimited travel for 24 hours throughout the entire city on   S-Bahn trains, trams and buses. S-Bahn network is included in Eurailpasses.

FOOD   Market is held at Schillerplatz and at Marktplatz (downtown) on

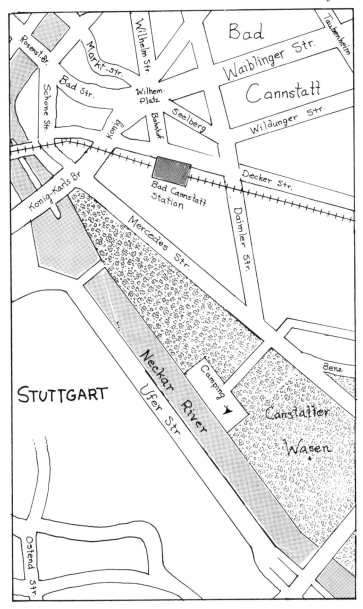

Tuesday, Thursday and Saturday from 7 am until noon.

SIGHTSEEING   Entry into most museums is free. Oberer Schlossgarten
contains the opera/ballet theater and drama theater of Wuerttemberg State
Theaters, State Parliament and sculptures "Reclining" by Henry Moore
(1960) and "Movement" by Bertoni (1960). Turn left as you leave the station
and walk along Arnulf-Klett-Platz and you will see the park on Schiller-
strasse. Stuttgart Municipal Art Gallery (Galerie der Stadt Stuttgart) is at

the Schlossplatz, four blocks from the station. Basically Swabian (regional) painting, 19th and 20th century sculpture and modern art are shown. Open Tu-Su 10-5, Wednesday to 7 pm. Free.

Staatsgalerie Stuttgart, Konrad-Adenauer-Strasse 32 --two blocks from station, shows notable Old Masters, an excellent early 20th century French collection and modern art. Shown are works by Manet, Renoir, Bonnard, Cezanne, Gauguin, Modigliani, Braque, Gris, Picasso, Leger, Kirchner, Nolde, Barlach, Beckmann, Klee, Feininger and more. Open Tu-Su 10-5, Tuesday and Thursday to 8 pm. Free.

A "must" excursion is to Ludwigsburg Palace, the largest Baroque palace in Germany. Open mid March-mid October daily 9-12 and 1-5, mid October-mid March there are tours at 10:30 am and 3 pm on M-F and at 10:30 am, 2 and 3:30 pm on SaSu. Take S-Bahn (S 5) from main station to Ludwigsburg. Palace is four blocks from the station. Ask the Stuttgart tourist office for its Ludwigsburg brochure which includes a map of the town.

Daimler-Benz Museum, Unterturkheim, is of interest to antique car enthusiasts. An appointment must be made with the Tour Service by calling 3022578 or by writing. Admission is free.

Baden-Wurttemberg State Trade Center, the Landesgewerbeamt, at Kanzleistrasse 19, functions as a design center for the area and exhibits high quality industrial goods including textiles, porcelain, glass, furniture, photo technology, radio and television. Open Tu-Su 11-6. Free. Take tram #9 or 14 from station and get off at "Universitaet" or walk the six blocks from the station.

Wurttembergisches Landesmuseum, Altes Schloss, in downtown area and six blocks from station, shows art and culture of Swabia beginning with the Stone Age, the Wuerttemberg crown jewels, and an excellent clock collection. Open Tu-Su 10-4, Wednesday to 8 pm. Free. Linden-Museum for Ethnology, Hegelplatz 1, six blocks from station, covers the Amazon, ancient Peru, New Guinea and Southern Africa. Open Tu-Su 10-5. Free. Television Tower (Fernsehturm) at Degerloch has an elevator that goes up 492 feet and costs adult/3 DM and student or child/1.50 DM. Take tram #10. Cannstatter Volksfest, a beer festival and carnival, starts the last Saturday in September and is near the campground.

READER'S SUGGESTION   "Train station has excellent shops and groceries. Wilhelmina Zoological and Botanic Gardens--beautifully arranged--best we'd ever seen. Take underground # 14." Frances Packer. Editor's note: we looked up information on the Wilhelmina and it is the only zoological-botanical garden in Germany and is visited each year by 1.5 million people which makes it the most popular attraction not only in Stuttgart but in the whole Baden-Wuerttemberg area. Nearby there are some celebrated mineral water swimming pools (a "champagne bath") in Leuze and Berg.

READER'S SUGGESTION

(Speaking of favorite places) "...And in Germany, its got to be Barental, but you either need a good topo map or you must ask to ever find the little camp on the slopes of the Drehkopf, from where hikes without end can be made all thru the Schwarzwald....." (Ray R. Rylander)

GREECE

Anyone with a railpass would be crazy not to go to Greece. Its islands, sand beaches, craggy landscapes with scrub pine, luscious cheap fruit and wonderful archaeological sites revealing its glorious history will leave Greece clearly etched in your mind long after your visit ends. Go to Athens, Delphi and the Peloponnese for classical history, to northern Greece for Byzantine and Hellinistic artifacts and to the 1,425 islands in the Aegean for the sheer joy of discovery! The Greek Tourist Office publishes a wonderful folder for each region and group of islands which give guidebook-quality details about archaeological sites, and also has good maps of the country, Athens, Thessaloniki, Rodos, Corinth, and Iraklion. Please get these folders and take the pertinent ones with you to read on the ferry to Greece and to be sure you have them while you're there. Many names of places are spelled several different ways. The most interchangeable letters are K for C, I for Y, E for AE, H for CH and F for PH. The second name on the list below is most commonly found on Greek maps.

A
Acrocorinth -Akrokorinthos
Aedipsos -Edipsos
Aegean -Egeo
Aegina -Egina
Aigion -Egio
Amphiaraeion -Amfiaraio
Amphiaraos -Amfiaraos
Alphios -Alfios
Antikythera -Antikithira
Antirrion -Antirio
Aphaia -Afea
Arakhova -Arahova
Arkalokhori -Arkalohori
Argolide -Argolida
Astypalaia -Astipalea
Athens -Athina
Attica -Atiki
Ayia Triada -Agia Triada
Ayiokambos -Agiokambos
Ayios Evstratios -Agios Efstratios

B
Bassae -Vasse
Boetia -Viotia
Bouleuterion -Vouleftirio

C
Cephallonia -Kefalonia
Chalcidice -Halkidiki
Chalkis -Halkida
Chalki -Halki
Chanea -Hania
Chios -Hios
Cnossos -Knossos
Corfu -Kerkira
Corinth -Korinthos
Cos -Kos
Crete -Kriti
Cyclades -Kiklades

D
Daphni -Dafni
Dodone -Dodoni
Delos -Dilos
Delphi -Delfi
Dodecanese -Dodekanissa

E
Elasson -Elassona
Eleusis -Elefsina
Epidaurus -Epidavros
Epirus -Ipiros
Epirus -Ipiros
Euboea -Evia

G
Glyfada -Glifada
Gytheion -Githio

H
Heraion -Ireo
Herakleia -Iraklia
Herakleion -Iraklio
Hermione -Ermioni
Hydra -Idra

I
Ialyssos -Ialissos
Istiaia -Isriea
Ithaca -Ithaki

J
Jannina -Ioanina

K
Kalavryta -Kalavrita
Kalymnos -Kalimnos
Kameiros -Kamiros
Kyllini -Kilini
Kymi -Kimi
Kythera -Kithira
Kythnos -Kithnos

L
Laconia -Lakonia
Lemnos -Limnos
Lesbos -Lesvos
Litokhoron -Litohoro
Levadhia -Livadia
Levkas -Lefkada
Levkimi -Lefkimi
Lycabettus -Likavitos

M
Macedonia -Makedonia
Marathon -Marathonas
Mycenae -Mikines
Mykonos -Mikonos
Myrina -Mirina
Mytilene -Mitilini

N
Nissyros -Nissiros
Nauplia -Nafplio
Navpaktos -Nafpaktos

O
Oia -Ia
Olympia -Olimpia
Olympus -Olimbos

P
Paiania -Peania
Palaiofarsala -Paleofarsala
Parnes -Parnitha
Parnassus -Parnassos
Pelion -Pilio
Pangaion -Pangeo
Peloponnese -Peloponissos
Paxoi -Paxi
Pella -Pela
Phaestos -Festos
Phareron -Faliro
Philippi -Filipi
Promahon -Promahonas
Phigaleia -Figalia
Platamon -Platamonas
Poligyros -Poligiros
Pylos -Pilos
Pyrgos -Pirgos
Patras -Patra
Piraeus -Pireas

R
Ramnous -Ramnouda
Rethymnon -Rethimno
Rhodes -Rodos

S
Salamis -Salamina
Salonika -Thessaloniki
Santorin -Santorini
Samothrace -Samothraki
Siteia -Sitia
Sparta -Sparti
Skyros -Skiros
Symi -Simi
Siphnos -Sifnos
Syros -Siros

T
Thebes -Thiva
Thera -Thira
Thessaly -Thessalia
Thrace -Thraki
Taygetos -Taigetos

Y
Ypati -Ipati
Yerontovrakhos -Gerodovrahos

V
Vravron -Vravrona
Vlykhada -Vlihada

Z
Zante -Zakinthos

CURRENCY   One dollar is worth about 56 drachma, and each drachma is worth about 2¢. One drachma equals 100 leptas.

WEATHER   Hot and crowded during July and August; spring and fall are best.

TOURIST INFORMATION   Besides offices of the National Tourist Organization of Greece (NTOG), many towns have Tourist Police (pronounced touristiki as-tee-no-mia) which function as tourist offices.

CAMPING   NTOG campgrounds are licensed by the National Tourist Organization and are generally large with numerous services₀ Rates in these campgrounds are usually adult/115 dr, child to 7/60 dr, tent/100 dr, hotplate/ 30 dr. High season is June 16 to September 16, middle season is March 16 to June 15, and low season is November 16 to March 15.   Hellenic Touring Club operates a chain of campgrounds and charges adult/35-50 dr, tent/35 dr. Camping is forbidden outside of organized campgrounds.

TRAINS   Trains in Greece (Grecia) are operated by the state Hellenic Railways Organization (O. S₀ E.), whose head office is at #1-3 Karolou Street in Athens₀ Main lines are northward from Athens to Thessaloniki and into Yugoslavia, Bulgaria or Turkey; and the Pelopponese line. Trains are fairly slow in Greece because of the terrain. A bus network makes up for the lack of railway density, and archeological sites can often be reached by combining train and bus₀ A book of train and bus schedules is sold for 60 dr. A supplement is charged on Eurailpasses for certain fast trains₀

entrance - eisodros   station - strathmo
exit -   exodhos   information - plirophoria

Included in Eurailpasses are ferry crossings on the Adriatica and Hellenic Mediterranean Lines between Patras, Greece and Brindisi, Italy. This is deck class--a reclining seat costs extra. A port charge of about 180 dr for adults must be paid in drachma upon embrakation. A reservation fee of $1.50 must be paid at the shipping line office. Between June 10 and Sept 30, a surcharge of $12 is made on Eurailpasses at the time the reservation is made. Before boarding, check in at the shipping line office at the pier. Hellenic Mediterranean Lines office in Athens is at Leoforos Amalias 28, near Syntagma Square. If a stopover is planned for Corfu, tell the agent when the reservation is made.

All year, a ferry leaves Patras at 9 pm, arrives Igoumenitsa at 7 am, Corfu at 9 am and Brindisi at 9 pm. If you don't wish to take the train to Patras from Athens, a connecting bus costing 365 dr leaves Athens at 1:30 pm from 28 Amalias Avenue. Between about June 10 and September 30, an extra ferry leaves Patras at 4 pm and arrives in Brindisi the next day at 8:30 am. The connecting bus leaves Athens at 9:30 am. During summer, the boats Appia and Egnatia make the 9 pm sailings, and Castalia and Espresso Grecia make the 4 pm sailings. During the rest of the year, Egnatia and Espresso Grecia alternate making the 9 pm trips.

Eurailpasses are also valid for a 30% reduction on Libra Maritime Line between Piraeus and Haifa or Ancona.

FOOD Food is much less expensive here than in the rest of Europe. As always, the open market is best. Typical Greek country salad is sliced tomatoes and cucumbers with olives and feta cheese, dressed with olive oil and lemon juice. Baked dishes such as "moussaka" are always good and reasonable. Throughout Greece, the custom is for the diner to go into the kitchen and select from what's on the stove.

POLLUTION   As long as you don't swim around the port city of Piraeus (or any closer than perhaps Glyfada), Corfu and other major ports, the Greek coastline and islands are free of pollution except for an occasional obvious oil slick washing ashore.

PELOPPONESE   (PELOPONISSOS)

Patras, arrival point for ships from Brindisi, Italy, is in the Peloponnese. The isle of Pelops, now connected by bridge at Corinth to mainland Greece, compactly presents 4000 years of history through its imposing ruins, archeological sites (some being currently excavated as at Corinth), and museums. Most attractions are accessible by train or bus. The most important sites from the second millennium B.C. are the Lion gate and bee-hive tombs at Mycenae, the Cyclopean walls at Tiryns, and Nestor's palace at Pylos. Also important are the Greek and Roman ruins in Olympia and Corinth, the theater in Epidaurus, the temple of Bassae, and the walls of Messini. Illustrative of later times are the medieval castles of AcroCorinth, Tornese and Karitena, and the Byzantine Mistra and Monemvasia. Still later in history and of less interest are the Venetian fortresses of Nauplion and Methoni.

Trains are operated by the Pelopponese branch of the Hellenic Railways. Diesel trains (automotrices) are comfortable and stop at main towns. Steam trains may be one car long and stop at villages. Trains make a circular tour of the island from Patras, Alfios, Kalamata, Tripolis, Argos and Corinth and then back to Patras along the northern shore. There are rail spurs off the main circular route at Kavassila for Killini and Loutra (NTOG camping Kyllini at nearby Vartholomio with bus stop within 500 meters, opern Apr-Oct); at Alfios for Olympia (camping); and at Kalonero for Kyparissia. At Zevgolatio, some trains go onward to Argos and others go to Messini and

Kalamata (camping 5 km from town, bus from Kalamata). Also a small rail
spur goes to Megalopolis。 Near Patras at Dhiakofto, the very scenic short
Kalavrita Railway goes to Zakhlorou where for a reasonable price a donkey
will carry you to see a monastery. Train leaves about 3 times daily for the
45 minute trip.

PATRAS   Ships from Brindisi, Italy, on which passage is included in
Eurailpasses arrive in Patras at either 12 noon or 6 pm。 A connecting bus
(365 dr) meets the ferry and drives to Athens arriving at 4 pm or 10 pm,
respectively, at 28 Amalias Avenue near Syntagma Square. There are also
trains.

Ayia (Aya) Patron Camping, a N.T.O.G. camp, is on the beach 5 km
from Patras. Open all year。 Bus from Patras stops at camp, but bus doesn't
run after about 5-6 pm. Hot showers, hotplates, restaurant. A smaller and
closer campground is on the beach about 2-3 km from Patras in the same
direction as Ayia Camping and is reported to be cheaper and more friendly.
Camping Rion is 8 km northeast of Patras on the beach, just south of the
ferry dock. Open Apr 1-Oct 31. Located 300 meters from ferry dock, 500
meters from the train station (Rion, Rio) and 500 meters from the village
market in Rion。 Hot showers, store, cafe equipped with a barbeque for
preparing souvlaki。 (See train schedules below.)

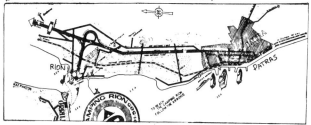

Trains leave Patras for Athens at 8:18 am (ar. 1:02 pm), 10:59 am (ar.
2:46 pm), 1:47 pm (ar。 6:34 pm), 5:02 pm (ar. 9:20 pm), and 6:58 pm (ar.
10:39 pm)。 These trains stop at towns enroute of any size, and the 8:18,
1:47 and 5:02 departures will stop at Rion if you notify the conductor in
advance (and similarly for other small towns usually).

To go to Delphi, take a train or bus the 8 km to the ferry terminal at
Rion (Rio)。 Then take the half-hourly ferry the short distance across to
Antiria (Antirion) and from there a bus for the final 120 km to Delphi. (See
Delphi, page 236。)

To Olympia, two through trains leave at 11:02 am (ar. 2:30 pm), and
3:00 pm (ar. 6:48 pm)。 Otherwise, take a train to Alfios and change trains
for Olympia. To Alfios, trains leave at 12:21 pm (ar。 2:15 pm), 3:08 pm
(ar. 5:23 pm) and 5:04 pm (ar. 6:50 pm)。 Trains leave Alfios for Olympia at
6:43 am, 10:04 am, 12:58 pm, 2:15 pm and 6:23 pm. About 1-1/2 hour trip.

OLYMPIA (Olimbia)   Birthplace of the Olympic Games, the sanctuary now within a 5000 acre national park is not in as good condition as that at Delphi or Mycenae, but remains worthwhile.   Camping Olympia (Arkhala Olimbia) is within walking distance of the train station, open all year, hot showers, 500 meters from store.   Trains leave Olympia for Alfios at 7:25 am (ar. 7:55 am), 10:36 am (ar. 11:01 am), 1:27 pm (ar. 1:52 pm), 4:31 pm (ar. 5:01 pm), and 6:51 pm (ar. 7:16 pm).   Trains leave Alfios to Kalamata at 1:16 pm (ar. 4:17 pm) and 5:23 pm (ar. 8:24 pm)。 To go to Mycenae, change at Zevgolatio enroute to Kalamata.   Trains leave Alfios for Patras at 8:59 am (ar. 10:54 am), 11:25 am (ar. 1:40 pm), 2:27 pm (ar. 4:58 pm) and 5:02 pm (ar. 6:54 pm)。 The last departure originates in Olympia.

MYCENAE (MIKINE)   Mycenae is 9 km from the main town of Argos on the Corinth-Argos train line.   Trains stop at Mikine (Mycenae).   The ancient city is half a mile from the village of Mycenae, and is open M-Sa 7:30 to sunset, Su 10-1 & 3-6.   Unusual beehive tombs and Lion Gate are the most famous relics but there is considerably more to be seen.   Bring along flashlight for the tombs.   Campground is within walking distance.   Trains leave for Corinth and Athens at 11:16 am, 12:54 pm, 2:52 pm, and 5:27 pm.

CORINTH (KORINTHOS)   Come to see the ancient city and Acrocorinth, the fortified citadel above it.   Camping Am Meer, Vrahos--5 km south of the isthmus on highway E 92, is served by bus from Corinth.   Open all year, store, restaurant, dancing。

ATHENS   (ATHINE)

What might be thought of as the "port" of Athens is actually Piraeus, another city, from which ferries depart for the islands.   The two main squares of Athens are Omonia and Syntagma.   Bus terminals change so please check information.

TRAIN STATIONS   Larissa Station (S. E. K.) serves trains going north to Thessaloniki and beyond and behind it is Peloponnese Station (S.P.A.P.) which serves trains to and from the Peloponnese. Trolleybus #1 (direction Kallithea) leaves from Delighianni Street outside Larissa Station and goes to downtown Athens via Omonia Square and Syntagma Square.   A Tourist Police office is at Larissa Station.

TOURIST INFORMATION   The most convenient branch is at 2 Karageorghi Servias Street inside the National Bank of Greece on Syntagma (Sintagma, Constitution) Square.   Ask for a leaflet on each town or island you will be visiting as well as a map of Athens, and ask them when ferries leave for the islands you plan to visit.   American Express is on this same square and its mail section has long lines and is closed 1-4 pm.   Hellenic

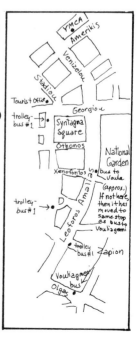

238

Mediterranean Line office is at Leoforos Amalias 28, near Syntagma, for reserving ferry passage back to Italy.

CAMPGROUNDS   Athens has good campgrounds, but please check these bus directions with tourist office. CAMPING ALIPEDON VOULAS, operated by NTOG, is 20 km from Athens on the beach at Voula on the road to Sounion. Take bus to Voula from entrance to the Royal Garden along Amalias St. just off Syntagma Square. Buses leave often from 5:30 am to 1 am. Buses to Vouliagmeni (farther than Voula) can be used and leave from the corner of Olgas

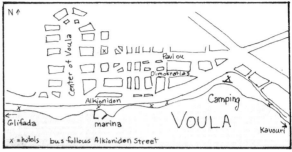

Avenue and Zappeion which is farther south along Amalias. From Piraeus, take bus #125 to Voula from terminal station. If camp is full, take bus #90 from camp for 7 km to another camp.   Hot showers, store, lounge.

CAMPING DAFNI is 10 km from Athens. Bus #100 from Koumoundourou Square (see map), which is about four blocks from Omonia Square, leaves every half hour to 11:45 pm and costs about 12 dr. Trip is 30 minutes. The campground has sit-down flush toilets and a pavillion for folk dances at night. During the wine festival at Dafni from mid-July to mid-September, the camp is crowded. At the festival, one entrance fee entitles you to sample wines from all over Greece.

CAMPING NEA KIFISIA at Nea Kifisia Eleon 12 about 12 km northeast of Athens can be reached by frequent buses from Kaningos Square (see map) which is about 4 blocks northeast of Omonia Square. Trip is 50 minutes. Or take the electric train (subway) to terminal station Kifissia and then short bus ride to Nea Kifissia. Ask driver to let you off at camping. The American Club in Kifissia has an information center and bulletin board, dining room, swimming pool and most importantly a bookstore where books and magazines are sold at American prices. It takes either Greek or American money. Market day in Kifissia is Wednesday.

PUBLIC TRANSPORTATION   Tourist office Athens map has buses and trolleys marked and lists routes. Trolleys are yellow and stops listing trolley number are yellow. Blue buses stop at blue signs. Enter rear door and pay conductor. Fare is about 12-18 dr. The electric train (subway) goes every few minutes between Piraeus - Neo Faliron - Kallithea - Thission - Monastiraki - Omonia - Victoria Square - Patisia - Nea Ionia - Neo Iraklion - Maroussi - Kifissia.

FOOD   Central market is under a roof between Eolou and Sokratous

Streets. XEN (YWCA) Cafeteria, 11 Amerikis Street (off Stadiou near
Syntagma Square) is patronized by both sexes, opens at 7 am, closes
between 3:30 and 5 pm and then reopens for dinner. Minion Department store
on Patission near Omonia Square has a supermarket and an eleventh floor
cafeteria.

SIGHTSEEING   The two important sights are the Acropolis with the
Parthenon, Temple of Athena Nike, Erechtheum and Acropolis Museum and
Agora area below the Acropolis, and the National Archaeological Museum
with its excellent chronologically presented displays. Both are free on Thurs-
days and Sundays as are other museums and monuments in Athens. The
Acropolis is open 9 to sunset. Take bus #16 from Amalias Street near
Syntagma Square. Whatever you do, you should come back to the Acropolis
at night, either during a full moon when it's open from 9 to midnight or in
the evening at 9 pm any night except Tuesday and Friday to see and hear
the Sound and Light show. Get off the #16 bus one stop beyond the Acropolis
for the show is seen from the Pynx hill above it. Get the cheapest seats,
about 60 dr and half-price for students. Show lasts about an hour.   Another
recommended evening excursion is to see the Temple of Poseidon at Cape
Sounion at sunset. This is most easily accomplished from Camping Voulas
which is a third of the way there. Otherwise from Athens, take a bus which
leaves from 14 Mavromateon at 20 minutes past the hour.

TRAIN SCHEDULES   Best train between Athens and Thessaloniki (reservation advised) is Akropolis Express which leaves Athens (Larissa Station) at
11:15 am and arrives in Thessaloniki at 6:50 pm. Other trains leave at
2:10 pm (ar. 9:34 pm), 7:30 pm (ar. 4:13 am), 9:40 pm (ar. 6:10 am) and
11:05 pm (ar. 7:30 am).

From Athens to Meteora take any northbound train from Larissa Station
but get off at Paleopharsalos and change to the Trikkala train and get off at
Kalambaka. Best departures from Athens are at 9:00 am (ar. Paleopharsalos
at 1:43 pm) and 11:15 am (ar. e:46 pm). Trains leave Paleopharsalos for
Kalambaka at 8:30 am, 12:55 pm and 4:10 pm. Trip is one hour, 45 minutes.

From Athens to Delphi, take a northbound train from Larissa Station
at 6:30 am, 9:06 am, 11:15 am, 2:10 pm or 3:30 pm, and get off in about two
hours at Livadia (Lavadhia, Levadia). Then take a bus for the remaining
47 km to Delphi.

From Piraeus and Athens for Corinth, trains leave Piraeus at 6:08 am,
6:56 am, 8:05 am, 9:15 am, 9:55 am, 11:33 am, 12:42 pm, 1:33 pm, 3:15 pm
and 4:05 pm for the approximately two-hour trip. Athens departures are
about 16 minutes later from Pelopponese Station.

From Piraeus and Athens to Patras, trains leave Piraeus at 8:05 am,
Athens at 8:22 am (ar. 12:15 pm); leave Piraeus at 9:55 am, Athens 10:22
(ar. 2:56 pm); leave Piraeus at 12:35 pm, Athens at 12:53 pm (ar. 5 pm);
leave Piraeus at 3:15 pm, Athens 3:42 pm (ar. Patras 7:56 pm). Trains
leave Athens from Pelopponese Station.

AEGEAN ISLANDS

The Aegean sea unites the Greek world, and historically its islands were stepping-stones between Eastern and Western civilization. Between July 15 and early September the Greeks themselves come for their vacations so boats and islands are less crowded at other times. August 15 is a religious celebration on Tinos and Paros and ferries to those islands are filled with pilgrims. The strong "meltemi" (etesian wind) blows in August making the seas very rough. During the last week in August and first week in September, boats are crowded with vacationers returning to Piraeus. Two days is minimum required to visit an island--one day to get there and spend the night and another to return late the next day. Boat schedules vary from week to week and up-to-date information can be obtained from the tourist office or the publication "What's On In Athens" sold at kiosks. The majority of boats leave from Piraeus. Always buy deck class fare (third class) and get to the boat early to stake out your space on the top deck. Bring food. The large car-ferries are comfortable.

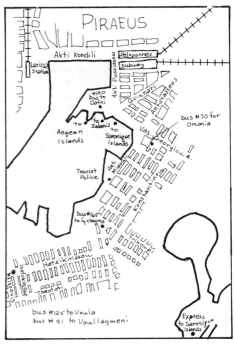

MYKONOS (Mikonos) is an extremely popular island with pelicans, windmills, whitewashed houses and narrow alleys. Boats generally leave three times a day for Mykonos: Apollon (good boat) at 7:30 am, Naias at 8 am and the Aegeon, Mimika or Elli in the afternoon. Check this information. The 7-hour trip costs about 250 dr deck class. (Boats leave Rafina--45-minute bus ride from Mavrommataion Street in Athens-- for Mykonos three times a week and the crossing is about 45 minutes less.) On Mykonos, campground is at Platys Yalos to which a bus goes from behind Taxi square in the town. People also camp at Paradise Beach (where there is also a nudist colony). You get there by boat from the town or it's a 30-minute walk beyond Platys Yalos. The nearby island of Delos, the political and religious center of the Aegean for 1,000 years, is reached by small boat leaving Mykonos each morning at about 8:30 am and returning about 12:30 pm for about 45 dr round trip. The time spent at Delos is far too short to see all the excavations properly unfortunately.

CRETE (Kriti), birthplace of the brilliant Minoan civilization which reached its zenith about 1600 BC, is about an 11-hour trip from Piraeus. Save time by taking one of the large overnight car-ferries such as Candia, Minos or Rethymnon to Herakleion (Iraklion), largest town on the island (deck class

645 dr, tourist 858 dr). On the island, you can get everywhere on the bus.
In Heraklion (Iraklion), see the Archaelogical Museum which contains
Minoan objects from the excavations and is considered the second-best
museum in Greece. Buses leave for the excavations at Knossos from
Kornarou Square twice an hour for the 20-minute ride. Camping Asimenia
Akti is 35 km from Heraklion on a beautiful white sugar-sand beach at Malia.
Take half-hourly bus from bus station which is 400 meters from the port of
Heraklion. The ride is an hour and costs about 75 dr. At Rethymnon, 78 km
from Heraklion, three beachfront campgrounds are east of town along the
Rethymnon -Heraklion national road. About four kilometers out are Camping
Arkadia and Camping Elizabeth (hot showers, supermarket, restaurant) and
at 15 km is Camping George. Two campgrounds at the town of Chania
(Khania) are Camping Shell which has a restaurant but is not on the beach
and Camping Gatt Alfredos. Covered market in Chania is on Venizelou
Square.

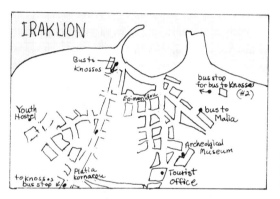

From Heraklion, boats
to Piraeus sail daily at
6:30 and/or 7 pm. On
Wednesday a boat goes
to Santorini, Ios,
Mykonos, Tinos and
Piraeus. On Wednes-
day and Sunday, a boat
goes to Santorini, Ios,
Naxos, Paros, Syros
and Piraeus. On Fri-
day a boat leaves for
Santorini, Ios, Paros
and Piraeus.

SKOPELOS ISLAND   Traveler Sara Dolph reports her favorite campground
in Greece was on Skopelos Island. To reach Skopelos, take the train to
Paleofarsalos, change trains for Volos, and then a boat to Skopelos. "On
Skopelos Island take the bus from Skopelos City To Agnontas Bay (last bus
leaves at 6:00 pm), then take boat around to Illuminasis Bay (last boat leaves
around 4:30 pm). The boat is free to the bay and 50 dr for return. However
there is a footpath, about a 25 minute walk, for the return trip to Agnontas.
The bus fare is 14 dr. The campground is on very uneven ground, but 100 dr
a night for two people and one tent. The beach is absolutely beautiful,
especially the clear water. The tourists all leave by 4:30 pm, only a few
campers are left. There is a cafe that serves dinner--moussaka, fish, or
lamb, and a Greek salad, plus retsina came to about 500 dr for 4 people each
night. The dinners were served after 9:00 pm and the atmosphere was very
friendly--the cook usually would sit down and have a glass of retsina with
you."

THESSALONIKI (SALONIKA)

New train station is about 18 blocks from the tourist office or take bus #1
from station to Aristotelous. Tourist Police office is at the station. Train

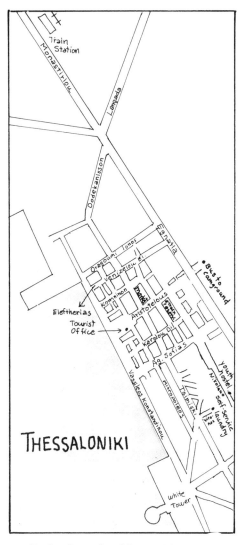

reservations office is on Aristotelous, 2 blocks from tourist office at 8 Aristotelous Square. Tourist office on Aristotelous Square is open M–F 8–8, Sa 8–2:30. A bus costs 10 dr in the city. Outside city fare is by distance. The closest campgrounds can be reached by bus #10 from the train station to Platia Dikastirion (marked on map), then bus #73 for Camping Aghia Triada which stops directly at the camp, or bus #69 to Epanomi N.T.O.G. campsite. Fare is 32 dr to Aghia and 44 dr to Epanomi. Camp Aghia Triada is very pretty with terraced sites facing the beach, and good facilities including hot showers, store, snack bar, laundry, and hotplates. Bus ride to camp is 25 minutes.

From train station, take bus #10, 11, 14, 17, 37 to Youth Hostel, Pring. Nikolaou 44.

Market is on V. Irakliou Street (see map).

Archeological Museum is open 9–3:15 except Su 10–5, closed Tu. Adult/50 dr, free Sunday. Folklore Museum, 10–2, closed Tu.

Self-service laundry, Canadian, is at Navarino Square #14, costs 130 dr a machine load.

Trains leave for Athens at 6:00 am, 8:10 am, 12:55 pm, 2:50 pm, 3:17 pm, 9:50 pm and 11:45 pm. Trip is about 8 hours.

DELPHI (DELFI)

Delphi Camping is 3-1/2 km in the direction of Amfissa from Delphi. When coming from Patras, ask the driver to let you off at the camp, which is on the highway, rather than going into town. Sanctuary entrance is about a 10 minute walk from Delphi. The museum within the Sanctuary is open Tu–Sa 8–1 & 3–8, Su 10–1 & 3–6, M 11–1 & 3–6.

METEORA

In the rivalrous 14th century, the towering rocks of Meteora were used as a safe refuge for monks who built their hermitages high among the inaccessible pinnacles. Originally ropes were lowered and raised to gain entrance to these refuges but in modern times steps have been built. The Meteora area is reached by the Trikkala train from Paleofarsalos on the Athens-Thessaloniki line. Kalambaka is the final stop on the Trikkala line and from there a bus goes to the village of Meteora near the monasteries. Two campgrounds are along the road between Kalambaka and Meteora. Buses run infrequently so you may wish to hitch or take a taxi for the few kilometers. Camping Kastraki is 500 meters from a store and a restaurant is nearby. Thessalia Camping Vrachos is 500 meters from Meteora and has a store and restaurant. From the campgrounds, you should be able to pick up a ride or hitch on the road to the monasteries. Or you can take a taxi for about 225dr round trip to St. Stephanos monastery plus about 15 dr per hour waiting time while you look. Going on foot, the monasteries are about a two-hour hike. Females need to have arms covered to be admitted to the monasteries. The view from St. Stephanos is best. Great Meteoron and Varlaam monasteries are within 300 meters of each other and roundtrip taxi fare would be about 175 dr. Tourist Police in Kalambaka is at 33 Rammidi Street.

From Paleofarsalos for Thessaloniki, trains leave at 1:43 pm, 3:46 pm, and 6:55 pm. To Athens, trains leave at 7:53 am, 9:18 am, 11:21 am, 4:04 pm, 6:05 pm, 6:28 pm. Trips are about 3 and 5 hours, respectively.

From Kalambaka to Paleofarsalos, trains leave at 6:00 am, 10:40 am, 3:09 pm and 6:35 pm. Trip is about 1 hour and 40 minutes.

CORFU (KERKIRA)

One ship from Brindisi stops at Corfu on its way to Patras. From your arrival dock, walk out to the main street and take a bus to Sanrocco or Theotoki Square. Tourist office is 2 blocks from here. To reach Camping Dionysus at Gouvia Bay, 8 km from town, take bus #7 from the main road in front of the ferry terminal. With your back to the sea, the bus should be going to your right, away from town. The bus also leaves from Sanrocco Square 2 blocks from the tourist office. Bus stops outside the campground. Hot showers/30 dr, store, restaurant, one-day laundry service, disco with Greek dancing, sandy beach, adult/100 dr, tent/100 dr. The campground caters to young people especially. There are also 5 other camps in the area.

Kontokali Youth Hostel is also reached by bus #7 in the same direction. Market is open 7-12 at the north end of S. Dessylla Street.

From May 15 to September 30, the Sound and Light (Son et Lumiere) show takes place in the Old Venetian Fortress in English. At the same spot, folk dances are performed before the show. Museum of Asiatic Arts and the Archeological Museum are open M-Sa 9:30-3:30, adult/25 dr.

See map next page.

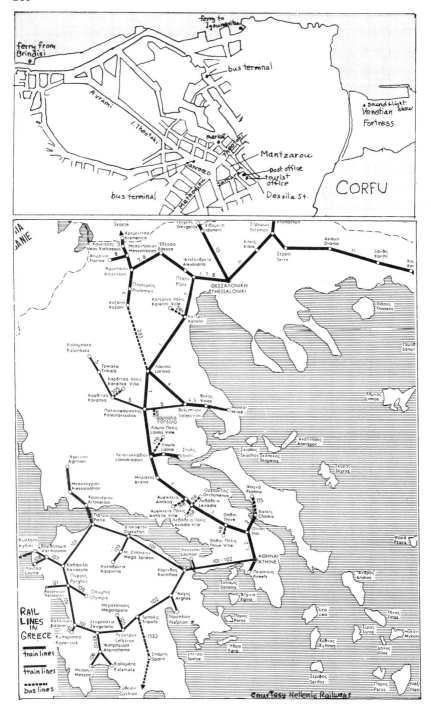

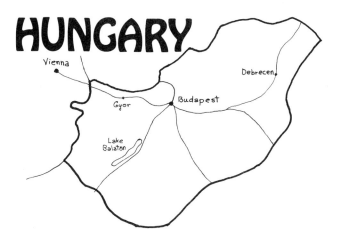

HUNGARY

Vienna
Debrecen
Gyor
Budapest
Lake
Balaton

An Eastern European tourist heads for Budapest as the Paris of the Eastern bloc. To western eyes, ears and palate, the resemblance may seem meager, yet the spirit is there and Budapest has much to offer at far less cost. Budapest occupies the geographical center of Europe being equidistant from Moscow and London, Kiev and Paris, and Stockholm and Istanbul. A trip to some cities might be put off, but Budapest is changing rapidly. The consumer revolution is on its way and the old standard of living is being eclipsed. The dollar is welcome in Hungary and it stretches way farther than in Western Europe. You must have a VISA to enter Hungary (see visas). If you failed to get one in the U.S., visit IBUSZ, the official Hungarian tourist agency, at 26 Karntnerstr. (3 blocks from the Opera) in Vienna. Eurailpass and Eurail Youthpass are valid only to the border, but at the border the ticket can be paid for in forints or purchased beforehand in Vienna with western currency.

CURRENCY   Hungarian forint. Each visitor is legally permitted to bring 100 forints in coins (no bills) with him into Hungary. It is to your great advantage to do so as forints can be legally purchased at any Viennese bank at a much better rate than in Hungary where it is government set artifically low. In Hungary exchange only the amount of dollars into forints that you will need as re-exchanging currency is difficult and time consuming. Save receipts from currency transactions to show customs when leaving.

BUDAPEST

Hydrofoil, train and bus bring travelers from Vienna to Budapest. Hydrofoil on the Danube takes four hours from Vienna to Danube quay at Duna-Intercontinental Hotel in Budapest. Inside hotel, IBUSZ desk clerk will change money and give information. This is an easier though a little more costly arrival than by train, which matters as Eastern Europe is not as well organized for receiving tourists as Western Europe.

TOURIST INFORMATION   Main organizations are IBUSZ, national tourist agency, and the city's Tourist Board. Both groups offer currency exchange, small amounts of tourist literature, sightseeing tours and hotel reservations. Tourist Board finds rooms in private homes from its offices at V. Roosevelt Ter, open 8 am-11 pm. IBUSZ main office is downtown at 5 Felszabadulas Ter with branch at 3 Tanacs Korut and in leading hotels. A hotel IBUSZ desk isn't crowded with the lines seen in the main offices. A hotel is also the easiest place to find a restroom. Addresses are: Duna Intercontinental, Danube Quay; Royal, 49 Lenin Blvd. (downtown with post office, souvenir store, pastry shop and cafe); Astoria, 19 Kossuth Lajos Utca; Szabadsag, 90 Rackoczi Ut, and Beke, 97 Lenin Korut.

CAMPGROUNDS   Budapest is divided into two parts. Buxom Buda is separated from plain Pest by the Danube River. Both campgrounds are on the hilly Buda side. Downtown is in Pest. HARSHEGY campground, Budakeszi Ut and Denes Utca, is the best. It has sixteen acres of park-like, grassy ground with a view of the city. Room for 1500 campers. Modern restrooms (220 v., 50 cycle current as in Western Europe), hot showers, grocery store, office with English-speaking clerk and safe deposit box, souvenir store, snack bar, indoor lounge, cooking facilities and cabins for rent. Take bus #22 from Moszkva Ter to Harshegy (check this). ROMAI-PART campground at Roman Beach (Romai-part or Romai Furdo) is next to the Danube River, Romai-part III. Flat and grassy site has similar facilities as Harshegy but with a barber and hairdresser (very cheap). Take suburban train from downtown Pest to station Romai-part across from campground.

CITY TRANSPORTATION   In addition to buses, there are tram, trolleybus, subway, cog-wheel railway and local train service in Budapest. A bus ticket costs 1.50 forints, and tram, trolleybus and subway cost 1 forint regardless of distance. All tickets must be bought in advance of boarding from bus or tram terminals, subway office, railway stations or tobacconists' shops. You punch your ticket in the machine after boarding. On the Metro (subway), a 1 forint coin must be dropped into the automat placed at the head of the escalator. Bus tickets can be used on the cog-wheel railway which goes to Szechenyi Hill--from which trails begin, or tickets can be bought at the railway terminals. For the Pioneer Railway tickets can be bought at the stops. HEV, the suburban train system, uses tram tickets up to the border of Budapest but after that supplementary tickets must be bought according to distance traveled. Trams are yellow, trolley-buses red, buses blue and the cars of HEV are green.

Rush hours are 7-9 and 4-5:30 and to be avoided. If you can't, be prepared to step lightly as drivers do not consider necessary more than one foot on board before departing. Buses and trolleys rattle along at a high clip and anarchy reigns. During a visit in 1969, a bus driver drove his bus into the Danube but this must have been a rare occurrence or it wouldn't have made the front page of "The Herald Tribune."

FOOD   Hungarian restaurants are the most atmospheric in Europe. Decor stretches from crystal chandeliers and remembrance of things past to gypsy style rooms with open hearths and dining al fresco. Usually there's at least one violinist! And you can afford to eat there if you brought in the legally allowed 400 forints at western exchange rates! Restaurants are classified by the government and charge accordingly. Quality of cooking has little to do with a restaurant's official classification, and you will be well fed anywhere. Hungarians eat at all hours and informal stand-up cafeterias are always open. Restaurants open at noon for lunch with most people eating at 1:00 pm or later. Dinner is at 7:00 pm or later, a leisurely affair considered the evening's entertainment. "Etterem" is restaurant. "Etlap" (menu) is printed in Hungarian and French with an English translation sometimes provided but not in cheaper places. The dish most frequently encountered is a form of stew with meat, green peppers, onions and paprika-flavored sauce, served with a salad of cucumbers and mild peppers.

Hungaria Cafe-Restaurant in Pest at VII Lenin Boulevard is a must for your visit. Though in need of restoration, it remains an elegant place with intimate multi-level interior making it possible for everyone to see and be seen. Built in 1894 with gold leaf everywhere and diagonally fluted columns, it served the aristocracy of the day admirably. You can order a full meal here or just pastry. Matyas Pince, Marcius 15 Ter near Duna Intercontinental has medieval atmosphere. Aranyszarvas, Szarvas Ter 1 (open 5 pm, closed Tuesday) is a game and venison specialty restaurant in a converted house. A sampler plate of 6-7 kinds of wild meat with characteristic strong flavor--children won't like them--is served. Budafolk Wine Vaults, southern edge of Budapest, has the underground restaurant Borkatakomba connected with vast wine cellars hewn from several miles of limestone. One of the three underground dining rooms, Szalonnasuto, has an open hearth where you assemble bacon, sausage and onion on a stick and roast-it-yourself. Address is 65 Nagytetenyi Ut in town of Budafok. Mini-buses leave from 4/6 Kigyo Utca on the hour from 5 pm.

We think Hungarians concoct even better desserts than the French and a cafe is the place to try some. Vorosmarty Cafe, Vorosmarty Ter in Pest (at end of Vaci Utca shopping street) serves a "chocolate creme" which is the quintessence of lightness in chocolate desserts. It's served in a parfait glass and there's also a strawberry version. The Cafe has several small rooms with faded brocade on the walls and faded ladies in the chairs with decor left over from an earlier more gracefully guilded age. Don't miss!

Public market (vasarcsarnok) locations are Tolbuhkin Korut next to Kalvin Square, and Rakoczi Ter off Grand Boulevard. Csemege Aruhaz at Lenin Korut and Rakoczi Ut is a large delicatessen which also stocks wines and liqueurs. Be certain to purchase a stick of Hungary's famous sausage. It's always available in Konsum-Turist stores in which you must pay in U.S. currency or travelers checks. If you happen to see it in a regular shop window, buy it then as it'll be gone by tomorrow. The sausage is lean, high quality and keeps without refrigeration. Water is safe to drink.

GUIDED SIGHTSEEING TOURS   It's harder to do it yourself in Eastern European countries. Tours are offered by both IBUSZ and City Tourist Board but itineraries and costs differ. City Tourist Board tours leave from its office at 5 Roosevelt Ter in Pest. Its City Tour is very reasonable, lasts 3 hours and covers Castle Hill and Buda, Acquincum, Margaret Island, National Gallery Museum, Gellert Hill and Citadella. Also offered are Buda

Hills Tour, Parliament and Museums Tour and Budapest by Night Tour.
IBUSZ tours leave from bus depot on Engels Square in Pest. (You will see
many buses in an open area surrounding a one-story ticket office.) Tickets
are sold at ticket office or beforehand at IBUSZ office. Offered is a 3 -hour
City Tour which visits People's Stadium, Castle of Vajdahunyad in City Park,
Heroe's Square, Opera House, Cathedral of St. Stephen and Parliament for
which there is an inside guided tour.

SIGHTSEEING ON YOUR OWN   Heroe's Square (Hosok Tere) and City Park
(Varosliget) are next to each other at end of avenue Nepkoztarsasag Utja in
Pest. Area includes a superb fine arts museum and the Vajdahunyad complex
of buildings. Heroe's Square, in the middle of lots of pavement, hosts a
semi-circular statuary of national heroes built in 1896-1929 as a Millenary
Memorial. Circular column in front depicts seven Hungarian Chieftains on
horseback, and colonaded semi-circle behind holds statues of 14 historical
figures. Fine Arts Museum, 41 Dozsa Gyorgy Ut (main street in front of
memorial), has works by Goya, Rembrandt, Titian, Raphael and other important artists including some French Impressionists. Mucsarnok (exhibition
museum) is next door in building resembling a Greek temple in granite. Behind Fine Arts Museum at Allatkerti Ut 2 is Gundel Restaurant, the Grand
Dame of olden times. Try lunch in the courtyard with flamed walnut crepes
for dessert.

City Park spreads behind the memorial and next to Gundel. Vajdahunyad Castle in the middle of the park is the most important sight. Park also
has a zoo, amusement area, restaurant, swimming pools, botanical gardens,
artificial lakes and fairgrounds. Castle of Vajdahunyad consists of 21 buildings on an island surrounded by an artificial lake and was built to celebrate
the Millenium with architects incorporating elements of previous historical
periods. Evolution of architecture through Baroque is demonstrated. An
interesting agricultural museum (Mezogazdasagi Museum) is in the Renais-
sance-looking building. Well-designed displays of Hungarian agriculture are
presented. Vajdahunyad Restaurant, next to castle at Kacson Pongract Ut,
has outside tables. "Ciganypecsenye" is steak, gypsy style. Zoo buildings
reflect eastern architecture. Swimming pools offer both plain and mineral
water--the former is in the three large outdoor ones. Vidam Park is the
amusement section with children's rides and a puppet show.

Castle Hill (Varhegy) in Buda is the site of the original settlement and
a good walking area of old houses. Fishermen's Bastion was part of the defence of the medieval city. This particular sector was manned by the fishermen's guild. Inside ramparts is Halaszbastya Restaurant. Across from
Fishermen's Bastion is Coronation Church (Matyastemplom) where kings
were crowned from 1309-1916. Also in the district is Castle Museum
(Varmuzeum), 2 Szentharomsag Utca, with things medieval. Royal Gardens
of yore is now a youth park (Ifjusagi Muvelodesi) where outdoor dances are
held in summer. Walking in the old town, you may come upon Ruszwurm
Cafe, Szentharomsag Utca 3, which started as a bakery in 1500. Fortuna
Restaurant, Hesz Andras Ter 4, is a small ancient palace, open 11 am.
Fehar Galamb, Szentharomsag Utca 9, features meats roasted in an open
fireplace. Regi Orszaghaz, Orszaghaz 17 north of castle, is atmospheric
with many small rooms.

Gellert Hill is what you come upon when crossing Elizabeth Bridge from downtown. On the right is Gellert Hotel, formerly the best hotel in Budapest. It's on Gellert Ter and offers numerous services including an outdoor swimming pool with artificial waves. The hotel's second class restaurant is good value--it's on the main floor and has a separate entry at far right of the hotel. You will see some tables set up outside and it's behind them. Nearby at Gellerthegy is Citadella, an old fort which was once part of the ramparts. Good view from top. Restaurant inside has a house specialty "magyaros izelito" which is a platter of pork, fish, sausage, foie gras and veal and mushroom omelet. Children's playground is on backside of Gellert Hill in Ifjusagi Park.

Acquincum is an excavated Roman town at 103 Szentendrei Ut on shore of Danube River in suburb of Obuda. Visitors can walk among the remains of this town which flourished from first century A.D.

SHOPPING   Stores are open weekdays 8-6 and to 1 pm on Saturday. Vaci Utca in Pest is main shopping street. Corvin Nagyuarhaz on Blaha Lujza Ter near Rakoczi Ut is largest department store. Special stores for tourists in which payment is made in hard currency such as dollars are called Konsum-Turist. Multi-lingual clerks sell articles of traditional interest to tourists such as embroidery, folk art, wine and salami. A Konsum-Turist is on Kigyo Utca. When a Hungarian wants to sell his own things which are antiques or of artistic merit, he consigns them to "bizomanyi boltok" shops. Some antiques and art works require an export permit. It's legal to take out three days supply of food, two liters of wine and one liter of spirits.

LE POTPOURRI   U.S. Consulate is at 12 Szabadsag Ter in area of Parliament in Pest. Offices and stores are closed on May 1 and August 20, Constitution Day.

HUNGARIAN

Leves	Soup
bableves	ham and bean soup
rantott leves	broth with croutons
korhely leves, kaposzta	cabbage soup
gulyas leves	meat and vegetable soup
Appetizers	Appetizers
pogacsa	pastry appetizers
libamaj	goose liver
langos	crepe appetizers
liptoi	cream cheese appetizer
Salata (fejes)	Salad (lettuce)
uborka	cucumber
ENTREE	ENTREE
csirke (paprikas)	chicken (stew)
rantott csirke	fried chicken
marhahus, vadas hus (gulyas)	beef (stew)
rostelyos	Swiss steak
borjuhus (paprikas)	veal (stew)
disznohus (pokolt)	pork (stew)
sonka	ham
kilbasz (virsli)	sausage (wiener)
borso, zoldbab, krumpli	peas, string beans, potatoes
VIZ (pronouned 'veez')	WATER

BEWARE SWIMMING IN THE MEDITERRANEAN

Though lovely to look at, the Mediterranean Sea has become so polluted that Jacques Yves Cousteau has been quoted as saying, "I've given up swimming in the Mediterranean." The "Coordinated Mediterranean Pollution Monitoring and Research Program" has been set up by countries bordering on the sea to deal with the problem before scientists' prediction of a "dead sea" by the end of the century comes true.

An important reason why the Mediterranean has come to be called the most polluted sea in the world is its slow-moving waters which prevent chemicals dumped into it by factories and tons of waste from coastal towns from being dispersed as it is in the Atlantic. The narrow Straits of Gibraltar is its only real exit and a complete change of water is estimated as taking 80 years.

There are still unpolluted places in the Mediterranean but they are becoming harder to find and would be away from large coastal towns. The area around Barcelona is considered heavily polluted and the romantic Bay of Naples is the most polluted area in Italy. Italy's National Research Council has estimated that the percentage of its country's beaches that are polluted to some extent is at least 60 percent. Deep in the Bay of Otranto in southern Italy is a sunken Yugoslavian ship with 909 metal drums of poisonous gasoline additives which are being recovered before they leak into the sea. Cholera, typhoid, dysentery, polio, viral hepatitis and other diseases live in the Mediterranean waters. The 1973 cholera epidemic in Naples was caused by contaminated mussels. A number of other diseases can be contracted by eating fish and shellfish.

IRELAND

Ireland is divided into Northern Ireland (Ulster), the six counties which are under British rule, and the South, which is called the Republic or Eire and is an independent country. The information given here refers to the South or Republic of Ireland.

CURRENCY   The Irish pound is divided into 100 pence (100p). The British pound is called the pound sterling。 One Irish pound is worth about $1.57 in 1981.

WEATHER   Always be prepared for the possibility of rain.

CAMPING   The Irish Tourist Board in the U.S. will send you a pamphlet, "Caravan and Camping Parks 1982," which lists and describes campgrounds. Usually the campground charges by tentsite and by person, or a flat fee per person。

TRAINS   CIE (Coras Iompair Eireann) operates the trains. Eurailpass and Eurail Youthpass are valid in Ireland。 These passes include ferry crossings on the Irish Continental Line between Rosslare, Ireland, and Cherbourg and LeHavre, France. Port taxes are extra and must be paid in Irish pounds. During July and August a reservation is advised. If a cabin is wanted, the cheapest is a berth in a 6-berth cabin on the ship, St. Killian. Otherwise the next cheapest berth is one in a 4-berth cabin on the lower deck which costs $10 and is available on both ships. There is a $5 reservation fee per berth. Between April 1 and September 30, a ferry leaves Rosslare for Le Havre every day except Monday and Friday, and a ferry leaves for Cherbourg on Mondays and Fridays. Departure time for both destinations is 5:00 pm. Arrival in Le Havre is 3:00 pm and in Cherbourg, 11:00 am the next day. Check-in time is one hour prior to sailing. From October 1 to March 31 the only sailings are from Rosslare to La Havre on Sunday, Wednesday and Friday. Meals on board cost about $6 for breakfast, $8 for lunch and $11 for dinner, however there is also a snack bar. Both car ferries also offer duty free gift shops, discotheque, lounges, and movies on closed circuit television.

CIE offers one day roundtrip tickets for train journeys for the price of one way (called "day excursion"). Weekend Travel tickets offer a discount for trips leaving on Friday, Saturday and Sunday and returning by the next Tuesday. A variation on Weekend Travel is an Eight Day Return Ticket that discounts a trip taken within 8 days. Reduced fares are given group travel. Rambler Tickets give unlimited travel by rail alone or by rail and bus for 8 or 15 days. Rail only for 8 days costs $58, 15 days--$84. Rail and bus costs $72--8 days, $102--15 days. Children under 15 pay half fare.

In Ireland public toilets are often classified in Gaelic--"Fir" is men's, "Mna" is women's.

IRELAND TO BRITAIN   The crossing from Rosslare to Fishguard, Wales, is one of the least expensive crossings. Only slightly higher is the route Dun (13 miles south of Dublin) to Holyhead, Wales. There is train service from all four towns.

SHOPPING   Value-added tax (VAT) is 25% and applies to items like furs, cameras, glassware and china. On some items the rate is 10% and no tax is assessed on clothing, food and shoes. VAT is always included in the displayed price. Merchandise sent out of the country or delivered to your plane can be sold free of VAT, but you must ask.

CORK

Cork City Caravan and Camping Park, located 2 miles southwest of the city center on Togher Road, is open April 1-Sept 30. Take bus #14 from downtown Cork which leaves every 20 minutes. Bus stop is in front of the campground. Hot showers, store, television lounge. Adult/ 30 p, tent/ £ 2.40

Cork Caravan Company Caravan and Camping Park is located 3-1/2 miles southwest of Cork on L42 road to Kinsale and Cork Airport. Open all year. Hot showers, television lounge, washing machine, 200 yards from supermarket. Adult/ 20 p, tent/£ 2.20.

DUBLIN

Dublin's suburban rail line goes north from Dublin Connolly Station and stops at Killester, Harmonstown, Raheny, Kilbarrack, Howth Junction,

Portmarnock, Malahide, Donabate, Rush & Lusk, Skerries and Balbriggan.
From Howth Junction, a rail spur goes to Bayside, Sutton and Howth.
South form Dublin Connolly Station, the train stops at Tara Street (Dublin),
Dublin Pearse Station, Landsdowne Road, Sidney Parade, Booterstown,
Blackrock, Monkstown & Seapoint, Dun Laoghaire, Sandycove, Glenageary,
Dalkey, Killiney, Shankill, Bray and Greystones.

Donabate Caravan Park is beside the sea in the village of Donabate.
Take suburban rail line to Donabate. Hot showers, store, television lounge.
Flat fee for tentsite/£3.25. Open May 1-Oct 1.

Shankill Caravan has 55 tent sites and is located just past the village of
Shankill on right hand side of Bray/Wexford Road. Take bus 45 or 84 from
Dublin, bus 45a from Dun Laoghaire, or train to Shankill plus a walk. Seaside town of Bray is 2 miles from campground. Hot showers, store, television lounge. Adult/30 p, tentsite/£2.30. Open Easter to Sept 30.

DUN LAOGHAIRE

The town is 13 miles south of Dublin, and is the arrival point for ferries
from Holyhead, Wales. Train line goes north to Dublin or south to Wexford
and Rosslare. Closest campground is Cromlech Caravan Park in Bally-
brack Village by town of Killiney. It is on the bus route to Bray. Open
Apr 16-Sept 19. Hot showers, store, television lounge. Adult/50 p, tent-
site/£3.00. Slightly further south is Shankill Caravan campsite listed under
Dublin.

GALWAY

Salthill Caravan Park, is 1/2 mile from village of Salthill. Take bus from
Station for Salthill and then walk. Open Apr 1-Oct 1. Hot showers, television lounge. Flat fee per tentsite/£3.50.

KILLARNEY

Three campgrounds are within 3-1/2 miles of Killarney. Closest is White
Bridge, located one mile east of Killarney off Cork Road. Entrance is 300
yards from road. Bus from Killarney. Open Easter-Sept 30. Hot showers,
store, washing machine, television lounge. Adult/20 p, tentsite/£3.00.

ROSSLARE

Irish Continental Line ferries, free with Eurailpasses, leave from Rosslare.
Starting from the water, the three train stations are called Rosslare Harbor
(pier), Rosslare Harbor (mainland) and Rosslare Strand (town).

In Rosslare Strand, Burrow Caravan Park is open all year. The camp
is mainly for trailers (caravans) but will take campers. Hot showers,
store, washing machine, take-out meals. Flat fee for tentsite/£3.00.

(See town of Wexford for another nearby campground.)

TRALEE

Bayview Caravan Park is one mile from Tralee on the road to Ballybunion.
Open Apr 1-Oct 31. Hot showers, television lounge. Adult/20 p, tentsite/
£1.60. Maximum stay of 2 nights for tents July 4-Aug 22.

WESTPORT

Parkland Camping is on the Westport House Country Estate, which offers pony rides, zoo park, the house itself, and bike rentals. No trailers are allowed, and there are 78 tent sites on 3 acres. Free membership in the holiday club is given to campers who stay 3 consecutive nights. Benefits include use of Westport House and discounts on facilities of the Estate. Hot showers, lounge, store, washing machine. Flat fee for tentsite £3.00. Open Apr 1–Sept 30.

      Roman Island campground is 1 mile from Westport at Westport Quay (dock). Open Easter–Oct 31. Hot showers, store. Tentsite £3.00.

WEXFORD

Ferrybank Caravan Park is located 1/2 mile from town on Dublin Road. Open last weekend in May to mid-Sept. Hot showers, store, washing machine. Flat fee tentsite £2.50.

Sightseeing is glorious, the food is good and you can camp somewhere in Italy the year around. But if you have a railpass and the railway workers are about to strike, get out fast. Rome, Venice, Florence and Naples are cities no one will want to miss and the bare minimum for a visit to Italy. Less well known but equally enjoyable is the island of Sicily to which an air-conditioned train down the boot of Italy will take you. We remind summer visitors destined for Greece to make ferry and connecting train reservations early. (Please see "trains" for details.)

CURRENCY   Italian lira (lire in plural) is the monetary unit. There are 1200 lire to one dollar in 1981. Conductors on international trains are allowed to change up to about $25 worth into lire at the official exchange rate. A small fee is charged just as at a bank and a receipt is given.

WEATHER   During July and August camping is best in the Alps and Dolomites and on the beaches and coasts. The main cities are rather warm in these months though they're still flooded with tourists much to the consternation of locals. Anything south of Naples is fairly warm unless tempered by sea breezes. Late spring and early fall are wonderful times to visit Italy, except for the northern mountainous regions. Fall color is spectacular while early spring vegetables and June raspberries are delicious. Best of all, there is no unbearable heat in Rome, Florence, Venice or Milan nor too many tourists. Sicily, so jampacked with attractions that it's called the archeological museum of Europe, is the place to head for a winter camping vacation. The sun shines an average of six hours a day then.

CAMPING Camping is well entrenched in Italy and prices are lower than in northern Europe. Tourist office will send you a map and campground list. The UPIM department store chain has reasonable camping equipment. Words in use at campgrounds are:

    campeggio - camping
    entrata - entrance
    uscita - exit
    venvenuti - welcome
    andate lentamente - drive slowly
    informazioni - information
    orario spaccio - hours open
    direzione - office
    tende - tent
    luce - child
    moto - motorcycle
    acqua potabile - drinking water
    acqua non potabile - don't drink water
    non sprecate l'acqua - don't waste water
    W.C. uomini - mens' toilets
    W.C. donne - womens' toilets
    non gettate gli assorbenti igienici nei W.C. - do not throw sanitary
        napkins in the toilet
    ma negli appositi recipienti - use the wastebasket
    docce - showers
    lavabo - handwashing sinks
    lavatoio stoviglie - dishwashing sinks
    vietato lavare - no washing
    lavatoio biancheria - clothes washing room
    rifiuti - garbage disposal
    spiaggia - beach
    noleggi sedie a sdraio, ombrelloni - deck-chairs, umbrellas for rent

TRAINS TEE trains operating solely in Italy are the Settebello (Milan-Bologna-Florence-Rome), Vesuvio (Milan-Naples) and Adriatico (Milan-Bari with connections to Brindisi and Lecce). Several more trains are on a par with TEE trains and carry only first class, such as the air-conditioned Peloritano on the route to Sicily. In general, fast trains are classified Rapido, Express (Direttissimo) and Fast (Diretto). Rapido trains carry a supplemental charge for ordinary ticket holders. A seat reservation costs 600 L.

    Tickets bought in the U.S. are good for six months and carry unlimited stopover privileges. Once in Italy, it's easier to buy tickets from a travel agent such as American Express than at the station as both charge the same price. Children 4-12 pay half and those under 4 ride free. Adults and children 12 and over in a family of four traveling together receive a 40 percent discount and children under 12 pay half fare. For each person beyond four in a family, one adult receives 50 percent off. Family discounts are available only at train stations in Italy. Group reductions are 30 percent discount for groups of at least 10 paying passengers, 40 percent off for groups of 25-100 paying passengers, plus one free ticket for groups of 15-50 paying passengers and two free tickets for groups of 51-100 paying passengers. A kilometric ticket is sold that is valid for 30 days and 20 trips totalling 3000 km maximum. It may be used by more than one person and costs $140 first class and $79 second class. For travel on Rapido or TEE trains, a supplement must be paid at the time a reservation is made. A "B. T. L. C." tourist ticket can be purchased in the U. S. or from border train stations in Italy. It gives unlimited travel on entire Italian State Railway (FS) system and free seat reservations from train stations in Italy. The first class pass includes TEE trains on the equivalent Italian Settebello, Ambrosiano, Vesuvio and Adriatico. Both first and second class passes include all Rapido trains, even those for which a supplement is normally charged. The pass must be used within six months of issue and the validity dates must be written by the train station personnel when the pass is first used. Cost is first class 8 days for $114, 15 days for $139, 21 days for $166 and 30 days for $202. Second class pass costs 8 days for $72, 15 days for $87, 21 days for $102 and 30 days for $127. Children under four ride free and those under 12 pay half. Kilometric and "Go Anywhere" tickets can be purchased through Italian State Railways, c/o CIT Travel Service, 5670 Wilshire Blvd., Los Angeles, Ca. 90036 or 500 Fifth Avenue, New York, N. Y. 10036.

Included in Eurailpass and Eurail Youthpass is the ferry crossing on the Adriatica and Hellenic Mediterranean Lines between Patras, Greece and Brindisi, Italy. Anyone with a railpass would be crazy not to go. Deck fare is what you get--a chair can be reserved by paying about $4 extra when the reservation is made and students receive a 30% reduction. The seat is of the reclining airline type but it's also possible to lay down your air mattress and sleeping bag and sleep on the floor. The car-ferry ships are one-class, air conditioned and have a lounge with television, snack bar, sundeck and swimming pool which is filled after leaving Corfu or thereabouts. The four ships are the Egnatia (6,185 tons, 980 passengers, 160 cars), Appia (8,026 tons, 1,130 passengers, 150 cars), Castalia (9,000 tons, 1600 passengers, 250 cars) and Espresso Grecia (7,322 tons, 1600 passengers, 300 cars). These ships are deluxe boats. Appia and Castalia are excellent boats. Egnatia is older than Appia and I don't know about Grecia. Be sure to bring food with you or be prepared to pay these prices: continental breakfast $2, lunch and dinner $7 on Egnatia and Castalia and $9 on Appia and Grecia. Food can also be bought from the snack bar. Two boats leave Brindisi each day from about June 10 to September 29. The Castalia and Grecia leave Brindisi on alternate days at 8 pm and sail directly to Patras, arriving there at 12 noon the next day. At Patras a connecting bus will take you to Athens for $7 which arrives in Athens at 4 pm. Otherwise trains and regular buses are available. The Egnatia and Appia leave Brindisi at 10:30 pm, arrive in Corfu at 7 am the next day, Igoumenitsa at 9 am and Patras at 6 pm from which a connecting bus brings passengers to Athens arriving at 10 pm. During the rest of the year, Grecia and Egnatia alternate on the sole 10:30 departure. The word is that you must make reservations for the ferry in advance or you may have to wait several days to get on in summer. This should be done as soon as you arrive in Italy at a Hellenic Mediterranean Lines or Adriatica Lines office whose address can be obtained from the tourist office. The reserva-

tion is free and can be obtained at Ufficio Passegeri de l'Adriatica S.P.A.M.,
11 Via Regina Margherita in Rome or at similar offices in most cities. If a
stopover in Corfu is planned, this should be indicated when the reservation
is made. A surcharge of $12 is made June 10 through September 30 and
paid when the compulsory reservation ($1.50 fee) is made. Also pay for a
seat, if wanted, at this time. Port taxes of about 4,000 L must be paid in
lira and are due upon actually boarding the ship. Before boarding, all
passengers must check in at the shipping line office at the pier in Brindisi.

It is advisable to make reservations on a connecting train for these
ships, but there is a risk as sometimes the trains are late and the ferry
leaves on schedule. The following schedules are for planning purposes only.
Please check departure times in Italy. From Milan, TEE leaves at 9:15 am
and arrives Brindisi at 9:08 pm (TEE goes as far as Bari and then a slower
train is taken). From Rome, leave 10:30 pm, arrive Brindisi 9:20 pm;
leave 10:30 pm, arrive Brindisi 6:43 am. From Naples (Central Station),
leave 2:06 pm and connect with the 12:30 pm departure from Rome at Caserta
and arrive Brindisi at 9:20 pm; leave Naples 10:40 pm (Central Station),
arrive Brindisi 6:43 am. From Messina on Sicily, leave (Marittima Station)
5:05 am, arrive Taranto 12:55 pm, change trains, leave Taranto 1:05 pm,
arrive Brindisi 2:21 pm or visit Taranto which is more worthy than Brindisi
and leave Taranto at 6:23 pm, arrive Brindisi 6:48 pm. Another train leaves
Messina (Marittima Station) 8:50 pm, arrive Taranto 6:18 am, visit the town
and take a later train to Brindisi.

Eurailpass and Eurail Youthpass entitle holders to reduced fares on
these steamship lines. A 20 percent reduction on first class fares on the
Eurailpass and on second class fares for Eurail Youthpass on the Tirrenia
Steamship Company boats between Naples and Palermo, Naples and Malta,
Syracuse and Malta and for crossings to Sardinia. A 20 percent reduction
on normal fares of DFDS Steamship Company between Genova and Tunis,
and Genova and Alicante and Malaga. A 30 percent reduction on published
fares of Libra Maritime for Eurailpass holders only, between Ancona and
Piraeus or Ancona and Haifa on the T.S.S. "Neptunia." A 30 percent reduc-
tion to Eurailpass and Eurail Youthpass holders on fares of the Adriatica
Line between Venezia (Venice), Piraeus and Alexandria on the M.S.
"Expresso Egitto." Contact local Adriatica offices for reservations.

When traveling by train in Italy, beware of the train that splits enroute.
This is especially true of trains leaving Rome where cars to both Milan and
Venice are strung together at the outset while later the cars to Venice are
detached and connected to another engine to turn east to Venice. Always
check the nameplate inside and outside the door of each car for its ultimate
destination.

FS - Italian State Railways	da, a - from, to
ferrovia - railway	data del viaggio - date of departure
binario - track	treni en partenza - departures
treno - train	treni en arrivo - arrivals
carozza - car	prenotazione - seat reservation
posta - seat	baglio a mano - baggage storage

DRIVING   Roads are classified (1) autostrade--freeways, most of which charge tolls based on mileage and horsepower of vehicle. Ticket is issued upon entering and payment is made at booth upon exiting. Portion between Salerno and Reggio Calabria is free. (2) Strade Statali (state roads). (3) Strade Provinciali (provincial roads). And (4) Strade Comunali (local roads). Gasoline discount coupons can be purchased by tourists who drive a car registered outside of Italy. Tourists with Italian rental cars do no qualify. The coupons give a 30 percent reduction on gasoline prices. Coupons are sold in 10 liter denominations for super or regular gas. Two allotments of 400 liters (106 gallons) per calendar year is maximum that can be bought. Coupons can be purchased from ACI (Automobile Club of Italy) offices at borders. Unused coupons may be refunded less 6 percent service fee by the Italian Government Travel Office, 630 Fifth Avenue, New York, N. Y. 10020. Coupon buyers are also given two coupons for free road service which includes towing up to 40 kilometers. Dial #116 from call box. On Autostrada del Sole (Milan-Naples), emergency call boxes are placed on right hand side of freeway every two kilometers. Drivers must not leave stalled car, but should hail a passing car to stop at a call box and call for you. If stalled car is blocking road, a triangular warning sign must be placed at least 30 meters behind.

Speed limits are 130 kmh (80 mph) on autostrade, 100 kmh (62 mph) on main roads and 50 kmh (31 mph) in cities and towns. Some roads have the reversible passing middle lane. Passing vehicle must signal in advance and leave signal on until returned to right-hand lane. At unmarked crossroads, vehicles coming from the right have priority. Trams and trains always have priority.

TOURIST OFFICE   E. P. T. are offices of the provincial tourist boards and A. A. S. T. are tourist offices operated by the city or town. "Carta" is map.

CITY TRANSPORTATION   Buses and trams are usually found but Milan and Rome have subways too. On buses and trams, enter by rear door, pay conductor and go out front. Check phone directory for map of routes. Always cross streets at the black and white striped crosswalks (passaggi zebrati). Watch the traffic signals (semafori).

FOOD   In 1981, one liter of milk sold for 500-600 L, 500 grams bread for 600-800 L and one whole hot cooked chicken for 5000-7000 L. The average Italian spends about 40 percent of his income on food and beverages. Though a few supermarkets exist, most is spent in the market and small food shops. To eat cheaply in Italy is to eat pasta (spaghetti, macaroni, etc.), salad, bread and fruit. Meat is relatively expensive, though veal and chicken are staples in this category. American-style beef is not found in Italy as grazing land is in short supply. Cheese is reasonable and good. Buy cheese, butter and meat by the "etto" which 100 grams or about three ounces. You can ask for a discount (sconto) on prices in the market and small shops (but you may not get any), but not in the supermarket. The important agricultural crops of Italy are wheat, much of which is the hard type used in pasta, olives and wine. Corn and citrus fruits are also important. Rice is grown too, the only place in Europe, and parboiled rice baked whole is available. Cheese is an important industry and both cow and goat cheese is made.

Pasta is the basic food and comes in numerous sizes and shapes and a couple of colors. Green is made from spinach flour. Macaroni is made from hard red wheat and boiling water. Many other varieties such as ravioli, canneloni, etc. have egg added to the macaroni dough. Pasta is not served as the

main course in Italy but as a separate first course following antipasto (appetizers). Lateria is the dairy, often found as an annex to a cafe, and it sells
pasteurized milk and usually keeps long hours from morning to midnight.
National brands are sold in sterilized, pasteurized, whole milk and skim
milk versions in sealed containers, often bottles. Ice cream is safe in all
large cities as it's made from pasteurized cream and also generally in small
towns where national brands have been trucked in.

Restaurants come in several types. The Ristorante ranges from deluxe
to reasonable. The Trattoria has a regular group of neighborhood customers,
more informal service, straight-forward decor and generally cheaper prices.
Aim for a noon to 2 pm lunch (colazione) and 7-9 pm dinner (pranzo) to get the
best freshly cooked food at both a ristorante and trattoria. The Pizzeria
serves quick simple meals and also pizza which is often baked in long, rectangular pans, cut into pieces and sold on the spot. Some offer take-out or
stand-up eating only. Others are self-service with sit-down tables. The
Tavola Calda is like our lunch counter, offering a wide range of food, some
of which is already prepared. The usual restaurant meal has four courses.
The meal begins with antipasto, appetizers which can be hot (caldo) or cold
(freddo). Usually a platter of small amounts of lightly dressed raw vegetables
and perhaps a slice of ham or pork sausage are served. Pasta or soup follow.
You always have a choice, often between a thick, vegetable (minestrone)
soup or a couple of kinds of pasta. A small dish of freshly grated parmesan
cheese is often served as garnishment. If the option of lasagne, cannelloni,
ravioli or tortellini is given for the pasta dish, choose it rather than the
usual spaghetti or macaroni because these items always contain a nicely sea-
soned meat and cheese mixture. A basic lettuce salad with oil and vinegar
dressing is sometimes served with the pasta or soup. The entree is usually
a meat, fowl or fish dish served with a vegetable or rice. Dessert is often
fruit, your choice between a peach or grapes perhaps. Sometimes a small
cake or portion of a special baked dessert is offered. Wine is normally taken
with the meal. Water is safe in all large cities. Use bottled water in rural
areas if you wish, but we never have.

Restaurants offer two kinds of set menus. The Prezzo Fisso is the
restaurant's daily special, and the restaurant sets policy for it. The Menu
Turistico is government controlled and required to have an appetizer, entree
with vegetable, dessert and beverage (1/4 liter wine, glass of beer or orange
pop, etc. or 1/2 bottle of mineral water). The quoted price includes bread,
cover, service and taxes. Cover charge is "pane e coperti," and service
charge is "servicio."

SIGHTSEEING   Italy is a bargain country for sightseeing. The usual
entry fee of a national museum is about 30¢. Museums are normally closed
on Monday and on Sunday afternoon. Italy has a plethora of public holidays
including Easter Sunday and the following Monday, April 25 (liberation day),
May 1 (labor day), Ascension Day, Corpus Christi, June 2 (national day),
June 29 (St. Peter and Paul) and August 15 (Ferragosto).

Italy has so many museums, art galleries, cathedrals and monumental
architecture that the traveler must be very selective. Try to include something from the following periods. (1) ETRUSCAN. Archaeological finds at
Tarquinia, Volterra, Cerveteri and Veio. Much of the uncovered art has
been removed to the Archaeological Museum in Florence, Etruscan Museum
in Rome and Municipal Museum in Bologna. (2) GREEK CIVILIZATION.

You needn't visit Greece to see ancient Greek architecture. Some of the most impressive examples are on Sicily and at Paestum, south of Naples.
(3) ROMAN. You will stumble upon many a remnant of the Roman Empire during your visit. Triumphal arches, colosseums and roads are prolific. Rome, Pompeii, Herculaneum and Ostia (suburb of Rome) host the most important excavations. Naples National Museum is the elite, but good examples are everywhere. (4) THE MIDDLE AGES. Sculpture and paintings are found in many museums and galleries. The Uffizi and Gallery of Ancient and Modern Art in Florence are two. (5) RENAISSANCE. Florence is the most notable for this period, but every large city has a collection. The best sightseeing guidebook to Italy is the Michelin green guide in English. Assuming you have this, we have included only minimal sightseeing information for each city.

POSTOFFICES   For poste restante in Italy, add "fermo in posta" after the name of the city. American Express is more reliable. Best to avoid mailing a package from Italy, but here is how if you must. (1) Pack the goods and tie a string around trying to leave as few loose ends as possible. (2) Go to the tobacconist and buy as many lead clamps as your package has loose ends. (Tobacco is a state monopoly and is sold in shops with the sign "Sale e Tabacchi." They also sell stamps, postcards, candy, etc. and many are open Sunday morning.) The clerk will press lead balls onto the string (the clamps prevent pilferage). (3) Go to the proper post office, fill out the form in triplicate and pay the fee. Our packages arrived safely.

BEACHES   Most beaches in Italy are private and require an entry fee. The charge is about 500-1200 L and includes a dressing room, umbrella and chair. Small stretches of public beach are found but they are crowded. You can enter the most deluxe hotel and use its beach and facilities by paying the entrance fee. Pollution is a problem on beaches near cities and towns and we advise not going in the water even though Europeans are doing so.

THEFT   While in Italy it is important to be especially careful about your railpass, money and travelers checks. Always keep them close to you. These items should not be kept in outside pockets of clothing or backpack. Rome, Brindisi and Naples are the spots to watch, but this is written so that a visitor will be careful--not to discourage him from touring this wonderful country.

BRINDISI

Brindisi is the ferry departure point for Greece. Main tourist office, Via Regina Margherita 12 at the port, is 14 blocks from Central Station (F.S.) and open 8:30-1 & 4:30-7:30 pm. Brindisi's other train station is Stazione Marittima which is at the port two blocks from the tourist office. Make reservations for ferry at Adriatica S.P.A.N., 11 Via Regina Margherita, located next to the tourist office. See "trains" at the beginning of this chapter for details. If you wish to stop over at Corfu or Igoumenitsa, this must be indicated when the reservation is made and can only be done on the 10:30 pm departure. A reader reports that all the agencies are after you to take their boat to Greece so be sure to take the boat that is included in the pass. You should not have to pay a surcharge or supplement greater than the equivalent of $12 plus a $1.50 reservation fee. An embarkation tax of 4,000 L per adult is levied at the port and must be paid in lira. Students should inquire about a reduction.

Remember to bring food for the ferry trip and the open market operates at Victoria Square by the Post Office daily except Sunday 6 am–1 pm.

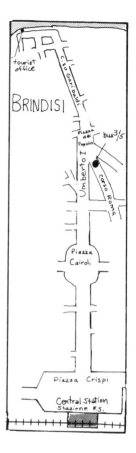

Camping Brin, in Materdomini five kilometers from downtown is open all year. Take bus # 3 or 5 from bus stop nine blocks from Central Station F.S. (see map). Bus ride is 25 minutes. Camp has store, snack bar, cooking facilities, beach, playgrounds, swimming pool and 18 modern cabins with kitchens for rent. Adult/ 1500 L, child/1100 L, tent/600 L, car/1000 L.

Here are train connections for people arriving at 8:30 am on the ferry from Greece. To Naples, leave Brindisi (Central Station) 11:02 am, arrive Naples (Central Station) 7:15 pm. To continue onto Rome, an all first class rapido train leaves Naples (Mergellina Station) 8:10 pm, arrives Rome 10:22 pm. To Milan, trains leave at 9:41 am and 10:55 am for Bari. Eurailpass holders could spend two hours exploring the "old city" in Bari and then take the 1:45 pm all first class rapido that arrives in Bologna at 9:46 pm and Milan at 11:45 pm. Those continuing on the 9:41 am departure from Brindisi will arrive in Bologna at 9:48 pm and Milan at 11:52 pm. To Sicily, leave Brindisi for Taranto 11:02 am, arrive Taranto 12:24 pm, change trains, leave Taranto 12:55 pm, arrive Messina Marittima 5:05 am.

If you have arrived in Brindisi at 5 pm, these train connections apply. To Naples, leave Brindisi 8:58 pm, arrive Naples (Central Station) 5:10 am. To continue to Rome, leave Naples (Garibaldi Station) 6:33 am, arrive Rome 9 am. For Milan and Bologna, leave Brindisi 6:25 pm, arrive Bologna 5:15 am and Milan 8:50 am. To Sicily, leave Brindisi 5:35 pm, arrive Taranto 6:52 pm. Visit Taranto, a one-star Michelin rated city with an attractive seafront promenade and a National Museum with a three-star collection of Greek pottery. Leave Taranto 10:33 pm, arrive Messina (Marittima Station) 7:45 am.

CREMONA

Famous for its violin makers--Stradivarius, Amati and Guarnerius, the town's International School of Violin Making carries on the tradition in the Piazza Marconi.

Colonie Padane-Camping Club, on the bank of the Po River, can be reached by bus #2 (Stazione-Bariera Po) from the train station. Then there is an 800 meter walk after getting off the bus. Hot showers, store, restaurant, adult/1400 L, tent/1000 L.

FLORENCE   (FIRENZE)

This lovely city of the Italian Renaissance is much visited by Americans. The train station (Stazione Centrale) is downtown. Tourist offices are Ente Provinciale per il Turismo (EPT) at Via Manzoni 16 and Azienda Autonoma di Turismo at Via Tornabuoni 15.

CAMPGROUNDS   Camp "ITALIANI E STRANIERI", 80 Viale Michelangelo, is on a hillside overlooking the Arno River and downtown Florence. Open Apr-Oct. From Central Station take bus #13 and get off at Viale Michelangelo in front of the camp. Bus fare is 100 L. Buses leave every 20 minutes. Bus #13 red follows the route: Stazione, Piazza dei Giudici and Piazzale Michelangelo. Bus #13 black goes from the Stazione to Porta Romana, Viale dei Colli and then Piazzale Michelangelo. It is an easy downhill walk from the camp to downtown. Camp has hot showers, store, snack bar with rotisseried chicken and fries, and post office. Adult/2300 L, child/1800 L, tent/free, car or camper/900 L.   Camping "VILLA CAMERATA", 2-4 Viale Augusto Righi, on youth hostel grounds (ostello della gioventu) requires a youth hostel card. Bus #17 from station and then a walk up a long private road.

FOOD   Public market is in the marble building diagonally across from the Medici Chapels. It's open 8 am-1 pm and here's where you'll find such foods as artichokes, beans, sweet peas, mushrooms and truffles. Tuscan olive oil from Lucca is high quality. Panforte of Siena, a cross between candy and cake in the shape of a large inch-high pancake, is unusual and very good. Self-service Grande Italia is on Piazza Stazione in front of the station. Self-service Restaurant, upstairs at 17 Via dei Pecori, off Via Vecchietti and 1-1/2 blocks from the Duomo, is open 12-3 & 7-10.

PUBLIC TRANSPORTATION   Buses cost 100 L. Machines dispense tickets.

SIGHTSEEING   If you haven't the Michelin guide or similar, stop by the tourist offices mentioned at the beginning and ask for their brochures and pamphlets. The important museums are the Accademia to see Michelangelo's works, Uffizi Gallery and Pitti Palace. Foremost church is the striking Duomo which can't possibly be missed as it forms part of Florence's most notable square.

READERS' SUGGESTIONS   "Camp Firenze, Florence, Italy (now called Italiani e Stranieri)--we loved the location of this campground--in an olive grove, near Piazzale Michelangelo, practically downtown, and on a bus line. The reason it isn't our unconditional favorite is that the bathrooms weren't very clean and the number of showers and sinks was inadequate for the large number of campers there. (It was filled and taking only those campers without cars.)" Linda Clark, Decatur, Georgia.   "In Florence we found a shop that would wrap packages to government standards so that you could send them home. They supply boxes, tape, packing paper (inside and out), and string. It's located at #27 Borgo SS Apostoli. This street is near the Ponte Vecchio, the bridge with all the shops on it. Costs: medium size box 2000 L and small box 1000 L. We don't recommend having anything breakable packaged here. We had a terricota tea set broken on arrival at home." Mr. and Mrs. Cooper, Batavia, Illinois.

TRAIN SCHEDULES   For Rome, TEEs leave Florence at 11:04 am (ar.

1:48 pm), 3:11 pm (ar. 5:46 pm) and first class only rapido leaves 2:25 pm (ar. 5:13 pm). Other trains leave at 8:02 am (ar. 12:06 pm), 9:48 am (ar. 1:18 pm), 10:23 am (ar. 2:50 pm), 11:52 am (ar. 3:05 pm), 1:30 pm (ar. 5:05 pm), 2:57 pm (ar. 6:50 pm), 3:51 pm (ar. 7:45 pm), 4:18 pm (ar. 7:15 pm), 4:43 pm (ar. 8:07 pm).

To Milan, TEEs leave Florence at 10:42 am (ar. 1:55 pm) and 2:23 pm (ar. 5:40 pm). Other trains leave at 9:15 am (ar. 1:45 pm, 10:15 am (ar. 2:40 pm), 1:27 pm (ar. 5:10 pm, 2:33 pm (ar. 5:40 pm), 4:55 pm (ar. 8:30 pm).

To Venice, trains leave Florence at 9:56 am (ar. Venezia-Mestre only (1:18 pm), 10:50 am (ar. Venezia S. L. 2:23 pm), 11:33 am (ar. Venezia S. L. 3:40 pm), 1:20 pm (ar. Venezia S. L. 4:37 pm), 2:58 pm (ar. Venezia S. L. 6:56 pm), 3:57 pm (ar. Venezia S. L. 7:16 pm), 4:28 pm (ar. Venezia S. L. 8:30 pm).

To Pisa, trains leave Florence at 7:25, 7:48, 8:30, 9:07, 10:58 am and 12:00, 12:50, 2:00, 2:23, 3:20, 4:10, 5:26, 6:16, 6:35, 7:08, 7:25 and 8:43 pm. Trip is about one hour.

To Ravenna, trains leave Florence at 6:00, 6:40, 8:15, 11:33 am and 1:15 and 4:52 pm. Trip is about 3 hours and 20 minutes.

To Sienna, trains leave Florence at 9:40 and 10:40 am, and 2:18, 3:26, 5:20, 6:45 and 8:10 pm. Trip is about two hours.

MILAN (MILANO)

Milan is Italy ringside and what's happening now. Heart of downtown is the pedestrians only area around Piazza Duomo.

TRAIN STATIONS Main station is Stazione Centrale. Make reservations to Rome at window #54. Others are Stazione Milano Garibaldi and Stazione Lamrate. Metropolitana (subway) line M 2 connects all three stations.

TOURIST INFORMATION An office is in Central Station and another at Piazza Duomo.

CAMPGROUNDS CAMPING AGIP is in suburban Metanopoli on Via Emilia at km 320 near the Autostrada (freeway). Open all year. No hot showers. Camp restaurant serves good reasonably priced food. Eric Wolterstorff writes "This camp is tricky to find the first time around. Take the clockwise ring-road tram 30, or from the station tram 9, around to Porta Romana, where the Corso di Porta Romana runs out of the center of town like the spoke of a wheel and on through the Roman gate. Walk one block down this street, away from town; it becomes Via Lodi. The stop for the suburban buses is at the next intersection. They'll be gray-and-blue, not orange like the city buses, and will be facing into town toward the Roman gate. Ask the driver or conductor for a bus going to San Donato. The buses run about every 15-20 minutes all day, slightly less often in the evening and on Sunday. In 1980 the fare was 450 L one way, and the ride took 10-12 minutes. Look for the sign on the right side of the road which says SAN DONATO, or ask the conductor to show you the stop, which is at the bus shelter immediately past the sign. Walk about 50 meters farther down the road, and cross the bridge over the concrete-lined gulley to the campground. Fees in 1980 were 3,100 L per night."

Campeggio Autodromo di Monza is in Parco Villa Reale next to the famous racing track in suburban Monza. Open Apr-Sept. From Central Station, take bus to Monza operated by Azienda Trasporti Municipali that leaves from Piazzale Duca d'Aosta in front of station. Bus stops 150 meters from camp. Monza is 12 kilometers from Milan and trains leave from Central Station at 9:35 am and 12:04, 2:05, 4:10, 5:40, 7:10 and 10:15 pm for the 11 to 21 minute trip. Trains leave for Monza from Garibaldi Station (P. G.) at 6:35, 8:15 am and 8:55 pm. Please check this campground with the tourist office before going there.

CITY TRANSPORTATION Buses, trams and metropolitana (subway) are operated by Azienda Trasporti Municipal (ATM). Single tickets can be bought from the yellow machines at most stops or at newstands with the yellow sign "Vendita Biglietti." Enter rear of bus or tram and cancel ticket in machine which marks the ticket with the time. Ticket is then good for one hour on all buses and trams except tram #1. Subway ticket is also good on buses and trams. For suburban buses, the ticket is bought on board. Tourist office and travel agencies sell a Tourist Ticket good for unlimited travel on city buses, trams and subway for one day.

SIGHTSEEING First priority is Italy's largest Gothic Cathedral located in the Plaza del Duomo, center of downtown Milan. Be sure to go up on the roof (free stairs or elevator 250 L) to see the statues. Brera Gallery, Pinacoteca di Brera, is the fine arts museum. Open Tu-Sa 9:30-4, Su 9:30-12:30 and Friday evening 9-11 pm.

TRAIN SCHEDULES To Brig (change for Zermatt), Lausanne and Geneva, TEE leaves Central Station at 8:30 am (ar. Brig 10:35 am Swiss time, Lausanne 11:58 am and Geneva 12:33 pm.) The portion between Brig and Martigny in the Alps is extremely scenic on this route. TEE Le Cisalpin leaves Milan Central Station at 2:48 pm (ar. Brig 4:44 Swiss time, Lausanne 6:10 pm and Paris 10:59 pm. Other trains on this route with cars destined also for Interlaken Ost and Bern are: leave Milan Central Station at 9:05 am (ar. Brig 11:51, Interlaken Ost 1:43 pm, Bern 1:47 pm, Lausanne 1:52 pm); 10:35 am (ar. Brig 1:03 pm, Interlaken Ost 2:50 pm, Bern 2:59 pm, Lausanne 2:53 pm); 12:35 pm (ar. Brig 3:27 pm, Interlaken Ost 5:58 pm, Bern 5:24 pm, Lausanne 5:49 pm); 3:05 pm (ar. Brig 5:51 pm, Interlaken Ost 7:55 pm, Bern 7:47 pm, Lausanne 7:46 pm); 5:15 pm (ar. Brig 7:40 pm, Interlaken Ost 9:34 pm, Bern 9:31 pm, Lausanne 9:31 pm.)

To Lugano and Zurich, TEE Gottardo leaves Milan Central Station at 5 pm (ar. Lugano 6:02 pm, Zurich 9:03 pm). Other trains on this basic Lugano, Zurich, Basle and Lucerne route leave about every hour or two with daylight arrivals in those cities as long as a morning or early afternoon train is taken.

To Monaco, Antibes, Marseille and Avignon, TEE Ligure leaves Milan (Central Station) at 6:45 am (ar. Monaco 11:07 am, Antibes 11:40 am, Marseille (St. Charles) 1:44 pm and Avignon 2:50 pm). Other trains on this route leave every one or two hours.

To Venice, Verona and Padua, first class only rapido trains leave Central Station at 6:55 am (ar. Verona 9:22 am, Padua 9:17 am, Venice S. L. 9:52 am) and at 9:35 am (ar. Verona 11:09 am, Padua 12:05 pm, Venice S. L.

12:34 pm). Other trains which also stop at Verona and Padua enroute to
Venice S. L. leave Milan (Central Station) at 7:20 am (ar. 11:00 am),
8:05 am (ar. 11:34 am), 8:40 am (ar. 11:50 am), 9:10 am (ar. 12:48 am),
11:36 am (ar. 3:06 pm), 12:38 pm (ar. 3:54 pm), 1:05 pm (ar. 4:35 pm),
2:48 pm (ar. 6:18 pm), 3:30 pm (ar. 7:02 pm).

To Florence and Rome, TEE trains leave Milan Central Station at
7:50 am (ar. Florence 10:59 am, Rome 1:48 pm) ana 11:50 am (ar. Florence
3:07 pm, Rome 5:46 pm). Other trains leave Milan Central Station at
7:55 am (ar. Florence 11:42 am, Rome 3:05 pm), 1 pm (ar. Florence
5:03 pm, Rome Tiburtina 8:48 pm.

NAPLES (NAPOLI)

Italian life gets louder and more animated the farther south you go. You
might think Naples the ultimate only if you haven't been to Palermo, Sicily.
Naples throbs with life and the survival of the fittest. It has very good campgrounds, exemplary pizza (herbal flavored rather than spicy), an important
archaeological museum and nearby Pompeii. To reserve space on the ferry
from Brindisi to Greece which is included in the railpasses, stop at either
of these offices: Adriatica, Piazza Bovio, or Hellenic Mediterranean Lines,
Via S. Nicola alla Dogana 15.

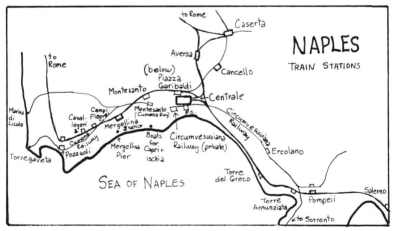

TRAIN STATIONS   Stazione Centrale (Napoli C.) is the main station and has
tourist office (Ente Turismo), seat reservations office and money change.
Many buses and trams leave from Piazza Garibaldi in front of Stazione Centrale. Beneath Stazione Centrale and Piazza Garibaldi is Stazione Garibaldi
(Napoli P. G.) which is reached through Stazione Centrale. Most trains arrive at Stazione Centrale but some stop only at the outlying stations Mergellina or Campi Flegrei. You need to know the arrival station for your train
to know when to get off--it is listed in the timetables at the stations. The
"metropolitana" subway is part of the state railway system (ferrovie dello

stato) and hence is included in railpasses. Its route is Napoli Gianturco - PIAZZA GARIBALDI (Central Station) - Piazza Cavour - Montesanto - Piazza Amedeo - Stazione MERGELLINA - Piazza Leopardi - Stazione CAMPI FLEGREI - Cavalleggieri Aosta (Citta Napoli Camping) - Bagnoli - Pozzuoli Solfatara. Circumvesuviana Railway which serves Ercolano, Pompeii, Vesuvious and Sorrento, and the Cumana Railway are both private railways and railpasses are NOT valid on them. Stazione Circumvesuviana is on Corso Garibaldi, about six blocks from Stazione Centrale, but the trains can be boarded at its other station, Stazione F.S. which is reached through Stazione Centrale. The Cumana Railway serves Marina di Licola and Torregaveta on the coast and leaves from its own Stazione Mergellina.

TOURIST INFORMATION   Ente Turismo (ENIT) offices are at both Central and Mergellina Stations. Ask for monthly publication "Carnet del Turista-Napoli" which lists sightseeing, restaurants, campgrounds, and train, bus and boat schedules.

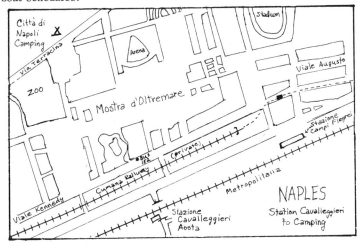

CAMPGROUNDS   CITTA DI NAPOLI (see map), Viale Giochi del Mediterraneo 75 is in Mostra d'Oltremare, a modern cultural center with swimming pool, stadium, sports arena, zoo and amusement park (Edenlandia). Open all year. If your train arrived at Stazione Campi Flegrei then the camp can be reached on foot. If you arrived at Stazione Mergellina, take the metropolitana to Stazione Cavalleggieri Aosta and from there walk to camp. From Central Station go down to Stazione Garibaldi beneath it and take the metropolitana to Stazione Cavalleggieri Aosta. OR take bus #152 from Corso Novara in front of Stazione Centrale. It leaves every 20 minutes and follows the route Corso Novara, Corso Garibaldi, the waterfront (Via Marina, Via Cristoforo Colombo), Vaile Augusto, Mostra d'Oltramare. Then the bus continues to Solfatara and Pozzuoli. NOTE: This camp is currently housing refugees from the 1980 earthquake and will not reopen until 1984.

    CAMPING SOLFATARA is near Pozzuoli beside the Solfatara Volcanic Crater. Open Apr 1-Oct 10. Follow bus directions above but remain on the bus until the Solfatara stop. The campground is in the woods about 100 meters from the bus stop. The metropolitana (subway) is faster. Follow

directions under Citta di Napoli on previous page but get off at Solfatara
Station. The campground is about a 15 minute partially uphill walk from
the station. Follow signs to Crater and the camp will be passed on the way.
The bus is recommended because it goes closer to camp but it takes more
time as the bus drives through downtown Pozzuoli. Store, restaurant, hot
showers (6 minutes-250 L), adult/2400 L, large tent/ 2150 L, small tent/
1100 L, car/1100 L, cabins/ 16,000 - 28,000 L.

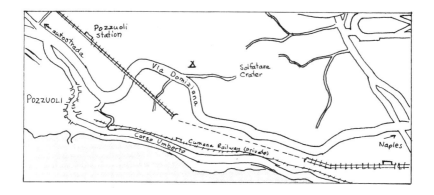

FOOD   Pizza was invented here and it's still made in the traditional
brick ovens. Basic pizza is Pizza Margherita, made of tomatoes, mozzarella cheese, olive oil and a leaf of fresh basil on top. Delicious! More
expensive pizzas have more ingredients such as Pizza Calzone to which
salami and cream cheese are added. Main food market is downtown not
far from Central Station but there are many neighborhood markets as well.

SIGHTSEEING Museums are half-price on Sunday. Most important is the
National Museum, Piazza Museo, which contains much of the sculpture and
decorations of Pompeii and Ercolano (Herculaneum). Open Tu-Sa 9-2, Su
9-1. Capodimonte National Museum and Gallery, Parco di Capodimonte, is
an exceptionally well-arranged museum in a beautiful palace within a park.
Bus #127, 110 from Central Station. Open Tu-Sa 9-2, Su 9-1 and in July
from 6-9pm also.
        Outside Naples, POMPEII is the famous excavated Roman town buried
by volcanic eruption in 79 A.D. Open daily 9 am to one hour before sunset.
Trains to Pompeii (direction Salerno) on Italian State Railways leave
Central Station at 6:50 am and 6:52 pm. Trip is 40 minutes. Trains leave
Pompeii for Naples at 6:09 am, 12:16 pm, 12:25 pm, 2:19 pm, 5:53 pm, and
10:14 pm. More frequent service is offered by the private Circumvesuviana
Railway whose trains leave about twice an hour from Circumvesuviana
Station and Station F.S. Station F.S. is connected to Stazione Centrale by
sort of an escalator which is called a travolator. Trip is 30 minutes.
ERCOLANO (Herculaneum) was more recently excavated and is an earlier
stop on the Circumvesuviana Railway.

GREEK TEMPLES AT PAESTUM. If you aren1t going to Greece, it would be a shame to miss the three beautiful Greek Temples at Paestum, 41 kilometers southeast of Salerno. Paestum was founded in the 6th century as a Greek colony and the ancient city stands all alone now in a grassy field inhabited only by crickets and lizards. Open 9 am-sunset. Take train to Battipaglia, 20 kilometers beyond Salerno, and change to a local to Paestum. Leave Naples Stazione Mergellina at 9 am or Stazione P. Garibaldi at 9:16 am and arrive in Battipaglia at 10:16 am. Change to a local train to Paestum here. Other Naples Central Station departures are 11:28 am, 12:55 pm, 1:05 pm and 2:50 pm. Check times to determine best connection. From Paestum Station, the temples, a campground (Villagio dei Pini), and cafe are a pleasant 20 minute walk down a tree-shaded country lane.

TRAIN SCHEDULES   To Sicily, the best train is the all first class Peloritano which leaves Napoli Mergellina Station at 12:33 pm, Napoli P. Garibaldi Station at 12:50 pm (ar. Messina Marittima 7:20 pm, Catania 9:01 pm, Syracuse 10:08 pm, Palermo 10:42 pm). A first and second class rapido train leaves Naples Mergellina at 9:00 am, P. Garibaldi at 9:16 am (ar. Messina Marittima 3:20 pm, Catania 5:22 pm, Syracuse 6:35 pm, Palermo 7:00 pm). There are other trains but these are the best.

To Rome, all first class rapido trains leave Napoli P. Garibaldi Station 6:33 am, Napoli Mergellina Station 6:51 am (ar. Rome Termini Station 9:00 am), Napoli Mergellina 8:00 am (ar. Roma Termini 9:58 am), Napoli Mergellina 3:30 pm TEE (ar. Rome Termini 5:25 pm), Napoli P. Garibaldi 4:00 pm, Mergellina 4:11 pm (ar. Rome Termini 6:00 pm), Napoli Mergellina 8:10 pm (ar. Rome Termini 10:22 pm). First and second class rapido trains which all leave from Centrale Station and arrive at Termini Station depart at 11:30 am, 1:00 pm and 2:00 pm; another train leaves from P. Garibaldi at 7:00 pm, Mergellina at 7:12 pm. Trip is about two hours and 20 minutes.

PISA

Stazione Centrale is outside the walls of the original settlement. Tourist office is on opposite side of the "old town" near the famous Campanile or leaning tower. Open M-Sa 9-12:30 & 3-7. Bus #1, 1, 3 and 6 leave every five minutes from the train station and go to the tourist office.

CAMPING PISA (Torre Pendente), Viale Delle Cascine #86, is several blocks outside the walls of the old town but within walking distance of the leaning tower. Open Apr-Oct. From station take bus #4 which leaves every 15 minutes. Ride is 15 minutes. Hot showers, store, snack bar.

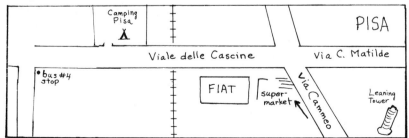

Public market is on Piazza Garibaldi near the River Arno, and is open
Monday to Saturday mornings. Self-service laundry, Via S. Maria, is one
kilometer from downtown and open M-F 9-12:30 & 3-7.

RAVENNA

Ravenna has the finest mosaics of early Christian art in Europe and became
the capital of the Roman Empire when Honorius left Rome for Ravenna in
402 A.D. Train station is about eight blocks from E.P.T. tourist office at
Piazza S. Franceso. City tourist office, A.A.S.T., is at Via Salara 8.
Eric Wolterstorff reports "at the kiosk opposite the train station one
can catch buses out to the Adriatic coast where there are many campgrounds. The roundtrip fare was 700 L in 1980, and the trip took about 30
minutes, as I recall. These camps, as huge and numerous as they are,
become jammed with beach people in August, and it may be difficult to find
a place to stay at that time of year. I talked my way into Camping Piombino,
on the left side of the road, away from the water. Cost for one night was
3,550 L (1980). Since these camps are geared to the beach and not the town,
the offices frequently don't open very early in the morning. They can't
understand why anyone would want to stay there without enjoying the sand and
sun. The prices also tend to be quite high."
Open market is in the center of town on Via Cavour. Ten kilometers
from Ravenna is the "International Center of Studies for the Teaching of
Mosaic Work" in Lido Adriano. Two week summer courses are offered.

ROME (ROMA)

The eternal city is monumental, huge, and you need at least five days to see
it. The frequently encountered letters "SPQR" stand for "Senatus
Populusque Romanus" or "The Roman Senate and People."

TRAIN STATIONS Most trains arrive at Stazione Termini (Terminal Station)
which is an enormous building with almost every conceivable service such
as tourist office, money exchange, eating establishments, and "albergo
diurno" which rents baths and showers. A few trains stop at Rome's
Tiburtina Station and don't come into Terminal Station and this is noted in the
train schedules. Beneath Terminal Station is the subway metropolitana.

CAMPGROUNDS About 14 campgrounds serve travelers visiting Rome.
CAMPING FLAMINIO, Via Flaminia Nuova, at Km 8.2, is a newer
camp. From Termini Station, take metropolitana A to Flaminio. Outside
the subway station is Piazzale Flaminio and the originating bus stop for
buses 202, 203 and 204. Take any of these buses and ride for about 15-20
minutes until you see the camp on the left side of the road, opposite a bus
stop. (See maps on following pages.) Shade, store, restaurant, free hot
showers, free washing machine (according to letter sent by management),
adult/2900 L, tent/1400 L. Address for camper's mail is Camping
Flaminio; Via Flaminia Nuova, km 8,200; 00191 Rome, ITALY.
CAMPING SEVEN HILLS, Via Cassia #1216, is north of Rome. From
Termini Station, take the metropolitana to Piazzale Flaminio (200 L). Outside the subway station is the originating bus stop for buses 202, 203 and

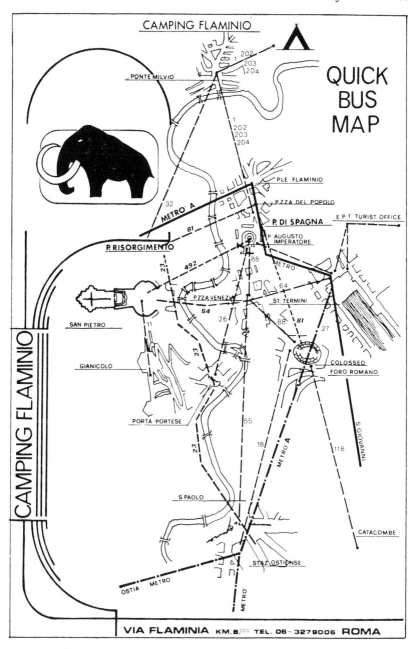

CAMPING FLAMINIO

QUICK
BUS
MAP

PONTE MILVIO

1 202
203
204

1
202
203
204

PLE FLAMINIO

P.ZZA DEL POPOLO

METRO A

81

E P T TURIST OFFICE

P. DI SPAGNA

P AUGUSTO
IMPERATORE

P. RISORGIMENTO

23

492

88

METRO

23

64

P.ZZA VENEZIA

ST TERMINI

54

SAN PIETRO

11

26

88

81

27

GIANICOLO

23

COLOSSEO
FORO ROMANO

PORTA PORTESE

55

23

18

METRO A

118

S GIOVANNI

S PAOLO

CATACOMBE

OSTIA METRO

METRO

STAZ OSTIENSE

VIA FLAMINIA KM.8.²⁰⁰ TEL. 06- 3279006 **ROMA**

CAMPING FLAMINIO

and 204. Take any of these buses and get off at Ponte Milvio which is just
after having crossed a river. Transfer to bus 201 at Ponte Milvio and get
off at Via Cassia (ask bus driver) from where the camp runs a mini-bus
service to the campground every half hour from 8 am to 7 pm. Office hours

272

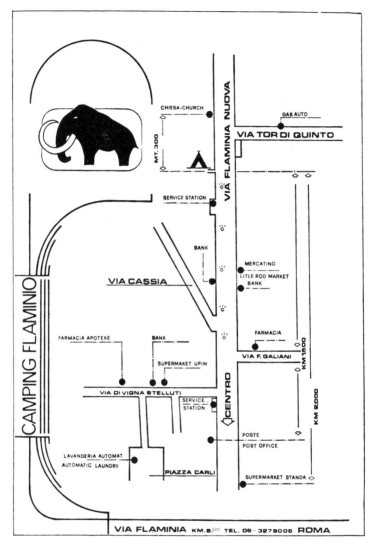

CHIESA-CHURCH

MT. 300

VIA FLAMINIA NUOVA

GAS AUTO

VIA TOR DI QUINTO

SERVICE STATION

BANK

VIA CASSIA

MERCATINO

LITLE ROD MARKET

BANK

FARMACIA APOTEKE

BANK

FARMACIA

VIA F. GALIANI

SUPERMAKET UPIM

KM 1500

CAMPING FLAMINIO

VIA DI VIGNA STELLUTI

SERVICE STATION

CENTRO

KM 2000

POSTE

POST OFFICE

LAVANDERIA AUTOMAT.

AUTOMATIC LAUNDRY

PIAZZA CARLI

SUPERMARKET STANDA

VIA FLAMINIA KM.8,200 TEL. 06- 3279006 ROMA

are 7 am - 11 pm, money exchange, store, restaurant, discotheque, mechanic, guided tours of Rome by bus, swimming pool, hot showers, rental cabins, no washing machine.   Send mail to campers at Camping Seven Hills; Via Cassia, 1216; 00189 Rome, ITALY.

CAMPING TIBER - ROMA, Via Tiberina Km 1,400, is in the district of Prima Porta.   From Terminal Station take metropolitana A to Piazzale Flaminio. From Piazzale Flaminio take the small train to Prima Porta (100 L) where the camp minibus (100 L) runs to the campground every ten minutes.   Drivers coming on A 1, the freeway from Florence, should about 20 meters after toll gates, turn right for Fiano Romano and continue along this road towards Rome for about 19 kms and the campground will be seen on your left. Alternatively you can pass through the toll gates and then continue straight towards Rome for about 21 km until you see a large sign on your right indicating "SS 4 Salaria, SS3 Flaminia, SS2 Cassia, SS1 Aurelia, Airport". Turn right onto the "Raccordo Anulare" (great ring road) and continue for about 5 kms until the road for Via Flaminia Terni. Leave the ring road and continue for about 2 kms until you see a sign on the right for FIANO. Turn right and after a kilometer you will see the campground on your right. From NAPLES, after passing through the toll

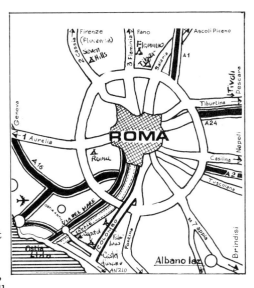

gates for the freeway (A 2), continue straight on for 4 kms until you see a large sign with "Raccordo: Casilina, Aquila, Tiburtina, Firenze, Cassia," and then bear right and take the "Raccordo Anulare" and continue along the ring road towards the freeway for Florence and SS 1 Via Flaminia Terni for about 22 kms. Exit the ring road at the sign for Via Flaminia and Terni. Go 2 kms and turn right for Fiano and in one more kilometer you will be at the campground.

Office is open 8-12 & 1-8, money exchange at bank rates, store, restaurant, discotheque (open 6 pm-1 am), english speaking, washing machine (1500 L or 2000 L including soap), guided bus tour of Rome, public bus from campground to downtown Rome, dormitories for groups, campers mail (send to Camping Tiber; Via Tiberina km 1,400; 00188 Prima Porta - Roma, ITALY.) Adult/2900 L, tent/2500 L, includes free hot showers and electricity. (Camp is 8 km north of Rome and 1.5 km from Prima Porta.)

ROMA CAMPING, Via Aurelia km 8.2, is within the great ring road and 4 km from the Vatican. From outside Terminal Station, take bus #64 to Ponte Vittorio. Change to bus #46 to Piazza Irnerio. Transfer to bus #246 and camp is visible on lefthand side before reaching bus stop. There is a half block walk to camp. Ride to camp takes one hour. Bus 246 runs infrequently on Sunday morning. By car, camp is 8 kilometers west of downtown. All roads entering Rome connect with the freeway, Gran Raccordo Anulare, which rings the city. Exit to camp is highway SS 1 (Aurelia). The camp is in terraces and has hot showers, store and snack bar. Several small restrooms are scattered throughout the camp. Adult/1700 L, tent/800 L (1980). This camp is cheaper than Camping Flaminio but not as nice and harder to reach.

The next three campgrounds are near the beach of Rome and reached by metropolitana line B Cristofo Colombo. CASTELFUSANO COUNTRY

CLUB, Piazza di Castelfusano, 1; 00124 Roma Casalpalocco, ROME; is 26 kilometers from Rome near Lido di Ostia on the sea. Kris and Ted Bushek write "Great campground ... private beach, good cheap restaurant, store, friendly staff. From train station go downstairs to underground and take Christopher Colombo to end station and then take first bus south--stops in front of campground. Train is 500 L round trip. Has large game room and playground for kids." Christopher Colombo is line B of the metropolitana (subway). Camp is 1.5 km from subway station. Hot showers, washing machine, swimming pool, adult/2000 L, tent/1000 L.

International Camping Pineta FABULOUS, Via Cristoforo Colombo km 18, is reached by metropolitana line B to station EUR FERMI. Outside subway station take busline ACOTRAL which stops 50 meters from camp. Shade, free hot showers, swimming pool, store, restaurant, adult/2400 L, tent/1200 L.

CAPITOL CAMPING CLUB, Via Castelfusano, 45; 00124 Roma-Casalpalocco, ITALY; is at Ostia-Antica. From the station, take metropolitana line B Christopher Colombo to Ostia, then a bus or 2 km walk. Shady, store, restaurant, swimming pool. Nearest self-service washing machines and dryers are in Ostia City, 2 km from campground. Adult/ 2400 L, tent/1200 L, hot shower/300 L.

Two campgrounds are near the town of Tivoli, 40 km from Rome. Trains to Pescara make their first stop at Tivoli and leave from Terminal Station at 1:10 am, 8:02 am, 2:08 pm and 6:05 pm and from Tiburtina Station at 11:08 am. Trip is about 40 minutes. Trains leave Tivoli for Terminal Station at 6:28 am, 8:40 am, 12:47 pm, 5:14 pm, 9:37 pm and 11:20 pm and for Tiburtina Station at 3:54 pm and 8:02 pm.

CAMPING CHALET DEL FIUME, Via Tiburtina-Valeria (km 34,500), 00019 Tivoli, ITALY, is right of the road to Avezzano behind the railroad tracks at the Aniene bank, and is 1.5 km from Tivoli. Take train to Tivoli (see above) and then outside station take bus #4 to the campground. Store, restaurant, hot showers (500 L), adult/1500 L, tent/800 L.

VILLAGGIO TURISTICO VILLA ADRIANA is right of Via Tiburtina, 5 km before Tivoli, near Villa Adriana. To get there take the train to Tivoli (see above) and then a bus to Villa Adriana. Store, hot showers, restaurant.

CITY TRANSPORTATION   Metropolitana is the subway which starts beneath Terminal Station. Buses wait at all subway stations. Bus fare is 100 L. A fare must be paid for luggage taken on a bus. Rome's two trams "ED" and "ES" circle the city in opposite directions and pass by the Colosseum, St. Paul's, St. Johns, Tiber River, area of Borghese Gardens and some of modern Rome.

FOOD   Main market is at Piazza Vittorio Emanuele, towards the rear of Terminal Station. Best meal value near station is Dopolavoro Ferroviario Mensa Tavola Calda (railway worker's restaurant) at 88 Piazza dei Cinquecento. From front of station, turn right and restaurant is in building on right-hand side of square, just to right of roadway passing through building. Open 12-9:30. Procedure is to first place the order with cashier (cassa) and pay. Take slip she gives you and sit down at a table with slip visible in front of you and a waitress will attend you.

TRAIN SCHEDULES   To Naples, trains leave Terminal Station on the hour and half-hour from 7 am to 10 pm. Of these, a TEE leaves at 6 pm (ar. Napoli Mergellina 8:10 pm), and a first class only rapido at 10:30 am (ar. Napoli P. Garibaldi 12:45 pm)。 Other rapido trains leave at 7:00 am (ar. Mergellina 9:00 am), 12:30 pm (ar. P. Garibaldi 2:55 pm), 4:00 pm (ar. Centrale 6:10 pm), 4:30 pm (ar。 Centrale 6:32 pm), 6:30 pm (ar. ⊢. Garibaldi 8:51 pm), 7:30 pm (ar. Centrale 9:34 pm)。
To Florence, TEE trains leave at 7:50 am (ar。 10:37 am), 11:27 am (ar. 2:13 pm) and 5:40 pm (ar. 8:24 pm). First class only rapido trains leave 1:00 pm (ar. 3:49 pm) and 7:12 pm (ar. 10:10 pm). Other trains leave at 8:05 am (ar。 11:17 am), 10:35 am (ar. 2:48 pm), 12:25 pm (ar. 4:18 pm), 1:45 pm (ar。 4:45 pm), 2:33 pm (ar. 6:08 pm), 4:05 pm (ar. 7:11 pm), 4:55 pm (ar. 7:56 pm) and 5:16 pm (ar. 8:10 pm) plus later trains.

VENICE (VENEZIA)

Venice is made of passageways, narrow waterways, curved footbridges, stone buildings and pigeons. St. Mark's Square, its focal point, is a paved plaza of football field dimensions extending forward from the great domed edifice Basilica San Marco (St. Mark's). No cars are allowed on Venice so the entire town is charming. Once an island, Venice is now connected to the mainland at Mestre by a three mile road and railway bridge built in 1933. Huge car parks are at the end of the road.

TRAIN STATION   Most trains to Venice stop first at Venice-Mestre Station before proceeding down the causeway to S. Lucia Station (Venezia S. L.) in Venice itself. A few trains stop only at Venice-Mestre and don't go into S. Lucia Station and you must know this in advance to be sure to get off there. It's usually just a short wait then for a train going into Venice. At S. Lucia Station, a tourist office is available. To reach St. Mark's from S. Lucia Station, go down the steps in front of the station to the water and board a boat.

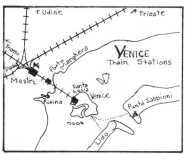

TOURIST INFORMATION   Besides the office at Venezia S. L. Station, there is one on St. Mark's Square.

CAMPGROUNDS   Jutting out from the Italian seacoast east of Venice, the Jesolo peninsula contains 27 campgrounds within a 30 minute vaporetto ride across the lagoon from Venice. To reach these campgrounds, take vaporetto (ferry boat) line #4 from in front of Venezia S. L. train station. The boat follows the Grand Canal to St. Mark's Square (San Marco). Get off at S. Zaccaria (stop #16) which is one stop beyond St. Mark's. Change to boat line #15, leaving from the next dock, Riva Schiavoni, and going to Punta Sabbioni on the Jesolo peninsula. A connecting bus at Punta Sabbioni drives the length of the peninsula coming within three or four blocks of all 27 campgrounds. But for convenience, we recommend staying at Camping Miramare located 500 meters from Punta Sabbioni and thus eliminating the bus.

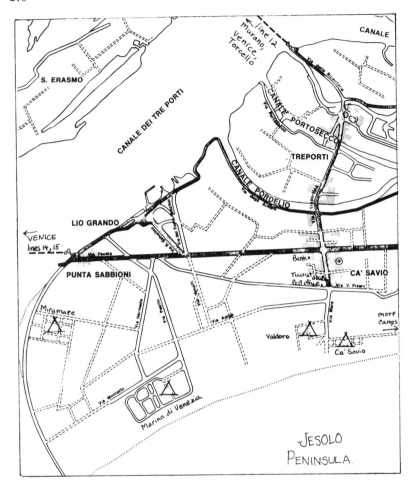

Camping Miramare has a shady tent area, hot showers, store, restaurant, playground, noon check-out time and costs adult/2200 L, tent/ 1300 L between 6/10 and 8/31, and adult/1800 L and tent/1000 L other times. Closed Oct-Mar.

Next closest camp is Camping Marina di Venezia, a larger camp with store, restaurant, pizza house, washing machines, minimum 3 day stay. Adult/2900 L, tent plus car/4500 L (6/15-8/31), adult/1700 L, tent plus car/2500 L otherwise. Closed Oct-Mar.

Main towns on the peninsula are Ca' Savio (tourist office, bank, post office), Treporti (Thursday open market), and Cavallino (Tuesday open market, post office, tourist office). Boats to Burano, Torcello and Murano leave from dock near Treporti

More campgrounds are located on the mainland around Mestre. Villa Tivan Camping, within the walls of a villa on left side of Via Terraglio, one kilometer north of Mestre, is an accessible camp not on a beach. Store, hot showers, restaurant, shady, bus stop for bus to Venice (300 L).

Camping Fusina is reached by bus #13 (300 L) from Mestre going to
the village of Fusina. Get off at last stop--Fusina-- and walk 150 meters
to camp. To reach Venice from Camping Fusina, a vaporetto (800 L) leaves
from dock 200 meters from camp and goes to Zattere, a ten minute walk
from St. Mark's in Venice. Hot showers, store, washing machine (2500 L
including detergent), adult/3000 L, tent/2500 L.

A reader suggests that "Venice is one of the few cities where anyone
not car camping is better off writing ahead for reservations to stay in a
hostel in town" because the campsites are time consuming to reach.

CITY TRANSPORTATION   Tourist office map gives boat routes. Fare
varies according to distance. Give name of destination as ticket is bought
and attendant will tell you the fare. A separate fare is payable for luggage.

FOOD   Market (erberia) is on left bank of Grank Canal. Take boat across
canal at Ca D'Oro dock. Near the train station, Mensa DLF (restaurant),
19 Fondamente S. Lucia, is to the right of the bottom of all those broad
steps in front of the station. Look for a plain modern structure not
resembling a commercial restaurant. The large institutional looking dining
room is operated by the railway workers union. First pay for your order
at the cashier and receive a meal ticket. Sit down and a waitress will serve
you. "Pranzo economical" includes three courses, bread, wine and service.
"Pranzo speciale" is similar but upgrades the entree and allows a soft
drink substitution for wine. A la carte is available.

SIGHTSEEING   Omitted by Michelin, Ca 'Pesaro Gallery and Guggenheim
Collection show modern art. Ca' Pesaro is near stop #5 on left bank of
Grand Canal. Open Apr-Sept 15, M-Sa 9:30-12:30 & 3-6, Su 9-1; Sept 16-
Mar, M-Sa 9-5, Su 9-12:30. Guggenheim Collection, Palazzo Venire dei
Leioni in vicinity of Accademia, stop #12 on the Grand Canal, is the resi-
dence of Miss Guggenheim and her personal collection is on view. Open
M, W, F, 3-5 pm, free.

TRAIN SCHEDULES   To Milan, first class only rapido trains leave Venezia
S. L. Station at 7:24 am (ar. 10:35 am), 11:14 am (ar. 2:43 pm), 2:00 pm (ar.
4:50 pm) and 6:35 pm (ar. 9:45 pm). Other trains leave at 8:54 am (ar.
12:32 pm), 10:32 am (ar. 2:04 pm), 11:14 am (ar. 2:53 pm), 3:00 pm (ar.
6:38 pm), 4:05 pm (ar. 7:35 pm) plus later trains.

To Florence and Rome, all first class rapido trains leave Venezia S.
L. Station at 8:05 am and 11:04 am. The trip takes about three hours to
Florence and six to Rome. Other trains leave at 10:20 am, 11:40 am,
12:42 pm, 2:04 pm plus later trains.

To Vienna, trains leave Venezia S. L. Station at 6:50 am (ar. Wien
Sudbahnhof 6:05 pm), 1:05 pm (ar. Venice-Mestre 1:14 pm, change trains,
leave Venice-Mestre 1:35 pm, ar. Wien Sudbahnhof 10:25 pm), 8:04 pm (ar.
Wien Sudbahnhof 6:52 am) and 10:55 pm (ar. Wien Sudbahnhof 9:32 am).

SICILY (SICILIA)

Fewer tourists go south of Naples but those who do are well rewarded. If the
weather is hot, the air-conditioned all first class Feloritano train will
assure your comfort. Next best is the Rapido train which carries both first
and second class. At Messina the train splits with each half circling the

island from the opposite direction. Rail travel is good to Palermo in one direction and Syracuse in the other, but after that it's fairly slow.

Sicily has seen a succession of rulers. The southern and eastern coasts were colonized by the Greeks who built fantastic cities with the aid of the native Sicels for five centuries until they were destroyed by Carthaginians who wanted to keep the western Mediterranean for themselves. Then came the Romans who first ruled from Rome until it fell, then continued their domination from Constantinople. Subsequent ruling Arabs, Moors, Spaniards and Saracens were succeeded in time by the well-liked Normans.

During the Middle Ages, numerous aristocratic landowners took control. Peasants reacted to years of foreign rule by banding together into secret societies of mutual aid. The structure of these organizations continued, but activities changed. Centers of Mafia activity are reportedly Monreale and Corleone but the visitor has no awareness of this presence.

WEATHER Camping is good the year around and half the campgrounds stay open all year. Main tourist season is April through October. February and March are the next most frequented months with November through January seeing the fewest visitors. July and August can be hot inland though the coast is always cooled by a breeze. Occasional rain and strong wind come outside the high season, though the sun shines through it all and swimming in the sea is possible even though skiers may be on Mt. Etna.

ALBERGHI DELLA GIOVENTU These are dormitories for young adults operated by local tourist offices at Agrigento, Catania, Syracuse, Trapani, Enna, Ragusa and Caltanissetta.

FOOD Sicilian specialties are wines, almonds, almond paste, early seasonal vegetables, lemons, oranges, mandarin oranges, tangerines, artichokes, apricots and a kind of celery (finocchio).

PALERMO This is Italy at its most expressive--a city of honking horns, transistor radios, animated conversations and fast-breaking life. The capital of Sicily has a variety of architecture reflecting past domination by Romans, Byzantines, Saracens and Normans, but the Saracen (Arab) influence predominates. Tourist office is in the train station.

Camping La Favorita is close to downtown in Parco della Favorita on Viale Diana and is marked on the tourist office map. Open Apr-Oct and can be reached by bus. Cold showers only, store, snack bar.

Camping Internazionale Trinacria , Via Barcarello, is 10 km from Palermo between monte Gallo and the bay of Sferracavallo. Open all year. Take bus #16 from the train station which runs every 30 minutes from 5 am to 11 pm. Fare is 150 L. This is a resort camp on the beach with shade, store, restaurant, hot showers (300 L), and rental cabins (25,000 L). A flat fee of 4500 L per adult is charged, all inclusive of tent, car, etc.

Market is at Via del Bosco (off Via Maqueda) and piazza Bellaro, in the square in front of the church.

For sightseeing, first see the center of town (quattro canti) at Via Maqueda and Corso Vittorio Emanule--you can't miss the walls. Next visit the exquisitely decorated Palentine Chapel in Palazzo dei Normanni, about 15 blocks from the city center. Chapel is upstairs on "first" floor. Open M-Sa 9-1 & 3-5, Su 9-12. Two blocks south of the Palace is the Church of

San Giovanni which has mosque-like domes. Catacombs in Convento di Cap-
puccini are some of the more startling ones to be seen. (Not for young
children.) Bodies have been mummified and are propped against the walls
in lifelike vertical position--babies, young children and adults. Heads are
not wrapped and have become basically skeletal as flesh has pretty much
dried. Other mummies rest in interminable rows of horizontal bunk bed
arrangement. Open 9-1 and 3:30 to one hour before sunset.

A huge Norman Cathedral is 14 kilometers away in Monreale. Benedictine Abbey and Cathedral form a large Norman church with overtones of
Arabic decoration. Abbey functioned as sort of a Camp David for royalty.
Highlight is the 12th century mosaics pictorially representing the story of
the old and new testaments. Also visit gardens and cloisters.

Train schedules. To Naples and Rome, the all first class Peloritano
leaves at 6:25 am (ar. Napoli Garibaldi 3:55 pm, Napoli Mergellina 4:11 pm,
Rome 6:00 pm). Next best is the first and second class rapido which leaves
at 8:55 am (ar. Napoli P. Garibaldi 6:55 pm, Napoli Mergellina 7:12 pm,
Rome 9:10 pm).

To Agrigento (139 km), trains leave at 8:11 am, 9:34 am, 12:28 pm,
2:26 pm, and 4:38 pm (change at Roccapalumba). Trip is 3-3 1/2 hours.
Trains also go to Trapani and then along the coast to Agrigento, Ragusa
and Syracuse where international standard trains begin again.

AGRIGENTO   Just outside town is the Valley of Temples (Vallata dei
Tempi) with five magnificent Greek Temples of the Doric order which are
best viewed at sunrise or sunset. Tourist office is by Jolly Hotel near the
train station. The bus to San Leone which goes to the Temples, also goes
to Camping San Leone (open Apr-Oct). Trains leave Agrigento for Palermo
at 8:16 am, 10:33 am (change trains at Termini Imerese at 1:13 pm),
12:51 pm, 2:30 pm, 4:57 pm and 7:28 pm. Trip is about 3-3 1/2 hours.
Trains go to Catania at 8:32 am, 9:56 am, 12:31 pm and 2:05 pm. Trip is
about five hours.

CATANIA   This is Italy's second largest town after Palermo. Camping
Jonio, 2 Via Villini A Mare, can be reached by bus #34 (200 L) from the
train station (see map). Bus tickets can be bought at the station newstand

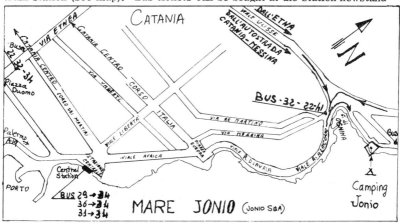

and campground. Shade, hot showers, store, restaurant, adult/1800 L,
tent/1000 L (6/15-8/31) or adult/1500 L, tent/850 L (9/1-6/14). Checkout
is 10 am. Trains leave Catania for Syracuse at 7:44 am, 10:56 am,
11:40 am, 2:23 pm, 3:24 pm, 3:51 pm, 5:26 pm, 6:22 pm. Trip is about one
hour and 40 minutes. Trains leave Catania for Agrigento at 8:10 am and
1:38 pm. Trip is about six hours.

SYRACUSE   (SIRACUSA)   A tourist office is in Central Station, at the
entrance to the archaeological area and in the historical center at Via
Maestranza 33. Camping Fontane Bianche is at Fontane Bianche about 14
km south of Syracuse. Linda Clark writes "the campground was in an
almond grove across the street from a beach with some of the most beautiful water I have ever seen." The noted archaeological area is on the hillside outside of town and is open 9 am to one hour before sunset. Most
notable is the 5th century B. C. Greek Theater (Teatro Greco) in such good
condition that classical plays are given there in spring and summer. The
original seats were hollowed out of rock and curved to fit the body, and are
still used. Nearby is a park-like area of five quarries (latomie) from which
most of the town was built. Orecchio di Dionisio (Ear of Denys) quarry's
acoustical properties enable a whisper from inside to be heard a great distance outside of the quarry. There are some catacombs but the ones in
Palermo are more fantastic.
    Trains leave Syracuse for Catania at 7:23 am, 9:18 am, 10:32 am plus
later trains. To Naples and Rome the all first class Peloritano leaves
Syracuse at 6:58 am (ar. Napoli Garibaldi 3:55 pm, Napoli Mergellina
4:11 pm, Rome Termini 6:00 pm). First and second class rapido leaves at
9:18 am (ar. Napoli Garibaldi 6:55 pm, Mergellina 7:12 pm, Rome Termini
9:10 pm). Plus there are other slower trains.

LUXEMBOURG

People who fly Icelandic and arrive in Luxembourg will be very grateful for
this information from Ray Rylander. "From the Flughaven (airport), don't
take the limo, and don't take the airlines bus to town. Wander down to the
parking lot and get on the blue and yellow city bus #9, leaving from the far
right hand side of the parking lot as you leave the new terminal. It gives you
a good city tour as it wends its way toward the train station. There you can
either leave immediately, or change to the #10 bus "Beggen." Ride it out to
Dommeldange and get off at the juncture of Rue d'Beggen and Rue d' Echternach, and there is a Shell station at the intersection. Cross the little
stream, the railway tracks and walk 1.5 km up the hill to the Camping Platz.
Or you can take a local train up to Dommeldange, and also at infrequent intervals there is local bus service to Echternach which will leave you direct
at the entrance to the camping place, thus saving that long walk. But both
this train service and the long distance bus service are not so regular and
frequent as the city bus service to Beggen. Camping Grunwald is a fair
camp, about average I guess."

NETHERLANDS

Holland is a wonderful compact country with good campgrounds near everything of interest and fast frequent train service to get there. Don't miss the
largest outdoor modern sculpture park in Europe at the Kroller-Muller
Museum near Arnhem.

CURRENCY   Guilders and Dutch cents. One guilder is worth 40¢. There
are about 2.4 guilders (florins or fl) to one U.S. dollar. Generally banks
charge about one guilder to cash travelers checks.

WEATHER   Similar to the Pacific Northwest. Expect cool evenings and
the possibility (though not probability) of rain. High season is mid-July
through August.

CAMPING   The tourist office publishes a combination map and campground directory, "Holland Camping '82," and the leaflet "Holland Camping
Houses and Farms." The latter brochure specializes in rural cabins and
farm campgrounds meant primarily for a week's stay. Many of these farms
operate primarily as a farm and most provide meals on request. No camping
carnet is necessary in The Netherlands. A few camps base the camping fee
on a 24-hour period rather than by the day.

YOUTH HOSTELS   The 54 youth hostels belong to Stichting Nederlandse
Jeugdherberg Centrale (NJHC), Prof. Tulpstraat 1-4, 1018 6X Amsterdam.
NJHC organizes all-inclusive tours for groups based on youth hostel accom-
modation for very reasonable prices. Write to them for information.

TRAINS   Dutch National Railways (NS) has built a dense network of
tracks with service half-hourly or hourly on most lines. The inter-city network introduced in 1970 provides express service between major Dutch cities.

Utrecht is the rail center of the country through which most trains pass. Unlimited stopovers are allowed on any ticket within the same day. Round trip tickets are valid for one day only. The round trip ricket (called an evening return) in which the return trip must be taken after 6 pm, costs the same as a one-way ticket plus 1.5 fl. On a weekend return ticket, you must leave on Saturday and return on Sunday, and are charged only the one day round trip price plus 1 fl. A group ticket gives a special price for groups of 2, 3, 4, 5 and 6 persons for unlimited traveling by train for one day. Only restriction is that no travel is allowed before 9 am, Monday through Friday. This "multirover" ticket costs about 53 fl for 2 persons, and 63 fl for 3 persons, for example. Three day and 7 day tickets are sold for unlimited rail travel, and cost about 55 fl and 75 fl, respectively. The purchaser is also entitled to buy a supplementary ticket for about 5 fl for 3 days and about 10 fl for 7 days of unlimited travel in city and town buses, subway and trams throughout Holland. A one-day ticket is sold for about 37.50 fl for train travel in the country, and includes the option to buy a supplementary ticket for unlimited travel in buses, trams and subways in towns in Holland for about 2.50 fl.

A Benelux Tourrail Pass allows 8 days of consecutive travel throughout The Netherlands, Belgium and Luxembourg within 16 days of the issue date. Cost is about 168 fl, second class. Those age 12-25, may purchase a Benelux Tourrail Junior ticket for about 99 fl, second class. Buy all tickets at train stations.

In train information offices, ask for the leaflet on day-excursions which are one day train tickets which include admission to sightseeing destinations. The booklet is full of good ideas for travel. On regular tickets, children under 4 ride free, and those 4-9 and senior citizens pay half. Train information office gives free timetables. International trains, marked D, are often crowded in The Netherlands. Arrival is "aankomst," departure is "vertrek," and track is "spoor."

DRIVING   Touristic itineraries are marked with six-sided signs. Tourist office in U.S. will send you some wonderfully helpful maps including one of signposted bulb and blossom routes throughout Holland, Tourist Road Map with 14 suggested itineraries, and Holland Monument Map which is the equivalent of a mini-guidebook with sketches and descriptions of types of architecture and windmills. Distances are quick and short in Holland: Amsterdam to The Hague is 35 miles, to Rotterdam 45 miles, to Arnhem 63 miles and to Eindhoven 75 miles. In cities, trams have priority over cars. In a circular multi-intersection, entering cars have priority over those already in it. When turning left, leave the policeman pedestal to your right. Speed limit is 30 mph in built-up areas. A priority road is indicated by diamond-shaped orange signs with white border.

TOURIST INFORMATION   This is its symbol, pronounced vay-vay-vay.

CITY TRANSPORTATION   All buses, trams and subways in the country have coordinated rates based on zones. A National Strip Ticket can be bought in train stations, offices of transport companies and in post offices for about 5.35 fl for 15 zones. One zone is about 4-1/2 km. Similar 6 to 8 strip tickets can be bought in buses and trams but these are proportionally more expensive. Transfers are included in single or strip tickets. Single tickets are often sold from vending machines at stops. Children have reduced rates. "Ingang" is entrance, and "uitgang" is exit.

FOOD   The open markets offer a mouth-watering array of vegetables and produce, and camp-cooking is recommended. However don't miss going to an Indonesian restaurant which has "rijsttafel" (pronounced rye-staf-fel), the Indonesian rice table consisting of many small deliciously sauced dishes served with steamed white rice. Rijsttafel comes in various prices depending on quantity and quality of food served, from the expensive and highly rated Bali to the many small Indonesian restaurants which you will come upon by yourself. One or two dishes may be very highly spiced, though delicious, but anyone with stomach problems may consider himself forewarned. In no way does 20th century Dutch cooking resemble those groaning board 17th century still-lifes where every last morsel glistens with appeal. However you can eat extremely well in Holland by staying with Indonesian restaurants or Dutch ones with definite gallic overtones. Avoid Dutch hotel restaurants, tea rooms and snack bars.

The Dutch are great milk imbibers and consume more than any other original member of the Common Market. Dutch cheese is very good and is some of the less expensive cheese in Europe. Edam and gouda are familiar names of milk cheeses produced here. A glass of beer costs less than a cup of coffee which costs twice as much as tea. Bread selection is extensive including a gingerbread (koek) and currant bread. Eel is available and good.

MODERN ART   The Netherlands is wonderful for modern art and reproductions are good buys. The tourist office in the U.S. publishes a superb 15-page booklet, "Holland, a Century of Form and Color," of color reproductions of paintings by Van Gogh, Mondrian, Appel and others and a short survey of modern art development in Holland. Free. The most important museums of modern art are the Vincent Van Gogh National Museum and Stedelijk (municipal museum) in Amsterdam; Kroller-Muller National Museum in Arnhem; Municipal Museum of The Hague with 251 works by Mondrian; and Van Abbe Municipal Museum in Eindhoven.

CARILLONS   The wristwatch put the carillons out of business, but originally the public told time by listening for the chimes to play briefly before the striking of the hours. Carillons are found in church clocks and towers of public buildings in Holland and Belgium.

AMSTERDAM

Of course you'll come to this city of canals, narrow gabled houses and modern art. Most of the city was built on piles because of the marshy soil.

SCHIPHOL AIRPORT   A new railway link is open between the airport and Amsterdam Zuid train station. From Amsterdam Zuid station, tram #5 goes to Central Station.

TRAIN STATION   Central Station anchors one end of the main street Damrak which leads to Dam Square, gathering spot for that portion of youth who like to congregate. Stationsplein, terminal for most buses and trams, is in front of Central Station. Inside station are luggage lockers costing .75 fl for small, 1.50 fl for large for 36 hours, attended baggage check costing

1.50 fl for 36 hours, and exchange office. Train information office is open M-F 8 am-11 pm, SaSu 9 am-6 pm, and will make reservations. Tourist Office (VVV) is opposite Central Station in a historical building on the waterfront.

Other minor stations are Amstel, Muiderpoort, Sloterdijk, RAI, and Zuid.

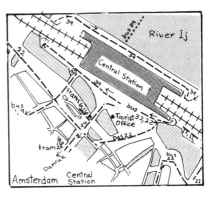

TOURIST INFORMATION   The office is on Stationsplein opposite Central Station. Open Easter - Sept 31, daily 8:45 am - 11 pm; Oct 1-Easter, M-Sa 9 am-10:30 pm, Su 10-1:30 & 2:30-5:30.

CAMPGROUNDS   HET AMSTERDAMSE BOS CAMPING, Kleine Noorddijk #1 (postal zip 1432 CC) is near Schiphol Airport and farthest from downtown. It is set within woods with canals, bridges and trails. From Station, take bus #9 or 19 to bus stop "Bosrandweg." After 6:30 pm, take bus #1 to bus stop "Schindeldijk." Three minute walk to camp. Hot showers (free), store, cold water in sinks, and used camping goods store where you can buy and sell equipment. Adult/5.15 fl, no charge for tent.

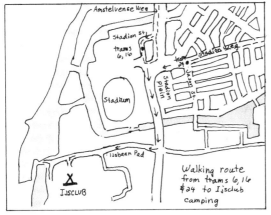

Walking route from trams 6, 16 $24 to IJsclub camping

AMSTERDAM IJSCLUB, IJsbaanpad 45 (zip 1076 CV) is close in by Olympic Stadium. From front of Central Station, go to the tram area near the canal, and take tram number 6, 16 or 24 to last stop. Then a five minute walk. From Station Zuid, it is about a 25 minute walk to camp. Camp is a large grass lawn and has hot showers (1 fl), store and cantine. Adult/3.60 fl, child under 10/free, tent/1.10 fl. Check-out time is noon. (See map next page for driving directions.)

CAMPING VLIEGENBOS, Meeuwenlaan 138 (zip 1022 AM), is primarily for students. Older adults and families will be happier at the two already mentioned. From station, take bus #32 or 39 (see map above). Camp is then a short walk (see map next page). Hot showers, store, adult over 30/4.50 fl, persons 14-30/3 fl, child under 14/1.50 fl, tent/free.

CAMPING ZEEBURG, IJdijk, is primarily for students. From Central Station, take bus #22 (direction Zeeburgerdijk) or tram #3, to Station Muiderpoort. Change to bus #36 or 38 to campground. Hot showers, store, person/3.50 fl, tent/free.

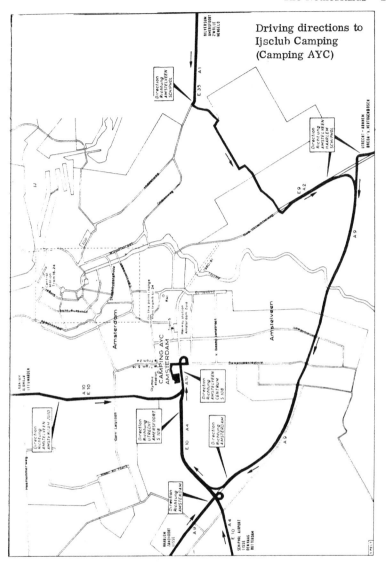

Driving directions to
Ijsclub Camping
(Camping AYC)

SLEEP-INN   For 7.50 fl per person, you can sleep at the Sleep-Inn I at
Rozengracht 180 which is open Easter and summer. Hot showers, lockers,
functions like a youth hostel but no card required. (Likely to be full.)

YOUTH HOSTELS   Vondelpark, Zandpad 5, sleeps 300, check-in 8-10 am
and 3:30-11:30 pm. Open all year, 14 fl including breakfast, tram 1 or 2
from Central Station. Stadsdoelen, Kloveniersburgwal 97, sleeps 190,
check in anytime to 11:30 pm, open Mar-Oct, 14 fl including breakfast, from
Central Station walk to Dam Square, or take any tram and get off at Dam
Square, then a walk.

286

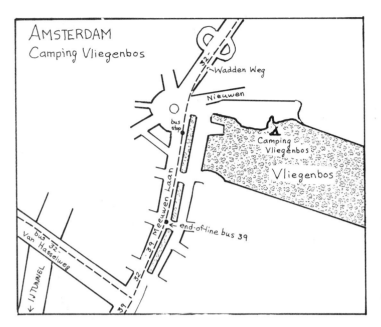

AMSTERDAM
Camping Vliegenbos

Wadden Weg
Nieuwen
bus stop
Camping Vliegenbos
Vliegenbos
Vliegenbos
Nieuwen Laan
end-of-line bus 39
Van Hasselweg
bus 32
IJ TUNNEL

CITY TRANSPORTATION   There are trams, buses and the Metro (subway).
The city is divided into zones and fare is calculated accordingly. The only
campground within the Central Zone (Centrum Zone) is IJsclub. There are
one, two and three day tickets good for unlimited travel on trams, buses
and Metro; and 6, 10 and 15 strip tickets which represent a discount over
buying individual tickets. These same tickets are good in other cities in
Holland. The one day ticket costs 4.75 fl and can be bought from the driver
of a tram or bus. If doing so, enter the vehicle from the front door. The
two and three day tickets cost 7 fl and 8.50 fl, respectively, but can only be
bought at the GVB ticket booth in front of Central Station and at the GVB
Central Office at Stadhouderskade 1. These offices also sell the one day
ticket. When using these tickets for the first time, stamp them in the
yellow stamping machines which are in the rear of a tram, and to the left
of the front door on a bus. (A one-day ticket can be bought from the ticket
machine in a Metro station, and one, two and three day tickets must be
stamped in a machine (near the stairs to the platform) before first use.
     Tram and bus drivers sell the 6-strip (2.85 fl) and 10-strip (4.75 fl)
tickets. At GVB ticket counters and postoffices, the 15-strip ticket can
be bought for 5.35 fl, which is the best deal. As many people as you want
can use the same strip ticket so long as sufficient strips are cancelled in the
machines. The ticket includes transfers to other tram, bus or Metro lines.
Stamped for 1 or 2 zones, your ticket is valid for 1 hour; for 3 zones, 2
hours. To use the ticket for one person who is traveling within the Central
Zone, start with the last ticket and fold your card between the last ticket
and the next to the last ticket. Then stamp the next to the last ticket in the
machine. For travel in 2 zones, you must stamp the third strip. You
always stamp one strip more than the number of zones.
     The three day ticket might be a good buy if you're staying at a camp

that's out of the central zone, but basically all you will need are two rides a day, leaving and returning to camp. Most tourist attractions are within the central zone.

Plain-clothes inspectors ride the buses and trams checking tickets for which violators must pay a 26 fl fine. To open a tram door, push the button marked "deur open." The door will close automatically. The lowest step controls the closing of the door which is automatic. To keep the door open, keep your foot on the lowest step. Doors to metro coaches open similarly to tram doors but never try to enter or leave a metro car after you hear the bell.

FOOD   A great market is M-Sa 9-4 at Albert Cuypstraat.

SIGHTSEEING   These four museums are top priority. RIJKSMUSEUM, 42 Stadhouderskade, is the national museum and one of the best fine arts museums in Europe. Open M-Sa 10-5, Su 1-5. Adult/3.50 fl, child to 17 and senior citizen/1 fl. On tram routes 1,2,3, 6, 7 and 16, and bus 26, 65 or 66. STEDELIJK MUSEUM, 13 Paulus Potterstraat, is a VERY outstanding museum of modern art. Open M-Sa 9:30-5, Su 1-5. Adult/2.50 fl, child/1.25 fl. It's within walking distance of Rijksmuseum or take tram #2, 3 or 16, or bus #26, 65 or 66. RIJKSMUSEUM VINCENT VAN GOGH, 7-11 Paulus Potterstraat, next to Stedelijk Museum, was new in 1973 and built especially for 200 paintings and 500 drawings by Van Gogh. Open M-Sa 10-5, Su 1-5. Adult/3.50 fl. Bring a sack lunch for the above three museums as there's plenty of lawn and benches but no inexpensive food in the area.   REMBRANDTHUIS (Rembrandt's House), 4 Jodenbreestraat, contains 200 of Rembrandt's etchings. Open M-Sa 10-5, Su 1-5. Adult/2 fl, child/.50 fl. Take tram #9, metro or 10 minute walk from Dam Square.

A traditional cheese market in the town of ALKMAAR is held on Friday mornings from 10-12 from mid-April to mid-September. Later in the morning, excursion buses leave from Alkmaar for a dike tour. Trains leave Central Station for Alkmaar at 8:11, 8:41 9:11 and 9:41; and a special Kaasexpres train leaves at 9:02 am between the third week in June and third week in August. Trip takes 32 minutes. Trains return from Alkmaar about twice an hour. A campground, Bergerweg 201, is reached by bus (direction Bergen) from the Alkmaar train station. Bus ride is 20 minutes and bus stops near the campground. To walk to camp from train station is about 40 minutes. Adult/ 3.10 fl (includes one shower), large tent/3.40 fl, small tent/2.10 fl. Trains leave Alkmaar for Haarlem at 22 and 52 minutes past the hour for the 48 minute trip. Trains leave Haarlem for Amsterdam every 20 minutes up to 12:24 am.

SELF-SERVICE LAUNDRY   Called "wasserette" and located near Central Station at Oude Doelenstraat 12, and at Herenstraat 24. Usual hours are M-F 8 am- 10 pm and Sa 8-4.

TRAIN SCHEDULES   To ARNHEM, TEE trains leave at 7:49 am and 1:55 pm and arrive about one hour later. Other fast trains leave at 8:19, 9:17 and 10:17 am, and 12:17, 1:17, 2:49, 4:55, 5:16, and 7:19 pm. Most of these departures are also good for DUISBURG, Germany and the trip takes just under two hours. Most of these trains continue onto Cologne, Germany which is another 45 minutes beyond Duisburg.

To BRUSSELS (Nord Station) and Paris (Nord Station), trains leave

Central Station at 7:48 am (ar. Brussels 10:42, Paris 1:52), 8:53 am (TEE)
(ar. Brussels 11:26 am, Paris 2:11 pm), 10:53 am (ar. Brussels 1:46 pm,
Paris 5:00 pm), 3:52 pm (ar. Brussels 6:46 pm, Paris 10:06 pm) and 5:53 pm
(TEE) (ar. Brussels 8:26 pm, Paris 11:11 pm). Above trains stop in
Brussels at both Nord and then Midi Stations, but not Central Station.

To HAMBURG and COPENHAGEN, the Holland-Scandinavian Express
leaves Central Station at 8:01 am (ar. Hamburg 2:15 pm, Copenhagen
9:09 pm), and the Nord-West Express leaves at 9:01 pm (ar. Copenhagen
8:09 am). These trains are crowded and a reservation is advisable. The
night train only operates between about May 28 and September 30.

ARNHEM

Two outstanding attractions are in this conveniently situated city on the
main rail line between Amsterdam and the German cities on the Rhine.
Kroller-Muller Museum owns 270 works by Van Gogh, and a large collection
of modern sculpture is erected in the surrounding woods. The National
Folklore Museum presents the past in a reconstructed village of peasant
houses and tradesmen's shops.

TRAIN STATION   The station is downtown and has an exchange office.

TOURIST OFFICE   VVV, Stationsplein 45 is on left of plaza in front of
train station. Open Apr-Sept daily 9 am-11 pm.

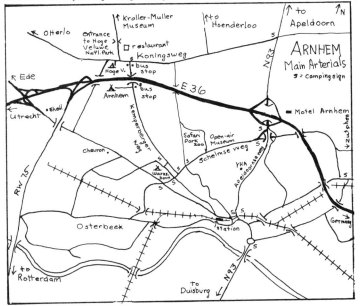

CAMPGROUNDS (See map.) CAMPING WARNSBORN, closest to town at
Bakenbergseweg 257, is on a large estate with trails in woods within a
wealthy residential area. This is the best camp for backpackers. Car-
campers might choose between it and Camping Arnhem. Open April-Sept 15.
From train station, take bus #8 (direction Schaarsbergen) across from sta-

tion. Buses leave every 30 minutes. Camping sign is visible from bus stop
one block from camp. By car, E 36 skirts Arnhem on the north and campgrounds, Kroller-Muller Museum and Folklore Museum can all be visited
without ever having to drive in downtown Arnhem. To get to Camping Warnsborn, take Arnhem-Hoge Veluwe exit when going east on E 36. Coming from
Germany on E 36, take Ede-Wolfheze exit. Then begin to follow signs to
Arnhem, except watch for "Arnhem-Oosterbeek War Cemetery" shield sign
and turn left at traffic lights. At next traffic lights, turn left again. Entering
Arnhem from the south on N 93 is slower because you have to go through
downtown Arnhem to reach the campgrounds which are all north or northwest
of town. As Camping Warnsborn is in the general vicinity of the zoo (Dieren-
park) and Folklore Museum (Openlucht Museum), follow these signs to get
through downtown. Then consult map above. Camp has
a store (open M-Sa 9-11, 3:30-5:30, 7-8, Su 10-12,
3:30-5:30), hot showers, trails, playground, bikes for
rent (6 fl a day) and charges per 24 hours adult/3 fl,
child to 12/ 2.25 fl, large tent/ 3 fl,   small tent/ 2 fl,
hot shower/.75 fl for 6 minutes, washing machine/5.50 fl, dryer/.75 fl.

    CAMPING ARNHEM (Kampercentrum), Kemperbergerweg 771, in
Gelegen woods is open Mar-Oct. From train station, take bus #8 (direction
Schaarsbergen) across from station. Bus stop closest to camp is on Zijpen-
daalse Weg and from there the camp is one kilometer down a narrow road
through the forest. By car, take the same exit from E 36 as for Camping
Warnsborn, but follow signs to Hoge Veluwe (see example of sign on previous
page). Immediately beyond entrance to Hoge Veluwe, turn off Koningsweg to
Kemperbergerweg. Turn right after underpass beneath E 36. Camp has hot
showers, store, swimming pool, snack bar (open M-F 2-11pm, Sa noon-
11pm, Su 10:30 am-9 pm), bikes for rent (5 fl a day, tandem/15 fl a day) and
charges adult/ 3.50 fl, tent/free.
    CAMPING HOOGE VELUWE (ho-kah vay-lu-vah), 14 Koningsweg in
Schaarsbergen and within five minute walk of entrance to Hooge Veluwe
National Park. Camp is open Apr-Sept. From train station, take bus #8
(direction Schaarsbergen) across from station to last stop. Camp is ten minute walk (see map). By car, take same exit off E 36 as for Camping Warnsborn. Then follow deer antler sign to De Hoge Veluwe as camp is half-block
from entrance to De Hoge Veluwe Park. Camp has store (open 9-1, 3-6, 7-8),
restaurant, play equipment. Hot showers, swimming pool and washing
machine are at far opposite end from camp entrance. Showers take .25 fl
coins. Adult pool (80'x32') and children's pool (32'x16') are open 9-7. To use
pool, you must wear a tag that you get from the office. Washing machine
takes a slug, sold at the office and costing about 6.00 fl including soap. A
dryer also takes a slug (1.25 fl).   Soap goes in top of washer, most in large
compartment on left and some in smaller hole on right. Set dial (round circle
on right) to 95 degrees for hot or 30 degrees for cold. Put in slug and machine
starts. Cycle takes 40 minutes. Then transfer clothes to centrifuge and place
evenly around center column making sure none are draped on top of column
as they get torn.   Camp charges adult and child/3.80 fl each, tent/
3 fl, car/3 fl, tax/.40 fl per person. We stayed here because it was late at
night and the first camp we came to but having checked out the other two, I
would recommend them because they are much cheaper and the grounds are

more wooded and private than this one which is flat and grassy with small
marked-off sites in rows.

SIGHTSEEING   RIJKS-MUSEUM KROLLER-MULLER shows modern art,
a few old masters and an exciting collection of sculpture within a beautiful
natural setting in De Hoge Veluwe (ho-kah vay-lu-vah) National Park. Open
M-Sa 10-5, Su 1-5. Sculpture Park opens early at 11 am on Sunday and
closes early every day at 4:30 pm. Museum is free but entry to the National
Park costs adult/5.00 fl. child 6-16/2.25 fl, car/5.00 fl. <u>Allow a minimum
of two hours</u> and three or four hours could easily be spent here. <u>No food is
available. Be sure to bring lunch or at least a snack.</u> There are benches in
sculpture garden.

How to get there. Museum is 8.8 km from Arnhem entrance to Hoge
Veluwe National Park (see map). The terrain is flat and you can rent a bike
for 5 fl at Warnsborn and Arnhem Camps. (If possible, reserve bike the night
before.) Or you can hitch from just inside the park entrance. Or from the end
of June to mid-August, a special yellow VAD bus leaves from behind the train
station every two hours, goes to the museum entrance, and costs adult/8 fl,
child to 17/5 fl. Otherwise a regular VAD bus #7 (direction Harderwijk)
leaves from across the station at 15 minutes past every hour on Monday
through Saturday and every other hour on Sunday. The ride takes 45 minutes
to the Otterlo entrance to the park where bikes can be rented or you can walk
the 3.5 km from the Otterlo entrance to the museum.

Inside the museum, some 250 works by Van Gogh form the nucleus of
the collection. His haunting self-portrait is here. Hepworth, Marini,
Mondrian, Picasso, Gris, Brancusi, Braque, Arp and Noguchi are represented by paintings and small sculpture. There is a small amount of pop art
such as a group of three garbage cans and five boxes graduated in size of
rocks, and a fascinating photography exhibit of unusual formations and
growths of trees. Galleries are brightened by fresh bouquets of flowers in
the corners. Allow at least an hour for the sculpture garden, whose entrance
is back of the sales desk by the cloak room. The wafting white sculpture in
the pond is by Hungarian-born Marta Pan and was commissioned especially
for the park to "represent the movement of nature." Its two sections move
independently of each other and its smaller upper piece swivels on a small
ball resting on the lower section. Bottom piece is stabilized by a lead keel
and appears to float in response to water movement at the same time the
lightweight top is moved by the wind. Elsewhere, a small rise is dominated
by a roughly hewed reclining female nude by Henry Moore. There are five
large lawns of sculpture with items such as a group of four brown canvas
and rope structures and a giant white pretzel. Huge purple and white rhodo-
dendrons serve as backdrops. "The best thing in the whole museum,"
according to our children is Jean Dubuffet's "Jardin d'Email"--a fanciful
play sculpture of moon-crater shape painted white with black maze-like
painted lines, the whole thing of tennis court dimensions.

The sales desk inside the Museum has excellent bargains. White
framed 10x12 reproductions of Van Gogh's works sell for about 15 fl and
unframed pictures are equally inexpensive such as a 10x12 for about 4.50 fl.
A catalog of Van Gogh's paintings is 9.75 fl, museum catalog is 5.50 fl and
postcards sell for about .50 fl. TOILETS and cloakroom are on side wall
behind sales desk. Extra time can be well spent exploring the surrounding

nature reserve which has trails and bicycle paths, and a "high stand" where male deer can be observed at close range.

OPENLUCHT MUSEUM (Folklore Museum) is a vast park with 70 farmhouses and buildings including an operating windmill, paper mill, treadmill and farm animals which all recreate country life of Holland of a bygone era. A unique herbal garden can be seen where medicinal plants and herbs are sown between rows of yellow stones in much the same manner as was done in medieval monasteries. During July and August, oldtime crafts are demonstrated. Open Apr-Oct M-Sa 9-5:30, Su 10-5:30. In April, September and October the park closes early at 5 pm. Adult/3 fl, child under 18/1.50 fl, family/7 fl. From train station take bus #3 (Alteveer), a 15 minute ride.

BURGERS ZOO and SAFARIPARK, Schelmseweg 85, next to Openlucht Museum are each self-contained. From train station take bus #3 (Alteveer), a 15 minute ride. Zoo entry is adult/5 fl, child to 10/2.50 fl. Combination zoo-safari park tickets are available. Safari Park entry is 15 fl per car. ZIJPENDAALSEWEG AQUARIUM shows Dutch fresh water and tropical fish. Bronbeek Museum covers East India and has a live exhibit of silk worm cultivation.

TRAIN SCHEDULES   Trains leave Arnhem for Amsterdam about three times an hour, and TEE trains leave at 9:35 am and 1:20 pm. Trip is about 1-1/4 hours. Trains leave south for Duisburg and Cologne, Germany, at 9:01 (TEE), 9:30 and 11:25 am, and 1:26, 2:25, 3:03 (TEE), 4:02, 6:03, 6:37, 7:25 and 8:25 pm. Trip to Duisburg is about one hour, to Cologne about two hours.

EINDHOVEN

Headquarters of the giant Philips Company, Eindhoven is on the main rail line in southern Holland near the Belgium border. Trains leave Amsterdam for Eindhoven on the hour and half hour and return from Eindhoven to Amsterdam at 6 and 36 minutes past the hour. The trip takes 1-1/2 hours. Tourist office is on Stationsplein in front of Station. Eurostrand Camping in Westerhoven is a vast vacation center with restaurant, store, lake with sailboats and pedal boats, mini-golf and a sportsfield. Eindhoven's main attraction is EVOLUON, museum of science and technology founded by the Philips Company. Take bus #2V (direction Veldhoven), #5 or 6 (direction Strijp) from bus station by train station--take Woensel exit. Museum is open M-F 10-6, Sa 10-5, Su 12-5. Free maps in entry hall, free checking, and portable tape cassettes for guided tour in English are available inside the entry. STEDELIJK VAN ABBE MUSEUM (Van Abbe Municipal Museum), Bilderdijklaan 10 is on bus route B (direction Stratum). Open M-Sa 10-5, Su 2-6, Tu also 8-10 pm. Entrance charge. Well endowed with works by important international artists, Eindhoven's museum of modern art gathered its collections together after 1945. Twentieth century painting and sculpture now occupy the neo-Romanesque building donated by industrialist and collector Henri van Abbe in 1936. Most every school of art since 1900 is represented here: Picasso, Braque, Kandinsky, Chagall, Kokoschka, Mondrian, Lissitzky (85 works), Appel, Vasarely and many important but not yet well known contemporary artists.

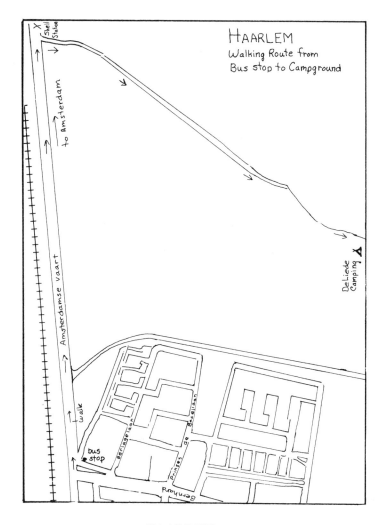

HAARLEM

A wonderful Frans Hals Museum is in this attractive town west of Amsterdam.
Train station is downtown. Tourist office, Stationsplein 1, is next to station.
Open Apr-Sept 1, M-Sa 9-8, Su 11-2 & 5-7; Sept-Mar M-Sa 9-6.

    CAMPING DE LIEDE, Liewegje 17 northeast of downtown, is open all
year. From train station, take bus #80 or 77 (direction Parkwijk) to Prins
Bernhardlaan bus stop, a 30 minute ride. (Four buses per hour.) Camp is
a 20 minute walk from bus stop (see map). Walk east from Prins Bernhardlaan two blocks to Amsterdamsevaart. Turn right to Shell Station. Turn
right onto Liewegie to campground. Hot showers/.50 fl, snack bar, store,
adult/3 fl, tent/3 fl.

    Same public transportation information for Amsterdam applies here.

Market is M-Sa 9-5 on Groote Markt, main square with Groote Church.
Frans Hals Museum, Groot Heiligland 62, downtown and 10 blocks from
train station is open M-S 10-5, Su 1-5. Adult/2 fl. Guided tours for groups
if arrangements are made three weeks in advance by writing. Perfectly set
within a beautiful 17th century mansion, the canvasses of Frans Hals and
other School of Haarlem painters are well displayed to recreate the mood of
the period. Period furniture completes the setting. Don't miss the formal
garden in the inner courtyard.
A self-service laundry, Hewi, is at Rustenburgerlaan 49 (open M-F 9-6)
and Speed Wash at Zijlweg 68 (M-F to midnight).

THE HAGUE   (DEN HAAG)

The Hague (rhymes with leg) is home of the Dutch government and the royal
residence. Trains from Amsterdam leave twice an hour and stop at Haarlem
enroute. Trip is about 50 minutes.

TRAIN STATION   Hollandse Spoor Station (Station HS) handles traffic to
Amsterdam, Rotterdam, Belgium and France. Its exchange office is open
M-Sa 7:30 am-10 pm, Su 9-8. Centraal Station (Station CS) carries traffic
towards Utrecht and Germany. Exchange office is open M-Sa 7:30 am-10 pm,
Su 9-8. Tourist office at Kon. Julianaplein 8 next to Centraal Station is open
Apr-mid-Sept M-Sa 8:30 am-9 pm, Su 10-6; and mid-Sept-Mar M-Sa 8:30-8,
Su 10-5.

TOURIST INFORMATION   Next to Centraal Station, on Groenmarkt in the
old quarter, and in Scheveningen next to the Europa Hotel. Map costs .50 fl.

CAMPGROUNDS   Camping Ockenburgh, Wijndaelerweg 25, is next to the
sea. Open Apr-Oct. From Station H.S., take bus #19 to last stop. Then 1000
meter walk. From Station CS, take tram #3 to last stop and change to bus
#19 and ride to last stop. Store, restaurant, money exchange, nudist beach,
separate area for tents, miniature golf, theater, recreation hall, youth
hostel adjacent. Adult/2 fl, child under 14/.80 fl, individual tent area/9.45 fl,
washing machine (includes soap and centrifuge)/5.25 fl, dryer/.50 fl, hot
showers/free.
Camping Duinrell is part of a large amusement park in Wassenaar.
Open all year. Take bus #90 from either station. Free hot showers, nearby
supermarket and laundromat. Adult and child 2 and over/4.50-6 fl, small
tent/2 fl, family tent/ 3.50 fl. Camp fee includes admission (normally 3.25-
6.00 fl) to recreation complex of swimming pool, trampolines, miniature
golf and playground. Extra charge for amusement rides.

FOOD   Market (markthof) is on Gedempte Gracht and Spui, downtown, and
open M 1-6, Tu-Sa 9-6. Supermarkets close Monday morning.

SIGHTSEEING   Mauritshuis and Gemeetemuseum are top attractions. Both
are easily seen by taking bus 4 from Central Station to farther out Gemeentemuseum. Then on return trip, take bus 4 stopping off at the Peace Palace if
you wish, or continuing downtown to Mauritshuis.
Gemeentemuseum, Stadhouderslaan 41, shows modern art including 250
works by Mondrian, ancient decorative arts and old musical instruments.
Take bus 4 from Central Station. Open M-Sa 10-5, Su 1-5, W 8-10 pm. Free.
Guided tours for groups available by writing to Department of Education.

Mauritshuis, Plein 29 between Het Plein and Het Binnenhof, is about 7 blocks from Central Station and 13 from Station HS. A 17th century mansion has been turned into an art museum of 15th, 16th and 17th century paintings by such artists as Rembrandt, Vermeer, Rubens, van Dyck and Holbein. The collection is nicely compact with only the best paintings shown. Take tram #8 or 9 from Station HS. Open M-Sa 10-5, Su 11-5, adult/3.50 fl, child under 18/1 fl. Restroom on main floor. Hour guided tour for groups if arranged in advance.

Peace Palace, Carnegieplein 2, was given by Andrew Carnegie for the International Court of Justice, Permanent Court of Arbitration and International Law Academy. Guided tour in English. Take tram #8 from Station HS and bus #4 from Station CS. Open M-Sa 10-12 and 2-4. Adult/2 fl, child under 14/1 fl.

Binnenhof, seat of Dutch government, is near Mauritshuis and offers tours. Open M-Sa 10-4, except July and August open 10-5. Adult/3 fl, child/ 2.50 fl.

Madurodam, a miniature town where everything is 1/25th of actual size, showcases houses, canals, bridges, a port and parliament. It's illuminated at night, and a two mile winding route lets you see it all. Tram #9 from Station HS or Mauritshuis, or bus #22 from Central Station. Open 9:30 am-10:30 pm except to 11 pm in July and August. Open 9:30-9:30 from Sept 1 - third Sunday in October. Adult/6 fl, child under 13/3 fl.

Gevangenpoort National Museum, Buitenhof 53 near Mauritshuis, shows historical instruments of torture. Children must be over 6. Tour each hour.

ROTTERDAM

Heavily bombed during the second world war, Rotterdam is now a modern city with an important seaport, which is easily seen on a day excursion from The Hague or Amsterdam. Tourist office is in Central Station, open 9 am-midnight. Immediately in front of station is the downtown area, and beyond that is the port.

Camping Rotterdam, Kanaalweg 84, is reached by bus 33 from Central Station. The bus leaves every 15 minutes and stops within 300 meters of the campground, which is 3-1/3 km from the station. Free hot showers, and washer and dryer available. Adult/3.25 fl per 24 hours, child to 12 years/ 1.80 fl, tent/3.25 fl.

Boymans-van-Beruningen Museum, Mathenesserlaan 18-20, shows masterpieces of Dutch painters from Van Eyck to Van Gogh including notable works by the imaginative and pictorial Bosch, some Italian and French Old Masters, and a large collection of modern art in the new wing of interchangeable halls built in 1972. Open M-Sa 10-5, Su 11-5, also W 7:30-10 pm. Guided tours for groups in English. Restroom in basement of new wing. "Nursery" in new wing.

UTRECHT

Rail-hub of The Netherlands, Utrecht is noted for its Cathedral which has the highest church tower in the country. Central Station is downtown and its exchange office is open daily to 9 pm. Tourist office is in station.

Camping De Berekuil, 5-7 Arienslaan, is open Apr-Sept. From bus station beside train station, take Centraal Nederland Company bus #50 to 55, 77-79, 81 or 85. Bus leaves every half hour. Ride to campground is 15 minutes and you get off at the last stop in Utrecht, then a five minute walk. Hot showers (.25 fl), store, snack bar, adult/3.50 fl, child 2-12/2.00 fl, tent/2.35 fl.

The National Travel Ticket (15 strip ticket) is sold at the GVB information booth at the bus station. Market is all day Wednesday and Saturday at Vredenburg. Connected to train station by covered passageway is the modern Hoog-Catharijne shopping center. Self-service laundry is at Zonstraat 102, open 9-6.

GRONINGEN

Groningen is capital of the Dutch northern "breadbasket" province. Train station is at edge of "old town" and has exchange office. Tourist office, Grote Markt, is on main square of old town, ten blocks from station. Walk or take bus #3 or 5. Open M-F 9-8, Sa 9-6, Su (July & August) 10-4.

Camping Stadspark, Campinglaan 6, within the major city park and recreational complex, is open Feb 15-Oct 15. Take bus #3 across from station which leaves every 15 minutes. Get off at Paterswoldseweg and there is a 10 minute walk to camp. During July and August only, the bus goes all the way to camp. Hot showers (.75 fl), store, snack bar, adult/3.50 fl, child under 12/2.00 fl, tent/2.50 fl.

Market, Westerhaven, is open Tu 9-4 and Sa 9-6. Market at Vismarkt is open W and F 9-4. Navigational Museum, 9 St. Walburgstraat, costs about adult/1 fl and child under 16/.50 fl. Self-service laundry, Clean Inn, is at Van Lenneplaang, De Wuert, and is open 7 am- 11 pm.

READER'S SUGGESTION

"If you're interested in windmills, don't miss Leiden, Holland. This small town has a fully functional windmill called "De Valk" that is a five minute walk from the train station. We were allowed to roam freely throughout and the cost was 2.5 fl each." Mr. and Mrs. Robert Cooper.

ATTENTION!!! The railway schedules given in this book are for planning purposes only. They are meant to give the reader some idea of train frequency and length of journey. Please check all departure times in a current timetable.

The directions given on how to reach campgrounds should be double-checked with the tourist office in the respective city. Sometimes a campground will have been closed or the bus or tram route changed.

Pronunciation of place names is given phonetically in parenthesis following the name.

PLEASE WRITE TO US!!!

If this guidebook helped you, we would appreciate your taking the time to help future travelers by writing and telling us about, particularly (1) errors in our information and (2) other towns that have a campground that can be reached on foot from the train station. We welcome any other information too.

We will send a copy of the next edition of this book to each person who writes to us or completes the "post-trip questionnaire" at the end of the book.

NORWAY

A land of spectacular fjords and snow-patched green mountains where a
fourth of Norwegian families maintain vacation homes, Norway beckons the
traveler far from the maddening crowds. To the American traveler weary
of the delights of big cities, Norway is the place for a recuperative mini-
vacation back to the soothing effect of forest, lake and mountain. English is
widely spoken due in part to the system of education in which compulsory
education ends at 16, but to proceed to the gymnasium (higher) level
requires passing exams in English, Norwegian, German and mathematics.
Hence for some travelers, Norway is the country of choice for a break
away from the capital city circuit into the countryside whether to stay at a
lakeside campground or to backpack into the lakes and forests. In this
respect, Norway has both the advantages of Switzerland, well-signed trails
and English-speaking people, without many tourists. Additionally, Norway's
scenery is equally spectacular and it's free with a train pass without having
to pay the stiff mountain train fares beyond the validity of the passes as in
Switzerland. However, being the only industrial country in Europe that's a

major exporter of oil has brought inflationary pressures to bear on the country. So far the government's plan for limiting oil production and allowing only half the oil revenue to feed back into the economy has slowed price rises. Norway is the most expensive of the Scandinavian countries.

CURRENCY Norwegian krone. One krone equals 100 ore. One krone equals about 18¢. There are about 6 kr to the U.S. dollar. Generally, a 2 kr fee is charged per currency exchange transaction.

WEATHER June, July and August are the best months but a shower may come anytime as for all of Scandinavia. In summer, it never gets really dark so it's easy to arrive late at a campground and set up a tent.

CAMPING Norway has excellent campgrounds and the Norwegians themselves are avid campers. Most are open June 15-August 25, except city camps are open longer. The Norwegian Camping Guide costs about 30 kr but only contains maps of Oslo's camps.

TRAINS Trains are very good and pass through spectacular scenery between the coast and Oslo. Get "Scandinavian Timetables and Fares" from tourist office in U.S. Children 4-12 travel at half price on tickets issued in U.S., but upper limit is 15 for tickets purchased in Norway. Reservations are made at ticket windows (billetter) and may be advisable in summer. Three main rail lines are the southern Railway which goes from Stavanger to Kristiansand and on to Oslo, the Bergen railway from Oslo, and the northern link from Oslo to Trondheim and on to Bodo. The train from Stockholm, Sweden goes to Narvik, Norway in the land of the midnight sun. Large size luggage lockers take 3 one kroner coins. Track is "spor," departures "avgaendetog," arrivals "ankommende tog," and windowseat "vindusplass."

DRIVING Roads around Oslo, the southern coast and eastern valleys, are flatter and straighter than the mountainous west or extreme north. On mountain roads, traffic uphill has the right-of-way. Descending drivers must wait in the provided turn-off area (moteplass). The following signs are found in addition to standard international road signs.

ferist - cattle grid	moteplass - passing turn-off
veiarbeide - road works	omkjoring - detour
kjor sakte - drive slowly	rasteplass - rest area
los grus - loose gravel	svake kanter - soft shoulder

Speed limit is 80 kph (50 mph) on highways and 50 kph (32 mph) in towns and built-up areas. Cappelen's Motoring and Touring Maps are good detailed maps, available in bookstores. Food and gas stations are infrequent in mountainous areas. Maintain a supply of 10 kr notes for automat gas stations in cities. Super grade gas costs about 4 kr per liter and diesel gas costs about half that. Blue camping gaz cylinders #904 and 907 can be exchanged at Progas Stations. Lower ferry fares are generally in effect before June and after August. On ferries, the driver's ticket is normally included in the price of fare for car. Obtain "Norway, Car Ferry Timetables" from tourist office in U.S.

FOOD In 1981, one liter milk cost 2.43 kr, 500 gram loaf of bread about 5 kr, one chicken about 26 kr. Fresh fish is always good in Norway. The country's catch of herring is one of the largest in the world. Herring is canned, its oil is used in production of margarine, fish scales yield a

chemical necessary for making artificial pearls and scraps and skin are
made into cattle feed. In restaurants, herring is served plain, smoked,
pickled, in sour cream and in wine. Trout and salmon are good though not
cheap. Lutefisk has a strong taste that Americans are not used to.

Few Norwegian families eat a hot breakfast. The usual children's
lunch is a glass of milk and open-faced sandwiches of egg, canned fish,
perhaps goat cheese or meat. People start work at 8:30 am and finish at
4:30 pm. They take a scant half-hour for lunch which is a snack brought
from home or "smorbord" in a restaurant. (Smorbord are open-faced sandwiches.) Restaurants begin serving dinner at 4 pm but 5:00 or 5:30 is a
more popular time. Some restaurants start to close up by 6:00 pm. $3.50-
$4.00 must be allowed for a cafeteria meal. This amount will cover fish
(always cheapest) or meat plus two vegetables (one is often boiled potatoes).
Any beverage will add 50-75¢ to the total so it's best to drink water when
dining out and buy a liter of milk at the grocery store for the same price as
a glass in a cafeteria. Whole milk is "helmelk," skim milk is "skummet
melk."

POST OFFICE   All postcards to U.S. go airmail for about 1 kr. Letters
under 5 grams go air mail for the surface rate of about 1.40 kr. but mark
them 5 gram on the outside. Printed matter is accepted up to 2,000 grams
weight for about 7.50 kr.

MIDSUMMER'S EVE   This June 23rd holiday ranks second in popularity
only to Christmas with the Norwegians. It's the shortest night of the year
and people stay up late, gather by the woods or lakes, build bonfires, sing,
dance and have fireworks.

HIKING   This is the best way to get to know Norway. Tourist huts are
found along the trails so only a towel, soap, clothing and personal items
need be carried. No one is turned away even if a hut is full. At the least you
will be provided with mattress and blanket on the floor. Included in the
nightly fee (about 65 kr) are dinner, breakfast, a sack lunch and a thermos
full of coffee or tea. Some huts are self-service for which a sleeping bag or
liner (blankets are stocked) must be carried and food is for sale. Others are
completely unstaffed and sleeping bag or liner and food must be brought.
Some campers prefer to carry their own tent and eat meals in the huts.
Trails and huts are coordinated by the Norwegian Mountain Touring Association (Den Norske Turistforening or DNT). DNT offices sell maps to a scale
of 1:100,000 and 1:50,000. Free rough maps of the area with suggested
routes and average hiking times are available to help decide what scale maps
will be needed. Some unstaffed huts are locked and require a standard key
from DNT. Conducted hikes of varying difficulty sponsored by DNT provide
a good introduction to hiking in Norway for the experienced hiker who can
keep up--in Norway, backpacking is a national sport. Oslo branch of DNT
is at Stortingsgaten 28, Oslo 1, Norway.   For area information contact:
Stavenger Turistforening, Turispaviljongen, 4000 Stavanger; Kristiansand
og Opplands Turistforening, Rutebilstasjonen, 4600 Kristiansand; Bergen
Turlag, C. Sundstsgt. 3, 5000 Bergen; or Trondhjems Turistforening, Hans
Hagerups gt. 1, 7000 Trondheim, Norway.   Hardangervidda, Hardanger Plateau, easily reached from the route of
Bergen-Oslo railway, is a popular hiking area with small lakes, good fishing
and wild reindeer. Tourist huts have been placed within a day's hike of each

300

other. Gateway towns are Hardanger, Numedal and Telemark. Itinerary and
topographical maps are available from Oslo DNT office. Lug or vibram-
soled hiking shoes or boots, warm jacket for chilly evenings and hiking experience are required for safety's sake. Trails are marked with red paint
on trees and signed at junctions, forks and bridges. Tourist office in U.S.
distributes the pamphlet "Mountain Hikes in Norway."

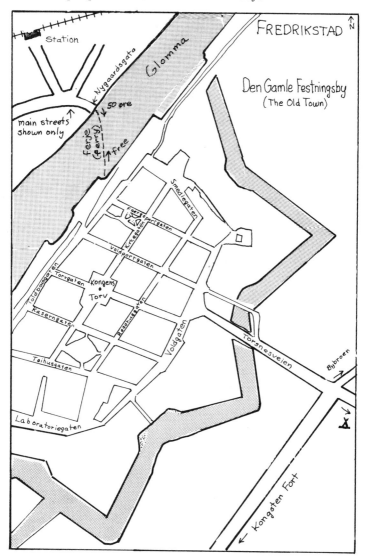

FREDRIKSTAD

Long overlooked by the traveler intent on making the Oslo-Goteborg run in
a day, Fredrikstad's three main attractions are worth your time. They are
the beautifully preserved fortified "old town" (Den Gamle Festningsbyen),

Kongsten Fort, and the PLUS organization of artists and craftsmen. These
are all located across the river from the new town. A passenger ferry
(ferje) crosses between the new town (at Nygaardsgata) and the old town.
Cost is 50 ore from new to old town and free in other direction. Train station
is in new town (see map) and if you walk to the ferry, cross over and walk
straight ahead, you will come to a campground in 20-30 minutes. Festningsbyen (old town) has guided historic tours June 14-Aug on Saturday at 11:30
and 1:30 and Sunday at 12:30 and 3:00 for adult/5 kr, child/2.50 kr. On
weekdays tours leave at 10:30, 12:30 and 2:15 for adult/ 7 kr, child/3.50 kr
and include workshops of the PLUS colony of artists in the old town. All
tours leave from Kongens Torv. Of course anyone can wander around the
old town on his own at any time. Kongsten Fort is within walking distance
of the old town. Tourist office is within Kreditkassen Bank in new town. Also
in the new town is an outstanding cafeteria within what is Scandinavia's biggest food center.

To reach Fredrikstad by train, the town is a stop off on the main rail
line from Copenhagen to Goteborg to Oslo. It is 1 hour and 23 minutes from
Oslo by train, and is the stop between Sarpsborg and Moss. By car, the
town is about a hour's drive south of Oslo--take Fredrikstad exit from E 6
Goteborg-Oslo.

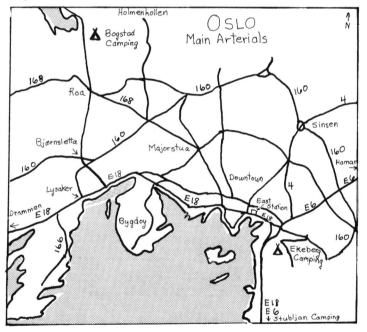

OSLO

Fjords were formed in the Ice Age when glaciers scooped out the granite
mountains in their pathway leaving very deep ocean beds behind. Oslo grew
beside Oslo fjord.

TRAIN STATIONS   Trains arrive from Denmark and Sweden at Oslo's East
Station (Ostbanestasjonen) and leave for Trondheim, Bodo and Bergen there.

Within the station are currency exchange (open June-Aug M-Sa 7 am-11 pm, Su 8-noon, shorter hours rest of year) and hotel reservations office (ink-vartering). There isn't a tourist office but campgrounds have free maps and information. Ostbanestasjonen anchors one end of Oslo's mainstreet, Karl Johans Gate. From Oslo's West Station (Veststasjonen) trains leave for Kristiansand, Stavanger, Drammen, Tonsberg and Rjukan.

TOURIST INFORMATION   Office is at Munkedamsv. 15 in general vicinity of Town Hall but a mite hard to find. Ask for "Oslo Guide."

CAMPGROUNDS   Ekeberg Camping, Ekebergsletta, is 4 km from downtown in a wooded residential area on a hillside overlooking central Oslo. Open June-Aug. From East Station (Ostbanestasjonen), take bus #24 or 72 in front of station to Jomfrubraten. Camp appears on right as bus travels uphill and stops half-block from camp entrance. Bus fare is adult/5 kr, child 3-15/2 kr. Returning from camp to town, the same buses can be taken. By car, camp is east of downtown Oslo. Heading north into Oslo from E 6/ E 18, an Ekeberg camping sign appears later after already having passed a Bogstad camping sign. The turn-off to Ekeberg camping comes before reaching downtown Oslo, however. Camp facilities are excellent with hot showers, cafeteria, grocery store, cooking facilities, clothes washing room, post office, money exchange, adjacent park with wading pool. Costs are flat fee: tent only/30 kr, tent and car/50 kr. This camp is the closest to downtown Oslo.

Bogstad Camping, 8 km from city center, open all year, has room for 800 tents. The camp is farther out than Ekeberg but has similarly good facilities. From East Station, take bus #41 (direction Sorkedalen) at 7:07 am and 7 minutes past each hour until 7:07 pm and then 9:07 pm and 11:07 pm. Route is Gronlands Torg, OSTBANEN (east station), Wessels plass, National theater, Solli plass, Frogner kirke and so on until bus arrives 32 minutes later at Woxen bus stop across street from Bogstad Camping. Bus fare is about adult/5 kr, child 3-15/2 kr. By car, pick up signs to camp on highway E 6/E 18. However camp is through downtown and across to other side of Oslo and traffic is heavy during rush hour. Camp has hot water in washbasins, hot showers (free), and hot water in dishwashing sinks. Post office and money exchange are in registration building. A separate large building contains laundry room with several washers and dryers, washers take 2 five-kroner coins, 50 ore for soap; free freezer in laundromat room for freezing ice packs, open for 15 minutes at 9 and 11 am and 1, 3, 5 and 7 pm; cookroom with coin-operated burners; cafeteria with outdoor terrace, open 9-9, serving chicken and fries, hamburger and fries, etc.; and grocery store, open M-Sa 8-12 and 3-8, which also sells souvenirs such as reindeer antlers for about 65 kr, beautiful reindeer skins for 330-360 kr and sheepskins for about 160 kr. Within the camp are playground, teenage pavillion with jukebox, 20 modern vacation cabins sleeping 4-5 for about 250 kr a day, but write to Bogstad Camping four months in advance for reservations. Gas station is at camp entrance. Same fees as Ekeberg.

Stubljan Camping, south of city, hot showers (5 kr), washing machine. Motorists driving north into Oslo on E 6/E 18 may prefer this camp which is on the right side of the highway and therefore the easiest to find. Otherwise, Ekeberg and Bogstad are closer to Oslo and have more facilities. Stubljan Camping can be reached by bus #75 (direction Ingierstrand) from East railway station.

CITY TRANSPORTATION   Basic fare is about adult/5 kr, child 3-15/2 kr.
A "trikkekort" is sold valid for 11 rides which offers a moderate savings
over buying individual tickets. Buy it on the bus or tram. Most buses stop
downtown at Wessels Plass. Free timetable is available from bus and tram
conductors. Subway is called tunnelbana, but some parts run above ground.
Stations are designated by a capital T. Main terminals are Jernbanetorget
by East Station and at National Theater downtown.

FOOD   Market is on Stortovet, the open plaza marked by the cathedral
that opens off Karl Johans Gate. Hours are Saturday 11-4. Fish market is
on docks in front of City Hall.   Pavilion Cafeteria of the luxury Hotel
Continental, downtown at Roald Amundsens gt. 2, is better and not any more
expensive than the campground cafeterias which serve mainly short-order
fried foods. As this hotel has several eating places on the premises, it's
important that you go to the Pavilion Cafeteria and not one of the more expensive restaurants. Once inside cafeteria entrance, continue upstairs to
the cafeteria. The modern elaborate decor will lead you to believe it's more
expensive than it is, but it's very reasonable for Norway. Menu is posted
in window outside and usually gives a choice of three entrees, the cheapest
being fish and the other two meat. When we were there, fried mackerel
plus vegetables, braised beef with boiled potatoes and green beans, and
two hindquarters of chicken in fricasee sauce with boiled potatoes and green
beans were the choices. The cost is 25-30 kr. A handy pour-it-yourself
water spout is provided just before the cash register. Important: the cafeteria line is open only from M-F 11-7, Sa 11-4 and Su 12-6. After that the
Pavilion operates as a more expensive restaurant.

SIGHTSEEING   The Viking Ships are Norway's most prized historical
possessions. These 9th century ships were grave-ships in which Viking
chiefs and queens were buried with their possessions. The bodies were
covered with a blue mud which helped to preserve them. When the ships
were recovered, workmen found chest-of-drawers, wood plates and cups,
hoes and iron scissors along with the bones. Three viking shops are in
Viking Ship Hall on Bygdoy Peninsula, open May-Aug daily 10-6, Sept daily
11-5, shorter hours rest of year, adult/4 kr, child/2 kr.   Take bus #30
(Bygdoy) from Wessels Plass or   half hourly ferry in summer from dock C
behind Town Hall (Radhusplassen). Ten minute ferry ride costs about 4 kr.

Norwegian Folk Museum, also on Bygdoy, is a collection of farm
buildings which recreate Norwegian life in earlier times. The 12th century
staved chruch, made entirely of wood with pieces being cut and fitted
together without nails, is the outstanding feature. The ends of the gabled
roof are decorated with ship's figureheads attesting to the workmen's
experience as shipbuilders, having only converted to Christianity a century
before. Folklore programs are given in summer. Open May 15-Aug M-Sa
10-6, Su 12-6; Sept 1-14 M-Sa 11-4, Su 12-3. Adult/4 kr child/2 kr. Directions as for Viking Ships above.

Also on Bygdoy is the Polar Expedition Ship 'Fram' used in 1893-96
and 1910-12, open 10:30-5:15, adult/4 kr, child/1.50 kr. The Maritime
Museum and Kon-Tiki Museum are here also, the latter containing the
raft used by Thor Heyerdahl as he and his companions drifted to see if the
South American Incas could have discovered the South Pacific. Summer

hours are 10-6, adult/4 kr, child/1.50 kr. Munch Museum, Toyengate 53, contains much of the lifetime output of the expressionist Edvard Munch, Norway's greatest contemporary painter. Hours are Tu-Sa 10-10, Su 12-10 pm, free. Take bus #29 from opposite National Theater or tunnelbana from in front of East Station to Toyen. Museum is east of downtown, beyond the Akerselva River and across the street from the Botanical Gardens. Playroom for children in basement is open Sunday noon to 3 pm. Across the street are the University's Natural History Museums, Sarsgate 1, Toyen. Paleontological Museum has collections of prehistoric plants and animals, open May-Oct Tu-Su 12-3 pm, free. Zoological Museum, recently modernized, has a good exhibit showing animals from beneath sea level on up to mountain plateau. Free, same hours as Paleontological Museum. There is also a Mineralogical Geological Museum.

National Gallery (Nasjonalgalleriet), 13 Universitetsgata, is open M-F 10-6, Sa 10-3, Su 12-3 and Wed. and Thurs from 6-10 pm, free. Gallery has works of Norwegian painters from 19th and 20th century and modern art with many Frenchmen represented. The 45 paintings by Munch give a good sampling of his gloomy outlook and forlorn sense of man's isolation, and of his expressive technique.

Henie-Onstad Art Center, Hovikodden, Baerum, is 12 km from downtown Oslo. The contemporary building sets on a small promonatory within a park. Only a small portion of the foundation's permanent collection is on view at any one time. Outside is a small undeveloped beach suitable for young children to play. Open daily 11-10, adult/8 kr, student and child/4 kr. Bus #32, 36 or 37 to Hovikodden from National Theater. Two buses an hour, 25 minute ride, bus fare about 5 kr. From Bogstad camping, transfer from bus #41 at Lysaker to bus #32 (Hovikodden) instead of going all the way into town. In this case, bus fare for #32 would be less. Bu car, follow E 18 towards Drammen.

Please consult free tourist office publication "Oslo Guide" for descriptions of additional museums.

SHOPPING   Arts and Crafts Center (Brukskunstsentret i Basarhallene A/L), Karl Johans Gate 11 in the arcades behind the cathedral, is open M-F 9-4, Sa 9-1. Forum, Rosenkrantzgate 7 across from Hotel Bristol is good. Norway Design, Stortingsgata 28 has furniture, rugs and jewelry. Christiania Glasmagasin, Stortovet, is good for glassware. The value added tax is deducted on purchases mailed out of the country.

OSLO - BERGEN RAILWAY

Three-fourths of Norway's land is covered by mountains and the Oslo-Bergen train ride gives a good idea of them. Trains leave Oslo East Station at 7:30 am (ar. 2:10 pm), 10:05 am (ar. 6:30 pm), 3:45 pm (ar. 10:30 pm) and 11:00 pm (ar. 7:45 am). Trains leave Bergen at 7:20 am (ar. 2:05 pm), 9:50 am (ar. 5:40 pm), 3:05 pm (ar. 10 pm) and 10:30 pm (ar. 7:00 am). Check all schedules. There are two very scenic rail spurs, one at Myrdal and the other at Voss, that can be taken by breaking the journey at those points. The train on the Myrdal-Flam line is equipped with five independent sets of brakes, which enables the tracks to decline 2,845 feet in only 12 miles. The train passes through sub-alpine mountains to sea level vegetation at Flam which nestles beside the fjord on the floor of a narrow canyon. Philip Jones

says his favorite town was "Flam, Norway--not crowded, unbelievable
scenery, campground only 100 yards from train station." Including the
Myrdal-Flam sidetrip on a day excursion is possible in the Bergen-Oslo
direction by leaving Bergen at 8:35 am (May-Aug) or 9:50 am (Sept), changing trains at Myrdal, and arriving Flam at 12:23 or 1:08 pm. Then you must
leave Flam at 2:55 or 3:25 pm, changing at Myrdal and arriving in Oslo at
10:00 pm. Check these schedules.

The Voss-Granvin sidetrip is next best and can be done on a day excursion in either direction. Leave Oslo East Station at 7:30 am, change at
Voss, and arrive Granvin at 2:10 pm. Or leave Bergen at 8:35 am (May-Aug)
or 9:50 am (Sept), change at Voss and arrive Granvin at noon. A train leaves
Granvin for Bergen at 3:55 pm (ar. 6:30 pm) and for Oslo at 3:30 pm (ar.
10 pm). Voss camping is situated close in by Vangsvatnet Lake near the
center of town--highly rated, room for 175 tents. Train reservations may be
necessary for Oslo-Bergen portions, preferably for a window seat on left
side when going to Bergen.

BERGEN

Bergen welcomes you with lush green parks, cobbled streets and a lively
waterfront. Train station is downtown, two blocks from bus station and eight
from tourist office.

CAMPGROUNDS   Midttun Camping is 13 km from Bergen. From train station, turn left as you come out and in about 100 meters, there is a sign to
your left "Bergen Busstadion." Catch bus #1 to Arna at "Perrong 1" to your
right as you enter. Fare is 8 kr. Free bus schedule "Lokalruter" can be had
from information office in bus station. Ride to camp is 20 minutes. Immediately after passing a small town, and where bus turns off main road, pull
the stop cord when you see the camping sign on the left. Camp is 100 meters
away and visible from bus stop. Hot water in sinks, hot showers, no store
or snack bar, camp closed between 11 pm and 8 am. Check out time is
3 pm.

Two other Bergen camps, Grimen near Helldal and Lone near Hauke-
land are farther on same bus route. Bus fare is 9 kr to Lone Camping, the
farthest.

Bus schedule: leave Oslo at 6:05, 6:30, 7:05, 7:35, 8:00, 8:40, 10:10, 11
11:00 am, noon, 1:00, 1:40, 2:10, 2:40, 3:10, 3:38, 4:10, 4:24, 4:45, 5:10,
5:50, 7:00, 7:25, 8:25, 9:10, 10:10, 11:10 pm and 12:10 am. Leave Midttun
at 6:23, 6:48, 7:08, 7:40, 7:58, 8:33, 9:15, 10:28 am, 12:08, 1:03, 1:50,
2:03, 2:30, 3:00, 3:43, 4:03, 4:35, 5:15, 6:28, 7:10, 8:20, 9:35, 10:30 and
11:30 pm. Some services omitted on Saturday and different schedule for
Sunday.

HOTEL ALREK   A lone traveler can do almost as well at the Alrek, a
modern dormitory of the University of Bergen where a single rents for
about 70-75 kr, which is handy to know in case it's raining. Linen is
supplied and sink is in each room. Season of hotel varies slightly each year
but it's usually open July 1-Aug 17. It's located 2 km from downtown at
Arstadveien 25, a 40 minute partially uphill walk or bus #2 from Kaltarveien.
(Turn right upon leaving train station and walk one block to Kaltarveien. Turn
right onto Kaltarveien--don't cross it—and bus stop is in third block.

TOURIST INFORMATION   At Torgalmenning. From train station walk 7 blocks straight ahead on main street Kaigaten to Torgalmenning. Open M-S 8:30 am-11 pm, Su 9:30 am-11 pm. Bergen Touring Club, 3 C. Sundtsgate, arranges hikes and can supply information on hiking huts and trails, open 9-4.

CITY TRANSPORTATION   Basic in-town fare is adult/5 kr, child 3-15/ 2 kr. A Tourist Ticket costs 28 kr for 48 hours but DOES NOT include bus line to campgrounds. Sold at Tourist office, hotels and travel agencies. Each in-town bus is signed with route number and terminus. Central Bus Station, 8 Stromgaten, is departure point for all buses serving the environs of Bergen and the Hardanger area. Campground buses leave from here. Ferry across Bergen harbor between Slottsgatan and C. Sundtsgt. costs 2 kr and has frequent service.

FOOD   Fish, fruit and vegetable market operates Monday through Saturday 8:30-3 at Torget on the waterfront. Fish market is exceptional and best in the morning.

SIGHTSEEING   Bryggen, the wharf lined with step roofed wooded ware- houses built when Bergen met success as a Hanseatic port is now home for the workshops of many artists and craftsmen. Hanseatic Museum, within a 16th century wooden building, displays merchant life in the Hansa days, open June-Aug 10-4, May & Sept 11-2, adult/4 kr, child/2 kr. Bryggen Museum shows archaeological and historical items, open in summer M-F 10-4, Sa-Su 11-3 and Tu and Th 6-8 pm, adult/4 kr.

Rasmus Meyer's Collection in central Bergen on Rasmus Meyer Alle, shows Norwegian paintings including works by Edvard Munch. Open May 15- Aug M-Sa 10-3, Su 12-3, Sept-May 14 daily 12-3 except Tuesday, free. Fishery Museum nearby is a good special interest museum. Same hours but adult/2 kr, child/1 kr. Museum of Arts and Crafts and Municipal Art Museum are here too.

Maritime Museum, Sydneshaugen, is a modern museum showing the development of shipping. Open daily 11-2, adult/1 kr, child/.50 kr. Aquarium on Nordnes Peninsula is a 10 minute walk from downtown or bus #6 from Town Hall. One of the best in Europe, it's open May-Sept daily 9-8, Oct-Apr daily 10-6. Admission charge.

Mount Floien (floy-en) is viewpoint and start of trails. Take funicular from downtown Bergen, open early morning to midnight, adult/7 kr. Gamle Bergen (Old Bergen), Elsesro, Sandviken, contains 30 buildings from 18th and 19th centuries grouped to form a town. Open May 8-Sept 17 daily 10-7. Guided tour each hour to 6 pm. Adult/5 kr, student and child/2 kr. Bus # 1 from downtown Bergen, departures every 8 minutes, bus fare 5 kr. Hill Farm Museum (Seter Museum) at Fanafjell shows how farmers used to do it. Also viewpoint. Adult/3 kr, child/1 kr. Bus from "perrong 15" at Central Bus Station, bus fare 9.50 kr. Fantoft Stave Church at Paradis is an excel- lent example of wood church completely built without metal nails. Open May 15-Sept 15 daily 3-6 pm and Tu, Th, Sa & Su also 10-1; July daily 10-1 and 3-6, adult/2.50 kr, child/1 kr. Bus from Central Bus Station to Paradis (direction Paradis or Saedal)--12 minute ride plus 10 minute walk--bus fare is 6 kr. Or take bus from campground which stops at Paradis.

TOILETS   All public toilets in Bergen require a 1 kr coin.

STAVANGER

Though the center of Norwegian North Sea oil exploration, Stavanger retains
its picturesque old quarter. Train station is downtown facing the lake.
Baggage checking is open 7:30 am-10 pm. Bus Station is next door..

Tourist information, "Reiselivslaget for Stavanger,"
is in modern glass building next to station. Turn left
upon leaving station. Open June 1-Aug 15 M-F 8:30-6,
Sa 8:30-2, Su 11-4; Aug 16-May M-F 9-4, Sa 9-1. Ask
for "Stavanger Guide."

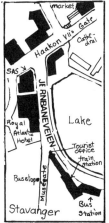

CAMPGROUNDS   Mosvangen Camping, Tjensvoll on
Lake Mosvatnet, is next to Mosvangen Youth Hostel.
From train station, turn left and bus stop for #10 bus
(yellow) is on the street "Musegate" behind the train
station.   (See map.) There are two buses each hour,
bus fare is 5 kr, and there is about a three minute walk
from bus stop to camp. You can walk from camp to
downtown in 30 minutes by walking on the gravel path
around Mosvatnet Lake and then following highway 510
into town.   Camp has hot water in sinks, hot showers,
grocery store, rental cabins, 200 tent capacity. Adult/
5 kr, child 5-12/1.50 kr, tent/15 kr.
     Vaulen Camping is on route #44, 5 km south of
Stavanger. From train station take bus NSB (blue)
from bus station beside and to rear of train station. Buses leave often.
Fare is 5-6 kr. No showers at camp, but swimming.
     Strandleiren Camping, Kolnes at Sola, is reached by bus to Sola from
SAS Royal Atlantic Hotel. Then 1f minute walk to camp. Showers, beach,
boat rental.

CITY TRANSPORTATION   City buses are yellow and cost 5 kr. Suburban
buses are blue-gray and leave from bus station beside and to rear of train
station. Circular route of city bus #10 (same bus as to Mosvangen Camping)
is suggested as an excellent unguided tour of Stavanger, passing by the most
interesting sights and taking in most parts of the city.

FOOD   Public market including tanks with live fish is near the cathedral
at Haakon VII's Gate and Skagenkaien. Open M-Sa until 3 pm. Eating out is
expensive in this oil town--you might try the Mosvangen Youth Hostel next
door to Mosvangen camp as it serves all three meals.

SIGHTSEEING   Old Stavanger (Gamle Stavanger) between Ovre Strandgate
and Nedre Strandgata has cobbled streets, gaslights and wooden buildings.
Iron Age Farm, Ullandhaug, is a reconstructed farm from about 350-550A.D.
on bus line #10 but farther than Mosvangen Campground. Guided tours for
groups can be arranged by contacting the Archaeological Museum, Musegt.
16. Ullandhaug Tower, telegraph company tower with public viewing platform, is also on bus route #10 (Gosen bus stop). Stavanger Museum, Musegt.
16, has archaeological, historical and zoological collections. Open June-Sept
Su-Fr 11-3, Sa 11-2, Sept-May Su 11-3. Adult/2 kr, child/1 kr.
     Pulpit Rock is a sheer cliff face 2,000 feet high above Lyse Fjord.
Sightseeing boats charge 60 kr for 3 hour tour but it can be done on your own
by taking local ferry to Lysebotn, which passes under the rock on the way.

Schedule from tourist office. Several do-it-yourself mountain forays into
the surrounding region of fjords and mountains are described in free tourist
office publication "Stavanger Guide." For example, by taking the Algard-
Oltedal bus, you can visit the Figgjo Fajanse pottery shop at Figgjo and
wool factories at Algard where prices are cheaper, and at the same time
see the Norwegian countryside. Bus fares total about 25 kr for adults and
12 kr for children.

SHOPPING   Shops are open M-F 8:30-4, Sa 8:30-1 with late 7 pm closing
on Thursday.

NARVIK

This far northern land of the midnight sun town is on the rail line from
Stockholm, Sweden. Narvik's fjord-side campground is a 10 minute walk
from the train station. Hot showers, grocery store, cooking facilities.

BODO

Bodo is across the Arctic Circle, and the midnight sun is visible from
June 3 to July 8. A favored viewpoint is from the restaurant on Mount
Ronvik. TRAIN STATION is downtown at edge of water. TOURIST OFFICE
is 3 blocks from train station. Turn right on Sjogata and tourist office is
in a corner of the open square.

CAMPGROUND Bodosjoen is 3 km from the train station, and can be
walked in about 40 minutes. From the train station turn left onto Sjogata
and continue walking on that street where eventually you'll see camping
signs. There is a bus about 150 meters from the train station which goes
within 150 meters of the campground. (See map.) The bus leaves every
half hour and the fare is about 5 kr. Camp has store (open 8:30 am-8 pm
daily), washing machines (15 kr), dryer (10 kr), and costs adult/5 kr,
child 4-12/1.50 kr, tent only/16 kr, tent and car/24 kr.

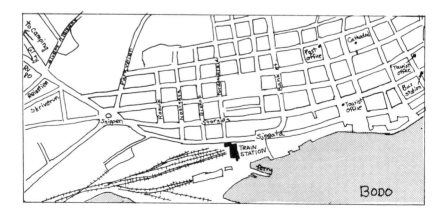

PORTUGAL

All year around the weather is fine for camping somewhere in Portugal. Prices are lower than northern Europe. Time is one hour earlier than Spain.

CURRENCY   Monetary unit is the escudo (es-HOO-dough), written 1$00. One escudo equals 100 centavos. Centavos are written to the right of the dollar sign. One escudo is worth about 16¢, or about 64$00 = $1.00.

WEATHER   Summer offers a mild coastline but finds the interior uncomfortably warm. Camping is pleasant in spring or fall, but with occasional rainfall. April is a noted tourist month because of the many folklore festivals. The Algave, southernmost province, is warm enough for winter camping though the season for swimming in the Atlantic or Mediterranean is March through October.

CAMPGROUNDS   Campgrounds are called "parque de campismo." A few camps require a camping card but most don't so this isn't a problem. Camping informally (not in a campground) is legal except in urban areas or less than one kilometer from a campground or public beach, and campers mustn't foul the water of springs and wells, build a fire or leave garbage behind. Tourist office pamphlet, "Portugal Camping," lists campgrounds according to area, distance from bus stop and train station. Camps are graded Tourist, first and second. Most camps charge less for a small tent than a large one.

pessoa - person	abastecimento - grocery store
tenda - tent	parque infantil - playground
cozinha - kitchen	informacoes - information
duche quente - hot shower	auto caravana - van
lava-loicas - washbasins	crianca - child
lava-roupas - laundry sinks	por noite - per night

Prices are very inexpensive: adults/ 25$00-45$00, child 4-10/ half-price,

310

child under 4/free, tent/from 30$00-40$00 according to size, car/30$00-
40$00, hot shower/12$00 for example. Prices drop to about half usually
from October to May.

TRAINS   Companhia dos Caminhos de Ferro Portugueses (EP) is the
Portuguese Railways. Best trains ply the international routes, such as SUD
Express, Lusitania Express and the best one, TER Lisbon Express.
Portugal does not have the fast inter-city trains of northern Europe but still
has good service along the coast north of Lisbon and good international con-
nections. Lisbon-Belem-Estoril-Cascais rail line is now part of the
Portuguese Railways. Children under 4 ride free and those 4-12 pay half.

estacao - station	guard de volumes de mao -
caminho de ferro - railway	luggage storage
chegadas - arrivals	informacoes - information
partidas - departures	sala des espera - waiting room
retrete - restroom	todos os dias - daily
deposito de volumes - luggage storage	domingos e feriados - Sundays
platforma - track	and holidays

Portuguese Railroads offer these special tickets. Kilometric Ticket is
issued for a minimum of 3,000 km, valid three months for 5,965$00 first
class and 3,975$00 second class for express trains, and 4,770$00 for first
class and 3,180$00 for second class for trains other than express. Two
children 4 to 12 years of age count as one adult. These tickets cannot be used
to travel from 12 noon to midnight on Fridays or the last working day of the
week or from 12 noon to midnight on Sundays or the last day of an official
holiday. The ticket must be validated at the station, or if there is none then
on the train, the first time the ticket is used. Tourist Ticket is good for
7, 14 or 21 days for unlimited travel and costs 7 days for 1,790$00, 14 days
for 3,050$00 and 21 days for 4,020$00. Family Tickets have the same ex-
clusions of when to travel as the kilometric ticket above. They are valid one
month and issued for a minimum of 150 km. The first member pays full
fare, all other members 12 years or over pay half fare and those 4 through
11 pay one quarter fare. A family can consist of parents and child under
21 years of age or single brothers and sisters under 21 provided they travel
together on the same train and class. Group Tickets are valid for groups of
10 or more on the same train for trips of 100 km minimum, valid for one
month. Tickets must be applied for four days before departure and confirmed at least two days before. For 10-14 people, the discount is 20%,
15-50 people get 20% discount plus one free ticket and groups over 50 people
receive 20% discount plus 1 free ticket for each 50 paying people. Children
of 4-12 pay half or two children count as one adult. Senior Citizen Ticket
gives 50% off regular fare for persons 65 years and over for trips of 50 km
minimum. Reduced rate is given when ticket is purchased.

FOOD   Portugal produces wheat, corn, rice, olives, tomatoes, grapes,
oranges, almonds, figs and sugar cane. Sardines and wine rank two and
three after cork on Portugal's list of exports. Fish is eaten ten times as
often as meat by the Portuguese and dried cod is very popular. The carob
plant, a short bushy evergreen, grows in the Algarve. A delicatessen
(mercearias) sells pasteurized milk. Check bottle cap for the original seal.
Tap water is safe in Lisbon, major towns and resorts, though the high mineral content in Lisbon's water bothers some. "Aqua de Lusa" is a

non-carbonated mineral water. House wine is "vinho de casa." "Prego" is
roast beef or thin filet steak on a bun which is served in cafes. Eggs are
incorporated into many dishes in restaurants and custard (flan) is on every
menu. Food is cooked in olive oil or groundnut oil.   For children, a half
portion is called "meia dose." Mealtimes are 1 pm and 8 pm. Foodstores
are open 9-1 and 3-7 and close at 1 pm on Saturday.

PRONUNCIATION OF PLACE NAMES   Aseitao (az-aye-TAN), Cascais
(kash-keish), Coimbra (KWEEM-bra), Estoril (ish-to-REEL), Evora
(a-VOO-ra), Faro (FA-roo), Fatima (FA-tee-ma), Oporto (oh-POR-toe),
Portimao (port-i-MAN), Praia da Rocha (PREE-a-da ROH-cha), Sagres
(SA-gresh), Setubal (se-TOO-bal), Sintra (SEEN-tra)

LISBON (LISBOA)

Lisbon has its own style with broad modern boulevards and Alfama, the old
quarter with steep cobbled streets and narrow alleys.

AIRPORT   Outside the entrance on the right is the bus stop. Bus #50 goes
directly to the campground. Bus #44 and 45 (both direction Cais do Sodre)
travel downtown to Rossio Train Station and the heart of Lisbon.

TRAIN STATIONS   Two important ones are Rossio, the central station and
focal point of the city, and Santa Apolonia, the main station which handles
international traffic. Gare Estoril-Cascais at Cais do Sodre and Gare do Sul
e Sueste (T. Paco) at Praca do Comercio are minor.   Santa Apolonia has
an exchange office open 9-12 and 2-6:30, combined train information, seat
reservations and tourist office (8:00 am-9:30 pm), and eating places. Bus
#9 and 9 A go to Rossio Station. Rossio Station serves Sintra, Vila Franca
de Xira and western lines but reservations for any train can be made here.
(Trains from nothern and eastern Portugal arrive at Santa Apolonia Station.)
"Servico International" window takes reservations for international trains.
Train information office is open 9 am-11 pm. Outside Rossio Station is Rossio
Square (Dom Pedro IV Square) with monument to Pedro IV of Portugal and
the national theater. Tourist office is nearby at Avenida de Liberdade. Metro
station: Rossio.   The charge for checking baggage is 10$00.

    Gare Cais do Sodre serves Estoril, famous resort, and Cascais which
has an interesting early morning fish auction. Station is next to Tagus River
on bus route #43 from campground or bus #1, 44 or 45 from Rossio Station.
Ride to Cascais is 30 minutes with Estoril and (on some trains) Belem as
intermediate stops. There are about four trains an hour. Sul e Sueste Station
(T. Paco), next to Praca do Comercio near waterfront, handles traffic going
south and southeast (Baizo Alentejo and Algave).   There is ferry service
from T. Paco Station to Barreiro on the other side of the Tagus where the
trains begin.

TOURIST INFORMATION   Offices are at Apolonia Station, on Avenida de
Liberdade near Rossio Station and at the campground. Ask for "Portugal
Welcomes You" which has a map of Lisbon, and "Lisbon, the Castle Neigh-
borhood" for its walking tour of Alfama, the old quarter.

CAMPGROUND   Municipal camp, Parque de Campismo, is in the north-
western corner of huge Parque Florestal de Monsanto which covers

one-sixth of Lisbon. The camp is outstanding. Open all year. From Rossio Station, walk across square in front and turn left onto Rua do Amparo to another square, Praca da Figueira. Take bus (carreira) #43 (direction Buraca) which leaves every 20 minutes. Ride is half-hour. Bus ride gives a good orientation to the city on its way to the campground. After leaving Praca da Figueira, bus follows R. da Prata straight through downtown to the waterfront (Praca do Comercio). It turns right on Av. 24 du Julho, passes Gare M. da Rocha and continues along shoreline on Av. da India to Belem. At Belem, the bus turns inland on Av. das Descobertas, passes through Parque Monsanto on Estr. de Queluz and finally reaches the campground. Then bus continues to Casa de Paulos and terminates at Buraca. From Apolonia Station (Estacao de Santa Apolonia), take bus #14 which stops in front of the campground. From Airport, take bus #50 (direction Alges) from front-right outside. Bus leaves every 15 minutes for the half-hour trip. After leaving airport, the bus travels on Avenida M. Carmona to Estadio da Luz (stadium), then enters Benfica district, goes by Alto Boa Vista and Casal de Paulos to campground. Then bus continues along E. Circunvalacao, road bordering Parque Monsanto, to Alges. Camp has hot showers (5$00), store, restaurant (white tablecloths and white-jacketed waiters), tourist office, post office, bank, hair dresser, automatic washing machines (42$00 without soap), swimming pool, tennis courts, playground, croquet and minigolf. Adult/20$00, child 4-10/10$00, small tent/20$00, large tent/30$00, car/20$00.

CITY TRANSPORTATION   Trams, buses and subway (metro) are good and inexpensive. Tram and bus fares are according to distance. Subway fare is a flat rate. Carris kiosks sell one-week ticket, and 12 ticket subway books.

FOOD   Main market, Av. 24 de Julho near Cais do Sodre Station, is open M-F 6 am-2 pm, Sa 6 am-5 pm. Fruit wholesale market is at Cais da Riviera near the river and open 6-11 am. Neighborhood markets are on R. Da Madalena below Castle of St. George, and between T. Maria da Fonte and R. Damasceno Monteiro northeast of downtown. Supermarket is on Rua de Dezembro next to Rossio Station.

SIGHTSEEING   Calouste Gulbenkian Museum (Fundacao Gulbenkian), Av. de Berna, is the gift of the Anglo-Armenian oil tycoon and one of the best in Europe. Collection includes representative items from Egyptian, Greek, Roman, Mesopotamian, Islamic and Oriental cultures in the form of paintings, sculpture, fabrics, pottery, furniture and jewelry. There is also a performing arts theater and library. Open T, Th, F, Su 10-5; W, Sa 2-8. Bus #31 (direction Moscavide) from Restauradores near Rossio Station. Buses leave every 10-20 minutes. Ride is 12 minutes to modern building on left side of street. From Praca da Figueira (terminus of bus #43 from camp) take subway to Palhava Station.
   The following museums are open at 10 am daily, except Monday. All are free or inexpensive. BELEM. Bus #43 from camp goes there. Jeronoimos Monastery, Praca do Imperio, masterpiece of Manueline architecture, was built in 16th century to celebrate success of voyages of Portugurese navigators. Next door is Naval Museum with model boats which show historical development of water-craft and a tiny seaplane in which first crossing of South Atlantic was made in 1922. Tower of Belem marks spot from which Portuguese navigators began their voyages. Folk Art Museum, Av. Brasilia,

exhibits handcrafts from the provinces, and the National Museum of Archae-
ology and Ethnology, Praca do Imperior, shows Roman mosaics, Egyptian
mummies, etc. Pier for boats crossing the river is in this area.

The 2,000 year old Castle of St. George crowns Lisbon's highest hill.
What you see now is the castle after its 16th century remodeling. Entrances
are on Largo do Chao da Feira and in the Alfama district, Largo do Menino
de Deus. Open 8 am-sunset. Alfama, the picturesque old quarter, is where
the Museum of Decorative Art, Lg. das Portas do Sol, shows 17th and 18th
century paintings set within a lovely palace. Adjacent is a craft school.
Downtown in Lisbon, the Cathedral, Lg da Se, was an Arab Mosque before
the 12th century. Bullfight season is Easter to October on Thursday evenings
in Campo Pequeno ring. Bull is not killed in Portuguese fights. Flea market
(Feira da Ladra) is on Campo de Santa Clara, Tu and Sa 9-6.

TRAIN SCHEDULES   To MADRID, a TER leaves S. Apolonia Station at
7:30 am (ar. Madrid Atocha 6:49 pm, Chamartin 7:02 pm). Reservation
required.   Another train leaves at 8:20 pm (ar. Atocha 9:10 am).

To PARIS, the SUD Express leaves S. Apolonia Station at 4:20 pm (ar.
next day Paris Austerlitz Station 8:54 pm).

To OPORTO, first class only trains leave S. Apolonia Station at
7:25 am, 8:25 am, 11:00 am, 2:25 pm, 5:00 pm and 8:15 pm, and arrive at
Campanha Station about 3 hours later. Other trains leave at 7:58 am,
8:50 am, 11:35 am, 3:30 pm and 7:00 pm.

To the ALGARVE and SEVILLE, a first class rapido train leaves T. de
Paco Station (which is actually a ferry which crosses the Tagus river and the
train is boarded on the other side) 2:25 pm M, W, F only plus Tu & Th from
June 15-Sept 15 and goes as far as Faro. At Faro, local trains run between
Faro, Tunes and Lagos. If continuing to Seville, change trains and leave
Faro at 7:21 pm and arrive at the border, Vila Real de Santo Antonio at 8 pm.
At the border, take the ferry to Ayamonte, Spain. Trip is 15 minutes, and
service is half-hourly from 9 am to 6 pm. Buses of Damas S.A. run twice
daily between Seville, Huelva and Ayamonte. Trains run three times daily.

PORTO (OPORTO)

Capital of the north and center of the port wine trade, Porto is 5 km inland
from mouth of Douro River on what once was Portucale in pre-Roman times.

TRAIN STATIONS Station Campanha is outside of downtown. Take bus "F"
to last stop at Praca de Almeida Garrett near Sao Bento Station downtown, or
bus #102 to downtown. Trindade Station serves coastal area around Porto.
To go to northern Spain or France, backtrack to Pampilhosa and take an
international express from there. For Madrid, go to Encontramento and
take TER Lisbon Express.

TOURIST INFORMATION   Office is at Praca Dom Joao I near Sao Bento
Station.

CAMPGROUND   Camping Prelada, Rua Monte dos Burgos, north of downtown in a public park, is operated by Santa Casa da Misericordia. Open all
year. Take bus #35 or 80 from Campanha Station to Praca Almeida Garrett
near S. Benito Station. Change to bus #6 at Praca de Liberdade. Hot

showers, store, restaurant, playground.

SIGHTSEEING   Tourist office has brochure on museums and churches. See the Moorish hall inside the Stock Exchange (Palacio de Bolsa), Praca Infante D. Henrique, for its tri-colored red, blue and gold ceiling and Arabesque interior of columns and arcades reminiscent of the Alhambra. Most port wine firms open their cellars to visitor, but Casa Ferreira and Sandemans even offer a boat cruise on the Douro River which passes by wine lodges where maturation takes place before wine is shipped. Shippers are in Vila Nova de Gaia which is across the river from Porto. Information from Instituto do Vinho do Porto, Rua Ferreira Borges.

TRAIN SCHEDULES   To LISBON, first class only trains leave Campanha Station at 7:15 am, 8:15 am, 11:00 am, 2:35 pm, 5:00 pm, 8:15 pm and 9:15 pm. Other trains leave Sao Bento Station at 6:57 am, and 4:00 pm. Other trains depart from Campanha Station at 9:25 am, 11:50 am, 3:30 pm and 6:45 pm.

THE ALGARVE

The extreme southern province is a sunny winter destination offering sandy beaches, fishing villages, and remnants of long past Arab occupation. Trains from Lisbon go to Tunes, where you must change trains for Lagos if going there, and continue from Tunes to Faro, Monte Gordo for which you must ask the conductor to stop, and Vila Real de Santo Antonio. Vila Real has two stations of which the second is Guadiana which is next to the Spanish border.

LAGOS, a fishing port with fine beaches, has Parque de Turismo de Lagos campground on the beach outside of town, between Porto de Mos and Ponta da Piedade. Open all year, hot showers, automatic washing machine, store, bus from Lagos, no camping carnet required.

FARO, largest town of the Algarve, has Camara Municipal de Faro campground in Praia de Faro, the beach reached by river ferry. Open all year, store, no camping card needed. Friday market is good in nearby Loule.

Two kilometers before Vila Real, Camara Municipal campground is in Monte Gordo, located 1500 meters from Monte Gordo train station or 200 meters from a bus stop. Not all trains will stop at Monte Gordo even if requested, in which case ride on to Vila Real and get off at the first station and take local train going to Monte Gordo or a bus. Camp is open all year, hot showers, store, playground.

SPAIN

Spain ranks with Italy, France and Greece in the degree of gloriousness of her past civilization. Possibly the best museum in Europe is in Madrid. The Prado shows only "la creme de la creme" and owns the only extensive collection of paintings and drawings by Goya. His drawings are humorous vignettes on the foibles of man and society and are even better than his paintings--perhaps because they weren't commissioned. Goya's seldomly reproduced paintings done on the walls of his house in his elderly years are the forerunners of Van Gogh's "Potato Eaters" and look strangely contemporary. Distances are great in this large and mountainous country, but the journey is emphatically worth it.

CURRENCY   Each peseta is worth about 1¢. About 92 pesetas (ptas.) equal $1.00. Travelers checks are cashed without fee at the Banco de Espana.

WEATHER   Spain is a mecca for the off-season camper and a non-summer traveler could make Spain the anchor of his itinerary. Best time for visiting all of Spain is spring or autumn, except the northern coast might be somewhat cold and rainy. May probably provides the best camping weather for an all-around itinerary, with September and early October next. In summer, the cities of Moorish background, Seville and Cordoba, are very warm. Madrid gets periodically hot in summer with an 84 degree average in July but temperatures can't be taken literally as weather varies from week to week and a heat wave sending temperatures soaring into the 90's can occur even in June. The trick to fitting Madrid into a summer itinerary comfortably is to keep plans flexible, watchdog the weather box in "The International Herald Tribune" (which gives yesterday's highs and lows for major cities) and be ready to move when the temperature is right. For a winter tour, camping is good along the Costa del Sol in southern Spain (of limited touristic interest) and on the islands of Majorca and Ibiza.

CAMPING   In contrast with the camps of Germany, Switzerland, France
and others which were first developed for their own countrymen, those of
Spain sprouted to meet the needs of tourists from the rest of Europe, notably
the traditional sun-seekers of Scandinavia, Britain and Germany. Because
of this, the most campgrounds are on the southern coast rather than in
Madrid or near the best sightseeing destinations. Some campgrounds on
Costa Brava and Costa del Sol in southern Spain are resort camps with
teams of cleaning ladies scouring the restrooms three times daily, resident
doctor, store, restaurant, shops and anything else a week-long vacationer
needs to enjoy himself. But the ones a train-camper will be using are more
modest, but with the usual facilities of restrooms with conventional toilets,
hot showers, store and snack bar. The tourist office publishes "Mapa de
Campings" which pinpoints each camp on a map of Spain and lists opening
times and government classification. Classifications are deluxe (lujo),
first, second and third class according to number of facilities and seaside
location. Foreign tourists come to the deluxe category camps, whereas
Spaniards know where the values are and visit the cheaper lower category
camps. From our experiences, we found camp classification to be unrelated
to restroom quality and, if anything, the smaller family-run camps seemed
tidier and more tightly managed. Before each season, the owners of each
campground are required by law to obtain a certificate of proof of water
quality to show that the water is drinkable. Non-drinking water may only be
used for irrigation and in the toilets. Each camp in Spain is required by law
to have a surrounding fence, watchman, running water, sinks, showers,
toilets, lighting, first aid box and fire extinguisher. "Tienda" is tent,
"coche" is car, "nino" is child.

TRAINS   Spanish State Railways (RENFE) operate Talgo and Ter trains
comparable with TEE and international express trains of northern Europe.
Distances are so great in Spain that trains have the habit of arriving late at
night which makes settling in more difficult. One way to minimize late
arrivals is to tour Spain from north to south. Stay overnight in Hendaye,
France at the French-Spanish border, and ride the E. L. T. which leaves
Hendaye/Irun at 7:55 am and arrives in Madrid (Chamartin Station) at
4:29 pm. Because Spaniards keep late hours, if you do arrive late at night
it's just as easy (and much cheaper) to find the campground as to hunt up a
hotel. The tracks of Spanish and Portuguese railways are of a broader
width than those in France and the rest of Europe (except Finland), so you
must change trains at French-Spanish borders except in a few cases where
trains are used whose wheels are adjustable in width. The best trains are
the Talgo, T. E. R. (Tren Espanol Rapido) and E. L. T. (Electrotren) which
have both first and second class and are air conditioned. Reservations are
strongly advised for these trains in summer--if you don't get one you aren't
likely to get on--but are not officially mandatory. But if you don't have a
reservation (which costs about 30 pesetas), it is mandatory that a free
boarding pass be obtained for the specific train departure at the train station
before you will be allowed on the train. The next fastest trains are "Rapido"
and a boarding pass is necessary for these too if you don't have a reservation. A boarding pass is not required for local and commuter trains nor for
slower long distance ones. Reservations are advised in summer for the fast
trains on the Madrid-Granada and Seville-Granada runs. One way to make

a seat reservation or obtain a boarding pass, is to first go to the train information window and tell the clerk what train you wish to take. She will give you a form to give to the clerk at the ticket or reservation window who will issue a boarding pass or reservation card.

Large Spanish cities tend to have more than one train station so be certain to go to the correct station, which is listed in parenthesis following the city name on train schedules. Stations generally have a tourist office and currency exchange. Lockers are less abundant but hand checking is always available. Sometimes there is a separate cashier to pay who issues a receipt before you proceed to the baggage line. Sometimes one line is for checking and another for retrieving.

estacion - station	Quiere darme un horario de trene? - May I have a time-table?
acceso andenes - to the tracks	
asiento - seat on train	
cambio - currency exchange	Deme un billete de ida para Madrid. - Give me a one-way ticket to Madrid.
la consigna - baggage check	
llegada - arrival	
sala de espera - waiting room	Cuanto tiempo paramos aqui? - How long does the train stop?
oficina de informacion - train information office	
oficina municipal de turismo - tourist information office	Esta ocupado este asiento? - Is this seat taken?
	senores, hombres, caballeros - men's toilet
horario de trene - train schedule	
trenes de salida - trains ready to depart	senoras, mujeres, damas - women's toilet
venta para hoy - tickets or reservations for trains leaving today	cerrado - closed
	abierto - open
venta anticipada - tickets or reservations for trains leaving after today	entrada - entrance
	salida - exit

lunes	- monday	jueves - thursday		domingo - sunday	
martes	- tuesday	viernes - friday		festivos - holidays	
miercoles	- wednesday	sabado - saturday		primero - first	

On Eurailpass and Eurail Youthpass, from June 13 to July 11, 1982 during the World Soccer Championship, a surcharge of $30 on Eurailpass and $20 on Eurail Youthpass will be made. The payment must be made in Spanish currency at a train station in Spain, for which a receipt will be issued valid for the entire period. During all times, supplements are charged Eurail Youthpass holders to ride Talgo, T. E. R. and E. L. T. trains. Eurailpass and Eurail Youthpass include a 20% reduction on the normal fares of the Transmediterranea Company on its ships sailing between Barcelona or Valencia and Palma de Mallorca, and between Algeciras and Tangiers, Morocco.

Spanish State Railways or RENFE (pronounced ren-fay) sell "Cheque-tren" booklets which give 15% discount on train fares for up to six people. It offers the reduction on 15,000 pesetas worth of travel. It works like script and is sold only in Spain through RENFE offices and at train stations. Senior citizens receive a 50% reduction on trips over 100 km when they purchase a Gold Card ("Tarjeta Dorada") for 25 pesetas. Buy it at RENFE ticket offices and train station. Present passport for proof of age.

DRIVING   Roads are good and the new "autopista" is a superhighway or freeway which starts from near the southern French border (La Junquera) and continues to Barcelona and south along the coast. The autopista is all toll. Upon entering you are given a card which is handed in at the exit and used to calculate the toll due. Each exit is marked, starting with Barcelona as "Salida 1." Maps, guidebooks, toys, newspapers, candy and souvenirs can be bought, currency exchanged, and tourist information obtained at Jacque Borel Restaurant/Cafeteria facilities which are accessible to both sides of the autopista via a pedestrian overpass. The baby-changing room near the women's restroom has sink, counter with pad, and diapers for sale. Restroom attendant unlocks the room and is tipped 10-15 ptas. In large cities, traffic is thick and numerous one-way streets make it almost faster to walk rather than drive to your destination.

A very nice and inexpensive campground is at Canet de Mar on the coastal highway north of Barcelona. It's not accessible to train-campers. At Camping La Llave, campsites are in rows, each site separated by a hedge on three sides. A covered storage areas is provided in the corner of each site. Facilities include individual sink compartments, conventional toilets without seats, no hot showers, store, swimming pool, cooked barbequed chickens, rental apartments, and the help speaks English.

FOOD   You can eat reasonably in Spain on seasonal fruits and vegetables, chicken, fish and cheese. Veal is good and cheaper than beef. Baby lamb costs less than in the United States. Sausage, rabbit and pork are commonly found. Milk and cream are pasteurized. There's also a "sterilized" milk that is safe. Good apple cider and juice come from the north of Spain. Tap water is generally safe but the popular and inexpensive Solares mineral water is only slightly effervescent and Font Vella brand is flat. Sherry is the usual aperitif and dessert wine. Valdepenas is the most popular reasonable red wine and is produced in central Spain. Open house wine is usually Valdepenas. Best and smoothest wines come from the Rioja region in north Spain. Better quality ones have the name of the vintner (bodega) on the label. A good sparkling Riojan white wine for a special occasion is made by Bodega Bilbainas.

The open market sells most everything and has considerably lower prices than the shops or supermarkets. A half kilo is "uno medio (MAY-dee-oh) kilo." A "panaderia" sells bread, "pasteleria" offers pastry, and milk and cheese are bought at a "lecheria." Go to a "bodega" for wine, liquor and soft drinks. Try an "ultramarinos" for canned food, vegetables, sausage, cooking oil and wine. Toilet paper, tissue and shampoo are sold at a "perfumeria." "Churreria" sells churros, rings of deep fried batter which Spaniards eat for breakfast. The tiny shops open and close in early morning to reopen later in the afternoon to cook and sell potato chips. Ice cream sold in restaurants, cafes and grocery stores is safe, but ice cream bars sold by vending carts, most of which have questionable means of refrigeration, are not safe.

Restaurants are officially classified into five categories from deluxe with a five fork symbol to a simple restaurant denoted by one fork. Each restaurant is required to offer a tourist menu (menu turistico) which includes three courses, bread, wine (1/4 liter) and service at a set price. The three courses are normally appetizer or soup, entree and dessert. A minimum of three choices are offered within each course. Some choices may carry a supplemental charge. Many restaurants offer a fixed price meal which

changes daily according to the offerings of the local market. This menu
is posted outside along with the tourist menu. It is often a better buy, but
doesn't necessarily include service or beverage. The best time to eat in a
restaurant is for the "noon meal" which is eaten about 2:00 pm. Sometimes
choosing a higher grade restaurant and ordering a la carte costs no more
and gives better value than ordering the tourist menu in an inferior place.
Reliability of cooking is often greater in a higher class restaurant unless a
specific recommendation is being followed. The Michelin red guide for Spain
is very reliable for restaurant suggestions. If you wish to avoid fried foods,
order a dish marked "a la parilla" (grilled) or "asado" (roasted). The evening meal is typically taken at 10:30 pm by a Spaniard, though restaurants
open earlier for tourists.

POLLUTION   The beaches near large cities and resorts are fine for sunbathing but the water is polluted.

PRONUNCIATION OF PLACE NAMES   Avila (AH-vee-lah), Cuenca
(KWANG-ka), Salamanca (sal-a-MANG-ka), Valencia (va-LEN-thee-ah).

BARCELONA

Try not to schedule your arrival in Barcelona for late at night. Best strategy
is to come from Madrid to Barcelona via Zaragoza. Talgo leaves Madrid
(Chamartin Station) at 10:55 am, arrives in Zaragoza at 2:54 pm, in Sitges at
6:35 pm, and Barcelona at Sants, P. Gracia, and at 7:27 pm, Termino Sta.

TRAIN STATIONS   Most important is called both Barcelona Termino and
Estacion de Francia and is used by most Talgo, TER, ELT and long distance
fast trains, and by trains coming from southern France. Station facilities

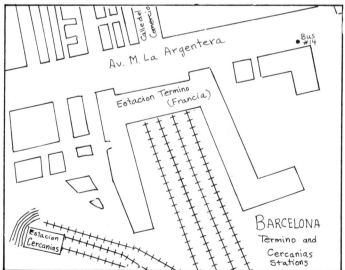

include tourist office, exchange office (open 7:30 am-11 pm), luggage check
and restaurant. Post Office is in adjacent building outside. Restrooms are
opposite the tracks. Seat reservations for same day departures can be made

in the station but you may have to find the central computer terminal to make reservations ahead of time. The "Oficina de Viajes de RENFE" is about a 15 minute walk from the station and is open M-F 8-1 & 4-7 and Sa 8-1. Reader board inside "acceso andenes" (entry to tracks) lists next departures from the station. Green light flashes next to departures currently loading. Below is an example of the reader board.

PROXIMAS SALIDAS (next departures)

Tren (train)	Destino (destination)	Hora (time of departure)	Via (track #)
Rapido Talgo	Madrid	10:00	7
Catalan Talgo	Ginebra	10:18	8
Electro Tren	Bilbao	12:35	not listed yet
Expreso	Malaga	12:48	" " "
Rapido Talgo	Madrid	13:50	2

Metro (subway) stop for Termino Station is Correos. Bus #14 in front of station (see map) travels Paseo Bonanova, Av. Marques de Argentera, Pl. Palacio, Correos, P. Colon, Atarazanas, Ramblas, Pl. Cataluna, Rda. y Pl. Universidad, Disputacion, Casanova, Santalo, Via Augusta, Gandaxer and Mandri.

Flanking the "Oficina Municipal de Turismo e Informacion" (tourist office window) in Termino Station are two large reader boards which list trains leaving from both the central (Termino) and Cercanias Stations. These two boards show Linea Villanueva and Linea de Mataro. Route is shown in red in diagram. Note time of next train going in the direction you want. Every train leaving from Cercanias Station stops at all towns on the map. Only "tranvia" and "semi-directo" trains leave from Cercanias Station. Trains leaving from Termino Station generally stop only at the largest towns but some departures stop at the small towns. LINEA de VILLANUEVA goes south of Barcelona and stops at Prat de Llobregat, Gava, Castelldefels, Playa de Castelldefels, Garraf, Vallcarca, Sitges, Villanueva, Geltru and farther up the coast. To get to Castelldefels, take a train in the direction of Taragona or Reus or one of the aforementioned stops. Trains leave about once an hour. LINEA de MATARO extends north of Barcelona up the coast towards France. Its trains stop at Pueblo N. , S. Adrian de B. , Badalona, Mongat, Montsolis, Masnou, Ocata, Premia, Vilasar, Mataro, Llavaneras, Caldetas, Arenys and so forth until it reaches Blanes. Then the train turns inland to Port-Bou and the Spanish border. Service is extremely frequent on this line, about every 15 minutes, with the last train departing at 23:00 (11 pm). DON'T take any train in the direction of Gerona VIA GRANOLLERS as that's the inland route.

To get to CERCANIAS STATION, use side door off the track area of Termino Station. From the tracks, pass the toilets and Cantina, turn left and follow signs to Cercanias Station (see map). Cercanias Station handles commuter trains and slow long distance ones. Reader boards in Termino Station are easier to read for Cercanias Station departures than those in Cercanias Station. But if you're already here, look for trains leaving under "Direccion Villanueva" for southern coastal towns and "Direccion Mataro" for departures for northern coastal towns towards France. These trains are free with railpass, or normal fare round trip (de ida y vuelta) between Barcelona and Monsolis for example is 30 ptas. In front of each track is a signpost listing:

VIA	01	(track # 1)
TREN		(type of train) TRANVIA
DESTINO		(final destination) Mataro
SALIDA		(departure time) 17:30 (5:30 pm)

Other Barcelona stations are Estacion del Norte (Vilanova), Cataluna Station and Paseo de Gracia Station. Termino, Norte and Cataluna are connected by metro. Metro is outside Estacion del Norte and inside Cataluna Station.

CAMPGROUNDS   Many camps are located south of Barcelona between the coast and the highway to Castelldefels. These are large, resort type deluxe camps with restaurant, supermarket, laundry, souvenir store and playground. The beaches are wide, sandy and unlittered. The camps are officially rated "deluxe" and charge the highest rates for Spanish campgrounds. These camps are especially recommended for families with a car or van. For details see Camping Ballena Alegre listing below. Smaller and cheaper campgrounds are situated north of Barcelona near the coast towards France. These are easily reached by train, free with railpass, and are recommended for backpackers because of the ease and convenience of using commuter trains. See listings for Camping Badalona-Playa and Camping Don Quijote.

CAMPING   "LA BALLENA ALEGRE" is 12.5 km south of Barcelona on highway to Castelldefels. From Termino Station, take bus #14 from right front of station (see map) to Calle de Aribau. Then walk two blocks to Diputacion-Enrique Granados on Calle (street) de Enrique Granados and take bus to Castelldefels. After about 40 minutes and beyond Barcelona, the bus takes the coastal highway and passes the first camp, El Toro Bravo, on the left. Don't get off here because this camp is a long walk from the highway to the coast whereas others are closer. Next camp, La Ballena Alegre, is immediately across the highway from the bus stop. (Bus stops are marked "parada.") The bus continues by several other camps before reaching Castelldefels. Alternatively, a train from Cercanias Station to Castelldefels can be taken, and then a bus to the camps. When coming from France by car, and progressing southwest through Barcelona, follow signs to airport and Castelldefels. Camps are on highway before Castelldefels. This camp is large with shady trees and a wide sandy beach. Currency exchange is open to 11 pm. Supermarket is open 8-1:30 & 4-8. Souvenir and camping store is open 9-1:30 & 4-8. Camp restaurant has mediocre food. Laundry is done for you and costs about 250 ptas a load which includes soap, washing and semi-drying in a spinner. Camp also has playground equipment, discotheque and chicken rotisserie, the latter two open only in July and August. Fees are about adult/160 ptas, child/110 ptas, car/160 ptas, tent/160 ptas. NOTE. The beautiful sunny weather of Barcelona is subject to sudden extremely heavy downpours. Be sure to pitch your tent on higher ground and permeable surface. We learned this the hard way as a water bed at least a foot deep formed beneath our unstaked tent within 15 minutes of the start of rainfall at 10 pm on an early June night. We hastily pulled our tent onto higher ground, and the next day we found the campground sunny and dry except for one area, and the lowest spot in that area on a clay surface was where we had unerringly pitched our tent.

CAMPING BADALONA-PLAYA, Apartado de Correos 77, is in Badalona, 7 km northeast of Barcelona. From Cercanias Station, take train to
"Estacion Badalona-Playa" (playa means beach), which is on P. Del
Caudillo. Walk one kilometer farther up (north) the coast on the seafront
to the campground. Camp can also be reached by bus "BS" departing from
Urquinaona-Plaza-Rda. San Pedro. Get off at bus stop when you see the
camping sign and follow the signs north for about one kilometer. The
bus runs day and night. Camping is in two straight lines of marked campsites with a reed roof above to filter the sun. Clean restrooms, sit-down
toilets without the seats, outdoor sinks for washing dishes, free hot
showers, beach in front, snack bar, and rental apartments (bath, kitchen,
bedroom for about 1,000 ptas a night--a bargain!). Adult/125 ptas, child/
85 ptas, tent/125 ptas, car/125 ptas.

CAMPING DON QUIJOTE, is northeast of Barcelona at Montsolis.
From Cercanias Station, take train to Montsolis. From Montsolis Station,
walk northeast farther up the coast paralleling the beach for one km. Camp
is on left side of road. Store, children's play area, some sun cover but not
as much as Camping Badalona. This is the cheapest camp in the area,
adult/ about 100 ptas, tent/free.

CAMPING - MASNOU is a more deluxe camp than the other two mentioned. It is 11 km from Barcelona in the town of Masnou which is the next
stop after Montsolis. Take the train from Cercanias Station to Masnou.
Trains leave every 20 minutes and Masnou Station is 200 meters from the
campground. (Also near the station is a beautiful modern yacht club and
marina.) A bus to Masnou which stops in front of the campground can also
be taken. Shade, hot showers, restaurant, store, swimming pool (100 ptas),
adult/170 ptas, child to 10/120 ptas, tent/160 ptas, car/160 ptas.

EVEN IF YOU ARRIVE IN BARCELONA LATE AT NIGHT, IT'S STILL
BETTER TO TAKE A TRAIN TO CAMPING MASNOU THAN TAKE A ROOM
IN BARCELONA BECAUSE EVERYTHING IS STILL GOING STRONG VERY
LATE.

Some readers have preferred to stay in the lovely resort town of Sitges
and commute to Barcelona. (See Sitges.)

FOOD   Public market (mercado de San Jose) is off Ramblas San Jose, next
to Iglesia (church) de Nuestra Senora de Belen.

PUBLIC TRANSPORTATION   Fares are inexpensive. Subway is 20 ptas.

SIGHTSEEING   MONTJUICH PARK is a stellar attraction with the Pueblo
Espanol (Spanish Village), Museum of Art of Catalonia and the new
Fundacion Joan Miro.   Spanish Village contains houses and workshops
reflecting different regional styles of architecture and decoration which are
grouped to form a small village. Opens at 9:00 am, admission charge. Also
worthwhile is the Museum of Art of Catalonia which shows the distinct style
of this area. The new museum honoring Joan Miro is open 11-8.

And if you like the Miro Foundation, you may wish to consider stopping
off at the town of Figueras on the Costa Brava towards France. Here is
where the Salvador Dali Museum is located. Designed by Dali, the museum
has a cupola painted inside by Dali who has foreshortened the characters

so they appear to be emerging towards you with very large feet.

PICASSO MUSEUM (Museo Pablo Picasso), Calle de Montcada 15, is open M-Sa 10-2 & 6-8, except it opens early at 4:30 pm in summer, Su 10-2. Adult/50 ptas., student and child/free. Free admission and guided tour for groups available by writing. Mansions and palaces mostly built in the 13th century line Calle de Montcada where beautiful medieval Aguilar Palace and Baron de Castellat Palace are now the Museo Pablo Picasso. Don't miss. The largest grouping in the world of Picasso's paintings, sculpture, etchings, lithographs and book illustrations is shown here. Picasso's friend and former secretary, Jaime Sabartes, donated his collection to the museum, and in 1968 and 1970, Picasso gave over 900 items as a memorial to Sabartes. "Las Meninas," a satire on Valazquez' famous painting in the Prado in Madrid, and consisting of 58 paintings done within five months, is here. So is Picasso's much reproduced "Harlequin." Restroom is near entrance. Sales counter sells good reproductions.

CATHEDRAL of the Sacred Family (Templo de la Sagrada Familia) by Gaudi, Calle Mallorca and Calle de Cerdena, is in no recognizable architectural style and somewhat strange, but monumental and worth seeing.

TRAIN SCHEDULES   To Montpellier, Cannes, Antibes and Nice, France, trains leave Barcelona Termino Station at 9:27 am (ar. Montpellier 2:13 pm, Cannes 6:39 pm, Antibes 6:50 pm, Nice 7:03 pm), 10:28 am (ar. Montpellier 4:39 pm, Cannes 9:36 pm, Antibes 9:57 pm, Nice 10:18 pm) and 7:00 pm (ar. Montpellier 2:56 am, Cannes 7:28 am, Antibes 7:49 am, Nice 8:05 am).

To Madrid, trains leave Barcelona Termino Station at 10:45 am (ar. Madrid Chamartin Station 7:23 pm), 2:15 pm Talgo (ar. Madrid Chamartin Station 8:10 pm), 3:05 pm Talgo (ar. Madrid Chamartin 11:31 pm), 10:00 pm (ar. Madrid Chamartin Station 8:19 am). (Complimentary meals are served on some Talgo and Ter trains in Spain.)

CORDOBA

Cordoba has both a wonderful old quarter and an attractive modern area. Tourist office (Oficina de Informacion de Turismo), Avenida del Gran Capitan and Avenida del Generalisimo is about four blocks from the station. With your back towards the station, turn left and walk one block, then turn right on Avenida del Gran Capitan and tourist office is in fourth block.

CAMPGROUNDS   CAMPAMENTO MUNICIPAL DE TURISMO, on Cordobe-Villaviciosa highway two km from central Cordoba is a first class site that is open all year. From train station, walk to tourist office (see above) but turn left on intersecting Avenida del Generalisimo and bus stop is in third block on right (south) side of street. Take bus #2 or 3. OR you can walk to the camp by turning left on Avenida de America upon leaving the station. Continue beside station for 2-1/2 blocks until you come to the street that crosses beyond railway tracks. Turn left and follow signs to camp. It's less than a two kilometer walk. Camp has hot showers, snack bar, store, swimming pool. Adult/85 ptas, child/65 ptas, small tent/60 ptas, large tent/85 ptas, car/85 ptas.

CAMPING CERCA DE LAGARTIJO, on Madrid-Cadiz highway, is four

324

kilometers from Cordoba. It's a first category camp with a capacity of 560
people but there is no bus transportation. Adult/110 ptas, child/60 ptas,
child/60 ptas, small tent/60 ptas, large tent/110 ptas, car/110 ptas.

FOOD   Market (mercado publico) is in Plaza de la Corredera, the public
square enclosed by walls, near Pedro Lopez (street).

SIGHTSEEING   Mosque (Mezquita-Catedral) is open Apr-Sept 10:30-1:30
& 4-8, Oct-Mar 10:30-1:30 & 3:30-6:00. Adult/50 ptas., child/25 ptas.
Tourist office pamphlet offers other sightseeing ideas, and a walk through
the old quarter is a must.

TRAIN SCHEDULES   Trains leave Cordoba for Seville (Plaza de Armas)
at 9:30 am (ar. 11:28 am), 1:55 pm (ar. 3:15 pm), 2:00 pm (ar. 3:54 pm),
5:00 pm (ar. 6:50 pm S. Bernardo), 6:06 pm ELT (ar. 7:26 pm), and 7:39 pm
Talgo (ar. 8:53 pm S. Bernardo).
    Trains leave Cordoba for Madrid Atocha Station at 9:15 am ELT (ar.
2:20 pm), 1:00 pm (ar. 8:51 pm), 5:09 pm talgo (ar. 10:15 pm), 5:44 pm
TER (ar 10:51 pm).

GRANADA

Linda Clark recommends "A trip to Granada is very enjoyable. The Alhambra is located there, which in my mind, is well worth the long train ride
from Madrid. We stayed at Camping "El Ultimo". It is just south of the city.
It is attractive with lots of trees and a swimming pool. It also has hot showers, lavatories, electricity, lighting, a restaurant and store. A bus stops
by the campground entrance every 15 minutes. We can't remember the camping fees, but being in Spain, I know they must have been nominal. To get to
the campground from the train station you take two buses. Walk one block
from the station down Av. Dr. Oloriz to Malaga Ave. Calvo Sotelo. Turn to
the left (not crossing the street) and walk several hundred feet to catch bus
#9. You ride this bus to the end of the line where you then catch bus #90
which stops in front of the campground. Or instead of taking bus #90, you
can walk down Al Camping for 15 minutes."
    "We would warn people, however, that we needed reservations on
trains both going to and leaving from Granada. The trains were very crowded
and even though we had first class Eurailpasses and made reservations the
day before, we had to get second class seats. Because we didn't make reservations early enough, we missed several trains leaving Granada and ended up
spending an extra day. We also were disappointed to discover we would have
had to go all the way back to Madrid in order to get to Lisbon."

TRAIN SCHEDULES   For Madrid Atocha Station, trains leave at 2:46 pm
talgo (ar. 9:47 pm), 6:30 pm 2nd class (ar. 7:09 am), 10:30 pm (ar. 8 am)--
all through trains. But, if you can't get a reservation, we would suggest
taking a train to Moreda, then changing if necessary for a train to Linares-
Baeza which puts you on the main Madrid-Cadiz run where trains including
the Talgo run more frequently.
    To Seville S. B. Station, trains leave at 12:35 pm (ar. 6:24 pm) and
5:51 pm TER (ar. 10:05 pm).
    To Algeciras, trains leave at 8:30 am (ar. 2:00 pm) and 12:35 pm
(ar. 8:02 pm).

MADRID

Home of the Prado Museum, Madrid also serves as an excursion base for
Toledo and El Escorial.

TRAIN STATIONS   Madrid has three. CHAMARTIN, the newest, handles
most international traffic. Its tourist information office has English language
brochures for all Spanish cities and towns. Also available are baggage check,
lockers, seat reservations (windows 1-8), exchange and post office. Bus #14
begins at Chamartin Station and follows the route D. Pastrana, Plaza de la
Habana, Plaza de la Castellana, Cibeles, Carlos V, Plaza M. Cristina and
Av. del Mediterraneo. Take this bus for going downtown. Alternatively, bus
#16 follows the route Chamartin, Av. Mnez. Campos and suburban Moncloa.

Chamartin Station is connected with Atocha Station
by shuttle train (apeadero) which is part of RENFE
and included in railpasses. Trains leave at 15
minute intervals and make two stops enroute, first
at Recoletos (Paseo Calvo Sotelo) and then at
Nuevos Ministerios (Avenida del Generalisimo).

Large ATOCHA station is in an area of hotels,
restaurants and pensions but away from the main
shopping area. Trains leaving from Atocha serve
Granada, Valencia, Seville, Cordoba, the Levant,
Extramadura, Toledo, Alcala de Henares, Guadala-
jara and Portugal. Inside is an exchange office and reservations office. Beside Atocha Station is small Atocha-Apeadero (Apd.) Station which is directly connected with the subway.   Estacion Norte is closed.

Seat reservations can be made at the station or RENFE office at
Alcala 44 downtown, open 9-1 and 4-6

TOURIST INFORMATION   Offices are at Chamartin Station, Torre de
Madrid, Plaza de Espana and Alcala 44 (open 9-7).

CAMPGROUNDS   Camping Osuna, 15 km from downtown, is on the highway
Ajalvir-Vicalvaro in the general vicinity of Barajas Airport. Open all year.
Take the subway to Ciudad Lineal Station, outside the station board bus #105,
then it is a short walk from where bus lets you off. Adult/120 ptas, child/80,
tent/120 ptas, car/120.   Hot showers, store, restaurant and swimming pool.
Madrid Camping, Cerro del Aguila, is closer at 7 km and the easiest to reach
from Chamartin Station. From Chamartin Station, walk to Plaza de Castilla
(5 minute walk), and there catch bus #129 marked MORALEJA, which
stops at Dominicos Church which is 900 meters from the campground. Hot
showers, store, snacks, adult/110 ptas, tent/110 ptas, car/110 ptas.

CITY TRANSPORTATION   Tourist office map of city includes subway map.
Bus route map (Plano de Lineas Itinerarios) is separate and distributed by
Banco Espanol de Credito. Besides regular buses, there are faster yellow
mini-buses which are privately owned, cost slightly more and don't allow
standing. Subway is called "metropolitano" and has five lines plus a suburban
line. Puerta del Sol (Sol) and Opera are main interchange (correspondencia)
stations. The inexpensive flat weekday fare includes all changes from one
line to another that you wish. Weekend fare is slightly more.

FOOD   In 1981, one liter milk cost about 60 ptas, 350 grams bread about

326

about 25 ptas, and one whole hot cooked chicken about 380 ptas. Market (mercado) is on Cava Baja, near interesting Plaza Mayor. Any entree with the word "pechuga" signifies chicken breast prepared in some manner and is reliably good.

SIGHTSEEING   MUSEO DEL PRADO is alone worth the trip to Madrid for its vast collection of the works of the incomparable Goya which show the real and fallible kings and queens of his time and comment on humanity in his cartoon etchings which include "The Disasters of War 1810-14." Also on display are the best works of El Greco, Velazquez, Zurbaran, Ribera, Murillo, Fra Angelico, Rafael, Bosco, Rubens, Titian, Breughel, Bosch, and van Dyke. Open M-Sa 10-6, Su 10-2.

   PLAZA MAYOR, a nicely proportioned square inaugurated in 1620, marks the heart of a good walking area in picturesque "old Madrid." Nearby are inexpensive food shops and the public market at Cava Baja. City Information office (Oficina Municipal de Informacion) is at Plaza Mayor 3, open M-F 10-1 & 4-7, Sa 10-1.

   ARCHEOLOGICAL MUSEUM, Serrano 13 (subway Moncloa), open daily 9-1:30, shows exact reproductions of prehistoric wall paintings from the Cave of Altamira near Santillana del Mar. Cave reopens later from 4-8 pm, entrance to left of main gate.

   TOLEDO, 92 km from Madrid and subject of El Greco's famous painting, can be seen on a day excursion from Madrid. (However, there is a good campground--see Toledo.)   Alcazar, Cathedral, El Greco's House and Museum, Transito Synagogue and Church of Santo Tome in which hangs El Greco's "Burial of the Count of Orgaz," are priority sights. Most of these open at 10 am and close for lunch from 2-3:30 pm. Trains classified "tranvia" and which have second class cars only, leave from Atocha Station at 7:40 am, 8:05 am, 10:00 am, 12:15 pm, 2:05 pm, 2:20 pm, 3:30 pm (change at Castillejo), 7:50 pm, 7:55 pm, 9:05 pm. Trip is about 1-1/2 hours. From the Toledo station, a bus goes to the "old town." Trains leave Toledo for Madrid (Atocha Station) at 7:46 am, 8:20 am, 9:14 am, 11:45 am, 12:52 pm, 2:45 pm, 3:59 pm, 5:32 pm (change at Castillejo), 8:08 pm, 8:36 pm, 10:06 pm.

   EL ESCORIAL, 52 km from Madrid, is the monastery built in the 16th century by Philip II. Open 10-1 & 3-6. El Escorial is on the train route to Avila. Trains leave Atocha-Apeadero Station at 8:30 am, 1:30 pm, and 6:30 pm, and pick up at Chamartin Station three minutes later. Trip is about one hour. Trains leave El Escorial at 4:28 pm, 8:49 pm and 10:22 pm.

   VALLE DE LOS CAIDOS (Valley of the Fallen), 13 km from El Escorial, commemorates those who died in the Spanish Civil War. The spectacular monument done in a stark modern style consists of a large cross on top of a mountain and a cavernous Cathedral carved out of the side of the mountain below. A bus from El Escorial leaves about 3:00 pm to the Valley and returns at about 5:30 pm.

SHOPPING   Department stores are El Corte Ingles at Preciados 3, Sepu at Avenida Jose Antonio 32, and Galerias Preciados at Preciados 28-30. El Rastro, flea market, operates Su 9-2 at Plaza de Cascorro (metro Tirso de Molino, line 1).

TRAIN SCHEDULES   To BARCELONA, trains leave Madrid Chamartin Station at 8:10 am (ar. 6:52 Barcelona Sants Station only), 10:55 am Talgo (ar. Barcelona Termino 7:27 pm), 2:25 pm Talgo (ar. Termino 10:19 pm), 8:05 pm (ar. Sants only 8:00 am), 9:25 pm (ar. Sants 7:48 am, Paseo de Gracia 7:55 am). Trains arriving at Termino Station stop first at Sants and Paseo de Gracia Stations.

For LISBON (Lisboa), the Lisboa Express-TER leaves Chamartin Station at 9:50 am, Atocha Station at 10:03 am and arrives in Lisbon S. Apolonia Station at 7:05 pm. The Lusitania Express leaves Madrid Atocha Station at 10:50 pm and arrives in Lisbon S. Apolonia Station at 9:35 am.

For PARIS Austerlitz Station, trains leave Chamartin Station at 7:55 am TER (ar. 11:36 pm), 3:15 pm Talgo (ar. 7:15 am), 6:08 pm (ar. 10:33 am).

For GRANADA, trains leave Atocha Station at 3:00 pm Talgo (ar. 10:40 pm), 10:15 pm (ar. 7:55 am), and 11:40 pm second class only (ar. 11:53 am). An alternative route would be to take a train going to Malaga but get off at Bobadilla and change trains to Granada. For example, leave Atocha Station at 9:45 am (ar. Bobadilla 7:09 pm, change trains, lv. Bobadilla 7:55 pm, ar. Granada 9:55 pm).

For CORDOBA and SEVILLE, trains leave Atocha Station at 8:45 am ELT (ar. Cordoba 1:50 pm, ar. Seville P. de Armas 3:15 pm), 9:45 am (ar. Cordoba 4:40 pm, Seville S. Bernardo 6:50 pm), 2:30 pm Talgo (ar. Cordoba 7:34 pm, Seville S. Bernardo 9:02 pm), 9:20 pm (ar. Cordoba 4:19 am, Seville S. Bernardo 6:55 am).

SANTANDER

CAMPING BELLAVISTA is 4 km from downtown Santander and the ferry terminal, on the road to El Sardinero resort. Open all year. Hot showers, washing machines, currency exchange, beach, adult/130 ptas, small tent/100 ptas, large tent/150 ptas.

SEVILLE   (SEVILLA)

Capital of Andalucia, Seville can be the hottest spot in all Spain with the average high reaching 93 degrees in summer. Seville's two train stations are San Bernardo and Plaza de Armas. RENFE office, 29 Zaragoza Street, takes reservations. Tourist information, Avenida Queipo de Llano 9 near the Cathedral, is about 14 blocks from San Bernardo Station, open M-F 9-2 & 4:30-7. Another office is at the Alcazar, Puerta del Leon.

CAMPGROUNDS near Seville can be reached by bus from bus station in Prado de San Sebastian. From San Bernardo Station, walk across plaza in front and head towards your left. Bus station is 3 blocks aways. Camping SEVILLA is 5 km from Seville on the highway to Cordoba and Madrid. Take bus to Carmona and ask driver to let you off at camp, then a 3 minute walk. Open all year, hot showers, swimming pool, snack bar, store, no washing machine, adult/120 ptas, small tent/100 ptas, large tent/120 ptas. Camping CLUB DE CAMPO is 12 km from Seville on the highway to Dos Hermanas which is the main Madrid-Cadiz highway. Take bus to Dos Hermanas and get off at camp. Open June-Oct, store, adult/130 ptas, small tent/120 ptas, large tent/130 ptas.

SIGHTSEEING--the top priority is the Cathedral, largest in Spain, and its accompanying tower, Giralda. Open all year 10:30-1, summer also

⅃ winter also 3:30-5:30. The Alcazar, a moorish (or more
⌐ mudejar) palace is open all year 9-12:45, summer also 4-6:30
and winter also 3-5:30₀ Santa Cruz is the picturesque old quarter.
TRAIN SCHEDULES   From Plaza de Armas Station, trains leave for
MADRID Atocha Station at 8:00 am ELT (ar₀2:20 pm), 11:00 pm (ar.8:05 am).
From S₀ Bernardo Station, trains leave for MADRID Atocha Station at
10:52 am (ar₀ 8:57 pm), 3:52 pm Talgo (ar. 10:15 pm), midnight (ar.9:14 am).
These same trains stop in Cordoba about 1-1/2 hours after leaving Seville₀

To PORTUGAL, trains leaves Plaza de Armas Station for the Spanish
border town Ayamonte at 7:35 am (ar. 11:17 am), and 11:20 am (ar₀ Huelva
12:55 pm, change trains, ar. Ayamonte 3:16 pm)₀ Between Ayamonte and
Vila Real in Portugal, ferry service operates on the half hour between
9:00 am and 6:00 pm--a 15 minute trip. From Vila Real, trains leave at
1:40 pm for Faro and Tunes on the Algarve, and at 3:55 pm for Lisbon
(ar. T. de Paco 10:20 pm). Plus there are later local trains.

SITGES

A resort town, Sitges is 41 km from Barcelona and on the main rail line
with fast (30-45 minutes) and frequent train service to all three train
stations in Barcelona₀ The most frequent departures to Sitges originate
at Sants Station in Barcelona, however. Kathy Carlson picked this camp as
her favorite because it is "a good cheap Mediterranean resort town with
good beaches." Tourist office is at Isla de Cuba 7, a street jutting perpendicularly from the train station. Two campgrounds within about 200 meters
of the station are Camping El Roca, Carretera S. Pedro Ribas; and Los
Almendros, Avenida Capellans. Jack Visscher says "this camp can be
found by getting off at the Sitges Station, walking over the tracks in the
walkover, and walking five minutes up the street. In fact there are two
campgrounds in this spot."
You come here for the sun, but there is one small museum, Cap-
Ferrat, with paintings and wrought iron work, which is located next to
"Raco de la Calma" above the ramparts. A coastline trip to Garraf, 9 km
away, is made by "Catalina" cruising boat.

TOLEDO

Camping Circo Romano is the nearest one to Toledo and the train station. Buses stop at the train station and go to main entrance of the town
which is where the tourist office is located. Bus fare is 17 ptas. From the
tourist office, it is a short walk of about 300 meters to the campground.
Signs indicate the route₀ Swimming pool, tennis courts, store, snack bar,
adult/125 ptas, small tent/90 ptas, large tent/125 ptas₀

SWEDEN

Sweden's Nobel Peace Prizes, smorgasbord and trolls, and its contribution to drama, science and film-making are well known. It practices a combination of social welfare programs and private capital with heavy emphasis on redistribution of wealth through taxation. Sweden's birth rate is so low the native population is no longer producing enough babies to replenish itself. Swedish citizens enjoy the highest standard of living in Europe and each receives a paid month's vacation by law!

CURRENCY   Swedish krona. Each krona is divided into 100 ore. There are about 5.5 kronor to the U.S. dollar. One krona is worth about 18¢.

WEATHER   June through the first half of September is the warmest period. Rain sometimes comes even in summer, just as in the Pacific Northwest. Days are long in Sweden where it may be light from 4 am until 10 pm and then only be semi-dark through the night. July is the most popular vacation month.

CAMPING   A few require a camping carnet or Swedish Camping Card. The latter can be bought at any campground requiring it for 7 kr. Most camps are open June through August except city camps remain open longer. Camping is permitted anywhere in the country, even on private land, as long as it's not too close to buildings or fenced land. The Swedish Camping Card is sometimes accepted in Portugal when a card is needed.

TRAINS   As in all of Scandinavia, second class is not much different from first class. If you haven't a train pass, going by bus is cheaper. On train fares, the longer the journey the cheaper each kilometer becomes.

Children between 6 and 12 travel at half price. Those under 6 ride free.
Same reductions on long distance buses. Family tickets are sold in Sweden
only, where the first adult pays full fare, second adult pays half fare, and
children 6-25 pay quarter fare. Persons 65 or older receive a 50% discount
on all rail tickets except during Easter, Christmas, and on weekends during
June, July and August.

Seat reservation costs about 5 kr. If train departure time is marked
with an "R," this is an "expresstag" and the conductor will collect double
the reservation fee on board if you don't have the required reservation!

Tourist office in U₀ S. will send "Scandinavian Railways Timetables and
Fares." "Snabbtag" are Swedish train schedules for individual runs that are
available free in Sweden. You can travel from Stockholm to Kiruna in
Swedish Lapland, and onward to Narvik in Norway by train. Swedish State
Railways are abbreviated "SJ."

ankomst	-	arrival	platsbiljetter	-	reservations
avgang	-	departure	spar	-	track
biljettluckan-ticket office			till sparen	-	to the platforms
jarnvagsstationen	-		utgang	-	exit
		train station	vaxelkontoret	-	money change
ingang	-	entrance			

Included in Eurailpass and Eurail Youthpass are ferry crossings
operated by Swedish and Danish State Railways between Helsingborg, and
Helsingor, Denmark; and ferry crossings operated by Stena Sessan Linjen
between Goteborg, and Frederikshavn, Denmark₀ A 50% discount is given
on normal fares for ferries operated by TT Saga Line between Malmo, and
Lubeck-Travemunde Hafen in West Germany.

Also included are Silja Line ferries between Stockholm and Helsinki,
Stockholm and Turku, and Stockholm and Mariehamn (Aland Islands). These
are large car-ferry boats on which the passes entitle you to deck class.
Cabin space, if wanted, is charged extra. (It's not necessary.) Silja Line
office in Stockholm is at Kungsgatan 2 for making reservations. To Helsinki,
a ferry departs Stockholm (Vartan) at 6 pm and arrives in Helsinki (South
Harbor) at 9 am. For Turku, ferries depart Stockholm (Vartan) at 8:30 am
(about May 16-Aug 31) and arrive 8:15 pm; at 7:30 pm (about June 1 - July
16) and arrive 8 am; and at 9:30 pm, arrive 8:45 am . The 8:30 am departure
stops enroute at 2:45 pm at Mariehamn, Aland Islands₀ Connecting trains
leave from Turku Harbor Station for Helsinki at 8:25 am (ar₀ 11:35 am), and
8:30 pm (ar. 11:32 pm).

DRIVING   According to law, seatbelts must be worn by driver and front
seat passenger. Don't drive after ANY drinking as Swedish law is very strict
on this₀ Main Swedish roads are two lane highways in excellent condition₀
Stretches of freeway appear near large cities. Some gas stations operate as
automats and take 10 kr notes. Stockholm to Goteborg is 300 miles, to
Malmo, 386 miles.

TOURIST INFORMATION   All "Turistbyra" will obtain a room costing 45 kr
in a private home. Swedish youth hostels (vandrarhem) often have family
rooms and the tourist office will call for you. No hostel card is required₀

FOOD   In 1981, 1 liter milk cost 2.70 kr, 500 gram loaf of bread cost 5 kr,
and 1 whole hot cooked chicken "to go" cost 20 kr. Food is high whether

buying raw ingredients or the prepared dish. Milk (excellent) and fish are reasonable. Meat, leafy vegetables and fruit are expensive. Carrots, beets, potatoes and other underground vegetables are reasonable. Soft drinks cost more than milk. Whole milk is "mjolk," skim milk is "skummjolk." Fruit juices usually have "saft" as the suffix, but any canned or bottled fruit juice or soft drink is expensive. "Frukost" is breakfast, usually an all-you-can-eat buffet --a good value often served in train stations, some hotels, and on ferries which cross a national border. "Middag" is dinner, the last meal. Smorgasbord is served in a few restaurants, usually at lunchtime.

HIKING   "Hiking in the Swedish Highlands" is stocked by the tourist office in the U. S. Hiking in Sweden differs from the Alps in the greater distances between huts, towns and villages--recommended for persons in good physical condition with previous hiking experience. Assistance is available from Swedish Touring Club; Stureplan 2, Fack; S-10380, Stockholm 7, Sweden.

MAIL   Ordinary rate mail not exceeding five grams goes by air without extra charge when marked "under 5 grams."

BODEN

Being both a rail junction and military town, it's not surprising that Boden offers an impressive military museum.

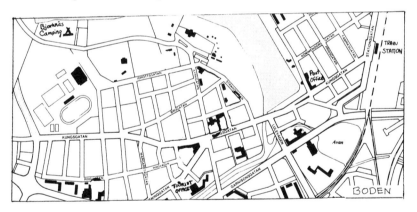

Tourist office is 10 blocks from train station. Bjorknas Camping is 17 blocks (800 meters) from station. (See map.) Hot showers, washing machine, flat fee for tentsite/20 kr.

GALLIVARE

This is a main town on the rail line to Narvik, Norway. Tourist office is 200 meters from train station, and open in summer M-Sa 8 am-8 pm, Su 12-3 & 4-8.   The municipal campground, Kvarnforsens, is open about June 15 to August 20, and is about a 10 minute walk from the station (see map). Hot showers, sauna and cooking facilities. No store at camp but the closest one, Nar-Oppet (open daily 9-8), is marked on the map. For sightseeing, try a

332

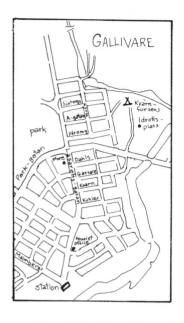

museum or the Lappish Church (Lapp-kyrkan), open M-Su 9-8.

GOTEBORG (GOTHENBURG)

It's a shame that some travelers drive or rail right through Goteborg without so much as a stop. The best maritime museum we saw in Europe is here and it's so good that even a person who didn't think he was interested in that sort of thing would be glad he came. The closest camp is excellent, but it was the only one on our entire trip that was full when we got there. Try to arrive before 3 pm if you're driving, especially on a weekend when lots of Swedish families arrive to take the children to Sweden's best amusement park, Liseberg.

TRAIN STATION   Centrally located downtown with a branch of the tourist office about 200 meters away (open daily 8-8). Stena-Sessan Line ships, free with railpass, leave Goteborg at 8 am, 12:30 pm, 4:15 pm and 10 pm, bound for Frederikshavn, Denmark. "The crossing is as follows when arriving by train. Go out the exit doors which are located near the information office. Cross the street and you will see the tram station. Take tram #3 to Stena-Sessan Line stop. If requested, the driver will announce the stop. Tram was free with Eurailpass. We felt this was too much of a walk (more than 10 minutes) and recommend the tram." Mr. and Mrs. Robert Cooper.

CAMPGROUNDS

Karralund Camping, open all year, is 4 km from downtown and has 310 tent sites. From train station, cross plaza and take tram #3 (direction Kalltorp) going towards your left when you have your back to the station. Driver sells tickets for 5 kr for the 20 minute ride. After getting off tram #3, walk about 300 meters in the direction the tram was

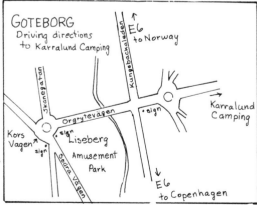

going. Then turn left off the main street at the small grocery store, continuing up this road, beyond the miniature golf, to the camp (a five minute walk). From downtown Goteborg, take tram #5 (direction Torp) which lets you off across from the grocery store and side road to camp. By car, E 6 goes through Goteborg and becomes a normal main street for the urban por-

tion. Don't leave E 6 until you see the camping sign (see map). The camp
is attractive with marked-off sites, hot showers, cooking facilities,
hot water for dishwashing, small store, snack bar, English spoken, free
maps and sightseeing information, marked trails in nearby woods. A flat
fee of 30 kr is made per tent. Other camps are further out--inquire at
tourist office. Because of the high cost of the campground and high cost of
the tram fare, it might be advisable to try to see the Maritime Museum on
a 3 hour layover between trains by taking tram 3 from the station, rather
than stay overnight here.

CITY TRANSPORTATION   A 24 hour ticket costs 10 kr and is sold by tram
drivers. Otherwise, a book of 19 coupons is sold for 25 kr. Two coupons
are needed for one ride but the same coupons (or individual ticket) can be
used on the return trip if taken between 9 am and 3 pm. Single ticket is 5 kr.
Railpasses are valid on tram #3 when changing from train to ship.

FOOD   Within the Nordstand shopping mall, two blocks from the station,
is Ahlens Department Store with supermarket, including a large delicatessen
section, in its basement. Restrooms are on top floor just outside elevators.
Good value is the all-you-can-eat breakfast served M-Sa 6:30-10:30 and Su
7-10:30 am in the train station restaurant for 20 kr. Open market is downtown at Kungstorget, M-F 8-6, Sa 8-1.

SIGHTSEEING   We thought the Maritime Museum (Sjofartsmuseet) to be
the best attraction in Goteborg. Three floors are loaded with all kinds of
ship models going way back to the Vikings. Excellent instructive dioramas
such as fishing boats set within a mock ocean to depict various kinds of gear
and techniques used in deep-sea fishing are provided. Located at Stigbergs-
storget. Open May-Aug daily 11-4, Sept-April M-F 12-3, Sa-Su 10-5. Adult/
5 kr, child over 5/2 kr. On ground floor is aquarium with separate identical
admission.
    Gotaplatsen is the cultural center of Goteborg marked by Carl Milles'
statue of Poseidon. Art Gallery (Konstmuseet) has a good selection of
modern Swedish artists, the most comprehensive group of French contemporary art in Sweden, and a few old masters. Open May-Aug daily 11-4,
Sept-April M-F 12-3, Sa-Su 10-5, adult/2 kr, child/1 kr.   Museum of
Industry (Industrimuseet), Art Exhibition Hall (Konsthallen), Concert Hall
and City Theater complete the square. Several blocks away but with walking
distance is the Rohsska Museet displaying Swedish design in furniture from
all periods, and on the third floor some Chinese art. Same hours as for
Konstmuseet, but free. Child's table, two chairs and box of toys are in the
"cafeteria" which is actually a plush lounge with automat.
    Liseberg Amusement Park, Orgrytevagen, is very popular with
Swedish out-of-towners. Free entrance during early part of day--most of
the rides and restaurants are closed then but a worthwhile half-hour can be
spent looking around the attractively landscaped grounds. There is a free
play equipment area for children. Otherwise admission is about adult/8 kr,
child/4 kr, child's ticket book of 8 rides/20 kr, single ride/3-4 kr. Adults
ride free on the merry-go-round when accompanied by a paying child.

PARKING   The multi-story parking garage attached to the Nordstand shopping mall waives the parking fee for an hour with a merchant's stamp. For
instance, the Ahlens Department Store central Cashier on each floor (there's

one just beyond the checkstands in the basement supermarket) will stamp
it upon showing receipts of 50 kr worth of goods.

SUBURBAN GOTEBORG   For those with a car, Kungalv has a campground
that usually has room when Goteborg's are full and the shopping center Obs!
at Backebol makes a good meal stop. Kungalve is 20 km north of Goteborg
near main highway E 6, Oslo- Goteborg. (Watch for Kungalv exit signs,)
Bohus Fortress (14th century) dominates the skyline. Open May-Sept 15 from
noon to 8 pm, adult/3 kr, child under 6/free. Kungalvs Camping, immediately across the old highway from the fortress, is a small grassy camp next to
the river with only restrooms (cold water) and play equipment. Open June 23
to Sept 8 and charges a flat fee of about 15 kr per tent.

    Backebol, between Kungalv and Goteborg, is reached by Backebol exit
from E 6. Obs! shopping center, visible from the road, closes at 8 pm. The
Swedish modern decorated cafeteria at the front of the store serves middag
(lunch) for about 17 kr. The menu is in the wall at the entry to the cafeteria
line and you push a button next to your selection as you enter the line. If you
choose the middag you are entitled to (1) 1 roll, 1 slice of bread, or 2
crackers, (2) butter, (3) milk or coffee, (4) middag entree-- ours was two
fried mackerel, two boiled potatoes and a side dish of herbed butter sauce,
and (5) salad which you serve yourself from the large bowl. The children's
menu (kottbuller) consisted of four small meat balls and mashed potatoes for
about 7 kr. The receipt is turned back in at the cash register for an ice
cream bar which comes with the children's menu. Other menu items
included two grilled weiners with fries and salad for about 15 kr but the
weiners were very spicy. Across from the check-out counters is a free
supervised playroom for children, ages 2-6, for a maximum of two hours.
Next to it is a do-it-yourself gift wrap counter with free paper, ribbon and
twine. The supermarket has hot grilled chickens for about 20 kr each.

TRAIN SCHEDULES   Trains leave for Oslo at 8:20 am, noon, and 5:13 pm for
the approximately 5 hour trip. Trains leave for Stockholm at 15 minutes past
each hour from 7:15 am to 7:15 pm, and these require a mandatory reservation for 5 kr. The conductor collects 10 kr on board from those who failed to
make a reservation. Trip is about 4-1/2 hours. Trains leave for Copenhagen at 8 am, 10 am, 12:40 pm, 2 pm and 6 pm.

KALMAR

Kalmar is the County seat in southeastern Sweden on the eastern coast, and
about a six hour train ride from Stockholm. In the early Middle Ages, it
was Scandinavia's capital city. The beautiful castle of Kalmar is the most
well known Renaissance castle of Sweden. Kalmar Turistbyra (tourist office)
is in the rear of the train station. Stenso Camping, 3 km from downtown,
can be reached by bus from the train station. Bus fare is about 2.50 kr.
Olands Bridge (6,070 m), longest bridge in Europe, stretches from Kalmar
to the very different island of Oland with its limestone bedrock, wildflowers
and birds, prehistoric ruins including stone passage graves, a medieval
church and 400 windmills. This is Sweden's sun-belt where Solliden, the
Royal Summer Home, was built outside the town of Borgholm. Many campgrounds. Take bus in Kalmar. Kalmar is the gateway city to the glass factories of Orrefors, Kosta and Boda which offer guided tours of their plants

and the opportunity to buy "seconds." Kalmar tourist office offers a guided
tour of the factories, or you can go by train from Kalmar for the hour ride
to the town of Orrefors which grew around the factory. Prices on goods are
about half of what they are in the stores, and the value added tax of about 23%
is deducted from anything mailed out of the country, which covers the postage
to the U.S. at least. If anything breaks, a replacement will be sent. This
replacement guarantee against breakage is offered throughout Scandinavia,
and we found it to be reliable as a broken glass ice cream dish--1 of a set of
6--was replaced without question and without having to return the broken dish.

KIRUNA

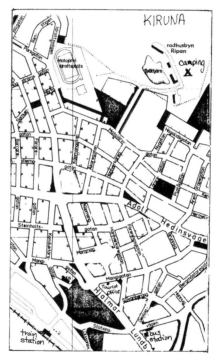

Situated 140 km north of the Arctic Circle, from May 28 to July 18, the sun
never goes down below the horizon in Kiruna. Night turning into day attracts
people to the best viewpoints--the top of Loussavaara or Kiirunavaara to
glimpse the northern lights and Aurora Borealis. But having come this far,
be sure to take the journey to Narvik, Norway, which can be done in one day
round trip from Kiruna if desired. The area between Kiruna and Narvik is
only accessible by train so motorists leave their cars in Kiruna and change
to the train. The railway travels through magnificent mountain scenery and
parallels Lake Torne-Trask for 44 miles. Once across the border into
Norway, the mountainsides drop steeply down into clear blue fjords until
finally reaching Narvik on the Atlantic Coast.

Swedish, Finnish and Lapp are all spoken in Kiruna, Lapps having given up their nomadic way of life many years ago. The Lapps still keep up many of their customs, and some still follow the annual trek of the reindeer herds up to the mountains in spring and summer for calving, and then back down to their grazing areas in the forest in late fall and winter. TRAIN STATION is at the edge of downtown. TOURIST OFFICE, Mangigatan 12, is near the other side of the park which is in front of the station. KIRUNA CAMPING is 1 km from the station, and is part of Radhusbyn Ripan, a "village" of 90 cottages that are rented to tourists. It is helpful to know that in the central building in the "village" is a laundry, small store, sauna, and snacks. Campground is open Mar-Aug 31. See map.

Kiruna grew up as a mining center and tours of the mine are offered daily in summer by the Kiruna Travel bureau. There is also an outdoor folk museum (Hembygdsgarden I Jukkasjarvi), open June 1-August 28 (11 am-8 pm), as well as some interesting artwork in the churches.

Trains leave for Narvik at 6:50 am, 10:50 am, 2 pm (F, Sa, some Su), and 7:15 pm. Trains leave Narvik for Kiruna at 6 am, 11 am (June 6-Sept 13, Sa and Su), 3 pm and 3:30 pm.

LUND

An old and beautiful town with a cathedral and outdoor museum of note, Lund is conveniently located 17 km from Malmo and makes a good day excursion from Copenhagen. Lund Touristtrafikforening (information office) is at S. Petri Kyrkogata 4, three blocks from the train station. No campgrounds, but three are 10 km away in Lomma on the coast. Take bus to Lomma from Lund bus station--fare is 7 kr, trip is one hour, and buses leave once an hour. Campsite costs 20 kr per tent (flat fee). Market is at Martens-torget, open M-F 7-1:30 and Sa 7-1.

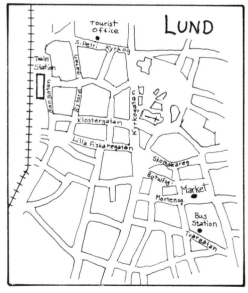

MALMO

Sibbarp Camping is situated 7 km south of Malmo. Take bus #41 from Central Station direct to the campground. Open 4/24-9/14. Hot showers, store, snacks, washing machine and dryer/ 6 kr together, tentsite/25 kr.

STOCKHOLM

An air of well-being pervades Sweden's capital. The city is built on thirteen islands within an archipelago of 24,000 making it hardly surprising that all four of Stockholm's campgrounds are near water.

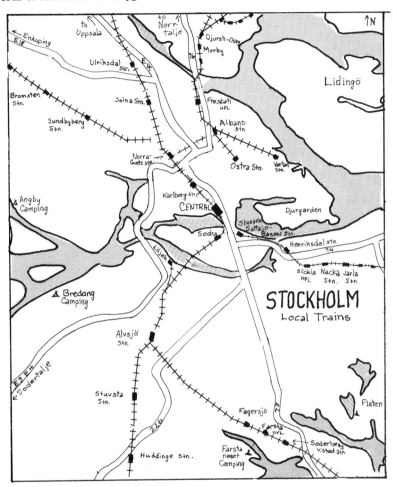

TRAIN STATION   Central Stationen, on Vasagaten downtown, forms part of an underground plaza of stores and services such as tourist office, money exchange, luggage lockers, grocery store, shops and T-Centralen subway station. Tourist Office (Hotellcentralen) is open June–Aug M-Sa 8-11:30 am and 12:30-11:30 pm, Su 2-11:30 pm, shorter hours rest of year. Train reservations are made in ticket office, "fardbiljetter platsbiljetter." Many commuter trains, free with railpasses, leave from Central Station and information is given on airport-type closed-circuit television screens in the station.

TOURIST INFORMATION   Stockholms Turisttrafikforbund, in Sweden House

338

(Sverigehuset) at Hamngatan 27, is 9 blocks from station. Open June 16-
Aug 9 8-7, shorter hours rest of year. Ask for map, "Stockholm Tourist
Information," subway map, and consider buying a 3-day tourist card.

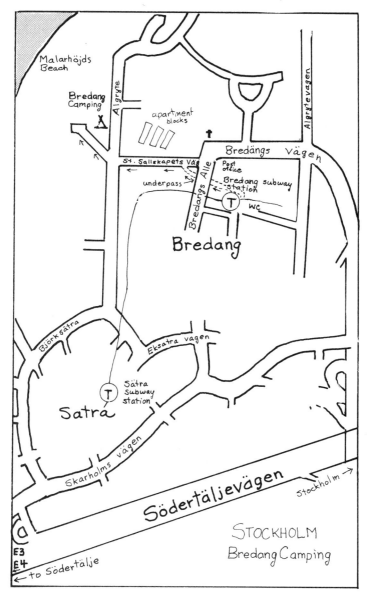

CAMPGROUNDS Bredang Camping is 10 km southwest of downtown Stockholm, and open Apr-Oct 15 (6 am-11 pm for new arrivals). From Central
Station, follow signs to T-Centralen tunnelbana (subway) station designated

by a large T. One way fare is 12 kr if a ticket is bought individually, which of course you shouldn't do. (See city transportation.) Board train #13 (direction Norsberg) or #15 (direction Satra). Frequent departures. Get off at Bredang Station, the 11th stop and a 20 minute ride. Walking out of Bredang Station you will see a Bredang (formerly called Satra) camping sign to the left. Turn left, follow pedestrian underpass, and once across, another camping sign directs you on the other side. Follow street Stora Sallskapets Vag straight to camp (see map). This street parallels subway tracks for most of the way--a ten minute walk. By car, the camp is easily reached from E3/E4 going north, and signed from Satra and Bredang exits. Camp has hot showers, sauna, burners for cooking, dishwashing room, store, snack bar, washing machine (5 kr, open 9-5), and dryer. Malarhojden Beach is nearby. Cost is flat fee: tent/35 kr, car extra/7 kr, van/35 kr. Camping card is needed, but any will do--even temporary Danish camping card, or they will sell you a Swedish Card for 7 kr.

ANGBY CAMPING is on Lake Malar, 12 km west of downtown Stockholm. Open June 15-Aug 31. From train station, follow signs to T-Centralen (subway) station. Board train #17 (direction Vallingby) or #18 (direction Hasselby Strand) and get off at Angbyplan Station, the 13th stop. Then it's about a 15 minute walk to camp. By car, this is the most convenient camp if entering city on E 18 from Enkoping. Exit onto Spanga-Krkvag. Hot showers, tent/26 kr, car/7 kr, van/30 kr.

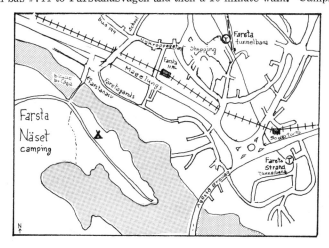

FARSTANASET CAMPING is on Lake Magelungen, 27 km south of downtown Stockholm. Open May 30-Sept. From Central Station, follow signs to T-Centralen (subway) station. Board train #18 (direction Farsta Strand) and get off at Farsta Station, the stop before Farsta Strand Station. From outside station, take bus #744 to Farstanasvagen and then a 10 minute walk. Alternatively, take trains # 19 or 29 to Hogdalen, and then bus #744 to Farstanasvagen and then a 10 minute walk. Campsite is a meadowland surrounded by pine trees. Chemical toilets, but cheap at only 7 kr for a tentsite, 3 kr for a car. Camp also has beach, playground and boat rentals.

FLATEN CAMPING is 17 km southeast of downtown Stockholm on Lake Flaten. Open May 30-Sept. From Central Station follow signs to T-Centralen (subway). Board train #27 (direction Hagsatra), #28 (Hokarangen) or #29 (Hogdalen). Get off at fourth stop, Skanstull Station. Outside station, take buses 811-817 and 828 from Ringvagen. From Slussen Station, take bus #401. Camp is mainly wooded pastureland. Chemical toilets, showers, water slide, rental boats, tentsite/7 kr, car/3 kr.

CITY TRANSPORTATION   Stockholm offers 24 hour, 72 hour and one month unlimited journey tickets, and discounted 20 coupon books. The entire greater Stockholm area is divided into zones. The same tickets are good on all forms of transportation. Tickets consist of coupons which cost 2 kr each when purchased from drivers or conductors. Half coupons which are used for children and senior citizens (pensioners) cost 1 kr each. Coupons are discounted when purchased in advance in 20-coupon books. One book costs 25 kr which reduces the price to 1.25 kr per coupon. (Children 7-16 and senior citizens pay half.) Coupon books are sold at newstands marked "pressbyran" which are commonly found in main subway stations including T-Centralen. The coupons can be shared among you.

A trip within one zone costs two coupons. Each additional zone costs one coupon for each zone. For trips late at night, two extra coupons are required. It doesn't matter if you change from bus to subway within the same zone, but if another zone is crossed another coupon is charged. However, changes must be made within one hour of the latest time stamp. The maximum fare is 8 coupons which if paid at the start, entitles you to three hours of unrestricted travel throughout the entire tansport area. The trip from Central Station to Bredang Camping is five zones. A ticket bought individually would cost 12 kr, or using the required 6 coupons from a coupon book the cost of the trip would be reduced to 7.50 kr.

Three kinds of tourist tickets (turistkort) are offered. All tourist tickets are valid for travel on the Djurgard ferries which ply between Rantmastart-rappan in Slussen and Allmanner Grand on island of Djurgarden at frequent intervals, and on the summer ferries which leave from Nybroplan (subway Nybroplan) for the same destination. They are also valid for admission to the Tramway Museum (Sparvagsmuseet). The 12 kr ticket is valid for 24 hours travel within Stockholm's inner city district only. The 20 kr ticket is valid for 24 hours travel throughout the entire greater Stockholm area which includes all campgrounds. The 40 kr ticket is valid for 72 hours travel plus admission to Skansen, Kaknastornet television tower, and Grona Lund amusement park. Children pay half fare.

In addition, a monthly season ticket is sold for 80 kr. It consists of a "base card" which requires a photograph--bring along an extra passport picture--and a monthly token. (Half price for children and senior citizens.) Monthly and tourist tickets and coupon booklets are sold at Pressbyran kiosks and other SL (Storstockholms Lokaltrafik) sales points such as tourist office and some agencies of Swedish State Railways.

FOOD   Public market (Hotorget Market or Haymarket) is at Hotorget Square in front of Concert Hall, and operates M-Sa 8-6. Take the subway to Hotorget or walk 8 blocks from Central Station. Another market is on Ostermalm storg Square near the Royal Dramatic Theater, and a third is at Kornhamn stora. Grocery stores in underground arcades at T-Centralen, Hotorget, Fridhemsplan and Ostermalmstorg subway stations close at 10 pm.

Restaurant on first level in Central Station serves an all-you-can-eat buffet breakfast (frukost) of rolls, bread, butter, jam, cheese, eggs, corn flakes, juice, milk, coffee and tea from 6:30-10 am for about 20 kr. Supermarket of Ahlens Department Store, next to train station, is open until 10 pm daily including Sunday. Its second floor cafeteria serves one-plate meals for about 20-30 kr.

SIGHTSEEING   Children under six usually receive free admission and those 6 through 11 and senior citizens pay half.   On Djurgarden are concentrated several attractions.   (Bus #47 from Central Station or ferry from Nybroplan.) SKANSEN, Stockholm's outdoor museum of reconstructed farms and dwellings from earlier times, is here. Buildings are open 11-5.   Free guided tours in English start on the hour from 11-4. Adult/10 kr, child/3 kr. WASAVARVET (Wasa Museum) shows the famous warship which sank soon after being launched in 1628. Open 9:30-7, adult/7 kr, student/5 kr, child/2 kr.   PRINS EUGENS WALDEMARSUDDE shows paintings including contemporary works, open Tu-Sa 11-4, Su 11-5 and W & F evenings 7-9, free. BIOLOGISKA MUSEET (Museum of Biology), open 10-4, adult/3 kr, child/1.50 kr.   LILJEVALCHS KONSTHALL (Liljevalch Art Gallery) houses special exhibitions, open Tu & Thu 11-9, W, F, Sa, Su 11-5.   GRONA LUNDS TIVOLI (amusement park), open M-F 7 pm-midnight, Sa 2 pm-midnight, Su noon-11 pm, except June 9-Aug 20 when it opens 2 pm weekdays, closed weekdays during first two weeks in Sept, closed for season Sept 15. Adult/10 kr, child/5 kr.

A good historical viking museum is Historiska Museet, Linnegatan and Narvavagen (subway Karlaplan), open 11-4, free.

On Skeppsholmen Island, the Moderna Museet (Modern Art Museum), formerly part of a naval station, was remodeled to become an uncluttered and spacious modern art gallery showing 20th century painting and sculpture. Open daily 11-9, adult/8 kr, child/free. Bus #46, 55 or 62 from Ostermalmstorg (subway station on lines 13 and 15). NATIONAL MUSEUM, on peninsula S. Blasieholmshamnen by Grand Hotel, is a five minute walk from Moderna Museet or bus #45, 55 or 62 from Ostermalmstorg. Here are paintings by Rembrandt, Rubens, Frans Hals, sculpture, graphic art, French Impressionists, craft items and an exhibit of modern Swedish design in home furnishings. Open daily 10-4 and Tu 10-9, adult/8 kr, Tuesday free.

ET NOGRAFISKA MUSEET (Ethnographical Museum), open daily 12-4, adult/5 kr, and TEKNISKA MUSEET (Museum of Technology), open M-F 10-4, Sa Su 12-4 pm, adult/5 kr, child/3 kr, family/10 kr, are close to each other on Djurgardsbrunnsvagen--take bus #69 or 69X from Ostermalmstorg. Four stops farther on, bus #69X brings you to Kaknastornet (Kaknas television tower), 508 feet high, open June-Aug, daily 9 am-midnight, Sept-May daily 10-7. Adult/5 kr, child/2.50 kr. Also, bus #69 goes within walking distance.

Downtown, STADHUSET (City Hall) near Central Station has guided tours daily at 11 am plus a noon tour on Sunday. Adult/3kr.

MILLESGARDEN at Lidingo is the former home of sculptor Carl Milles.

Take subway train #13 or 14 to Robsten Station, then bus #203. Open May-Aug M-Sa 11-4, Su 12-4; Apr, Sept, Oct daily 1-3 pm. Palace: adult/5 kr, child/3 kr; Chinese Pavilion: adult/5 kr, child/3 kr; Court Theater and Museum: adult/10 kr, child/5 kr.

SHOPPING   Third floor of AHLENS Department Store by Central Station contains restrooms, baby changing room, supervised playroom (barnparkering) camping equipment and toys. Shipping is on street floor and value added tax of about 20% is deducted from purchases sent out of the country. Parking for cars is on third and fourth levels underground. Street floor and all lower levels are open Sundays and evenings until 10 pm.

TRAIN SCHEDULES (* = reservation mandatory) To OSLO, trains leave at 7:00 am* (ar. 1:25 pm), 4:00 pm* (ar. 10:08 pm) and 11:05 pm (ar. 7:55 am).
     To COPENHAGEN, trains leave at 7:22 am*, 9:22 am*, 10:22 am, 12:22 pm, 2:22 pm* Trip is 9-1/2 hours.
     To NARVIK, Norway, a train leaves at 4:10 pm* (ar. Boden 6:58 am, ar. Kiruna 10:44 am, ar. Narvik 2:00 pm), and 8:10 pm (ar. Narvik 10:20 pm next day but remember that it's still light.)
     To UPPSALA, there are about 30 trains a day for the 45 minute trip.

UPPSALA

Viking burial mounds can be seen in this old and famous university town in historical Sweden. TRAIN STATION is downtown on Kungsgatan. TOURIST INFORMATION office is nearby at Kungsgatan 44. Open June-Aug M-F 9-7, Sa 9-1, Su 10-2. GRANEBERG CAMPING, 20 minutes from town by bus #20 which leaves from Nybron by the river (towards right of station). Bus leaves on the hour and half-hour and costs 5 kr. Flat fee of 17 kr for a tentsite. Also rents two bed cabins for 24 kr per night. YOUTH HOSTELS are Sunnersta Herrgard (May 1-Aug 31), bus #20; and Fritidsgarden Glanten (June 28-August 16), bus #6 or 7.
     SIGHTSEEING Burial grounds in Gamla Uppsala are reached by bus #24 from Kungsgatan to right of station. Disagarden in Gamla Uppsala is a museum of old original Swedish farmhouses. Other sights are the Cathedral, castle, anatomical theater in Gustavianum and Upplands Museum, St. Erikstorg 10, which shows local history.
     FOOD MARKET is "Saluhall" and is held indoors at St. Erikstorg.

SWITZERLAND

Entering Switzerland from southern Europe makes you feel as if you've come home. Many Swiss speak English, the atmosphere is low-keyed, food is unit priced per 100 grams in the lavish supermarkets, and toilet paper is furnished in campground restrooms. The traveler who camps and confines his eating to M Restaurants (cafeterias) in Migros Supermarkets will find the country manageable financially.

There are four official languages but German is predominant with 73 percent of the population speaking it. French is spoken by 21 percent, Italian by 5 percent and Romansh by 1 percent.

A commonly heard greeting is "gruezi," pronounced roughly "gru-at see" but very fast.

In 1981, Swiss voters adopted an equal rights amendment to their constitution. providing that "men and women are equal in rights...particularly in the domains of family, instruction and employment...."

CURRENCY   Strong and getting stronger. The Swiss call their money francs just like the French but one Swiss franc equals 55¢. There are about 1.8 francs to the U.S. dollar. Each franc is divided into 100 rappen.

WEATHER   Except for Ticino (around Lugano), temperatures are never uncomfortably hot in summer. Rather an occasional cold or rainy day can be expected. July and August are the most crowded months, with the first week in August the most popular. School children are on vacation from mid-July through August. September weather is usually better than June. Weather varies from one region to another in Switzerland more than you would think possible for such a small country. Valais (around Zermatt) and the Engadine have least rainfall. Grapes, apricots and peaches grow in Valais. Lugano in southern Switzerland has relatively mild winters with sunshine and pleasant camping in May and October. Vegetation in the Ticino area is reminiscent of the Mediterranean. Lakes of Lucerne and Thun have relatively warm weather starting in April because of the "fohn" wind which makes mountain areas highly uncomfortable, but becomes warm and dry by the time it reaches these two lakes. Lucerne, Basel, Zurich, Fribourg, Berne and all cities of the central plateau have fairly warm weather through October although rain can be expected. This is the lowland area which spreads between the Alps and the Jura mountains. Geneva is warmer and less rainy than Zurich or Lucerne though. Always expect cool evenings, even in summer, and occasional rainfall in mountain areas.

CAMPING   Campgrounds are well kept and found in all touring areas. Toilet paper is provided in camp restrooms. A small visitor's tax is often charged in addition to camp fees. Swiss Federation of Camping Clubs (FSCC) and Swiss Touring Club (TCS) are the main camping organizations. Brochure with map "Camping Holidays in Switzerland," and similar Youth Hostel folder which includes bus and tram numbers, are free from tourist office in U.S.

TRAINS   Swiss Federal Railways (SBB) operate one of the best networks in Europe. Swiss trains go virtually everywhere and reservations cannot be made for travel within Switzerland. Also a reservation is not compulsory on TEE trains L'Arbalete, Bavaria and Roland for travel within Switzerland and to Italy. For local train travel within Switzerland on these trains, a reservation cannot be made but the TEE train can be used if you can find a seat. Unlimited stopovers are allowed on all tickets without having them stamped. Ordinary one-way tickets are valid for 2 days and ordinary round trip tickets are valid for 10 days with renewals possible when purchased in Switzerland. Tickets purchased in U.S. are valid 6 months. Seat reservation fee is 3 F but you shouldn't need any. Rail tickets can be used on corresponding lake steamer. Children under 6 travel free and those 6-15 inclusive pay half. Reduction for round trips (return tickets) is 25 percent.

Swiss Tourist Office in U.S. sells these special tickets. Swiss Holiday Card gives unlimited travel on trains, postal motor coaches and lake steamers and 25-50% off on cog-wheel railways and private railways which are generally very expensive. Cost for second class is $56 for 4 days, $71 for 8 days, $93 for 15 days and $129 for 1 month. Children 6-15 inclusive pay half. Pass must be purchased outside Switzerland. Send name and passport number to order. Regional Holiday Season Tickets are obtained at any rail station in the region in which they are valid. The regions are Montreux/Vevey (50 F); Bernese Oberland, includes Interlaken and Zermatt (70 F); Lake Lucerne (80 F); Grisons (66 F); Locarno/Ascona (40 F); and Lugano (42 F). The first four regions mentioned sell tickets good for 15 days, on your choice of five of those days you get unlimited rail, boat, bus travel on designated lines and for the other 10 days you pay half fare. In addition, for 15 days you get a 25% or 50% reduction on such adjoining lines as lifts, and cog-wheel trains. Half Fare Travel Card costs $27 for 15 days and $34.50 for 1 month and allows purchase of tickets on railways, steamers and postal buses and private railways like Zermatt-Gornergrat and the Jungfraujoch in Switzerland for 50% off. There is also a Half Fare Travel Card for persons from 16 to under 26 for $16 for one month which is valid only on Swiss Federal Railways trains. Buy it at Swiss train stations. Need passport and picture. Senior Citizen Half Fare Travel Card is good for one year, costs about $52 and gives 50% reduction on all public transportation and off-season discounts at some hotels.   Men must be over 65 and women over 62. Send photo, date of birth and date on which pass should start. Group discounts are given for groups of 6 or more. One free ticket for groups of 15 paying passengers is given. Groups of 25 persons under 21 receive 35% off. For families, 1 adult pays full fare and the rest pay half. Contact Swiss Tourist Office for more information.

Best rail map is in "The Swiss Holiday Card" brochure from U.S. tourist office. Many narrow gauge and cog-wheel trains which climb moun- tains are privately owned and very expensive. Postal service operates a system of bus routes through the most scenic areas--rates are similar to the train but routes are seldom duplicated. Tickets are bought from the post office which is also the point of departure. Baggage can be checked through to another city for a moderate charge by getting it to the station at least an hour ahead to register it. Baggage lockers and checkroom cost 1 F for 24 hours. Free timetables are available at train information offices. Or you can buy the 376 page "Amtliches Kursbuch" for about 7.50 F from train infor mation offices which lists all public, private railways, cog-wheel railways, buses and steamers in the country as well as international train schedules.

Eurailpass and Eurail Youthpass include use of regular steamer ser- vices on the lakes of Geneva, Lucerne, Thun, Brienz, Zurich, Neuchatel, Biel, Murten and on the Rhine from Schaffhausen to Kreuzlinger and on the Aare River from Biel/Bienne to Solothun. When the steam ship company or railway offers escorted tours via train or boat, a railpass holder can join these free of charge--inquire at tourist office of city you're in for brochure. If a private railway or lift is involved, the cost of these must be paid but not the rest.

DRIVING   Freeways are signed in green, main roads in blue. Vehicles coming from the right have priority in cities, towns and on secondary roads. Trams have right of way over other traffic. Speed limit is 100 kmh (60 mph) on main roads except freeways and 60 kmh (36 mph) in cities, towns and built up areas unless otherwise posted. Mountain passes are open June to October and the most important are kept open all year or else there is a tunnel. The San Bernardino auto tunnel (Thusis-Bellinzona) is free. The toll charge for the S. Bernard tunnel (Martigny-Aosta) is from about $7-16 de- pending upon cylinder capacity of car. Special rail facilities are provided for motorists wishing to transport their cars through the Alpine rail tunnels of the Gotthard, Simplon and Loetschberg. The car is put on the train and costs $22 for Simplon, $23.50 for Loetschberg and $39 for Simplon- Loetschberg. Zurich to Paris is 355 miles, Munich 192 miles, Milan 188 miles, Berne 80 miles and Lucerne 35 miles. Berne to Basel is 62 miles, Interlaken 34 miles and Lucerne 57 miles.

TOURIST INFORMATION   These are called "Office du Tourisme," "Associazone per il Turismo" or "Verkehrsverein" in this tri- lingual country. Usual hours are 8-12 and 2-6.

FOOD   Quality of processed Swiss foodstuffs is very good. Food is priced differently than in surrounding countries because Switzerland is not in the Common Market so does not follow the market's agricultural policies and price supports. Swiss agricultural output is very substantial for a country which is half mountainous and whose crops must be carefully pursued in a small amount of cultivable land. Eighty per cent of agricultural output consists of dairy products. Flocks and herds make good use of the mountainous parts by being taken into the Alps during summer for grazing. Accordingly, fresh milk, cheese, butter, ice cream, powdered milk and milk chocolate are high quality. A specially processed form of milk can be found in unrefrigerated counters (marked UP). This means that if unopened, it can be kept for several months. "Magermilch" is skim milk; "milchdrink" is two percent. "Tafelbutter" is table butter; "kochbutter" is unpasteurized.

Fondue and raclette are two national main courses of cheese commonly served in the French-speaking parts of Switzerland. Served in cold weather, raclette consists of chunks of cheese melted on a stick over a fire and then scraped onto potatoes on a plate. Bundnerfleisch, viande seche or viande de Grisons, is wafer-thin air-dried beef characteristic of the Grisons. Leberspiessli is liver wrapped in bacon on a skewer. All of these specialties plus fondue bourguignonne are fairly expensive.

Swiss restaurants are very expensive. The saving grace of campers is the country-wide chain of M Restaurants (cafeterias) that are found in Migros (MEE-gros) Markets (supermarkets). Not all Migros Markets have one so remember upon arrival to ask at the tourist office for the location. M Restaurants are very modern and attractive cafeterias with good food and reasonable prices and the best value in Switzerland. Apple juice (apfelsaft), grape juice (traubensaft) either red (rot) or white (weiss), and milk are sold in all Swiss restaurants and cafeterias.

Migros Markets (supermarkets) have good prices, especially on their house brands of chocolate and weekly specials. These and public markets are the cheapest places to buy food in this rather expensive country. Groceries have a "use by" date and are unit priced per 100 grams or per liter.

HIKING   Switzerland is well organized with regularly maintained and regulation signed trails traversing the country. Tourist office distributes an excellent 68-page booklet "On Foot Through Switzerland" describing with diagrams 42 hikes including six cross country ones and a route map. Official sectional maps are published by the Swiss Topographical Service and can be ordered in advance from the tourist office. They're called "Landeskarte Carte Nationale" series with a scale of 1:50,000 (3/4 mile per inch).

Trails are maintained by the Swiss Footpath Protection Association (Schweizerische Arbeitsgemeinschaft fur Wanderweg), except for the Jura Ridge trail which is looked after by the Swiss Jura Association. You have 42,000 miles of trails from which to choose. Signing is standardized. Basic sign is yellow with black lettering on white signpost. On post are location and altitude. A yellow sign points to nearest fork, farm, village, mountain hut or trail junction. Secondary lettering beneath indicates a more distant destination of the trail. According to regulations, this point should be within six hours walking time. Sometimes a sign will carry directions for several trails, in which case a black line separates the information. Secondary signs are placed along the trail to indicate where the path continues if unclear. These are yellow. Additionally, small yellow diamond, rectangular or arrow-shaped markings are placed on rocks and trees along the route.

All trails in the central lowlands are marked by all yellow signs. This area between the truncated Jura Mountains and higher Alps is filled with meadows, lakes, forests and small hills, but also farms, villages and commercial and industrial cities. This region is the economic heart of Switzerland where most Swiss live. Trails pass through some towns and villages, but in most cases skirt them. Only a picnic lunch need be carried because meals can be bought at village inns and campgrounds. Basic central lowlands trail starts at Romanshorn on Lake Constance (Bodensee--shared by Switzerland, Austria and Germany), passes through Zurich, Berne, Fribourg and Lausanne to end in Geneva. Any section can be done without hiking the entire distance.

Half of Switzerland is taken up by Alps, and signs for these mountain trails are specially marked with a white tip on a yellow sign with red stripe in the middle. A hiker should be prepared for sudden rain and cold in the mountains before venturing very far on this type of trail. Boots or shoes with lug soles and waterproof jacket should be worn on mountain paths if you're going for more than a hour's walk from a hut. Small white directional markers with red middle stripe in diamond, arrow or rectangular shape, help show the way.

A separate category is the Jura Ridge Trail that follows the Jura mountains, a low mountain range flanking the central lowlands, in northern Switzerland. Signs are yellow with half red and half white tip. Trail begins in Zurich and ends at Lake Geneva.

Main difference between hiking in Switzerland and the Pacific North-west is not having to carry lots of food. In some cases, such as the central lowlands trail, you needn't even camp but can stay in guesthouses and inns on the outskirts of small towns along the route. Even on mountain trails, the route is punctuated with guesthouses and mountain huts which provide a night's lodging for about $5 and/or prepared meals. A picnic lunch can be bought at a hut to see you through the following day until another is reached. There are climber's huts throughout the Alps which are maintained by the Swiss Alpine Club (Schweizer Alpen Club or Club Alpin Suisse). Charge is about 8.50 F per night for non-members. No food is available. Most mountain huts are staffed with a married couple who provide beds, dormitory style, and cook food. You can eat in a hut without staying there, however don't camp on grass being grown for hay. Guidebooks describing routes, meals, inns and campgrounds are available for some trails. Ask at the tourist office in the locale of the trail when you get there.

PRONUNCIATION OF PLACE NAMES   Appenzell (AHP-uhn-tsel), Davos (dah-VOHS), Grindelwald (GREEN-dul-vault), Lake Maggiore (mahd-JOH-ra), Lausanne (loh-ZAN), Leysin (LAY-zann), Montreux (mon-TRUH), St. Moritz (san mah-RITS), Ticino (tee-CHEE-no), Valais (va-LEH)

LE POTPOURRI   Swiss post offices are excellent and easy to use. Most are near the train station and are open 7:30-12 and 2-6, weekdays and 7:30-11 am on Saturday. Shops are open 8-6:30 weekdays but some close earlier on Saturday and remain closed until Monday afternoon. "Don't Miss the Swiss" is the people-to-people program offered by the Swiss Tourist Office in which you complete an application giving occupation and interests and are matched with a Swiss family and invited to their home for coffee and cookies. Get an application blank before you go. Daycare for children is well organized and extensive. Tourist office leaflet "Child Care in Swiss Holiday Resorts" has a listing. Lakes of Lucerne, Lugano and Maggiore sometimes have problems and closed beaches are so marked. Lakes of Geneva and Zurich are clean.

BASEL (BASLE)

Switzerland's second largest city, Basel is situated on the Rhine River at the confluence of the frontiers of France, Germany and Switzerland.

TRAIN STATIONS   Basel Station has two parts. SNCF Station serves trains to and from France while SBB Station handles other international services and local trains to Germany and the Swiss interior. If you are going into France, allow time to clear customs at the station before boarding. If your train is passing through Basel from France, you may have to debark at SNCF Station, go through customs and board in SBB Station. SBB Station is the most important with post office, exchange office and tourist office. Basel Baden Bahnhof or Bad Bahnhof D.N.B. is a minor German Station across the river. Coming from Germany, the train stops there first before continuing to SBB Station.

TOURIST OFFICE   At Blumenrain 2 and SBB Station.

CAMPGROUND   Camp Waldhort Basel is closed and there is no other camp in the Basel area. We suggest commuting by train across the border to the good campground in Mulhouse, France. (See Mulhouse, France.)

YOUTH HOSTEL   A new Youth Hostel opened in 1980 at St. Alban-Kirchrain 10. From Basel SSB /SNCF train station, the hostel is a 15 minute walk in the direction of the Rhine River. From Basel Baden Bahnhof (Badischer Bahnhof) take tram #2 to Kunstmuseum and then walk 5 minutes. Hostel offers hot showers, hairdryer, washing machine and dryer.

CITY TRANSPORTATION   Trams and buses are operated by Basler Verkehrs-Betriebe. Tickets are sold from machines at stops. No conductors on board. Single tickets cost according to zone. Yellow zone is .60 F, white zone is .90 F and blue zone 1.50 F. Map on ticket machine indicates zones. Children 6-15 inclusive (dogs and strollers!) pay .60 F regardless of zone. Children under 6 ride free. Each ticket carries unlimited transfer privileges within a certain time period as follows: 30 minutes on .60 F ticket, one hour on .90 F ticket and 1-1/2 hours on 1.50 F ticket and child's ticket. Ticket books, giving 11 tickets for price of 10, cost 15 F for 1.50 tickets, 9F for .90 F tickets and 6 F for .60 F tickets. Ticket machines work by pressing button corresponding to ticket price, depositing correct change (no return) and removing ticket. If you do it wrong, press button "Irrtumtaste" which means error and releases the money. One day pass is sold and costs 4 F. Bus and tram map is given by tourist office. Unique cable ferry boats cross the Rhine River for a .50 F fare. One is near Munster Cathedral.

FOOD   Public market on Marktplatz next to Rathaus (city hall) in vicinity of Mittlere Rhein bridge is open M-Sa 7 am-noon. Take tram #1 or 7 from SBB Station to reach downtown.

SIGHTSEEING   Museum of Fine Arts, Kunstmuseum, is the finest in Switzerland and a top European museum. Open June-Sept Tu-Su 10-5, Oct-May Tu-Su 10-12 & 2-5. It's located on St. Alban-Graban, a six block walk from SBB Station or take tram #2 from SBB Station to third stop. Adult/2 F, free on Sat, Sun and in the afternoon on Wednesday. First floor shows the largest collection of Hans Holbein's works and other European masters. Elsewhere is an excellent contemporary section with Braque, Klee, Leger, Chagall, Picasso, Arp, Mondrian and others represented.

Basel zoo is renowned for success in breeding endangered species in captivity. Animals roam separated by moats. Open daily 8-6:30. Adult/6 F. It's an 8 minute walk from SBB Station. A modern sculpture by Arp stands in the courtyard of the new School of Applied Arts on Vogelsangstrasse (south of Bad Bahnhof D. B.). Take tram #1 from SBB Station. Elevator of Swiss Navigation Company is open Mar-Oct daily 10-12 and 2-5 and offers a panoramic view from its Silo Terrace, adult/1 F, child/.50 F. For a nice walk, follow Oberer Rheinweg along the right bank. Other attractions include Museum of Natural History and Anthropology, Kirschgarten Palace --18th century private mansion with period furniture, and Munster Cathedral--a landmark of Basel made of red sandstone in Romanesque and Gothic style with a tiled roof and twin towers. Erasmus' tomb is there. A cable ferry crosses the Rhine nearby.

TRAIN SCHEDULES   Trains leave for Lucerne,; Zurich and Berne almost every hour and the trip to Lucerne and Zurich takes a little over an hour, to Berne about 1-1/2 hours.

BERNE (BERN)

A capital city of red roofs and arcaded sandstone buildings, Berne is a good choice for visiting a Swiss city and makes a good base for day trips to other towns.

TRAIN STATION   Station is downtown facing Bahnhofplatz. Bus terminal is above train station. Two banks have branches inside, open daily 6:10 am-10 pm. Tourist office in station is open M-Sa 8-6:30, Su 10-5. Train information office is open daily 7:30 am-8:30 pm. Post office (hauptpost) nearby is open 6 am-11 pm.

CAMPGROUNDS   Camping Eichholz on Aare River in Wabern district is 3 km southeast of downtown. Open May-Sept. From square in front of train station at tram stop with "Wabern" on the sign, take tram #9 (yellow sign) direction Wabern. Fare is .80 F. Get off at last stop, Wabern. Walk back one block past Co-op grocery store and post office to Eichholzstr. Turn right and follow signs to campground, a 10 minute downhill walk. By car, in general follow signs to Belp or Flugplatz (airport) unless entering Berne from the south. Coming from Basel or Zurich on N 1, you have to go through downtown to get to the campground. Follow signs to Belp until camping signs appear. Camp has exclusive use of one section of a public park within a good residential area. The camp is especially nice for backpackers as cars are prohibited from camping area which is a beautiful lawn. (Tents have to be moved once a week to preserve the lawn.) Adjacent parking area is provided for cars and vans. Office, open 8-12 and 2-8 pm, gives a good free map of Berne. Hot showers (.20 F), 3 outdoor nooks equipped with 2 burner coin-operated gas stove and sink, tables and chairs nearby, and a free freezer for ice bags are provided. Ask at office to use washing machine inside room with red door, 3.50 F including soap. Lines for drying. No store, but small bread store (boulangerie) and grocery store (epicerie) are three blocks away. Restaurant at camp with counter service and outdoor tables under cover closes at 10 pm but kitchen closes earlier. Restaurant offers two weiners (wienerli) with roll (mutschli) and mustard (senf) for about 3.50 F, 1/4 liter milk for about 1.10 F (get at window on left), fries for about 3 F, green salad for about 2 F and half chicken and fries for about 9.50 F. Two wading pools (one with slide), small sandy beach area and cold water shower are in park area. Trail along Aare River leads to downtown Berne from Camp in about 40 minutes. Trail also goes to zoo (tierpark) across the river on a footbridge. Camp fees are adult/3.50 F, student/2.80 F, child to 16/1.50 F, tent/1.50 F, car/1 F, room in cabin for one night/10 F.

    Camping Eymatt on road to Wohlen is 5 km northwest of city center. Open all year. Take bus from station above train station. Bus leaves once an hour, bus fare is about 2 F. Get off at bus stop "Eymatt." Store, same fees as Camping Eichholz but less convenient and fewer facilities.

CITY TRANSPORTATION   Trams cost between .80 F and 1 F per ride. A 24 hour card (Tagescarte) for the municipal transport system costs 4 F and is sold at SVB Ticket Office, 5 Bubenbergplatz--the tram terminal across from station, and at tobacco-newspaper stands in station. Parking meters downtown cost 1 F for 60 minutes except are free between Sa 5 pm - Mon 7 am.

FOOD   Public market is Tuesday and Saturday morning on Bundesplatz in front of Houses of Parliament, three blocks from station. Meat and dairy products market is held on same days on Munstergasse, about six blocks further east. Migro Market on Marktgasse, open M 11-6:30, Tu-W 8-6:30, Th 8 am-9 pm, F 8-6:30, Sa 8-5, is a very large supermarket that has everything including a tank with live trout. M Restaurant (cafeteria) upstairs opens at 6:30 am and has very modern orange decor, all sit-down tables and 2 highchairs. It's a quick and efficient self-service operation with various food stations rather than one long line. Of the two stations for hot plates, one serves the daily special exclusively while the other has a grill and cooks hamburgers and fries on the spot but heats up previously cooked chicken. Hamburger and fries cost about 4.30 F, half chicken and fries about 5.40 F. There is a salad bar with many salads, some meat and hard-boiled eggs, all priced at about 1.80 F per 100 grams. Help yourself and your plate is weighed at the cashier's to determine charge. Be careful here though as cost mounts quickly. Daily special is best value. At the drink station, milk, chocolate milk, and carbonated apple juice cost about .85 F a glass. Dessert costs a minimum of about .85 F for a small petit four and more for caramel custard, cake or soft ice cream in a parfait glass.

    For drivers, there is a Co-op Supermarket just before the bridge on way from camp to Natural History Museum which has free parking behind the store and a good delicatessen section. Hot whole rotisseried chicken costs about 6.50 F, salads (grated carrots, cucumbers, etc) for about 1 F per 100 grams and bologna for about 1.40 F per 100 grams. Store also carries Nuk pacifiers and good inexpensive (for Switzerland) toys.

SIGHTSEEING   Besides exploring the old town which centers on Marktgasse and visiting the bear pits at Barengraben which have drawn travelers since the 15th century (open 7-6, bring carrots to feed them), Berne offers the following attractions.

    Kunstmuseum, Hodlerstr. 12, has the most extensive collection of Klee's works in the world (he was born here) including 40 paintings, 150 gouaches and watercolors and 2500 drawings. The museum also has the Rupf Foundation which purchased mostly cubist works of Picasso, Braque, Gris and Leger. Open Tu-Su 10-12 & 2-5 and 8-10 pm Tuesday. During special exhibition: adult/5 F, student/2.50 F, child 7 and over/1 F. Other times prices are lower. Good 9x12 reproductions sell for 6 F. Toilets are on main floor to right of entrance and first floor up. Museum is five blocks from station.

Naturhistorisches Museum (Natural History Museum) is at Bernastr. 15. Don't miss--one of the best in Europe. Open M-Sa 9-12 & 2-5, Su 10-12 & 2-5. Twenty minute walk by trail from camp. Adult/1 F, student, child 6 and over and groups of 10/.50 F. Modern building, cool inside, check room, lots of seating in foyer. Restrooms are on left beyond ticket seller and on first, second and third floors at top of stairs. The museum shows nicely done dioramas of stuffed animals in natural settings. Ground floor: African species including Aardvark, rhinoceros, pigmy hippopotamus. First floor: fish, lizards, birds, wall board display showing dung of various species, rows of nests with eggs and feathers, stuffed animals such as bats and shrews, mole in cross-section of earth showing his habitat, stuffed llamas, camels, hedgehogs, armadillo, anteater and other kinds of animals not often found in zoos. Also skull, antler and teeth collection, whale skeleton sus - pended from ceiling, model of whale heart and display of stomach contents of whale. Second floor: birds, reptiles, beautiful python skeleton, shells, insects, room devoted to honeybees showing assorted hives and large model of a bee. Top floor: rocks, crystals, fossils, prehistoric room. A very modern wonderful museum! Nearby are Swiss Alpine Museum, Art Gallery, Berne Historical Museum and Swiss Rifle Museum.

Parlamentsgebaude, Parliament, on Bundesplatz. To learn about the workings of Swiss democracy, take a free guided tour at 9, 10, 11 am, 2, 3, or 4 pm daily except 4 pm tour is omitted on Sunday. No tours are given when parliament is in session in March, Jun, September and December. Tour lasts 45 minutes.

Clock Tower does its thing at four minutes before each hour just as it has been doing since 1530. Crowing rooster, jester, carousel of bears and golden knight. At Theaterplatz.

Gurten--take funicular from tram stop near Camping Eichholz stop which climbs to viewpoint with children's fairyland (miniature railway), snack bar and restaurant. Adult/3 F, child 6-16/1.50F. Be sure the sky is clear.

Zoo (Tierpark Dahlholzli) is across the river from Camping Eichholz, a 10 minute walk. Follow riverside trail north to footbridge. Bring bread to feed deer. Free entrance. Just inside zoo grounds are pony rides and donkey cart rides for .50 F, half-franc coins required. Nearby are baby goats, guinea pigs and play equipment. Entry to zoo birdhouse is adult/1.50 F, child 6 and over/.50 F. Toilets inside.

Murten, a compact medieval walled town 30 km west of Berne, makes a good train excursion. Fribourg's market days are Wednesday and Saturday when local costumes are worn.

DAYCARE Berne branch of Franz Carl Weber toy stores, Markt gasse 52-54 beside Migros Market, offers daycare for 3-7 year olds on Tuesday, Thursday and Friday from 1:30-5 pm. Reasonable prices. Tourist office says daycare is also available at Loeb and Ryfflihof, both near train station.

CHUR

Ray Rylander has contributed a map
of how to get to Camping Au in
Chur which is near Davos. He says
"no bus--must walk from station
down to campingplatz, about 2 km."
Washing machine, store, hot
showers, adult/3.60 F, tent/1 F.

GENEVA

Center of French-speaking Switzerland and an international crossroads
of Europe, Geneva is home base for
such international organizations as
the Red Cross, sections of the
United Nations and European
branches of U.S. Corporations.
"Fetes de Geneva," local celebration of three days in mid-August,
causes campgrounds to fill fast.
Water shooting upwards in the lake
is Jet d'eau, highest water spout in
the world at 400 feet.

TRAIN STATIONS Gare de Cornavin
is main station and is across the
river from main shopping area. It
has exchange office, post office,
automatic lockers and baggage check.
Outside is Place Cornavin from
which buses and trams depart.
CGTE, the public transportation
company, has a kiosk on Place
Cornavin and gives tram and bus
information. Smaller Eaux Vives
Station in northeastern part of city
handles trains for a part of France, particularly the Haute Savoie such as
Chamonix and Evian. From Gare Cornavin, take bus #5 to "Rond Point de
Rive" and transfer to tram #12 to Eaux Vives Station.

TOURIST OFFICE   This is at 2 rue des Moulins on "Pont de I'lle" (island
bridge), only a 5 minute walk from Cornavin Station. From Station, take
Mont-Blanc street until the river where you'll turn right following the river.
Tourist office is on fourth bridge.

CAMPGROUNDS   Camping Sylvabelle, 10 Chemin de Conches, in Conches
district. From Cornavin Station, take bus #5 to Rive, then #8 or 88 (Vey-
rier). Open all year, hot showers, snacks, cabins for rent, adult/3 F,
child/1.50 F, tent/2 F, car/2 F.

Camping Pointe a la Bise is in Vesenaz next to the lake. From Cornavin Station, take bus #5 to "Rond Point de Rive" and transfer to bus #9.

This is a resort camp with hot showers, store, restaurant, playground and wading pool, and nicer than Sylvabelle. Adult/3.60 F, tent/2-4 F, car/2 F.

CITY TRANSPORTATION   Information, map and tickets are available from CGTE kiosk on Place Cornavin in front of station. Tickets are sold from machines at bus stops. For a distance of three bus stops or less, a 60 centime ticket is required. A one franc ticket is good for more than 3 stops and includes free transfers in the city (reseau urbain) during one hour. Children 6-12 purchase a 50 centime ticket regardless of how many stops. There is a 6 trip card for 5.50 F including free transfers and a 7 trip card for 4 F for trips over 3 bus stops in length. A 7 trip card for children 6-12 costs 3 F. These cards must be punched in the machines before getting on board. One day card called "journee" costs 4 F. For buses outside of Geneva, tickets can be bought on the bus. The small boats which cross the lake are called "Mouettes." They stop at various points within the city. The cost is 1 F to cross the lake and leave from docks marked "Mouettes." They also go further up the lake and the cost varies according to the distance. Railpasses are not valid on Mouettes but only on the big boats belonging to the CGN. A copy of the tours on the lake operated by CGN can be obtained from the tourist office. The CGN boats stop at two docks: "Mont-Blanc" and "Jardin Anglais." These tours are operated by CGN and are free with rail-passes. (1) One Hour Cruise--leave Mont Blanc dock at 1:30 pm and 4:25 pm, leave Jardin Anglais dock at 1:34 pm and 4:30 pm. (2) Noon Cruise--leave Jardin Anglais at 12:30 pm weekdays only. (3) Short Lower Lake Cruise--leave Jardin Anglais dock at 10:15 am and 2:45 pm, leave Mt. Blanc dock at 10:20 am and 2:40 pm for 1 hour and 40 minute cruise. (4) Lower Lake Cruise--leave Mont Blanc dock at 9:15 am and 5:10 pm, leave Jardin Anglais dock at 2:30 pm and on Sunday in July and August 7:00 pm. (5) Complete Tour of the Lake--leave Mont Blanc dock at 9:15 am, leave Jardin Anglais dock at 8:00 am and 10:45 am. This is an all day tour with a stop of your choice at Lausanne, Montreux or Castle of Chillon. (6) Evian-Lausanne--leave Mont Blanc dock at 9:15 am and 2:00 pm, leave Jardin Anglais at 10:45 am. This is an all day trip. (7) Montreux - Castle of Chillon--leave Mont Blanc dock at 9:15 am, leave Jardin Anglais dock 10:45 am, return by boat or rail. (8) Dancing Cruise--leave Thursday and Saturday from Mont Blanc dock at 8:30 pm, return 11:30 pm.

FOOD   Wednesday and Saturday morning markets are Eaux-Vives at Boulevard Helvetique and Cours de Rive, Placette on rue Coutance and place Grenus (six blocks from Cornavin Station), and Carouge on place du Marche in suburban Commune de Carouge. Smaller markets are on Fusterie, place de la Fusterie downtown; and L'ile on pont de l'ile, island in middle of Rhone River where tourist office is located. Most important Tuesday and Friday morning market is Plaine de Plainpalais, avenue Henri Dunant, outside of downtown near Rond-Point de Plainpalais on bus lines #1 and #12. Two smaller ones are at Place des Alpes, two blocks from Lake Geneva on Cornavin Station side; and Rue Beulet which is off Rue St. Jean away from downtown. Small Monday and Thursday markets are at Rue Liotard, eight fairly long blocks from Cornavin Station; Mairie on Pre l'Eveque northeast of Place des Eaux-Vives; and Petit Saconnex on rue de Vermont and rue du Vidollet, nine long blocks south of Palais des Nations.

354

Plaza Migros, 5 rue de Chantepoulet--four blocks from Cornavin
Station, has a cafeteria and supermarket.

SIGHTSEEING   United Nations, Palais des Nations, is open June 15-Aug
9-5, Sept-June 14 M-F 9-12 & 2-4:30, SaSu 10-11:30 & 2-4:30. Take bus
"F" or "O" from Cornavin Station or if you have more time a pleasant hour
and a half walk will get you there by following the waterfront promenade,
passing through Parc Mon Repos and adjacent Parc Barton, then turning
inland on Avenue de la Paix which leads to the U. N.

TRAIN SCHEDULES   To Chamonix, trains leave Eaux-Vives Station in
Geneva at 9:30 am, 12:20 pm, 3:05 pm and 5:53 pm for the approximately four
hour trip. A change of train is made at St. Gervais de Fayet (St. Gervais).

INTERLAKEN AND THE BERNESE OBERLAND

Berne, Brig and Lucerne are rail gateway cities to Interlaken and the
magnificent Bernese Oberland.   Its magnet is the ascent of the Jungfraujoch (YUNG-fraw-yuk), which at 11,333 feet is the highest mountain station
in Europe. (The mountain itself is 13,642 feet.) There are also other lifts
in the area that don't go as high, but are less expensive yet still give a
good view of the fabulous mountains. Numerous excellent campgrounds are
near the villages and well-marked trails traverse the area. The Jungfraujoch trip is not advised for persons with health problems as oxygen is rather
thin at that altitude. Also, save your money if the weather isn't clear. The
Eurailpasses are only valid as far as Interlaken. After that the private
railways, cog-wheel railways and lifts get you. Actually there is a lot of
breathtaking mountain scenery between Brig and Visp on the regular rail-
line without paying the king's ransom on mountain routes.
    Ferry boats on Brienz and Thuner Lakes are included in Eurailpasses.
Lake Brienz boats depart near Interlaken Ost Station, Lake Thuner boats
by Interlaken West Station.

TRAIN STATIONS   Interlaken Ost (east) is the main station and handles
international traffic and local trains within the region. Interlaken West
Station is downtown in Interlaken and Migros supermarket and cafeteria are
across from side of station. Migros is open M-Sa 9-6:30 and Friday until
9 pm. Some international trains only stop at Interlaken Ost, while others
stop at both. The mountain railways depart from Interlaken Ost. Both
trains and buses connect the two stations.

TOURIST INFORMATION   Tourist Office Interlaken, Hoheweg 37, is four
blocks west of Interlaken West Station.

CAMPGROUNDS   Interlaken and the small towns of the Bernese Oberland
are saturated with good campgrounds. Nine camps are accessible from
Interlaken Ost or West Stations, by bus or on foot. Both stations have
information on bus departures. A visitor's tax is charged at all camps.
    From Interlaken West Station,   closest camp is Camp Jungfrau in
Unterseen which is one kilometer from the station, and easily walked.
(See map.) Open all year, hot showers, washing machine, cooking burners,
adult/3.50 F, child/2 F, tent/2 F. All camps charge about the same.

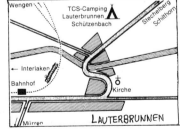

INTERLAKEN

From <u>Interlaken Ost Station,</u> Camping TCS Tiefenau (Sackgut) in Tiefenau district is 1.5 km from downtown Interlaken and half a kilometer from Interlaken Ost Station. (See map。) Hot showers, washing machine, store, snacks, adult/3.20 F, tent/2-4 F。 One km from Interlaken Ost Station, outside the town of Boningen, is Camping TCS Bonigen (Seeblick) near Lake Brienz. Hot showers, washing machine, store, adult/3.40 F, tent/2-4 F. Both Tiefenau and Bonigen are half a kilometer from the ferry on Lake Brienz。 A bus to Bonigen from Interlaken Ost Station goes within half a kilometer of Bonigen Camp. Camping Seiler in Boningen is cheaper but not as good as these other camps.

In an outstanding setting is Camping TCS <u>Lauterbrunnen</u> (Schutzenbach) in the village of Lauterbrunnen which is a station on the rail line leading to the Jungfraujoch。 The walk is 1 km from Lauterbrunnen station, and if possible we advise not stopping in Interlaken but instead breaking your journey in this town which is a higher altitude and in the mountains. Hot showers, individual sink cubicles, washing machine, store, adult/3.40, tent/2 F.   The camp offers a 24% discount on morning trains of the Jungfrau and Schilthorn Railway.   The rail line to Lauterbrunnen is not included in Eurailpasses.   The town's altitude is 2,640 feet and easier hiking trails start from here. (See map.)

Grindelwald, 3393 feet, and recommended by Bonnie and Doug Robinson as "fantastic scenery, great hiking...our campsite "Sands Camping" was directly under the North face of the Eiger。" This picturesque resort is on a private rail line and is an alternative route for the ascent of Jungfraujoch. Or do as Philip Jones suggests, " Mountain fares are murder in Switzerland。 When in Interlaken, instead of going all the way up to Jungfrau, take the train to Grindelwalk and then chairlift up to "First." The chair is in four stages and ascends to 7,200 feet. In summer the last departure is at 6:00 pm from First。 Be sure to buy a round trip ticket (hin- und ruckfahrt) which is only a little more than a one-way ticket. The chairlift to First is much less than the cog-wheel train to Jungfraujoch, and the village of Grindelwald is very attractive。

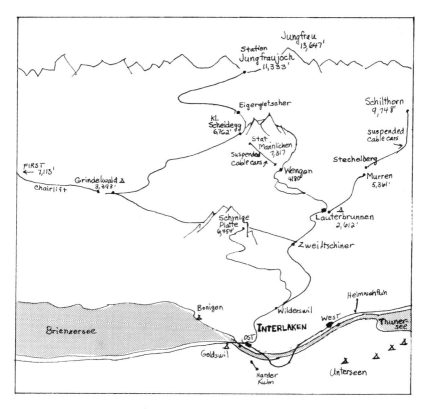

BERNESE OBERLAND SEASON TICKET   This ticket is valid 15 days, out
of which you receive unlimited travel for five of those days on certain lines
and half price travel for ten days on certain lines. In addition, on those
lines not covered by the pass, a discount of 25% or 50% is given. "Free"
travel lines are those from Interlaken Ost as far as Murren, Stechelberg,
Kleine Scheidegg and First. A 25% reduction is given from Kleine Scheidegg
to Jungfraujoch, Kleine Scheidegg to Lauterhorn, and Murren to Schilthorn.
More lines adjacent to the Interlaken area are included in both unlimited and
reduced travel, the most notable being 50% discount from Brig to Zermatt
and 25% discount from Zermatt to Gornergrat. The price of the ticket is
70 F, second class. Buy at train station.

JUNGFRAU EXCURSION TICKET   This ticket is valid three days
for stopovers, represents about a 25% reduction, and is a round-trip ticket
from Interlaken Ost-Wilderswil-Lauterbrunnen-Wengen-Kleine Scheidegg-
Jungfraujoch. It can also be routed in one direction via Grindelwald. The
restriction is on the journey up, only certain trains between Kleine
Scheidegg and Jungfraujoch can be taken. They are the first part of the
morning trains and the late afternoon trains. This means that you must
catch an 8:00 am or earlier train out of Interlaken Ost if you plan to do the
trip in one day. TCS campgrounds say they will sell you a reduced rate
ticket (about 24%) for the Jungfraujoch and Schilthorn trips, (this may be

this same excursion ticket.) (Also to be considered is forgoing the Jungfrau trip and taking the much cheaper chairlift from Grindelwald to First, unless you mind dangling.)

JUNGFRAU TRIP   Bring warm clothing and sunglasses. Trains leave Interlaken Ost in the valley and climb mountains passing by Wilderswil, Lauterbrunnen, Wengen and Wengenalp until finally reaching the top station of the Wengernalp Railway, Kleine Scheidegg (6,673 feet). This is also a good starting point for trails through alpine meadows that don't necessarily involve too much uphill trekking. Transfer to Jungfrau Railway which reaches Eigergletscher and enters a four-mile tunnel to eventually emerge at the mountaintop. On top are ice skating rink, restaurant, sleigh rides pulled by husky dogs and souvenir stands. Of course, great view of glaciers and highest mountain peaks up there on a clear day.

SCHILTHORN CABLEWAY (9,748 feet) is the longest cableway in the alps and takes you to top of Schilthorn mountain, site of Piz Gloria, revolving restaurant. The coach is suspended from the cable.

SCHYNIGE PLATTE (6,454 feet) is a splendid vantage point giving a wide view of the Bernese Alps, and site of an alpine botanical garden with over 500 different plants.

FIRST (7,113 feet) is a wonderful viewing station reached by chairlift from Grindelwald.

HEIMWEHFLUH is a funicular that is located a 6 minute walk from Migros Market in Interlaken West. Here is a view of Eiger, Monch, Jungfrau, Interlaken, and lakes of Thun and Brienz. Model railway on top.

HARDER KULM (4,337 feet) has its lower station near Interlaken Ost rail station. From top station to restaurant is about a 20 minute walk. Good view of Interlaken and Bernese Alps.

LUCERNE (LUZERN)

A well-placed resort city, Lucerne has good train access to Zurich, Berne and Basel.

TRAIN STATION   Located downtown and facing Lake Lucerne, it has exchange office, post office and bicycle rentals. Main post office is on Bahnhofplatz just left of station.

TOURIST INFORMATION   Main office, Pilatusstrasse 14, is on street that juts out from left side of station as you face the lake, in third block   on side nearest river.   Lucerne Season Ticket is sold for about adult/16 F, child/8 F which gives free admission to museums, four bus rides, one boat ride and three mountain railway trips.

CAMPGROUND   Camp Lido Lucerne is at Lido (Bruelmoos) near the beach on the opposite side of Lake Lucerne from the station. Bus #2 from station travels across Seebrucke bridge and follows lakeshore to camp. Ten minute ride. Bus stop is at Swiss Transport Museum before the camp appears. Walk one block farther and camp can be seen within a fence on the left, while Lido swimming beach and parking area are on right. Or, a railpass holder can take a ferry from dock across plaza in front of station and

towards the right, and save the bus fare. Only board a ferry which lists
"Lido" as a destination. Boats leave at 9:30 am, 12:05 pm, 1:25, 3:07 and
5:30 pm on way to Fluelen. (Return from Lido is at 10:08 am, 12:35 pm,
1:45, 2:40 and 6:15 pm.) Boats also leave from across from station at
10:25 am and 4:15 pm enroute to Alpnachstad. Trip from station to Lido is
ten minutes. Camp Lido is flat and grassy and you pitch your tent where-
ever there's room. Camp has hot showers, store, laundromat, cabins for
rent, and snack bar from which you order a rotisserie chicken in the morning and pick it up hot off the spit with french fries for dinner. Camp costs
about adult/3.50 F, child under 16/1.75 F, tent/1.50 F. Fee includes admission to Lido beach across the road. Lucerne draws lots of British so you'll
find plenty of English-speaking companions. In July and August, camp is
often filled to capacity. Lucerne hosts a music festival from mid-August to
first week in September. If you wish to attend, order tickets through tourist
office in U.S. and make reservations at Camp Lido (minimum of five nights):
Camp Lido Lucerne, Lidostr. 6008, Lucerne, Switzerland.

CITY TRANSPORTATION   Bus terminal is Bahnhofplatz in front of station.
Ticket buying instructions are given in English at bus stops. Motor launches
(Vierwaldstattersee) are slower than buses but free with train pass. They
leave from Bahnhofquai--a pier in front of station. Boats also travel
between station and downtown (Schweizerhofquai) but this can easily be
walked. Boats for the Lido pick up at both station and Schweizerhofquai
before stopping at the Lido. From Lido stop, boats go to Seeburg.

FOOD   Public market is at Unter der Egg on northshore of Reuss River.
"Unter der Egg" is not written on tourist office map, but is between Reuss
bridge and Reuss-Steg. Migros Market, Hertensteinerstrasse 46--the street
behind boat dock Schweizerhofquai--, has a stand-up cafeteria, Imbiss Ecke.

SIGHTSEEING   Lucerne has a picturesque old quarter. You can't miss the
roofed Chapel Bridge (Kapell-Brucke) with octagonal water tower made of
wood in 1333 (Gothic). Each roof section is a painting which was donated by
different leading families of Lucerne at the time. Town Hall, Kornmarkt,
was built in 1602-1606. Its roof is characterized as Swiss hip-roof. All
around are the winding streets of the old quarter. In the background can be
seen nine defence towers which comprise Musegg Wall, 14th century fortifi-
cations. Schirmer Tower, sixth from river, and some surrounding ramparts
are open to the public. Spreuer Bridge, fifth bridge from the lake, dates
from 1408 and is similar to Chapel Bridge.
    On Mt. Pilatus is an observation platform at 7,000 feet. There are
three ways to get there. Take ferry from dock by station to Alpnachstad
(free with railpass), a 1-1/2 hour trip, and then Pilatus Railway (private)
to the top (40 minutes). Or take bus #1 to Kriens (about 2.40 F) and aerial
cableway to top (50 minutes total time). Or take ferry or train to Hergiswil
(both free with railpass), then hike 4-1/2 hours on marked trail by way of
Brunni Hotel to top.
    For Rigi Mountain Ridge, take ferry to Fluelen (included in railpass)
and get off at Weggis, Vitznau or Gersau. Ferry leaves Bahnhofquai at
6:30 am, 7:05, 8:30, 9:30 (this one picks up at Lido at 9:40 am), 10:40 am
and 12:05 (Lido at 12:15 pm), 1:25 (Lido at 1:35), 2:25, 3:07 (Lido at 3:17),
5:10, 5:30 (Lido at 5:40) and 7:10 pm. From Weggis, Vitznau and Gersau,
a trail begins that climbs up to Rigi mountain ridge in about three hours

walking time. From Vitznau, there is also a private mountain railway that gets there in 35 minutes. Once on top, many good trails begin through meadows and forests.

Back in Lucerne, Glacier Garden is between downtown and camp-- about 8-10 blocks from the lake, and shows glacier potholes dating from the Ice Age and historical geology and natural science exhibits. Open 8-6, adult/ 3.50 F. Swiss Transport Museum with planetarium is next to camp at Lido- strasse 5, and is the largest and most modern transport museum in Europe. Displays encompass road, railway track, airplanes and boats. Open 9-6. Museum of Swiss Folk Costumes is out of town at Utenberg and within walk- ing distance of Glacier Garden. Adult/2.50 F.

Schwyz is a village with nice old houses reached by ferry to Brunnen (direction Fluelen). Transfer to tram for 20 minute ride to Schwyz, or take train to Schwyz from Lucerne. From Brunnen, ferry continues to Rutli where a 15 minute walk brings you to the meadow which figured prominently in Swiss history. The natural rock monument near the dock is dedicated to Schiller, author of "William Tell." If you go all the way on the ferry, in three hours you will arrive in Fluelen, town where William Tell shot the apple from his son's head. Train service back to Lucerne.

LUGANO

What? Palm trees in Switzerland? Once over St. Gotthard Pass, the canton of Ticino emerges where southern Europe begins. Its warm climate make Lugano (lu-GAH-no) the best bet for a stop in Switzerland during May or October. July and August are punctuated by sudden brief but heavy rainfall. Largest town in Ticino (tee-CHEE-no), Lugano combines a beautiful lakeside situation, Swiss solidity, Italian effervescence and a charming old quarter with cobbled streets replete with worn stone grooves from cart wheels. Lugano's yearly calendar lists a spring International Show of Art and Culture, International Biennial of Graphics and Drawings and late July "Festival on the Lake."

TRAIN STATION   Funicular (cog-wheel railway) travels between Stazione FFS and downtown. Fare is .30 F. Bus #9 leaves the station and follows the route: city center, La Santa and Viganello. Bus #10 follows same route in reverse.

CAMPGROUNDS   None in Lugano but several camps are nearby. Five are at Agno, fourth town on train line Lugano to Ponte Tresa. Trains leave once or twice a hour. Fifteen minute ride. Camps are about a 5-10 minute walk from station. All charge about adult/3.50 F and from 2 F per tent at Eurocampo to 5 F per tent at Tropical (except prices at Piodella were not reported.)

Maroggia, between Lugano and Mendrisio on Gotthard train line, has several campgrounds. Trains leave Lugano about hourly.

FOOD   Grapes, corn, tobacco, peaches, almonds, walnuts and figs are
important agricultural crops. Public market is Tuesday morning in Piazza
della Riforma, the main square and city center. Nuovi Grandi Magazzini
(department store), Via Nassa, has a cafeteria open noon-1 pm.

SIGHTSEEING   Villa Favorita in nearby Castagnola has a good collection
of paintings by Rubens, Holbein, Durer, Goya, Titian, El Greco, Valesquez,
van Eyck, Rembrandt and others set within an attractive villa. Open Apr-
Oct F-Sa 10-12 & 2-5, Su 2-5. Take bus #2 from main square near fountain
in Lugano. Ask conductor to stop at Villa Favorita. Fare is about .80 F.
Lugano municipal park offers morning concerts and summer evening folklore
performances. Santa Maria degli Angioli Church has a huge mural depicting
the crucifixion with angels, soldiers and large crowd scene, done by
Bernardino Luini. There are good ferry trips to Gandria (half-hour), an old
fishing village, and Morcote (one hour) but train passes are not valid.
Swissminiature in Melide, 5 km by train, reproduces Switzerland's most
notable sights to 1/25th scale. Open May 11-Oct 3 daily 7:30-7 and to 10 pm
in July and August. Open Sunday rest of year. Hiking in the Sottoceneri on
well marked trails is possible. Tourist office has maps.

RAPPERSWIL

Harold Parkerson offers these directions for reaching Campingplatz Lido-
Rapperswil.   "From train at Bahnhof, go into tunnel under the tracks. Go
out the end of tunnel towards the Technical Institute and away from the main
street. Turn left out of tunnel along Oberseestrasse past Knie Kinder Zoo
on the right, soccer field on the right, and to the grocery store (Mitzgerei
and Gemuse), which is also on the right. Turn right at grocery store. Walk
approximately two city blocks to campground. Campground has cooking
room with two electric hotplates (.20 F) and shower (1 F). Area is on Lake
Zurich. The campground is small, and has a small store and small
restaurant. (About 11 F a night.)"   In the town on a short street called
"Muhlegase," there is an automatic washing machine and a centrifuge spin
dryer which leaves clothes damp.

SCHAFFHAUSEN

"In Schaffhausen, take the trolleybus toward Neuhausen and get off at
Scheidegg. Campingplatz is down the hill and under the railroad tracks and
right on the river. 'So-so'--about average," reports Ray Rylander. TCS
Camping Strandbad Rheinwiesen charges adult/3.20 F, tent/2 F, and has hot
showers, individual sink cubicles, store, and snack bar. Camp is located
2 km from Schaffhausen.

SIERRE

"We took a beautiful hike... it was well worth it. Take the train to Sierre
and then a bus to Chandolin. It is 13.60 F for the bus strip up a mountain,
but the scenery is well worth it. When at Chandolin, take the hike to Bella-
Tola, about four hours up and three back. A hut with food and lodging is
half way up. At the top is an incredible view of the Alps with snow and
glaciers." (Lee Diamond)

Sierre is near Brig on the train line Brig-Geneva. Bus ride from Sierre to Chandolin takes 1 hour and 10 minutes and departs 5 times daily.

Camping Sierre-Ouest (Siders-west) is open Apr-Oct 15. Camp is west of town, 1 km from train station. Walk up main street, then turn left and walk through town until reaching Hotel Atlantic. Then turn left onto a little road along a little river and walk to campsite. Or, take bus #3 which departs every half hour from the station, costs .50 F, and stops at the campground. Hot showers, individual com-

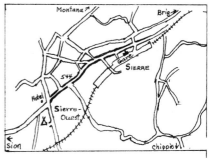

partments with sink, store, snack bar, adult/4.50 F, child to 14/2.25 F, tent/1.50 F.

VISP

Tourist office is 2 blocks from train station. Harold Parkinson reports that Camping Muhleye "is good and reasonable and close to the station--a 10-15 minute walk." Camp has hot showers and a washing machine.

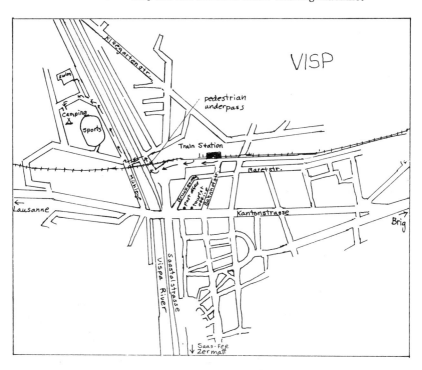

ZERMATT

Gateway to the Matterhorn, the village of Zermatt (tzair-MAHT) nestles
below the towering peak in an alpine valley. A popular ski resort in
winter, glacier skiing and hiking through meadows and forests occupy its
guests during summer. Zermatt is reached via the towns of Brig and
Visp. The 28 km between Visp and Zermatt are covered by privately owned
narrow-gauge railway in 1-1/4 hours. Eurailpasses are not valid. Cars
are parked outside Zermatt and not allowed in the town.

Tourist office is near the train station, and sells an aerial map showing trails. Closest campground is Camping Spiss, 500 meters from the
station, and reportedly below average for Switzerland. It has hot showers
for about 1 F. Migros Market with M Restaurant (closed Sunday) is a
budget-saver in this resort town. Number one sightseeing excursion, the
Gornergrat, gives a closer look-see at solitary majestic Matterhorn for a
hefty price. The 50 minute cog-wheel railway ride ends at Gornergrat at
10,289 feet. A cheaper way is to hike up through a pine forest on trails
beginning at Rifflealp and Riffelberg. Hiking down, an alternative route
goes by way of Obere Kelle, Frunsee (lake) and base of Findelen Glacier.
Consult office for map. Alpine Museum near post office exhibits memorabilia of first scaling of Matterhorn, and shows evolution of climbing equipment (open 4-6:30 pm, admission fee).

ZURICH

Switzerland's largest city and financial center, Zurich probably has better
train connections than any other Swiss city.

TRAIN STATIONS   Hauptbahnhof is the main one. Exchange office is in
main passageway leading to entrance, open 6:30 am-11:15 pm. Reservations
office is towards rear of station, open daily 8 am-10 pm. Tourist office is
outside entrance to the left, on other side of post office. Shopping area
starts immediately across Bahnhofplatz in front of station. Buses and trams
leave from Bahnhofplatz. Tram #11 travels main street, Bahnhofstrasse to
Schifflande Bahnhofstrasse, the pier on Zurich-See (Lake Zurich) from
which ferries depart, free with train pass. Pick up a copy of "Zurich
Excursions" from either the tourist office or train information because it
contains suggested rail excursions which you can duplicate with a rail pass
or join upon payment of non-railpass covered charges.

CAMPGROUNDS   Camping Seebucht, 3 km from downtown at See-Str. 559
on west side of Lake Zurich, is in the suburb of Wollishofen. Open May-Sept.
There are two ways to get there. Take tram #11 from station for four stops
to Burckliplatz, next to lake. Then change to bus #61 or 65 to bus stop
"Stadtgrenze platz" near camp entrance. Buses leave at 20 minute intervals
with last departure at 11:30 pm. Tram and bus fare is adult/1.20 F. Or you
can take a local train to suburban station Wollishofen and camp is a 15
minute walk. Campsite is an attractive parklike area often filled in summer.
Reservations not accepted. Mailing address is Camping Zurich-Seebucht,
Sesstr. 557, 8038 Zurich, Switzerland. Camp has hot showers, automatic
washer, clothes line, store and snack bar serving breakfast and light meals.
Prices are about adult/4 F, child 6-16/2 F, tent/2 F.

Tourist office has details on other camps accessible by public transportation within 10-20 km of Zurich. Ray Rylander contributes: "In Zurich, you lay awake all night listening to the trains and trucks and foghorns, and other people talking. Quieter than Seebucht is Camping Sihlwald, and to get here, you must take the Sihltalbahn from Bahnhof Selnau (take tram #8). Get off at Station Sihlwald, about 15 or 20 km from town, cross the river and go about 200 meters upstream along the road. It's a beautiful camp, right on the river, and they allow camp fires. And to be sure, you are out in the country!"

CITY TRANSPORTATION   A one day pass costs about 4.50 F. Buses and trams cost .80 F for a 1-4 stop ride and 1.20 F for a five or more stop ride to the city limits. Ticket books are also sold. Single tickets are sold and cancelled by machines at stops. Each suburb has a local train station and these trains are included in railpasses. Some international trains stop at suburban Enge Station which is connected to Hauptbahnhof by train or tram #7.

FOOD   Market is Tuesday and Friday, 7-11 am, at Stadthausanlage on lakeshore near Burckliplatz where you take buses #61 and 65 to camp. Another market, same days and hours, is further out at Helvetiaplatz, on other side of Sihl River.

Bahnhofstrasse, perpendicular to station entrance, is lined with restaurants, department stores and shops. One block down is Bell's butcher shop and delicatessen selling top quality hot dogs (bratwurst) for about 3 F and rotisseried chicken in foil-lined bag to go. Jelmoli (yell-mo-lee) department store on Bahnhofstrasse has a basement supermarket and third floor restaurant serving hot plates for about 8-12 F and a breakfast smorgasbord for about 8 F of nine kinds of bread, five kinds of meats, butter, cereal and eggs. Migros Market, Lowenstrasse and Silhlbrucke-strasse has a stand-up cafeteria (Teller Service) serving hot plates for about 6 F and breakfast for about 3.50 F. Other Migros Markets are located at Limmatplatz (east of river), Kreuzplatz (eastside of lake), Folkenstrasse and Lowenstrasse. Anahof deparment store on sidestreet Fussli, off Bahnhofstrasse, has a cafeteria.

Specialties of Zurich include "Zurcher ratsherrentopf" which we know as hamburger, macaroni and tomato sauce casserole, and "geschnetzeltes nach Zurcher art," ground veal in cream sauce.

SIGHTSEEING   Summer hours are given below. Opening hours are restricted during rest of year.

Landesmuseum (Swiss National Museum) is conveniently located behind the train station. After exiting, turn left and walk to corner of station building. Turn left again and museum is across the street. The museum presents a large group of Swiss art and chronologically presented exhibits on the country's cultural development beginning with prehistoric times. Open T-Su 10-5, M 12-5, free, brochure in English/1 F.

Rietberg Museum is in Rieterpark at Gablerstrasse 15 near Seestrasse and a five minute walk from Bahnhof Zurich-Enge or tram #7 or 10 from main station. Shown is a private collection of non-European art from India, Africa, South America, East Asia, China and Japan. Open Tu-Su 10-5, and Wednesday evening 8-10 pm. Free.

E. G. Buhrle Art Collection, 172 Zollikerstrasse in Riesbach across
the lake from campground, exhibits a large collection of French Impressionists (14 Cezannes). Get there by ferry, train to Bahnhof Zurich-Tiefen-
brunnen or tram #4 from station. Open Tu and Fri 2-5 pm, adult/4.40 F,
student/2.20 F.

Kunsthaus (fine arts museum), Heimplatz 1, shows a group of 13th to
20th century paintings and sculpture plus graphic art. Modern section is
particularly large and important, and includes 100 works by the sculptor
Giacometti. Open Tu-F 10-9, SaSu 10-5, M 2-5. Adult/5 F, reduction for
students, children and groups. Restrooms on ground and "first" floors.
Museum is about a 15 minute walk from the station.

Old quarter of Zurich is off Limmat-Quai, main street across the
river from the station. Grossmunster on Zwingliplatz is the most important
Romanesque Cathedral in Switzerland. Here is where Zwingli first began to
talk of reformation in 1519. Though construction began in the 13th century,
the modern bronze reliefs on the portal were done by Otto Munch and
Giacometti created the church windows in 1932. Haus zum Rechberg,
Hirschgraben 40, is a beautiful rococo patrician house. Guildhouses from
the 15th to 18th centuries include Zur Meisen (rococo), Munsterhof 20; Zur
Waag (15th century gabled), Musterhof 8; Zur Ruden (now a restaurant with
curious carved barrel vault in its Gothic room), Limmatquai 42; and Zur
Saffran (Baroque), a restaurant at Limmatquai 54. Across the river can be
seen the Schipfe, which refers to a group of elegant old houses with interesting facades and gables.

Huge Zurichberg Park has many trails, a zoo and a miniature railway.
Zoo is open daily 8-6, adult/4.40 F, child/1.65 F. From station, take tram
#6 and transfer at stop "Kirche Fluntern" to tram #5. On Sunday, tram #6
goes right through to the zoo.

In Winterthur, 22 km east of Zurich, the Art Gallery, Museumstrasse
52, shows some modern paintings.

READERS' SUGGESTIONS FOR SWITZERLAND

FILISUR (between Davos and St. Moritz on a main rail line). "My favorite
place in Switzerland is Filisur (you can see the camping platz from the station.) In SCHAFFHAUSEN, take the trolleybus toward Neuhausen and get
off at Scheidegg. Campingplatz is down the hill and under the railroad
tracks and right on the river. 'So-so" about average. " (Ray Rylander)
TCS Camping Strandbad Rheinwiesen charges adult/3.20 F, tent/2 F, and has
hot showers, individual cubicles with sinks, store and snacks. It is 2km
from Schaffhausen.

DISTANCE FROM TRAIN STATION AND BUS STOP
OF CAMPGROUNDS IN SWITZERLAND

(Information compiled from the Swiss Touring Club Camping Caravanning
guidebook. The book gives details including prices on 450 sites and provides
maps and photos of STC sites. For a copy, send 12 international reply
coupons obtainable at any U. S. postoffice to Swiss Federation of Camping-
Caravanning, Section for Tourisme, Habsburgstrasse 35, Postfach 24;
CH-6000 Luzern 4/Switzerland. The book is revised annually and costs 10 F.)

365

town	kms station	bus stop	town	kms station	bus stop	town	kms station	bus stop
Aarburg	2	.3	Champex-Lac	8	.8	Goldau	2	2
Acquarossa	13	1	Chateau-d'CEx	6	.3	Gordevio	10	1
Adelboden	14	.2	Chevroux	10	.2	Grandson	.5	.5
Aeschi	5	-	Cheyres	.5	.5	Grenchen	3	.3
Agarn	2.3	.2	Chiggiogna	.5	-	Grindelwald	1.3	-
Agno	1	-	Chur	2	.5	Gryon	1	-
Agnuzzo	2	-	Claro	.5	1	Gstaad	10	.1
Aigle	1	1	Colombier	3	.1	Gsteig b/		
Altenrhein	1.5	1	Conthey	.8	.1	Gstaad	10	.1
Altnau	.1	.1	Corcelettes	2.5	1.5	Gstein-Gabi	-	.5
Andeer	12	5	Cossonay-Gare	.3	.3	Gudo	1	-
Arbon	2	2	Courgenay	2	-	Gwatt-Thun	1	.1
Ardon	.5	.2	Cudrefin	7	2			
Ascona	-	-	Cugnasco	2	.5	Harkingen	1.5	.8
Auslikon	1.9	-	Cureglia	5	.1	Haute-Gruyere	.8	.8
Avegno	-	.2				Horw-Luzern	1	.1
Avenches	3	3	Dardagny	5	-			
			Davos-Dorf	1	1	Igis-Landquart	3	.3
Baden	2	-	Davos	5	.3	Innertkirchen	1	.3
Bad Ragaz	.8	.8	Delemont	2	1	Interlaken	.5	-
Ballens	.2	-	Disentis	2	.5			
Basse-Gruyere	7	1				Jakobsbad	.3	-
Bellavista	1	.2	Egnach	1.5	1	Jaunpass	11	.1
Bendern	2	.2	Engelberg	1	-			
Bern-Eymatt	5	.1	Enney	.8	.8	Kaiseraugst	1	-
Biasca	1.5	.5	Erlach	3	.5	Kandersteg	1	-
Bischofszell	2.5	-	Eschenz	.8	-	Kehlhof	1	.1
Blumenstein	8	.1	Estavayer-			Klontal	10	.1
Bonigen	1	.5	le-Lac	2	-	Krattigen	5	.3
Bois de Finges	1	.2	Evionnaz	1	1	Kreuzlingen	1.4	-
Bois-Noir	2	-	Evolene	25	.5	Krummenau	.3	-
Bonnefontaine	-	.4						
Blumenstein	8	.1	Fanel-Strand	2	-	La Chaux-de-		
Bramois	8	.2	Filisur	1	.6	Fonds	1.5	.5
Brenzikofen	.3	8	Flaach	5	.3	Lac Noir	-	.3
Brienz	1.5	-	Flims	-	.5	La Crois/		2
Brig	1	.5	Forel-Lavaux	.6	2	Lutry	2	.5
Brigerbad	4.5	-	Frauenfeld	2.3	-	La Fouly	13	.8
Brunnen	2	-	Frick	1	1	La Medettaz	.1	.3
Buchs	1.5	.3	Frutigen	1.5	1.5	Landquart	3	.3
Bullet-Les						Langwiesen	1	3
Cluds	6	2	Gadmen	19	.1	La Sarraz	.5	.5
Buochs	1	-	Gambarogno	1	.2	Lauerz	1.5	1.5
Burgdorf	1.5	-	Gampel	.3	-	Lausanne-Vidy	4	.2
			Gampelen	2	-	Lauterbrunnen	.8	.8
Cadenazzo	.5	.5	Gemmiblick	2.3	.2	Lavey-les-Bains	2	.2
Chalet-a-			Geneve-Vesenaz	8	.5	Lawena	6	.4
Gobet	8	.2	Giswil	2	-	Le Bouveret	.5	-

town	station (kms)	bus stop
Le Locle	2	.5
Lenk	.6	.5
Lenzerheide	.3	-
Le Rocheray	.1	-
Les Evouettes	1	-
Les Iles	2	.1
Les Marecottes	.1	.8
Les Paccots	2.4	2.4
Leukerbad	17	.7
Leutwsil	1.5	1
Lignieres	1	-
Locarno	5	4
Losone	1	-
Lotschental	1	1
Lugano	2	-
Lungern	2	-
Luzern	3	.1
Maloja	-	3
Maroggia	-	.2
Martigny	1	-
Matten	.5	.2
Maur	4	2
Maurholz	4	2
Meinisberg	4	.2
Meiringen	1	.5
Melano	1	-
Meride	5	.1
Mezzovico	1	.1
Mohlin	2	2
Molinazzo	4	.5
Montana	4	2
Montecu	-	.4
Montmelon-Dessous	2	-
Morges	1	-
Morgins	15	.5
Mosen	.1	-
Moudon	1	-
Mustair	-	.6
Murg	.3	-
Murten/ Morat	.3	-
Muster	2	.5
Muzzano	2	-
Nax	-	1

town	station (kms)	bus stop
Neue Ganda	3	.3
Noranco	5	-
Nottwil	1	1
Noville	2.5	1.5
Nyon	2	1
Oberiberg	-	1
Obervaz	-	.3
Oey-Diemtigen	.5	-
Orbe	2	1
Ottenbach	4	.5
Pambio	5	-
Payerne	1.2	-
Penthalaz	1.3	.3
Piodella	2	-
Pointe a la Bise	8	.5
Pointe Bleue	7	1
Pontresina	1.5	-
Porrentruy	1	-
Poschiavo	.2	-
Post Crusch	8	3
Preles	1.5	.1
Primadengo	2	.5
Punt-Muragl	.1	.1
Raron	.4	-
Reckingen	1	-
Ricken	.1	5
Ringgenberg	.4	.2
Roche	1.5	1.5
Rolle	1	1.5
Roveredo	-	1
Saanen	.5	.5
Saas-Fee	-	.5
Saas-Grund	-	.1
Sachseln	2	-
Saint-Aubin	1	.2
Saint-Cergue	1	1
Saint-Leonard	.8	.5

town	station (kms)	bus stop
Saint-Maurice	2	-
Salavaux	5	1
Saland	1	-
Salvan	6	.1
Samedan (Punt Muragl Station)	.1	-
Sarnen	2	-
Savognin	3	.5
Schaffhausen	1	3
Schonengrund	5	.2
Schupfheim	2	.1
Scuol/ Schuls	2.5	1
Sembrancher	.5	.5
Sempach	1.3	-
Sent	8	3
Sierre	1	.2
Sihlwald	.5	-
Silvaplana	5	.3
Sion	.5	.1
Sisikon	.5	-
Sorens	11	3
Spiez	5	-
Splugen	25	.5
Staad	3	.3
Stafa	1	.1
Staldbach	1.5	-
Stampa	-	3
Stechelberg	7	.1
Steckborn	1	-
Steg	1.4	-
Stein am Rhine	1.5	-
Steinen	1	-
St. Gallen	2	.2
St. Moritz	3	.1
Strada	-	.1
Sur En	8	3
Sursee	1	-
Susten	2	-
Tasch	.2	-
Tannay	.5	-

town	kms station	bus stop	town	kms station	bus stop	town	kms station	bus stop
Tenero	.7	.7	Vesenaz-			Werdenberg	1.5	.3
Thorishaus	1.5	-	Geneve	8	.5	Wetzikon	1.9	-
Thun-			Vetroz	1	1	Wildberg	2.5	-
Gwatt	1	.1	(Arden Station)			Wilderswil	3	1
Thusis	.5	.5	Vex	8	.2	Wildhaus	1	-
Tiefenau	.5	.5	Villeneuve	.8	.8	Willerzell	4	.5
Triesen	3	.2	Vira-			Wollishofen	1	-
Trun	.5	-	Bellavista	1	.2			
Tschierv	27	.2	Viscoso-			Yverdon	1	1
			prano	-	.3	Yvonand	2	2
Ulrichen	.3	.3	Visp	1	-	Yvorne	1.5	1.5
Unterageri	-	1.2	Vissoie	16	.4			
Unterseen	2	1	Vitznau	-	1	Zernez	.5	-
Uttwil	1	-	Vorderthal	8	.1	Zinal	28	1
						Zurich	3	1
Vaduz-			Wabern	2	.6	Zug	2	.5
Sud	3	.2	Wagen-			Zurzach	1.3	-
Vallorbe	.5	-	hausen	1	1	Zweisim-		
Vals	-	1.5	Walenstadt	1	1	men	1.5	-
Vers-			Weissen-					
l'Eglise	.8	-	burg	1	-			

YUGOSLAVIA

LJUBLJANA

Ray Rylander says: "In Ljubljana, for Autocamp Jezica, walk two blocks west from station to main north-south street in town, Totova cesta. Catch trolleybus #6 or 8 and ride to next-to-last stop. Good camp is on the right - free hot showers. And Yugoslavia is pretty."

Kris and Ted Bushek recommend for Eastern Europe: "We also brought 4 function calculators which were cheap on sale at home for gifts to helpful folk in Eastern Europe."

FRENCH

Good day	Bonjour*	(bohn-ZHOOR)
Good evening	Bonsoir*	(bohn-SWAH)
Goodbye	Au revoir*	(aw-ruh-VWAR)
Yes, no	Oui*, Non*	(we), (nor'n)
Please	S'il vous plait*	(seel-voo-PLAY)
Thank you	Merci*	(mayr-SEE)
How much?	Combien?	(kawn-bee-AHN)
Where is?	Ou est?	(oo-a) --as in you-hay
I would like	Je voudrais	(zjhuh-voo-DRAY)
Do you go to?	Allez-vous vers?	(allay-voo-ver)
Camping, toilet	Camping, toilettes	(kahng-peeng) (twah-LEHT)
Is it within walking distance?	Est-il possible d'y aller a pied?	(eel po-SEEBL dah-LAY ah pee-A?)
Thank you, that was a very good meal*.	Merci, c'etait tres bon*.	(mayr-SEE, say-TAY tray bawng)

*append monsieur, madame or mademoiselle

1	un	(uhn)	6	six	(sees)	11	onze	(awnz)
2	deux	(duh)	7	sept	(set)	12	douze	(dooze)
3	trois	(twah)	8	huit	(weet)	13	treize	(trehz)
4	quatre	(caht)	9	neuf	(nuff)	14	quatorze	(kah-TORZ)
5	cinq	(sank)	10	dix	(dees)	15	quinze	(cans)

100 grams   cent gramme   (sahnt grahm)

service compris - service included
eau potable (oh po-tahbl) - water
lait (leh) - milk
pain (pang) - bread
pain complet (pang kawn-pleh)wholegrain
beurre (burr) - butter
oeuf (urf) - egg
potage - soup
crudites - raw marinated vegetables
  chauds, froids - hot, cold
assiette de charcuterie - coldcuts
salade - salad
  laitue, tomate - lettuce, tomato
poisson - fish
quenelle - fish mousse (superb!)
anguille - eel
fruits de mer - seafood
poulet - chicken
coq au vin - chicken in wine sauce
boeuf - beef
bifteck - steak
hache - hamburger
pot-au-feu - stew

veau - veal
porc - pork
jambon - ham
saucisse - sausage
foie - liver
legumes - vegetables
petit pois - peas
champignons - mushrooms
pommes frites - french fries
pommes de terre - potatoes
haricots verts - green beans
choucroute - sauerkraut
riz - rice
en croute - in pastry crust
fromage du pays - local cheese
fromage du chevre - goat cheese
glace (glass) - ice cream
creme chantilly - whipped cream
fraises - strawberries
framboise - raspberry
pomme - apple
peche - peach

GERMAN

W is pronounced as V. Many German words are pronounced much the same as our English such as butter, fisch, haus, glas, tee and kaffee.

Good day	Guten tag	(GOO-ten-tawk)
Goodbye	Auf wiedersehn	(owff-VEE-dayr-zayn)
Yes, no	Ja, nein	(yah) (nine)
Please	Bitte	(BIT-tuh)
Thank you	Danke schon	(DAWHN-keh shen)
How much?	Wieviel kostet?	(vee-FEEL KAW-stet)
Where is?	Wo ist?	(voh eest)
I would like	Ich mochte	(ik mersh-tah)
Do you go to?	Gehen sie nach?	(gay-en-see nark)

1	eins	(eintz)	6	sechs	(zecks)	11	elf	(elf)
2	zwei	(tzvai)	7	sieben	(zeeben)	12	zwolf	(tzverlf)
3	drei	(dry)	8	acht	(ahkht)	13	dreizehn	(dry-tsayn)
4	vier	(fear)	9	neun	(noyn)	14	vierzehn	(fear-tsayn)
5	funf	(fewnf)	10	zehn	(tsayn)	15	funfzehn	(fewnf-tsayn)
						100	hundert	(hoon-dert)

wasser -(vahs-ser)- water
milch - milk
brot - bread
schwarzbrot - ryebread

suppe - soup
vorgerichte - appetizers
salat - salad
kopsalat - lettuce salad
gemischter - mixed salad
gurkensalat - cucumber salad

huhn - chicken
brathuhn - roast chicken
rindfleisch - beef
rinderbraten - roast beef
Deutsches beefsteak - hamburger steak
kalbfleisch - veal
schweinefleisch - pork
schweinebraten - roast pork
schinken - ham

wurst - sausage
leber - liver
aufschnitt - cold cuts
aal - eel
thun fisch - tuna fish

gemuse - vegetables
erbsen - peas
pilze - mushrooms
kohl - cabbage
kartoffeln - potatoes
grune bohnen - string beans
reis - rice
kase der gegend - local cheese
ziegenkase - goat cheese
sahneneis - ice cream
schlagsahne - whipped cream
erdbeeren - strawberries

ITALIAN

Good day	Buon giorno	(bwahn JOR-noh)
Goodbye	Ciao	(chow)
Goodbye	Arrivederla	(ah-ree-va-dair-lah)
Yes, no	Si, no	(see) (no)
Please	Per favore	(payr fah-VOR-ay)
Thank you	Grazie	(GRAHTS-zee)
How much?	Quanto?	(KWAN-toh)
Where is?	Dov'e	(doh-vay)
I would like	Vorrei	(voh-ray)
Do you go to	Dov'e vay	(doh-vay var-ee)
I am having a wonder-ful time	Mi diverto molto	(me dee-vair-toh mohl-toh)

1	uno	(oo-noh)	6	sei	(say)	11	undici	(oon-dee-chee)
2	due	(doo-ay)	7	sette	(set-tay)	12	dodici	(doh-dee-chee)
3	tre	(tray)	8	otto	(aw-toh)	13	tredici	(tray-dee-chee)
4	quattro	(kwah-troh)	9	nove	(noh-vay)	14	quattordici	(kwah-tor-)
5	cinque	(cheen-kway)	10	diece	(dee-ay-chee)	15	quindici	(kween-etc.)
						100	cento	(CHAYN-toe)

aqua (AH-quah) - water
latte - milk
pane - bread
burro - butter

zuppa, brodo - soup
antipasto, struzzichini - appetizers
insalata - salad
pollo - chicken
carni di manzo - beef
vitello - veal
vitello cotoletta - veal cutlet
vitello al forno - roast veal
carne di maiale - pork
prosciutto - ham
salsiccia - sausage
fegato - liver

legume, verdura - vegetables
carcioti - artichokes
piselli - peas
melanzana - eggplant
funghi - mushrooms
patate - potatoes
fagiolini - string beans
pomodori - tomatoes
riso, risotto - rice
formaggio della regione - local cheese
formaggio di capra - goat cheese
gelato - ice cream
panna montata - whipped cream

SPANISH

Good day	Buenos dias	(BWAY-nose DEE-ahs)
Goodbye	Adios	(ah-dee-OHS)
Yes, no	Si, no	(see) (noh)
Please	Por favor	(pore-fah-BORE)
Thank you	Gracias	(GRAH-thee-ahs)
How much?	Cuanto?	(KWAHN-toe)
Where is?	Donde esta?	(DOHN-day es-TAH)
I would like	Quiero	(kee-YER-oh)
Do you go to?	Va usted a?	(var oos-TED ah)
I am having a good time.	Me estoy divirtiendo mucho.	(may ess-TOY dee-ver-tee-END-do MOO-choh)

1	uno	(OO-noh)	6 seis (sayss)	11 once	(OWN-thay)
2	dos	(dose)	7 siete (see-A-tay)	12 doce	(DOH-thay)
3	tres	(thrace)	8 ocho (OH-choh)	13 trece	(TRAY-thay)
4	cuatro	(KWAH-troh)	9 nueve (NWAY-bay)	14 catorce	(kah-TOR-thay)
5	cinco	(THEEN-koh)	10 diez (dee-AYTH)	15 quince	(KEEN-thay)
				100 cien	(thee-EN)

aqua (AH-qwah) - water
leche (LAY-chay) - milk
pan - bread
mantequilla (mawn-tay-KEY-ya) - butter

sopa - soup
entremeses - appetizers
hot - calientes
cold - frios
atun - tuna
pollo - chicken
carne de vaca - beef
filete - steak
albondigas - meatballs
ternera - veal
chuletas - veal cutlets
cerdo - pork
jamon - ham
salchicha - sausage
higado - liver

legumbres - vegetables
alcachofas - artichokes
guisantes - peas
berenjena - eggplant
patatas - potatoes
judias verdes - string beans
arroz - rice
queso - cheese
queso de cabra - goat 'cheese
helado - ice cream
nata - whipped cream

DANISH

J is pronounced as a Y. In Danish, Norwegian and Swedish the definite article is placed after the noun: en mann means "a man" but "the man" is mannen.

Good day	God dag	(go th-day)
Goodbye	Farvel	(fahr-vel)
Yes, no	Ja, nej	(ya) (nigh)
Please	Vaer saa god	(vayr saw go)
Thank you	Tak	(tahk)

1	en	(een)	6	seks	(secks)	11	elve	(el-vuh)
2	to	(toe)	7	syv	(sue)	12	tolv	(tahlv)
3	tre	(tray)	8	otte	(oh-tuh)	13	tretten	(trett-un)
4	fire	(fee-rah)	9	ni	(nee)	14	fjorten	(fyawr-tun)
5	fem	(fem)	10	ti	(tee)	15	femten	(fem-tun)

vand - water
maelk - milk
franskbrod - white bread
rugbrod - rye bread
smor - butter
aeg - egg
sild - herring
cod - torsk
helleflynder - halibut
kylling, hons - chicken
svinekotelet - pork chop
kalvesteg - roast veal
kodboller - meatballs

stegt - fried
roasted - ovnstegt
kartofler - potatoes
kartoffelmos - mashed potatoes
Franske kartofler - french fries
aerter - peas
svampe - mushrooms
bonner - green beans
agurk - cucumber
tomater - tomatoes

NORWEGIAN

Good day	God day	(goo dog)
Goodbye	Adjo	(ah-YER)
Yes, no	Ja, nei	(yah) (nay)
Please	Var so god	(vair suh goo-duh)
Thank you	Mange takk	(mahng-uh tahk)

1	en	(ayn)	6	seks	(secks)	11	elleve	(all-vuh)
2	to	(toh)	7	syv	(soo-eva)	12	tolv	(tahl)
3	tre	(trec)	8	otte	(ah-tuh)	13	tretten	(tret-uhn)
4	fire	(free-ruh)	9	ni	(nee)	14	fjorten	(fyawr-tun)
5	fem	(fem)	10	ti	(tee)	15	femten	(fem-tun)

vann - water
melk - milk
franskbrod - white bread

rostbiff - roast beef
svinekotelett - pork chop
lammestek - roast lamb

rugbrod - rye bread
smor - butter
egg - egg

sild - herring
al - eel
torsk - cod
halibut - kveite
kylling, hons - chicken
kjottboller - meatballs

erter - peas
sopp - mushrooms
poteter - potatoes
potetpure - mashed potatoes
kokte - boiled potatoes
bonner - string beans
tomater - tomatoes
ris - rice

SWEDISH

Good day	God dag	(goo dah)
Goodbye	Adjo	(ah-YER)
Yes, no	Ja, nej	(yah) (nay)
Please	Var snalloch	(var snell ohk)
Thank you	Tack sa mycket	(tahk sah micket)
How much?	Hur mycket kostar?	(hur micket KO-star)
Where is?	Var ar	(var air)
I would like	Jag vill ha	(yog vil ha)
Toilet	Toaletten	(too-ah-LAH-ten)
To your health!	Skal!	(skol!)
I am having a good time.	Jag har trevligt	(yog hahr tray-uh-vleekt)

1	ett	(et)	6	sex	(sex)	11	elva	(el-vah)
2	tra	(tvoh)	7	sju	(shoo)	12	tolv	(tawlv)
3	tre	(tray)	8	atta	(awt-tah)	13	tretton	(tret-tawn)
4	fyra	(fee-rah)	9	nio	(nee-yoh)	14	fjorton	(fyoor-tawn)
5	fem	(fem)	10	tio	(tee-yoh)	15	femton	(fem-tawn)

vatten - water
mjolk - milk
vitt brod - white bread
knackebrod - Swedish bread
smor - butter
agg - egg

stromming - fresh herring
flundra - flounder
torsk - cod
al - eel
kyckling, hons - chicken
kottbullar - tiny meatballs
kottfars - hamburger
flaskkotlett - pork chops

arter - peas
svamp - mushrooms
kokt - boiled potatoes
flottystekt - french fries
brutna bonor - green beans
ris - rice
surkal - sauerkraut

GREEK

Hello (how do you do)	(pooze ees thay)
Good day (how do you do)	(ka-li-mer-a)
Yes, no	(nay) (oh he)
Please	(pah-ra kah-LOH)
Thank you	(eff-hahr-ee-STOW)
I am having a wonderful time.	(ta pare now or ray ah)

1 (ay nuh)   3 (tree oh)   5 (pen tay)   7 (ep tuh)   9 (enn tay uh)
2 (dee oh)   4 (tess er-ruh)   6 (ex he)   8 (ok toe)   10 (decks)

water   (nee-ROH)
mezedakia, meze - appetizers
 (olives, cheese, sausage)
melitzanossalata - eggplant salad
lathera - marinated vegetables
avgolemono - egg and lemon soup
fassolada - bean soup
marides - smelt
sinagrida - bream (fish)
barbouni - mullet

moussaka - ground meat and eggplant casserole
pastitsio - noodles and gound meat
 casserole
dolmas - grape leaf wrapped ground
 meat and rice mixture
youvarlakia - ground meat, rice and
 egg sauce
arni - lamb
kotopoulo - chicken

Post-Trip Questionnaire

Dear European Traveler,

    We know you have discovered many things that a new European traveler would benefit by knowing. Would you please complete this questionnaire and mail to Ariel Publications, Box 255, Mercer Island, Washington 98040. Thank you.

First a few vital statistics: age__ sex__ occupation_____
How many days were you in Europe?   Which months?
Who did you travel with? (circle) alone spouse friend family
  If family, please give ages of children:
How did you get to Europe:
Did you buy a (circle) Eurailpass Eurail Youthpass Other?

Excluding air and train fare, how much did the rest of your trip cost?   This is for how many people?
For car and van-campers--how much did gas cost you?

What was your favorite campground? Why?

What was your favorite city, town or resort? Why?

What would you have left out if you knew before your trip what you know now?

What would you have done differently?

What are your recommendations regarding campgrounds, food, cities, trains, car-camping, sightseeing and this guidebook that would help future campers in Europe? (Please use additional pages if necessary."

What inaccuracies or misleading statements did you find in this guidebook?

Thank you very much!

Lenore Baken

EXCERPTS FROM LETTERS

"Bring a skirt and shorts--I only brought a skirt and wish I had shorts for hiking and in Greece (hot hot there but great). Bring youth hostel card and save hotels, bed and breakfasts and hostels for rainy days and cold weather. We camped most of the time but stayed in Bed and Breakfasts in Ireland in mid-October and a hotel in Paris due to the cold. Fall is a good time to tour Europe but be sure to hit the Northern countries first--we toured England and Scandinavia in August. To do differently, we would have spent more time in Ireland and visited in August and September, not October like we did. We also would have hiked more in Austria and Switzerland." Bonnie and Doug Robinson

"We would have left our small white gas backpack stove at home and bought one that uses butane. White gas stoves are illegal in Germany and Switzerland. Even with Eurailpass, if you are planning to ride many buses or mountain railroads in Switzerland, the Swiss 1/2 Fare Card can save you a lot of money. We almost paid for ours on the trip to Jungfraujoch." Clyde and Mary Anna Anderson

"We would have spent the time we did in Scotland in Wales which is absolutely gorgeous and not so heavily tourist. We recommend getting about $25 in every country's currency before leaving the U.S. Many times we entered a country at a time when the only change place open would be the train station--needless to mention the long lines." Robert Rubin

"We had a backpack (30 to 40 pounds) and a small duffle (10-15 pounds) each. Next time, a 20-30 pound pack total! This was by no means my first trip, but was the first time since 1971 when prices of hotels were reasonable. I would simply have taken less bulk and weight, having no hotel room to stash things in. It was otherwise a flawless trip, cheap! but as fun as any big-budget trip could be. We recommend being willing to camp to the exclusion of any hotels or other "roofed" accommodations. We slept on trains, boats and in fields, averaging about three paid nights (i.e. campgrounds) per week, just enough for showers and to save time in urban areas." from Eugene, Oregon

"I would not have taken Cook's Timetable. I threw it away. Rail information is available everywhere I went. I wrote to Optimus in Europe to find out where the #802 cartridge is available in Europe and found out it's only merchandised in the U.S." Harold Parkerson

"I would recommend taking a xerox copy of passport as ours were in the Hungarian Embassy and we would not have been able to cash travelers checks without it. Take cheese and fruit with you on trains. We skipped a few meals because of delayed trains in Italy. I'm not a camper but I love trains. Scenery was terrific and you don't have the hassle of traffic and parking." Peggy Redelfs

(Excerpted from a newspaper article by Cathy Reiner) "We have only two regrets about our recent European trip. It was too short, and we should have camped more. Camping was without question the best part of the trip. Surprisingly, the inconvenience of carrying all that extra gear was more than compensated for by the delightful experiences we had and people we met."

"...Inside our packs we crammed a four-pound nylon tent with rain fly, two tiny sleeping bags (we couldn't find small-enough ones, so I made ours by tracing our bodies on a layer of mylar-backed curtain lining, then encasing it in nylon ripstop closed with Velcro hook-loop fasteners, an alcohol stove, flashlights, candles, cups, spoons, toiletries (including bug repellent and liquid soap), rope, cameras, a small AM radio (for music and English-language news,) guidebooks, maps and notebooks."

"That didn't leave much room for clothes. We limited ourselves each to two pairs of jeans, two long and two short-sleeved shirts, two sweaters, two tee shirts, four sets of underwear and socks, a nylon raincoat, a pair each of tennis and leather walking shoes, thongs, a wool cap and a bathing suit."

"Other necessities included alarm-clock watches (invaluable), small nylon packs (used when we would check our big packs in train stations and set out to explore), sturdy cotton money belts (to wear under our clothes and keep traveler's checks, passports, tickets, etc.,) hand towels, plastic sacks and supplies of coffee, cocoa, soup, spices and dried fruits."

"In the weeks before we left we piled every potential trip item into our packs. We soon found that most of the things we wanted to take would not fit. The last week I remember night after night of repacking to eliminate extras so everything would fit. Fortunately, we got rid of extra clothes, and the camping gear stayed." (The author traveled during autumn.)